# ILLUSTRATED ATLAS
## OF WORLD HISTORY

## Table of Contents

## Introduction

This illustrated atlas contains dramatic maps and vibrant pictures and graphs to bring your study of world history to life. You can use these pages to compare regions or to make connections between past and present. The atlas has been placed at the front of your book, so you will have it as a ready reference throughout the year.

WORLD DESK
REFERENCE
Click here to ● select a country

Prentice Hall

*Get up-to-date information about any country in the world. Use the World Desk Reference Online, to learn about the world today, practice critical thinking skills, and get updated statistics and data.*

# THE WORLD: PHYSICAL

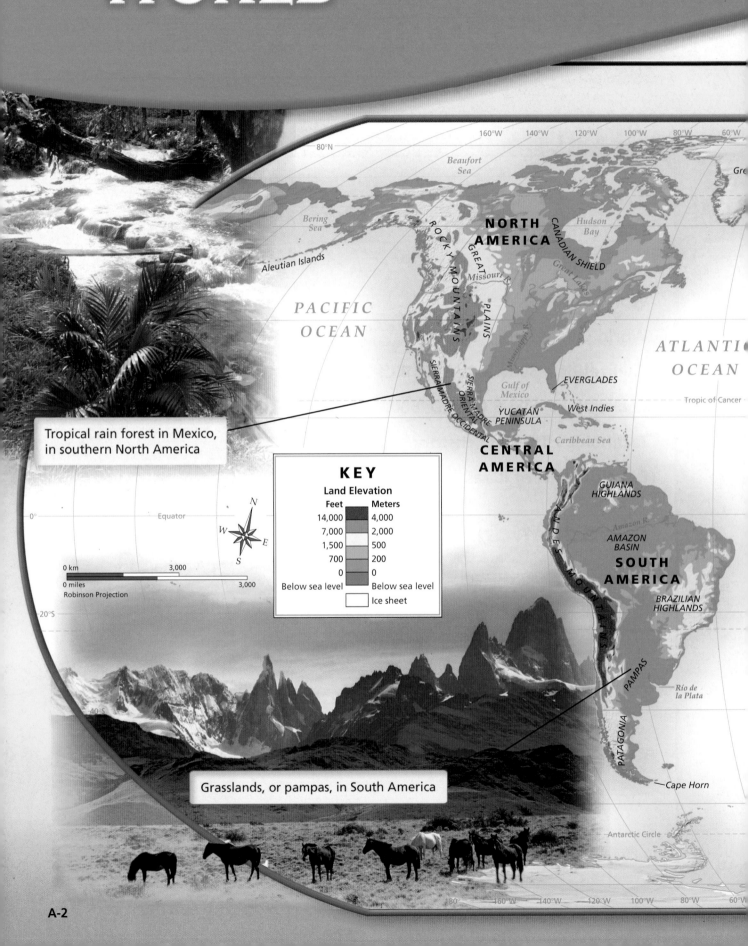

Tropical rain forest in Mexico, in southern North America

Grasslands, or pampas, in South America

## KEY

**Land Elevation**

| Feet | Meters |
|------|--------|
| 14,000 | 4,000 |
| 7,000 | 2,000 |
| 1,500 | 500 |
| 700 | 200 |
| 0 | 0 |
| Below sea level | Below sea level |
| Ice sheet | |

0 km    3,000
0 miles    3,000
Robinson Projection

N
W E
S

Equator

Beaufort Sea

Bering Sea

Aleutian Islands

PACIFIC OCEAN

NORTH AMERICA

ROCKY MOUNTAINS

GREAT PLAINS

Missouri R.

Hudson Bay

CANADIAN SHIELD

Great Lakes

Mississippi R.

Gulf of Mexico

SIERRA MADRE OCCIDENTAL

SIERRA MADRE ORIENTAL

YUCATÁN PENINSULA

EVERGLADES

West Indies

Caribbean Sea

CENTRAL AMERICA

ATLANTIC OCEAN

Tropic of Cancer

GUIANA HIGHLANDS

Amazon R.

AMAZON BASIN

SOUTH AMERICA

ANDES MOUNTAINS

BRAZILIAN HIGHLANDS

PAMPAS

Río de la Plata

PATAGONIA

Cape Horn

Antarctic Circle

Gre

The Himalayas, in south central Asia

**ARCTIC OCEAN**

Arctic Circle

20°W  0°  20°E  40°E  60°E  80°E  100°E  120°E  80°N

eland

SCANDINAVIAN PENINSULA

British Isles

North Sea

NORTH EUROPEAN PLAIN

**EUROPE**

ALPS

IBERIAN PENINSULA

Volga R.

BALKAN PENINSULA

Danube R.

Black Sea

CAUCASUS MTS.

Strait of Gibraltar

ATLAS MTS.

Mediterranean Sea

PLATEAU OF IRAN

ZAGROS MTS

Caspian Sea

URAL MTS.

Ob R.

WEST SIBERIAN PLAIN

Yenisey R.

Lena R.

Aral Sea

**ASIA**

TIAN SHAN

KUNLAN SHAN

HIMALAYAS

TIBETAN PLATEAU

GOBI DESERT

NORTH CHINA PLAIN

Sea of Japan

40°N

**PACIFIC OCEAN**

East China Sea

Nile R.

Niger R.

Red Sea

**SAHARA**

**AFRICA**

Persian Gulf

Arabian Sea

INDIAN PENINSULA

DECCAN PLATEAU

Ganges R.

Bay of Bengal

South China Sea

INDOCHINA PENINSULA

20°N

MICRONESIA

Philippine Sea

Philippine Islands

MELANESIA

**INDIAN OCEAN**

ETHIOPIAN PLATEAU

Congo R.

Victoria

GREAT RIFT VALLEY

KATANGA PLATEAU

Zambezi R.

**ATLANTIC OCEAN**

Sumatra

Borneo

East Indies

Celebes

New Guinea

0°

Madagascar

Tropic of Capricorn

KALAHARI DESERT

Cape of Good Hope

**AUSTRALIA**

GREAT DIVIDING RANGE

Darling R.

40°S

Sahara, a desert in northern Africa

**SOUTHERN OCEAN**

**ANTARCTICA**

20°W  0°  20°E  40°E  60°E  80°E  100°E  120°E  80°S

# THE WORLD: POLITICAL

100°W    80°W    60°N
*Greenla* (Den.)

*Alaska* (U.S.)

60°N

CANADA

**NORTH AMERICA**

Ottawa ⊛

40°N

**UNITED STATES**    ⊛ Washington, DC    *Bermuda (U.K.)*

Tropic of Cancer

See inset map

*Hawaii* (U.S.)

**ATLANTIC OCEAN**

*Gulf of Mexico*

20°N

**MEXICO**

Mexico City ⊛

*Caribbean Sea*
Caracas

**VENEZUELA**    **GUYANA**
Paramaribo

Bogotá ⊛    Georgetown ⊛    ⊛ Cayenne
**COLOMBIA**    *French Guiana* (Fr.)
**SURINAME**

*Galápagos Is.* (Ecuador)    ⊛ Quito
**ECUADOR**

0°    Equator

**SOUTH AMERICA**

**PERU**    ⊛ Lima    **BRAZIL**

**PACIFIC OCEAN**

**SAMOA**

*American Samoa (U.S.)*

**TONGA**

*French Polynesia* (Fr.)

*Cook Is.* (N.Z.)

**BOLIVIA**
⊛ La Paz    Brasília ⊛
Sucre ⊛

20°S

*Pitcairn I.* (U.K.)

**PARAGUAY**

Tropic of Capricorn

Asunción ⊛

*Easter Is.* (Chile)

**CHILE**

Buenos    **URUGUAY**
Aires ⊛    ⊛ Montevideo

Santiago ⊛

International Date Line

40°S

**ARGENTINA**

*Falkland Is.* (U.K.)

60°S

**SOUTHERN OCEAN**

Antarctic Circle

**ANTARCTICA**

---

## Central America and the Caribbean

**UNITED STATES**

0 km    300
0 miles    300
Azimuthal Projection

*Gulf of Mexico*

30°N

N
W    E
S

Tropic of Cancer    Havana

Nassau ⊛

B A H A M A S

**CUBA**

*Br. Virgin Is.* (U.K.)

**DOMINICAN REPUBLIC**    *Puerto* Rico (U.S.)

20°N

**HAITI**

Kingston ⊛    Port-au-Prince    Santo Domingo    *Virgin Islands (U.S.)*

**MEXICO**

⊛ Belmopan

**BELIZE**

**JAMAICA**

**ANTIGUA AND BARBUDA**

*Guadeloupe* (Fr.)

**GUATEMALA**    **HONDURAS**
Guatemala ⊛    ⊛ Tegucigalpa
San Salvador ⊛

**ST. KITTS AND NEVIS**

**DOMINICA**

**ST. LUCIA**    *Martinique* (Fr.)

**EL SALVADOR**    **NICARAGUA**    Managua ⊛

*Caribbean Sea*

*Neth. Antilles* (Neth.)
*Aruba* (Neth.)

**ST. VINCENT AND THE GRENADINES**

**BARBADOS**

**GRENADA**

10°N

**COSTA RICA**    San José ⊛

**TRINIDAD AND TOBAGO**

*PACIFIC OCEAN*

**PANAMA**    ⊛ Panamá

Caracas ⊛    Port of Spain ⊛

*ATLANTIC OCEAN*

**COLOMBIA**    **VENEZUELA**    60°W

80°W    70°W    **GUYANA**

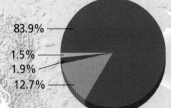

**Northern America**

- 83.9%
- 1.5%
- 1.9%
- 12.7%

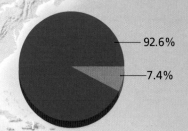

**Latin America**

- 92.6%
- 7.4%

## Religious Affiliations of World's Population

World Population: 6.3 billion*

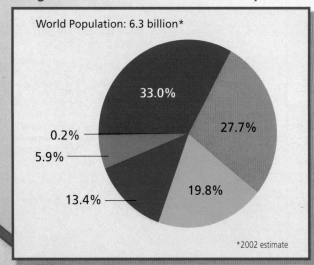

- 33.0%
- 27.7%
- 19.8%
- 13.4%
- 5.9%
- 0.2%

*2002 estimate

Sources: *The World Almanac* and *CIA Factbook*

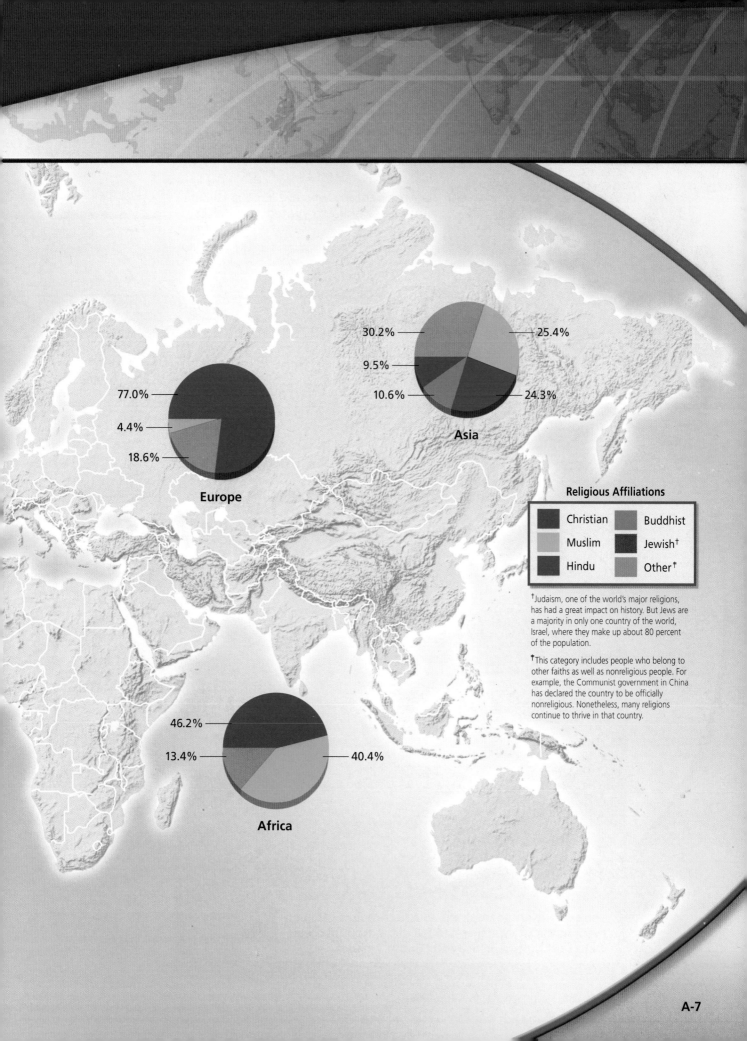

Europe

77.0%

4.4%

18.6%

Asia

30.2%

9.5%

10.6%

25.4%

24.3%

Africa

46.2%

13.4%

40.4%

## Religious Affiliations

- Christian
- Muslim
- Hindu
- Buddhist
- Jewish[†]
- Other[†]

[†]Judaism, one of the world's major religions, has had a great impact on history. But Jews are a majority in only one country of the world, Israel, where they make up about 80 percent of the population.

[†]This category includes people who belong to other faiths as well as nonreligious people. For example, the Communist government in China has declared the country to be officially nonreligious. Nonetheless, many religions continue to thrive in that country.

# WORLD CLIMATE REGIONS

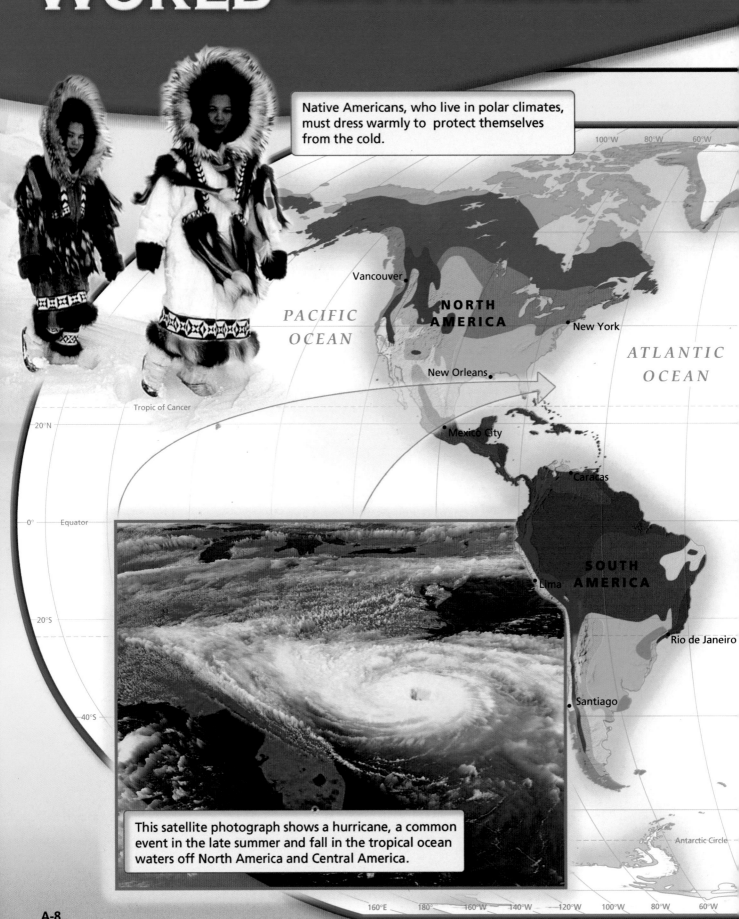

Native Americans, who live in polar climates, must dress warmly to protect themselves from the cold.

This satellite photograph shows a hurricane, a common event in the late summer and fall in the tropical ocean waters off North America and Central America.

PACIFIC OCEAN

NORTH AMERICA

ATLANTIC OCEAN

Vancouver

New York

New Orleans

Mexico City

Caracas

SOUTH AMERICA

Lima

Rio de Janeiro

Santiago

Tropic of Cancer

Equator

Antarctic Circle

100°W    80°W    60°W

20°N

0°

20°S

40°S

160°E    180°    160°W    140°W    120°W    100°W    80°W    60°W

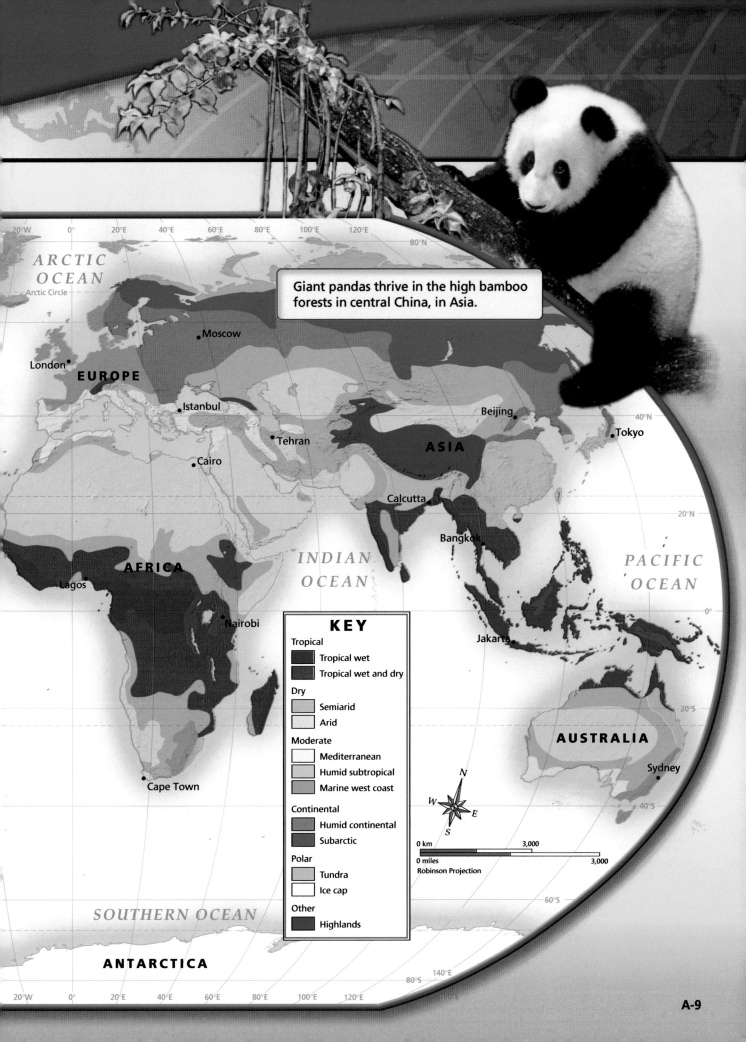

Giant pandas thrive in the high bamboo forests in central China, in Asia.

**ARCTIC OCEAN**

Arctic Circle

20°W  0°  20°E  40°E  60°E  80°E  100°E  120°E

80°N

Moscow

London

**EUROPE**

Istanbul

40°N

Tehran

Beijing

Cairo

Tokyo

**ASIA**

Calcutta

20°N

Bangkok

**INDIAN OCEAN**

**PACIFIC OCEAN**

**AFRICA**

Lagos

Nairobi

Jakarta

0°

**KEY**

**Tropical**
- Tropical wet
- Tropical wet and dry

**Dry**
- Semiarid
- Arid

**Moderate**
- Mediterranean
- Humid subtropical
- Marine west coast

**Continental**
- Humid continental
- Subarctic

**Polar**
- Tundra
- Ice cap

**Other**
- Highlands

**AUSTRALIA**

20°S

Cape Town

Sydney

40°S

N
W        E
S

0 km          3,000
0 miles          3,000
Robinson Projection

**SOUTHERN OCEAN**

60°S

**ANTARCTICA**

20°W  0°  20°E  40°E  60°E  80°E  100°E  120°E  160°E

80°S

140°E

# WORLD CIVILIZATION
## 3000 B.C. - 500 B.C.

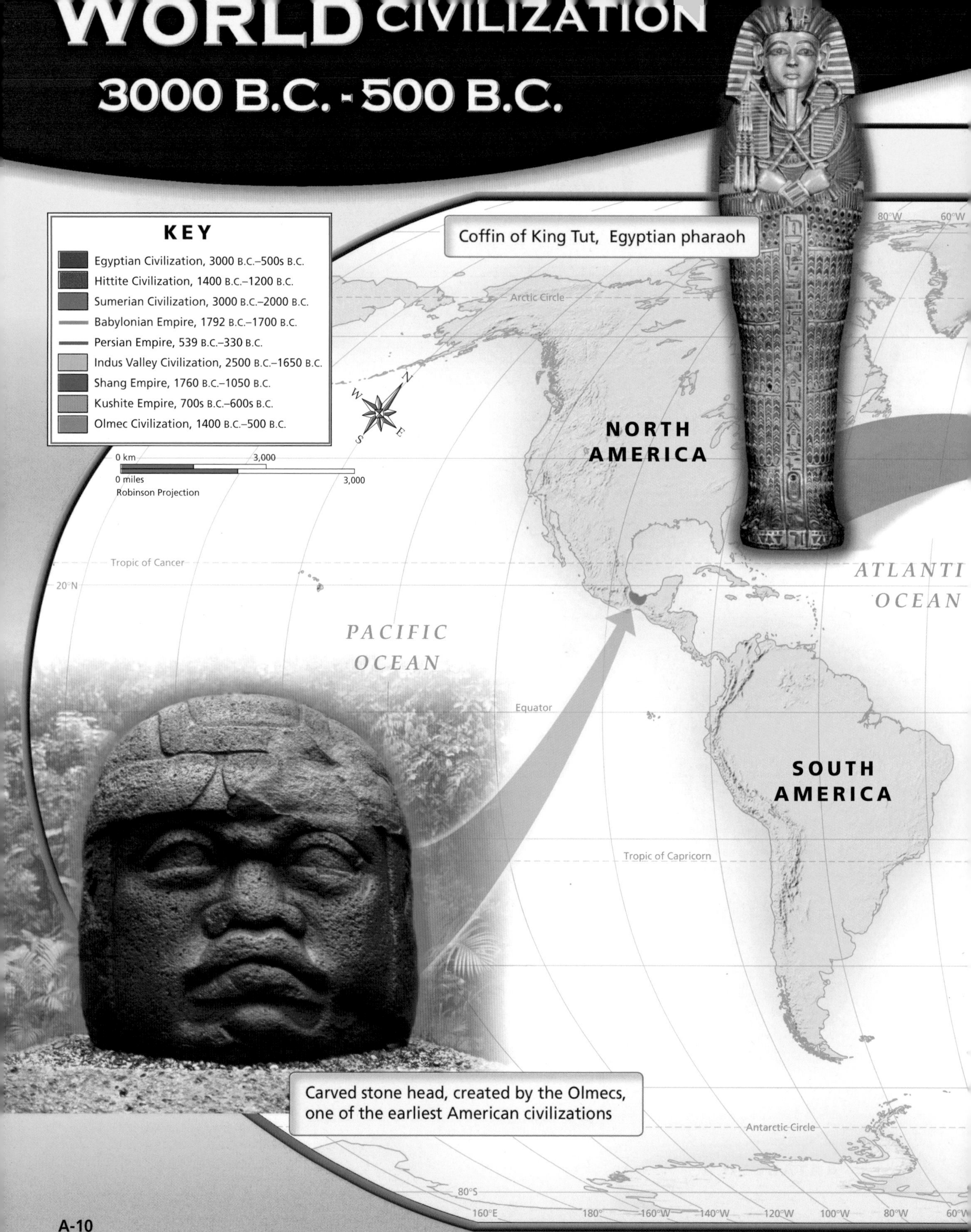

**KEY**

- Egyptian Civilization, 3000 B.C.–500s B.C.
- Hittite Civilization, 1400 B.C.–1200 B.C.
- Sumerian Civilization, 3000 B.C.–2000 B.C.
- Babylonian Empire, 1792 B.C.–1700 B.C.
- Persian Empire, 539 B.C.–330 B.C.
- Indus Valley Civilization, 2500 B.C.–1650 B.C.
- Shang Empire, 1760 B.C.–1050 B.C.
- Kushite Empire, 700s B.C.–600s B.C.
- Olmec Civilization, 1400 B.C.–500 B.C.

0 km      3,000
0 miles      3,000
Robinson Projection

Coffin of King Tut, Egyptian pharaoh

Arctic Circle

NORTH AMERICA

ATLANTIC OCEAN

Tropic of Cancer

20°N

PACIFIC OCEAN

Equator

80°W   60°W

SOUTH AMERICA

Tropic of Capricorn

Carved stone head, created by the Olmecs, one of the earliest American civilizations

Antarctic Circle

80°S

160°E   180°   160°W   140°W   120°W   100°W   80°W   60°

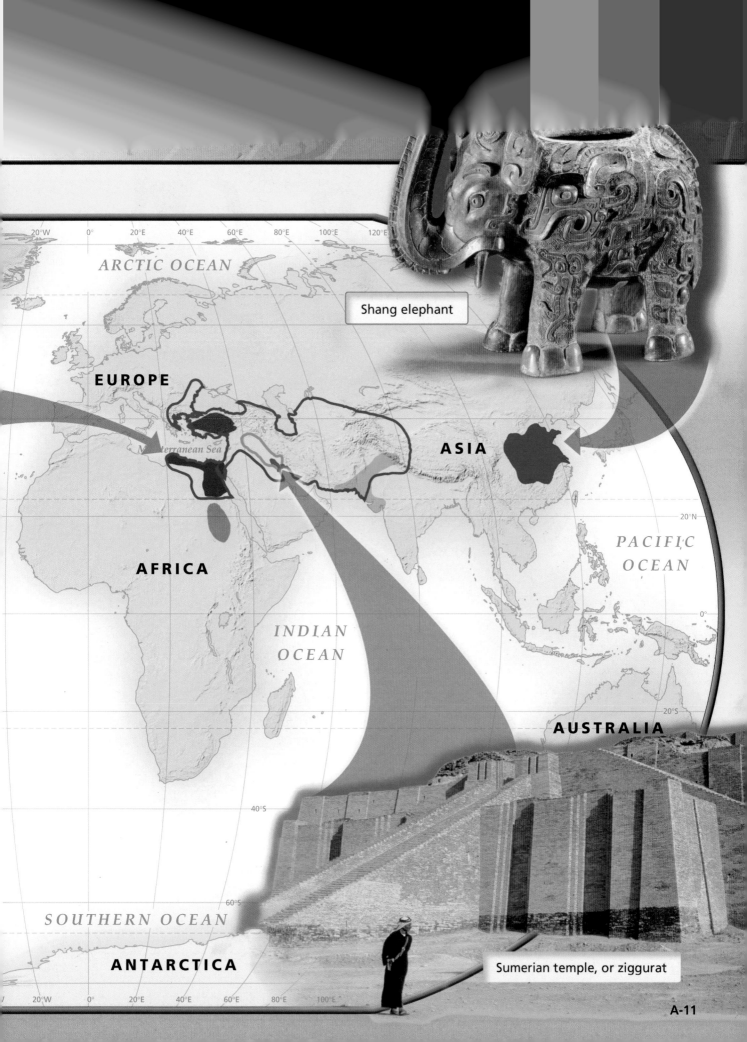

ARCTIC OCEAN

EUROPE

Shang elephant

Mediterranean Sea

ASIA

AFRICA

PACIFIC OCEAN

INDIAN OCEAN

AUSTRALIA

SOUTHERN OCEAN

ANTARCTICA

Sumerian temple, or ziggurat

20°W  0°  20°E  40°E  60°E  80°E  100°E  120°E

20°N

0°

20°S

40°S

60°S

20°W  0°  20°E  40°E  60°E  80°E  100°E

# WORLD CIVILIZATION
## 500 B.C. - A.D. 500

**KEY**

| | |
|---|---|
| | Greek Civilization, 750 B.C.–30 B.C. |
| | Roman Empire, 200s B.C.–A.D. 476 |
| | Gupta Empire, A.D. 335–A.D. 540 |
| | Maurya Empire, 321 B.C.–185 B.C. |
| | Qin Empire, 221 B.C.–206 B.C. |
| | Han Empire, 206 B.C.–A.D. 220 |
| | Maya Civilization, A.D. 250–A.D. 900 |

0 km    3,000
0 miles    3,000
Robinson Projection

PACIFIC OCEAN

**NORTH AMERICA**

ATLANTIC OCEAN

**SOUTH AMERICA**

Antarctic Circle

Sculpture of a woman athlete in Sparta, a region in the Greek civilization

Ruins of Palenque, a religious center built by the Mayas

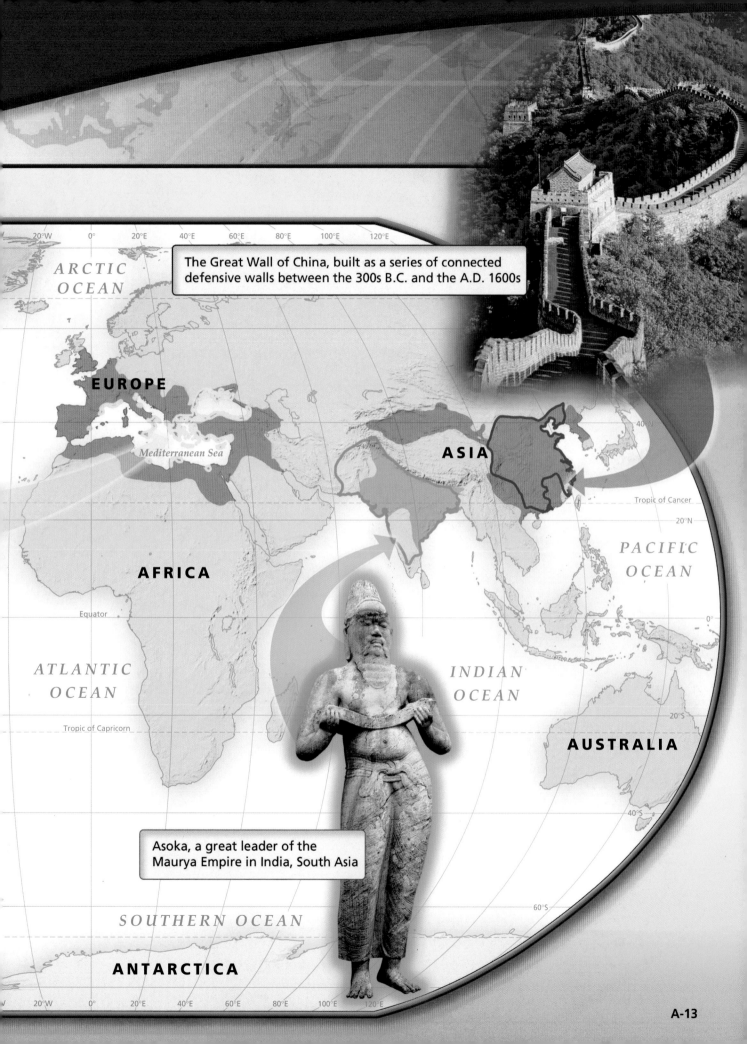

The Great Wall of China, built as a series of connected defensive walls between the 300s B.C. and the A.D. 1600s

ARCTIC OCEAN

EUROPE

Mediterranean Sea

ASIA

40°N

Tropic of Cancer

20°N

AFRICA

Equator

PACIFIC OCEAN

ATLANTIC OCEAN

INDIAN OCEAN

Tropic of Capricorn

20°S

AUSTRALIA

0°

40°S

Asoka, a great leader of the Maurya Empire in India, South Asia

SOUTHERN OCEAN

60°S

ANTARCTICA

20°W    0°    20°E    40°E    60°E    80°E    100°E    120°E

# TECHNOLOGY AND HISTORY

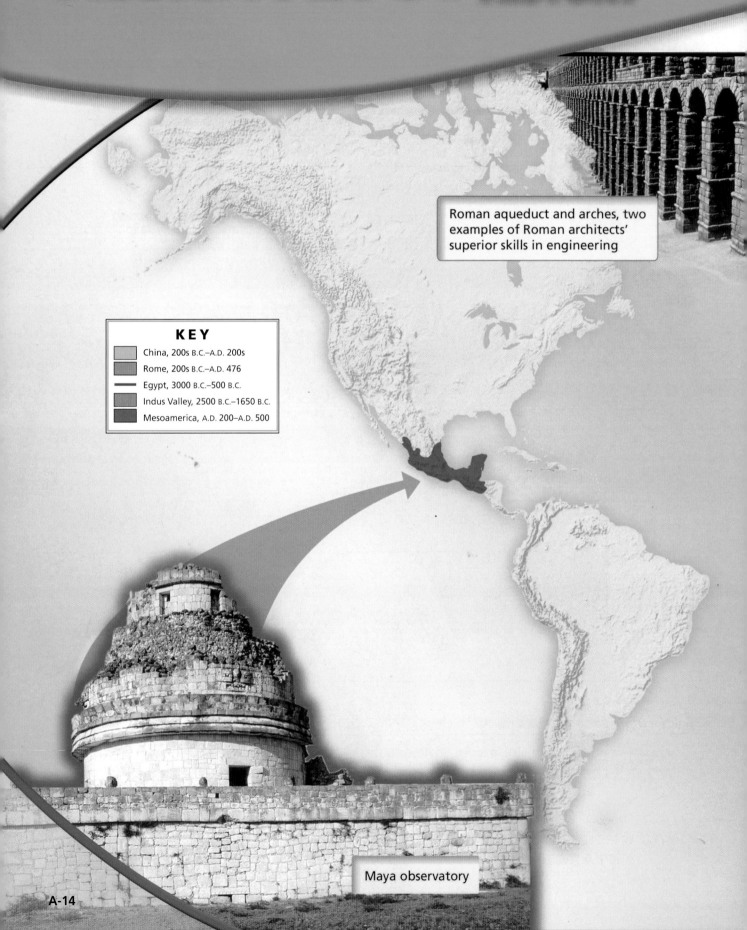

Roman aqueduct and arches, two examples of Roman architects' superior skills in engineering

**KEY**

- China, 200s B.C.–A.D. 200s
- Rome, 200s B.C.–A.D. 476
- Egypt, 3000 B.C.–500 B.C.
- Indus Valley, 2500 B.C.–1650 B.C.
- Mesoamerica, A.D. 200–A.D. 500

Maya observatory

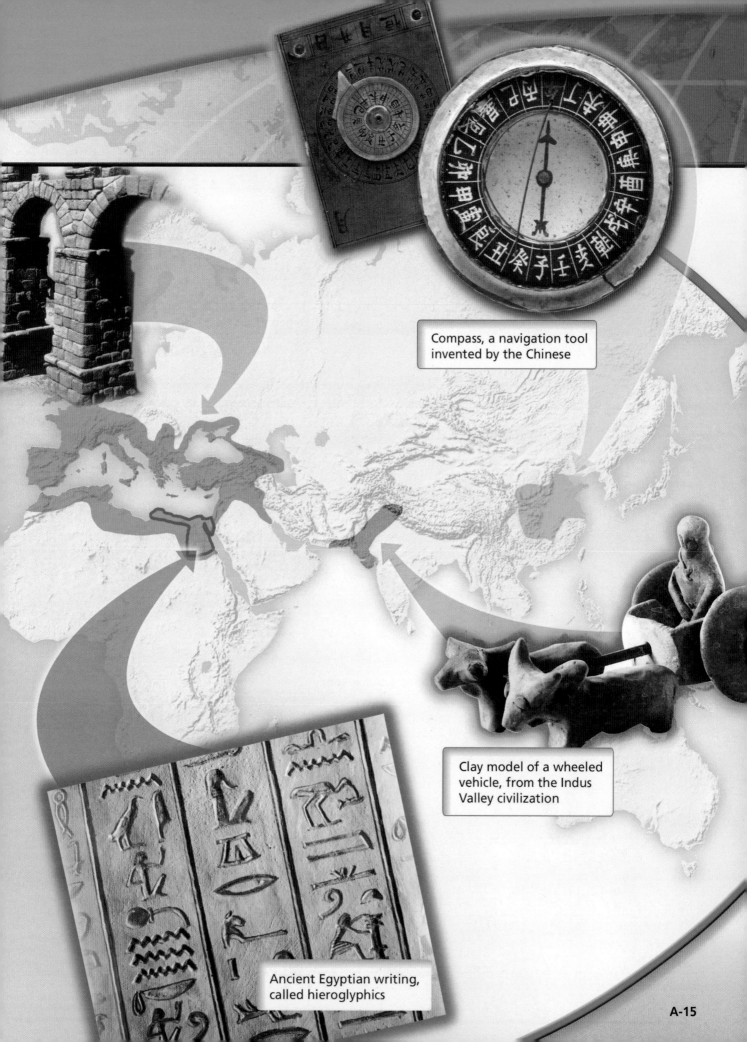

Compass, a navigation tool invented by the Chinese

Clay model of a wheeled vehicle, from the Indus Valley civilization

Ancient Egyptian writing, called hieroglyphics

# DEVELOPMENT OF IDEAS

## Greece (950 B.C. – 325 B.C.)

Democracy, Mathematics,
Architecture, Art

Greek pottery

Roman aqueduct

## Rome (500 B.C. – A.D. 500)

Republicanism, Engineering, Court System
and Written Law Code

Roman coin, saying,
"Senate and the People"

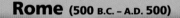

Maya numbers

## Maya (A.D. 250 – A.D. 900)

Astronomy, Mathematics

## China (550 B.C. – A.D. 300)

Confucianism, Civil Service,
Currency

Confucius

Herbs for medicine

## India (325 B.C. – A.D. 540)

Mathematics, Astronomy, Medicine

Ginger for medicine

| 900 B.C. | 600 B.C. | 300 B.C. | A.D. 300 | A.D. 600 | A.D. 900 |

CALIFORNIA

# Prentice Hall
# ANCIENT
# CIVILIZATIONS

PEARSON

Prentice Hall

Upper Saddle River, New Jersey
Needham, Massachusetts

*Author*
Diane Hart

Acknowledgments appear on page 650, which constitutes an extension of this copyright page.

ISBN 0-13-181746-9

1 2 3 4 5 6 7 8 9 10    09  08  07  06  05

# Author

## Diane Hart

Diane Hart is a writer and consultant in history and social studies. She earned bachelor's and master's degrees in history from Stanford University and was a Woodrow Wilson Fellow.

As a former teacher at the elementary, secondary, and college levels, Ms. Hart remains deeply involved in social studies education through her active participation in both the National and California Councils for the Social Studies. She has written a number of textbooks for middle school students.

# Senior Reading Consultants

## Kate Kinsella

Kate Kinsella, Ed.D., is a faculty member in the Department of Secondary Education at San Francisco State University. A specialist in second-language acquisition and adolescent literacy, she teaches coursework addressing language and literacy development across the secondary curricula. Dr. Kinsella earned her master's degree in TESOL from San Francisco State University and her Ed.D. in Second Language Acquisition from the University of San Francisco.

## Kevin Feldman

Kevin Feldman, Ed.D., is the Director of Reading and Early Intervention with the Sonoma County Office of Education (SCOE) and an independent educational consultant. At the SCOE, he develops, organizes, and monitors programs related to K–12 literacy. Dr. Feldman has a master's degree from the University of California, Riverside, in Special Education, Learning Disabilities, and Instructional Design. He earned his Ed.D. in Curriculum and Instruction from the University of San Francisco.

# Table of Contents

# Unit 1 The Beginnings of Humankind . . 1

**Standards Preview**

## History-Social Science

**6.1** Students describe what is known through archaeological studies of the early physical and cultural development of humankind from the Paleolithic era to the agricultural revolution.

**6.2** Students analyze the geographic, political, economic, religious, and social structures of the early civilizations of Mesopotamia, Egypt, and Kush.

**6.3** Students analyze the geographic, political, economic, religious, and social structures of the Ancient Hebrews.

Liu River, China

# Explore the past through the power of technology.

**MAP MASTER**

Develop geographic literacy through dynamic map skills instruction. Learn map skills and interact with every map online and on CD-ROM.

**Discovery School Video**

Visit the times and places you are studying in world history with a high-impact video program, created to enhance your experience with this book by our partner Discovery School.

**PRENTICE HALL StudentEXPRESS**
Learn · Study · Succeed

Activate your learning with a suite of tools online and on CD-ROM:
• Interactive Textbook
• Reading and Notetaking Study Guide
• Social Studies Skills Tutor
• Web Resources

**History Interactive**

Launch into an interactive adventure online—using special graphics in this book as jumping-off points—to extend your understanding of world history.

# Table of Contents

CALIFORNIA **Standards Preview**

**History-Social Science**

**6.2** Students analyze the geographic, political, economic, religious, and social structures of the early civilizations of Mesopotamia, Egypt, and Kush.

**6.3** Students analyze the geographic, political, economic, religious, and social structures of the Ancient Hebrews.

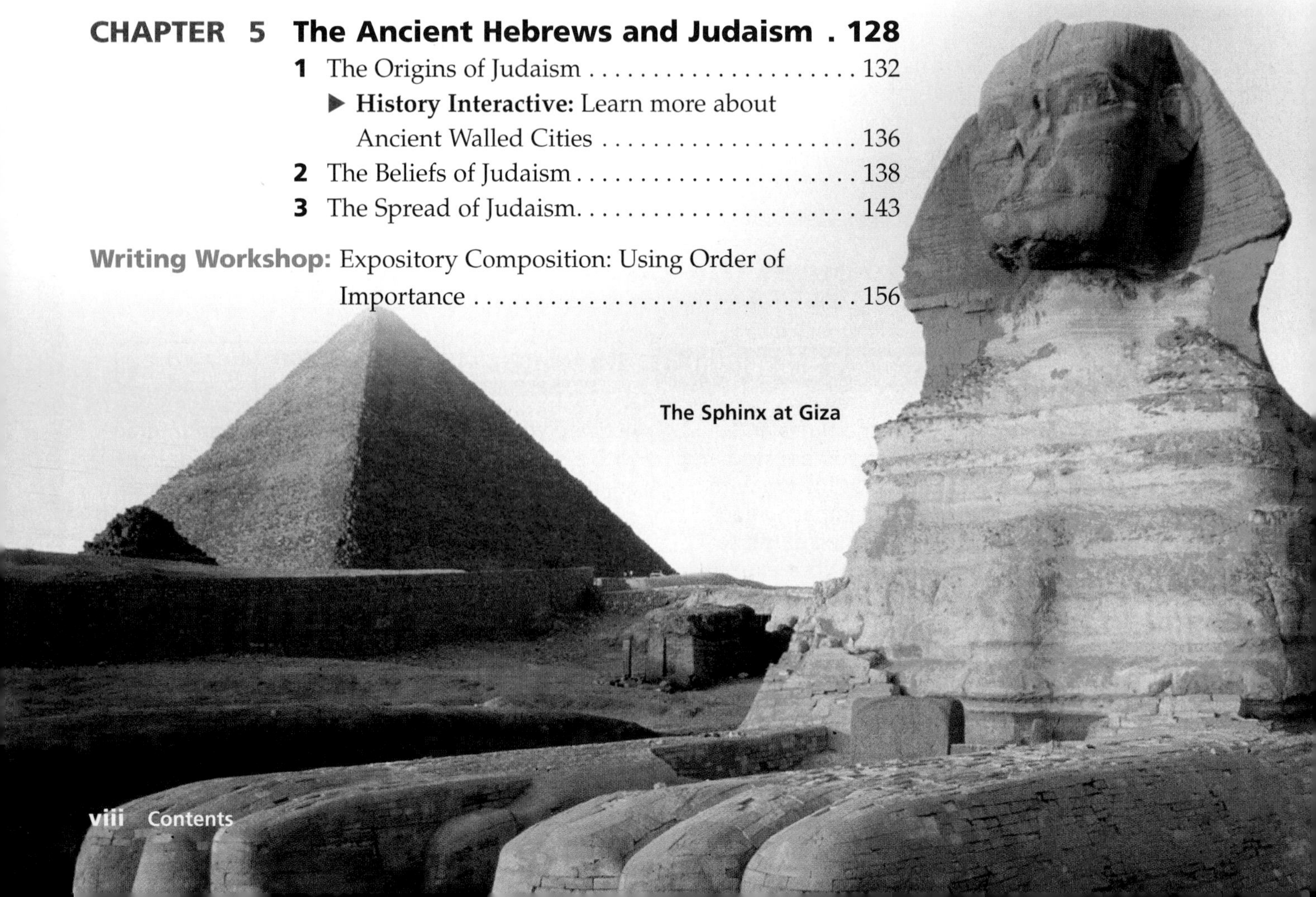

**The Sphinx at Giza**

**History-Social Science**

**6.5** Students analyze the geographic, political, economic, religious, and social structures of the early civilizations of India.

Visitors to a Hindu temple in India

Postage stamp honoring Chandragupta Maurya

4.00 चन्द्रगुप्त मौर्य **INDIA**
CHANDRAGUPTA MAURYA

# Table of Contents

**Standards Preview**

**History-Social Science**

**6.6** Students analyze the geographic, political, economic, religious, and social structures of the early civilizations of China.

**Great Wall of China**

# Unit 5 Ancient Greece............ 352

**Standards Preview**

**History-Social Science**

**6.4** Students analyze the geographic, political, economic, religious, and social structures of the early civilizations of Ancient Greece.

Greek vase

The Parthenon, Athens

# Table of Contents

**Standards Preview**

## History-Social Science

**6.7** Students analyze the geographic, political, economic, religious, and social structures during the development of Rome.

The Colosseum, Rome

# Special Features

## History Reading Skills

Enhance your ability to read and understand textbooks by building reading skills.

## Analysis Skills

Build skills that will help you analyze world history content.

## Writing Workshop

Develop your writing skills through step-by-step instruction and practice.

## Literature

Experience world history through works of literature.

# Special Features (continued)

## Discovery School Video

Visit the past through these high-impact video stories.

## Citizen Heroes

Meet people who have made a difference in the lives of others.

Search for answers to mysteries about key people in world history.

Ruth

Confucius

# History *Interactive*

**Launch into an interactive adventure to extend your understanding of world history.**

# LIFE AT THE TIME

**Learn more about how people lived at different places and times.**

**Activate Your Learning:**
**History Interactive** Launch into an interactive adventure to extend your understanding of world history. Go online to explore each chapter's History Interactive. Use the Web Code provided to gain direct access to these activities.

**How to use the Web Code:**
1. Go to **www.PHSchool.com**
2. Enter the **Web Code**
3. Click go!

# Maps

## MAP★MASTER™

**Interact with world history maps in your textbook and online.**

## MAP★MASTER™ INTERACTIVE

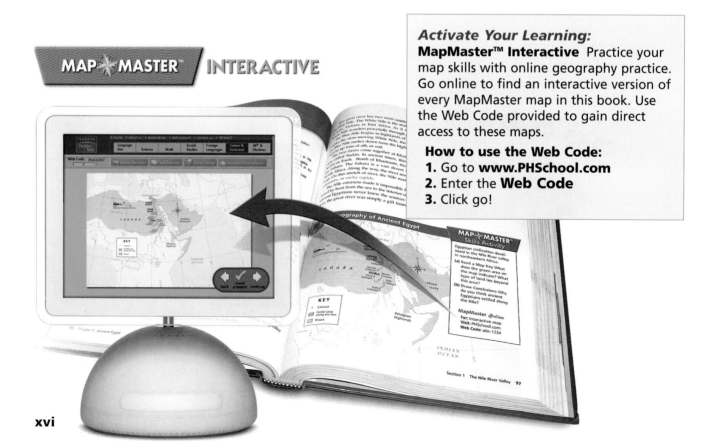

**Activate Your Learning:**
**MapMaster™ Interactive** Practice your map skills with online geography practice. Go online to find an interactive version of every MapMaster map in this book. Use the Web Code provided to gain direct access to these maps.

**How to use the Web Code:**
1. Go to **www.PHSchool.com**
2. Enter the **Web Code**
3. Click go!

## Illustrated Atlas of World History

Understand your world by comparing maps of the world today with historical maps.

## Origins of Agriculture

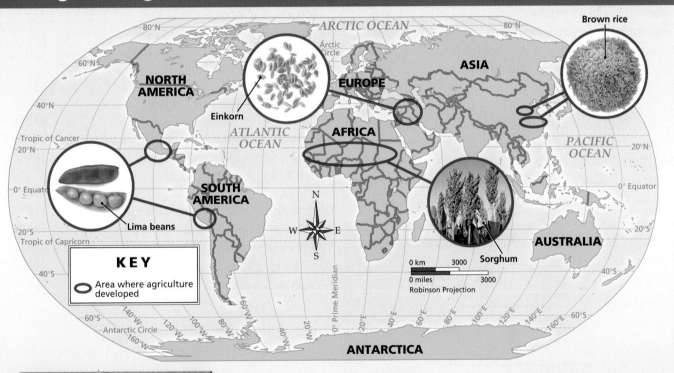

**KEY**

⬭ Area where agriculture developed

## MAP★MASTER
### Skills Activity

Early people learned to farm in many different parts of the world.

**(a) Identify** Where did early farmers grow sorghum?

**(b) Distinguish Relevant Information** Which continents had the greatest number of areas where people learned to farm? Which had the fewest?

**MapMaster ●nline**

**For:** Interactive map
**Visit:** PHSchool.com
**Web Code:** abc-1234

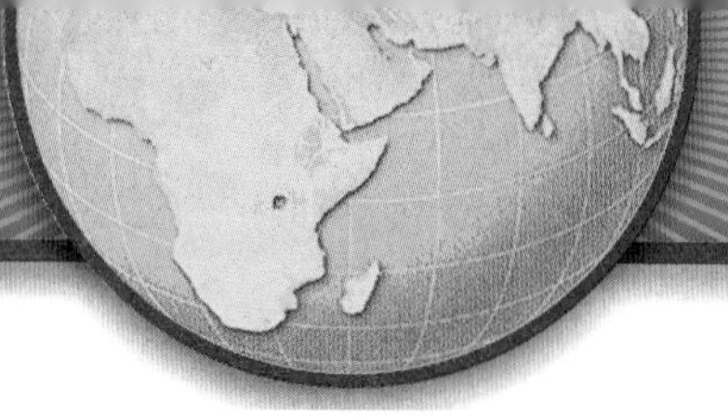

# Charts and Graphs

## Charts, Graphs, and Diagrams

**Expand your knowledge of world history by analyzing data and information.**



**Egypt's Social Pyramid**

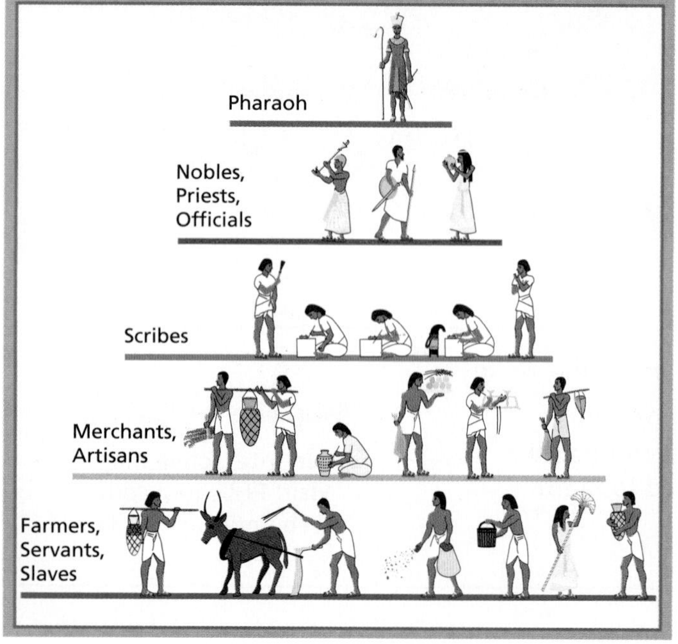

Pharaoh
Nobles, Priests, Officials
Scribes
Merchants, Artisans
Farmers, Servants, Slaves


## Timelines

# In-Text Sources

Gain insights by examining documents, eye-witness accounts, and other sources as you read the chapters of this textbook.

**❝** Every man make up his mind to fight
And move on his enemy! Strong as I am
It's hard for me to face so many men
And fight with all at once . . .
And yet I will! **❞**

—Homer, *Iliad*

*continued*

# Primary Sources (continued)

> **"**This soul of mine within the heart
> is smaller than a grain of rice. . . .
> This soul of mine within the heart
> is . . . greater than the sky. . . .**"**
>
> —The Thirteen Principal Upanishads

# **Primary** Sources

**Connect to the past through primary sources and literature in the Reference Section.**

Shi Huangdi

# History-Social Science Standards Guide for Students

Here is a complete list of the Grade 6 History-Social Science Standards so that you know what you will learn this year.

## CONTENT STANDARDS

**6.1** Students describe what is known through archaeological studies of the early physical and cultural development of humankind from the Paleolithic era to the agricultural revolution.

### What It Means to You

Early humans were not very fast or strong, but they were smart enough to create tools. Early humans gradually spread across Earth. They also learned how to farm and how to raise animals. These amazing accomplishments made our way of life today possible.

| California Standards | What You Will Learn |
|---|---|
| 6.1.1 Describe the hunter-gatherer societies, including the development of tools and the use of fire. | You will learn how the earliest humans ate what they could hunt and gather. In particular, you will learn how using fire and making tools helped change their lives. |
| 6.1.2 Identify the locations of human communities that populated the major regions of the world and describe how humans adapted to a variety of environments. | You will learn where early peoples settled in different parts of the world. You will see that early peoples lived in many types of surroundings. In each area, they learned how to live in the natural environment and how to use available resources. |
| 6.1.3 Discuss the climatic changes and human modifications of the physical environment that gave rise to the domestication of plants and animals and new sources of clothing and shelter. | Several ice ages changed the land and climate. You will see how early peoples learned to farm and learned how to domesticate animals. This led to new ways of making clothes and building homes. |

**6.2** Students analyze the geographic, political, economic, religious, and social structures of the early civilizations of Mesopotamia, Egypt, and Kush.

**What It Means to You**

Three early civilizations—Mesopotamia, Egypt, and Kush—arose in Africa and in southwest Asia. The peoples of these lands made major contributions to the world that we can still see today. They built incredible structures, such as the Egyptian pyramids. They created the world's first law codes. And they developed methods of writing that made it possible to keep records. Because of these records, we have been able to learn a great deal about the lives of these ancient peoples.

| California Standards | What You Will Learn |
| --- | --- |
| 6.2.1 Locate and describe the major river systems and discuss the physical settings that supported permanent settlement and early civilizations. | You will study the Nile and Tigris-Euphrates river valleys, where early civilizations grew. You will discover why these valleys were good places to live. |
| 6.2.2 Trace the development of agricultural techniques that permitted the production of economic surplus and the emergence of cities as centers of culture and power. | You will see how farmers learned to control river water and to irrigate the land. You will also discover how growing more food led to the growth of the first cities. |
| 6.2.3 Understand the relationship between religion and the social and political order in Mesopotamia and Egypt. | In Mesopotamia and Egypt, rulers claimed to be gods or servants of gods. Everyone else was expected to serve these god-kings. |

Today, shepherds still raise sheep.

| California Standards | What You Will Learn |
|---|---|
| **6.2.4** Know the significance of Hammurabi's Code. | You will learn that a ruler named Hammurabi created one of the first known law codes. |
| **6.2.5** Discuss the main features of Egyptian art and architecture. | You will learn about the temples and the great Age of Pyramids in Egypt. You will also learn about Egyptian painting and sculpture. |
| **6.2.6** Describe the role of Egyptian trade in the eastern Mediterranean and Nile valley. | You will learn how trade grew. Egyptians traded food for goods produced in other lands. |
| **6.2.7** Understand the significance of Queen Hatshepsut and Ramses the Great. | You will find out how two powerful rulers—Queen Hatshepsut and Ramses the Great—worked to expand the power of Egypt. |
| **6.2.8** Identify the location of the Kush civilization and describe its political, commercial, and cultural relations with Egypt. | The Kush civilization was located south of Egypt. These two neighbors traded with each other, had cultural exchanges, and sometimes fought each other. |
| **6.2.9** Trace the evolution of language and its written forms. | You will learn that writing began as a way to keep records, first as simple drawings and later as an alphabet of letters. |

**Abu Simbel, a temple built by Ramses II**

**6.3** Students analyze the geographic, political, economic, religious, and social structures of the Ancient Hebrews.

## What It Means to You

The ancient Hebrews developed Judaism, the first religion based on a belief in one God. The belief in one God was also the foundation of two later world religions: Christianity and Islam. The beliefs and values of Judaism have contributed to many of the key ideas of Western civilization.

| California Standards | What You Will Learn |
| --- | --- |
| 6.3.1 Describe the origins and significance of Judaism as the first monotheistic religion based on the concept of one God who sets down moral laws for humanity. | You will learn that unlike their neighbors who worshiped many gods, the ancient Hebrews believed that there was one God who set rules of what is right and good. |
| 6.3.2 Identify the sources of the ethical teachings and central beliefs of Judaism (the Hebrew Bible, the Commentaries): belief in God, observance of law, practice of the concepts of righteousness and justice, and importance of study; and describe how the ideas of the Hebrew traditions are reflected in the moral and ethical traditions of Western civilization. | You will learn about the main beliefs and practices of Judaism. You will see how the Jewish concepts of right and wrong and the importance of learning continue to influence people even today. |
| 6.3.3 Explain the significance of Abraham, Moses, Naomi, Ruth, David, and Yohanan ben Zaccai in the development of the Jewish religion. | You will learn about some important men and women in Jewish history. |
| 6.3.4 Discuss the locations of the settlements and movements of Hebrew peoples, including the Exodus and their movement to and from Egypt, and outline the significance of the Exodus to the Jewish and other people. | You will learn where the early Hebrews lived. You will see why they settled in Egypt but later fled from there in a migration known as the Exodus. You will learn why the Exodus is a major event in Jewish history. |
| 6.3.5 Discuss how Judaism survived and developed despite the continuing dispersion of much of the Jewish population from Jerusalem and the rest of Israel after the destruction of the second Temple in A.D. 70. | You will learn how Jews were able to continue practicing their traditions and religion even after they were forced to leave their homeland in A.D. 70. |

**6.4** Students analyze the geographic, political, economic, religious, and social structures of the early civilizations of Ancient Greece.

## What It Means to You

Many ideas that are important to us today had their start in ancient Greece. These include the ideas of democracy and citizenship and the notion that things can be proved through human reasoning and logic.

| California Standards | What You Will Learn |
| --- | --- |
| **6.4.1** Discuss the connections between geography and the development of city-states in the region of the Aegean Sea, including patterns of trade and commerce among Greek city-states and within the wider Mediterranean region. | You will learn that geographic obstacles divided the Greeks and led to the creation of separate independent city-states. Geographic conditions helped the Greeks carry on trade by traveling the seas around their islands. |
| **6.4.2** Trace the transition from tyranny and oligarchy to early democratic forms of government and back to dictatorship in ancient Greece, including the significance of the invention of the idea of citizenship (e.g., from *Pericles' Funeral Oration*). | You will learn that the Greeks practiced different forms of government. Power might be held by a single person, by a small group of people, or by all citizens. The Greeks of some city-states increased the role of ordinary people in government. |
| **6.4.3** State the key differences between Athenian, or direct, democracy and representative democracy. | You will learn the difference between a democracy in which citizens make laws themselves and a democracy in which citizens elect others to make laws for them. |

**The coastline of Greece**

| California Standards | What You Will Learn |
|---|---|
| 6.4.4 Explain the significance of Greek mythology to the everyday life of people in the region and how Greek literature continues to permeate our literature and language today, drawing from Greek mythology and epics, such as Homer's *Iliad* and *Odyssey*, and from *Aesop's Fables*. | The Greeks told stories of gods and heroes to explain how the world worked, to teach lessons, and to entertain. Tales of Zeus, Athena, Hercules, and others are familiar to us today because ancient Greek mythology remains an enduring part of Western literature. |
| 6.4.5 Outline the founding, expansion, and political organization of the Persian Empire. | You will learn how the Persians created an empire by conquering other lands. You will also learn how Persian rulers governed their vast empire. |
| 6.4.6 Compare and contrast life in Athens and Sparta, with emphasis on their roles in the Persian and Peloponnesian Wars. | You will examine Sparta, a warrior state, and Athens, a democracy. You will learn how these city-states joined forces to battle the Persians but later went to war against each other. |
| 6.4.7 Trace the rise of Alexander the Great and the spread of Greek culture eastward and into Egypt. | Alexander built an empire by conquering Persia, Egypt, and other lands. He spread Greek culture eastward and mixed it with the cultures of the lands that he conquered. |
| 6.4.8 Describe the enduring contributions of important Greek figures in the arts and sciences (e.g., Hypatia, Socrates, Plato, Aristotle, Euclid, Thucydides). | You will become acquainted with some of the Greeks whose names are still remembered for their work in mathematics, science, philosophy, and history. |

**6.5** Students analyze the geographic, political, economic, religious, and social structures of the early civilizations of India.

### What It Means to You

The ancient Indians made major contributions to world history, including two major world religions—Hinduism and Buddhism—and important developments in medicine and in mathematics. Today, more than one billion people live in India. It is the world's largest democracy and second-most populous country after China.

| California Standards | What You Will Learn |
|---|---|
| **6.5.1** Locate and describe the major river system and discuss the physical setting that supported the rise of this civilization. | You will learn that the earliest civilization in India developed in the Indus River valley, where there was water and fertile soil for farming. |
| **6.5.2** Discuss the significance of the Aryan invasions. | You will learn that Aryans from the north invaded India. Cultural blending occurred. The Aryans produced a thriving civilization with achievements in the arts, sciences, and religion. |
| **6.5.3** Explain the major beliefs and practices of Brahmanism in India and how they evolved into early Hinduism. | You will learn how Brahmanism, an ancient religion in India, laid the foundation for Hinduism. |
| **6.5.4** Outline the social structure of the caste system. | The Hindu caste system divided people according to who their parents were and the kind of work they did. It became a strict class system in which people were born into a certain class that they could not change. |

| California Standards | What You Will Learn |
|---|---|
| 6.5.5 Know the life and moral teachings of the Buddha and how Buddhism spread in India, Ceylon, and Central Asia. | You will learn that Buddha adapted Hindu traditions to develop a new religion. Buddhism declined in India, but it spread through Asia, becoming one of the major world religions. |
| 6.5.6 Describe the growth of the Maurya empire and the political and moral achievements of the emperor Asoka. | You will find out about Maurya, the first great Indian empire. Its leader, Asoka, rejected violence and helped unite the people of his empire. |
| 6.5.7 Discuss important aesthetic and intellectual traditions (e.g., Sanskrit literature, including the *Bhagavad Gita;* medicine; metallurgy; and mathematics, including Hindu-Arabic numerals and the zero). | You will learn that India made many advances in medicine, metalworking, and mathematics. You will also read about Indian literature, including a famous work called the *Bhagavad Gita.* |

**The Buddha teaching at Deer Park**

**6.6** Students analyze the geographic, political, economic, religious, and social structures of the early civilizations of China.

**What It Means to You**

Today, China's one billion people make up about one fifth of the world's population. The nation has a growing economy and is ruled by a communist dictatorship. Understanding the geography of China and the origins of Chinese culture will help you understand this people, who have a significant influence in the world today.

| California Standards | What You Will Learn |
| --- | --- |
| 6.6.1 Locate and describe the origins of Chinese civilization in the Huang-He Valley during the Shang Dynasty. | Like other early civilizations, China's first civilization developed in the fertile river valleys that could support large populations. |
| 6.6.2 Explain the geographic features of China that made governance and the spread of ideas and goods difficult and served to isolate the country from the rest of the world. | You will learn that geographic barriers made it difficult for the people of ancient China to trade with people of other lands. Geographic obstacles also made it hard for Chinese rulers to govern outlying regions. |
| 6.6.3 Know about the life of Confucius and the fundamental teachings of Confucianism and Daoism. | You will learn about the ideas of Confucius, which have influenced the Chinese for thousands of years. You will also learn about Daoism, a religion whose followers try to live in harmony with nature. |
| 6.6.4 Identify the political and cultural problems prevalent in the time of Confucius and how he sought to solve them. | About 500 B.C., China faced many problems, including war and poor government. You will learn how Confucius said that leaders and their people should behave so as to bring peace and order. |

| California Standards | What You Will Learn |
|---|---|
| **6.6.5** List the policies and achievements of the emperor Shi Huangdi in unifying northern China under the Qin Dynasty. | You will learn how the emperor Shi Huangdi unified China. He urged people to use one type of money and one writing system. He directed construction of the Great Wall. |
| **6.6.6** Detail the political contributions of the Han Dynasty to the development of the imperial bureaucratic state and the expansion of the empire. | You will learn how the Han Dynasty introduced a new way of choosing people for government jobs. You will also learn how it strengthened and expanded the empire through war and trade. |
| **6.6.7** Cite the significance of the trans-Eurasian "silk roads" in the period of the Han Dynasty and Roman Empire and their locations. | You will trace the route of the Silk Road that linked China to southwestern Asia and beyond. The Silk Road allowed for the exchange of trade goods and ideas. |
| **6.6.8** Describe the diffusion of Buddhism northward to China during the Han Dynasty. | You will trace how Buddhism spread to China during the Han Dynasty. The Chinese people took these ideas and created their own form of Buddhism. |

**A Buddhist statue**

**6.7** Students analyze the geographic, political, economic, religious, and social structures during the development of Rome.

## What It Means to You

The Roman Empire left many lasting contributions, including advances in ways of building that you can still see in large structures today. Also, Roman ideas about government strongly influenced the writers of the United States Constitution, the basis of our nation's government.

| California Standards | What You Will Learn |
|---|---|
| **6.7.1** Identify the location and describe the rise of the Roman Republic, including the importance of such mythical and historical figures as Aeneas, Romulus and Remus, Cincinnatus, Julius Caesar, and Cicero. | You will locate Rome on the map and see how its central location helped it expand in the Mediterranean. You will also learn about historical and legendary people who were important to the rise of the Roman Republic. |
| **6.7.2** Describe the government of the Roman Republic and its significance (e.g., written constitution and tripartite government, checks and balances, civic duty). | You will learn that in the Roman Republic, the people had some say in government. The Roman Republic encouraged leaders to share power and tried to prevent them from gaining too much power. |
| **6.7.3** Identify the location of and the political and geographic reasons for the growth of Roman territories and expansion of the empire, including how the empire fostered economic growth through the use of currency and trade routes. | You will find out that Rome acquired an empire by expanding in every direction through war and trade. Through control of trade routes, Rome became wealthy and powerful. |

Caesar crosses the Rubicon

| California Standards | What You Will Learn |
|---|---|
| **6.7.4** Discuss the influence of Julius Caesar and Augustus in Rome's transition from republic to empire. | You will learn about Julius Caesar's career as a military leader and dictator. You will also learn about Augustus, who laid the foundation for a powerful government under the rule of emperors. |
| **6.7.5** Trace the migration of Jews around the Mediterranean region and the effects of their conflict with the Romans, including the Romans' restrictions on their right to live in Jerusalem. | You will learn that Jews rebelled against Roman rule. The Romans forced them to leave Jerusalem. Jewish people settled throughout the region around the Mediterranean Sea. |
| **6.7.6** Note the origins of Christianity in the Jewish Messianic prophecies, the life and teachings of Jesus of Nazareth as described in the New Testament, and the contribution of St. Paul the Apostle to the definition and spread of Christian beliefs (e.g., belief in the Trinity, resurrection, salvation). | You will examine Jesus' early life and his teachings, as they are described in the New Testament. Paul and others helped spread Jesus' teachings so that Christianity eventually became a world religion. You will learn about the main beliefs of Christianity. |
| **6.7.7** Describe the circumstances that led to the spread of Christianity in Europe and other Roman territories. | You will learn about the conditions that helped Christianity spread through the Roman Empire's lands in Europe, Africa, and Asia. |
| **6.7.8** Discuss the legacies of Roman art and architecture, technology and science, literature, language, and law. | You will learn how Roman civilization still influences the world today. Roman law is the basis of legal systems in Europe, Latin America, and the United States. English and other modern languages owe much to Latin, the language of the Romans. The Romans also developed skills in building that we still rely on today. |

# HISTORICAL AND SOCIAL SCIENCES ANALYSIS SKILLS
## Chronological and Spatial Thinking

| California Standards | What You Will Learn |
| --- | --- |
| **1.** Students explain how major events are related to one another in time. | You will learn how to relate events to one another in terms of when they took place. This will help you see how some events cause other events. |
| **2.** Students construct various time lines of key events, people, and periods of the historical era they are studying. | Working with timelines will help you understand the order of events, the amount of time between events, and the role people played in the events. |
| **3.** Students use a variety of maps and documents to identify physical and cultural features of neighborhoods, cities, states, and countries and to explain the historical migration of people, expansion and disintegration of empires, and the growth of economic systems. | Maps and historical documents help you understand historical events and see patterns. They help you draw conclusions from what you see and read. You will use different kinds of maps to identify places and their features. You will use visuals and documents to trace the movements of people, the rise and fall of empires, and the growth of economic systems. |

# Research, Evidence, and Point of View

| California Standards | What You Will Learn |
| --- | --- |
| **1.** Students frame questions that can be answered by historical study and research. | You will learn to ask questions about people, places, and events and why they are important. This will help you study and do research more easily. |
| **2.** Students distinguish fact from opinion in historical narratives and stories. | You will learn to tell the difference between statements that can be proved and statements that express an opinion. |
| **3.** Students distinguish relevant from irrelevant information, essential from incidental information, and verifiable from unverifiable information in historical narratives and stories. | Not all information has the same importance. Minor details may be interesting, but they may not be important to the main idea. You will learn to separate main ideas and important details from minor ideas and unimportant details. You will also learn to tell the difference between information that can be proved and information that cannot be proved. |
| **4.** Students assess the credibility of primary and secondary sources and draw sound conclusions from them. | You will read primary sources, which are created by eyewitnesses to an event, and secondary sources, which are created later by people who did not witness the event. You will learn to detect exaggerations, distortions, biases, and missing details that reduce the reliability of sources. You will analyze the sources to come up with your own valid interpretations of the past. |
| **5.** Students detect the different historical points of view on historical events and determine the context in which the historical statements were made (the questions asked, sources used, author's perspectives). | You will learn to identify points of view or opinions of people in history. You will learn to tell the difference between facts and opinions and to look for clues that show a one-sided view. You will learn to think about how the writer's experiences and way of life affect his or her point of view. |

# Historical Interpretation

| California Standards | What You Will Learn |
|---|---|
| **1.** Students explain the central issues and problems from the past, placing people and events in a matrix of time and place. | You will learn to explain the main issues and problems in history. Knowing where and when people lived and where and when events took place will help you do this. |
| **2.** Students understand and distinguish cause, effect, sequence, and correlation in historical events, including the long- and short-term causal relations. | You will learn to see the relationships between events. These include cause-and-effect connections. You will see that some effects happen soon and that others happen only after a long time has passed. Finally, you will see that sometimes, although one event happened before another event, the first event did not cause the second event. |
| **3.** Students explain the sources of historical continuity and how the combination of ideas and events explains the emergence of new patterns. | You will learn to analyze trends and patterns of events and to make predictions. Sometimes things continue as they have been, and sometimes new patterns appear. |

| California Standards | What You Will Learn |
|---|---|
| 4. Students recognize the role of chance, oversight, and error in history. | You will learn that, in history, sometimes things go wrong. They may go wrong because of a chance event, such as a severe storm; because a person fails to do something that he or she should have done; or because a person simply makes a mistake, which changes the way things turn out. |
| 5. Students recognize that interpretations of history are subject to change as new information is uncovered. | You will learn that our understanding of the past is always changing. Whenever new information is uncovered, historians must rethink their ideas about what happened and why it happened. |
| 6. Students interpret basic indicators of economic performance and conduct cost-benefit analyses of economic and political issues. | You will learn how to evaluate the health of an economy on the basis of its economic data. Throughout history, people have had to solve problems and make decisions. To do this, they had to judge whether the good effects that could result from a decision would outweigh any bad effects that might result. |

# Tools to help you along the way...

## Taking Notes

In history, there's a lot to read about and a lot to understand. Taking good notes is one way to help you remember key ideas and to see the big picture. This program has two ways to help you.

You can keep your notes in the *Interactive Reading and Notetaking Study Guide*. Or you can go online to take your notes. Either way, you will be able to record what you are learning. And, by the end of the year, you'll have created a perfect study tool.

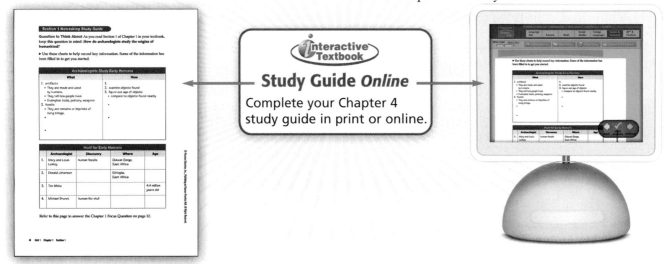

**Study Guide *Online***

Complete your Chapter 4 study guide in print or online.

## Monitor Your Progress

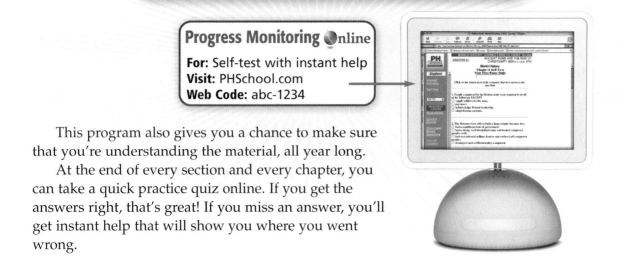

**Progress Monitoring Online**

**For:** Self-test with instant help
**Visit:** PHSchool.com
**Web Code:** abc-1234

This program also gives you a chance to make sure that you're understanding the material, all year long.

At the end of every section and every chapter, you can take a quick practice quiz online. If you get the answers right, that's great! If you miss an answer, you'll get instant help that will show you where you went wrong.

# Historian's Toolkit

## Introduction: Studying Our Past

This year, you will learn about the great civilizations of the ancient world. You will find out who built the great pyramids of Egypt, how the rulers of China and Rome conquered huge empires, and why powerful ideas such as the Ten Commandments and Greek democracy shaped the world.

But why should you study history? One American historian, David McCullough, warns that not knowing about the past is "like a creeping disease."

> **❝Everything we have, all our great institutions, hospitals, universities, libraries, this city, our laws, our music, art, poetry, our freedoms, everything is because somebody went before us and did the hard work. . . . Indifference to history isn't just ignorant, it's rude. It's a form of ingratitude.❞**
>
> — David McCullough, *Why History?*

Historians like McCullough use many methods to help us learn from the past. They do not simply collect names and dates. Instead, they explore important questions and issues of the past in order to find out how people lived and why they made the decisions they did. Historians also consider how the past is linked to our lives today.

In the next few pages, you will learn to think like a historian. You will also have the chance to try some of the tools historians use. Your Historian's Toolkit can make your study of ancient history easier and more rewarding.

**Egyptian mummy case**

## Historical Evidence

Historians use many types of evidence to learn about the past. This evidence can be divided into primary sources and secondary sources.

**Primary Sources** A primary source is firsthand information about people or events. Primary sources include official documents, such as laws and public speeches, as well as eyewitness accounts, such as diaries, letters, and autobiographies. Primary sources may also include visual evidence, such as news photographs or videotapes.

Another type of primary source is an artifact. This is an item left behind by people in the past. An artifact could be a statue, a tool, or an everyday object.

Primary sources are valuable because they were created at the time an event occurred. This does not necessarily make them "true," though. Primary sources are created by people and may simply reflect the point of view of those who created them. The source might have been made to impress someone or to make the creator seem to be an expert or for some other personal reason. So, you can see that even primary sources must be evaluated carefully and considered in relation to other sources on the same subject.

**Secondary Sources** Historians also use secondary sources. These are sources created by someone who did not actually witness the events. Secondary sources include news articles and biographies. This textbook, too, is a secondary source. The author gathered information from many sources to reach an understanding of what happened and why it happened. Then, she wrote her interpretation of events.

## Types of Historical Sources

| Type of Source | Description | Examples |
|---|---|---|
| **Primary Sources** | • Direct evidence about event<br>• Limited viewpoint<br>• May be reliable or unreliable<br>• Includes objects left behind by people | • Official documents<br>• Letters and diaries<br>• Speeches and autobiographies<br>• Photographs<br>• Artifacts:<br>  • Tools and weapons<br>  • Religious objects<br>  • Statues and other art |
| **Secondary Sources** | • Secondhand information about event<br>• Uses primary sources to create broader picture<br>• May be reliable or unreliable | • History books<br>• Biographies<br>• Encyclopedias and other reference works<br>• Internet Web sites |

# Using Historical Sources

Learning about history starts with asking questions. You, as a student, might be accustomed to the types of questions you are asked in your textbook or by your teacher. But historians ask questions the way a detective would. Each answer is a clue that leads to another question. The questions and answers will bring the historian to an understanding of events in the past.

Consider this situation: Jake visited a nearby history museum with his family. In one display case, he saw a very old letter, written in a language he couldn't read. Beside the letter was a copy that had been translated into English.

Reading the letter, Jake asked himself many questions. Some of his questions are shown at right. Trying to find the answers to the questions is the same sort of thinking that historians use to find out about the past.

Dear Aunt Lavinia,

Everyone is telling me not to be afraid, but I think they are foolish. The Huns are at the gates of Rome, threatening to enter at any moment.

We hear stories of death and destruction wherever the invading armies go. They have already sacked many villages. Food is becoming scarce because they have ripped up the fields. There remains only the grain stored in our own storehouse.

Mother and Father are not sure that the Emperor's armies can protect us. They have packed a box with our most precious things so that we can escape quickly. Please be ready to receive us, if we can get away from here with our lives.

Your loving niece,
Portia

← Who are the Huns?

← What happens when armies "sack" a city?

← Where could the family go to escape from Rome?

Jake may follow several steps to find the answers to his questions:

■ **Read and observe.** Jake can search for further information about the Huns in primary and secondary sources. He might look on a map to discover where Portia lived and where she wanted to flee.

■ **Speculate.** Jake might make some guesses, called hypotheses, about the answers to his questions, to help him get started.

■ **Evaluate evidence.** As Jake uncovers more information, he will test his hypotheses against the information he finds. He can always change his hypotheses as he learns more.

■ **Draw conclusions.** Jake states what he believes are the final answers to his questions.

To start his search, though, Jake will first go to the library media center. On the next pages, you will see what he finds there.

> From the encyclopedia, Jake finds out that the Huns invaded the Roman Empire, which had lasted more than 500 years and ended around the year 476.

> Jake's search in the atlas will probably reveal the fact that the Huns began to invade Rome in the year 434. This raises a new question. The encyclopedia said that the Roman Empire ended around the year 476. Does this mean that the Huns beat the Romans and ended their empire?

The library media center will have many types of sources to help Jake find the answers to his questions.

Jake might start with an encyclopedia in print or on the Internet to get some basic information. An encyclopedia is organized like a giant index. The topics are listed in alphabetical order. To learn more about Portia's letter, he might look up Huns, the invaders named in the letter.

The library media center also contains books, magazines, newspapers, and other references, such as atlases and books with statistics. Jake might look in a historical atlas, such as the one shown below, to find maps of the Roman Empire. This may help him discover where the Huns came from and the routes they used. He might even be able to figure out where Aunt Lavinia lived.

Jake might also find books about the Roman Empire and the invaders. He can use the library's catalog to find which books are available in the library media center. The catalog may be cards in drawers or an index on the computer. Either way, he can look up a topic and find books that are available.

The books that are listed may be nonfiction or fiction. To find information about Portia's letter, Jake probably should start with nonfiction, or a factual account of events. Fiction books, such as stories and novels, will be interesting, but they may contain information that was created by the writer to make the story more dramatic.

Map in a historical atlas

The library media center also has magazines and newspapers. These may be available in hard copy or in an electronic format, such as microfilm. Magazines and newspapers are organized differently from books. They do not contain chapters. Instead, they contain articles and special features. They may also contain advertisements.

To make the best use of these sources, Jake will need to practice his skills of reading like a historian and using maps. The next pages will help you review some of these skills.

Before you can borrow books from the library, you will need a library card. You must fill out an application to get the card. The application might look something like this:

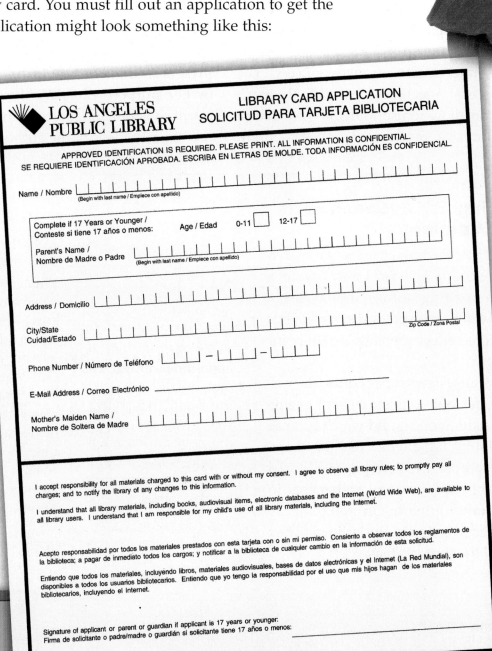

LOS ANGELES PUBLIC LIBRARY

LIBRARY CARD APPLICATION
SOLICITUD PARA TARJETA BIBLIOTECARIA

APPROVED IDENTIFICATION IS REQUIRED. PLEASE PRINT. ALL INFORMATION IS CONFIDENTIAL.
SE REQUIERE IDENTIFICACIÓN APROBADA. ESCRIBA EN LETRAS DE MOLDE. TODA INFORMACIÓN ES CONFIDENCIAL.

Name / Nombre
(Begin with last name / Empiece con apellido)

Complete if 17 Years or Younger /
Conteste si tiene 17 años o menos:     Age / Edad     0-11 ☐     12-17 ☐

Parent's Name /
Nombre de Madre o Padre
(Begin with last name / Empiece con apellido)

Address / Domicilio

City/State
Cuidad/Estado                                                                    Zip Code / Zona Postal

Phone Number / Número de Teléfono

E-Mail Address / Correo Electrónico

Mother's Maiden Name /
Nombre de Soltera de Madre

I accept responsibility for all materials charged to this card with or without my consent. I agree to observe all library rules; to promptly pay all charges; and to notify the library of any changes to this information.

I understand that all library materials, including books, audiovisual items, electronic databases and the Internet (World Wide Web), are available to all library users. I understand that I am responsible for my child's use of all library materials, including the Internet.

Acepto responsabilidad por todos los materiales prestados con esta tarjeta con o sin mi permiso. Consiento a observar todos los reglamentos de la biblioteca; a pagar de inmediato todos los cargos; y notificar a la biblioteca de cualquier cambio en la información de esta solicitud.

Entiendo que todos los materiales, incluyendo libros, materiales audiovisuales, bases de datos electrónicas y el Internet (La Red Mundial), son disponibles a todos los usuarios bibliotecarios. Entiendo que yo tengo la responsabilidad por el uso que mis hijos hagan de los materiales bibliotecarios, incluyendo el Internet.

Signature of applicant or parent or guardian if applicant is 17 years or younger:
Firma de solicitante o padre/madre o guardián si solicitante tiene 17 años o menos:

# Read Informational Texts

Reading a magazine, an Internet page, or a textbook is not the same as reading a novel. The purpose of reading nonfiction texts is to acquire new information. On page HT 9, you'll read about some ⊙ **History Reading Skills** that you'll practice as you read this textbook. Here, we'll focus on a few skills that will help you read nonfiction with a more critical eye.

## Analyze the Author's Purpose

Different types of materials are written with different purposes in mind. For example, a textbook is written to teach students information about a subject. The purpose of a technical manual is to teach someone how to use something, such as a computer. A newspaper editorial might be written to persuade the reader to accept a particular point of view. An author's purpose influences how the material is presented. Sometimes, an author states his or her purpose directly. More often, the purpose is only suggested, and you must use clues to identify the author's purpose.

## Distinguish Between Facts and Opinions

Active reading enables you to distinguish between facts and opinions when reading informational texts. Facts can be proved or disproved, but opinions reflect someone's own point of view.

Because newspaper editorials usually offer opinions on current events and issues, you should watch for bias and faulty logic when reading them. For example, the newspaper editorial at right shows factual statements in blue and opinions in red. Highly charged words are underlined. They reveal the writer's bias.

More than 5,000 people voted last week in favor of building a new shopping center, but the opposition won out. The margin of victory is irrelevant. Those <u>radical</u> voters who opposed the center are obviously <u>self-serving elitists</u> who do not care about anyone but themselves.

This month's unemployment figures for our area are 10 percent, which represents an increase of about 5 percent over the figures for last year. These figures mean that unemployment is getting worse. But the people who voted against the mall probably do not care about creating new jobs.

## Identify Evidence

Before you accept a writer's conclusion, you need to make sure that the writer has based the conclusion on enough evidence and on the right kind of evidence. A writer may present a series of facts to support a claim, but the facts may not tell the whole story. For example, the writer of the newspaper editorial on the previous page claims that the new shopping center would create more jobs. But what evidence is offered? Is it possible that the shopping center might have put many small local stores out of business? This would increase unemployment rather than decreasing it.

## Evaluate Credibility

Whenever you read informational texts, you need to assess the credibility of the writer. In other words, you have to decide whether the writer is believable. This is especially true of sites you may visit on the Internet. All Internet sources are not equally reliable. Here are some questions to ask yourself when evaluating the credibility of a Web site:

☐ Is the Web site created by a respected organization, a discussion group, or an individual?

☐ Does the Web site creator include his or her name as well as credentials and the sources he or she used to write the material?

☐ Is the information on the site balanced or biased?

☐ Can you verify the information using two other sources?

☐ Is there a date telling when the Web site was created or last updated?

# Build Vocabulary

One of the most important steps in reading informational texts is to make sure you understand the key vocabulary used by the writer. This textbook uses two devices to help you understand important vocabulary terms:

## Key Terms

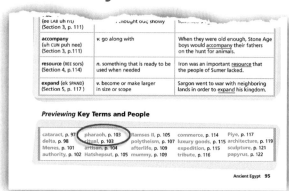

**1** Key social studies terms for each chapter are introduced in the chapter opener.

## High-Use Academic Words

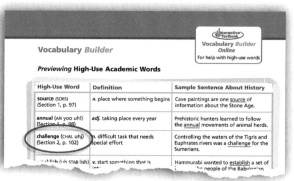

**4** High-Use Academic Words appear on the chapter opener in a chart. The chart gives a sample history sentence using each high-use word.

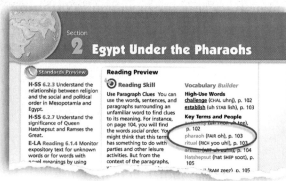

**2** They are then listed at the beginning of the section in which they will be used.

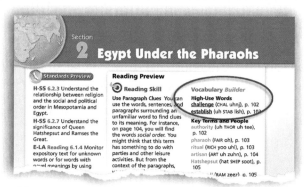

**5** The high-use words are then listed at the beginning of the section in which they will appear.

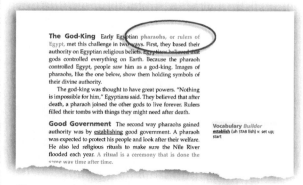

**3** Notice that they are always shown in blue type. Their definitions are also in blue.

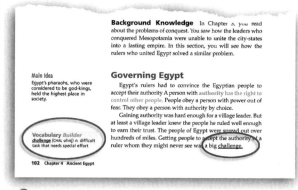

**6** High-use words are underlined in the text and defined in the margin.

# History Reading Skills

The History Reading Skills introduced on this page are important in helping you read and understand the information in this book. Each chapter introduces a reading skill. As you learn to use these skills, you will find that you can apply them to other books you read. Developing these skills is key to becoming a successful reader.

**Understand Text Structure** You can use text elements such as headings, punctuation, or boldface print to understand how information is organized. You will practice this skill in **Chapter 1.**

**Read Fluently** Learning to read text easily at a steady pace will help you understand and remember what you have read. You will practice this skill in **Chapter 2.**

**Clarify Meaning** As you read this textbook, you will recognize ideas that you have explored in earlier chapters or even in other books. When using this skill, you first identify main ideas and then connect these ideas to other sources. You will also practice using summaries, using outlines, and taking notes to help identify main ideas and supporting details. You will practice the many aspects of this skill in **Chapters 3, 5, 8, 10, and 16.**

**Use Context** As you read, you will practice using context clues to help you understand the meaning of unfamiliar words and words with more than one meaning. You will practice this skill in **Chapters 4, 7, 9, 12, and 19.**

**Word Analysis** You can analyze words to determine their meanings. You will practice using word parts (such as roots and prefixes) and recognizing word origins in **Chapters 6, 13, and 17.**

**Make Comparisons and Contrasts** When you compare, you examine the similarities between things. When you contrast, you look at the differences. You will practice analyzing comparisons and contrasts in **Chapters 11, 14, and 18.**

**Evaluate Information** As you read to find information, you need to determine what the author's purpose is and whether the author gives evidence to support his or her conclusions. You will practice this skill in **Chapters 15 and 20.**

**MAP★MASTER™**

## CONTENTS

**Go Online** PHSchool.com  The maps in this book can be found online at **PHSchool.com**, along with map skill practice.

## Geography and History

Historical information is presented not only in written sources. Maps are often a key to understanding what happened and why.

Do you remember when Jake was asking questions about Portia's letter? (See page HT 3.) In addition to using primary and secondary sources, Jake could have used a map to locate Rome, the Roman Empire, and the routes of the invading Huns.

To get the most out of maps as sources, you may need to build your geography map skills. In the next few pages, you can review some of the basic tools historians use to understand maps and geography.

The Nile River was the key geographic feature of ancient Egypt.

# Five Themes of Geography

Studying the history and geography of the ancient world is a huge task. You can make that task easier by thinking of geography in terms of five themes. The five themes described below are tools you can use to organize geographic information and to answer questions about the influence of geography on human history.

## Location

1 The exact location of a country or city is expressed in terms of longitude and latitude. (See the next page.) Relative location defines where a place is relative to other places. The exact location of the city of Athens, Greece, is 37° north (latitude) and 23° east (longitude). Its relative location could be described as "on the Aegean Sea" or "north of Egypt."

## Place

2 Location answers the question Where is it? Place answers the question What is it like there? You can identify a place by such features as its landforms, its climate, its plants and animals, and the people who live there. Much of the history of ancient Egypt was shaped by the fact that it was a narrow strip of fertile land in the middle of a desert.

## Regions

3 Areas that share at least one common feature are known as regions. Some regions are defined by geography. For example, the modern nations of India and Pakistan are part of the same region because they are both located on a large peninsula in South Asia. Other places are part of cultural regions, where people share the same language, the same religion, or the same background.

## Movement

4 Much of history has to do with the movement of people, goods, and ideas from place to place. In Portia's letter, the Huns moved to attack Rome, while Portia's family hoped to travel south to escape the invasion. In ancient times, Chinese traders traveled hundreds of miles across desert and mountains to carry silk to markets in southwest Asia.

## Interaction

5 Human-environment interaction has two parts. The first part has to do with the way an environment affects people. For example, people in the harsh deserts of North Africa developed very different ways of life from those living in the rich farmlands of Italy. The second part of interaction concerns the way people affect their environment. Even in ancient times, people found ways to bring water from rivers to farms or to build roads across mountains.

### Practice Geography Skills

Describe the area in which you live, using each of the five themes of geography.
- Where is it located?
- What are its features as a place?
- What regions is it part of?
- How do people and goods move in and out?
- How do people interact with the environment?

## Globes

A globe is a model of Earth. It shows the actual shape, size, and location of each landmass and body of water.

Globes divide Earth into lines of latitude and longitude. Latitude measures distance north or south of the Equator, which is an imaginary line around the widest part of Earth. Longitude measures distance east or west of the Prime Meridian, which is an imaginary line running from the North Pole to the South Pole. The diagram below shows how lines of longitude and latitude form a grid pattern on a globe.

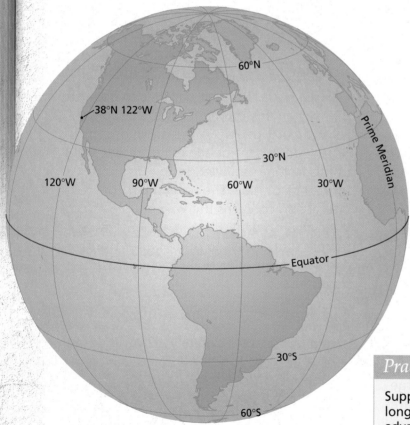

Using lines of latitude and longitude, you can locate any place on Earth. The location of 38° north latitude and 122° west longitude is written as 38° N/122° W. Only one place on Earth has this location: the city of San Francisco, California.

*Practice* **Geography Skills**

Suppose that you wanted to plan a long trip. What would be some advantages and disadvantages of using a globe?

# Map Projections

Globes are accurate, but they are not easy to carry around, and they are not useful for showing smaller areas of Earth in detail. So mapmakers had to develop methods to show the curved Earth on a flat surface. These methods are known as map projections. All map projections distort Earth in some way. Below are two common types of map projections.

## Mercator Projection

In the 1500s, ocean travelers relied on the Mercator projection, named after mapmaker Gerardus Mercator. The Mercator projection accurately shows direction and the shape of Earth's landmasses. However, it distorts distance and size.

## Robinson Projection

The Robinson projection shows the correct shape and size of landmasses for most parts of the world. However, it does not show directions as well as a Mercator projection does. It also distorts the size of the North Pole and South Pole.

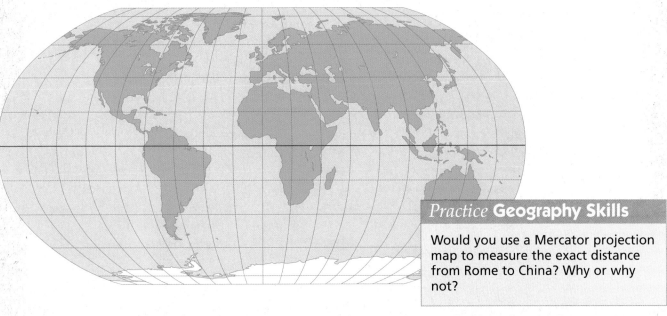

### Practice Geography Skills

Would you use a Mercator projection map to measure the exact distance from Rome to China? Why or why not?

# How to Use a Map

MAP MASTER™

Mapmakers provide several clues to help in understanding the information on a map. Maps provide different clues, depending on their purpose or scale. However, most maps have several clues in common.

**Locator globe**
Many maps are shown with locator globes. They show where on Earth the area of the map is located.

**Compass rose**
Many maps show direction by displaying a compass rose with the directions north, east, south, and west. The letters N, E, S, and W are placed to indicate these directions.

**Title**
All maps have a title. The title tells you the subject of the map.

**Key**
Often a map has a key, or legend. The key shows the meaning of the symbols and colors used on the map.

**KEY**
⊛ National capital
• Major city
─ National border

Western Europe

# Maps of Different Scales

Maps are drawn to different scales, depending on their purpose. Here are three maps drawn to very different scales. Keep in mind that maps showing large areas have smaller scales. Maps showing small areas have larger scales.

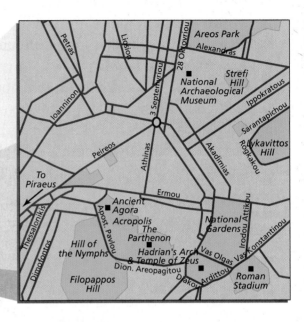

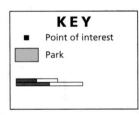

▲ **Greater Athens**
Find the gray square on the main map of Western Europe (left). This square represents the area shown on the map above. It shows the city of Athens and the features around the city. This map can help you find your way from the airport to the center of town.

▲ **Central Athens**
Find the gray square on the map of Greater Athens. This square represents the area shown on the map above. This map moves you closer into the center of Athens. Like the zoom on a computer or a camera, this map shows a smaller area but in greater detail. It has the largest scale (1 inch represents about 0.6 mile). You can use this map to explore downtown Athens.

**KEY**
- ■ Point of interest
- ▨ Park

**KEY**
- ⊛ National capital
- • Town or neighborhood
- ✈ Airport
- — City or county border
- ▨ Built-up area

**Scale bar**
A scale bar helps you find the actual distances between points shown on the map. Most scale bars show distances in both miles and kilometers.

## Practice **Geography Skills**

1. What part of a map explains the colors used on the map?
2. How does the scale bar change depending on the scale of the map?
3. Which map would be best for finding the location of the National Gardens? Why?

## Political Maps

MAP MASTER™

Historians use many different types of maps. On the next four pages, you will see four maps that show the same part of the world: southern and eastern Asia. Each map shows this area in a different way and for a different purpose.

One of the most familiar types of map is the political map. Political maps show political divisions, such as borders between countries or states. Colors on a political map help make the divisions clear. Political maps also show the location of cities. This map shows South Asia and East Asia today.

### Practice Geography Skills

- Identify two countries that border India.
- What city is the capital of Pakistan?

New Delhi, capital of India

# Physical Maps

Physical maps show the major physical features of a region, such as seas, rivers, and mountains. Many physical maps, such as the one below, use colors to indicate elevation. Elevation is the height of the land above sea level. Relief, indicated by shading, shows how quickly the land falls or rises. On a relief map, mountains seem to rise off the page.

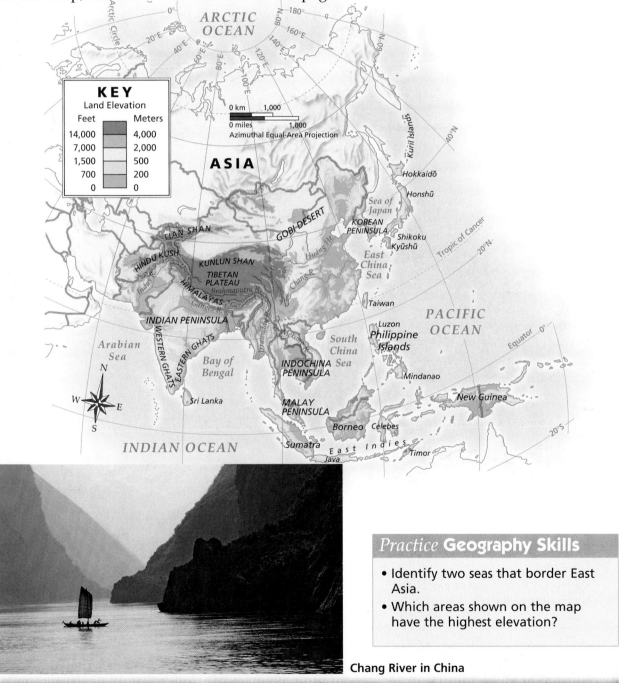

**KEY**

Land Elevation

| Feet | | Meters |
|------|---|--------|
| 14,000 | | 4,000 |
| 7,000 | | 2,000 |
| 1,500 | | 500 |
| 700 | | 200 |
| 0 | | 0 |

0 km 1,000
0 miles 1,000
Azimuthal Equal-Area Projection

### Practice Geography Skills

- Identify two seas that border East Asia.
- Which areas shown on the map have the highest elevation?

**Chang River in China**

**MAP MASTER**

## Special-Purpose Maps: Trade Routes

In addition to political maps and physical maps, there are different types of special-purpose maps. These range from road maps to weather maps to election maps. Some special-purpose maps use arrows to show the movement of people and goods from place to place. The map below shows some of the trade routes merchants used in Asia about the year 100.

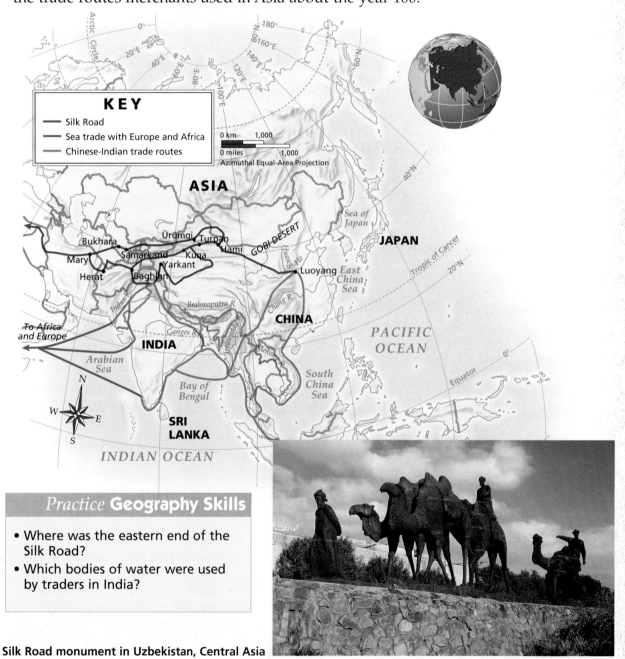

**KEY**

— Silk Road
— Sea trade with Europe and Africa
— Chinese-Indian trade routes

0 km    1,000
0 miles    1,000
Azimuthal Equal-Area Projection

### Practice Geography Skills

- Where was the eastern end of the Silk Road?
- Which bodies of water were used by traders in India?

**Silk Road monument in Uzbekistan, Central Asia**

# Special-Purpose Maps: Cultures

Other special-purpose maps show cultural, or human, characteristics of a region. One map might show the different languages spoken in Europe or in North America. Another might show where the wealthiest people and the poorest people in a city live. The map below shows the major religions in South Asia and East Asia today. You will learn about some of these religions in your study of ancient history this year.

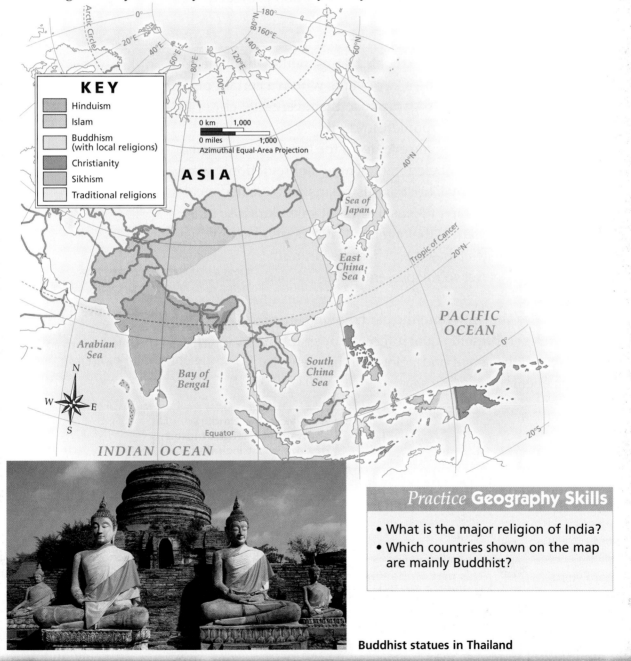

**KEY**
- Hinduism
- Islam
- Buddhism (with local religions)
- Christianity
- Sikhism
- Traditional religions

0 km 1,000
0 miles 1,000
Azimuthal Equal-Area Projection

ASIA

Sea of Japan

East China Sea

Tropic of Cancer

PACIFIC OCEAN

Arabian Sea

Bay of Bengal

South China Sea

N W E S

Equator

INDIAN OCEAN

Buddhist statues in Thailand

## Practice Geography Skills

- What is the major religion of India?
- Which countries shown on the map are mainly Buddhist?

# Read Visual Information

In this textbook, the information you need to know is presented in written form. Often, though, key information is also summarized in chart form. Charts organize facts and ideas in a visual way that may make them easier to understand.

The next four pages review some of the basic types of charts you will find in this textbook. Building your chart skills will help you get the most from the information provided.

## Timelines

Every chapter in this textbook begins with a timeline. A timeline is a chart that shows key events within a certain period of time. Timelines are organized so that events get closer to the present as you read from left to right.

You will notice that some events on the timeline are labeled B.C. and others are labeled A.D. These abbreviations were developed long ago by Christian historians who created a calendar based on the life of Jesus. Different calendars also exist, but this dating system is the one most commonly used by historians today. Dates labeled B.C. decrease in number as they get closer to the present. Dates labeled A.D. increase.

The dates shown within the bar (shown here in black circles) represent equal intervals, or spans of time. The dates above and below the bar refer to specific events.

### Practice Chart Skills

- When did Alexander the Great conquer Persia?
- Which came first: the death of Jesus or the unification of China?

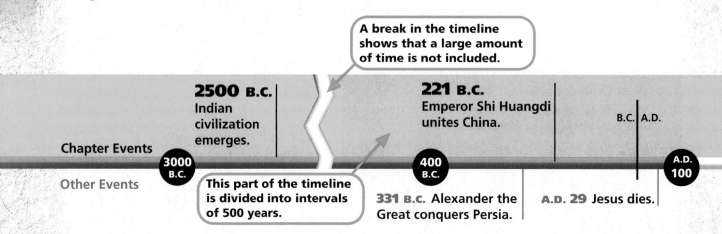

A break in the timeline shows that a large amount of time is not included.

**2500 B.C.** Indian civilization emerges.

**221 B.C.** Emperor Shi Huangdi unites China.

B.C. A.D.

Chapter Events

Other Events

3000 B.C.

This part of the timeline is divided into intervals of 500 years.

400 B.C.

331 B.C. Alexander the Great conquers Persia.

A.D. 29 Jesus dies.

A.D. 100

# Tables

Tables provide a simple way to organize a large amount of information graphically. A table is arranged in a grid pattern. Columns run vertically, or from top to bottom. Rows run horizontally, or from left to right.

Look at the sample table below. It summarizes some basic facts about four early civilizations. The four civilizations are listed in the column on the far left, at the beginning of each row. The categories of information given about each civilization are listed at the head of each column. To find information, you must read both horizontally and vertically. For example, if you want to find where the Egyptian civilization was located, go to the row labeled *Egypt*, and then read across to the column labeled *Location*.

Tables can be very large. You may have seen computer spreadsheets that include dozens of rows and columns. Yet all tables follow the basic grid pattern shown here.

## Four Ancient Civilizations

| Civilization | Location | River(s) | Emerged |
|---|---|---|---|
| Mesopotamia | Southwest Asia | Tigris and Euphrates | about 3000 B.C. |
| Egypt | Northeast Africa | Nile | about 2700 B.C. |
| India | Indian subcontinent | Indus | about 2500 B.C. |
| Shang China | East Asia | Huang | about 1650 B.C. |

### *Practice* Chart Skills

- When did Shang China emerge?
- On which river did Egypt depend?

## Flowcharts

As you have read, a timeline is a special type of chart that shows when things happened. A flowchart is a special type of chart that shows how one thing leads to another.

Many flowcharts show a process, or a series of steps that follow one another. To understand a flowchart, begin by reading the first box. Then, follow the arrows to the next event or stage in the process. Sometimes the arrows will lead you back to where you started. This shows that the events are a cycle, or a series of events that keeps repeating.

The flowchart below illustrates a process that occurred over and over again in ancient China. As you read, notice how one step leads to another.

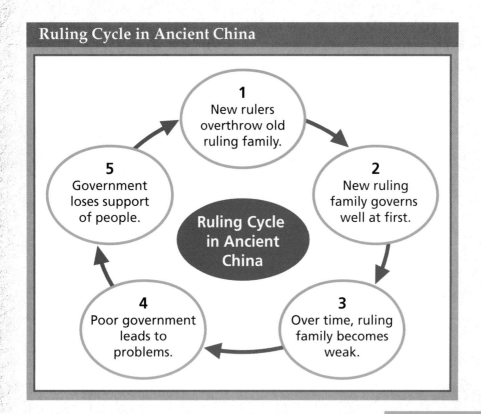

**Ruling Cycle in Ancient China**

1 New rulers overthrow old ruling family.

2 New ruling family governs well at first.

3 Over time, ruling family becomes weak.

4 Poor government leads to problems.

5 Government loses support of people.

Ruling Cycle in Ancient China

### Practice **Chart Skills**

• Without reading the chart, how can you tell that it describes a cycle?

• How did step 3 lead to step 4? How did step 4 lead to step 5?

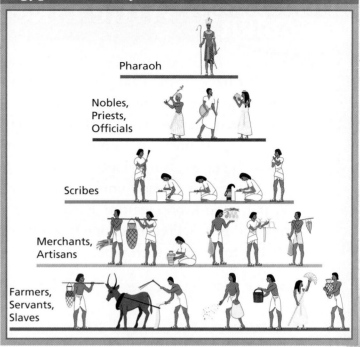

## Social Pyramids

The civilizations you will study in this textbook all had strict social orders. Certain classes, or groups, of people had more power and prestige than did other classes.

A special type of chart shows how such societies are organized. This chart is called a social pyramid. In a social pyramid, the person or persons with the highest rank are shown at the top. The persons with the lowest rank are shown at the bottom. Social pyramids get wider as you go from top to bottom. This design shows that the highest classes usually had the smallest number of people.

The social pyramid here shows how Egyptian society was organized. Between 1500 B.C. and 500 B.C., Egypt was ruled by pharaohs. Below the pharaoh, the other people in society each had a place.

### *Practice* **Chart Skills**

- Which group of people was most respected in Egyptian society?
- Who was more important: farmers or merchants?

## Roman Currency Collapse

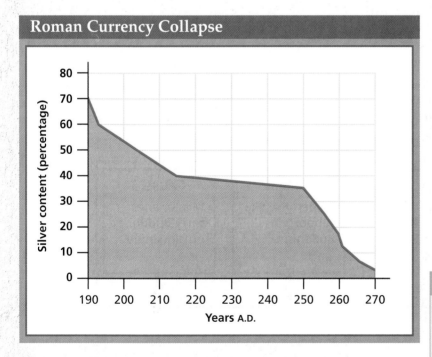

## Graphs

One common type of visual is the line graph, such as the one shown here. Line graphs indicate changes over time. They are useful for showing information such as population growth or government expenses. In studying ancient times, though, historians have very few exact numbers to work with.

### *Practice* **Chart Skills**

Why would there be more line graphs in today's newspapers than in a textbook on ancient history?

# Write Like a Historian

You have learned how to use a historian's tools to learn about the past. The next step is to write about what you have discovered. Historians share their findings in a variety of ways, including expository compositions, historical narratives, research papers, and persuasive compositions or speeches.

At the end of each unit in this textbook, you will find a Writer's Workshop feature. Each Writer's Workshop presents detailed instruction about one type of writing. You will have a chance to practice each type.

## Expository Compositions

An expository composition is writing that explains something in detail. You will learn to write specific types of expository compositions in Units 1–3.

**❶ Select and Narrow Your Topic**

Define exactly what you want your composition to do. Do you want to describe a process? Will you rank things in order of importance? Will you choose to compare and contrast two ideas? You cannot plan your composition until you know what you want to do.

**❷ Gather Evidence**

Prepare a graphic organizer that identifies details to include in your composition, such as the one shown here.

**❸ Write a First Draft**

Write a topic sentence, and then organize the composition on the basis of what you are trying to do. If you are describing a process, write about the steps of the process in the correct order. If you are comparing and contrasting two events, describe each event and then point out similarities and differences.

**❹ Revise and Proofread**

Make sure that all the details support your topic sentence.

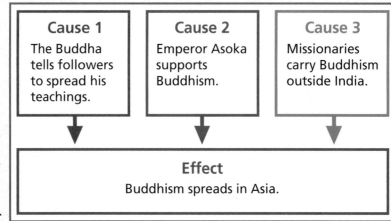

| Cause 1 | Cause 2 | Cause 3 |
|---------|---------|---------|
| The Buddha tells followers to spread his teachings. | Emperor Asoka supports Buddhism. | Missionaries carry Buddhism outside India. |

**Effect**
Buddhism spreads in Asia.

**If you were writing a cause-and-effect composition, you might create a chart like this to help you organize your ideas.**

## Narrative Compositions

History is like a story. It has characters, both leaders and ordinary people. It has a setting, in which events occur. It even has a plot, in which events unfold, conflicts arise, and resolutions take place.

### 1 Select and Narrow Your Topic

In this textbook, you will be asked to write narratives about the past. You might be asked to imagine a setting and describe how it affects what is happening. You might be asked to take the point of view of one of history's characters. Or you might be asked to explain the conflict or resolution of a historical situation. First, you must understand what you are being asked to do or who you are asked to be.

Suppose you are asked to picture yourself as a Roman soldier. You can use your imagination and your knowledge of history to create a narrative. For example, would a Roman soldier write proudly about conquering new territory for Rome? Would the soldier complain about the hardships of marching hundreds of miles on foot? Identifying your viewpoint will help you plan your narrative.

### 2 Gather Details

Brainstorm for a list of details you would like to include in your narrative.

### 3 Write a First Draft

Start by writing a simple opening sentence that conveys the main idea of your narrative. Continue by writing a colorful story that has interesting details. Write a conclusion that sums up the viewpoint presented in your narrative.

### 4 Revise and Proofread

Check to make sure that you have not begun too many sentences with the word *I*. Replace general words with more specific, colorful words.

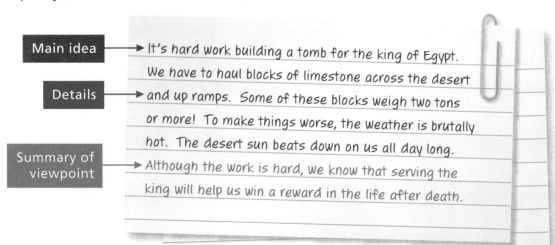

Main idea → It's hard work building a tomb for the king of Egypt.

Details → We have to haul blocks of limestone across the desert and up ramps. Some of these blocks weigh two tons or more! To make things worse, the weather is brutally hot. The desert sun beats down on us all day long.

Summary of viewpoint → Although the work is hard, we know that serving the king will help us win a reward in the life after death.

## Research Papers

Research papers present information that you have found about a topic. You will have a chance to practice writing a research paper in Units 4 and 5.

### ❶ Select and Narrow Your Topic

Choose a topic that interests you, one that is not too broad. For example, don't write a report on Africa. Focus instead on the gold-salt trade in West Africa.

### ❷ Acquire Information

The library and Internet are good sources of information about a topic. But be sure to evaluate the reliability of each source.

For each resource, prepare a source index card. Then, record each detail or subtopic on a separate card, noting where you found the information. Use quotation marks when copying exact words from a source.

### ❸ Make an Outline

Use an outline to organize your information. Sort your index cards in the same order.

### ❹ Write a First Draft

Write an introduction, a body, and a conclusion. If you prepare your first draft on paper, leave plenty of space between lines so you can add more details later.

### ❺ Revise and Proofread

Be sure to include transition words between sentences and paragraphs. Here are some examples:

- To describe a process: *first, next, then*
- To show a contrast: *however, although, despite*
- To point out a reason: *when, because, if*
- To signal a conclusion: *therefore, as a result, so*

Introduction

Burning the Books

Emperor Shi Huangdi did a shocking thing. He ordered his soldiers to burn almost all of the books in China. Shi especially wanted to get rid of the writings of the philosopher Confucius. Why would China's great ruler want to destroy the work of China's great thinker?

Conclusion

So Shi Huangdi failed in the end. His empire fell apart soon after his death. However, the ideas of Confucius continued to influence China for hundreds of years.

## Persuasive Compositions

A persuasive composition is writing that supports a position or an opinion. You will learn more about writing persuasive compositions in Unit 6.

**1 Select and Narrow Your Topic**

Choose a historical topic that has at least two sides or two interpretations. Choose a side. Decide which argument will best persuade your audience to agree with your point of view.

**2 Gather Evidence**

Design a chart that states your position at the top and then lists the pros and cons for your position below, in two columns. Predict and then address the strongest arguments against your viewpoint.

**3 Write a First Draft**

Write a strong thesis statement that clearly states your position. Continue by presenting the strongest arguments in favor of your position and acknowledging and refuting opposing arguments.

**4 Revise and Proofread**

Check to make sure that you have made a logical argument and that you have not oversimplified the argument.

## Practice Your Writing

In this textbook, you will have many opportunities to practice your writing skills. The chart below shows how you can build writing skills in each section, chapter, and unit of the textbook.

| Check Your Progress: Writing (end of every section) | Review and Assessment: Writing (end of every chapter) | Writing Workshop (end of every unit) |
| --- | --- | --- |
| Helps you build writing skills you will need to complete the unit-level Writing Workshop | Helps you practice the skills from Check Your Progress and build toward the unit-level Writing Workshop. | Helps you learn and practice the steps in a type of writing— expository, research, or persuasive. |
| *Examples:* • List similarities. • List differences. • Use a Venn diagram to organize similarities and differences. | *Example:* • Write a paragraph describing one similarity and one difference. | *Example:* • Expository Composition: Comparison and Contrast |

# Unit 1

**History-Social Science**

**6.1** Students describe what is known through archaeological studies of the early physical and cultural development of humankind from the Paleolithic era to the agricultural revolution.

 What You Will Learn

## Early People

Scientists called archaeologists have learned about the development of humankind through the study of fossils and artifacts. Over a very long time, groups of early peoples migrated to many different parts of the world.

## The Beginning of Civilization

The development of farming led people to establish permanent settlements. Eventually, such settlements grew into the earliest cities.

 **Quick View** Video

**Discovery School Video** View *The Beginnings of Humankind* for a quick preview of the main ideas of this unit.

**The Li River in China**

# The Beginnings of Humankind

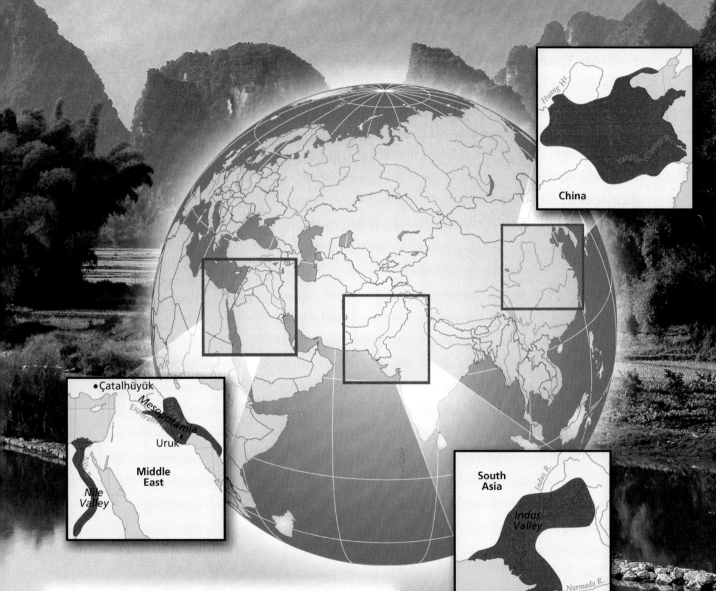

China

Çatalhüyük

Mesopotamia

Euphrates

Uruk

Middle East

Nile Valley

South Asia

Indus R.

Indus Valley

Narmada R.

## *Think* like a historian

This map shows areas of the world in which several early civilizations appeared.

**As you read this unit, think about this question:**
*What is civilization and how did it begin?*

## Chapter 1

# Early People

## (PREHISTORY–30,000 B.C.)

## Prepare to Read

 **Chapter Standards**

### History-Social Science

**6.1** Students describe what is known through archaeological studies of the early physical and cultural development of humankind from the Paleolithic era to the agricultural revolution.

| | |
|---|---|
| **Section 1,** pp. 6–11 | **What You Will Learn** |
| **Studying the Distant Past** | Archaeologists study artifacts and fossils to learn about the physical and cultural development of humankind. Archaeological studies suggest that humankind began more than 4 million years ago. |
| **Section 2,** pp. 12–15 | |
| **Hunter-Gatherer Societies** | Early humans were hunter-gatherers who moved from place to place in search of food. The development of tools and the use of fire helped these groups improve their chances for survival. |
| **Section 3,** pp. 18–23 | |
| **Populating the Earth** | Modern humans formed communities in many regions of the world. As they moved to new places, these people had to adapt to their new environments. |

Modern human carving

**2.5 Million B.C.**
Paleolithic Era begins.

**200,000 B.C.**
Neanderthals, a Stone Age people, live in Germany.

**100,000 B.C.**
*Homo sapiens*, the first modern humans, appear.

**Chapter Events**

2.5 million B.C.

200,000 B.C.

100,000 B.C.

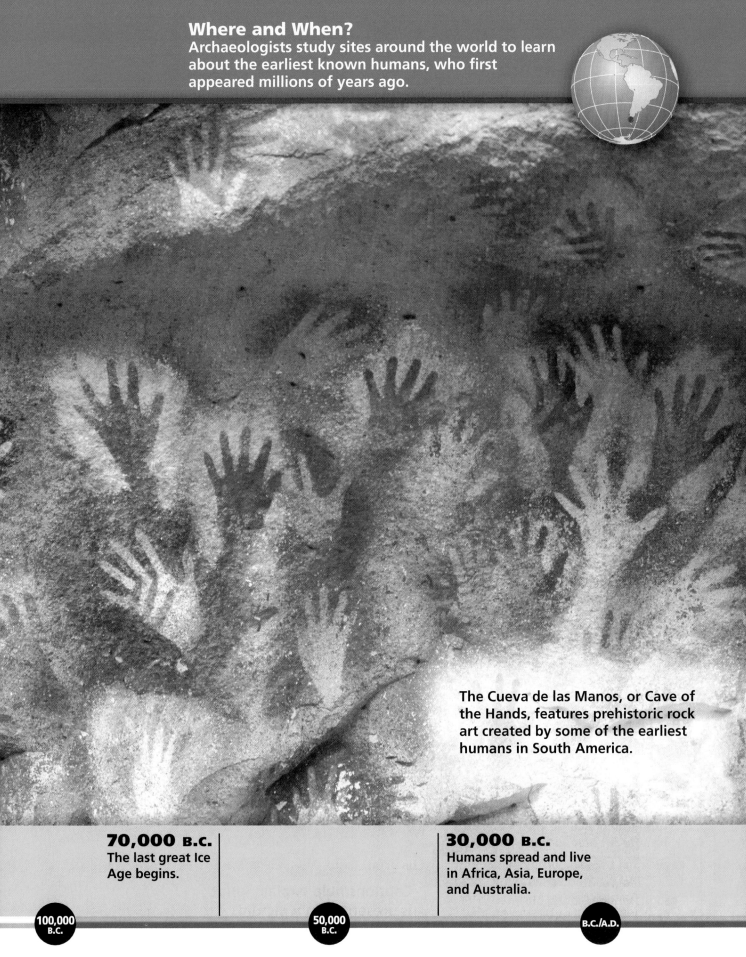

## Where and When?
Archaeologists study sites around the world to learn about the earliest known humans, who first appeared millions of years ago.

The Cueva de las Manos, or Cave of the Hands, features prehistoric rock art created by some of the earliest humans in South America.

**70,000 B.C.**
The last great Ice Age begins.

**30,000 B.C.**
Humans spread and live in Africa, Asia, Europe, and Australia.

100,000
B.C.

50,000
B.C.

B.C./A.D.

# How to Read History

## History Reading Skill

### *Previewing* Use Text Features

Media such as magazines, newspapers, and online information can be helpful to you as you study. Prepare to use these popular media by learning about their features as you read your textbook. Both your textbook and these other sources have structural features that can help you locate information.

**Chapter Standards**

**English-Language Arts**

**Reading 6.2.1** Identify the structural features of popular media (e.g., newspapers, magazines, online information) and use the features to obtain information.

---

**1** The article below appears at an online news site. It has many structural features that give you information.

> A sidebar provides you with or tells you where to look for additional information.

> Bold face text briefly tells you the subject of the news story.

Address:

MAIN PAGE
WORLD
U.S.
WEATHER
BUSINESS
SPORTS

### Ancient Egyptian tomb found

November 18, 2001 Posted: 12:17 PM EST (1717 GMT)

**CAIRO, Egypt – Egyptian archaeologists have discovered a 2,500-year-old limestone tomb in a densely populated area of apartment blocks in Cairo.**

"This is an amazing discovery because . . . between the houses of downtown Cairo in an area called Ain Shams . . . (we) have found this tomb," said Zahi Hawass, antiquities chief for the Giza Pyramids area, told Reuters on Sunday.

---

**2** This article uses photographs and captions to give you information. Some popular media will also use graphs or charts.

> Titles tell you what information you will find in an article.

Men's NCAA Tournament March 18-April 5

> Photos help you visualize information in text.

Gonzaga's Blake Stepp wants to build on his past heroics at the tournament.

> Captions help explain what is presented in a picture, chart, or graph.

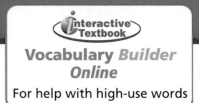
## Vocabulary *Builder*

### *Previewing* High-Use Academic Words

| High-Use Word | Definition | Sample Sentence About History |
|---|---|---|
| **layer** (LAY er) (Section 1, p. 7) | *n.* single thickness, coat, or fold | The object was found buried beneath several <u>layers</u> of soil and rock. |
| **material** (muh TIR ee uhl) (Section 1, p. 8) | *n.* what a thing is, or may be, made of | Birds use <u>material</u> such as sticks and twigs to build their nests. |
| **intelligent** (ihn TEHL uh juhnt) (Section 2, p. 15) | *adj.* having or using intelligence | A person's skill at solving problems can show that he or she is <u>intelligent</u>. |
| **symbol** (SIHM buhl) (Section 2, p. 15) | *n.* written or printed mark, letter, or abbreviation that stands for something else | The sign used a <u>symbol</u> of a person walking to show that it was safe to cross the street. |
| **debate** (dee BAYT) (Section 3, p. 19) | *n.* discussion or argument on a subject that people express different opinions about | The two scientists shared their differing views during the <u>debate</u>. |
| **expose** (ehk SPOHZ) (Section 3, p. 21) | *v.* to allow to be seen; reveal; display | The group shoveled away the snow to <u>expose</u> the sidewalk below. |

### *Previewing* Key Terms and People

**Mary Leakey**

prehistory, p. 6
archaeology, p. 6
artifact, p. 7
fossil, p. 7
Mary and Louis Leakey, p. 8
Donald Johanson, p. 10

Michael Brunet, p. 10
hunter-gatherer, p. 12
innovation, p. 12
nomad, p. 13
culture, p. 13
Neanderthals, p. 14

*Homo sapiens,* p. 14
populate, p. 18
migration, p. 19
environment, p. 20
adapt, p. 20

**Louis Leakey**

# 1 Studying the Distant Past

**H-SS 6.1** Students describe what is known through archaeological studies of the early physical and cultural development of humankind from the Paleolithic era to the agricultural revolution.

**E-LA Reading 6.2.1** Identify the structural features of popular media (e.g., newspapers, magazines, online information) and use the features to obtain information.

## Reading Preview

 **Reading Skill**

**Recognize Text Features** Textbooks, like magazines or newspapers, organize information to help you find what you need. This textbook uses boldface blue type to point out new words, as well as larger type to show titles. Special information appears alongside the main text. For example, you will find definitions and main ideas in sidebars. Captions offering further explanation appear with pictures, graphs, and charts.

**Vocabulary** *Builder*

**High-Use Words**
layer (LAY er), p. 7
material (muh TIR ee uhl), p. 8

**Key Terms and People**
prehistory (pree HIHS tuh ree), p. 6
archaeology (ahr kee AHL uh jee), p. 6
artifact (AHRT uh fakt), p. 7
fossil (FAHS uhl), p. 7
Mary and Louis Leakey (LEE kee), p. 8
Donald Johanson (joh HAHN suhn), p. 10
Michael Brunet (broo NAY), p. 10

**Background Knowledge** Many people enjoy learning about their families' histories and how their relatives lived in years past. Scientists known as archaeologists look much farther back in time. They are interested in the origins of humankind—or human beings in general. In this section, you will read about the ways in which archaeologists study the distant past and what they have learned about the development of humankind.

**Main Idea**
The work of scientists who study the distant past provides information about the early development of humankind.

## Studies of Early Humans

Studying the origins of humankind is not easy. Until about 6,000 years ago, humans had no way to write things down. This time before written records is called **prehistory.** The scientists who study prehistory are called archaeologists. **Archaeology** is the study of human life in the past through the examination of the things that people left behind.

**Searching for Artifacts** Archaeologists study the development of humankind by looking for places where people may have lived long ago. Old campsites and settlements often lie buried beneath <u>layers</u> of dirt. Archaeologists excavate, or uncover, these sites to learn about the people who once lived there.

As archaeologists dig up a site, they look for artifacts such as tools, pottery, or weapons. **Artifacts are objects made and used by humans.** The artifacts found in an ancient campsite can help archaeologists understand how the people who once camped there hunted for food or what types of plants the people ate.

Some questions about early humans, however, are difficult to answer by studying artifacts. For example, archaeologists excavating old campsites have found animal bones carved with strange designs. Archaeologists can identify the animals from which the bones came and describe the tools used to carve the designs. But they cannot explain the thoughts and ideas of the people who created these fascinating artifacts.

**Hunting for Fossils** Artifacts have taught archaeologists a great deal about people who lived thousands of years ago. The earliest humans, however, lived millions of years ago. The artifacts they created have mostly disappeared. For these people's story, archaeologists depend mainly on fossils. **Fossils are the remains or imprints of living things that existed millions of years ago.** These remains may include parts of plants, feathers, bones, and even footprints.

**Vocabulary** *Builder*
<u>layer</u> (LAY er) *n.* single thickness, coat, or fold

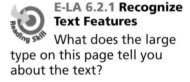

**E-LA 6.2.1 Recognize Text Features** What does the large type on this page tell you about the text?

**Archaeological Sites**
At sites such as this one in South Africa, archaeologists search for evidence of the people who lived there long ago. **Critical Thinking: Draw Conclusions** *Why do you think these workers are filling bags with dirt from the site?*

**Vocabulary *Builder***

<u>material</u> (muh TIR ee uhl) *n.* what a thing is, or may be, made of

Fossils form only under special conditions. After a living thing dies, it must become quickly covered by sand or mud. Once covered, the soft parts of the plant or animal rot away quickly. The harder parts, such as bones, teeth, or woody stems last much longer. Over many years, minerals from the soil slowly replace this once-living <u>material</u>, leaving a rocklike copy of the original.

Fossilized bones of early humans are rare. A whole fossil skeleton is even more unusual. Fossil hunters usually find a bone here or a tooth there. Still, examining a fossil tooth can show what kind of food an early human ate. Fossil bones might indicate the size and features of an early human's body.

**Dating Fossils and Artifacts** Archaeologists use several methods for determining the ages of artifacts and fossils. One method is to compare objects found in similar layers of rock or soil. Objects found in lower layers are likely to be older than those found in upper layers. Archaeologists may also compare an object with a similar fossil or artifact whose age is already known.

Radioactive dating is another method for determining the age of very old objects. Both living things and rocks contain radioactive elements that decay or disappear over time. By measuring the amount of radioactive material left in an object, scientists can tell when it was formed. Other dating methods use different types of physical or chemical tests to determine the age of objects.

**Checkpoint** How do scientists study the distant past?

**Main Idea**
Archaeologists study fossils to better understand the beginnings of humankind.

# The Hunt for Early Humans

Where did people first appear on Earth? This was one of the first questions asked by scientists studying the development of humankind. For a long time, no one knew the answer. Then, in 1959, archaeologists **Mary and Louis Leakey** discovered human fossils at a place called Olduvai Gorge in East Africa. A piece of a skull found by Mary Leakey featured large molars, or rear teeth, which suggested the individual ate mostly plant foods.

Tests showed that the fossils found by the Leakeys were at least 1.75 million years old. From that point on, the search for the origins of humankind centered on Africa.

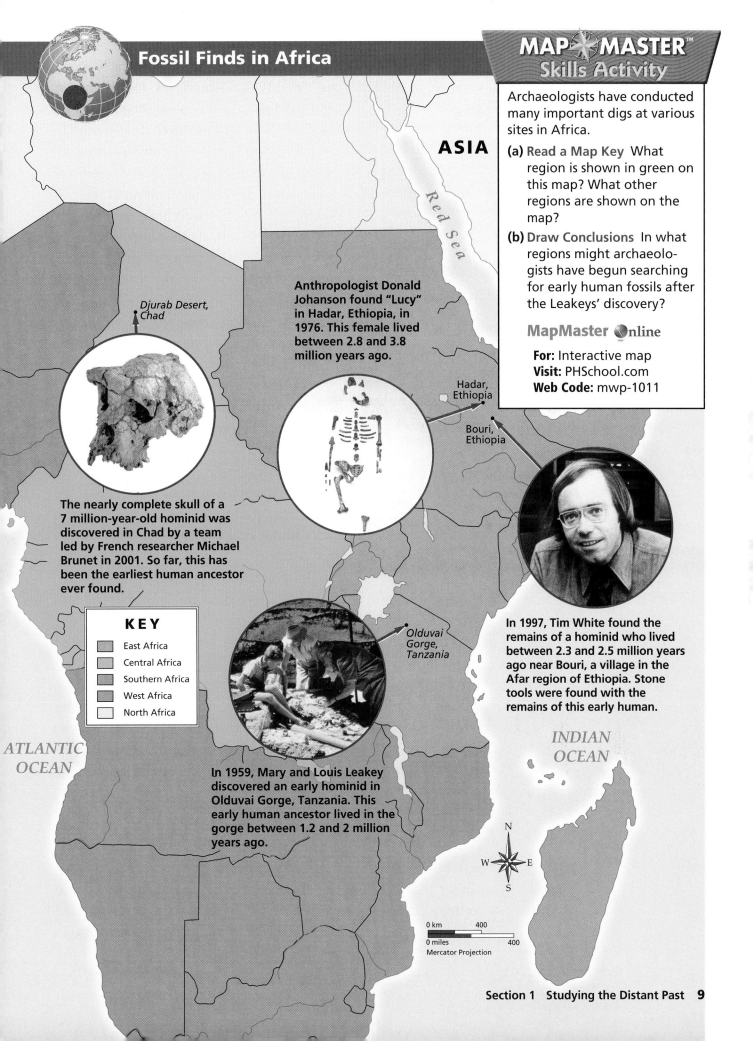

ASIA

Red Sea

### MAP MASTER™
### Skills Activity

Archaeologists have conducted many important digs at various sites in Africa.

**(a) Read a Map Key** What region is shown in green on this map? What other regions are shown on the map?

**(b) Draw Conclusions** In what regions might archaeologists have begun searching for early human fossils after the Leakeys' discovery?

**MapMaster Online**

**For:** Interactive map
**Visit:** PHSchool.com
**Web Code:** mwp-1011

*Djurab Desert, Chad*

Anthropologist Donald Johanson found "Lucy" in Hadar, Ethiopia, in 1976. This female lived between 2.8 and 3.8 million years ago.

Hadar, Ethiopia

Bouri, Ethiopia

The nearly complete skull of a 7 million-year-old hominid was discovered in Chad by a team led by French researcher Michael Brunet in 2001. So far, this has been the earliest human ancestor ever found.

**KEY**

- East Africa
- Central Africa
- Southern Africa
- West Africa
- North Africa

*Olduvai Gorge, Tanzania*

In 1997, Tim White found the remains of a hominid who lived between 2.3 and 2.5 million years ago near Bouri, a village in the Afar region of Ethiopia. Stone tools were found with the remains of this early human.

*ATLANTIC OCEAN*

*INDIAN OCEAN*

In 1959, Mary and Louis Leakey discovered an early hominid in Olduvai Gorge, Tanzania. This early human ancestor lived in the gorge between 1.2 and 2 million years ago.

N
W E
S

0 km       400
0 miles       400
Mercator Projection

## How did Lucy get her name?

*Fast Facts*

**Who:** Lucy

**What:** A 3.5-foot-tall female fossil skeleton

**When:** About 3.2 million years ago

**Where:** Present-day Ethiopia

**Why important:** Lucy's discovery showed that our human ancestors walked on two legs before their brain size increased or toolmaking began. Walking upright seems to have been one of the earliest steps in the process of becoming human.

*Fast Find*

**How:** Go online to find out how Lucy got her name.

**Biography**
**Online**

**For:** More about Lucy
**Visit:** PHSchool.com
**Web Code:** mwe-1011

Lucy

**African Beginnings** On November 30, 1974, American fossil hunter Donald Johanson woke up feeling lucky. For three years, Johanson had been searching for evidence of early humans in Ethiopia, a country in East Africa. By noon, the temperature had risen to almost 110° F, making it too hot to search any further.

On his way back to camp, Johanson took a detour through a dry gully. There, he saw a tiny bone sticking out of the dirt. That one small forearm bone led to more bones—including those from a skull, leg, pelvis, and jaw.

After searching another two weeks, Johanson and his team had uncovered hundreds of pieces of bone. The pieces, which all belonged to a 3.5-foot-tall woman, made up about 40 percent of her skeleton. Johanson named her Lucy. Johanson's team determined that all of the bones belonged to one individual because they did not find two examples of any one type of bone.

The bones of Lucy's legs, pelvis, ankle, and spine suggest that, like humans today, she walked upright on two legs. However, she lived an amazing 3.2 million years ago!

Since the discovery of Lucy, even older fossils have been found in Africa. In the 1990s, an American fossil hunter named Tim White found fossils of early humans who lived in Ethiopia at least 4.4 million years ago. The back of one skull found by White's team was badly crushed. White guesses that a hippopotamus or an elephant may have stepped on the skull after the individual died.

**The Search for the "Oldest One"** The discovery of Lucy and other older fossils led many scientists to conclude that humankind began in East Africa about 4.5 million years ago. But not everyone agrees. One such person is French fossil hunter Michael Brunet. In 2001, Brunet found in the African country of Chad a worn brown humanlike skull. Tests showed the skull to be nearly 7 million years old. That makes it, says Brunet, "the oldest one."

Brunet's discovery has raised many questions. Chad is in Central Africa. Did humankind begin there rather than in East Africa? The skull Brunet found is much older than all the other human fossils discovered so far. Does this mean that humankind is older than scientists once thought? The skull found in Chad looks more apelike than other early human skulls. Does this mean that it may not be an early human skull at all?

Scientists are still looking for answers to these questions. Meanwhile, the search for ancient human fossils continues. "This is the beginning of the story," says Brunet of his work in Chad, "just the beginning."

 **Checkpoint** Why do scientists believe that humankind began in Africa?

**Looking Back and Ahead** In this section, you have read about archaeological studies of the development of humankind. You have learned that humans first appeared in Africa more than 4.5 million years ago, and that scientists continue to search for fossils older than those already discovered. In the next section, you will find out how these early humans lived and how they continued to develop.

## Discovering the Past

**1955 A.D.**

— **1959** Human fossils found at Olduvai

— **1974** "Lucy" discovered in Ethiopia

**1980 A.D.**

— **1990s** Human fossils dated 4.4 million years discovered

— **2001** Fossil dated nearly 7 million years discovered in Chad

**2005 A.D.**

### Discovery Dates
This time line shows the dates of several key discoveries related to early people. **Critical Thinking: Understand Sequence** *How many years passed between the discovery at Olduvai and that of Lucy?*

---

## Section 1 Check Your Progress

**Progress Monitoring** ⏻nline

**For:** Self-test with instant help
**Visit:** PHSchool.com
**Web Code:** mwa-1011

**Standards Review** H-SS: 6.1; E-LA: Reading 6.2.1

### Comprehension and Critical Thinking
1. **(a) Describe** What types of evidence do scientists use to study prehistoric times?
   **(b) Draw Inferences** What are some problems with these types of evidence?

2. **(a) Identify** Where do most scientists believe that humankind first appeared?
   **(b) Make Predictions** What new evidence could change this conclusion?

### Reading Skill
3. **Recognize Text Features** Look back at the first paragraph under Studies of Early Humans. What information does the side-column note for this paragraph provide you?

### Vocabulary *Builder*
Complete each of the following sentences so that the second part further explains the first part and clearly shows your understanding of the highlighted word.

4. The time before about 6,000 years ago is called prehistory; _____.

5. We can learn about the past through archaeology; _____.

6. Scientists study early human fossils; _____.

### Writing
7. Review the text and take notes detailing some of the important steps in archaeologists' search for the earliest humans. Include in your notes examples and descriptions of important discoveries in this search.

## Standards Preview

**H-SS 6.1.1** Describe the hunter-gatherer societies, including the development of tools and the use of fire.

**E-LA Reading 6.2.1** Identify the structural features of popular media (e.g., newspapers, magazines, online information) and use the features to obtain information.

## Reading Preview

### Reading Skill

**Use Text Structure to Obtain Information** This textbook organizes the text to help you find information. Main headings suggest the general topic of the text that follows. Smaller headings further break down these passages. Use such headings to pinpoint which paragraphs contain specific information. Use the placement of pictures, graphs, and charts to determine how these visuals connect to the main text.

### Vocabulary *Builder*

**High-Use Words**
intelligent (ihn TEHL uh juhnt), p. 15
symbol (SIHM buhl), p. 15

**Key Terms and People**
hunter-gatherers (HUHNT er GATH er erz), p. 12
innovation (ihn uh VAY shuhn), p. 12
nomad (NOH mad), p. 13
culture (KUHL cher), p. 13
Neanderthals (nee AN der thawlz), p. 14
*Homo sapiens* (HOH moh SAY pee ehnz), p. 14

**Background Knowledge** Archaeologists believe that human beings first appeared in Africa millions of years ago. These early humans were **hunter-gatherers.** They lived by hunting small animals and gathering plants. In this section, you will read about the societies that these people formed and the developments that improved their chances for survival.

## How Early Hunter-Gatherers Lived

**Main Idea**
The development of new skills gave hunter-gatherer societies improved chances for survival.

Archaeologists know very little about the lives of early hunter-gatherers like Lucy. But they do know that their lives often proved difficult. Many groups appeared for a time and died out.

**The Development of Tools** About 2.5 million years ago, early humans developed a useful new skill. They learned how to make tools out of stone. This **innovation, or new way of doing things,** was so important that archaeologists call this period the Paleolithic Era, or the Old Stone Age.

At first, the tools made by early humans were simple. Toolmakers split stones to make cutting tools for chopping down small trees, cutting meat, or scraping the flesh off an animal skin.

Over time, Stone Age toolmakers became more skillful, making thinner and sharper stone blades. Some blades were used to make spears and arrows. Toolmakers began using bones and antlers, and some added decoration and color to their work.

**Primary** Sources

See "Ancestors: In Search of Human Origins" in the Reference Section at the back of this book.

**The Use of Fire** The Stone Age lasted from about 2.5 million to 10,000 years ago. Sometime during this period, people learned how to use fire. With fire, people could have light on the darkest nights. They could cook meat and plants and use flames to scare off dangerous animals. Fire also allowed them to live in places where it would have otherwise been too cold to survive.

**Wandering Bands** Stone Age hunter-gatherers lived in small groups, or bands. A band probably included ten or twelve adults and their children. Most of these people were **nomads. They moved from place to place with the seasons.** After gathering food in one area, they moved on to a new campsite. These wandering bands often used caves as shelters. If they stayed in one place for a while, they built tents or huts in which to live.

The **culture,** *or way of life,* of early hunter-gatherer societies was simple. Most of their time was spent looking for food. Women and girls usually gathered fruit, grains, seeds, and nuts. They collected eggs and honey, and caught small animals such as lizards or fish. They also may have picked herbs for medicine.

Hunting was probably an important task for men. At first, they hunted mostly small animals. As their skills and weapons improved, Stone Age hunters probably turned to larger animals such as deer.

Checkpoint **What new skills did early humans develop during the Stone Age?**

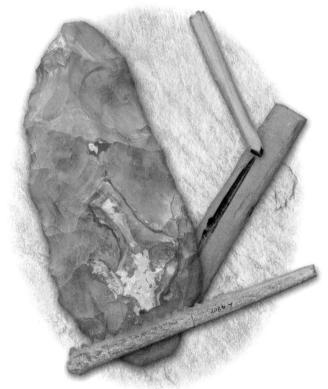

**Early Tools**
Tools such as the stone object pictured here allowed early humans to cut materials more easily. A wooden object like that on the right could start fires. The tool on the bottom is a harpoon point used for hunting.
**Critical Thinking: Distinguish Relevant Information**
*Which of these tools would be relevant to a discussion of how Stone Age peoples built their shelters?*

# Late Stone Age Peoples

Toward the end of the Stone Age, two groups of larger-brained humans appeared. Both groups had more-developed cultures than earlier peoples, but only one of these groups would survive.

**Neanderthals** A group known as Neanderthals appeared in Europe and parts of Asia about 200,000 years ago. Their name comes from the Neander Valley in present-day Germany, where their fossil remains were first found.

Neanderthals were the first people to bury their dead at times. They carefully arranged bodies in graves, as if for sleeping. On some occasions, they sprinkled a dead person with flowers and colored clay. They then buried the body along with food and tools.

Archaeologists do not know why Neanderthals did these things. It might have been to protect the bodies from harm. This may mean that Neanderthals held beliefs about life after death.

**Modern Humans** About 100,000 years ago, the last new group of humans appeared. The scientific name of this group is *Homo sapiens,* which means "wise people." Homo sapiens were the first modern humans—or people like you.

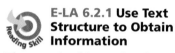
**E-LA 6.2.1 Use Text Structure to Obtain Information**
The text in this section is structured in chronological order. Which subheading discusses the earlier group of people?

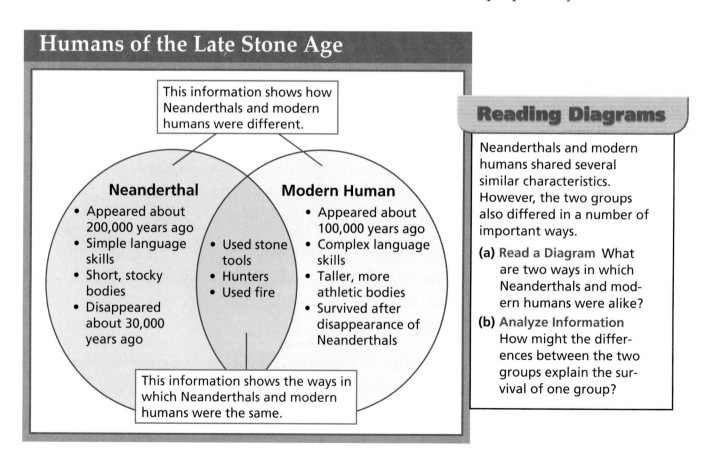

## Humans of the Late Stone Age

This information shows how Neanderthals and modern humans were different.

**Neanderthal**
- Appeared about 200,000 years ago
- Simple language skills
- Short, stocky bodies
- Disappeared about 30,000 years ago

- Used stone tools
- Hunters
- Used fire

**Modern Human**
- Appeared about 100,000 years ago
- Complex language skills
- Taller, more athletic bodies
- Survived after disappearance of Neanderthals

This information shows the ways in which Neanderthals and modern humans were the same.

**Reading Diagrams**

Neanderthals and modern humans shared several similar characteristics. However, the two groups also differed in a number of important ways.

**(a) Read a Diagram** What are two ways in which Neanderthals and modern humans were alike?

**(b) Analyze Information** How might the differences between the two groups explain the survival of one group?

These people were like Neanderthals in some ways. Both groups made tools, used fire, and hunted animals. Both were <u>intelligent</u>. But modern humans were taller and more athletic. And they had a powerful new tool—complex language.

With language, modern humans could better communicate their ideas. They could organize a hunt or pass knowledge on to the younger people in their groups. This ability to use words and <u>symbols</u> gave them a great advantage in the struggle to survive.

For thousands of years, Neanderthals and modern humans lived near one another, but the Neanderthals eventually disappeared. Some archaeologists believe they fought with the newcomers and lost, while others think the groups mixed together. Whatever the cause, fossils suggest the Neaderthals did not live past about 30,000 years ago.

**Vocabulary** *Builder*
<u>intelligent</u> (ihn TEHL uh juhnt) *adj.* having or using intelligence

**Vocabulary** *Builder*
<u>symbol</u> (SIHM buhl) *n.* written or printed mark, letter, or abbreviation that stands for something else

 **Checkpoint** What new advantage did modern humans develop?

**Looking Back and Ahead** In this section, you have read about Stone Age hunter-gatherer societies and their improved ability to survive. In the next section, you will learn how early peoples survived long periods called ice ages.

# Section 2 Check Your Progress

**Progress Monitoring** ⊕nline
**For:** Self-test with instant help
**Visit:** PHSchool.com
**Web Code:** mwa-1012

**Standards Review** H-SS: 6.1.1; E-LA: Reading 6.2.1

**Comprehension and Critical Thinking**

**1. (a) Explain** What were three ways that modern humans were different from Neanderthals?
**(b) Apply Information** Which of these differences was most important to the future of humankind? Explain.

**2. (a) Recall** When did modern humans appear?
**(b) Compare** How might the development of language have helped modern humans survive?

**Reading Skill**

**3. Use Text Structure to Obtain Information** Refer to the feature on pages 16–17. What is its title? How does this separate text connect to the main text? Why does it appear after Section 2?

**Vocabulary** *Builder*
Read each sentence below. If the sentence is true, write YES. If the sentence is not true, write NO and explain WHY.
**4.** Neanderthals struggled to survive because they were not <u>intelligent</u>.

**5.** Modern humans learned to use <u>symbols</u> to communicate their ideas.

**Writing**
**6.** Write a topic sentence for a paragraph that will discuss the ways in which hunter-gatherer societies developed over time.

# Maroo of the Winter Caves

by Ann Turnbull (born in 1943)

## Prepare to Read

### Standards Preview

**H-SS 6.1.1** Describe the hunter-gatherer societies, including the development of tools and the use of fire.

**E-LA 3.1** Identify the forms of fiction and describe the major characteristics of each form.

### Reading Skill

**Analyze Historical Fiction** If an author makes up a story, it is considered fiction. The selection below is a kind of fiction called *historical fiction*. Historical fiction features imagined characters and events, but a real *setting*, or time and place in which the story takes place. As you read, note how the selection shows what life was like for Ice Age people.

### Vocabulary *Builder*

As you read this literature selection, look for the following underlined words:

**feigned** (FAYND) *adj.* not real; pretended

**flaying** (FLAY eeng) *v.* stripping off the skin

**carcass** (KAHR kuhs) *n.* dead body of an animal

**renowned** (rih NOWND) *adj.* well known; highly thought of

▶ **BACKGROUND**

The story in this book takes place in Europe during the last Ice Age. In this episode, the main character, a young girl named Maroo, along with her brother Otak and sister Nimai, greet a group of hunters led by their father, Areg, and another hunter named Tevo. The hunters have returned with a bison for the people to eat.

They ran faster, delighted to be first to greet the hunters. When they reached them, they stood, breathless, unable to speak.

Tevo said modestly, "We have not had much luck. Just this small animal."

Otak and Maroo smiled. They knew that such modesty was <u>feigned</u>, merely the politeness expected of hunters who have made a magnificent kill. Their father made a joke of it, pretending to stagger under the weight of the beast. The children shouted with laughter, but Tevo gave Areg a disapproving look.

Otak signaled to the distant group of women who had gathered by the lakeside. He put his hands to his forehead, curving them like horns. The women knew this meant a bison. They began to move back up the slope toward the cave.

Behind Tevo and Areg came the other hunters. Areg's brother, Vorka, carried the spears. Otak chattered to Vorka, and the young man told him about the hunt as they walked back to the cave.

Everyone was waiting at the cave mouth. The women helped to lower the great animal onto the flat ground outside the cave, and immediately began <u>flaying</u> it with sharp stone knives. Blood was collected in a bowl made from a deer's skull, and passed around for the hunters to drink. Old Mother, meanwhile, had made the fire hot and was giving drinks of herb-flavored water to the women and children.

One of the elders, Keriatek, brought out a small drum and began to tap a rhythm. The women sang as they worked. Maroo and an older girl were given stone scrapers and set to cleaning every scrap of flesh from the flayed skin. It was hard work, but they joined in the singing and thought of the feast to come. The liver and other soft parts were cut out and eaten raw, but the children had none: the hunters came first.

Before long the <u>carcass</u> was jointed, and chunks of meat were stuck on sticks and roasting over the fire. Fat splashed, sizzling, into the flames. Maroo, still scraping at the hide, felt limp with hunger.

At last enough meat was cooked for the feast to begin. Old Mother called everyone to stop working and come to eat. Maroo was handed a meaty bone. It was so hot she almost dropped it. But she was too hungry to care about getting burned, and began tearing at the hot flesh with her teeth.

The feast lasted all day. They did not eat all the time, but stopped to talk and sing and tell stories. The hunters were tired and stretched, yawning, by the fire, but Nimai made sure her father did not fall asleep. She climbed onto his knees and giggled as he tossed her about and fed her tidbits. Vorka smiled quietly at Areg's games; he lived in his elder brother's shadow.

Soon Vorka slipped away to the back of the cave and came back with Areg's drum. He offered it to his brother, who was a <u>renowned</u> drummer. Nimai squealed as Areg swung her down and took the drum. He began to experiment with a rhythm. The small drum was made of hide stretched over bone and decorated with fox-fur pompoms on thongs that spun outward as Areg tossed and caught the drum and tapped a complex rhythm. Everyone began to clap and sing.

—From *Maroo of the Winter Caves,* by Ann Turnbull.
© 1984, Clarion Books.

**Prehistoric carving of a bison made from a reindeer antler**

E-LA 3.1 **Analyze Historical Fiction**
In this piece of historical fiction, information about the past is presented very differently from the way it is within the sections of the chapter. How do these two forms of writing about history differ? Do you think that historical fiction helps people better understand history? Why or why not?

**Checkpoint** What clues tell you that this story took place a very long time ago?

## *Analyze* LITERATURE

Maroo's people prepared the bison and held a huge feast. People today prepare food and have similar celebrations to mark certain special occasions. Write a short paragraph that describes important similarities and differences between Ice Age feasts and feasts of today.

If you liked this story about early humans, you might want to read another work of historical fiction about early humans, ***Malu's Wolf*** by Ruth Craig. *Puffin Books, 1997*

**H-SS 6.1.2** Identify the locations of human communities that populated the major regions of the world and describe how humans adapted to a variety of environments.

**E-LA Reading 6.2.1** Identify the structural features of popular media (e.g., newspapers, magazines, online information) and use the features to obtain information.

## Reading Preview

 **Reading Skill**

**Use Structural Features** This textbook includes pictures, maps, graphs, and charts. These visuals contain important information that adds to the main text. You can use these visuals by reading their titles and labels, studying the captions or map legends, and looking for names or facts that link the items to the main text. Ask yourself: How does this information make the main text clearer to me?

**Vocabulary** *Builder*

**High-Use Words**
debate (dee BAYT), p. 19
expose (ehk SPOHZ), p. 21

**Key Terms and People**
populate (PAHP yoo layt), p. 18
migration (mi GRAY shuhn), p. 19
environment (ehn VI ruhn muhnt), p. 20
adapt (uh DAPT), p. 20

**Background Knowledge**   Over millions of years, many groups of early humans appeared and then died out. *Homo sapiens,* or modern humans like us, were the last of these groups to appear. As you will read, scientists still have much to learn about the development of the first modern humans. But one fact is clear: These large-brained "wise people" were often on the move. Over many thousands of years, they spread out to **populate,** or become inhabitants of, every region of the world.

**Main Idea**
Soon after their appearance, modern humans populated the world's major regions.

## The Human Migration

Modern humans appeared late in the history of humankind. Most archaeologists agree that *Homo sapiens* have walked Earth for only about 100,000 years. But they do not agree on where modern humans came from or how they spread around the world. In fact, scientists continue to study both fossils and genetic information, or the qualities that living things pass from one generation to the next, in order to learn more about the movement of early humans.

Some scientists in this <u>debate</u> think that *Homo sapiens*, like other early humans, originated in Africa. From there, they argue, *Homo sapiens* began a long migration to other regions of the world. A **migration** is the movement of people from their homeland to other places. These scientists suggest that as modern humans moved to new places, they gradually replaced the older groups already living there.

Other scientists disagree. They believe that large-brained groups of humans evolved in many parts of the world. These scientists argue that as regional populations mixed together, the different groups eventually became the one group known today as *Homo sapiens*.

Wherever *Homo sapiens* first appeared, they spread fairly rapidly across Earth. By about 30,000 years ago, these modern humans lived in Africa, Asia, Europe, and Australia. By at least 12,500 years ago, they had reached North America and South America.

✔ Checkpoint  **In which regions did modern humans appear?**

**Vocabulary *Builder***
<u>debate</u> (dee BAYT) *n.* discussion or argument on a subject that people express different opinions about

## The First Great Migration

Early humans gradually migrated to many parts of the world over time. How did they reach these locations? This map shows some of the routes by which early humans may have traveled. **Critical Thinking: Draw Conclusions** *Why do you think South America would be one of the last areas to which early humans migrated?*

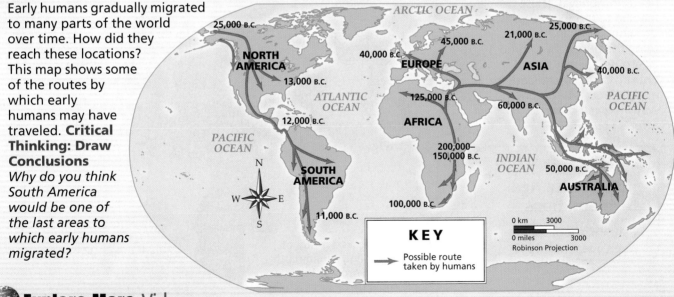

**Explore More** Video

**Discovery School Video**
View *The First Great Migration* to learn more about the migration of early humans around the world.

# Adapting to Varied Environments

As modern humans migrated, they settled in a variety of **environments,** or surroundings. Each new place had its own climate, plants, and animals.

With each move, people had to **adapt,** or change their way of life, to suit their new environment. They had to find out which plants could be eaten. They had to learn to hunt different animals and to find new materials for tools and shelters.

**A Changing Climate**  People also had to adapt to changes in Earth's climate. Over the past two million years—including most of the Stone Age—Earth experienced four long ice ages. The last great Ice Age began about 70,000 years ago, soon after modern humans appeared.

During this period, thick sheets of ice, called glaciers, spread across large regions of Earth. Glaciers covered the northern parts of Europe, Asia, and North America. Parts of the Southern Hemisphere were also under ice.

**Ice Age Adaptation**
Ice Age climate change caused people of the time to adapt to their surroundings. This visual shows some of the ways in which they used their environment to meet their needs for survival. These people learned to produce food, clothing, tools, and shelter using the things they found all around them. **Critical Thinking: Analyze Cause and Effect**  *What is one way in which climate affects your life?*

**History** *Interactive*
**Explore Ice Age Adaptations**

**Visit:** PHSchool.com
**Web Code:** mwp-1013

This image shows a group of hunters attacking a mammoth. By working in groups, Ice Age people could more successfully hunt such animals. Also working together, they could construct huts from the bones of mammoths.

With so much of Earth's water frozen in the glaciers, rainfall decreased. Areas that had once been well-watered grasslands became deserts. Sea levels dropped, <u>exposing</u> "land bridges" where ocean waters had once been. With these changes, many animals had to migrate to find food. The people who depended on these animals for food had little choice but to follow.

**Vocabulary** *Builder*
<u>expose</u> (ehk SPOHZ) *v.* to allow to be seen; reveal; display

**Staying Warm**   Ice Age hunter-gatherers adapted to climate change in many ways. As winters grew longer, people learned to use whatever materials they could find to build warm shelters. In Eastern Europe, for example, people built huts out of mammoth bones. Mammoths were huge furry elephants that lived during the Ice Age. These huts were covered with animal skins to keep out the winter wind and snow.

People also found other ways to stay warm. Using bone needles, they sewed snug clothing from animal skins and furs. They kept fires burning in their hearths day and night.

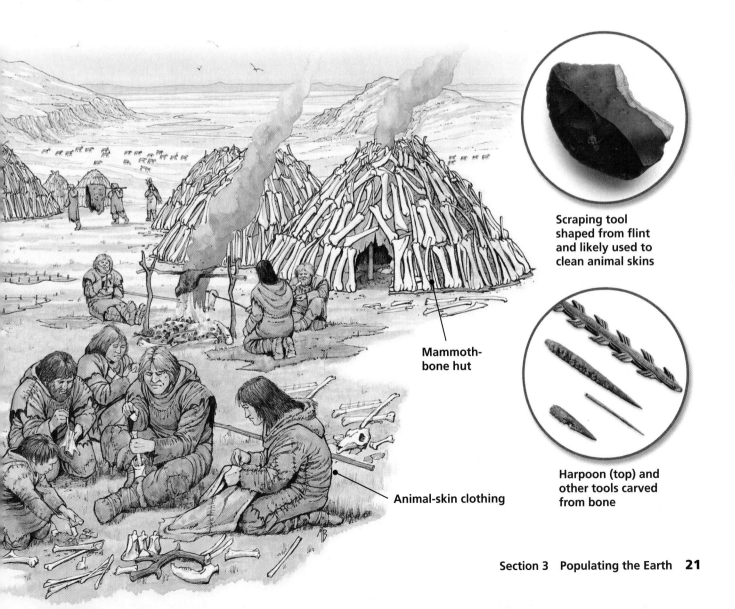

Scraping tool shaped from flint and likely used to clean animal skins

Mammoth-bone hut

Harpoon (top) and other tools carved from bone

Animal-skin clothing

**Early Artists**
The cave paintings at Lascaux Grotto in France depict approximately 600 animals and symbols in a variety of colors. The stone figure shown is an example of a fertility symbol created by modern humans. **Critical Thinking: Frame Questions** *What questions might an archaeologist ask after studying the painting and the stone figure?*

**E-LA 6.2.1 Use Structural Features**
What does the group of images above show you? How do these images help you understand the text?

**Main Idea**
New art forms, burial practices, and beliefs suggest that Ice Age cultures became more complex over time.

**Forming Larger Communities** Some groups adapted to change by forming larger communities. In larger groups, hunters could work together to kill animals such as mammoths. They could also better defend their communities from attack.

In time, communities began to trade with one another for special stones or shells. They likely also traded information about finding food during hard times.

✔**Checkpoint** How did people adapt to the changing conditions of the last Ice Age?

## Developing Complex Cultures

Over many years, the culture of Ice Age communities became more complex. *Complex* means having many parts that connect with one another.

In Europe, Ice Age hunters produced early examples of art. They painted the walls and ceilings of caves in present-day Spain and France with images such as the ones that you see on this page. Although the meanings of these paintings are not known, artists may have hoped that painting an animal would give them power over the animal during a hunt.

Ice Age artists also carved small statues of animals and pregnant women. Some of these items may have been created to bring good luck to hunters or to women about to give birth.

Burials became more complex as well. An Ice Age grave found in present-day Russia contained the bodies of two children, a boy about 13 years old and a girl about 8 years old. Both children were covered with thousands of ivory beads. The boy wore on his chest an ivory pendant carved in the shape of a mammoth. The girl wore a bead cap and an ivory pin at her throat.

Discoveries like these suggest that modern humans may have been trying to explain things that they found mysterious, such as birth and death. They may have developed ideas about powerful beings that humans could not see. Their beliefs would represent the beginnings of religion.

 **Checkpoint** **What is one way in which the culture of Ice Age people grew more complex?**

**Looking Back and Ahead** In this section, you have read how humans populated the major regions of the world. You also have learned how people adapted to new environments and to climate change. In the next chapter, you will find out what happened when people learned how to grow their own food.

---

## Section 3 Check Your Progress

**Progress Monitoring** Online
**For:** Self-test with instant help
**Visit:** PHSchool.com
**Web Code:** mwa-1013

 **Standards Review** H-SS: 6.1.2; E-LA: Reading 6.2.1

### Comprehension and Critical Thinking

1. (a) **Identify** What were the last two major regions of the world to be settled by modern humans?
   (b) **Apply Information** Use the map on page 19 to help explain the migration of people to these parts of the world.

2. (a) **Explain** How did the environment change during the last Ice Age?
   (b) **Evaluate Information** How did these changes lead to further migration?

### Reading Skill

3. **Use Structural Features** Look at pages 18–19. Identify the text and structural features on this page. Explain what information they provide.

### Vocabulary *Builder*

4. Write two definitions for each word: populate, migration, environment, and adapt. First, write a formal definition for your teacher. Second, write a definition in everyday English for a classmate.

### Writing

5. Make a simple outline that organizes in chronological order information from the section about the spread of human populations across the world. Include in your outline supporting details for each of your main points.

# Identify Main Ideas

When reading about history, you must identify the main ideas, or decide what information is most important. Learning to identify the main idea of a passage will help you understand what you have read.

 **Chapter Standards**

**English-Language Arts**
Reading 6.2.3 Connect and clarify main ideas by studying their relationships to other sources and related topics.

Ice Age hunter-gatherers moved from place to place in the spring and summer months while following migrating animals. During the long, cold winters, they often stayed in one place. Throughout the year, however, these people needed shelters to protect them.

As they moved in the spring and summer, the hunter-gatherers favored simple shelters that were easy to put up and take down. A tent made from hides provided good shelter during these seasons.

When cold temperatures came, hunter-gatherers required sturdier shelters that gave more protection from snow and wind. As a result, caves offered good places to live during the winter. Other Ice Age people built huts from stone or mammoth bones, while some constructed huts in shallow pits.

**Learn the Skill** *Follow these steps to learn how to identify main ideas.*

1. **Find and state the main idea of the introductory paragraph.** Topic sentences often state the main idea of a paragraph.

2. **Identify the main ideas of the remaining paragraphs.** For those with no topic sentence, find the main idea by identifying the key point made by the details of the paragraph.

3. **Identify what the main ideas have in common.** Connecting the main ideas of the paragraphs in a passage can help you clarify the main idea of the entire passage.

4. **Use these connections to state the main idea of the passage.** Identifying a main idea helps you understand why the information presented in a passage is important.

**Practice the Skill** *Answer the following questions about the passage above.*

1. **Find and state the main idea of the introductory paragraph.** What is the topic sentence of the first paragraph?

2. **Identify the main ideas of the remaining paragraphs in the passage.** Do the second and third paragraphs have topic sentences? What are their main ideas?

3. **Identify what the main ideas have in common.** What connections can you make between the main ideas of the paragraphs?

4. **Use these connections to state the main idea of the passage.** What is the main idea of the complete passage?

**Apply the Skill**
*See page 27 of the Review and Assessment.*

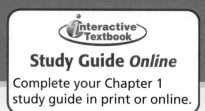

**Study Guide** *Online*
Complete your Chapter 1 study guide in print or online.

## Chapter Summary  H-SS: 6.1; 6.1.1; 6.1.2

### Section 1  Studying the Distant Past

- Archaeologists study prehistoric times by examining things that early peoples left behind.
- The study of fossils has helped archaeologists learn about the lives of the earliest humans.
- Archaeological studies suggest that the earliest humans lived in Africa millions of years ago.

### Section 2  Hunter-Gatherer Societies

- Hunter-gatherer societies moved from place to place, hunting small animals and gathering plants for food.
- The development of tools and the use of fire helped the people in hunter-gatherer societies improve their lives.
- Modern humans developed the ability to use language, which helped them to survive.

### Section 3  Populating the Earth

- By about 12,500 years ago, modern humans had spread to many regions of the world, including Africa, Asia, Europe, Australia, North America, and South America.
- Modern humans adapted to Ice Age conditions by building shelters and making warm clothing.
- By forming larger groups, modern humans adapted in order to better hunt and defend themselves.

**Ice Age hunters**

## Standards Practice  H-SS: 6.1; 6.1.1; 6.1.2

## Vocabulary *Builder*

### High-Use Words

Draw a table with three rows and three columns. In the first column, list the following high-use words from this chapter: <u>layer</u>, <u>symbol</u>, and <u>debate</u>. In the next column, write the definition of each word. In the last column, make a small illustration that shows the meaning of the word.

### Key Terms

Decide whether each highlighted word is used correctly. If it is, explain why. If not, rewrite the rest of the sentence to make it logical.

1. Scientists study **fossils,** such as pieces of pottery, to learn about early humans.

2. Because they learned to use tools, early hunter-gatherers were called **nomads.**

3. *Homo sapiens* began a **migration** from their homes to other parts of the world.

4. Modern humans have often had to **adapt** in order to live in changing surroundings.

##  Apply Reading Skills

**Use Structural Features** Review the contents of pages 2–3. Identify the text and structural features shown on these pages, and explain what information they provide.

## Comprehension and Critical Thinking

**1. (a) Explain** Describe the conditions under which fossils can form.
**(b) Apply Information** What types of information can archaeologists expect to learn from studying fossils?
**(c) Draw Conclusions** In which parts of the world might archaeologists continue their search for the oldest human fossils? Why?

**2. (a) Recall** How did the development of tools prove useful for early humans?
**(b) Analyze Cause and Effect** How would such a development have improved these people's chances for survival?
**(c) Link Past and Present** What is one recent development that has similarly improved the lives of people today?

**3. (a) List** What two major groups of humans appeared around the end of the Stone Age?
**(b) Compare** In what ways were these two groups similar?
**(c) Evaluate Information** State one explanation given for the disappearance of the first group. Describe a piece of evidence that would support that explanation.

**4. (a) Detect Points of View** Explain the two views in the debate regarding the migration of modern humans.
**(b) Draw Inferences** How did the migration of modern humans encourage the development of their tools, shelters, and cultures?

## Researching

**Archaeological Studies** The work of archaeologists has provided a great deal of information about the lives of early people. In this activity, you will use the Internet and the library media center to research and report on the work of archaeologists. Choose a task below to work on. Post your project on an "Archaeological Studies" bulletin board in the classroom. Make a list of the resources you used for your project.

**Scientists:** Make a map that shows the locations of major archaeological sites in California. Include on your map labels and captions that briefly identify and describe each site.

**Journalists:** Write a short article reporting on an archaeological site you discover through your research. Your article should detail topics such as who is working at the site and what they have found or hope to find.

> **Researching Online**
> **For:** Help in starting this activity
> **Visit:** PHSchool.com
> **Web Code:** mwe-1013

## Writing

**1. Write a paragraph on the following topic.** Modern humans have often had to adapt to changing environments. Explain how modern humans adapted to Earth's changing climate during the last Ice Age.
**Your paragraph should:**
- describe the types of environments facing modern humans.
- give specific examples of adaptation.
- begin with a clear topic sentence.
- give evidence or examples to support the topic sentence.

**2. Write a short narrative.** Imagine you are Donald Johanson. Write a few sentences describing your discovery of "Lucy."

# Apply Analysis Skills

Use the text entitled Developing Complex Cultures in Section 3 to answer these questions:

1. Read the first paragraph. What is its main idea?

2. What is the main idea of the second paragraph? What is the main idea of the third paragraph?

3. Does the fifth paragraph have a topic sentence? What is the main idea of this paragraph?

4. What do the main ideas of each of the paragraphs in this passage have in common?

5. What is the main idea of the whole passage?

# Test Yourself

1. **To which of the following continents did humans migrate last?**
   A Asia
   B Africa
   C Europe
   D South America

2. **What was one major factor that influenced the migration of early humans?**
   A changing climate
   B common language
   C cultural innovation
   D radioactive material

**Refer to the quotation below to answer Question 3.**

3. **Why would Michael Brunet make this statement about his fossil discovery?**

   *"This is the beginning, just the beginning."*

   A to claim that no older fossil will be discovered
   B to disprove the findings of other archaeologists
   C to suggest that more research be conducted
   D to debate the human features of the fossil

4. **Hunter-gatherer societies**
   A built cities.
   B ate only plants.
   C used fire and tools.
   D could read and write.

**Refer to the image below to answer Question 5.**

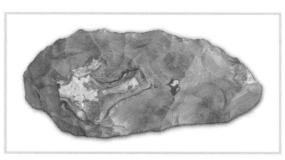

5. **Stone Age people may have used a tool such as this to**
   A start fires.
   B cut materials.
   C build land bridges.
   D construct brick shelters.

6. **Which of the following shows that *Homo sapiens* developed language?**
   A clothing made from animal skins
   B Neanderthal graves
   C symbols in cave paintings
   D stone tools

## Chapter 2

# The Beginning of Civilization (10,000 B.C.–A.D. 250)

## Prepare to Read

 **Chapter Standards**

### History-Social Science

**6.1** Students describe what is known through archaeological studies of the early physical and cultural development of humankind from the Paleolithic era to the agricultural revolution.

**Section 1,** pp. 32–37
### Early Agriculture

**Section 2,** pp. 40–45
### Cities and Civilizations

**Section 3,** pp. 46–51
### The Maya Civilization

 **What You Will Learn**

When people began to farm, they established permanent settlements. Ways of living and working changed dramatically.

Some farming villages grew into the world's first cities. Because farmers produced extra food, city residents were free to create specialized jobs and develop complex societies.

The Maya farmed and built cities in present-day Mexico and Central America. Their achievements include an advanced writing system, many scientific discoveries, and highly developed arts.

Sculpture of a Sumerian man

**Chapter Events**

**10,000 B.C.**
The last Ice Age ends.

**8000 B.C.**
People begin to grow their own crops.

10,000 B.C.

7500 B.C.

5000 B.C.

**Where and When?**
About 13,000 years ago, people in the Indus River valley of South Asia, as well as in the Middle East and Africa began to farm and to establish permanent settlements.

About 4,500 years ago, farming and trade flourished at Mohenjo-Daro, a city of about 35,000 people in the Indus River valley.

**3500 B.C.**
The world's first cities appear in the Middle East.

**3000s B.C.**
The first civilizations develop in river valleys.

**A.D. 250**
Maya civilization takes shape.

**5000 B.C.**

**2500 B.C.**

**B.C./A.D.**

# How to Read History

## History Reading Skill

### Previewing **Read Text Fluently**

Reading fluently means reading smoothly, without stumbling. When you read fluently, you will "hear" the text and understand the meaning more easily. Look at the examples below for suggestions on how to read fluently.

**Chapter Standards**

**English-Language Arts**

**Reading 6.1.1** Read aloud narrative and expository text fluently and accurately and with appropriate pacing, intonation, and expression.

**❶** Read each sentence in groups of words that go together. In the sentence below, this means pausing at natural breaks in ideas. The underlined groups of words show these pauses.

More often, fossil hunters find a bone here or a tooth there.

> **Pause at the comma.** **Pause to show different ideas.**

**❷** In this example, it is important to read accurately. Otherwise, you may not understand how old the fossils were.

Tests showed that the fossils found by the Leakeys were at least **1.75 million years old.**

> **Read as "one point seven five million."**

**❸** Most sentences need to be read with expression. Others have words that should be stressed. When you read with expression, you put the meaning of the sentence into your voice. Try reading aloud to find the right expression.

> **The second sentence tells you how exciting the discovery of fire must have been. Show that excitement in your voice as you read the first sentence.**

Sometime during this period, people learned how to use fire. **This was a wonderful discovery.** Over time, Stone Age toolmakers became **more** skillful. Their stone blades became **thinner and sharper.**

> **Stress this word.**

> **Adding stress to these words makes clear how the tools changed.**

# Vocabulary *Builder*

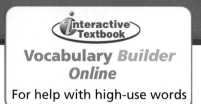

**Interactive Textbook**

**Vocabulary** *Builder* **Online**

For help with high-use words

## *Previewing* **High-Use Academic Words**

| High-Use Word | Definition | Sample Sentence About History |
|---|---|---|
| **shrink** (shringk) (Section 1, p. 32) | *v.* to become smaller; to contract | The size of the lake began to <u>shrink</u> as less water was available. |
| **benefit** (BEHN uh fiht) (Section 1, p. 35) | *n.* good effect or advantage | Fire was a great <u>benefit</u> to early peoples. |
| **found** (fownd) (Section 2, p. 40) | *v.* to start a city or an organization | Some early peoples <u>founded</u> large communities so that everyone could work together. |
| **maintain** (mān TĀN) (Section 2, p. 44) | *v.* to provide what is needed to make something continue | Hunter-gatherers used stone for tools to <u>maintain</u> their way of life. |
| **structure** (STRUHK cher) (Section 3, p. 49) | *n.* how parts connect to form a whole | We do not know the <u>structure</u> of human groups during the last Ice Age. |
| **impressive** (ihm PREHS ihv) (Section 3, p. 51) | *adj.* causing admiration | Mary and Louis Leakey made an <u>impressive</u> discovery of human fossils in Africa. |

## *Previewing* **Key Terms and People**

**Maya hieroglyph**

## Standards Preview

**H-SS 6.1.3** Discuss the climatic changes and human modifications of the physical environment that gave rise to the domestication of plants and animals and new sources of clothing and shelter.

**E-LA Reading 6.1.1** Read aloud narrative and expository text fluently and accurately and with appropriate pacing, intonation, and expression.

## Reading Preview

### Reading Skill

**Read Fluently** You can use punctuation and clue words to help you read fluently. Punctuation tells you when one group of ideas ends and another begins. For example, the sentence might be "About 12,000 years ago, the last Ice Age ended." The comma tells you to pause after *ago.* Clue words such as *but* or *and* also connect one group of ideas to another.

### Vocabulary *Builder*

**High-Use Words**
shrink (shringk), p. 32
benefit (BEHN uh fiht), p. 35

**Key Terms**
domesticate (doh MEHS tih kāt), p. 33
revolution (rehv uh LOO shuhn), p. 36
surplus (SER pluhs), p. 37
specialize (SPEHSH uhl īz), p. 37

**Background Knowledge** As you have learned in Chapter 1, most people lived as hunter-gatherers and moved to follow their food supply. After the last Ice Age ended, people had to adapt to a changing environment in order to survive. In this chapter, you will find out how this change in climate set the stage for the birth of farming.

**Main Idea**
People began to farm in the Middle East about 10,000 years ago.

**Vocabulary *Builder***
shrink (shringk) *v.* to become smaller; to contract

## The Birth of Farming

When the last Ice Age ended, about 12,000 years ago, a long period of global warming began. Temperatures rose around the world, and rainfall patterns changed. Glaciers that had covered so much of Earth began to <u>shrink</u>, and ocean levels rose.

Most plants and animals adapted to these changes. Cold-loving fir trees spread north into once-icy regions. Some large Ice Age animals did not adapt to a warmer world, and many species died out. People who had hunted some of these animals for food had to find something else to eat.

**Modifying the Environment** Some people adapted to these changes by searching for new sources of food. They found smaller animals to hunt. People living near rivers and lakes began to depend more on fish for food.

Others sought ways to modify or change their environment so that it would produce more food. For example, people cleared trees and bushes by setting an area on fire. The grasses that grew back attracted grazing animals such as deer. People also found ways to encourage the growth of wild food plants.

**Domesticating Plants and Animals** Over time, people began to domesticate the plants and animals that they used for food. To **domesticate** means to change the behavior of a population of animals or plants in ways that are useful for humans. The domestication of plants and animals marked the birth of farming.

At first, there was little difference between wild and domesticated plants and animals. Year after year, people selected the seeds of the plants that produced the best crops to sow again. As a result, domesticated plants began to produce more abundant food of higher quality. A wild tomato, for example, is the size of a cherry, but the domesticated tomato is the size of an orange. In contrast, some breeds of domesticated goats, pigs, and cattle are smaller than their wild ancestors. Smaller animals may have been easier to manage.

**E-LA 6.1.1 Read Fluently**
How does punctuation show you where to pause in the fourth sentence of this paragraph?

**Herding Sheep**
This shepherd in present-day Tunisia watches over his animals in much the same way as early farmers did. **Critical Thinking: Draw Inferences** *Why do you think a shepherd must watch over domesticated sheep as they graze?*

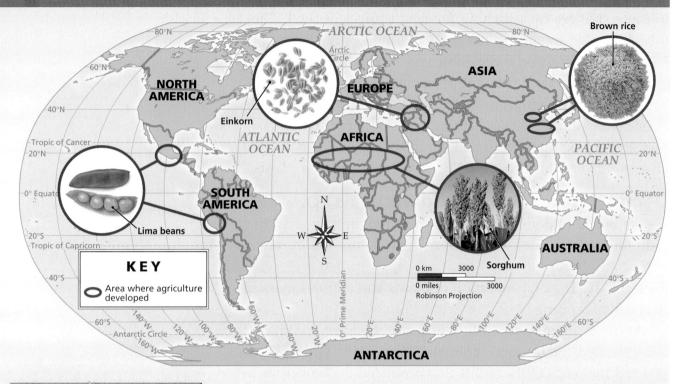

**KEY**

⬭ Area where agriculture developed

## MAP★MASTER
### Skills Activity

Early people learned to farm in many different parts of the world.

**(a) Identify** Where did early farmers grow sorghum?

**(b) Distinguish Relevant Information** Which continents had the greatest number of areas where people learned to farm? Which had the fewest?

**MapMaster** ◉nline

**For:** Interactive map
**Visit:** PHSchool.com
**Web Code:** mwd-1021

## The First Centers of Agriculture

The Middle East became the first center of agriculture, or farming, about 10,000 years ago. There, scientists have unearthed seeds buried long ago from domesticated wheat plants. The seeds are similar to wild varieties of wheat that still grow in the area.

As the map on this page shows, farming spread from the Middle East westward into Africa. It may also have spread northward into Europe and eastward into the Indus River valley of South Asia.

The map also shows that other centers of agriculture appeared independently in different areas of the world. For example, farming began with the growing of wheat and barley in southwestern Asia. These crops then spread to Egypt. In the southern part of present-day China, farming began with the domestication of rice. Farther to the north, a grain called millet was the first crop to be domesticated.

Farming started in the Americas with the domestication of maize, or corn, in present-day Mexico. Farther north, farmers domesticated the sunflower. In South America, people learned to grow potatoes, beans, and squash. In Africa, farming began with crops such as sorghum and yams.

**The Costs and Benefits of Farming** Wherever centers of agriculture developed, people had to decide whether to live as nomadic hunter-gatherers, or as farmers. Each way of life had costs as well as benefits.

**Vocabulary** *Builder*
benefit (BEHN uh fiht) *n.* good effect or advantage

Some of the costs of shifting to farming were clear. First, farming took much time and energy for planting crops and herding animals. Second, farming was risky. If a crop failed, a family might starve. Third, farming could be dangerous. Bands of nomads might attack farmers and steal their food.

Agriculture also offered many benefits. Farming produced far more food and required less land than hunting and gathering. One historian estimated that a Stone Age farm family needed 25 acres of land to raise enough food for a year. In contrast, a hunter-gatherer family needed about 20,000 acres on which to find enough food for a year.

Another benefit of farming was that people could build permanent homes and villages. People used a mixture of mud and straw to form walls. The sun baked and hardened the mud mixture. People then placed poles and branches across the tops of the walls and covered them with mud, forming a roof.

Farming also provided new sources of material for clothing. People used fibers from animals and plants to make cloth. Wool and other animal hair provided fibers that people used to form yarn or thread. People also wove cloth from plant fibers such as cotton and flax.

Some groups tried farming and then returned to hunting and gathering. But in the end, most people chose farming.

**✓ Checkpoint** How did most people become farmers?

## Farming and Hunting-Gathering

1 square ■ = 25 acres

A hunter-gatherer family needed 20,000 acres of land in order to find enough food for a year.

A farm family needed 25 acres or less to raise enough food for a year.

**Reading Diagrams**

Hunter-gatherers and farmers used land differently and needed different amounts of land for survival.

**(a) Read a Diagram** Which group needed large areas of land, farmers or hunter-gatherers?

**(b) Identify Benefits** Why did people mainly choose farming as opposed to hunting and gathering?

## Çatalhüyük

Çatalhüyük once was a busy community with many houses built close together. The picture below shows what the site looks like today. Archaeologists have excavated the site to learn about Çatalhüyük. **Critical Thinking: Draw Conclusions** *Why might people want to build their houses close together?*

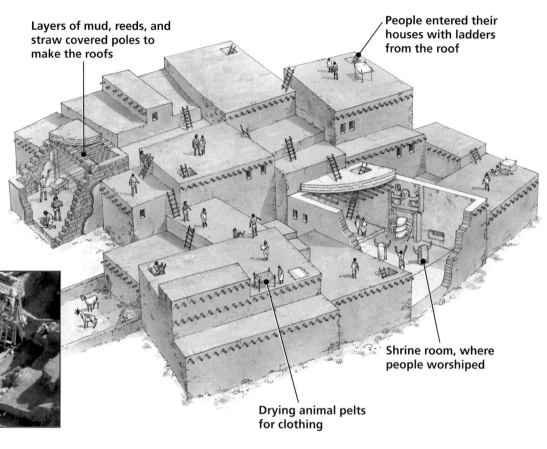

Layers of mud, reeds, and straw covered poles to make the roofs

People entered their houses with ladders from the roof

Shrine room, where people worshiped

Drying animal pelts for clothing

# New Ways of Living

Farming changed the ways that people lived. Nomads stopped wandering and settled in one place. They learned to plan for the next harvest. These changes took place over a 2,000- to 4,000-year period. Historians call the shift from hunting to farming the birth of agriculture. It is also known as the Neolithic agricultural revolution. A **revolution** is a complete change in ways of thinking, working, or living.

**New Kinds of Shelter**  Farming enabled nomads to build permanent shelters and fill their homes with furniture, tools, clay pots, and other goods. These items would have been too heavy to move from one campsite to another.

One of the oldest known farming settlements is a village called Çatalhüyük (cha tal hu YOOK). This village stood in present-day Turkey more than 8,000 years ago. The people of Çatalhüyük lived in two-story houses made of mud and reeds. Houses were so close together that people used the rooftops for streets. A few thousand people may have lived in this new kind of community.

**Surpluses and Specialization**   As crops and herds improved, the amount of food that farmers could produce each year increased. Some families raised a **surplus,** or more than they needed to feed themselves. When there was a surplus of food, not everyone in a village needed to farm. Some people could **specialize,** or spend most of their time working at a craft. They could then trade the goods they made for the surplus food grown by farmers.

Çatalhüyük supported many specialists. Skilled toolmakers turned stone into polished axes and knives. Potters shaped clay into bowls. Weavers wove sheep's wool into cloth. A few people also became skilled at metalworking. Early metalworkers heated ore to extract, or remove, such metals as copper and tin.

 **Checkpoint**  In what ways did life change after people began to farm?

**Looking Back and Ahead**   In this section, you have read about how the change in climate conditions led to the Neolithic agricultural revolution. You have learned how new farming changed the ways that people lived. In the next section, you will learn how farm villages grew into cities and civilizations.

## Section 1 Check Your Progress

**Progress Monitoring** Online
**For:** Self-test with instant help
**Visit:** PHSchool.com
**Web Code:** mwa-1021

**Standards Review**  H-SS: 6.1.3; E-LA: Reading 6.1.1

**Comprehension and Critical Thinking**

1. **(a) Recall**  When and where did farming first begin?
   **(b) Apply Information**  How did farming spread from one place to another?

2. **(a) Explain**  What were farming settlements like?
   **(b) Draw Conclusions**  How did having a surplus of food change how people worked?

**Reading Skill**

3. **Read Fluently**  Read this sentence. Then, write the sentence and use slashes (/) to show pauses between groups of words: Skilled toolmakers turned stone into polished axes and knives.

**Vocabulary** *Builder*

4. Write two definitions for each word: domesticate, specialize. First, write a formal definition for your teacher. Second, write a definition in everyday English for a classmate.

**Writing**

5. List in chronological order the steps that led to the development of farming.

# Tilling the Soil

About 12,000 years ago, people began to farm. The ability to grow plants and raise animals meant that people did not have to rely on hunting and gathering. The invention of farming made civilization possible. Farming allowed people to stay in one place all year long. It allowed them to produce more food and to feed more people. As a result, populations increased. Towns began to develop. Over time, towns became cities, and cities became civilizations.

**History-Social Science**

**6.2.2** Trace the development of agricultural techniques that permitted the production of economic surplus and the emergence of cities as centers of culture and power.

**Historical Interpretation 3** Students explain the sources of historical continuity and how the combination of ideas and events explains the emergence of new patterns.

Flint cutting edge (c. 4000–2300 B.C.) in modern handle

**1 Clearing the Ground**
In some areas with trees, farmers used axes like this one to clear huge areas of land for their fields.

Bronze cutting edge

Reproduction handle

Iron cutting edge

**2 The First Harvest**
Einkorn wheat grows wild in present-day Turkey and Iran. It was first cultivated, or planted and grown by people, in those areas.

**3 Backbreaking Task**
Cereal crops were cut with sickles. These three sickles represent the three "Ages" of prehistory: Stone, Bronze, and Iron.

### ◀ 4 Threshing

This Iron Age farmer is beating stalks of wheat to remove the grain.

Quern

Stone held in hand used for grinding

Grain ready for grinding

### 5 ▶ From Grain to Flour

This is a stone quern, or hand mill used for grinding grain. This type of quern was used about 4,000 to 6,000 years ago. Grain was placed on the flat surface of the quern and ground into flour with the stone.

### ◀ 6 Bread

Bread made in the Stone Age was flat because it was made without yeast.

### *Analyze* LIFE AT THE TIME

You are a farmer in the ancient Middle East, and you have used a bronze sickle for the first time. Write a short paragraph that explains the benefits of a metal sickle. In what ways will it help you produce more food crops?

# 2 Cities and Civilizations

**H-SS 6.2.1** Locate and describe the major river systems and discuss the physical settings that supported permanent settlement and early civilizations.

**E-LA Reading 6.1.1** Read aloud narrative and expository text fluently and accurately and with appropriate pacing, intonation, and expression.

## Reading Preview

### Reading Skill

**Read Accurately** Social studies text includes many facts, such as dates and place names. Slow down when you see a date or place name. Look at this sentence: "The world's first cities appeared in the Middle East around 3500 B.C." Read the place name *Middle East* as one term. Read the date *3500 B.C.* as "three thousand five hundred bee cee." Notice the word *first*, which gives key information about when events happened.

### Vocabulary *Builder*

**High-Use Words**
found (fownd), p. 40
maintain (mān TĀN), p. 44

**Key Terms**
economy (ih KAHN uh mee), p. 41
civilization (sihv ih luh ZĀ shuhn), p. 42
resource (REE sors), p. 42
established religion (ih STAB lihsht rih LIHJ uhn), p. 44
social class (SOH shuhl klas), p. 44

**Background Knowledge** In Section 1, you have read about hunter-gatherers who changed their nomadic ways of life. As farming spread across the Middle East, many small, permanent settlements appeared. In time, some of these villages grew into cities. In this section, you will read about early cities and how they led to the rise of early civilizations.

**Main Idea**
Farming villages grew into cities with large populations.

## The First Cities

The world's first cities began as farming villages in the Middle East around 3500 B.C. As the villages grew, the people of one village began to trade with people of other villages. Trade, like farming, became an important source of wealth.

**Vocabulary** *Builder*
found (fownd) *v.* to start a city or an organization

**The City of Uruk** Many historians consider Uruk to be the world's first city. It was founded around 5000 B.C. in present-day Iraq and had houses, gardens, and large public buildings such as temples. Uruk was not the oldest city in the Middle East.

Çatalhüyük and other villages were older, but Uruk was different from these older villages.

One difference was Uruk's size. When the city was at its largest, more than 40,000 people lived there. Uruk covered an area of nearly 1,000 acres. In comparison, Çatalhüyük covered about 32 acres and was home to no more than 6,000 people.

Another difference was Uruk's form of government. Villages such as Çatalhüyük had little need for government. People behaved according to ancient village customs. A village council settled most disputes. A city such as Uruk was too large to manage that way. Uruk had a strong, well-organized government. The city's first rulers were probably temple priests. Later, powerful military leaders ruled Uruk as kings. These rulers had far more power than a village council did.

## Centers of Wealth

A city such as Uruk also had a more complex economy than did Çatalhüyük and other villages. An economy is the production, distribution, and use of goods and services. Çatalhüyük's economy was based mainly on farming. Uruk's economy, in contrast, was based on both -farming and trade. Workshops that produced all kinds of goods lined the city's streets. Traders from Uruk traveled widely. Archaeologists have found pottery and other trade goods from Uruk in many places in the Middle East.

**E-LA 6.1.1 Read Accurately**
Reading Skill

What words in the third sentence of this paragraph are the most important to read accurately?

**The World's First City**
Many artifacts, such as the one shown here, have been found where the ancient city of Uruk once stood in present-day Iraq. **Critical Thinking: Draw Inferences** *What can the remains of Uruk tell archaeologists about how the people lived?*

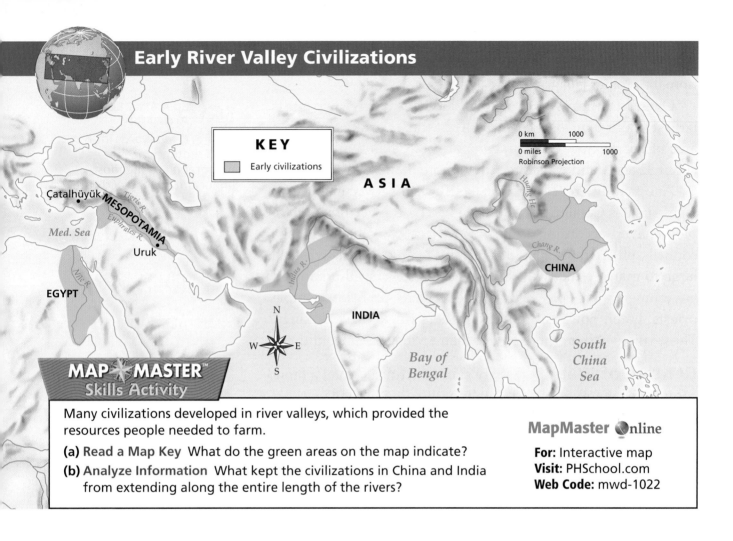

**KEY**

☐ Early civilizations

0 km    1000
0 miles    1000
Robinson Projection

ASIA

Çatalhüyük
MESOPOTAMIA
*Tigris R.*
*Euphrates R.*
Med. Sea
Uruk

*Nile R.*

EGYPT

*Indus R.*

*Huang He*

*Chang R.*

CHINA

INDIA

Bay of
Bengal

South
China
Sea

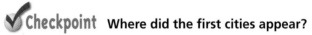
**MAP★MASTER**
*Skills Activity*

Many civilizations developed in river valleys, which provided the resources people needed to farm.

**(a) Read a Map Key** What do the green areas on the map indicate?

**(b) Analyze Information** What kept the civilizations in China and India from extending along the entire length of the rivers?

**MapMaster ●nline**

**For:** Interactive map
**Visit:** PHSchool.com
**Web Code:** mwd-1022

---

The wealth in Uruk and other cities attracted many people. Farmers and others living in the countryside began to move into the cities. Many early cities built walls to protect themselves from raiders. Uruk, for example, was surrounded by a wall 18 feet thick that stretched for 6 miles around the city. This wall was a sign that Uruk was a wealthy city worth protecting.

✓**Checkpoint** **Where did the first cities appear?**

**Main Idea**
Cities gave rise to civilizations, which had common features.

## The Rise of Civilizations

As early cities grew in size and power, some of them gave rise to civilizations. A **civilization** is a society that has cities, a well-organized government, and workers with specialized job skills. The word *civilization* comes from the Latin word *civis*, meaning "resident of a city."

The rise of early civilizations depended on the creation of a food surplus. Creating that surplus, in turn, depended on the ability of people to manage their resources well. A **resource** is a supply of something that can be used as needed.

The most important resources that people needed were soil, water, and seeds. However, these resources were worth little if people could not provide the labor and tools needed to produce enough food. Managing these resources well required a level of planning and organization that marked a new stage in human society.

**Settings of Early Civilizations** The first civilization also appeared in the Middle East. You will read more about this civilization in Chapter 3. In time, other early civilizations appeared in different parts of the world. You can see the locations of these early civilizations on the map on page 42.

Four of these early civilizations developed in major river valleys. River valleys provided a good setting for permanent settlements. Each year, the rivers rose and flooded the nearby land. When the floodwaters went down, a fresh layer of fertile soil remained that farmers could use to grow crops. Not all early civilizations began in river valleys, however. The Maya civilization, for example, started in the rain forests of present-day Mexico and Central America. The Inca civilization began in the Andes Mountains of South America.

**Features of Civilizations** In general, early civilizations shared seven features. The first of these shared features was cities. Cities served as centers of religion, government, and culture.

The second shared feature of an early civilization was a well-organized government. One benefit of government is managing society's resources. Another is organizing workers to build public works, such as roads, water systems, and city walls. A strong government can also form and train an army to defend a society from attack or to expand its borders. The rulers who governed early civilizations usually claimed that their right to rule came from the gods. A Chinese emperor, for example, called himself the "Son of Heaven."

**Rivers and Civilization**
Workers in Egypt today raise water from the Nile using methods similar to those used by workers from the river valley civilizations. **Critical Thinking: Link Past and Present** *Why might these methods still be used today?*

## Shared Features of Civilizations

Government

Cities

Religion

**Civilization**

Job specialization

Social classes

Culture

Writing

### Reading Graphs

Most civilizations share the seven features shown in the web.

**(a) Read a Graphic Organizer** What is the main topic of this web?

**(b) Apply Information** How do governments contribute to the development of civilization?

A third common feature of a civilization was an **established religion,** or a set of religious beliefs shared by everyone in a society. In most early civilizations, people shared a belief in many gods that they believed controlled most events in their lives. Priests led prayers and offered sacrifices, hoping to keep the gods happy. In return, people hoped that their gods would protect them from harm.

Job specialization was a fourth feature that was common to civilizations. Most people in early civilizations were farmers. They produced enough food to support many kinds of specialized workers, such as priests, rulers, soldiers, craftsworkers, and others. Priests specialized in religious activities. Rulers and soldiers specialized in keeping order in a society. Skilled craftsworkers specialized in producing goods. Traders and merchants specialized in buying and selling goods. Job specialization allowed people within a society to develop the many skills and talents needed to create and maintain a civilization.

A fifth feature of early civilizations was the development of social classes. **Social classes are groups of people that occupy different ranks or levels in society.** The highest social class in most early societies was made up of priests and rulers. The people at these ranks or levels were the people with the most power. The social classes in the middle included farmers, merchants, and skilled workers. Slaves usually made up the lowest social class.

**Vocabulary** *Builder*

maintain (mān TĀN) *v.* to provide what is needed to make something continue

A highly developed culture was a sixth feature of most early civilizations. People in early civilizations produced great works of art, music, and literature. They built magnificent temples, tombs, and palaces. People studied the movement of the stars and developed such sciences as mathematics and medicine.

The final common feature of most early civilizations was a system of writing. At first, writing was used mainly to record numbers. Eventually, however, people used writing to record all kinds of information. Historians have learned much about early civilizations from the written records that these peoples left behind.

 **Checkpoint** **Along what geographic locations did many early civilizations develop?**

**Looking Back and Ahead** In this section, you have read about the rise of cities and civilizations. You have also learned about the seven common features of most early civilizations. In the next section, you will see how those features took shape in the Maya civilization of present-day Mexico and Central America.

---

Section **2** **Check Your Progress**

**Progress Monitoring** **Online**
For: Self-test with instant help
Visit: PHSchool.com
Web Code: mwa-1022

 **Standards Review** H-SS: 6.2.1; E-LA: Reading 6.1.1

**Comprehension and Critical Thinking**

1. **(a) Identify** In what part of the world did many of the earliest cities and civilizations arise?
   **(b) Analyze Cause and Effect** What two key conditions led to the birth of civilization?

2. **(a) Recall** What are the seven common features of a civilization?
   **(b) Draw Conclusions** Why would social classes be a sign of civilization?

**Reading Skill**

3. **Read Accurately** Read the sentence below. Then, write the sentence, and underline the words that must be accurately read. "You will see how those features took shape in the Maya civilization of present-day Mexico and Central America."

**Vocabulary** *Builder*
Complete each of the following sentences so that the second part explains the first part and clearly shows your understanding of the highlighted word.

4. Çatalhüyük had a complex economy; _____.

5. People could create a food surplus by carefully managing their resources; _____.

6. Cities were home to people of different social classes; _____.

**Writing**

7. Write three sentences describing the rise of cities. Make use of the transitions *first, next, then, as a result,* and others that indicate development over time.

**Standards Preview**

**H-SS 7.7.5** Describe the Meso-American achievements in astronomy and mathematics, including the development of the calendar and the Meso-American knowledge of seasonal changes to the civilizations' agricultural systems.

**E-LA Reading 6.1.1** Read aloud narrative and expository text fluently and accurately and with appropriate pacing, intonation, and expression.

## Reading Preview

### Reading Skill

**Read With Expression** Words that answer the questions *Where? When? How much? How fast?* and so on can help you read with expression. You can then show that importance in your voice when you read. For example, a sentence might say, "You will see whether those features were part of one of the most advanced early civilizations of the Americas." Emphasizing the word *most* when you speak shows that you understand the ideas in the sentence.

### Vocabulary *Builder*

**High-Use Words**
structure (STRUHK cher), p. 49
impressive (ihm PREHS ihv), p. 51

**Key Terms**
hieroglyph (HĪ er oh glihf), p. 50
astronomy (uh STRAHN uh mee), p. 50
architecture (AHR kuh tehk cher), p. 51
pyramid (PIR uh mihd), p. 51

**Background Knowledge** Historians first identified the shared features of early civilizations by studying the river valley civilizations of the Middle East, North Africa, South Asia, and East Asia. In this section, you will see whether those same features were part of one of the most advanced early civilizations in the Americas.

**Main Idea**
Unlike early river valley civilizations, the Maya civilization started in tropical rain forests.

## The Geographic Setting

The Maya civilization arose in the tropical rain forests of Mesoamerica. Mesoamerica is the region of the southern part of present-day Mexico and northern Central America. This civilization reached its height between A.D. 250 and A.D. 900.

The geographic setting of the Maya civilization was not like that of the river valley civilizations. Those civilizations arose on fertile soil beside large rivers. The Maya had no such rivers. They built their civilization on thin soil in dense rain forests.

More than 2,000 years ago, Mesoamerican farmers learned how to clear patches of rain forest to raise food. Because rain washed away the thin forest soil, farmers built raised fields for planting. They also dug canals to bring water to their fields in the dry season. Their main crop was maize, or corn. In addition to corn, they grew beans, squash, and other foods. They also domesticated animals such as dogs and turkeys.

✔ **Checkpoint** How did the Maya farm in tropical rain forests?

# Features of Maya Civilization

Maya civilization shared many of the features of other civilizations. However, the Maya did not form a united group under a single government. Instead, Maya civilization was made up of different groups living in separate, independent cities.

**Main Idea**
The Maya civilization shared the main features of other civilizations.

**Maya Cities** People in the cities depended on the food supplied by Maya farmers. At the center of a Maya city were splendid stone buildings, wide plazas, and courts for playing ball games. Some Maya cities were home to as many as 100,000 people. Officials lived in the city's stone buildings, but farmers and workers lived in simple wooden houses.

Ball games drew large crowds into a city. The object of the game was to keep a hard rubber ball in the air without touching it with hands or feet. Although players wore protective pads on their arms, knees, and hips, injuries were common.

**Maya Government** Each Maya city had its own well-organized government. At the highest level of government was the ruler. The position of ruler was handed down from father to son within a family. Beneath the ruler were various officials of different ranks, or levels. High-ranking officials advised the ruler. Low-ranking officials had jobs such as collecting taxes.

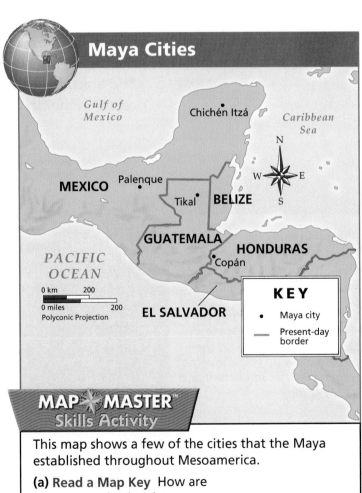

**Maya Cities**

Gulf of Mexico
Chichén Itzá
Caribbean Sea
MEXICO
Palenque
Tikal
BELIZE
GUATEMALA
HONDURAS
Copán
PACIFIC OCEAN
0 km 200
0 miles 200
Polyconic Projection
EL SALVADOR

**KEY**
• Maya city
— Present-day border

**MAP MASTER**
**Skills Activity**

This map shows a few of the cities that the Maya established throughout Mesoamerica.

(a) **Read a Map Key** How are present-day borders shown on the map?

(b) **Apply Information** Which cities are located near mountains? Which are not?

**MapMaster** ●nline
**For:** Interactive map
**Visit:** PHSchool.com
**Web Code:** mwd-1023

The Maya believed that their rulers had godlike powers. A ruler was expected to use these powers to help his people. In one ceremony, the ruler offered his blood to the gods. In return, he asked the gods to provide sunshine and rain for the crops.

**Maya Economy**  Maya farmers raised enough food to support people in other jobs. In addition to government officials, the Maya had many skilled craftsworkers and artists.

Traders traveled from city to city with such goods as animal skins and jade, a beautiful green stone. They also traded dried fish, honey, and cacao, or cocoa beans. Cacao, which was used to make a chocolate drink, was so valuable that the Maya sometimes used cocoa beans as a form of money.

**Maya Religion**  The Maya worshiped many gods. Most of their gods represented natural forces, such as the sun, the moon, and rain. Religion was part of daily life. People might make offerings or say prayers to ask for health or good crops. During the year, religious events were held to please the gods. These activities usually took place in a temple located in the center of the city.

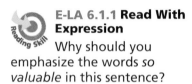

**E-LA 6.1.1 Read With Expression**
Why should you emphasize the words *so valuable* in this sentence?

**Double-headed jaguar throne from the Temple of the Jaguar**

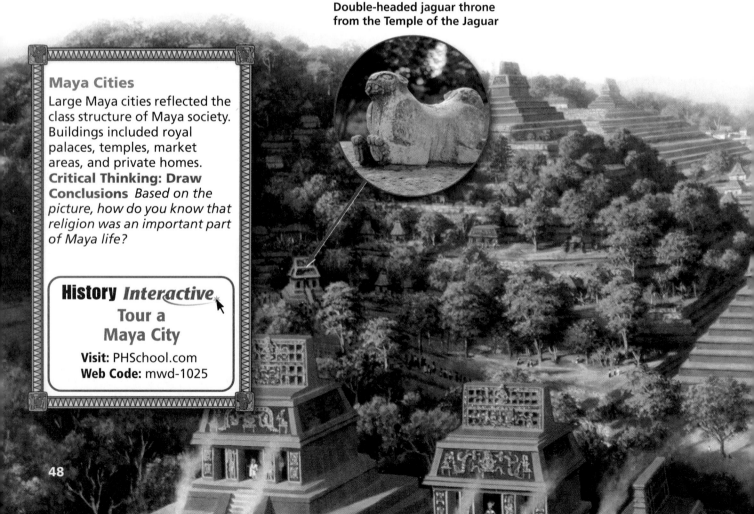

**Maya Cities**
Large Maya cities reflected the class structure of Maya society. Buildings included royal palaces, temples, market areas, and private homes.
**Critical Thinking: Draw Conclusions** *Based on the picture, how do you know that religion was an important part of Maya life?*

**History** *Interactive*
Tour a
Maya City

**Visit:** PHSchool.com
**Web Code:** mwd-1025

48

The city's ruler was the most important religious official. Many priests assisted him. The priests were in charge of marking time. In other words, it was their job to know the exact day when festivals and ceremonies honoring each of the gods should take place.

## Maya Social Structure

At its height, the Maya civilization was divided into several social classes. The top class was made up of the ruler, high-ranking officials, and priests. These people held important positions in the government and in business. Lower-ranking officials, traders, and skilled workers formed the middle class. Farmers stood at the bottom of this social <u>structure</u>.

Warfare was part of Maya life. Powerful rulers often raised large armies and fought other cities. One goal of warfare was to take prisoners. Farmers and workers who were captured in battle became slaves, or captive workers. High-ranking prisoners were sacrificed to the gods.

**Vocabulary Builder**
<u>structure</u> (STRUHK cher) *n.* how parts connect to form a whole

✔ **Checkpoint** How was the Maya civilization different from other early civilizations?

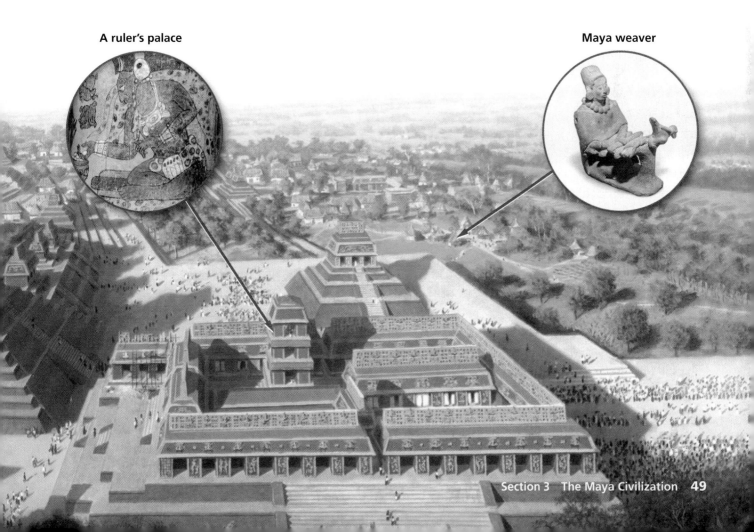

A ruler's palace

Maya weaver

## Maya Achievements

There was more to Maya life than work, worship, and warfare. The Maya were interested in history, science, art, and architecture as well.

**A System of Writing**  The Maya invented one of the most advanced writing systems in the ancient world. The Maya carved their writing on giant stone blocks. They recorded information about rulers, ceremonies, and wars. They created books that described their history, religion, and culture. These books also included information about the stars and planets.

The Maya used a writing system based on hieroglyphs. A hieroglyph is a symbol that can represent a word, an idea, or a sound. A hieroglyph that represents a word or an idea is like one of the numerals that we use to represent a number. Anyone who knows the numeral 5, for example, understands what 5 means. This is true whether a person speaks English, Russian, or Japanese.

**Discoveries in Science**  Maya priests made brilliant discoveries in astronomy—the study of the stars and planets. They plotted the movements of the sun, the moon, and the planet Venus. They also made great advances in mathematics. They figured out the concept of zero long before it was known in most of the rest of world.

With their knowledge of mathematics and astronomy, the Maya could make very accurate calendars. Like other people in Mesoamerica, the Maya used several calendars with different lengths of time. They used a 365-day calendar based on the solar year. A solar year is the time it takes Earth to orbit the sun. The Maya also used a 260-day calendar, mainly for religious purposes. Their longest calendar, called the Long Count, covered a period of about 5,128 years.

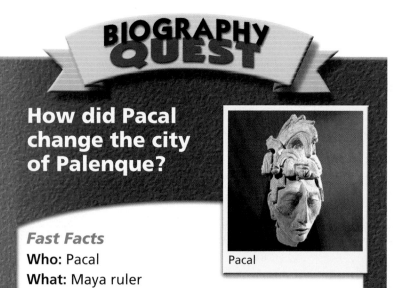

### BIOGRAPHY QUEST

## How did Pacal change the city of Palenque?

Pacal

**Fast Facts**

**Who:** Pacal

**What:** Maya ruler

**When:** A.D. 615–A.D. 683

**Where:** Palenque

**Why important:** Pacal was one of the greatest rulers of the Maya. He gained power and wealth for Palenque by conquering neighboring lands.

**Fast Find**

**How:** Go online to find out what Pacal achieved and how he changed Palenque.

**Biography Online**

**For:** More about Pacal
**Visit:** PHSchool.com
**Web Code:** mwe-1023

### Main Idea
The Maya made advances in writing, science, art, and architecture.

**Art and Architecture**  The Maya were highly skilled in many arts. They crafted fine pottery, bone carvings, and jewelry from gold and jade. They also painted beautiful scenes on the walls of palaces and temples. These paintings show high-ranking Mayas dressed in fine clothing. Many wear large head coverings with the feathers of tropical birds.

The Maya developed their own style of architecture, or building design. They constructed buildings from large blocks of stone, which were often carved with complex designs. Many buildings were topped with a roof comb, or a stone carving that made the building look taller and more <u>impressive</u>. The most important Maya buildings were temples and palaces. Many temples were built on the tops of great pyramids. A pyramid is a structure with a flat base and sides shaped like triangles. The ruins of such Maya cities as Tikal, Copan, and Palenque are among the wonders of the ancient world.

**Vocabulary** *Builder*
<u>impressive</u> (ihm PREHS ihv) *adj.*
causing admiration

**Checkpoint**  What advances did the Maya make in science and architecture?

**Looking Back and Ahead**  In this section, you have read about the Maya civilization and its key features. In the next chapter, you will learn about the first civilization that arose in the ancient Middle East.

# Section 3 Check Your Progress

**Progress Monitoring** ●nline
**For:** Self-test with instant help
**Visit:** PHSchool.com
**Web Code:** mwa-1023

**Standards Review**  H-SS: 7.7; 7.7.5; E-LA: Reading 6.1.1

## Comprehension and Critical Thinking

**1. (a) Explain** Describe the social classes that made up Maya society.
**(b) Analyze Information** How did each social class contribute to the development of Maya civilization?

**2. (a) List** List three key achievements of Maya civilization.
**(b) Draw Conclusions** How would writing have helped in the development of Maya science?

## Reading Skill

**3. Read With Expression** Which words must be emphasized in the following sentence in order to read it with expression? The most important Maya buildings were temples and palaces.

## Vocabulary *Builder*

Decide whether each highlighted word is used correctly. If it is, explain why. If not, rewrite the rest of the sentence to make it logical.

**4.** The Maya used hieroglyphs to record information about their traditional songs.

**5.** Maya architecture included buildings with carved stones and roof combs.

**6.** Each Maya pyramid had a flat base and square sides.

## Writing

**7.** Write three sentences describing the contributions of the Maya civilization. Your final sentence should be a strong concluding sentence.

# Create Concept Webs

Concept webs enable you to present key information and ideas clearly. The main idea and details of a text are shown visually. Concept webs also show how the details are related to the key topics.

 **Chapter Standards**

**History-Social Science**

Reading 6.2.4 Clarify an understanding of texts by creating outlines, logical notes, summaries, or reports.

The ancient town of Jericho lies near the Dead Sea. In 8000 B.C., Jericho was a hub of activity. The surrounding fields yielded huge crops of wheat and barley. The nearby wilderness provided a good supply of meat. Gazelles and ibexes were plentiful. With this agricultural surplus, Jericho was able to support a population of up to 3,000 people.

Traders did a brisk business in Jericho. People came from near and far to trade salt, obsidian, and semiprecious stones.

Jericho was well protected against attack. There was a high stone wall around the town. There was also a broad ditch and a watchtower almost 30 feet high.

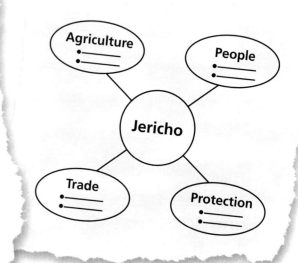

**Learn the Skill** *Follow these steps to learn how to create a concept web.*

1. **Identify the subject of the text, and put it in the center circle.** The subject of a text is its main concept or topic. In this case, the subject of the text is Jericho.

2. **Identify the key concepts related to the subject, and place them in circles linked to the center circle.** Look for the major concepts or topics that expand on the subject, rather than the details. In this passage, the key concepts are *Agriculture, People, Trade,* and *Protection.*

3. **Place details in circles linked to the concept they support.** Reread the text to find details about the key concepts.

4. **Continue placing related details into linking circles.** Make sure that the details in the linked circles relate to the correct concepts.

**Practice the Skill** *Complete the following steps to add links to the concept web above.*

1. **Identify the subject of the text.** Where is the subject of the text placed in the concept web?

2. **Identify the key concepts related to the subject, and place them in circles linked to the center circle.** In which paragraphs of the text do the key concepts appear?

3. **Place details in circles linked to the concept they support.** Find at least two details for each key concept.

4. **Continue placing related details into linking circles.** For each circle linked to *Agriculture,* find two additional details.

**Apply the Skill**
*See page 55 of the Review and Assessment.*

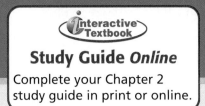
**interactive Textbook**
**Study Guide** *Online*
Complete your Chapter 2 study guide in print or online.

## Chapter Summary  H-SS: 6.1.3, 6.2.1, 7.7.5

### Section 1  Early Agriculture

- Over a long time, hunter-gatherers domesticated plants and animals, and most groups became farmers.
- Although the Middle East was the first center of agriculture, farming appeared in several other parts of the world.
- Permanent farming settlements developed, and surplus food allowed some people to become craftsworkers.

### Section 2  Cities and Civilizations

- Some farming villages grew into cities with large populations and large land areas.
- Wealth from farming and trade created powerful cities that gave rise to civilizations.
- The shared features of most civilizations are cities, a well-organized government, an established religion, job specialization, social classes, a developed culture, and a system of writing.

### Section 3  The Maya Civilization

- Unlike river valley civilizations, the Maya civilization arose in the rain forests of Mesoamerica.
- The Maya lived in separate, independent cities, but their civilization shared many of the features of other civilizations.
- Maya achievements include a system of writing, knowledge of astronomy and mathematics, and highly developed arts and architecture.

**Ancient city of Uruk**

## Standards Practice  H-SS: 6.1.3, 6.2.1, 7.7.5

## Vocabulary *Builder*

### High-Use Words

Decide whether each underlined word is used correctly. If it is, explain why. If not, rewrite the rest of the sentence to make it logical.

1. One of the **benefits** of farming is that it could be dangerous if bands of nomads attacked the farmers and stole their food.

2. The city of Uruk was **founded** in what is now the country of Iraq.

3. The Maya style of architecture featured small, **impressive** mud buildings.

### Key Terms

Answer the following questions in complete sentences that show your understanding of the Key Terms.

1. How did the domestication of plants and animals change the way early people lived?

2. What are the differences between the economies of Uruk and Çatalhüyük?

3. What did the Maya priests do when they studied astronomy?

## Apply Reading Skills

**Read Fluently, Accurately, and With Expression** On a sheet of paper, copy the section Discoveries in Science on page 50. Read the second paragraph silently. Underline groups of words that should be read together. Circle words that must be read accurately so that the meaning will be understood. Draw a box around words that you should emphasize through expression. Then, read the paragraph aloud to a partner.

## Comprehension and Critical Thinking

**1. (a) Explain** How did climate change help farming get started?
**(b) Evaluate Information** Why did the shift to farming take place over a long time?
**(c) Draw Conclusions** How did farming affect the way people lived and worked?

**2. (a) Recall** What was the Neolithic-agricultural revolution?
**(b) Apply Information** What role did surplus food play in the Neolithic-agricultural revolution?
**(c) Link Past and Present** How does modern society reflect changes that began during the Neolithic-agricultural revolution?

**3. (a) Explain** What was the link between cities and civilization?
**(b) Apply Information** Why did most ancient civilizations develop in river valleys?
**(c) Contrast** How do modern civilizations differ from ancient ones?

**4. (a) Describe** Describe the Maya social structure.
**(b) Analyze Cause and Effect** How did religion influence the social structure?

## Researching

**The Effects of Farming** The development of farming affected people's lives dramatically and offered many benefits. In this activity, you will use the Internet and the library media center to research and report on some of those changes. Choose a task below to work on. Share your work by displaying it in the classroom. Include in your materials a list of the resources you used.

**Scientists:** Create a chart that shows as many types of plants and animals as possible that were raised in one of the centers of agriculture discussed in the chapter.

**Journalists:** Choose two or three kinds of domesticated plants or animals, and write a feature article about the ways in which people have used them over time. You might focus on one type of use, such as medicine or food.

> **Researching Online**
> **For:** Help in starting this activity
> **Visit:** PHSchool.com
> **Web Code:** mwe-1024

## Writing

**1. Write a paragraph on the following topic.** Describe in chronological order the changes that hunter-gatherers experienced as they began to farm.
**Your paragraph should include:**
- Transition words such as *first, next, then, as a result,* and others that show development over time.
- A strong concluding sentence summarizing the benefits and costs of farming as opposed to hunting and gathering.

**2. Write a short narrative.** Suppose that you and your family lived in a large Maya city. Write a short narrative describing some of the buildings and other features of the city.

**Progress Monitoring** ⏻nline

**For:** Self-test with instant help
**Visit:** PHSchool.com
**Web Code:** mwa-1024

## Apply Analysis Skills

**Create a concept web based on the text at right by answering these questions:**

1. What is the subject of the text?

2. What are the key concepts related to the subject? Which details support the key concepts?

3. How would you include in the web how thinner, sharper stone blades were used?

> ❝Early humans developed the useful skill of making tools out of stone. First, people used simple, sharp-edged rocks to chop down small trees, cut meat, or scrape the flesh off animal skins. Later, people developed more advanced tools. Thinner, sharper stone blades were used on spears and arrows. Bones and antlers were also used. Some people added decoration and color to their work.❞

## Test Yourself

1. **Which helped the development of farming?**
   A formation of glaciers
   B erupting volcanoes
   C global warming
   D nomadic living

**Refer to the image below to answer Question 2.**

2. **Farmers used tools such as this stone quern to**
   A hunt large animals.
   B fish in rivers.
   C grind grain.
   D clear trees from land.

3. **Achievements by the Maya in astronomy and mathematics are evident in their**
   A hieroglyphics.
   B social structure.
   C 365-day calendar.
   D religious ceremonies.

4. **What enabled many early civilizations to develop in river valleys?**
   A well-organized governments
   B fresh water and fertile soil
   C high mountains and plentiful rain
   D social classes

5. **The Maya civilization arose in**
   A river valleys.
   B dry plains.
   C tropical rain forests.
   D very high mountains.

**Refer to the map below to answer Question 6.**

6. **Which Maya city was located in the country that is now Honduras?**

   A Chichén Itzá
   B Palenque
   C Tikal
   D Copán

# Writing Workshop

**History-Social Science**

**6.1** Students describe what is known through archaeological studies of the early physical and cultural development of human-kind from the Paleolithic era to the agricultural revolution.

**English-Language Arts**

**Writing 6.2.2** Write expository compositions (e.g., description, explanation, comparison and contrast, problem and solution).

## Expository Composition
## Explanatory Essay

### ▶ Introduction

In an explanatory essay, you inform your readers about one particular subject. You might tell them what the subject is, how it works, or why it happened. Many explanatory essays describe a historical sequence. For example, you might trace the chain of events that took place as early humans began to grow their own food. An explanatory essay that analyzes events in a historical sequence should demonstrate the following characteristics:

- The essay outlines a series of events that took place in a clearly defined order.
- The thesis statement explains why the series of events is significant.
- The details describe the events and show how one event led directly to the next.
- The events are placed in chronological order, and the relationships between events are explained.

**Assignment** On the following pages, you will learn how to write an explanatory essay that uses chronological organization. You will get step-by-step instructions. Each step includes an example from a sample essay that explains how farming began.

First, read the instructions and the examples. Then, follow each step to plan and write a 500–700 word essay on this topic:

> **Explain the sequence of events in which civilizations developed in cities.**

For a review of the steps in the writing process, see the **Historian's Toolkit, *Write Like a Historian.***

### ▶ Prewriting

**Clarify the assignment.** Often, you will be asked to explain how a particular sequence of events occurred. Make sure you understand which events your essay should cover.

**Gather information.** Think about the individual events in the historical sequence that you are going to explain. How does this sequence begin and end? What event happens in between? List the events from start to finish, and make sure you understand how each one leads to the next.

**Sample Assignment:** Describe the events that led early humans to change from hunter-gatherers to farmers.

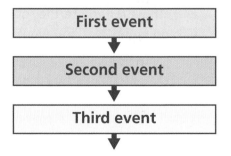

**Create a working thesis.** After you have explored your topic, write a sentence that states your main idea. This "working thesis" can change as you go along, but it should guide your planning.

> **Sample working thesis:** Changes in the environment led to the development of farming.

## ▶ Drafting

**Use chronological organization.** An essay analyzing historical sequence uses chronological organization. This means that events are presented in the order in which they occurred.

Challenges to the hunting and gathering way of life set the stage for the birth of farming.

A. When the ice age ended, people adapted by eating smaller animals and fish.

B. People changed their environment.
  1. Cleared fields with fire
  2. Allowed wild grains to grow
  3. Attracted smaller animals

C. People domesticated plants and animals.
  1. Selected seeds from better plants
  2. Bred animals that were easier to care for

> Each paragraph should discuss one major point. Paragraphs should be arranged in sequence.

> Details in each paragraph should also be arranged in sequence.

**State your thesis.** Write an introductory paragraph that explains the importance of the sequence of events and generally describes how this sequence took place.

**Support your thesis with examples and details.** Discuss the events in the sequence as concretely and specifically as possible. Use time-order transition words such as *first, next, then, before, after, as a result, finally,* and *in the end* to clarify the relationships between events.

**Write a strong conclusion.** In your final paragraph, show the reader how the evidence supports your thesis.

# Writing Workshop *continued*

## ▶ Student Model

Read the following model of a sequence-analysis explanatory essay. Notice how it includes the characteristics you have studied.

### Early Farming

During the last ice age, humans populated the Earth. Most lived as hunter-gatherers. About 12,000 years ago, the Earth's climate changed. All living things had to adapt to a new environment. Challenges to the hunting and gathering way of life set the stage for the birth of farming.

During the ice age, hunter-gatherers moved around each season as they followed large animals. Then, the ice age ended. Rising temperatures caused many of the larger animals to die out. When this happened, people adapted by hunting smaller animals and adding more fish to their diets.

Some people changed their environment to attract more animals and grow more food. First, people cleared fields by burning trees and brush. Then, grains and grasses grew in the fields. In turn, these plants attracted small animals that were easy to hunt.

Over time, people also learned to domesticate plants and animals. These early farmers learned to select the seeds of plants. As a result, domesticated plants produced larger and tastier food. People also bred smaller animals, probably because these animals were easier to manage. Farming enabled groups of people to settle together in one place.

Humans have a great capacity for adaptation. When some animals died out after the ice age, humans responded by changing their ways of getting food. The birth of farming marks a major change in the human way of life.

> The opening paragraph contains the thesis statement.

> Within each paragraph, the events should be in the correct sequence. Use transitions such as *first, next,* and *as a result.*

> The events described in each paragraph follow the events described in the previous paragraph.

> The last paragraph should contain a strong conclusion about the long-term effects of the development you discussed.

# ▶ Revising

After completing your draft, read it carefully to find ways to improve your writing. Here are some questions to ask yourself:

## Revise to heighten interest
- Does the first paragraph capture the reader's attention?
- Can you use more specific words to describe the events?
- Did you include any information that does not support your main points and so should be deleted?

## Revise to clarify the process
- Are the events in the correct order?
- Did you leave out any information that readers will need to be able to understand the order of the events?
- Are the relationships between the events clear? Can you add any transitions to make these relationships clearer?

## Revise to meet Standard English conventions
- Are all sentences complete, with a subject and a verb?
- Are all words spelled correctly?
- Are all proper nouns capitalized, including names of people and places?
- Did you use proper punctuation? Check punctuation within sentences as well as at the ends of sentences.

*#*
*Overtime people also learned to
domesticate plants and animals.
These early farmers learned to first
select the seeds of plants. As a
result, domesticated plants
produced larger and tastier food.
People also bred smaller animals,
probably because they were easier
to manage. Farming enabled
groups of people to settle Eventually
together in one place. ☉*

# ▶ Rubric for Self-Assessment

*Use this rating scale to evaluate your sequence-analysis explanatory essay.*

|  | Score 4 | Score 3 | Score 2 | Score 1 |
|---|---|---|---|---|
| **Organization** | Uses chronological organization correctly and presents time relationships clearly | Uses chronological organization and presents most time relationships clearly | Chooses an organization not suited to an explanatory essay | Shows lack of organizational strategy |
| **Presentation** | Develops ideas with relevant facts, details, or examples; links all information to the process being analyzed | Develops most ideas with facts, details, or examples; links most information to the process being analyzed | Does not develop most ideas in depth; some information is not linked to the process | Does not provide facts, details, or examples to support ideas |
| **Use of Language** | Varies sentence structure and vocabulary; has very few mechanical errors | Uses some variety in sentence structure and vocabulary; has few mechanical errors | Uses repetitive sentence structure and vocabulary; has many mechanical errors | Shows poor use of language; generates confusion; has many mechanical errors |

# Unit 2

**Chapter Standards**

**History-Social Science**

**6.2** Analyze the geographic, political, economic, religious, and social structures of the early civilizations of Mesopotamia, Egypt, and Kush.

**6.3** Analyze the geographic, political, economical, religious, and social structures of the Ancient Hebrews.

## What You Will Learn

 **Quick View** Video

**Discovery School Video** View *The Ancient Middle East* for a quick preview of the main ideas of this unit.

The head and shoulders of the Great Sphinx at Giza, Egypt were carved from one solid block of stone about 2600 B.C.

# The Ancient Middle East

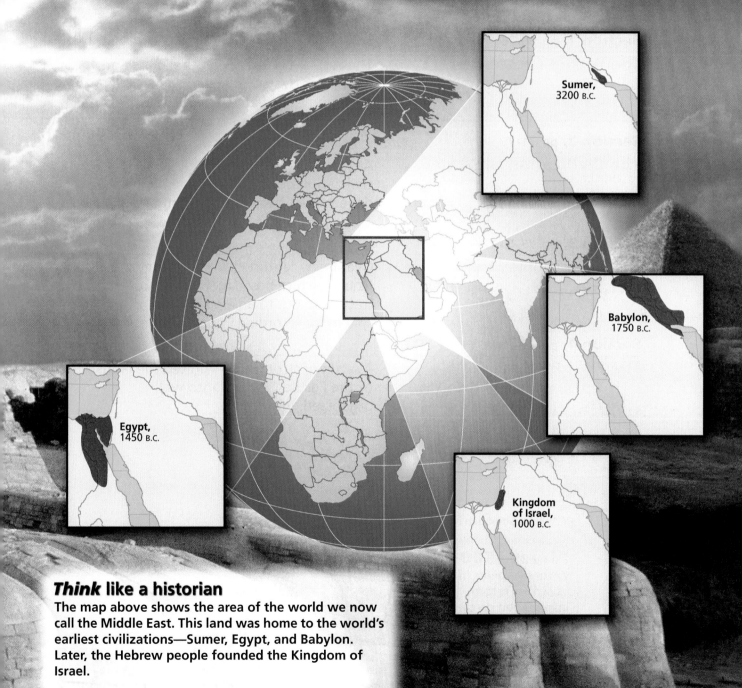

Sumer,
3200 B.C.

Babylon,
1750 B.C.

Egypt,
1450 B.C.

Kingdom
of Israel,
1000 B.C.

## *Think* like a historian

The map above shows the area of the world we now
call the Middle East. This land was home to the world's
earliest civilizations—Sumer, Egypt, and Babylon.
Later, the Hebrew people founded the Kingdom of
Israel.

# Chapter 3
# Ancient Mesopotamia (3500 B.C.–1792 B.C.)

## Prepare to Read

### Chapter Standards

**History-Social Science**

**6.2** Students analyze the geographic, political, economic, religious, and social structures of the early civilizations of Mesopotamia, Egypt, and Kush.

| | |
|---|---|
| **Section 1,** pp. 66–70 | ✔ **What You Will Learn** |
| **The Fertile Crescent** | The fertile land between the Tigris and Euphrates rivers supported the development of early civilizations. |
| **Section 2,** pp. 71–75 | |
| **The Civilization of Sumer** | As settlements grew into cities, civilization became more complex, and government became more important. |
| **Section 3,** pp. 76–80 | |
| **The Development of Writing** | Over many centuries, writing developed from a picture-based method for keeping track of goods to an alphabet-based system for recording important ideas. |
| **Section 4,** pp. 81–86 | |
| **The First Empires** | A series of strong rulers united the lands of the Fertile Crescent into well-organized empires. |

Ancient Sumerian helmet

**About 3500 B.C.**
Writing appears in Sumer as scribes record information on clay.

**About 3000 B.C.**
Cities emerge in Mesopotamia.

**Chapter Events**

**3500 B.C.**    **3000 B.C.**    **2500 B.C.**

**Other Events**

**3000 B.C.** Upper and Lower Egypt unite under one ruler.

**2600s B.C.** Building of the Great Pyramid at Giza begins.

**Where and When?**
The earliest civilizations emerged in the Middle East over 6,000 years ago.

This reconstruction of an ancient Sumerian temple at Ur shows how it might have looked over 4000 years ago.

**About 2350** B.C.
Sargon the Great creates Mesopotamia's first empire.

**About 1792** B.C.
Hammurabi becomes king of Babylon.

**2500** B.C.

**2000** B.C.

**1500** B.C.

**2500** B.C. Mohenjo-Daro is a large city with 40,000 residents.

**1650** B.C. Chinese civilizations develop in Asia.

**History Reading Skill**

*Previewing* **Clarify and Connect Main Ideas**

Social studies reading is filled with new ideas and information. You can use what you have already learned to understand these new ideas. Look for ways to connect new ideas to one another and to other knowledge about social studies. Use these connections to help you clarify, or understand, the new ideas. Look at the steps outlined below.

 **Chapter Standards**

**English-Language Arts**

**Reading 6.2.3** Clarify and connect main ideas by identifying their relationship to other sources and related topics.

**1** First, identify the main idea or concepts in a paragraph. Here, the main idea appears in the first sentence. Read it, then say it in your own words.

Not all early civilizations began in river valleys, however. The Maya civilization, for example, arose in the rainforests of Mexico and Central America. The Inca civilization took root in the Andes Mountains of South America.

**2** Next, make sure you have not confused the main idea with any supporting details. Check your main idea statement from Step 1. If all the details don't support the main idea, you may need to review it.

Not all early civilizations began in river valleys, however. The Maya civilization, for example, arose in the rainforests of Mexico and Central America. The Inca civilization took root in the Andes Mountains of South America.

> **Both give examples of cities not in river valleys.**

**3** Finally, connect new main ideas to those from earlier readings. For example, you can link those identified above to main ideas in Chapter 1.

The geographic setting of the Maya was not like that of the river valley civilizations. Those civilizations arose on fertile soil beside large rivers. The Maya had no such rivers. They built their civilizations on thin soil in dense rainforests.

Connect the underlined main idea to the main idea from paragraph #1. Notice that it gives more information about that earlier main idea.

# Vocabulary *Builder*

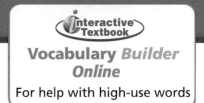

**Interactive Textbook**

**Vocabulary** *Builder*
**Online**

For help with high-use words

## *Previewing* **High-Use Academic Words**

| High-Use Word | Definition | Sample Sentence About History |
|---|---|---|
| **method** (MEHTH uhd) (Section 1, p. 66) | *n.* a way of doing something | People in Asia developed a <u>method</u> for growing rice. |
| **challenge** (CHAL uhnj) (Section 1, p. 67) | *n.* something that calls for special effort | Ancient hunters faced a <u>challenge</u> when the large ice-age animals began to die out. |
| **achievement** (uh CHEEV muhnt) (Section 2, p. 71) | *n.* something that is done through hard work | One <u>achievement</u> of Uruk was a strong, well-organized government. |
| **predict** (prih DIHKT) (Section 2, p. 73) | *v.* to say in advance something that will happen | Priests of ancient cities often studied the stars to <u>predict</u> important events. |
| **sketch** (skehch) (Section 3, p. 78) | *v.* to draw quickly | Hieroglyphic writing was often based on a <u>sketch</u> of the object being represented. |
| **creation** (kree AY shun) (Section 3, p. 79) | *n.* the act of making something | Maya artists were responsible for the <u>creation</u> of many beautiful paintings. |
| **occupy** (AH kyuh pī) (Section 4, p. 82) | *v.* to live in and take control of a place | Maya warriors often captured prisoners, but they did not often <u>occupy</u> the towns and cities they conquered. |
| **series** (SIHR eez) (Section 4, p. 85) | *n.* a group of similar events that happen one after the other | The development of farming began a <u>series</u> of changes in the way most people lived. |

## *Previewing* **Key Terms and People**

irrigation, p. 68
population, p. 69
city-state, p. 69
barter, p. 70
polytheism, p. 72

scribe, p. 72
kingship, p. 73
law code, p. 74
technology, p. 74

cuneiform, p. 76
cultural borrowing, p. 77
pictograph, p. 78
alphabet, p. 79

conquest, p. 82
empire, p. 82
chariot, p. 82
barbarian, p. 82

# 1 The Fertile Crescent

**H-SS 6.2.2** Trace the development of agricultural techniques that permitted the production of economic surplus and the emergence of cities as centers of culture and power.

**E-LA Reading, 6.2.3** Connect and clarify main ideas by identifying their relationships to other sources and related topics.

## Reading Preview

### Reading Skill

**Identify Main Ideas and Concepts** The main idea of a paragraph is the most important idea, the one that brings all the details and information in the paragraph together. Often you can find the main idea in the first or last sentence of a paragraph. At other times you must ask yourself: What is this paragraph mostly about? The answer will be the main idea. Once you find the main idea, restate it in your own words.

### Vocabulary *Builder*

**High-Use Words**
method (MEHTH uhd), p. 66
challenge (CHAL uhnj), p. 67

**Key Terms**
irrigation (ihr uh GAY shuhn), p. 68
population (pah pyuh LAY shuhn), p. 69
city-state (SIH tee stayt), p. 69
barter (BAHR tuhr), p. 70

**Vocabulary *Builder***
method (MEHTH uhd) *n.* a way of doing something

**Background Knowledge** When people first learned to farm, their farming methods were simple. But over many years, these methods improved. In this section, you will read about some of these improvements. You will also learn how better farming methods led to the rise of cities and the world's first civilization in a land known as Mesopotamia.

**Main Idea**
The Tigris and Euphrates rivers were part of a fertile land that helped early civilizations grow.

## The Land Between the Rivers

The first civilizations arose on a wide, flat plain between two great rivers, the Tigris (TĪ grihs) and Euphrates (yoo FRAY teez). These rivers flow from the mountains of present-day Turkey into the Persian Gulf. In ancient times, this plain was called Mesopotamia (mehs uh puh TAY mee uh). The name comes from a Greek word that means "land between the rivers."

Mesopotamia was part of a larger region that historians call the Fertile Crescent. This area of fertile land stretched in a large curve from the Persian Gulf to the Mediterranean Sea. The Fertile Crescent gave birth to the world's first farming communities.

According to many scholars, a people known as Sumerians (soo MIHR ee uhns) migrated to Mesopotamia thousands of years ago. The land they settled became known as Sumer (SOO muhr).

**A Challenging Place to Farm**   Mesopotamia offered the Sumerians fertile soil for farming. The Tigris and Euphrates both carried fine, fertile soil called silt down from the mountains. Each year, the rivers flooded their banks. Floodwaters carrying this silt spread across the plain. When the floodwaters finally went down, they left behind a fresh layer of moist, rich earth.

However, Mesopotamia's geography also posed <u>challenges</u> to Sumerian farmers. The same spring floods that brought fresh soil also brought danger. In years of heavy flooding, whole villages might be swept away by the floodwaters.

In addition, most of the region beyond the rivers was a desert. During the summer, the ground baked rock-hard in the hot sun. With no rain for months, plants withered and died. Winds blowing out of the mountains whipped up dust and sand into gritty clouds that turned day into night.

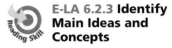

**E-LA 6.2.3 Identify Main Ideas and Concepts**

Which sentence tells the main idea in this paragraph?

**Vocabulary** *Builder*

**challenge** (CHAL uhnj) *n.* something that calls for a special effort

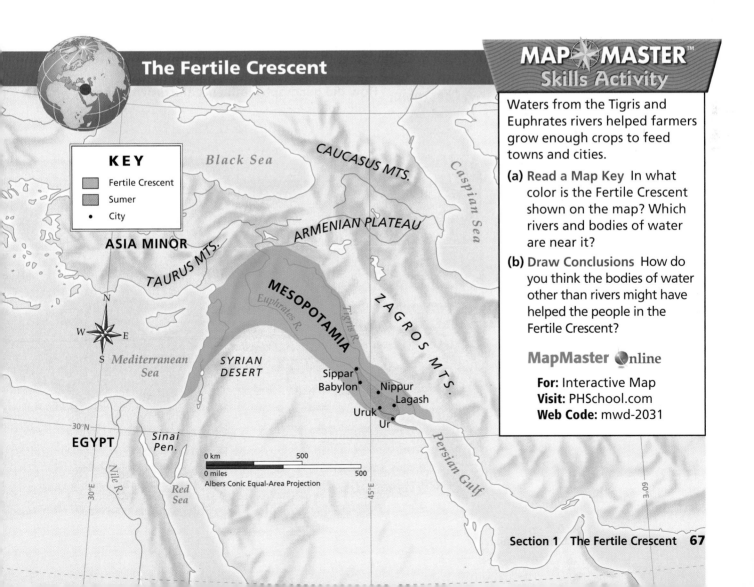

**The Fertile Crescent**

**MAP MASTER™**
**Skills Activity**

**KEY**
- Fertile Crescent
- Sumer
- • City

*Black Sea*

CAUCASUS MTS.

*Caspian Sea*

ARMENIAN PLATEAU

**ASIA MINOR**

TAURUS MTS.

MESOPOTAMIA

*Euphrates R.*

Tigris R.

ZAGROS MTS.

N W E S

*Mediterranean Sea*

**SYRIAN DESERT**

Sippar
Babylon
Nippur
Lagash
Uruk
Ur

30°N

**EGYPT**   *Sinai Pen.*

0 km       500
0 miles       500
Albers Conic Equal-Area Projection

*Nile R.*

*Red Sea*

*Persian Gulf*

30°E   45°E   60°E

Waters from the Tigris and Euphrates rivers helped farmers grow enough crops to feed towns and cities.

**(a) Read a Map Key**  In what color is the Fertile Crescent shown on the map? Which rivers and bodies of water are near it?

**(b) Draw Conclusions**  How do you think the bodies of water other than rivers might have helped the people in the Fertile Crescent?

**MapMaster** ●**nline**

**For:** Interactive Map
**Visit:** PHSchool.com
**Web Code:** mwd-2031

**New Agricultural Techniques** Despite these challenges, the Sumerians turned Mesopotamia into productive farmland. Two new agricultural techniques made this possible.

The first of these techniques was **irrigation, or a system for watering crops.** With irrigation, farmers could keep their crops alive through the hot, dry summer. The Sumerians dug many miles of irrigation canals to carry water from the rivers to their fields. These canals allowed them to plant crops far from the rivers.

The second technique was a new way of preparing the ground for planting by using a plow. Before Sumerian farmers invented the plow, they used digging sticks to poke holes in the damp ground. Then they dropped seeds into these holes. Sowing seeds in this way was hard, slow work.

A farmer using a plow cut a long, shallow furrow, or trench, in the earth. It was much easier to drop seeds into this furrow than into small holes. The plow also loosened the soil so that roots could grow more quickly. By hitching oxen to their plows, the Sumerians made this invention even more useful. A farmer using an oxen-powered plow could prepare much more land for planting each spring than could a farmer using a digging stick.

✓Checkpoint How did geography influence the growth of early civilizations?

**An Ancient Feast**
The Standard of Ur is a mosaic from about 2500 B.C. One side shows activities of war; the other shows activities of peace. **Critical Thinking: Draw Conclusions** *Why do you suppose the people are shown in different sizes?*

ⓐ Ruler leading feast (shown largest)
ⓑ Servants serving guests (shown smallest)
ⓒ Musician playing a lyre
ⓓ People bringing food, live-stock, and goods to the feast

# The Emergence of Cities

Improved agricultural techniques helped the Sumerians produce a food surplus. With a dependable food supply, families increased in size. Over time, the **population, or number of people,** in farm settlements increased. Villages that began as groups of mud huts grew into towns of neat mud-brick houses.

Around 3000 B.C., the Mesopotamian plain saw the emergence of cities. As you have read in Chapter 2, Uruk was the first of these cities. It had a population of as many as 40,000 people. But Uruk was soon joined by other cities such as Ur, Lagash, Sippar, Nippur, and Babylon.

**The Sumerian City-States** As cities continued to grow, some became powerful city-states. **A city-state is made up of a city and the surrounding land and villages that it controls.** Each Sumerian city-state was independent of its neighbors. It had its own government and laws. Its people worshiped gods that were special to that city.

Each city-state was also a center of trade. Although Mesopotamia was rich in fertile soil, it lacked wood, stone, and metals. Sumerian traders traveled far to find these resources and bring them back to their cities.

Two advances made such widespread trade possible—the wheel and the sail. With wheeled carts and sailing ships, Sumerians could carry their surplus grain and wool over long distances. They could also bring home heavy trade goods like lumber, metals, and precious stones. Trade gave Sumerians access to products that were not produced in Mesopotamia.

Most trade was done by barter. **Barter** is a trading system in which people exchange goods directly without using money. By bartering their farming surplus for needed resources, the Sumerian city-states grew in wealth and power. Increased travel also meant that ideas traveled faster from one community to another.

 **Checkpoint** How did villages in Sumer became cities?

**Looking Back and Ahead** In this section you have read about the Sumerians who settled in Mesopotamia. You have learned that the Sumerians developed agricultural techniques that allowed them to produce a food surplus. With that surplus, they built the world's first cities and city-states. In the next section, you will learn more about the civilization created by Sumerians in the Fertile Crescent.

**Sumerian Shipping**
Early Sumerians load wood on boats to trade for other goods. **Critical Thinking: Identify Benefits** *How might trade have benefited the economy of Sumer?*

---

## Section 1 Check Your Progress

**Progress Monitoring** Online
**For:** Self-test with instant help
**Visit:** PHSchool.com
**Web Code:** mwa-2031

**Standards Review** H-SS: 6.2.2; E-LA: Reading 6.2.3

**Comprehension and Critical Thinking**

1. (a) **Explain** How did farming develop in Sumer?
   (b) **Draw Conclusions** How would life in Sumer have been different without its rivers?

2. (a) **Recall** What two inventions helped Sumerian city-states to trade over long distances?
   (b) **Apply Information** Why was trade important to Sumer's city-states?

**Reading Skill**

3. **Identify Main Ideas and Concepts** Choose a paragraph from Section 1. Find its main idea. Write the sentence that contains the main idea, if it is directly stated. Then write the main idea in your own words.

**Vocabulary** *Builder*
Complete each of the following sentences so that the second part explains the first part and clearly shows your understanding of the highlighted word.

4. Irrigation was important to Sumerian farmers; _____.

5. The food surplus allowed the population of villages to grow; _____.

6. Trade between different communities usually depended on barter; _____.

**Writing**

7. Create a list of the new techniques that made farming more productive for Sumerians.

# 2 The Civilization of Sumer

**Standards Preview**

**H-SS 6.2.3** Understand the relationship between religion and the social and political order in Mesopotamia and Egypt.

**E-LA Reading, 6.2.3** Connect and clarify main ideas by identifying their relationships to other sources and related topics.

## Reading Preview

 **Reading Skill**

**Clarify Main Ideas** Paragraphs have a main idea and supporting details. The supporting details provide examples or additional facts that tell more about the main idea. You can focus on the main idea by organizing the supporting details. Ask yourself what all the details have in common.

**Vocabulary** *Builder*

**High-Use Words**
achievement (uh CHEEV muhnt), p. 71
predict (prih DIHKT), p. 73

**Key Terms**
polytheism (PAHL ih thee ihz um), p. 72
scribe (SKRĪB), p. 72
kingship (KIHNG shihp), p. 73
law code (law kohd), p. 74
technology (tehk NAH luh jee), p. 74

**Background Knowledge** When Sumer was a land of small villages, it had a simple social and political order. Most people were roughly equal in rank and had similar roles in their community. Villagers chose their leaders. The social order of a Sumerian city-state was more complex. In this section you will read about Sumerian society. You will learn how religion and government supported the social order of Sumer. You will also learn about some of the achievements of the Sumerian civilization.

**Vocabulary** *Builder*
achievement (uh CHEEV muhnt) *n.* something that is done through hard work

## Sumerian Society

The Sumerian city-states developed a social order with three social classes. People of each class took on more distinct roles. The upper class consisted of the ruler, his top officials, powerful priests, wealthy merchants, and large landowners. Average people like farmers and skilled workers made up the middle class. The lowest class was made up mostly of slaves. This social order was supported by both the Sumerian religious beliefs and by the governments of the city-states.

**Main Idea**
Sumerian society developed social classes, and religion played a key role.

**Ancient Sumerian statue**
Many of the earliest Sumerian statues seem to have religious significance. This statue probably represents a man praying. **Critical Thinking: Draw Inferences** *What does this statue tell you about Sumerian beliefs?*

**Primary** Sources

See "School Days" in the Reference Section at the back of this book.

**Sumerian Religious Beliefs**   Religion was important in Sumer. People looked to the gods for answers to their most basic questions. Would it rain? Would the harvest be good? Sumerians believed that the gods played an active role in their lives, so it was important to keep the gods happy.

Sumerians practiced **polytheism,** that is, they worshiped many gods. Some gods represented elements of nature, such as rain and wind. Others represented objects, such as the plow. In addition, each city had its own special gods.

Sumerians believed that their gods behaved much like people. They believed that the gods ate, drank, slept, and married. However, unlike people, the gods lived forever and had great power. If the gods were happy with people's prayers and offerings, they might bring good fortune to the city. If not, they might bring war, floods, or other disasters. Because the Sumerians believed this, they wanted to please their gods.

**The Power of Priests**   Sumerians depended on their priests to tell them what the gods wanted. Only priests knew how to communicate with the gods. Only they knew when religious events or ceremonies should take place. This knowledge made priests very powerful people in Sumerian society.

Priests ran the temples where the gods were worshiped. In larger cities, the temples were grand structures known as ziggurats (ZIHG oo rats). The largest ziggurats were seven stories tall. They rose upward in steps, with each level smaller than the one below. Some temples were decorated inside with beautiful paintings and statues. The temples also owned large amounts of farmland. They stored their surplus grain and other goods in large storehouses.

**The Development of Writing**   To keep track of all these goods, the priests made marks on tablets of wet clay. At first they drew simple pictures to stand for different items. By 3000 B.C., however, Sumerian priests had developed a writing system that could record far more than numbers of objects. Writing was so useful that priests set up schools to train scribes. A **scribe** is a person who was trained to write and keep records in ancient times. One student who was training to become a scribe wrote that he had gotten into trouble in school, but his teacher admired his hard work.

**✓ Checkpoint**   How did religion affect social order in Sumer?

**Ziggurat at Ur**
This model of a ziggurat shows how the structure probably looked when it was first built. **Critical Thinking: Draw Inferences** *What does the size of this structure say about its importance to the people of Ur?*

# The Rise of Kings

At first, the city-states of Sumer were ruled by priests, but then the city-states expanded and began to come into conflict with one another. As a result, the way cities were governed, or ruled, changed.

**Conflict Among City-States** When cities first appeared in Sumer, they had room to grow. Eventually, expanding city-states began to argue over the ownership of land and the control of water. These conflicts sometimes led to war. A Sumerian proverb, or saying, described these conflicts in this way: "You go and take the field of the enemy; the enemy comes and takes your field."

In times of war, priests tried to <u>predict</u> who would be the best leader to lead the city into battle. After the war was over, this leader was expected to return to normal life. Some of these military leaders, however, held on to the position of ruler of the city even in times of peace. This was the beginning of the idea of **kingship,** or government headed by a king.

**Main Idea**
Conflict among city-states helped kings come to power and spread written laws.

**Vocabulary *Builder***
<u>predict</u> (prih DIHKT) *v.* to say in advance something that will happen

## Kings and Priests

To stay in power, the kings needed the support of the priests. So kings were careful to respect their rights. Priests, in return, declared that the king had been sent from heaven to rule the city. This idea that kings were chosen by the gods became common in Sumer.

Kings and priests also worked together to create religious ceremonies that supported royal power. One such ceremony was the New Year's festival. On this day each year, the king "married" the city's chief goddess. This annual marriage ceremony was supposed to bring good fortune to the city.

The New Year's festival was a happy event. People wore their finest clothes, and music filled the air as people moved toward the temple. Street stalls overflowed with food. Such ceremonies made people feel close to their ruler and to one another.

**King Ur-Nammu**
This figurine from about 2000 B.C. shows a Sumerian king. **Critical Thinking: Apply Information** *Was this statue created before or after the invention of writing?*

## Kings and Laws

Sumerian kings took over many of the jobs once done by priests. They built new canals, temples, and roads. Each king also served as his city's chief lawmaker and judge.

Some rulers collected the laws of their city into a **law code,** or written sets of laws. The earliest known law code was issued by Ur-Nammu (uhr NAHM oo), the king of Ur, around 2100 B.C. The Ur-Nammu law code fixed the amount of silver a man had to pay to a person he had injured in some way. One law read, "If a man knocks out the eye of another man, he shall weigh out 1/2 a mina of silver."

## Advances in Technology

Under the rule of priests and kings, Sumerians produced many advances in technology. **Technology** is the application of human intelligence to problems to create new and better ways of doing things.

You have read about the Sumerians' use of the plow, the wheel, the sail, and a system of writing. The Sumerians also invented the potter's wheel, a machine used to make clay jars and pots. The potter's wheel enabled potters to make many jars and pots much more quickly than they could simply shaping the clay by hand.

Sumerians also discovered how to make glass out of sand. They were also the first people to mix copper and tin to make bronze. Bronze is harder than copper. It is therefore better for making tools and weapons.

**Advances in Learning** The Sumerians also made impressive advances in learning. They wrote the first mathematics books. Their number system, based on units of 60, is still used today for telling time and measuring circles.

The Sumerians invented the science of astronomy. From their study of the stars, they developed a calendar that helped them predict the best times for planting and harvesting their crops. Such achievements helped make Sumer a wealthy and advanced society.

**Bronze Bowl**
This Sumerian bowl shows bronze-making skills. **Critical Thinking: Draw Inferences** *Why might bronze bowls be more practical than pottery bowls?*

Checkpoint  **How did kings gain power in Sumer?**

**Looking Back and Ahead** In this section, you have read about Sumerian religion, government, and society. You have also learned that Sumerians made great advances in technology and learning. In the next section, you will read about the invention of writing in Sumer and in other parts of the world.

## Section 2  Check Your Progress

**Progress Monitoring Online**
**For:** Self-test with instant help
**Visit:** PHSchool.com
**Web Code:** mwa-2032

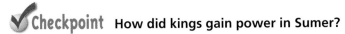
**Standards Review** H-SS: 6.2.3; E-LA: Reading 6.2.3

**Comprehension and Critical Thinking**

1. (a) **Summarize** Describe Sumerian religious beliefs.
   (b) **Apply Information** How did fear of the gods influence life in Sumer?

2. (a) **Explain** What part did priests play in the rise of Sumerian kings?
   (b) **Apply Information** Why would the kings need religious support?

**Reading Skill**

3. **Clarify Main Ideas** Read the first paragraph under the heading **Kings and Laws.** Identify the main idea and supporting details. Then tell how the supporting details help you understand the main idea.

**Vocabulary Builder**
Answer the following questions in complete sentences that show your understanding of the Key Terms.

4. How does a code of laws help a government to be fair to its citizens?

5. What sort of tools might a scribe use on the job?

6. What are some technologies that first developed in ancient Sumer?

**Writing**

7. Write four sentences about two Sumerian achievements in mathematics.

# The Development of Writing

**H-SS 6.2.9** Trace the evolution of language and its written forms.

**E-LA Reading, 6.2.3** Connect and clarify main ideas by identifying their relationships to other sources and related topics.

## Reading Preview

 **Reading Skill**

**Connect Main Ideas** You can connect the main ideas in the paragraphs you read. There are several ways to connect ideas. You might look for ways that the ideas are similar or different. You might explore whether one idea tells more about another idea. You might question whether the events described by one main idea caused or affected those discussed in the other main ideas.

**Vocabulary** *Builder*

**High-Use Words**
sketch (skehch), p. 78
creation (kree AY shun), p. 79

**Key Terms**
cuneiform (kyoo NEE uh fawrm), p. 76
cultural borrowing (KUHL chuhr uhl BAHR oh ihng), p. 77
pictograph (PIHK tuh graf), p. 78
alphabet (AL fuh beht), p. 79

**Background Knowledge** Of all the Sumerians' inventions, the most important was probably writing. As you read in Chapter 2, written language is a key feature of a civilization. In this lesson, you will find out where writing began. You will also see how it evolved, or changed, over time.

**Main Idea**
Writing was invented in more than one place. It developed slowly into the modern writing systems.

## The Origins of Writing

Around 3500 B.C., scribes in Sumer recorded information by pressing wedge-shaped marks into clay. Today the written language of Sumer is known as cuneiform. The word cuneiform comes from a Latin term that means "wedge-shaped."

For a long time, cuneiform was thought to be the first written language. Recent discoveries have cast doubt on that belief. At a tomb in Abydos (uh BEE dahs), Egypt, archaeologists have found signs of even older writing. It may be that writing developed first in Egypt, but there is not enough evidence yet to be sure. Historians do agree that the earliest writing was first invented in the ancient Middle East.

**Other Writing Systems**  A system of writing was also invented in at least one other place. The Maya created a writing system based on hieroglyphs (HĪ er uh glihfs) in Mesoamerica. Archaeologists are sure that the Maya developed writing independently because the Americas were cut off from the rest of the world in ancient times.

Most historians believe that writing was invented a third time in China, but they are not certain. Although China had a system of writing as early as 1300 B.C., the idea of writing may have come to Asia from Mesopotamia. If so, this would be an example of **cultural borrowing.** This term means the transfer of ideas or customs from one culture to another.

E-LA 6.2.3 **Connect Main Ideas**
How does the main idea in this paragraph connect with the main idea in the preceding paragraph?

**Inventing a Written Language**  You may be wondering why writing was invented in so few places. The answer may be that inventing a written language is difficult. It would be even more difficult if you had never seen or heard of writing.

Consider the steps needed to invent a written language. First, you would have to think about how to break up a spoken language into words and sounds. Then, you would have to find a way to represent those words and sounds with symbols. Next, you would have to develop some way of recording these symbols. For your written language to be useful, you would also have to teach others how to read and write your symbols.

✔**Checkpoint**  **Where was the earliest writing invented?**

**Mesopotamian Scribe and Tablet**
Many early scribes kept records by pressing marks into clay. **Critical Thinking: Apply Information** *How might this technique cause the shape of letters to be different, compared with using a pen or pencil?*

# The Evolution of Writing

After writing was invented, its use spread from one people to another. Each group that adopted a writing system changed it to fit their needs. In this way, writing went through a gradual evolution over time.

**Pictures for Words** Writing began as **pictographs, or pictures that represent objects.** To record the number of fish given to a temple, for example, Sumerian priests <u>sketched</u> a fish shape. Then they added marks to show how many.

Sumerian scribes simplified these pictographs into symbols that were easier to press into wet clay. They also created new symbols to stand for other objects and ideas. As a result, the number of cuneiform symbols grew to more than 2,000. This was a large number of symbols for one scribe to learn.

**Symbols for Syllables** Some of the symbols Sumerians used for words evolved over time into symbols for sounds. For instance, the Sumerian word for *arrow* was pronounced *tih.* Thus, the cuneiform symbol for an arrow could also be used to represent the syllable *tih* in any word with that sound.

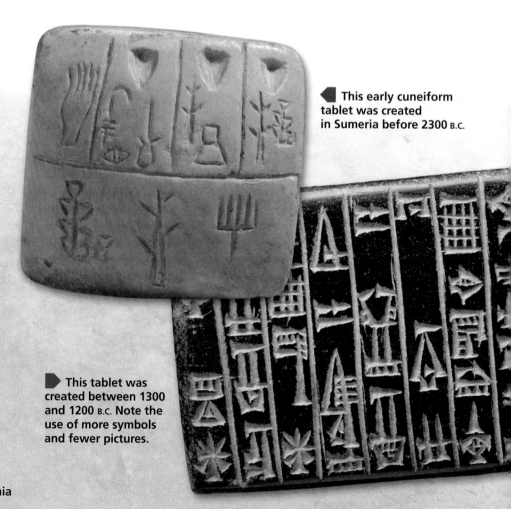

This early cuneiform tablet was created in Sumeria before 2300 B.C.

**Writing Evolved**
Both cuneiform and hieroglyphics changed as symbols were used to represent sounds instead of pictures. **Critical Thinking: Apply Information** *On the basis of what you have read, which examples show writing based on sounds as opposed to writing based on pictures of ideas?*

**History** *Interactive*
**Learn more about Ancient Writing**
**Visit:** PHSchool.com
**Web Code:** mwp-2033

This tablet was created between 1300 and 1200 B.C. Note the use of more symbols and fewer pictures.

Once the Sumerians developed symbols for every syllable in their language, they could string these symbols together to write words. This change allowed Sumerians to reduce the number of symbols they used to about 600.

**Letters for Sounds** The next step in the evolution of writing was the creation of an alphabet. **An alphabet is a small set of letters, or symbols each of which stand for a single sound.** By combining these few symbols in different ways, a writer can record any word. That makes an alphabet a very flexible system of writing.

**Vocabulary *Builder***
**creation** (kree AY shun) *n.* the act of making something

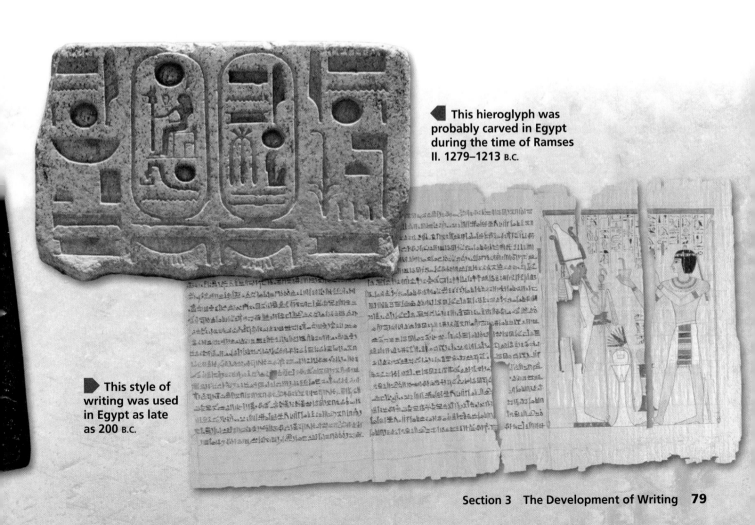

Our alphabet has its roots in ancient Egypt. Around 3000 B.C., the Egyptians created a written language based on hieroglyphs. These symbols stood for objects, ideas, and sounds. With hundreds of hieroglyphs to memorize, learning to read and write Egyptian was no easier than learning cuneiform.

In time, the Egyptians developed a simpler writing system. This system used 24 symbols to stand for consonants such as *b*, *d*, and *t*. All alphabets used today evolved from this one set of symbols.

This hieroglyph was probably carved in Egypt during the time of Ramses II. 1279–1213 B.C.

This style of writing was used in Egypt as late as 200 B.C.

| Phoenician | Greek | Roman |
|---|---|---|
| ⴹ | ᐱ | A |
| ⴑ | Ᏸ | B |

**The changing alphabet**
As the alphabet evolved, letter shapes gradually changed. **Critical Thinking: Link Past and Present** *Why do you suppose that our letters have kept the same basic shape since printing was invented?*

**Our Modern Alphabet** Other groups in the Middle East borrowed the Egyptian symbols to create their own alphabets. One was a sea-going people known as Phoenicians (fuh NIHSH uhns). Phoenician traders traveled the Mediterranean Sea. Some of their trading partners adopted the Phoenician alphabet, including the people of ancient Greece.

The Greeks made more changes to the alphabet. Around 500 B.C., they added letters for vowels to the consonants. They also gave the letters names. The word *alphabet* comes from the first two letters in the Greek alphabet—*alpha* and *beta.*

Around 100 B.C., the Romans adopted the Greek alphabet. The Romans changed some letters. The result was an alphabet that looks very much like the one we use today.

**✔ Checkpoint** How did early writing develop into the modern alphabet?

**Looking Back and Ahead** In this section, you have read about the evolution of writing. You have learned that writing was invented independently at least twice, but the alphabet seems to have been invented only once. In the next section, you will see how writing helped unite Mesopotamia.

## Section 3 **Check Your Progress**

**Progress Monitoring ⊕nline**
**For:** Self-test with instant help
**Visit:** PHSchool.com
**Web Code:** mwa-2033

**Standards Review** H-SS: 6.2.9; E-LA: Reading 6.2.3

**Comprehension and Critical Thinking**

**1. (a) Recall** When did writing first appear?
**(b) Apply Information** Why do you think writing first developed in the Middle East?

**2. (a) Explain** How did written language develop from pictures?
**(b) Drawing Conclusions** Why did writing take so long to develop?

**⟳ Reading Skill**
**3. Connect Main Ideas** Read the first two paragraphs under the heading **Inventing a Written Language.** Explain the connection between the two main ideas.

**Vocabulary *Builder***
**4.** Draw a table with three rows and three columns. In the first column, list the key terms about writing from this section: alphabet, cuneiform, and pictograph. In the middle column, write the definition of each word. In the last column, make a small illustration that gives a sample of each word.

**Writing**
**5.** List the ways in which the development of writing affected life in ancient Mesopotamia. Then decide which effect was the most important.

Section

# 4 The First Empires

 **Standards Preview**

**H-SS: 6.2.4** Know the significance of Hammurabi's Code.

**E-LA Reading, 6.2.3** Connect and clarify main ideas by identifying their relationships to other sources and related topics.

## Reading Preview

 **Reading Skill**

**Connect Main Ideas to Previous Sections** You can connect main ideas in current reading to those in earlier reading. For example, you can take a main idea from this section and connect it to a main idea from Sections 1–3. You will look for the same kinds of connections that you would find between ideas in the same section.

**Vocabulary** *Builder*

**High-Use Words**
occupy (AH kyuh pī), p. 82
series (SIHR eez), p. 85

**Key Terms**
conquest (KAHN kwest), p. 82
empire (EHM pī), p. 82
chariot (CHAIR ee uht), p. 82
barbarian (bahr BEHR ee uhn), p. 82

**Background Knowledge** Each city-state in Sumer had its own government and gods. Conflict among the city-states often led to war. For hundreds of years, the city-states of Sumer fought among themselves. In this section, you will learn how strong rulers finally conquered the city-states to create the world's first empires. You will also read how a ruler named Hammurabi (hah muh RAH bee) tried to unite Mesopotamia under one law code, or set of laws.

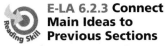 **E-LA 6.2.3 Connect Main Ideas to Previous Sections**
In Section 3, you read that writing became more widespread through the region. As you read this section, look for ways this idea continues to be important.

## The Conquest of Sumer

Around 2450 B.C., the Sumerian city-states of Umma and Lagash (LAY gash) went to war. Soldiers on both sides were armed with bronze axes and long spears with sharp metal points. By the end of the battle, thousands lay dead on the battlefield. The soldiers from Lagash celebrated their victory by looting and burning Umma. Then they returned to Lagash, herding prisoners to be sold as slaves.

Many other wars occurred between Sumerian city-states. However, centuries would pass before the soldiers from one city-state would take permanent control of another city-state.

**Main Idea**
Although Sumerian city-states were originally independent, they were in time unified by strong rulers.

War between city-states was common in Sumer. However, these battles rarely resulted in conquest. **Conquest occurs when one people defeats and controls another.** Achieving conquest was never as easy as winning a battle.

**Vocabulary** *Builder*
**occupy** (AH kyuh pī) *v.* to live in and take control of a place

**The Problems of Conquest**   To achieve conquest, a victorious king had to take control of the city he defeated. He could do this by ordering part of his army to <u>occupy</u>, or live in, the defeated city. But such a plan carried risks. If he left too few soldiers, they might not be able to keep the occupied city under control. If he left too many troops, he might not have enough soldiers to protect his home city from attack.

Few rulers wanted to take these risks. After a battle, the victorious king usually returned home with his army. As a result, no one Sumerian ruler was able to conquer all the city-states.

**Sargon the Great**   Around 2350 B.C., a leader known as Sargon (SAHR gahn) the Great came out of Akkad (AK ad). Akkad was a region just north of Sumer. One by one, Sargon conquered the Sumerian city-states. Then he united them under his rule to create Mesopotamia's first empire. **An empire is a group of countries or peoples who are ruled by one government.**

The secret of Sargon's success was his large, well-equipped army. Charging into battle on **chariots, or wheeled war vehicles,** his troops crushed all rivals. But feeding a large army was not easy. Sargon and his troops were always on the move looking for fresh supplies of food.

**The Akkadian Empire**   Sargon ruled his Akkadian Empire for more than 50 years. At first, Sumerians looked on the Akkadians as **barbarians, or people without civilization.** The Akkadians, however, quickly borrowed many features of Sumerian culture. They adopted Sumerian farming techniques, cuneiform writing, and even religion. Wherever Sargon and his army went, they carried these seeds of civilization with them.

# BIOGRAPHY QUEST

## Where did Sargon live?

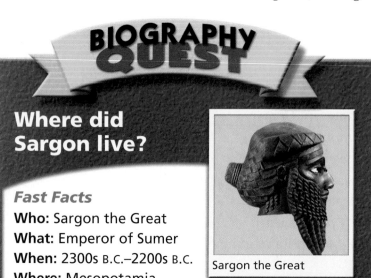

Sargon the Great

### Fast Facts

**Who:** Sargon the Great
**What:** Emperor of Sumer
**When:** 2300s B.C.–2200s B.C.
**Where:** Mesopotamia
**Why Important:** Sargon was the first ruler to unite the city-states of Sumeria into one empire. He also helped people from the Sumerian and Akkadian cultures learn from each other.

### Fast Find

**How:** Go online to learn the name of the city that Sargon built and ruled from, as well as what historians know about its location.

**Biography** **⚉**nline

**For:** More about Sargon
**Visit:** PHSchool.com
**Web Code:** mwd-2034

When Sargon died, his empire began to weaken. Fierce barbarians from the north overthrew the last Akkadian king. With that defeat, the empire of Sargon the Great fell apart.

**Ur-Nammu Unites Sumer** Around 2100 B.C., Sumer was united once again, this time by a ruler named Ur-Nammu. As you have read in Section 2, Ur-Nammu issued the first known law code in Ur. After Ur-Nammu's death, however, his kingdom fell apart. Then around 2000 B.C., barbarians attacked and destroyed Ur. A poet from Ur wrote of those dark times:

**❝That "law and order" cease to exist . . .
That cities [are] destroyed . . .
That rivers flow with bitter water . . .
That the mother care[s] not for her children . . .
The fate decreed by [the gods] cannot be changed.
Who can overturn it?❞**

—quoted by S. N. Kramer in *Cradle of Civilization*

✔**Checkpoint** How was Mesopotamia first united into one empire?

**Military Might of Sumer**
Bronze weapons and new techniques enabled early Sumerian empires to conquer much of Mesopotamia.
**Critical Thinking: Draw Conclusions** *How might new weapons such as bronze spear tips and armor have changed the way that armies fought?*

Sumerian warriors advancing with shields and spears

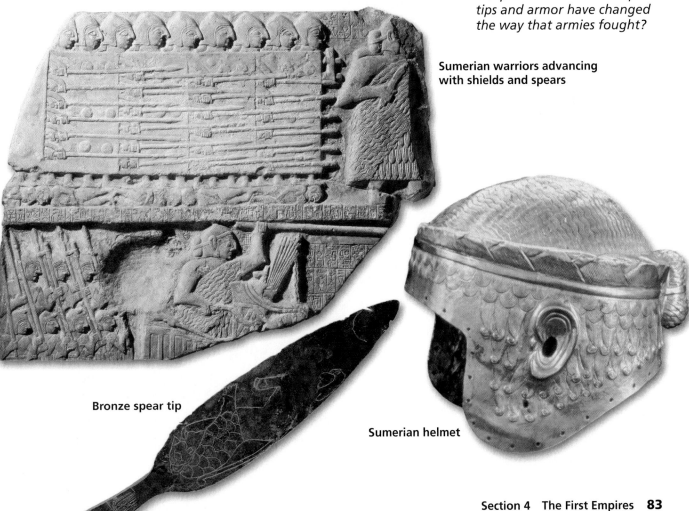

Bronze spear tip

Sumerian helmet

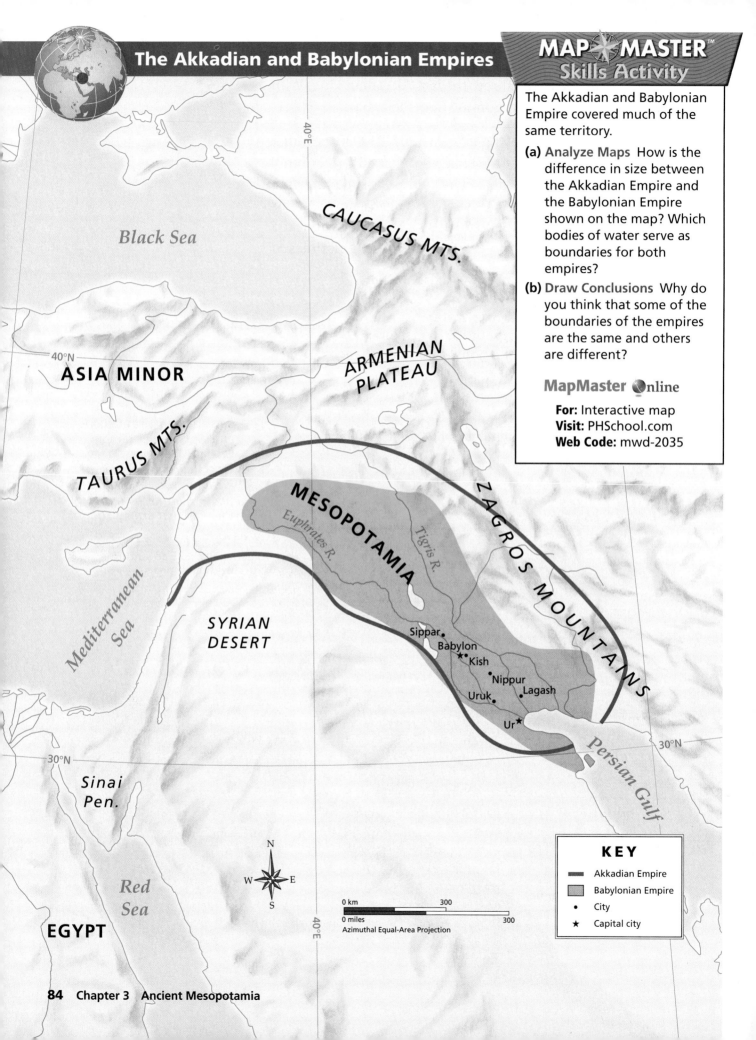

MAP☆MASTER™
Skills Activity

The Akkadian and Babylonian Empire covered much of the same territory.

(a) **Analyze Maps** How is the difference in size between the Akkadian Empire and the Babylonian Empire shown on the map? Which bodies of water serve as boundaries for both empires?

(b) **Draw Conclusions** Why do you think that some of the boundaries of the empires are the same and others are different?

**MapMaster ◉nline**

**For:** Interactive map
**Visit:** PHSchool.com
**Web Code:** mwd-2035

Black Sea

CAUCASUS MTS.

40°E

40°N

**ASIA MINOR**

ARMENIAN
PLATEAU

TAURUS MTS.

MESOPOTAMIA

Euphrates R.

Tigris R.

ZAGROS MOUNTAINS

Mediterranean Sea

**SYRIAN
DESERT**

Sippar
Babylon ★ • Kish
• Nippur
Uruk • • Lagash
Ur ★

30°N

Persian Gulf

Sinai
Pen.

30°N

Red
Sea

N
W ⊕ E
S

40°E

0 km          300
0 miles          300
Azimuthal Equal-Area Projection

**EGYPT**

**KEY**

━━━ Akkadian Empire

▨ Babylonian Empire

• City

★ Capital city

# The Empire of Hammurabi

**Main Idea**
Under Hammurabi, Babylon became an important empire that was noted for its written laws.

After the destruction of Ur, many groups invaded Sumer. One of them, the Amorites (AM uh rīts), came from the deserts of Arabia. The Amorites took control of several Sumerian cities, including Babylon (BAB uh lahn). At that time, Babylon was a small city of little importance. Under a king named Hammurabi, however, Babylon became the center of a new Mesopotamian empire.

**The Babylonian Empire** Hammurabi became king of Babylon around 1792 B.C. For more than 30 years, he built up his army. Then he launched a <u>series</u> of all-out attacks against his rivals. Within a few years he had united Sumer and northern Mesopotamia into a new Babylonian (bab uh LOH nee uhn) Empire.

**Vocabulary** *Builder*
**series** (SIHR eez) *n.* a group of similar events that happen one after the other

Hammurabi found new solutions to the problems of conquest. Rather than keep a large army around him as a sign of his power, Hammurabi spread his forces over his empire. This made it easier to feed his troops because they could obtain food locally. But he also kept careful written records of which troops went to each location. This allowed him to call his army together quickly when needed.

**Hammurabi's Law Code** Hammurabi also tried to create a government strong enough to hold his empire together. He sent his own governors, tax collectors, and judges to distant cities. He issued one code of laws for all his people to follow. Some of his laws defined crimes and punishments. Others dealt with trade, marriage, adoption, daily wages, and the rights of landowners. There were even laws to protect patients and doctors.

**Hammurabi's Code**
This is a carving of Hammurabi receiving laws from the Babylonian god of justice.
**Critical Thinking: Identify Benefits** *Why would having the same laws throughout an empire be better than each region having its own laws?*

Hammurabi had his law code carved in stone for people to see. He wanted people to know the laws that they were to live by. In the introduction to his code, Hammurabi wrote that his aim was this:

> **❝to bring about the rule of righteousness in the land,
> to destroy the wicked and the evil-doers;
> so that the strong should not harm the weak—
> so that I should . . . further the well-being of mankind.❞**
>
> —from Code of Hammurabi

Hammurabi's Code was important, in two ways. First, it marked the first known attempt by a ruler to use laws to unite an empire. Later rulers would follow Hammurabi's example. Second, his law code has provided historians with a great deal of information about life in Mesopotamia.

**The Lasting Influence of Sumer** Despite Hammurabi's efforts to create a strong government, his empire, like Sargon's, collapsed after his death. In the years that followed, the once-great civilization of Sumer slowly faded away.

The influence of Sumer, however, did not fade. The many peoples who had come into contact with this civilization learned from it. They took ideas and customs from Sumer back to their homelands. In this way, Sumerian advances in farming, technology, writing, learning, and the law lived on.

 **Checkpoint** Why did Hammurabi issue his famous law code?

**Looking Back and Ahead** In this section, you have read about the first empires in Mesopotamia. You also read how Hammurabi tried to unite his empire under a single code of laws. In the next chapter, you will read about the rise of the Egyptian civilization in the Nile River valley of North Africa.

# Section 4 Check Your Progress

**Standards Review** H-SS: 6.2.4; E-LA: Reading 6.2.3

## Comprehension and Critical Thinking

1. **(a) Describe** How did Sargon unite Mesopotamia?
   **(b) Evaluate Information** Why was Sargon's empire a great achievement?

2. **(a) Explain** What part did writing play in Hammurabi's rule?
   **(b) Apply Information** What were Hammurabi's main strengths as a ruler?

## Reading Skill

3. **Connect Main Ideas to Previous Sections** Read the text under **Kings and Laws** in Section 2. Connect the main ideas in the section to what you learned about Hammurabi in Section 4.

## Vocabulary *Builder*

4. Write two definitions for each word: barbarian, chariot, conquest, and empire. First, write a formal definition for your teacher.

Second, write a definition in everyday English for a classmate.

## Writing

5. Write a brief paragraph about one empire of ancient Mesopotamia. Begin your paragraph with a topic sentence that will describe what paragraph will say.

# Citizen Heroes

**History-Social Science** 6.2.4 Know the significance of Hammurabi's Code.

| Respect | Caring | Responsibility | **Fairness** | Honesty | Civic Virtue |

# Hammurabi Law-Giver

**One mark of a good citizen is showing obedience to the law. In the eighteenth century B.C., King Hammurabi created a system of laws so that everyone in Babylon would know what laws they needed to obey.**

**Hammurabi** said that the god Marduk had called upon him ". . . to bring about the rule of righteousness in the land, . . . so that the strong should not harm the weak. . . . "

Hammurabi's code included laws about all aspects of life. It even described how people should be punished for certain crimes. The Code of Hammurabi was carved into a stone pillar and put on display so everyone could learn about their laws.

## Connect to Today

**Martin Luther King, Jr.,** was born in Georgia in 1929. The law there did not protect African Americans the same as it protected white people. African Americans were not allowed to play in the same parks, eat at the same restaurants, or go to the same schools as white people.

Martin Luther King, Jr. fought against these unfair laws. He organized people to resist them without using violence. In 1963, he gave a famous speech to a quarter of a million people in Washington, D.C. In it, he said, "I have a dream that one day this nation will rise up and live out the true meaning of its creed; 'We hold these truths to be self-evident, that all men are created equal.'"

## *Analyze* CITIZEN HEROES

Can you list at least three laws that were made to protect people? Then write down how life would be different if those laws only protected certain people, but not everyone. Write down whether you think that would be fair or not, and why you think so.

When you read history, you may some-times find it hard to keep track of what happened when. One way to understand the order of events is to look for "time word" clues like *first*, *before*, and *later*. Another way to keep track of dates and events is to make and use timelines.

**Chapter Standards**

**History-Social Science**

**Analysis Skill C&ST 2** Students construct various timelines of key events, people, and periods of the historical era they are studying.

**Ancient History of the Wheel**

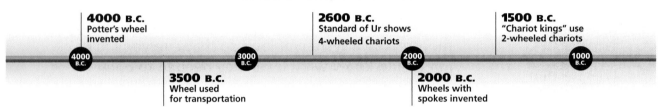

**4000 B.C.** Potter's wheel invented

**3500 B.C.** Wheel used for transportation

**2600 B.C.** Standard of Ur shows 4-wheeled chariots

**2000 B.C.** Wheels with spokes invented

**1500 B.C.** "Chariot kings" use 2-wheeled chariots

**4000 B.C.  3000 B.C.  2000 B.C.  1000 B.C.**

❝The history of the wheel dates back thousands of years. The first wheel was probably a potter's wheel, invented about 4000 B.C. It made working with clay easier. The earliest surviving potter's wheel was found at Ur, in Sumeria.

Around 3500 B.C., Sumerians were using wheels for transportation. The wheels were solid wooden disks.

Soon, wheeled vehicles were being pulled by animals. Wheels came to be used in war vehicles. By 2600 B.C. Sumerians were using four-wheeled chariots in battle.

Spoked wheels were first used on war chariots around 2000 B.C. By around 1500 B.C., "chariot kings" were using two-wheeled chariots in fierce battles.❞

**Learn the Skill** *Follow these steps to learn how to sequence events in time.*

1. **Identify the topic and the time span.** The topic of this passage is the early history of the wheel. The time span of this passage is 4000 B.C. to 1500 B.C.

2. **Place the events in time order, with a date next to each event.** Look for clues to identify the dates and events.

3. **Use the information to make a timeline.** The timeline should
   a) have a title
   b) include a beginning and ending date
   c) be divided into equal sections
   d) have labels identifying each event.

**Practice the Skill** *Answer the following questions about the timeline above*

1. **Identify the topic and the time span.**

2. **Identify the events that relate to the topic.**
   • What events are about transportation?
   • What events are about military uses?

3. **Use a timeline to calculate time differences.**
   • About how many years passed between the first potter's wheel and the use of a wheel for transportation?
   • How many years passed between the first use of the wheel for transportation and the first wheels with spokes?

**Apply the Skill**
*See page 91 of the Review and Assessment.*

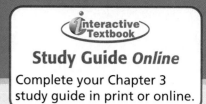

## Chapter Summary  H-SS: 6.2.2, 6.2.3, 6.2.4, 6.2.9

### Section 1  The Fertile Crescent

- As people began to farm the fertile soil near the Tigris and Euphrates rivers, new methods of farming began to develop.
- Eventually, cities emerged and became powerful centers of trade and government.

### Section 2  The Civilization of Sumer

- With the growth of cities, government became more important, and different social classes emerged.
- Writing may have begun at religious structures such as temples and ziggurats, to keep records of goods that were received.
- Learning in math and science also became important.

### Section 3  The Development of Writing

- Writing began in Sumeria as a way to keep track of goods in the temple.
- Writing began with pictographs. Then some symbols began to be used to represent syllables. Eventually some symbols began to represent individual sounds.
- Our modern alphabet is based on an alphabet that began in the Middle East.

### Section 4  The First Empires

- As civilization advanced, strong rulers united city-states into empires.
- Sargon the Great created Mesopotamia's first empire.
- Hammurabi united the Babylonian Empire. He also created a written law for his people.

## Standards Practice  H-SS: 6.2.2, 6.2.3, 6.2.4, 6.2.9

## Vocabulary *Builder*

### High-Use Words

Look at the following words to see whether you understand their meanings: method, occupy, series, and predict. Then use one of those words in each of the following sentences to complete the sentence.

1. The _____ of plowing enabled farmers to plant crops more quickly.

2. A king might _____ the territory he had conquered.

3. The people of ancient Sumeria used astronomy to _____ the best time to plant crops.

4. Writing developed in a _____ of changes.

### Key Terms

Finish each sentence in a way that shows that you understand what each highlighted word means.

1. Sargon was able to achieve his conquest of Mesopotamia because _____.

2. A city-state protected and governed _____.

3. To earn a living, a scribe _____.

4. Irrigation helped farmers because _____.

## Apply Reading Skills

**Clarify and Connect Main Ideas** Think about what you have learned in this chapter. Choose a main idea from each section and explain a way to connect it to the following section.

## Comprehension and Critical Thinking

**1. (a) Recall** Describe the geography of Mesopotamia.
**(b) Apply Information** Why did farming develop there?
**(c) Analyze Cause and Effect** How did farming contribute to the growth of city-states in Sumer?

**2. (a) Explain** What was Sumerian religion like?
**(b) Apply Information** How were religion and government linked in Mesopotamia?
**(c) Draw Inferences** How might the religion of ancient Mesopotamia have helped city-states to grow into empires?

**3. (a) Identify** What was cuneiform?
**(b) Evaluate Information** How did cuneiform become more important to Mesopotamian society over time?

**4. (a) Recall** Who founded the Akkadian and Babylonian empires?
**(b) Draw Conclusions** Why were these empires significant?
**(c) Link Past and Present** What influence did Hammurabi's Code have on the modern world?

## Researching

**The Empires of Mesopotamia** In addition to the Sumerian and Babylonian Empires discussed in this chapter, Mesopotamia has been home to empires such as the Assyrian, the neo-Babylonian, and the Persian. Use the Internet and library media center to learn more about each empire. Choose a task below to work on. Share your work with the class by creating a Mesopotamian bulletin board display.

**Historians:** Create a timeline that shows about when each empire came into existence and when it fell. To accompany the timeline, create a map showing the approximate area covered by each empire.

**Artist Researchers:** Research the kind of art created during each empire. Make a poster with drawings showing similar art from each empire.

---

**Researching Online**

**For:** Help in starting this activity
**Visit:** PHSchool.com
**Web Code:** mwd-2036

---

## Writing

**1. Write a paragraph on the following topic.** New technologies, such as irrigation, sailing, and chariots, led to the growth of cities and empires. Explain how one technology helped people move toward the next stage in civilization.
**Your paragraph should**
• state a purpose for writing
• explain the subject you are writing about
• offer details to support your explanation
• conclude with a short summary.

**2. Write a short narrative.** Imagine you were a visitor to ancient Sumer who has just ridden a sailboat for the first time. Write a short narrative describing the experience.

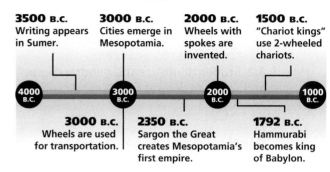

**H-SS:** C&ST 2, 6.2.2, 6.2.3, 6.2.4, 6.2.9

# Apply Analysis Skills

Use the timeline at the right to practice working with timelines.

1. **Identify the topic and the time span.**
   - What is the topic of the time line?
   - What is the time span?

2. **Identify the events that relate to the topic.**
   - What events are about wheels?
   - What events are about emperors?

3. **Use a timeline to calculate time differences.**
   - How many years passed between the
     invention of writing and the first use of
     wheels for transportation?
   - How many years passed between the
     emergence of cities in Mesopotamia and
     the first Mesopotamian empire?

**Ancient Achievements**

**3500 B.C.** Writing appears in Sumer.

**3000 B.C.** Cities emerge in Mesopotamia.

**2000 B.C.** Wheels with spokes are invented.

**1500 B.C.** "Chariot kings" use 2-wheeled chariots.

4000 B.C. — 3000 B.C. — 2000 B.C. — 1000 B.C.

**3000 B.C.** Wheels are used for transportation.

**2350 B.C.** Sargon the Great creates Mesopotamia's first empire.

**1792 B.C.** Hammurabi becomes king of Babylon.

# Test Yourself

1. **Which improvements for farming were devel-
   oped by the Sumerians?**
   
   A bridges and terraces
   
   B irrigation and plows
   
   C ziggurats and pyramids
   
   D fences and digging sticks

2. **What was the relationship between religion
   and government in Mesopotamia?**
   
   A The priests elected the king.
   
   B The king appointed the priests.
   
   C The people elected the king and the priests.
   
   D The king and the priests shared responsibilities.

**Refer to the reading below to answer
Question 3.**

3. **According to this quote, one reason for
   Hammurabi's code was**

   *". . . to bring about the rule of righteousness
   in the land, . . . so that the strong should not
   harm the weak . . ."*

   A to make priests more important.
   
   B to make his son the next ruler.
   
   C to protect the weak from the strong.
   
   D to make people pay their taxes.

**Refer to the image below to answer Question 4.**

4. **The wedge-shaped impressions on this clay
   tablet tell you that its writing style is**

   A cuneiform.
   
   B alphabetic.
   
   C hieroglyphic.
   
   D Egyptian.

5. **Cities grew because of trade, increased
   population, new technology and**
   
   A the development of social classes.
   
   B conquests between neighboring kingdoms.
   
   C the invention of the alphabet.
   
   D farming methods that brought about a
   food surplus.

## Chapter 4

# Ancient Egypt

### (3500 B.C.–500 B.C.)

## Prepare to Read

**Chapter Standards**

### History-Social Science

**6.2** Students analyze the geographic, political, economic, religious, and social structures of the early civilizations of Mesopotamia, Egypt, and Kush.

| | |
|---|---|
| **Section 1,** pp. 96–99 |  **What You Will Learn** |
| **The Nile River Valley** | Egyptians depended on the Nile River for their survival. Most Egyptians settled in the fertile strip of land beside the river. |
| **Section 2,** pp. 100–105 | |
| **Egypt Under the Pharaohs** | The pharaohs ruled Egypt as both political and religious leaders. Egypt was a stable society in which everyone had a place. |
| **Section 3,** pp. 106–110 | |
| **Egypt and Nubia** | Egypt and Nubia interacted through trade and conquest. They borrowed ideas and skills from each other's cultures. |
| **Section 4,** pp. 111–115 | |
| **Life and Death in Ancient Egypt** | Religion played a key role in Egyptian life. The Egyptians believed in life after death. |
| **Section 5,** pp. 118–123 | |
| **Art, Architecture, and Learning in Egypt** | The people of ancient Egypt made important contributions in art, architecture, and learning. |

A Nubian soldier

**3000 B.C.**
Upper and Lower Egypt are united under one ruler.

**2600s B.C.**
The building of the Great Pyramid at Giza begins.

**Chapter Events**

**Other Events**

**4000 B.C.**

**3000 B.C.**

**2000 B.C.**

**3000 B.C.** The Sumerians invent a system of writing.

**2000 B.C.** Chinese civilizations begin to grow in Asia.

## Where and When?
More than 5,000 years ago, ancient Egyptian civilization emerged in the Nile River valley.

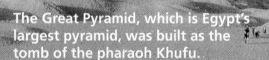

The Great Pyramid, which is Egypt's largest pyramid, was built as the tomb of the pharaoh Khufu.

**1292 B.C.**
Ramses II becomes Pharaoh of Egypt.

**700s B.C.**
Piye, King of Kush, invades the Egyptian city of Hermopolis.

**2000 B.C.**

**1000 B.C.**

**B.C./A.D.**

**1700 B.C.** Hammurabi establishes the first set of written laws.

**790 B.C.** City–states begin to develop in Ancient Greece.

## History Reading Skill

### *Previewing* Clues to Determine Meaning

Social studies reading often contains unfamiliar words. When you are reading, use clues in the text to figure out what these words mean. You can find clues in the word itself, in the surrounding words and sentences, and even in how the word is printed on the page. Read the information below to learn about these clues and how to use them to determine word meanings.

 **Chapter Standards**

**English-Language Arts**

**Reading 6.1.4** Monitor expository text for unknown words or words with novel meanings by using word, sentence, and paragraph clues to determine meaning.

**Secondary Source**

Writing began as **pictographs**. . . . To record the number of fish given to a temple, for example, Sumerian priests sketched a fish shape. Then they added marks to show how many.

Sumerian **scribes simplified these first pictographs into symbols that were easier to press into wet clay.** At the same time, they created new **symbols to stand for other objects and ideas.** As a result, the number of cuneiform symbols grew to more than 2,000. This was a large number of symbols for one scribe to learn.

— *Ancient Civilizations* by Diane Hart.
Copyright © 2006, Prentice Hall

**Unfamiliar Word**

**Surrounding words that help explain the unfamiliar word**

This unfamiliar word is made up of word parts that you have seen before. "Pict" is related to "picture," and "graph" means "to write or draw." Do you think that the word might mean something like "picture writing"?

**Unfamiliar Word**

**Surrounding words that help explain the unfamiliar word**

# Vocabulary *Builder*

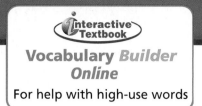

**Vocabulary** *Builder*
*Online*
For help with high-use words

## *Previewing* **High-Use Academic Words**

| High-Use Word | Definition | Sample Sentence About History |
|---|---|---|
| **source** (sors) (Section 1, p. 97) | *n.* place where something begins | Cave paintings are one <u>source</u> of information about the Stone Age. |
| **annual** (AN yoo uhl) (Section 1, p. 98) | *adj.* taking place every year | Prehistoric hunters learned to follow the <u>annual</u> movements of animal herds. |
| **challenge** (CHAL unj) (Section 2, p. 100) | *n.* difficult task that needs special effort | Controlling the Tigris and Euphrates was a <u>challenge</u> for the Sumerians. |
| **establish** (eh STAB lish) (Section 2, p. 101) | *v.* set up; start | Hammurabi wanted to <u>establish</u> a set of laws for the Babylonians. |
| **region** (REE juhn) (Section 3, p. 108) | *n.* large and indefinite part of Earth; district | The nomads covered a wide <u>region</u>. |
| **expand** (ek SPAND) (Section 3, p. 109) | *v.* become or make larger in size or scope | The ruler wanted to <u>expand</u> his territory around the world. |
| **site** (sīt) (Section 4, p.114) | *n.* piece of land considered from the standpoint of its use for a specific purpose | The fertile valley was an excellent <u>site</u> for farming. |
| **accurate** (AK yoor it) (Section 5, p.121) | *adj.* correct; without mistakes | Early lunar calendars were not completely <u>accurate</u>. |
| **document** (DAHK yoo mehnt) (Section 5, p. 122) | *n.* anything printed or written that contains information or is relied upon to record or prove something | The archaeologist confirmed the historic value of the <u>document</u>. |

## *Previewing* **Key Terms and People**

cataract, p. 97
interior, p. 97
delta, p. 98
double-crop, p. 99
Menes, p. 99

authority, p. 100
pharaoh, p. 101
ritual, p. 101
artisan, p. 102
Hatshepsut, p. 103

Ramses II, p. 104
commerce, p. 106
luxury goods, p. 107
expedition, p. 107
Snefru, p. 107

tribute, p. 108
Piye, p. 109
underworld, p. 112
afterlife, p. 113
mummy, p. 113

Imhotep, p. 118
sculpture, p. 120
anatomy, p. 121
papyrus, p. 122

Section

# 1 The Nile River Valley

## Standards Preview

**H-SS 6.2.1** Locate and describe the major river systems and discuss the physical settings that supported permanent settlement and early civilizations.

**E-LA Reading 6.1.4** Monitor expository text for unknown words or words with novel meanings by using word, sentence, and paragraph clues to determine meaning.

## Reading Preview

 **Reading Skill**

**Use Word Clues to Determine Meaning** Many unfamiliar words contain meaning clues. You can add the meaning of word parts—suffixes and prefixes—to familiar words within the unfamiliar word to build new meaning. You can also use a word's part of speech—noun, adjective, verb—to determine meaning.

**Vocabulary** *Builder*

**High-Use Words**
source (SORS), p. 97
annual (AN yoo uhl), p. 98

**Key Terms and People**
cataract (KAT uh rakt), p. 97
interior (in TIR ee uhr), p. 97
delta (DEL tuh), p. 98
double-crop (DUB uhl krahp), p. 98
Menes (MEE neez), p. 99

**Background Knowledge** A Greek historian once called Egypt "the gift of the Nile." The people of ancient Egypt would have agreed. All life in Egypt depended on this river. As you learned in Chapter 2, the world's first civilizations emerged in the fertile valleys near major rivers. In this section, you will follow the journey of the Nile from its source to the sea. You will also see how the Nile supported permanent settlements in the middle of a desert.

**Main Idea**
The Nile River strongly affected life in ancient Egypt.

## The Journey of the Nile

"Hail to you, O Nile, who flows from the Earth and comes to keep Egypt alive." Some 3,000 years ago, the Egyptians wrote poems and hymns like this to the river that made their lives possible. The Egyptian people knew that without the Nile, their world would be nothing but a sunbaked desert land of bright blue skies and dry sand.

**Sources of the Nile** The Nile is the world's longest river. It begins in Central Africa and flows about 3,500 miles north to the Mediterranean Sea.

This great river has two main <u>sources</u>—the White Nile and the Blue Nile. The White Nile is the main stream. It flows out of Lake Victoria in East Africa. The Blue Nile rushes down from the highlands of present-day Ethiopia. The two rivers meet at Khartoum, in the country now called Sudan. In ancient times, this land was known as Kush, or Nubia.

North of Khartoum, the Nile winds through the Sahara, a vast desert that covers much of North Africa. Along the way, the river roars through six sets of rocky rapids called cataracts. The cataracts made it impossible for people to travel by ship from the sea to the interior of Africa. The interior of a continent is the area away from the coast. Therefore, the people of ancient Egypt never knew the sources of the Nile.

**Upper and Lower Egypt** Beyond the cataracts, the Nile travels another 700 miles through the land known as Egypt. For much of the way, the river flows through a narrow valley lined with cliffs. This region is known as Upper Egypt because it is upstream from the Mediterranean Sea.

**Vocabulary *Builder***
<u>source</u> (SORS) *n.* place where something begins

**E-LA 6.1.4 Use Word Clues to Determine Meaning**
What words show you that this sentence is giving you a definition for the word *cataracts*?

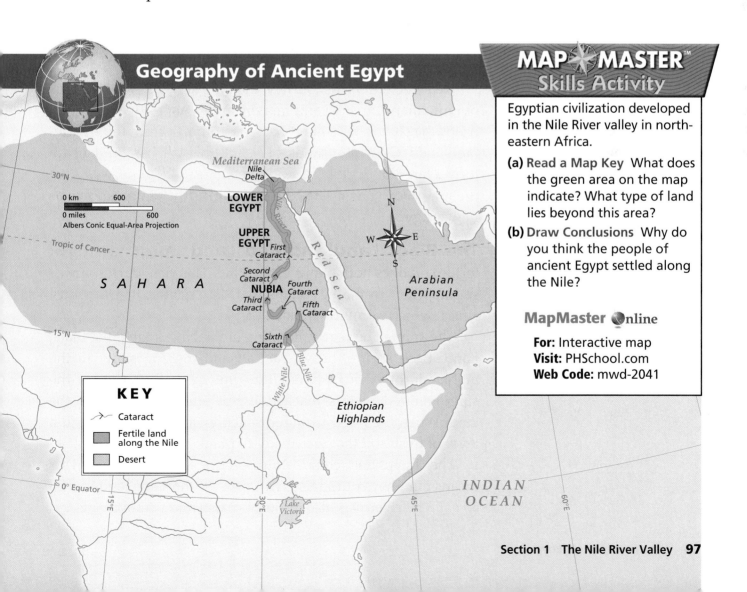

**Geography of Ancient Egypt**

Mediterranean Sea
Nile Delta
LOWER EGYPT
Nile River
30°N
0 km 600
0 miles 600
Albers Conic Equal-Area Projection
Tropic of Cancer
UPPER EGYPT
First Cataract
Second Cataract
S A H A R A
NUBIA Fourth Cataract
Third Cataract
Fifth Cataract
Red Sea
N
W E
S
Arabian Peninsula
15°N
Sixth Cataract
White Nile
Blue Nile
Ethiopian Highlands

**KEY**
Cataract
Fertile land along the Nile
Desert

0° Equator
15°E
30°E
Lake Victoria
45°E
60°E
INDIAN OCEAN

MAP MASTER
Skills Activity

Egyptian civilization developed in the Nile River valley in northeastern Africa.

**(a) Read a Map Key** What does the green area on the map indicate? What type of land lies beyond this area?

**(b) Draw Conclusions** Why do you think the people of ancient Egypt settled along the Nile?

**MapMaster** ⬤nline

**For:** Interactive map
**Visit:** PHSchool.com
**Web Code:** mwd-2041

# The Nile Gives Life

**Black Land and Red Land**
This photograph shows the contrast between the "Black Land" of the Nile Valley and the "Red Land" of the Sahara. **Critical Thinking: Draw Inferences** *Based on this picture, which type of land would be more attractive to settlers? Explain.*

## Explore More Video

**Discovery School Video** View *The Nile Gives Life* to learn more about the importance of the Nile to the people of ancient Egypt.

**Vocabulary** *Builder*
<u>annual</u> (AN yoo uhl) *adj.* taking place every year

Near the end of its journey, the Nile slows down and fans out into many streams and marshy areas. As it slows, the river drops the silt, or soil, that it has carried north from the African highlands. Over thousands of years, this silt has built up to form a large river delta. A **delta is an area of soil deposited at the mouth of a river.** The Nile delta forms the region known as Lower Egypt.

**The Black Land and Red Land**  A narrow strip of fertile soil lines both banks of the Nile. This rich, dark soil was so important to the Egyptians that they named their country *Kemet*, which means "the Black Land."

The <u>annual</u>, or yearly, flooding of the Nile created the Black Land. Each spring, heavy rainfall and melting snow in the highlands of Africa poured into the river. By summer, the surging flood waters reached Egypt and spread across the land. When the flood waters drained away, they left behind a layer of fresh soil that was ready to plant.

The Egyptians could **double-crop** this rich soil. This means that they could raise two crops on the same land within a year. The river was also a source of fish and useful plants.

On either side of the Black Land lay the endless Sahara. Egyptians called this desert "the Red Land." Unlike the Black Land, the Red Land was a deadly place of hot, burning sands.

 **Checkpoint** How was the Nile River important to life in Egypt?

## Uniting Upper and Lower Egypt

As settlements in the Nile River valley grew, two kingdoms developed. The kings of Upper Egypt, who wore white crowns, controlled the Nile River valley. The kings of Lower Egypt, who wore red crowns, ruled the delta. According to Egyptian legend, a king called Menes united the two kingdoms in about 3000 B.C. Egypt was united under one ruler who wore a double crown of red and white and was known as the "Lord of the Two Lands."

 **Checkpoint** Why did the Lord of the Two Lands wear a double crown?

**Looking Back and Ahead** In this section, you have learned how important the Nile was to the settlement of Egypt. You read that about 5,000 years ago, Egypt was united under one ruler. In the next section, you will read about the amazing civilization that developed along the Nile.

**Main Idea**
Upper Egypt and Lower Egypt united into one kingdom.

---

## Section 1 Check Your Progress

**Progress Monitoring** Online
**For:** Self-test with instant help
**Visit:** PHSchool.com
**Web Code:** mwa-2041

 **Standards Review** H-SS: 6.2.1; E-LA: Reading 6.1.4

**Comprehension and Critical Thinking**

**1. (a) Explain** Where does the Nile River begin and end?
**(b) Apply Information** Explain the relationship between the Nile River and Egypt's "Black Land."

**2. (a) Identify** Which areas of land were included in Upper and in Lower Egypt?
**(b) Draw Conclusions** Why would a ruler want to control both Upper and Lower Egypt?

**Reading Skill**

**3. Use Word Clues to Determine Meaning** Read this sentence. Then write the meaning of *surging* by using sentence word clues. Tell what clues you used.
By summer, the *surging* flood waters reached Egypt and spread across the land.

**Vocabulary Builder**

**4.** Write two definitions for each word: interior, delta. First, write a formal definition for your teacher. Second, write a definition in everyday English for a classmate.

**Writing**

**5.** Write three sentences with supporting details about the Nile River's importance to the people of ancient Egypt.

Section

# 2 Egypt Under the Pharaohs

## Standards Preview

**H-SS 6.2.3** Understand the relationship between religion and the social and political order in Mesopotamia and Egypt.

**H-SS 6.2.7** Understand the significance of Queen Hatshepsut and Ramses the Great.

**E-LA Reading 6.1.4** Monitor expository text for unknown words or words with novel meanings by using word, sentence, and paragraph clues to determine meaning.

## Reading Preview

 **Reading Skill**

**Use Sentence Clues** Unfamiliar words that are important to understand the text in this book are printed in blue. The definition is provided in the sentence or in a nearby sentence. Look at this example: "Early Egyptian pharaohs, as the rulers of Egypt were called, met this challenge in two ways." The blue text helps you find the unfamiliar word, which is then restated in a different way.

**Vocabulary** *Builder*

**High-Use Words**
**challenge** (CHAL uhnj), p. 100
**establish** (eh STAB lish), p. 101

**Key Terms and People**
authority (uh THOR ih tee), p. 100
pharaoh (FAIR oh), p. 101
ritual (RICH yoo uhl), p. 101
artisan (ART uh zen), p. 102
Hatshepsut (hat SHEP soot), p. 103
Ramses II (RAM zeez) the Second, p. 104

**Background Knowledge** In Chapter 3, you read about leaders with armies strong enough to conquer Mesopotamia's city-states. But the leaders were not able to unite those city-states into a lasting empire. In this section, you will see how the rulers who united Egypt solved a similar problem.

**Main Idea**
Egypt's pharaohs, who were considered god-kings, ruled the land and held the highest place in society.

## Governing Egypt

The first ruler of a united Egypt ruled by conquest. For Egypt to remain united, however, a ruler needed more than military power. He needed to persuade the Egyptian people to accept his **authority.** A person with authority has the right to control other people. People obey a person with power because of fear. They obey a person with authority by choice.

A village leader usually gained authority over the people he hoped to control because he knew them. The people of Egypt were spread out over hundreds of miles. It was a <u>challenge</u> to get so many people to accept the authority of a ruler whom they did not know and would probably never see.

**Vocabulary** *Builder*
**challenge** (CHAL uhnj) *n.* difficult task that needs special effort

**100** Chapter 4 Ancient Egypt

**The God-King**   Early Egyptian pharaohs, as the rulers of Egypt were called, met this challenge in two ways. First, they based their authority on Egyptian religious beliefs. Egyptians believed that gods controlled everything that happened on Earth. Because the pharaoh controlled Egypt, people naturally saw him or her as a god-king. They believed that after death a pharaoh joined the other gods to live forever. Rulers prepared for life among the gods by building large tombs, filling these with items that they might need after death.

**Good Government**   The second way that pharaohs gained authority was by providing Egypt with good government. One of the most important responsibilities for a pharaoh was to lead religious rituals to make sure that the Nile River flooded each year. A ritual is a ceremony enacted in the same way time after time. The ruler was also expected to protect his people and look after their welfare. The pharaohs established a well-run government to carry out these responsibilities. Priests and officials carried out the pharaoh's orders up and down the vast stretches of the Nile. They enforced laws, collected taxes, and organized building projects.

**E-LA 6.1.4 Use Sentence Clues**   What words in the sentence, or in a nearby sentence, help you understand the word *tomb*?

**Vocabulary *Builder***
establish (eh STAB lish) *v.* set up; start

The cobra stood for the pharaoh's power to protect Egypt from its enemies.

The crook, or shepherd's stick, meant that the pharaoh would look after his people like a shepherd looked after his sheep.

The flail, or whip, showed that the pharaoh was the heavenly guardian of his people.

**Symbols of Royal Authority**
This mummy case of a pharaoh shows several symbols of his authority as a god-king.
**Critical Thinking: Draw Conclusions**  *Why would a king want to be compared to a shepherd?*

## Egypt's Social Pyramid

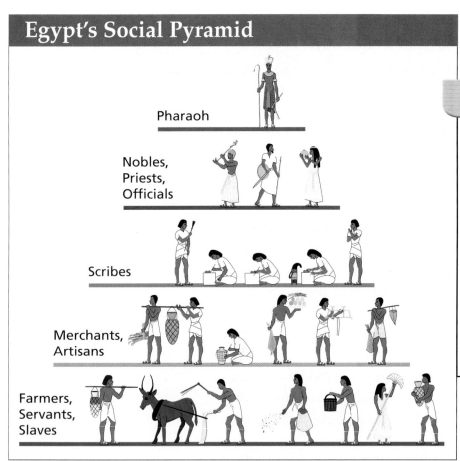

Pharaoh

Nobles, Priests, Officials

Scribes

Merchants, Artisans

Farmers, Servants, Slaves

### Reading Diagrams

The pharaoh stood alone at the top of Egyptian society. Beneath him were the people who made his government work.

**(a) Read a Diagram** What people were at the bottom levels of the pyramid?

**(b) Analyze Information** How did the people at the bottom support those at the top? What do you think the people at the bottom received in return?

**The Egyptian Social Order** To maintain the pharaoh's authority, he or she needed the loyalty and labor of his people. Egypt's social order provided both.

Egyptian society was shaped like a pyramid. The pharaoh was at the top of that pyramid. In the level below were nobles, priests, and officials. They helped the pharaoh govern Egypt. So did soldiers, who fought battles for their ruler, and scribes, who kept records for the government and the temples.

Merchants and artisans made up the next level. Artisans are skilled workers who practice a trade or handicraft. In Egypt, painters, stonecutters, and builders spent their entire lives working on palaces, temples, and tombs.

Farmers, servants, and slaves were at the bottom of the social pyramid. During the growing season, farmers raised Egypt's food. For the rest of the year they worked as laborers on the pharaoh's building projects. Most did so willingly as a form of religious devotion. They believed that if they helped the god-king in life, they would be rewarded after death.

✓ **Checkpoint** How did Egyptians view their rulers?

# Two Pharaohs in Power

Pharaohs ruled Egypt for more than 3,000 years. Not all of them were good leaders. Some lost their power to foreign invaders. But each time that happened, a new pharaoh rose up to drive the foreigners out. Queen Hatshepsut and Ramses II are two of Egypt's most famous rulers. Each used the pharaoh's power in a different way.

**The Queen-King** Hatshepsut was one of the few women to rule Egypt. She was the daughter of one pharaoh and the Great Royal Wife of another. When her husband, Thutmose II, died in 1504 B.C., he left a son who was too young to rule. Instead, Hatshepsut made herself Egypt's new pharaoh. One of her officials wrote

**❝The god's wife Hatshepsut governed the land and the Two Lands were under her control. People worked for her, and Egypt bowed its head.❞**

—from *Great Civilizations of Africa*

Some Egyptians did not want to bow to a woman. To gain their support, Hatshepsut carried out all of the rituals expected of a king. Her statues showed her dressed as a king. She even wore the false beard that was a symbol of the pharaoh's power. The picture at right shows Hatshepsut with a false beard.

Hatshepsut's rule was peaceful. She was often called "Good Queen Hatshepsut." Hatshepsut built Egypt's wealth and power through trade. She sent traders by sea to a land called Punt in East Africa. They returned with precious wood, ivory, gold, and perfumes. Hatshepsut had the story of their journey carved on the walls of an enormous temple that she built near the city of Thebes.

At some time, Hatshepsut's name and images were chipped out of carvings and many of her statues were smashed. Who did it? History may never know the true story.

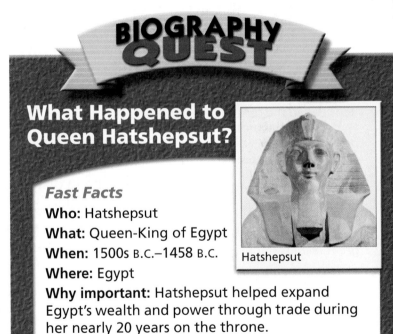

## BIOGRAPHY QUEST

### What Happened to Queen Hatshepsut?

Hatshepsut

**Fast Facts**
**Who:** Hatshepsut
**What:** Queen-King of Egypt
**When:** 1500s B.C.–1458 B.C.
**Where:** Egypt
**Why important:** Hatshepsut helped expand Egypt's wealth and power through trade during her nearly 20 years on the throne.

**Fast Find**
**How:** Go online to find out what historians think happened to Hatshepsut.

**Biography Online**

**For:** More about Hatshepsut
**Visit:** PHSchool.com
**Web Code:** mwe-2042

**Abu Simbel**

Abu Simbel is a temple built by Ramses II in the central part of Nubia, near the present-day border of Sudan. Four massive (65 feet high) statues of Ramses guard either side of the entrance. **Critical Thinking: Link Past and Present** *What are some present-day statues that depict great leaders?*

**The Warrior King** Ramses II, who ruled about 200 years after Hatshepsut, was a different kind of pharaoh. What Hatshepsut had tried to do through trade, Ramses chose to do through war. He spent the first half of his reign, or rule, fighting in distant lands.

In 1274 B.C., King Ramses led his army against the powerful Hittites. The two armies met in a place called Qadesh in present-day Syria. According to Ramses, he won a great victory at Qadesh without much help from his soldiers. Later King Ramses had these words, scolding his troops, carved on a temple wall:

> ❝None of you was there. . . . None rose to lend me his hand in my fight. . . . None of you came later to tell the story of his heroic deeds in Egypt. . . . The foreigners who saw me, praise my name to the end of all lands. . . . Since ancient times a man was honored for his fighting abilities. But I will not reward any of you, as you abandoned me when I was alone fighting my enemy.❞

—Ramses II on the Battle of Qadesh

In fact, Ramses lost many of his soldiers to the Hittites in the Battle of Qadesh. Rather than lose the rest of his army, King Ramses headed home.

Ramses II was Egypt's greatest builder. During a reign of more than 60 years, he built more monuments than any other pharaoh. One of his many projects was the temple at Abu Simbel, pictured on page 104. This huge temple was carved from a rock cliff. Four statues of Ramses, each more than 65 feet tall, guard the entrance. Not surprisingly, Ramses II is remembered as Ramses the Great.

 **Checkpoint** **How were Hatshepsut and Ramses II different in their rule of ancient Egypt? How were they alike?**

**Looking Back and Ahead** This section began with a problem: How could one person gain the authority needed to rule a country as large as Egypt? In this section, you have learned that Egypt's rulers solved that problem in two ways. First, Egypt's pharaohs claimed to be gods. Second, they created a government strong enough to carry out their orders. In the next section, you will read about Egypt's relationship with Nubia, its neighbor to the south.

**Symbol of Life**
Only gods and pharaohs could carry the *ankh*, an Egyptian symbol of life. **Critical Thinking: Draw Conclusions** *Why do you think pharaohs carried a symbol associated with the gods?*

---

## Section 2 Check Your Progress

**Progress Monitoring** Online

**For:** Self-test with instant help
**Visit:** PHSchool.com
**Web Code:** mwa-2042

 **Standards Review** **H-SS: 6.2.3, 6.2.7; E-LA: Reading 6.1.4**

### Comprehension and Critical Thinking

**1. (a) Recall** In what two ways did Egypt's rulers establish their authority?
**(b) Link Past and Present** In what ways did the pharaoh's authority differ from that held by the president of the United States?

**2. (a) Identify** What groups made up the level below the pharaoh on the social pyramid in Egypt?
**(b) Draw Inferences** Why do you think priests and scribes held such high rank?

### Reading Skill

**3. Use Sentence Clues** Read this sentence from Section 2: Early Egyptian pharaohs, as the rulers of Egypt were called, met this challenge in two ways. What does the word *pharaohs* mean? Use sentence clues to define this word.

### Vocabulary *Builder*

Complete each of the following sentences so that the second part explains the first part and clearly shows your understanding of the highlighted key term.

**4.** The pharaoh had authority over the people: _____.

**5.** Queen Hatshepsut carried out rituals: _____.

**6.** Artisans in ancient Egypt included painters, stonecutters, and builders: _____.

### Writing

**7.** Write three sentences describing how Egypt's rulers were able to rule a country as large as Egypt. Include a thesis statement identifying which way was more effective.

Section

# 3 Egypt and Nubia

**Standards Preview**

**H-SS 6.2.6** Describe the role of Egyptian trade in the eastern Mediterranean and Nile River valley.

**H-SS 6.2.8** Identify the location of the Kush civilization and describe its political, commercial, and cultural relations with Egypt.

**E-LA Reading 6.1.4** Monitor expository text for unknown words or words with novel meanings by using word, sentence, and paragraph clues to determine meaning.

## Reading Preview

### Reading Skill

**Use Paragraph Clues** Often you can find definition clues in the sentences around an unfamiliar word. One clue type is the example. Examples sometimes appear in addition to an actual definition. Look at this example: "Merchants and artisans made up the next level. In Egypt, this group included painters, stonecutters, and builders." Examples like these help you understand what the word *artisan* means.

### Vocabulary *Builder*

**High-Use Words**
region (REE juhn), p. 108
expand (ek SPAND), p. 109

**Key Terms and People**
commerce (KAHM ers), p. 106
luxury goods (LUK shur ree gudz), p. 107
expedition (eks puh DISH uhn), p. 107
Snefru (SNEF roo), p. 107
tribute (TRIB yoot), p. 108
Piye (PĪ yee), p. 109

**Background Knowledge**   The civilization of Egypt was widely admired across the Mediterranean world. In Section 2, you read how Queen Hatshepsut tried to expand Egyptian trade. Other pharaohs also sent traders to the south, north, and east. Much less was known about the second civilization to take root in the Nile valley. In this section, you will read about the Kush, or Nubian, civilization. You will also learn about the relationship between Nubia and its neighbor, Egypt.

**Main Idea**
Egypt traded goods with many lands to get useful resources and beautiful finished goods.

## The Role of Trade in Egypt

Trade brought Egypt and Nubia together. Egypt was rich in sunshine and soil, but it lacked forests, minerals, horses, and other useful resources found in Nubia and other places. People in ancient Egypt had to get these resources through commerce with the country's neighbors. **Commerce** is the buying and selling of goods and services.

As their country grew in wealth, Egyptians were eager to buy luxury goods from other lands. **Luxury goods** were goods that they did not need, but that made life more enjoyable in some way. Such goods included animal skins, precious stones, and perfumes.

## Trade in the Eastern Mediterranean

The pharaohs organized expeditions to open trade with other lands. An **expedition** is a journey or trip taken for a special purpose. All trade goods brought back to Egypt by these expeditions belonged to the pharaoh. Around 2500 B.C., a pharaoh named **Snefru** ordered expeditions to the eastern Mediterranean Sea.

**E-LA 6.1.4 Use Paragraph Clues**
What words in a nearby sentence give you examples that help define the term *luxury goods*?

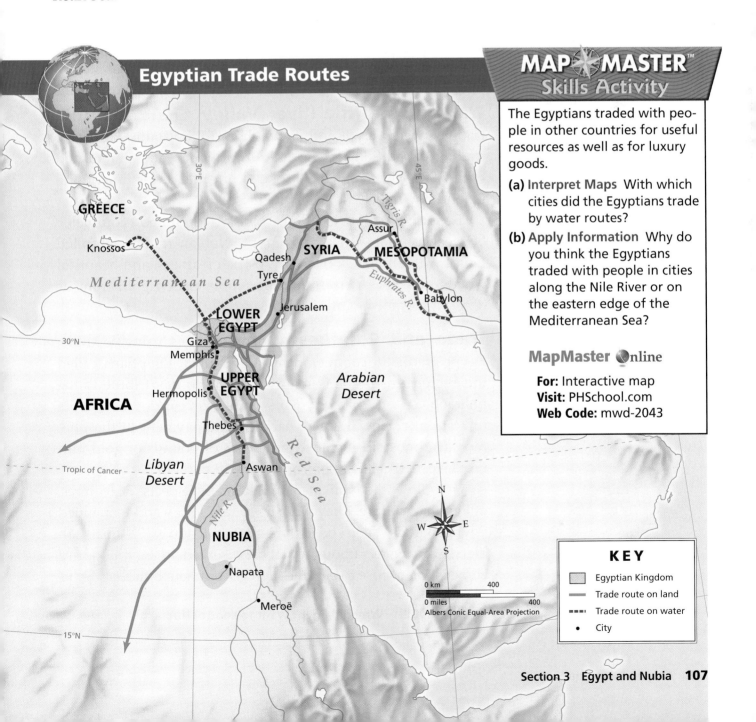

**Egyptian Trade Routes**

**MAP MASTER**
**Skills Activity**

The Egyptians traded with people in other countries for useful resources as well as for luxury goods.

**(a) Interpret Maps** With which cities did the Egyptians trade by water routes?

**(b) Apply Information** Why do you think the Egyptians traded with people in cities along the Nile River or on the eastern edge of the Mediterranean Sea?

**MapMaster Online**

**For:** Interactive map
**Visit:** PHSchool.com
**Web Code:** mwd-2043

GREECE
Knossos
Mediterranean Sea
Qadesh
SYRIA
Tyre
Assur
MESOPOTAMIA
Tigris R.
Euphrates R.
Babylon
Jerusalem
LOWER EGYPT
Giza
Memphis
UPPER EGYPT
Hermopolis
Arabian Desert
AFRICA
Thebes
Libyan Desert
Aswan
Red Sea
Nile R.
NUBIA
Napata
Meroë
Tropic of Cancer

**KEY**
Egyptian Kingdom
Trade route on land
Trade route on water
City

0 km 400
0 miles 400
Albers Conic Equal-Area Projection

**Nubia Pays Tribute to Egypt**

For centuries, Egypt ruled Nubia. This Egyptian wall painting shows Nubian princes bringing tribute to the pharaoh. **Critical Thinking: Apply Information** *According to this painting, what were some of the goods that Nubians brought to Egypt as tribute?*

**Vocabulary** *Builder*
**region** (REE juhn) *n.* large and indefinite part of Earth

**Trade in the Nile River Valley** Snefru also started trade between Egypt and its neighbor to the south. He sent a trading expedition up the Nile into Nubia, and it returned with 7,000 slaves and 200,000 head of cattle. Over time, trade up and down the Nile Valley increased.

Because of its location, Nubia controlled commerce between central Africa and Egypt. Nubian traders supplied Egypt with animal skins, ivory, ostrich feathers, and beautiful woods from the African interior. Nubia traded gold from its desert mines for Egyptian wheat.

**Trade and Conquest** To protect this valuable trade, Egypt gradually conquered most of Nubia. Egyptians called this region Kush. The Nubians also had to pay tribute to the pharaoh. Tribute is a payment made by a conquered people to a stronger power. One year's tribute payment to the pharaoh Thutmose III included hundreds of pounds of gold, cattle, slaves, ostrich feathers, and ivory from Nubia.

Over time, the Nubians adopted many aspects, or features, of Egyptian culture. They wore Egyptian clothes and worshiped Egyptian gods. They spoke the Egyptian language. Nubian soldiers, who were famous as archers, served in Egypt's army. Some Nubians rose to become high government officials.

✓ **Checkpoint** Why did Egypt want to control Nubia?

# Relations Between Egypt and Kush

After the rule of Ramses II, Egypt's government collapsed. Rival leaders in different cities were so busy fighting one another that they forgot about maintaining Egypt's control of Kush. This was a costly oversight. Left on its own, Kush became an independent kingdom ruled by Nubian kings.

**Main Idea**
Kush broke away from Egypt and later conquered and ruled Egypt.

**Kush Conquers Egypt** In the mid-700s B.C., a Nubian king conquered the Egyptian town of Thebes. The next ruler of Kush, a king named Piye, expanded the Kushite empire by conquering one Egyptian city after another. The city of Hermopolis, however, refused to surrender. Piye issued these orders: "Surround the city and capture its people. Let not the peasants go forth to the field, and let not the plowman plow."

**Vocabulary** *Builder*
expand (ek SPAND) *v.* become or make larger in size or scope

For five long months Hermopolis held out against Piye's army. But when the city's food supply ran out, its people began to starve. A horrible odor filled the city as dead bodies rotted in the heat. Only then did Hermopolis surrender. When the city fell, Piye declared himself the new pharaoh of a united Egypt and Kush.

**Egypt Under Kush** Pharaohs from Kush ruled Egypt for almost a century. The rulers from the south encouraged an Egyptian-style culture. They built temples to honor Nubian and Egyptian gods. They dotted the desert with hundreds of tombs. Like earlier pharaohs, they encouraged trade between Africa and the lands around the Mediterranean Sea.

The rulers from Kush might have remained in power longer if they had been content to govern only Egypt. Instead, they tried to expand their power. They went to war with the Assyrians, skillful warriors who had recently conquered the Fertile Crescent. This error in judgment led to the Nubians' downfall. Assyrian troops invaded Egypt in 663 B.C. After suffering many losses in battle, the Nubians retreated from Egypt to Kush.

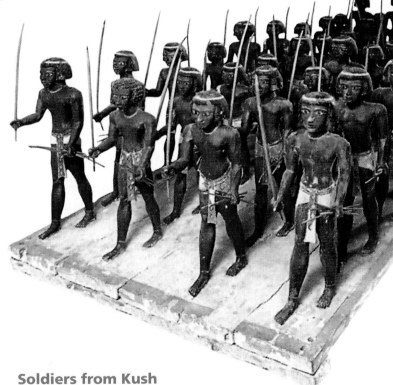

**Soldiers from Kush**
In the 700s, King Piye of Kush marched his armies northward to conquer Egypt. Compare this picture with the one on page 108. **Critical Thinking: Contrast** *How do the two pictures show the changing relationship between Egypt and Kush?*

**Iron Vessel from Meroë**
A vessel, or container, made from Meroë iron **Critical Thinking: Apply Information** *Why did items from Meroë last for hundreds of years?*

**Iron Working at Meroë**   Around 200 B.C., the rulers of Kush moved their capital south to the city of Meroë (mehr oh WEE). Meroë received more rain than did most of Nubia. The city was also located on trade routes from Central Africa. Historians believe that the main reason for moving the capital here was the iron ore deposits located near Meroë. For the next 900 years, Meroë thrived as a center of trade and culture.

The Nubians turned Meroë into Africa's first ironworking center. Iron tools and weapons made there were much stronger than the soft bronze tools made in Egypt. Knowledge of ironworking spread from Meroë to other parts of Africa.

✔**Checkpoint**   **What area did the pharaohs of Kush rule?**

**Looking Back and Ahead**   In this section, you have read that Egypt depended on trade to obtain useful resources and luxury goods. You have also learned that Egypt and Kush came together as partners in trade and rivals in war. In the next section, you will read about another key aspect of Egyptian civilization. You will learn about the importance of religion in Egyptians' lives.

---

## Section 3 **Check Your Progress**

**Progress Monitoring** ⏻nline
**For:** Self-test with instant help
**Visit:** PHSchool.com
**Web Code:** mwa-2043

 **Standards Review**   H-SS: 6.2.6, 6.2.8; E-LA: Reading 6.1.4

**Comprehension and Critical Thinking**
1. **(a) Recall** What kinds of goods did Egypt get from Nubia in trade?
**(b) Apply Information** What aspects of Egyptian society helped encourage the development of trade?

2. **(a) Explain** What made it possible for Kush to conquer and rule Egypt for a time?
**(b) Analyze Cause and Effect** In what ways did Egyptian culture affect that of Kush? Did the culture of Kush have the same effect on Egypt's culture?

**◉ Reading Skill**
3. **Use Paragraph Clues** Choose a blue Key Term from the section. Write a short paragraph containing the word. Include examples to define the word in your paragraph.

**Vocabulary *Builder***
Read sentences 4–6 below. If the sentence is true, write YES. If the sentence is not true, write NO and explain WHY.
4. Commerce is another word for goods that people do not need, but that make life more enjoyable.

5. An expedition is an area where something is placed, or its position.
6. A tribute is payment made by conquered people to a stronger power.

**Writing**
7. Write three sentences describing Egyptian trade, beginning with a general statement and ending with the important details.

**Standards Preview**

**H-SS 6.2.3** Understand the relationship between religion and the social and political order in Mesopotamia and Egypt.

**E-LA Reading 6.1.4** Monitor expository text for unknown words or words with novel meanings by using word, sentence, and paragraph clues to determine meaning.

## Reading Preview

 ### Reading Skill

**Use Sentence Clues** In this textbook, unfamiliar words are often defined with appositives. An appositive restates a word in a different way. It follows the unfamiliar word and is introduced by a comma and the word *or.* Look at this example: "He spent the first half of his reign, or rule . . ." *Rule* restates the unfamiliar word *reign.*

### Vocabulary *Builder*

**High-Use Words**
site (sīt), p. 114

**Key Terms and People**
underworld (UHN der wurld), p. 112
afterlife (AF tuhr līfe), p. 113
mummy (MUH mee), p. 113

**Background Knowledge** Like other early civilizations, the Egyptians had an established religion. Egyptian religious beliefs affected how people behaved in life. Those same beliefs had a powerful impact on how the Egyptians viewed death. In this section, you will read about the Egyptians' religious beliefs. You will also learn about the daily life of the Egyptian people.

## Egyptian Religious Beliefs

Like the Sumerians, the Egyptians accepted polytheism, or belief in many gods. *Poly* is a Greek word meaning "many," while *theism* comes from the Greek word for "gods."

Religion played an important role in the daily life of the people of Egypt. They believed that their gods controlled every aspect of life, from the flooding of the Nile River to the death of a child. Their gods could be kind or dangerous. To keep the gods happy, Egyptians built temples for the gods and offered them prayers and gifts. Many villages had their own special gods.

**Main Idea**
Egyptians worshiped many gods and believed that life continued after death.

### The Egyptian Gods

Egyptians worshiped hundreds of gods, many of whom were associated with animals. Statues or other works of art often show a god with the head or body of a lion, a crocodile, or some other creature. Egyptians believed that gods shared the qualities of these animals, such as their strength, speed, or bad temper.

The most important god was Amon-Re, the sun god. Egyptians believed that Amon-Re made a daily journey across the sky. Each night, he died in the west and the land grew dark. Each morning, he was reborn in the east as the sun rose.

### Osiris, Isis, and Horus

Other popular Egyptian gods were Osiris, Isis, and Horus. Osiris was the god of the underworld, or the world of the dead. According to Egyptian legend, Osiris was killed and chopped into pieces by a rival god named Seth. Isis, the wife of Osiris, was the mother goddess of Egypt. She moved heaven and earth to help her husband. Isis found the pieces of Seth's body and brought her husband back to life. Isis represented love, caring, and protection. Egyptians looked to Isis for protection in both life and death.

Horus was the son of Isis and Osiris. Egyptian legends tell of great battles between Horus and Seth. When Horus defeated Seth, he united the two lands of Egypt. Because of these stories, every pharaoh was thought to be Horus in human form.

**Egyptian Gods and Goddesses**

Religious beliefs supported Egypt's social and political order. The Egyptians believed that gods and goddesses controlled every aspect of life. **Critical Thinking: Apply Information** *Which of the gods and goddesses shown here would be especially important to Egyptian farmers?*

**a** **Horus** Linked to the pharaoh

**b** **Osiris** God of the underworld

**c** **Isis** First taught women to grind corn, spin cloth, and care for children

**d** **Khnum** Controlled flooding of the Nile

**e** **Thoth** God of wisdom, patron of scribes

**f** **Amon-Re** Sun god; creator of the world

**g** **Anubis** Directed the preparation of dead bodies for the afterlife

**Life After Death** Egyptians believed that they, like Osiris, could overcome death. Life on Earth could lead to an **afterlife, or life after death.** Egyptians would then enjoy all of the things that they had loved in life. But they had to prepare.

The first way to prepare for the afterlife was to live well. Egyptians believed that Osiris decided who would enter the afterlife. Those who had lived good lives would be allowed to live forever, but those who had lived sinful lives would be destroyed.

**Preserving the Dead** The second way that Egyptians prepared for the afterlife was by having their bodies preserved after death. Egyptians believed that a person had two spirits. One was *Ka,* or the life force. The other was *Ba,* or the soul. For a person to live forever, the *Ka* and the *Ba* had to be united with the body after death.

Egyptians went to great efforts to preserve the bodies of their dead. Poor people were buried in the desert, where the hot sand quickly dried out their bodies. Wealthy Egyptians had their bodies made into mummies. A **mummy is a body preserved by a special process.** From these preserved bodies, scientists today have learned a great deal about life and death in ancient Egypt.

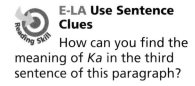

**E-LA Use Sentence Clues**
How can you find the meaning of *Ka* in the third sentence of this paragraph?

✔**Checkpoint** **How did Egyptians prepare for the afterlife?**

e f g

# How Egyptians Lived

Although religion was important, it did not keep Egyptians from enjoying themselves. Temple priests carried out most of the important religious rituals. Meanwhile, life for ordinary Egyptians centered on their homes.

**Staying Cool**  Most Egyptians lived in houses built with bricks made from Nile mud. The fertile Black Land along the Nile was farmland, too valuable to build on. Towns sprang up on higher ground set back from the river or in the desert near building sites.

Egyptian homes were designed to help people stay cool in the desert heat. Homes were built with thick walls and small windows to keep out the burning sun during the day. Stairs led to a flat roof where people could sleep during hot nights. Wealthy people relaxed in gardens with cooling pools and shade trees.

**Eating Well and Having Fun**  Wherever they lived, Egyptians usually ate well. No matter how elaborate the dinner, people ate with their fingers. Barley and wheat were their most important foods. These crops were turned into beverages and bread or cakes. Sometimes these items were accompanied by dates or honey.

Vegetables and fruits grew well along the Nile. The river also provided good catches of fish. However, cropland was so precious that very little of it was used for raising animals. Therefore, Egyptians ate meat only on special occasions.

Most Egyptians worked hard but still found time to play. Children ran, wrestled, swam, and played ball games. They played with dolls, wooden animals, and other toys.

**Egyptian House**
A clay model of an early Egyptian home, showing its very small windows and flat roof. **Critical Thinking: Distinguish Relevant Information** *How did Egyptian homes remain cool in the hot desert heat?*

Egyptians enjoyed festivals and banquets. No matter how special the dinner, people ate with their fingers. Music and dancing usually accompanied a meal. Egyptian paintings of the period show that songs were accompanied by musicians playing harps, flutes, drums, and other instruments.

**Personal Care** Egyptians loved beauty and fashion. Many women's names included the word *nefer,* which means "beautiful." Examples include Nefret and Nefertiti. Both men and women wore eye paint and wigs to make themselves more attractive. On special occasions, a person might tie a cone filled with perfumed animal fat over the wig. The fat slowly melted, filling the air with perfume as it ran down the wig.

**Checkpoint** **Describe the daily life of an ordinary Egyptian.**

**Looking Back and Ahead** In this section, you have learned that Egyptians believed in many gods. They also believed that life could continue after death for those who were prepared. In the next section, you will read about Egyptian achievements.

**Women of Ancient Egypt**
Upper-class women like the one pictured here used many types of cosmetics. **Critical Thinking: Draw Conclusions** *Do you think that most Egyptian women lived like the woman shown here? Explain.*

---

**Section 4 Check Your Progress**

**Progress Monitoring** Online

**For:** Self-test with instant help
**Visit:** PHSchool.com
**Web Code:** mwa-2044

**Standards Review** H-SS: 6.2.3; E-LA: Reading 6.1.4

**Comprehension and Critical Thinking**

1. **(a) Summarize** Summarize the basic ideas of Egyptian religion.
   **(b) Apply Information** How did the Egyptians' beliefs influence their customs surrounding death and burial?

2. **(a) Recall** Where were most Egyptians' homes located?
   **(b) Analyze Cause and Effect** Give two examples of ways that geography affected the daily life of Egyptians.

**Reading Skill**

3. **Use Sentence Clues** Read this sentence from Section 1: As it slows, the river drops the silt, or soil, it has carried north from the African highlands. Use sentence clues to define *silt.*

**Vocabulary *Builder***

4. Write two definitions for each term: underworld, afterlife, and mummy. First, write a formal definition for your teacher. Then, write a definition in everyday language for a classmate.

**Writing**

5. In four sentences, describe how Egyptians prepared for the afterlife. In your writing, use transition words such as *therefore* and *however* and terms of comparison such as *greater, more, less,* or *least.*

# Journey to the Afterlife

What happens to us after we die? The Egyptians believed that they could live on after death, but first they had to journey through the underworld. If they could recite the right spells, they might complete the journey unharmed. Then, they faced the final test—the judgment of Osiris in the Hall of Two Truths.

**History-Social Science**

**6.2.3** Understand the relationship between religion and the social and political order in Egypt.

**Historical Interpretation 4** Recognize the role of chance, oversight, and error in history.

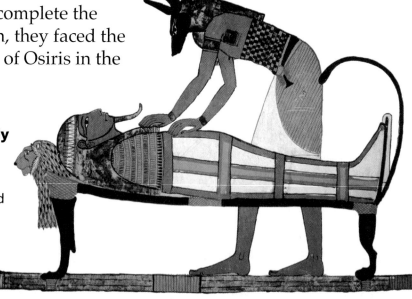

**1 Preparing the Body**

To prepare for the afterlife, Egyptians had their bodies specially preserved. They hoped that their mummified bodies would last forever so that their spirits would always have a home.

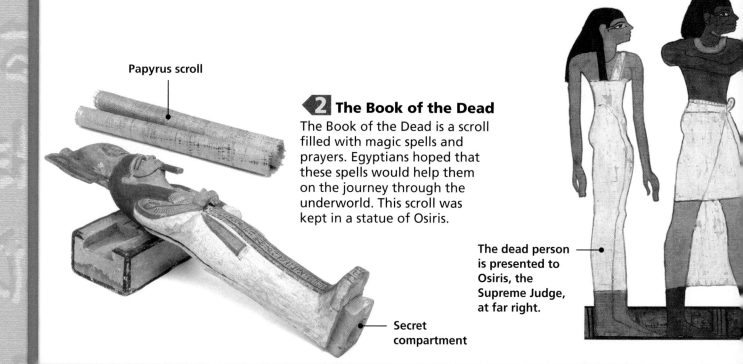

Papyrus scroll

**2 The Book of the Dead**

The Book of the Dead is a scroll filled with magic spells and prayers. Egyptians hoped that these spells would help them on the journey through the underworld. This scroll was kept in a statue of Osiris.

The dead person is presented to Osiris, the Supreme Judge, at far right.

Secret compartment

**Anubis** leads a person to judgment.

**Thoth,** the god of wisdom, records the results.

**Horus,** watching the weighing of the heart.

### 3 The Hall of Two Truths

In the Hall of Two Truths, a person's heart was weighed against the Feather of Truth to see whether the heart was heavy with sin. A heart free of sin passed. A heart heavy with sin was eaten by the monster Ammit, and the person ceased to exist.

The dead person's heart

The Feather of Truth

**Osiris** makes his final judgment.

### 4 The Final Judgment

The final judge of the dead person's soul was Osiris, god of the underworld. Osiris ruled the heavenly kingdom where Egyptians wished to live after death. They believed that this kingdom was a perfect version of the best place they knew on Earth—Egypt.

*Analyze* **LIFE AT THE TIME**

Egyptians believed that if they successfully completed the steps shown here, they would have a happy afterlife. But what might go wrong along the way? For each step in the journey, write a sentence describing what might keep an Egyptian from entering the afterlife.

## Standards Preview

**H-SS 6.2.5** Discuss the main features of Egyptian art and architecture.

**H-SS 6.2.9** Trace the evolution of language and its written forms.

**E-LA Reading 6.1.4** Monitor expository text for unknown words or words with novel meanings by using word, sentence, and paragraph clues to determine meaning.

## Reading Preview

 ### Reading Skill

**Use Paragraph Clues** Paragraphs will often say what a word is like or what it is *not* like. These comparisons and contrasts help you build meaning for an unfamiliar word. Look at this example: "The result is known as the Step Pyramid. Later architects made the sides smoother to create a true pyramid." The last sentence tells you that a Step Pyramid does *not* have smooth sides and is different from a true pyramid.

### Vocabulary *Builder*

**High-Use Words**
accurate (AK yoor iht), p. 121
document (DAHK yoo mehnt), p. 122

**Key Terms and People**
Imhotep (ihm HOH tehp), p. 118
sculpture (SKUHLP cher), p. 120
anatomy (uh NAT uh mee), p. 121
papyrus (puh PĪ ruhs), p. 122

**Background Knowledge** For 3,000 years, the Egyptian civilization was admired throughout the ancient world for its power and wealth. Furthermore, as you will read, this civilization also produced great buildings, art, and learning.

**Main Idea**
We have learned much about the people of ancient Egypt from their temples, tombs, and other artwork.

## Homes for the Dead

One of the most important types of Egyptian buildings were temples. Most were built of mud or from stone that was quarried, or mined, far away, and then transported over long distances. The Egyptians created temples for their gods and tombs for their pharaohs.

**Tombs for the Pharaohs** Tombs of early rulers were underground chambers, or rooms. The burial chamber contained items that the ruler might want in the afterlife.

An architect named **Imhotep** designed a new kind of tomb for his pharaoh, with six stone mounds, one on top of the other. The result is known as the Step Pyramid. Later architects made the sides smoother to create a true pyramid.

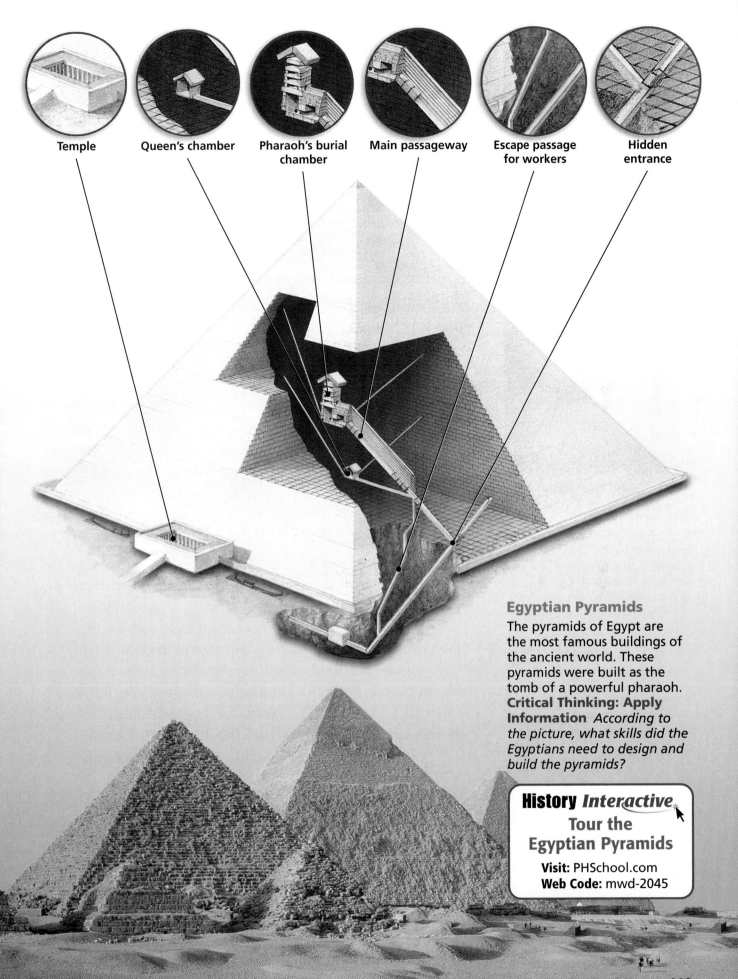

Temple

Queen's chamber

Pharaoh's burial chamber

Main passageway

Escape passage for workers

Hidden entrance

**Egyptian Pyramids**

The pyramids of Egypt are the most famous buildings of the ancient world. These pyramids were built as the tomb of a powerful pharaoh. **Critical Thinking: Apply Information** *According to the picture, what skills did the Egyptians need to design and build the pyramids?*

**History** *Interactive*
**Tour the Egyptian Pyramids**

**Visit:** PHSchool.com
**Web Code:** mwd-2045

Three enormous pyramids were built at Giza by King Khufu, his son Khafre, and his grandson Menkaure. The tallest of these is the Great Pyramid of Khufu. For more than 4,000 years, this pyramid was the world's tallest building. Nearby stands the famous statue known as the Sphinx. The Sphinx guarded the road to Khafre's pyramid.

The great age of pyramid building ended about 2200 B.C. Pharaohs who ruled after that time carved tombs from the cliffs in the Valley of the Kings and the Valley of the Queens.

**Painting and Sculpture**   Egyptians were skilled artists as well as builders. Much of what we know about life in Egypt comes from paintings found on the walls of tombs. Although these paintings show Egyptians at work and at play, their purpose was not decoration. The paintings were created to provide the person buried in the tomb with all of the objects and pleasures shown on the walls.

Egyptian artists also created wonderful sculptures. A **sculpture** is a statue made of clay, stone, or other materials. Most Egyptian sculptures were statues of people or gods. Colossal statues of gods stood in temples. Smaller statues of once-living Egyptians were placed in tombs along with their mummies. If the person's mummy was destroyed, the statue could replace it as a home for the dead person's spirit.

**Checkpoint**   **Why did the Egyptians build pyramids?**

**The Great Sphinx**
The Great Sphinx, with a lion's body and a king's head, rises between two pyramids in Giza.
**Critical Thinking: Draw Inferences** *Why do you think the Great Sphinx had the body of a lion?*

# Advances in Knowledge

The Egyptians advanced knowledge in many areas. From their work with mummies, for example, they learned much about human anatomy. Anatomy is the study of the body and its organs. Egyptian doctors also studied diseases and developed medicines to treat them.

**Measuring Time** The Egyptians developed the first accurate calendar. Like most early peoples, they first measured time by the cycles of the moon. The result was a lunar, or moon-based, calendar of about 360 days.

This lunar calendar worked adequately for many purposes, but it was not accurate enough to predict the regular flooding of the Nile. Egyptians developed "Nilometers"—a form of calendar based on the height of the Nile's flooding. To improve their predictions, the Egyptians developed a 365-day calendar, which was the first calendar based on the solar year. Every four years the Egyptians added an extra day to keep their solar calendar accurate.

**Main Idea**
Egyptian contributions include advances in technology, medicine, and science.

**Vocabulary** *Builder*
accurate (AK yoor iht) *adj.* correct; without mistakes

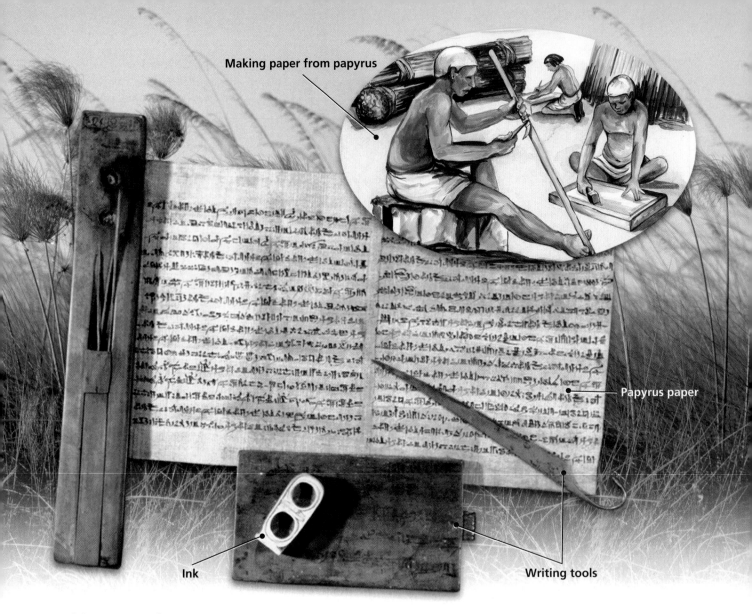

Making paper from papyrus

Papyrus paper

Ink

Writing tools

## Making Paper from Papyrus

Egyptians made paper from the papyrus plant. **Critical Thinking: Link Past and Present** *Are there any similarities with how the Egyptians wrote and how people of today write? Explain.*

**Vocabulary** *Builder*

<u>document</u> (DAHK yoo mehnt) *n.* anything printed or written that contains information or is relied upon to record or prove something

**Early Egyptian Writing**   As you have read in Chapter 3, the Egyptians created a writing system around 3000 B.C. In 1995, two archeologists discovered what may be even older Egyptian writing.

John and Deborah Darnell discovered an ancient tableau, or picture, carved into the side of a cliff. The Darnells believe the carving shows the victory of a legendary ruler. "We do feel that this is the earliest known historical <u>document</u>," said John Darnell. "It may not be 100 percent writing . . . but the tableau is able to impart [communicate] the who, what, where of an event."

Not all archeologists agree on what the carving shows, but some do agree that the tableau dates to about 3250 B.C. This was before Egypt was united.

**The First Paper** Egyptians invented the world's first paper. They made paper from papyrus, a reed that grows along the Nile. Our word *paper* comes from the Greek word *papyrus.* Scribes wrote in ink on papyrus sheets. This was much easier than pressing letters into wet clay as the Sumerians had done. Papyrus sheets were also easier to transport than pieces of stone.

Papyrus sheets had another important quality. They could last a very long time. Many documents written on papyrus—including medical books, calendars, stories, poems, and prayers—have survived to the present. Wall paintings may show us how Egyptians lived; however, it is only from written records that we can learn what was in their hearts and minds.

 **Checkpoint** What contributions did Egyptians make to technology?

**Looking Back and Ahead** In this section, you have read about some of Egypt's gifts to the world in art, architecture, and learning. In the next chapter, you will meet a people whose legacy, or lasting contribution, was something very different. They developed the first of the world's major religions.

## Section 5 Check Your Progress

**Progress Monitoring** Online
**For:** Self-test with instant help
**Visit:** PHSchool.com
**Web Code:** mwa-2045

 **Standards Review** H-SS: 6.2.5, 6.2.9; E-LA: Reading 6.1.4

**Comprehension and Critical Thinking**

1. **(a) Analyze** What do their temples and tombs tell us about the people of ancient Egypt?
   **(b) Link Past and Present** What might architecture someday tell people about life in our country today?

2. **(a) Recall** What contributions did the Egyptians make to art? To architecture? To learning?
   **(b) Apply Information** How did each of these contributions affect the lives of Egyptians?

**Reading Skill**

3. **Use Paragraph Clues** Read the following paragraph from Section 3, Trade and Conquest: Over time, the Nubians adopted many aspects, or features, of Egyptian culture. They wore Egyptian clothes and worshiped Egyptian gods. They spoke the Egyptian language. What clue words help you understand *aspects* in these sentences?

**Vocabulary *Builder***
Answer the following questions to show your understanding of the Key Terms.

4. What did most of the Egyptian sculptures show?

5. How did the people of ancient Egypt contribute to our knowledge of anatomy?

6. How was the papyrus plant used?

**Writing**

7. Write four sentences describing the important contributions that the people of ancient Egypt made to our knowledge of art, architecture, and paper making. Include a strong concluding statement.

Maps can show you the world. They can help you plan a trip, find your way around a strange city, or figure out the weather for the next day. They can also help you understand history. In this skill, you will learn to read historical maps by using the tools provided by the *cartographer,* or mapmaker.

## Chapter Standards

### History-Social Science

**Analysis Skill C&ST 3** Students use a variety of maps and documents to identify physical and cultural features of neighborhoods, cities, states, and countries and to explain the historical migration of people, expansion and disintegration of empires, and the growth of economic systems.

### E-LA Standards

**5.2.1** Understand how text features (e.g., format, graphics, sequence, diagrams, illustrations, charts, maps) make information accessible and usable.

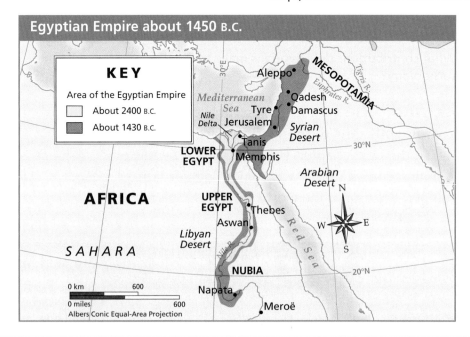

**Egyptian Empire about 1450 B.C.**

**KEY**

Area of the Egyptian Empire

About 2400 B.C.

About 1430 B.C.

**Learn the Skill** *Follow these steps to use the different parts of a map.*

1. **Read the map title.** The title tells you the topic of the map.

2. **Be aware of both physical and cultural features.** Physical features are rivers, mountains, or other natural things. Cultural features are things created by people.

3. **Relate the features on the map to information in the text.** Maps in textbooks usually show things described in the text. They may add more information.

**Practice the Skill** *Answer the following questions about the map above.*

1. **Read the map title.** What is the topic of the map?

2. **Be aware of both physical and cultural features.** Name two physical features shown on the map.

3. **Relate the features on the map to information in the text.** Did the Egyptian Empire grow or shrink between 2000 B.C. and 1430 B.C.? What actions by pharaohs caused that change?

**Apply the Skill**
*See page 127 of the Review and Assessment.*

## Chapter Summary  **H-SS:** 6.2.1; 6.2.3; 6.2.5; 6.2.6; 6.2.7; 6.2.8; 6.2.9

### Section 1  The Nile River Valley

• Egypt and Nubia rose in the valley of the Nile River, which flows from central Africa to the Mediterranean Sea.

• Early farmers grew crops in the fertile "Black Land" of the Nile Valley, but no crops could grow in the deadly "Red Land" of the Sahara.

• Around 3100 B.C., Upper Egypt and Lower Egypt were united into one kingdom.

### Section 2  Egypt Under the Pharaohs

• Pharaohs based their authority on Egyptian religious beliefs. The pharaoh was believed to be a god.

• A strong government carried out the pharaoh's orders and provided for the needs of the people.

### Section 3  Egypt and Nubia

• Egypt traded with lands around the Mediterranean Sea and in Africa.

• At first, Egypt gained control over Nubia. Later, Nubia, called Kush by the Egyptians, conquered Egypt.

### Section 4  Life and Death in Ancient Egypt

• The ancient Egyptians believed in many gods and goddesses.

• The Egyptians believed in an afterlife and carefully preserved the bodies of their dead.

### Section 5  Art, Architecture, and Learning in Egypt

• Egyptian architects built huge pyramid tombs and temples for the worship of gods.

• Paintings and statues in tombs were meant to provide for the dead in the afterlife.

## Standards Practice  **H-SS:** 6.2.1; 6.2.3; 6.2.5; 6.2.6; 6.2.7; 6.2.8; 6.2.9

## Vocabulary *Builder*

### High-Use Words

Decide whether each underlined word is used correctly. If it is, explain why. If it is not, rewrite the sentence to make the word fit logically.

1. The **annual** flooding of the Nile happened every other year.

2. Survival in the harsh desert was a **challenge** for the Egyptians.

3. The Egyptian empire **expanded** when the pharaohs lost control of Nubia.

4. Because their calendar was **accurate**, the Egyptians could not predict when the Nile would flood.

### Key Terms

Answer the following questions in complete sentences that show your understanding of the Key Terms.

1. How did the cataracts affect travel on the Nile?

2. How was the Nile delta formed?

3. What kinds of work did artisans in ancient Egypt do?

4. What are some examples of Egyptian luxury goods?

5. How did the Egyptians use papyrus?

## Apply Reading Skills

**Use Sentence Clues to Determine Meaning** Use sentence clues to determine what the word *rituals* means in this sentence: One of the pharaoh's most important duties was to lead rituals to make sure that the Nile River flooded each year.

## Comprehension and Critical Thinking

**1. (a) Recall** Describe the location of ancient Egyptian civilization.
**(b) Analyze Cause and Effect** How did the flooding of the Nile affect Egypt?
**(c) Predict** What do you think would have happened to Egyptian society if the Nile had failed to flood annually?

**2. (a) Recall** Describe Egypt's social order.
**(b) Apply Information** How did the figure at the top of the social order get the authority to rule?
**(c) Draw Conclusions** Do you think that a ruler can stay in power without providing good government? Explain.

**3. (a) List** What kind of luxury goods did Egypt get from Nubia?
**(b) Draw Conclusions** Why do you think such goods were valued?
**(c) Link Past and Present** List three items that you think of as luxury goods today.

**4. (a) Summarize** What contribution did Egyptians make to writing?
**(b) Contrast** How did Egyptian writing differ from Sumerian writing?

## Researching

**The Gifts of the Nile** About 2,500 years ago, the Greek historian Herodotus described Egypt as "the gift of the Nile." In this activity you will use the library media center or other resources to research and report on some of those gifts. Choose one of the following tasks. Share your work with the class on "Gifts of the Nile" day. Make a list of the resources you used to go with your presentation.

**Geographers:** Create a farming calendar for ancient Egypt. On your calendar, show how farmers along the Nile timed the planting and harvesting of their crops.

**Economists:** In 1971, a huge dam was built across the Nile River at Aswan. It is known as the Aswan High Dam. Create a two-column T chart on the impact of the dam. On one side, list the benefits of the Aswan High Dam. On the other side, list the costs of the dam.

> **Researching Online**
> **For:** Help in starting this activity
> **Visit:** PHSchool.com
> **Web Code:** mwa-2045

## Writing

**1. Write a paragraph on the following topic.** In early civilizations, religion and government were closely linked. Explain one way in which ancient Egypt's religious beliefs affected its government.
**Your paragraph should:**
• contain a clear topic sentence.
• use transition words, as needed.
• offer evidence, or details to support your explanation.

**2. Write a short narrative.** Imagine that you are a Nubian, seeing the Great Pyramid for the first time. Write a short narrative describing the experience.

**Progress Monitoring** :globe: nline
**For:** Self-test with instant help
**Visit:** PHSchool.com
**Web Code:** mwa-2045

# Apply Analysis Skills

**Use the map at right to answer the following questions.**

1. What is the topic of the map?

2. Name one physical feature and one cultural feature on the map. Explain how they are related.

3. Describe the extent of the Egyptian Empire around 1450 B.C. Why did the empire expand into these areas?

Egyptian Empire about 1450 B.C.

# Test Yourself

1. **Which of the following geographic features had the greatest influence on ancient Egypt?**
   A the Mediterranean Sea
   B the Red Sea
   C the Ethiopian Highlands
   D the Nile River

**Refer to the image below to answer question 2.**

2. **Why were the buildings shown in this picture built?**

   A as tombs for the pharaohs
   B to hold surplus grain
   C to protect Egypt from invasion
   D as homes for artisans

3. **Because of Nubia's location between Egypt and Central Africa, Nubia was**
   A destroyed by the Egyptians.
   B a center for trade.
   C never very wealthy.
   D the first sea empire.

4. **Which statement is true about Hatshepsut?**
   A She used her power to build trade with other lands.
   B The empire fell apart during her reign.
   C She was a great military conqueror.
   D She was the last pharaoh of Egypt.

**Refer to the reading below to answer question 5.**

5. **Why might an person from ancient Egypt have learned these words?**

> Oh, great Osiris . . . .
> I have not caused pain,
> I have not caused tears.
> I have not killed . . . .
> I have not held back water in its season,
> I have not dammed a flowing stream. . .

   A to honor the sun god
   B to gain favor with the pharaoh
   C to win admission to the afterlife
   D to protect against illness and death

## Chapter 5
# The Ancient Hebrews and Judaism (1800 B.C.–A.D. 100)

## Prepare to Read

### Chapter Standards

**History-Social Science**
**6.3.** Students analyze the geographic, political, economic, religious, and social structures of the Ancient Hebrews.

**Section 1,** pp. 132–137

**The Origins of Judaism**

**Section 2,** pp. 138–142

**The Beliefs of Judaism**

**Section 3,** pp. 143–149

**The Spread of Judaism**

### ✔ What You Will Learn

An ancient Mesopotamian people known as the Hebrews grew into a nation that was known for its belief in a single god.

Judaism is based on the belief in one God and in the teachings found in the Hebrew scriptures and other writings.

From early kingdoms of ancient Israel to many Jewish communities today, Jews have retained and built on their ancient traditions and practices.

This case protects a scroll containing Hebrew scriptures

**About 1800 B.C.**
Early Hebrews journey from Ur to Canaan.

**About 1250 B.C.**
Israelites escape from slavery in Egypt.

Chapter Events

Other Events

**2000 B.C.**

**1500 B.C.**

**1000 B.C.**

**About 1792 B.C.**
Hammurabi becomes King of Babylon.

**About 1300 B.C.**
The Chinese have a system of writing.

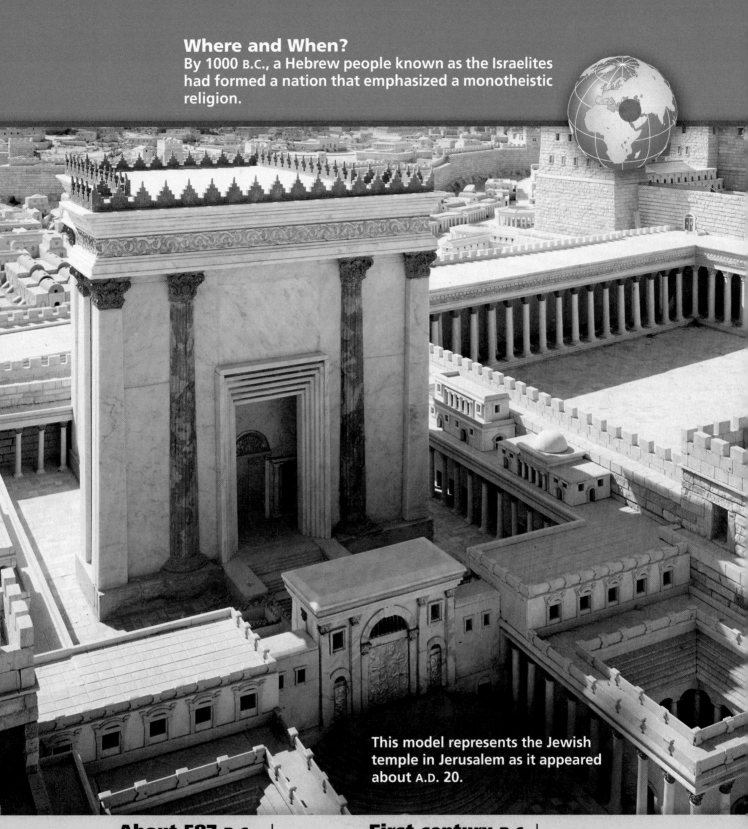

**Where and When?**
By 1000 B.C., a Hebrew people known as the Israelites had formed a nation that emphasized a monotheistic religion.

This model represents the Jewish temple in Jerusalem as it appeared about A.D. 20.

**About 587 B.C.**
Nebuchadnezzar's army destroys Jerusalem.

**First century B.C.**
Judah becomes part of the Roman Empire.

1000 B.C.

500 B.C.

B.C./A.D.

**About 500 B.C.**
The Greeks add vowels to their alphabet.

**About 100 B.C.**
Ancient Romans adopt the Greek alphabet.

## History Reading Skill

### *Previewing* Clarify Texts

When you understand something you have read in social studies, you can explain its important ideas clearly and accurately. Use strategies to find and organize the important ideas and to summarize the information they contain. Read the steps below to learn how.

**Chapter Standards**
**English-Language Arts**
**Reading 6.2.4** Clarify an understanding of texts by creating outlines, logical notes, summaries, or reports.

**1** Outline the main idea of each paragraph. Add two key details for each.

**Having Fun**
    **A.** Egyptians enjoyed leisure time.
        **1.** Children swam, wrestled, played ball games.
        **2.** Adults played board games.

**2** Next, summarize the main points from the outline. State them in your own words and include a few details.

( **main point** )        ( **important detail** )

The people of Ancient Egypt liked to have a good time. Their children played ball games, and adults enjoyed board games.

**3** Link main points from many sections to summarize the historical information or events discussed. A concept web can help:

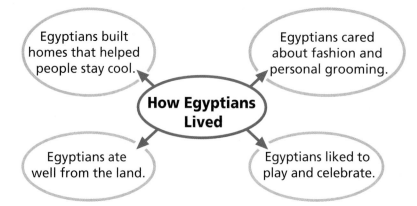

Now you can summarize this way: The life of Egyptians was full and varied. It included the work of growing food and staying cool and the fun of fashion and celebrations.

# Vocabulary *Builder*

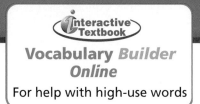
## *Previewing* **High-Use Academic Words**

| High-Use Word | Definition | Sample Sentence About History |
|---|---|---|
| **migration** (mī GRAY shuhn) (Section 1, p. 136) | *n.* movement of a large group of people from one area to another | The Fertile Crescent's river valleys encouraged the <u>migration</u> of people looking for farmland. |
| **approach** (uh PROHCH) (Section 1, p. 136) | *v.* to move closer to something | Egyptian slaves were allowed to <u>approach</u> the Pharaoh with food and gifts. |
| **tradition** (truh DISH uhn) (Section 2, p. 139) | *n.* a belief or custom that is very old | Egyptian religion included a <u>tradition</u> of preparing goods to take to the afterworld. |
| **interpret** (ihn TUHR priht) (Section 2, p. 140) | *v.* to explain the meaning | The Sumerian priests claimed that they could <u>interpret</u> the will of the gods. |
| **author** (AW thuhr) (Section 3, p. 144) | *n.* person who creates a written work | Hammurabi was the <u>author</u> of a famous law code. |
| **rebel** (rih BEHL) (Section 3, p. 145) | *v.* to oppose someone in authority | After Ramses II died, the Nubians <u>rebelled</u> against the Pharaoh. |

## *Previewing* **Key Terms and People**

**Ruth**

monotheism, p. 132
ethical, p. 132
covenant, p. 134
commandment, p. 135

scriptures, p. 138
prophet, p. 139
rabbi, p. 140
justice, p. 142

judge, p. 143
exile, p. 146
Diaspora, p. 147
synagogue, p. 147

**Seder Meal**

**Charity Box**

Section

# 1 The Origins of Judaism

## Standards Preview

**H-SS 6.3.1** Describe the origins and significance of Judaism as the first monotheistic religion based on the concept of one God who sets down moral laws for humanity.

**H-SS 6.3.4** Discuss the locations of the settlements and movements of Hebrew peoples, including the Exodus and their movement to and from Egypt, and outline the significance of the Exodus to the Jewish and other people.

**E-LA** Reading 6.2.4

## Reading Preview

 **Reading Skill**

**Clarify Understanding** As you read a section of text, find the main ideas. Headings can help you identify these ideas. Use headings and the subheadings beneath them to create an outline of the section. List key ideas in each part of the section, along with a few important details. Then choose the three most important ideas. Outlining in this way will help you clarify and understand the text.

**Vocabulary** *Builder*

**High-Use Words**
**migration** (mī GRAY shuhn), p. 136
**approach** (uh PROHCH), p. 136

**Key Terms and People**
monotheism (MAH nuh thee ihz uhm), p. 132
ethical (EH thih kuhl), p. 132
covenant (KUH vuh nuhnt), p. 134
commandment (kuh MAND muhnt), p. 135

**Background Knowledge** In Chapters 3 and 4, you learned about early empires of the Fertile Crescent. Great rulers controlled large areas of Egypt and Mesopotamia and the lands between them. At the same time, many smaller groups of people were migrating throughout the region. One of those groups, the Hebrews, developed beliefs and traditions that affected many aspects of world history.

**Main Idea**
The religious ideas of the Hebrews developed into the religion known as Judaism.

## The Worship of One God

The Hebrews were related to other Mesopotamian peoples, but they developed a unique culture.

Although they were surrounded by cultures that worshiped many gods, Hebrews practiced **monotheism,** or the belief that there is only one God. They also followed a tradition of **ethical** behavior; that is, behavior based on ideas of right and wrong.

**132** Chapter 5 **The Ancient Hebrews and Judaism**

These practices and beliefs became known as Judaism, the religion of the Jewish people. Judaism is one of the world's oldest religions and one of the most influential.

 Checkpoint **How did beliefs of the Hebrews differ from those of other cultures?**

# A Wandering People

The early history of the Hebrews is a story of travels. These travels took place in the region between two centers of civilization—Egypt and Mesopotamia. Most of what we know about this history comes from ancient Hebrew writings such as those in the Torah (TOH ruh). The Torah includes the first five books of the Hebrew Bible. (These are also the first five books of the Christian Old Testament.) In addition, histories written in Egypt and Mesopotamia at about the same time give details about some events.

**The Patriarchs** The leaders of the Hebrews were Abraham, his son Isaac, and Isaac's son Jacob. These early leaders are known as patriarchs, or the forefathers of their people. The stories of these men were told for centuries long before they were written down in Genesis (JEH nuh sihs), the first book of the Torah. Abraham's grandson Jacob was later renamed Israel, from which his descendants would receive the name Israelites.

**Main Idea**
According to the Torah, the Israelites were descendants of one family that moved from Mesopotamia to Canaan.

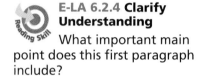 **E-LA 6.2.4 Clarify Understanding** What important main point does this first paragraph include?

**Abraham's Travels**
The Hebrew leader Abraham brought his family and servants far from their home in Mesopotamia. **Critical Thinking: Apply Information** *What details in this painting show that Abraham and his family were prepared for a long voyage through hot, dry lands?*

## Abraham's Journey

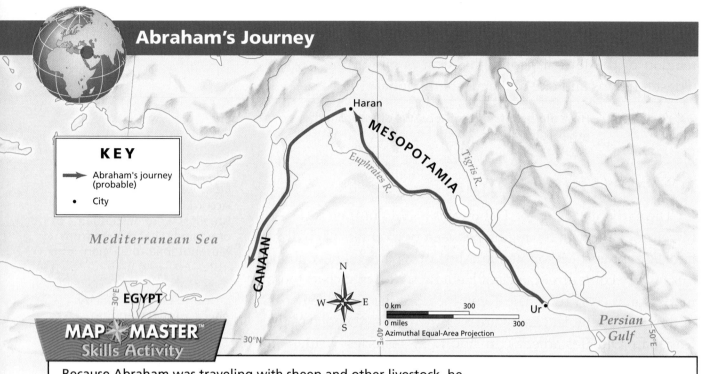

**KEY**

→ Abraham's journey (probable)

• City

*Mediterranean Sea*

EGYPT

MESOPOTAMIA

Haran

*Euphrates R.*

*Tigris R.*

CANAAN

Ur

*Persian Gulf*

0 km 300
0 miles 300
Azimuthal Equal-Area Projection

**MAP MASTER**
*Skills Activity*

Because Abraham was traveling with sheep and other livestock, he probably tried to stay close to rivers during his journey.

**(a) Identify** Which direction did Abraham first take from Ur? In which direction did he approach Canaan from Haran?

**(b) Draw Conclusions** Why do you suppose it would have been difficult for Abraham to travel in a straight line from Ur to Canaan?

**MapMaster ●nline**

**For:** Interactive map
**Visit:** PHSchool.com
**Web Code:** mwd-2051

**Abraham's Journey** The patriarch Abraham probably lived about 1800 B.C. He and his people were nomads who herded flocks of sheep, goats, and other livestock. Their home was Ur in Mesopotamia.

According to the Book of Genesis, Abraham's God told him to leave his home in Ur. Abraham eventually led his family and servants to a land called Canaan (KAY nuhn) on the eastern coast of the Mediterranean Sea. Genesis also says that God then made a **covenant, or binding agreement,** with Abraham. He promised that Abraham would be the father of many nations. The land of Canaan would belong to Abraham's descendants, so it became known as the Promised Land.

Abraham's family grew slowly at first, but Abraham's grandson Jacob had twelve sons, one daughter, and many servants and grandchildren. In time, each of Jacob's sons would become the ancestor of a large family called a tribe. However many years would pass before Abraham's descendants would rule Canaan.

 **Checkpoint** According to the Hebrew Bible, what land did God promise to Abraham?

# The Exodus

The last chapters of Genesis describe a famine that occurred in Canaan. Because Egypt had great storehouses of grain, Jacob's family moved there and continued to grow.

The Book of Exodus (EKS uh duhs) comes after Genesis in the Torah. According to Exodus, as Jacob's descendants became more numerous, Pharaoh, the ruler of Egypt, became mistrustful of them. Exodus describes how Pharaoh enslaved and mistreated the Israelites.

**Moses**  The Book of Exodus then describes the early life of Moses (MOH zuhz). He was an Israelite who grew up in Pharaoh's palace. As an adult, Moses came to believe that God was leading him to rescue his people from Pharaoh's control.

Moses asked Pharaoh for permission to lead the Hebrews out of Egypt, but Pharaoh refused. Exodus describes terrible hardships that came to Egypt, including sicknesses and swarms of insects. Still Pharaoh would not change his mind. The last and worst punishment for the Egyptians was the death of every firstborn son in Egypt. Moses told the Israelites to avoid this punishment by marking their doorways with the blood of a lamb. This event is now celebrated as the feast of Passover, because the punishment "passed over" Israelite homes and families.

Finally, Pharaoh demanded that the Israelites leave Egypt. Moses led the Israelites to the Sinai (SĪ nī) Peninsula, out of Pharaoh's reach. This liberation of Jacob's descendants from slavery in Egypt is called the Exodus.

**The Ten Commandments**  Exodus says that the Israelites stopped at the foot of Mount Sinai while Moses went up the mountain to meet with God. Moses returned with the laws known today as the Ten Commandments. A commandment is an order to do something. In addition, Moses received many other laws.

The commandments and other laws told the Israelites how to behave toward God and one another. These laws are still important to Jews and to many other people today.

**The Ten Commandments**
According to the Torah, Moses brought stone tablets containing the Ten Commandments down from Mount Sinai. **Critical Thinking: Compare**  *How do you think the Ten Commandments were different from Hammurabi's Code?*

## The Wilderness Experience

**The Wilderness Experience** The Exodus probably occurred about 1250 B.C. According to the Torah, after the descendants of Jacob left Egypt, they lived in the desert for forty years while God prepared the people for <u>migration</u> into the Promised Land. During this time, they learned more about God's commandments. They also prepared many items, such as altars, that they would use in worshiping their God.

Occasionally, the Israelites battled other peoples who considered the Israelites to be a threat. Gradually, the Israelites began to <u>approach</u> Canaan.

Finally, they began a war of conquest against several kingdoms near Canaan. Some of the Israelites liked areas that they had conquered that were just outside of Canaan, and they asked Moses whether they could settle there. Moses agreed that they could, as long as they helped other Israelites with their battles in the Promised Land first.

Moses himself, however, was not to enter the Promised Land. When Moses died, his assistant Joshua led the armies of Israel.

**Vocabulary** *Builder*
<u>migration</u> (mī GRAY shuhn) *n.* movement of a large group of people from one area to another

**Vocabulary** *Builder*
<u>approach</u> (uh PROHCH) *v.* to move closer to something

### Walled Cities

Many of the smaller kingdoms that the Israelites battled used walled cities for defense. Some of the defenses used in Canaan were still in use two thousand years later. **Critical Thinking: Draw Conclusions** *Why do you think walled cities were so useful for defense?*

**History** *Interactive*
**Learn more about ancient walled cities**

**Visit:** PHSchool.com
**Web Code:** mwp-2051

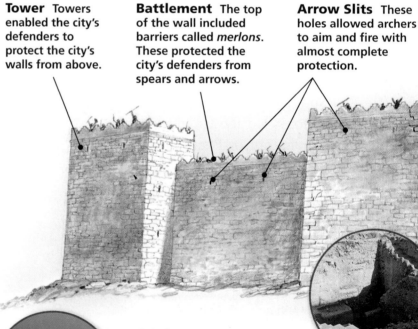

**Tower** Towers enabled the city's defenders to protect the city's walls from above.

**Battlement** The top of the wall included barriers called *merlons*. These protected the city's defenders from spears and arrows.

**Arrow Slits** These holes allowed archers to aim and fire with almost complete protection.

**Brick from Jericho** Dried mud bricks like this one are still used throughout much of the Middle East. They hold up well to most natural forces, but not earthquakes.

**Ruins of Jericho** This wall once towered over the surrounding countryside.

**The Conquest of Canaan**  According to the Book of Joshua in the Hebrew Bible, the Israelites entered Canaan from the east under Joshua's leadership. One of the first cities they conquered was the high-walled city of Jericho (JEHR ih koh). After the defeat of Jericho, the Israelites went on to conquer several small kingdoms. Then the descendants of each of Jacob's sons settled in a different part of Canaan. The descendants of Judah, Simeon, and Benjamin settled in the south, near the Dead Sea. The other tribes settled to the north and east. The initial settlements of the Israelites in Canaan are shown in the map on page 145.

 **Checkpoint** **According to the Torah, who led the Israelites out of Egypt?**

**Looking Back and Ahead**  You have read about the early history of the Hebrews under the patriarch Abraham and about how these people came to Egypt. You have also learned about how Moses led the Hebrews out of Egypt and taught them about the Ten Commandments. In the next section, you will learn how the beliefs of Judaism continued to develop from the laws and teachings of Moses.

# Section 1 Check Your Progress

**Progress Monitoring** Online
**For:** Self-test with instant help
**Visit:** PHSchool.com
**Web Code:** mwa-2051

**Standards Review** H-SS: 6.3.1, 6.3.4; E-LA: 6.2.4

**Comprehension and Critical Thinking**

1. **(a) Identify** Who were the patriarchs? After which patriarch are the Israelites named?
   **(b) Apply Information** Why are the journeys of the patriarchs important to the Jewish people?
2. **(a) Recall** To what event does the name of the book Exodus refer?
   **(b) Apply Information** Why is the Exodus significant in the history of Israel?

**Reading Skill**

3. **Clarify Understanding** Write an outline of Section 1. Then indicate the three main ideas.

**Vocabulary** *Builder*
Complete each of the following sentences in a way that shows that you understand the highlighted term.

4. The Israelites practiced monotheism because they believed _____.
5. According to the Torah, God made a covenant with Abraham that _____.
6. The ethical teachings of Judaism tell people what is _____.

**Writing**

7. Write two or three sentences in which you describe one important geographic region in the history of the Hebrews. The first sentence should be a strong topic sentence.

Section

# 2 The Beliefs of Judaism

## Standards Preview

**H-SS 6.3.2** Identify the sources of the ethical teachings and central beliefs of Judaism (the Hebrew Bible, the Commentaries): belief in God, observance of law, practice of the concepts of righteousness and justice, and importance of study; and describe how the ideas of the Hebrew traditions are reflected in the moral and ethical traditions of Western civilization.

**E-LA Reading 6.2.4** Clarify an understanding of texts by creating outlines, logical notes, summaries, or reports.

## Reading Preview

 **Reading Skill**

**Summarize Main Points** A section of text may have several main points. You can summarize these points to clarify your understanding. Remember that a summary includes the main points and a few important details. It is created in your own words and does not simply repeat the text. As you did with outlining, use headings and subheadings to focus on the main topics and ideas in the text. Then summarize the material.

### Vocabulary *Builder*

**High-Use Words**
**tradition** (truh DISH uhn), p. 139
**interpret** (ihn TUHR priht), p. 140

**Key Terms and People**
scriptures (SKRIHP chuhrs), p. 138
prophet (PRAH fuht), p. 139
rabbi (RABI), p. 140
justice (JUHS tihs), p. 142

---

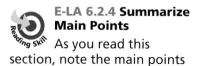 **E-LA 6.2.4 Summarize Main Points**
As you read this section, note the main points and create a brief summary.

**Main Idea**
From ancient times, the Israelites and their descendants have treasured their religious writings.

**Background Knowledge** You have read about the ancient Hebrews and their belief in one God. You have also read about how the Ten Commandments and the teachings of Moses became important as the Israelites journeyed to Canaan. In this section, you will learn more about these writings and others that are important to Judaism.

## Religious Writings

The written tradition is very important in Judaism. Jews greatly value scholarship and learning. In fact, they have been called "People of the Book." The Scriptures, or sacred writings, of the Jews are known as the Hebrew Bible. The Bible is more than stories of war and slavery and exile. For believers, it is the story of God's will as revealed through the prophets and carried out in human events. This shared story unites Jews all over the world in common belief.

**The Hebrew Bible** Many of the events in the Hebrew Bible are far older than the written text itself. Scholars believe that many sections were passed down by word of mouth for centuries before they were put into writing. By <u>tradition</u>, the books of the Hebrew Bible are divided into three sections.

As you have learned, the first five books of the Hebrew Bible are called the Torah. These books are also called the Law of Moses, because they contain not only the Ten Commandments but also many rules that explain the Ten Commandments in more detail. The Torah also tells the history of the Hebrews' covenants with God, up to the death of Moses.

The next section of the Hebrew Bible is called the Prophets. In Jewish tradition, a **prophet** is a person chosen by God to bring truth to a ruler and the people. The prophets were preachers, poets, and reformers. They reminded people to obey God's laws. In so doing, they told people how they should relate to God, to other people, to the land in which they lived, and even to themselves.

The last section of the Hebrew Bible is the Writings. This section includes great Hebrew literature such as the Psalms (sahlmz) and Proverbs. The Book of Psalms is a collection of songs praising God. Proverbs contains wise sayings. Many give advice to young people, such as this example:

> **❝A wise son brings joy to his father;
> A dull son is his mother's sorrow.❞**
>
> —Proverbs 10:1

**Vocabulary** *Builder*
<u>tradition</u> (truh DISH uhn) *n.* a belief or custom that is very old

**Primary** Sources

See Psalm 23 in the Reference Section at the back of this book.

**The Torah**
This Torah has been copied by hand. A reader would unroll the Torah from right to left, using the handles to avoid touching the scroll itself. A pointer called a *yad* is used to follow the line being read. **Critical Thinking: Draw Conclusions** *Why might readers of the Torah be so careful to avoid touching the scroll itself?*

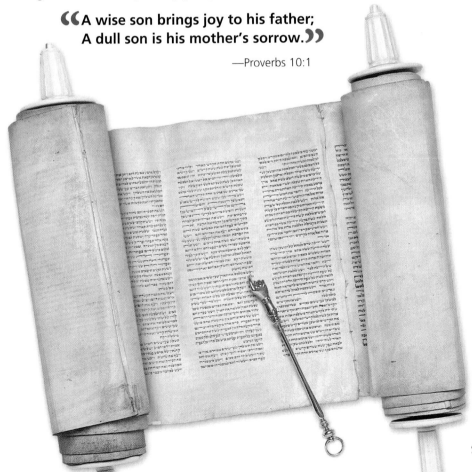

Specially made ink

Quill from a Kosher bird (one that, according to Jewish laws, may be eaten)

## A Scribe at Work

Many centuries ago, when all books were copied by hand, Jewish scribes adopted strict rules for copying the Torah. The rules included the kind of materials to use and instructions for avoiding mistakes. Because of this care, the wording of the Torah has remained essentially the same since ancient times. **Critical Thinking: Draw Inferences** *Why might Jews believe it is important to keep every copy of the Torah free from mistakes?*

**Vocabulary** *Builder*

**interpret** (ihn TUHR priht) *v.* to explain the meaning

Other Writings tell stories about heroes like Esther, Job (johb), and Daniel. All of the books of the Hebrew Bible are also in the Old Testament of the Christian Bible, but they are in a different order.

**Laws and the Talmud** Respect for God's laws is basic to Judaism. The great leader Moses is known as "Moses the Law-giver." The Torah contains many laws that explain and add to the Ten Commandments. Many of these laws give directions for religious rituals. Others describe how to wage war, how to have a fair society, and even how to protect the health of the community by cleanliness and sanitation.

Many centuries after the time of Moses, prominent Jewish teachers recorded oral laws that they believed had come down from the teachings of Moses. Other teachers, called rabbis, (RA bīz), discussed how laws should be interpreted in certain situations. Eventually, they wrote down their discussions about the laws. These writings are collected in the Talmud (TAHL mood), a text that Jewish scholars still study and discuss.

✔ **Checkpoint** Why do Israelites value their religious writing?

# Basic Beliefs

The Jews' idea of God was new in the ancient world. In other early religions, people worshiped many gods and thought that each god lived in a special place. These gods were usually represented by statues made of wood, stone, pottery, or brass. In contrast, the God of the Hebrews did not live in stones, rocks, or the sea. He did not take a human or an animal form. He was invisible, and yet he was everywhere.

The God of the Jews expected the people to follow his laws. He was strict, but he was also just, or fair. He punished the wicked but forgave people who showed that they were truly sorry for doing wrong.

**One God**   After the Exodus, the religion of Judaism became even more specific. According to the Bible, God gave humans a written code of laws, the Ten Commandments, at Mount Sinai. The Ten Commandments begin with one basic belief:

> **❝I the Lord am your God who brought you out of the land of Egypt, the house of bondage. . . .❞**
>
> —Exodus 20:2–3

The prophets declared that there was only one true God. They insisted that people honor God, behave in a moral way, and treat one another fairly. Some prophets predicted that the Israelites would be driven from their land in Canaan if they did not follow God's laws. However, they also predicted that any Israelites who were driven from their land would return one day if they were once again obedient to God's commands.

**A Covenant with the People**   According to the Torah, God's first covenant with the Hebrews was made with Abraham. The second, at Mount Sinai, was made with all of the Israelites. That led to another basic belief of Judaism—that the covenant had made Israel a nation. According to the Torah, God had a special relationship with the Israelites. In return, the Israelites believed that they had a responsibility to serve God, to treat one another fairly, and to protect the land that God had given them.

**Star of David**

As a symbol, this six-pointed star represented Judaism in many lands for many centuries.
**Critical Thinking: Draw Conclusions**
*Why might a symbol such as this star be important to a group of people who are spread out across many nations and continents?*

**A Charity Box**
Boxes like this one are used to collect spare change and other donations for giving to people with needs. **Critical Thinking: Draw Conclusions** *Why is helping people in need considered ethical behavior?*

**Ethical Behavior** Knowing the difference between right and wrong is an important part of Judaism. Jewish religious writings describe principles of behavior toward God, one's parents, and other people. The prophets also emphasized moral actions and behavior in society. For example, they reminded people that they needed to be honest and kind to each other. They criticized rulers who were cruel to the poor and weak. They urged people to work for justice, or fair treatment, for everyone. Jewish teachers also expected everyone to help those in need. Many of these ideas have influenced modern thinking about human rights and the need to be concerned for the welfare of others.

 **Checkpoint** **What beliefs of Judaism are shared with other religions today?**

**Looking Back and Ahead** In this section, you have read about the basic Scriptures of Judaism and how they have affected the practice of Judaism. In the next section, you will learn how the ancient nation of Israel was established and how the Israelites were eventually scattered to many parts of the world.

## Section 2 Check Your Progress

**Progress Monitoring Online**
**For:** Self-test with instant help
**Visit:** PHSchool.com
**Web Code:** mwa-2052

**Standards Review** H-SS: 6.3.2; E-LA: 6.2.3

**Comprehension and Critical Thinking**

1. **(a) Identify** What is the first main section of the Hebrew Bible?
   **(b) Evaluate Information** In what way do the writings of the Prophets expand on the laws recorded in the Torah?

2. **(a) Explain** What is ethical behavior?
   **(b) Identify Benefits** How does the idea of ethical behavior benefit the Jewish community?

**Reading Skill**

3. **Summarize Main Points** Use your own words to summarize the main points from this section. Be sure to include three main points and several important details.

**Vocabulary Builder**
Read each sentence below. If the sentence is true, write YES. If the sentence is not true, write NO and explain WHY.

4. A person who practices justice tries to treat everyone fairly.

5. Prophets are the sons of Jacob who migrated to Egypt.

6. Scriptures are people who are chosen by God to bring truth to the people.

**Writing**

7. Write two sentences in which you describe two important beliefs of Judaism. Put the most important belief in your second sentence. Add a transition that shows the relationship between these points.

Section

# 3 The Spread of Judaism

## Standards Preview

**H-SS 6.3.3** Explain the significance of Abraham, Moses, Naomi, Ruth, David, and Yohanan ben Zaccai in the development of the Jewish religion.

**H-SS 6.3.5** Discuss how Judaism survived and developed despite the continuing dispersion of much of the Jewish population from Jerusalem and the rest of Israel after the destruction of the second temple in A.D. 77.

**E-LA Reading 6.2.4** Clarify an understanding of texts by creating outlines, logical notes, summaries, or reports.

## Reading Preview

 **Reading Skill**

**Summarize Events** History is filled with significant events. To better understand and accurately remember these events, summarize them. Use the same strategy that you used to summarize main points. Look for and identify the important information along with a few key details. Then combine the information in your own words.

**Vocabulary** *Builder*

**High-Use Words**
<u>author</u> (AW thuhr), p. 144
<u>rebel</u> (rih BEHL), p. 145

**Key Terms and People**
judge (juhj), p. 143
exile (EHK sīl), p. 146
Diaspora (dī AS puh ruh), p. 147
synagogue (SIH nuh gahg), p. 147

**Background Knowledge** In Sections 1 and 2, you learned how the descendants of Jacob came to be known as the Israelites and how the Hebrew Scriptures and teachings affected Jewish thought and life. In this section, you will learn what happened to the Israelites after they settled in Canaan.

## Judges and Kings

After the death of Joshua, the Israelites had no centralized leadership. For about two centuries, they suffered from attacks by other peoples. Their enemies included the Philistines, a seafaring people who settled along the Mediterranean shore.

In times of distress, the Israelites often rallied around leaders called judges. A judge was usually a warrior or a prophet who could inspire an army of volunteers to defend their land.

Judges would often remain in leadership during times of peace, but they did not pass leadership to their descendants.

**Main Idea**
A kingdom eventually emerged in Israel. Unfortunately, it later split and was defeated by strong enemies.

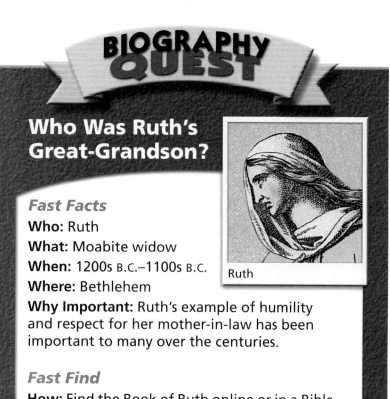

# BIOGRAPHY QUEST

## Who Was Ruth's Great-Grandson?

Ruth

### Fast Facts

**Who:** Ruth
**What:** Moabite widow
**When:** 1200s B.C.–1100s B.C.
**Where:** Bethlehem
**Why Important:** Ruth's example of humility and respect for her mother-in-law has been important to many over the centuries.

### Fast Find

**How:** Find the Book of Ruth online or in a Bible, and look in the last chapter.

**Biography Online**

**For:** More about Ruth
**Visit:** PHSchool.com
**Web Code:** mwe-2053

**Vocabulary** *Builder*

<u>author</u> (AW thuhr) *n.* person who creates a written work

**E-LA 6.2.4 Summarize Events**
Summarize the event that this section describes.

*Reading Skill*

At least two women became well-known during the time of the judges. One well-known judge was the prophet Deborah, who inspired an army to win a great battle. Another well-known woman is described in the Book of Ruth. Ruth married a man from Israel. When her husband died, Ruth followed her mother-in-law Naomi back to Israel. There she accepted Naomi's religion and became an important member of the tribe of Judah.

According to the Hebrew Bible, the time of the judges came to an end when the warrior Saul won a great victory. Saul became the first king of Israel.

**David and Solomon** One of King Saul's best fighters was David, a young shepherd and musician from the tribe of Judah. After Saul died in a war with the Philistines, David became the next king, about 1000 B.C.

David captured Jerusalem and made it his capital. He made the city the center for worship, and he donated land and goods for the religious leaders of Israel to use. He also extended the borders of his kingdom, making the Israelites safe from attack.

David is also well-known because he wrote many beautiful songs. He is thought to be the <u>author</u> of many psalms that are still used in synagogues and churches around the world.

During the rule of David's son Solomon, the kingdom prospered. Solomon built a great temple in Jerusalem. He also had a reputation for great wisdom. Solomon is considered the author of many of the wise sayings in Proverbs.

**A Divided People** After Solomon died, probably about 928 B.C., the kingdom split into two parts. The descendants of Solomon continued to rule the southern kingdom from Jerusalem. This area became known as the kingdom of Judah. From this name, the religion of the Israelites came to be known as Judaism, and the descendants of the Israelites came to be known as Jews.

A rival kingdom was set up in the north. Both kingdoms were caught in conflicts between Egypt and a new Mesopotamian empire, Assyria (uh SIR ee uh). About 722 B.C., the Assyrians conquered the northern kingdom. The Assyrians were brutal rulers who believed that they could keep conquered people from rebelling by resettling them in other parts of the empire. Thousands of Israelites were sent to distant parts of the empire, and other people were brought in to replace them. Many other Israelites avoided capture by fleeing south to Judah.

Over a century later, the city-state of Babylon, located in present-day Iraq, <u>rebelled</u> against Assyrian leaders and began the second Babylonian Empire. Babylon's greatest emperor, Nebuchadnezzar (nehb yuh kuhd NEHZ uhr) conquered Judah. According to the Bible, he brought some of the leaders and their families back to Babylon. A few years later, the Jewish leaders remaining in Jerusalem rebelled against Nebuchad-nezzar's rule. About 587 B.C., the emperor's armies returned and destroyed the city, as well as the temple that Solomon had built.

**Vocabulary** *Builder*
<u>rebel</u> (rih BEHL) *v.* to oppose someone in authority

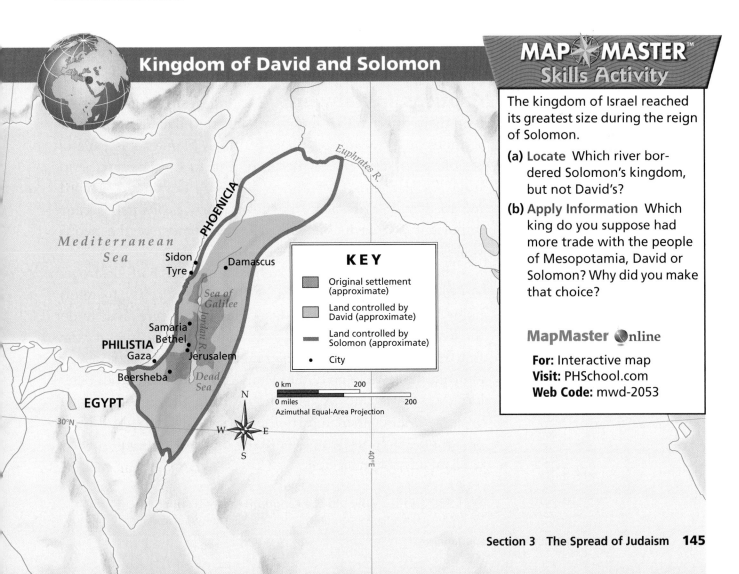

## Kingdom of David and Solomon

*Mediterranean Sea*

PHOENICIA

Sidon
Tyre
Damascus
Sea of Galilee
Jordan R.
Euphrates R.

Samaria
Bethel
PHILISTIA
Gaza
Jerusalem
Beersheba
Dead Sea

EGYPT

30°N
40°E

**KEY**

■ Original settlement (approximate)
■ Land controlled by David (approximate)
▬ Land controlled by Solomon (approximate)
• City

0 km 200
0 miles 200
Azimuthal Equal-Area Projection

N
W E
S

**MAP MASTER™**
*Skills Activity*

The kingdom of Israel reached its greatest size during the reign of Solomon.

**(a) Locate** Which river bordered Solomon's kingdom, but not David's?

**(b) Apply Information** Which king do you suppose had more trade with the people of Mesopotamia, David or Solomon? Why did you make that choice?

**MapMaster** Online

**For:** Interactive map
**Visit:** PHSchool.com
**Web Code:** mwd-2053

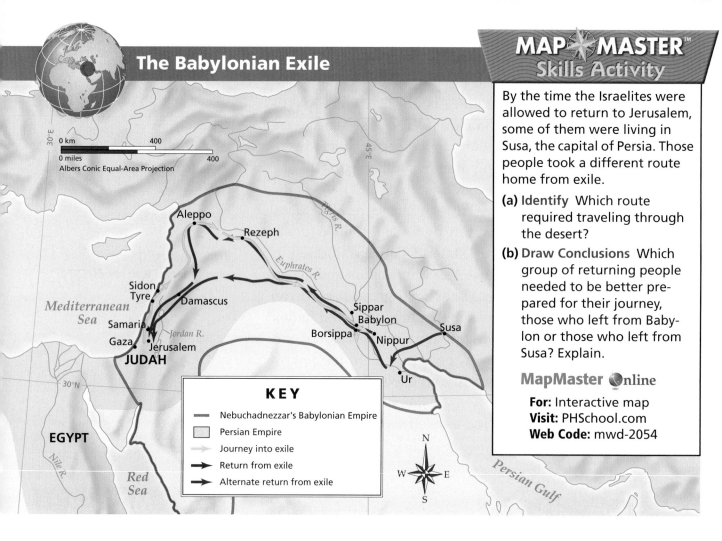

By the time the Israelites were allowed to return to Jerusalem, some of them were living in Susa, the capital of Persia. Those people took a different route home from exile.

**(a) Identify** Which route required traveling through the desert?

**(b) Draw Conclusions** Which group of returning people needed to be better prepared for their journey, those who left from Babylon or those who left from Susa? Explain.

**MapMaster ●nline**

**For:** Interactive map
**Visit:** PHSchool.com
**Web Code:** mwd-2054

**KEY**

— Nebuchadnezzar's Babylonian Empire
▢ Persian Empire
→ Journey into exile
→ Return from exile
→ Alternate return from exile

**Captives in Babylon** After the destruction of Jerusalem, many more of the Jews were taken to Babylon, hundreds of miles away. Many prophets of Judah blamed this exile on people who were not living according to the Hebrew Scriptures. Exile means separation from one's homeland. According to the Bible, some of the Jews, such as Daniel, became important people in Babylon. However, most of the people wished to return to their homeland.

About fifty years after Nebuchadnezzar had destroyed Jerusalem, many of the Jews had the opportunity to return home. The last and greatest Mesopotamian empire arose under the leadership of Cyrus the Great, king of Persia (present-day Iran). The Persian Empire tolerated other religions, so Cyrus allowed the Jews to go home. Many traveled home from Babylon. Another group traveled home from the Persian capital Susa. Soon after their return, the Jews began to build the second temple in Jerusalem. Eventually they began rebuilding the walls of Jerusalem as well.

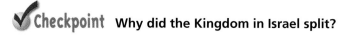

**Checkpoint** Why did the Kingdom in Israel split?

# The Diaspora

The Babylonian exile was a turning point in Jewish history. Communities of Jews were now living all over the Middle East. They lived in Egypt, Syria, Greece, and other trade centers. The communities of Jews living away from their ancient homeland came to be called the **Diaspora** (dī AS puh ruh), the Greek word meaning dispersion, or scattering. By the first century A.D., about 5 million Jews were living outside their homeland. Nonetheless, Jews everywhere still looked to Jerusalem as their spiritual home.

**A New Way to Worship** The Diaspora brought changes in the way Jews worshiped. Many Jews lived too far from Jerusalem to return for worship. However, their religious leaders urged them to follow the laws God had given them, no matter where they lived.

Some Jews had already been used to gathering in a **synagogue, or meeting place.** There they could pray, read, and discuss the Scriptures. Often, someone who knew the Scriptures well acted as the group's rabbi, or teacher. During periods of exile, the synagogues became even more important.

When most Jews had lived near the temple at Jerusalem, many had returned there for special festivals. Because of the Diaspora, however, Jewish leaders taught people to celebrate their festivals and practice their faith wherever they were.

**Main Idea**
Since ancient times, many Jews have remained faithful to their beliefs, even though they have lived far from Jerusalem.

**Passover Today**
The Seder meal is eaten by Jews throughout the world to commemorate the first Passover. **Critical Thinking: Link Past and Present** *Why are such festivals still important to Jews today?*

Bitter herbs–symbolize the bitterness of slavery

Lamb's shank– symbolizes the lamb sacrifice

Charred egg–symbolizes burnt sacrifices made in ancient times

Sweet vegetable–dipped in salt water to symbolize the tears of the slaves

Charoset (a nut and fruit paste)–symbolizes the mortar used by Jewish slaves

Bitter vegetable–symbolizes the bitterness of slavery

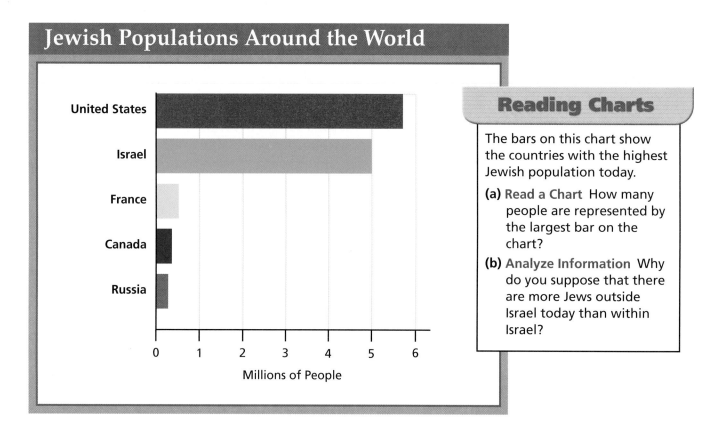

## Jewish Populations Around the World

United States
Israel
France
Canada
Russia

0 1 2 3 4 5 6
Millions of People

### Reading Charts

The bars on this chart show the countries with the highest Jewish population today.

(a) **Read a Chart** How many people are represented by the largest bar on the chart?

(b) **Analyze Information** Why do you suppose that there are more Jews outside Israel today than within Israel?

**More Dispersions** In the centuries after the Babylonian Exile ended, the Jews in Judah tried hard to live according to their religion in spite of harsh rulers in the Greek and Roman Empires. They also revolted against foreign rule several times. During the second century B.C., a family of rebels known as the Maccabees won Jerusalem the right to govern itself for a time.

In the first century B.C., Judah became part of the Roman Empire. Later, the Jews rebelled against Rome. As a result, in A.D. 70, the Romans attacked Jerusalem and destroyed the temple.

During the attack, a teacher named Yohanan ben Zakkai (yoh HAN uhn behn ZA kī) secretly visited the Roman general Vespasian (ves PAY zhehn). He received permission to set up a center for Jewish scholars in another town. The temple was gone, but learning survived and remained important to Jews.

Checkpoint  **Why did synagogues become more important to Jews in the Diaspora?**

**Main Idea**
Today, many faiths and cultures respect ideas that were first put forth in Judaism.

## The Legacy of Judaism

Today, nearly 13 million Jews live throughout the world. In addition to the Jewish state of Israel, many live in North America and parts of Europe. More than 5 million live in the United States.

Judaism today has several branches. The members of each branch interpret traditions in different ways.

Judaism gave the world the idea of one supreme, invisible God who had created everything. It became the first truly monotheistic religion. Both Christianity and Islam honor the writings of Moses in the Torah and share the Jewish belief in a single God. The ethical teachings of Judaism have also affected spiritual leaders in all parts of the world. So has the Jewish idea of service to the community.

The Bible is another legacy of Judaism. Its beautiful language makes it a classic of world literature, as do its dramatic stories of unforgettable characters such as Moses, Esther, and Solomon.

 **Checkpoint** What is one major legacy of Judaism?

**Looking Back and Ahead** You have learned how the Israelites returned to Canaan and formed a kingdom. You have also learned that Jewish people have settled in many parts of the world, and that the legacy of Judaism has influenced many aspects of modern civilization. In the next unit, you will learn about two more of the world's major religious traditions.

**The Ten Commandments**
This Christian version of the Ten Commandments includes Roman numerals and reads left to right. **Critical Thinking: Link Past and Present** *How does Christian use of the Ten Commandments show the influence of Judaism on other religions today?*

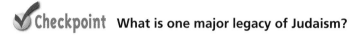

Section **3** **Check Your Progress**

**Progress Monitoring** ⏸nline
For: Self-test with instant help
Visit: PHSchool
Web Code: mwa-2053

**Standards Review** H-SS: 6.3.3, 6.3.5; E-LA: 6.2.4

**Comprehension and Critical Thinking**

1. (a) **Explain** Where did the Jews go after the Babylonian exile?
   (b) **Analyze Cause and Effect** How did the Babylonian exile affect the way Jews lived and worshiped?

2. (a) **Explain** What do Christianity and Islam have in common with Judaism?
   (b) **Link Past and Present** How do Jewish ideas about ethical behavior and community service influence people today?

**Reading Skill**

3. **Summarize Events** Summarize the events discussed in this section. Describe the events, and explain their importance.

**Vocabulary** *Builder*

4. Write two definitions for each word: judge, exile. First, write a formal definition for your teacher. Second, write a definition in everyday English for a classmate.

**Writing**

5. Write two sentences in which you describe two ways that the term Diaspora may be used in describing the history of the Jewish people. Put the most important way in your second sentence. Add a transition that shows the relationship between these points.

# Daniel and the Lion's Den
from The Book of Daniel

## Prepare to Read

### Standards Preview

**H-SS 6.3.2** Identify the sources of the ethical teachings and central beliefs of Judaism (the Hebrew Bible, the Commentaries): belief in God, observance of law, practice of the concepts of righteousness and justice, and importance of study; and describe how the ideas of the Hebrew traditions are reflected in the moral and ethical traditions of Western civilization.

**E-LA 3.2** Analyze the effect of the qualities of the character (e.g., courage or cowardice, ambition or laziness) on the plot and the resolution of the conflict.

### Reading Skill

**Analyze Character** Characters in stories, like people in real life, have many different qualities. They can be strong or weak. They can be kind or mean. They can be lazy or hard-working. In literature, what a character is like often affects what happens in the story. This is especially true in Bible stories. As you read, pay attention to how the characters' qualities affect what happens to them.

### Vocabulary *Builder*

As you read this literature selection, look for the following underlined words:

**province** (PRAWV ihns) *n.* a large division of a country

**criticize** (KRIH tuh sīz) *v.* to find fault

---

### BACKGROUND

The Book of Daniel, from the Hebrew Bible, tells the story of a young Jewish man who was taken to Babylon as a prisoner. He became an important official who served several rulers in Babylon and Persia.

Darius the Mede decided to divide the kingdom into 120 provinces, and he appointed a prince to rule over each <u>province</u>. The king also chose Daniel and two others as administrators to supervise the princes.

Daniel soon proved himself more capable than all of the other administrators and princes. Because of his great ability, the king made plans to place him over the entire empire. Then the other administrators and princes began searching for some fault in the way Daniel was handling his affairs, but they couldn't find anything to <u>criticize</u>. He was faithful and honest and always responsible. So they concluded, "Our only chance of finding grounds for accusing Daniel will be in connection with . . . his religion."

So the administrators and princes went to the king and said, ". . . Your Majesty should make a law that will be strictly enforced. Give orders that for the next thirty days anyone who prays to anyone, divine or human—except to Your Majesty—will be thrown to the lions. And let Your Majesty issue and sign this law so it cannot be changed. . . ." So King Darius signed the law.

But when Daniel learned that the law had been signed, he went home and knelt down as usual in his upstairs room, with its windows open toward Jerusalem. He prayed three times a day, just as he had always done, giving thanks to his God. The officials went together to Daniel's house and found him praying and asking for God's help. . . .

Then they told the king, "That man Daniel . . . still prays to his God three times a day."

Hearing this, the king was very angry with himself for signing the law. . . . He spent the rest of the day looking for a way to get Daniel out of this predicament. In the evening the men went together to the king and said, "Your Majesty knows that according to the law of the Medes and the Persians, no law that the king signs can be changed."

So at last the king gave orders for Daniel to be arrested and thrown into the den of lions. The king said to him, "May your God . . . rescue you." . . . Then the king returned to his palace and spent the night fasting. He . . . couldn't sleep at all that night.

Very early the next morning, the king hurried out to the lions' den. When he got there, he called out in anguish, "Daniel, . . . Was your God . . . able to rescue you from the lions?"

Daniel answered, ". . . My God sent his angel to shut the lions' mouths so that they would not hurt me, for I have been found innocent in his sight. . . ."

The king was overjoyed and ordered that Daniel be lifted from the den. . . . Then the king gave orders to arrest the men who had maliciously accused Daniel. He had them thrown into the lions' den. . . . The lions leaped on them and tore them apart before they even hit the floor of the den.

Then King Darius sent this message to the people of every race and nation and language throughout the world: . . . "I decree that everyone throughout my kingdom should tremble with fear before the God of Daniel. . . ."

So Daniel prospered during the reign of Darius and the reign of Cyrus the Persian.

—From *The New Living Translation.*
Tyndale House Publishers, 1976.

**Daniel in the lion's den**

**E-LA 3.2  Analyze Character**
Early in this selection, we learn that Daniel is very responsible. Why does that displease his enemies at the same time that it pleases his ruler?

If you liked this story about Daniel, you may want to read other stories about people in the Hebrew Bible in *Children's Bible Stories: From Genesis to Daniel,* by Miriam Chaikin.
*(Dial Books, © 1993)*

## Analyze LITERATURE

The story of Daniel illustrates the Jewish belief that it is important to do what is right before both people and God. Do you think that doing right was important to Daniel's enemies? Write a paragraph describing how Daniel's enemies were similar to and different from Daniel.

# Analysis Skills
# Locate Information in a Library Media Center

Social studies books are good starting points for learning about a topic. However, when you want to know more about a subject, you need other sources. This lesson will help you use your library media center to locate books about topics you choose.

**Chapter Standards**

**History-Social Science**

E-LA 6.1.4 Use organizational features of electronic text (e.g., bulletin boards, databases, keyword searches, e-mail addresses) to locate information.

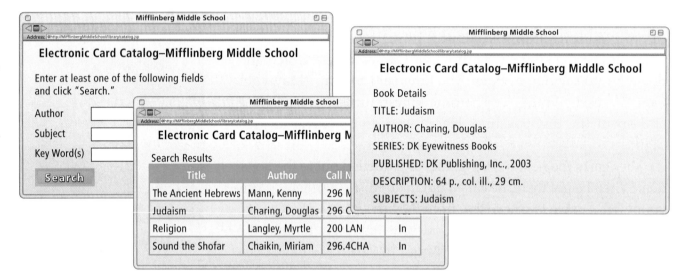

**Learn the Skill** *Follow these steps to learn how to locate information in a library.*

1. **Identify the topic you want to research.** Think of a keyword that describes the topic. For example, you could start your search by using the keyword *Judaism.*

2. **Use the library catalog to identify several sources.** The second screen shows what happens after you enter the keyword *Judaism* into a library's online catalog.

3. **Use the list to identify the books you want to look at.** The third computer screen shows information about the book *Judaism,* including information to help you locate the book.

4. **Locate the book and decide whether it is a good information source.** Look at the table of contents and the index to see if the book contains the information you need.

**Practice the Skill** *Find information in a library.*

1. **Identify the topic you want to research.** For example, to learn more about Jewish religious festivals, you may enter the word *festival,* the word *Jewish,* or both.

2. **Use the library catalog to identify several sources.** Enter the keyword you have chosen into your library's computerized catalog.

3. **Use the list to identify the books you want to look at.** Select a book that seems likely to have the information you need.

4. **Locate the book and decide whether it is a good information source.** Examine the table of contents and index.

**Apply the Skill**
*See page 155 of the Review and Assessment.*

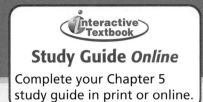

**i**nteractive Textbook

**Study Guide** *Online*
Complete your Chapter 5 study guide in print or online.

## Chapter Summary  H-SS: 6.3.1, 6.3.2, 6.3.3, 6.3.4, 6.3.5

### Section 1 The Origins of Judaism

- According to the Torah, ancient Hebrews left Mesopotamia for Canaan under the leadership of the patriarchs.
- Centuries after the Israelites entered Egypt, Moses led them out of slavery.
- The Israelites received many commandments in the wilderness.
- Then the Israelites began the conquest of Canaan.

### Section 2 The Beliefs of Judaism

- The commandments that were received at the time of Moses make up the first part of the Hebrew Bible.
- Other religious writings and traditions continue to guide Jews today.

### Section 3 The Spread of Judaism

- After reaching Canaan, the Israelites were led first by judges, and then by kings.
- After the kingdom weakened, many people were taken captive into other lands. This was the beginning of the Diaspora.
- Many Jews were able to return to Jerusalem from Babylon and Persia. However, many centuries later, Roman officials again drove many Jews away from Jerusalem.
- Today Jews live all over the world. Judaism has affected many religions and cultures.

**Star of David**

## Standards Practice  H-SS: 6.3.1, 6.3.2, 6.3.3, 6.3.4, 6.3.5

## Vocabulary *Builder*

### High-Use Words

Read each sentence below. If the sentence is true, write YES. If the sentence is not true, write NO and explain WHY.

1. The history of Judaism includes the history of a **migration** from Egypt.

2. King David is considered an **author** of part of the Hebrew Bible.

3. Some rabbis have **interpreted** the teachings of Moses.

4. Leaders in Jerusalem **rebelled** against Egyptian authority.

### Key Terms

Complete each of the following sentences so that the second part further explains the first part and clearly shows your understanding of the highlighted word.

1. The **ethical** teachings of Judaism explain how to _____.

2. The **monotheism** of the people of ancient Israel set them apart from their Canaanite and Philistine neighbors because _____.

3. The **Scriptures** of the Jewish people include _____.

4. The **Diaspora** of the Jewish people continues today because _____.

## Apply Reading Skills

**Clarify Understanding** Review the main ideas and events of Chapter 5. Then create a concept web to show these ideas and how they connect to one another. Fill the bubble for each with a very short summary of its main ideas.

## Comprehension and Critical Thinking

**1. (a) Identify** Who led the Hebrews out of Egypt in the Exodus?
**(b) Recall** What persuaded the Pharaoh to let them go?
**(c) Draw Conclusions** Why might the Exodus be an important symbol for non-Jews as well as for Jews?

**2. (a) List** What are the three main sections of the Hebrew Bible?
**(b) Recall** Which section includes the Exodus and the Ten Commandments?
**(c) Apply Information** Which section, the Writings or the Prophets, provides more history and stories about heroes? Explain your answer.
**(d) Draw Conclusions** Which section, the Writing or the Prophets, is likely to contain more ethical teachings? Explain your answer.

**3. (a) Recall** What is the Talmud?
**(b) Understand Sequence** Was the Talmud written before or after the Torah?
**(c) Draw Inferences** Why are the contents of the Talmud important to Jews who wish to keep the commandments in the Torah?

## Researching

**The Importance of Learning** For thousands of years, learning has been important to Jews. Initially, many Jews learned to read so that they could study the Scriptures. However, learning about other subjects is also important. Use an encyclopedia and library resources to learn more about important Jewish scholars and thinkers. Choose a task below to work on. Share your work with the class by creating a bulletin board about Jewish thinker's.

**Artists:** Create a portrait of an ancient Jewish thinker. On an attached page, list where and when the person was born and where he or she lived. Then list the person's contributions.

**Scientists:** Create a list of important contributions made by Jewish scientists.

> **Researching Online**
> **For:** Help in starting this activity
> **Visit:** PHSchool.com
> **Web Code:** mwe-2053

## Writing

**1. Write a paragraph on the following topic.** The Hebrews of ancient times were distinguished more by what they believed than by where they lived. Discuss two factors in Jewish history that explain why Judaism has outlasted most other religions of ancient times.
**Your essay should:**
• have a thesis statement that identifies both factors.
• describe the least important factor first and the most important factor last.
• use transitions that show the relationship between your points.

**2. Write a short narrative.** Imagine you were with the Israelites when Moses led them from Egypt. Write a short narrative describing what you did on Passover night and how you felt when you left Egypt.

**H-SS:** 6.3, 6.3.1, 6.3.2, 6.3.3, 6.3.4, 6.3.5; **E-LA:** 6.1.4

**Progress Monitoring** ●nline
**For:** Self-test with instant help.
**Visit:** PHSchool.com
**Web Code:** mwa-2054

# Apply Analysis Skills

Use your school library to find a good book about a topic of your choice. The topic should relate in some way to the information in Chapter 5. Follow these steps, and answer the questions.

1. What topic do you want to find out about?

2. What keyword should you use to start your search?

3. List the names and authors of three books that you found in the library catalog.

4. Name the book you chose.

5. Decide whether the book is a good source. Explain your decision.

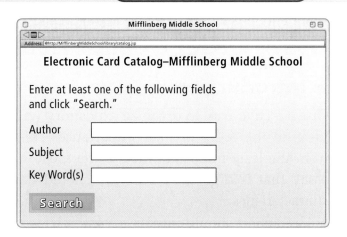

# Test Yourself

1. The first people to have a religion with a belief in only one god were the

   A Hebrews.

   B Philistines.

   C Sumerians.

   D Canaanites.

Refer to the image below to answer Question 2.

2. Which of the following statements about the Torah is/are correct?

   A It is still copied by hand.

   B It is written left to right.

   C It is written in Greek.

   D A and B

3. The first king of Israel was

   A Moses.

   B Saul.

   C Jacob.

   D David.

Refer to the reading below to answer Question 4.

4. What does this quote about the Babylonian exile signify?

   *"By the waters of Babylon, there we sat down and wept. . . . If I forget you, O Jerusalem, let my right hand wither! Let my tongue cleave [stick] to the roof of my mouth, if I do not remember you, if I do not set Jerusalem above my highest joy!"*

   A The Israelites have escaped from Egypt.

   B The second temple has been destroyed.

   C The Jews in Diaspora wish to return.

   D Cyrus has become emperor of Persia.

5. Which of the writings of the Jewish people repeat and explain the ethical teachings of the Torah?

   A The Talmud

   B The Prophets

   C The Writings

   D The Ten Commandments

# Writing Workshop

## History-Social Science

**6.2** Students analyze the geographic, political, economic, religious, and social structures of the early civilizations of Mesopotamia, Egypt, and Kush.

## English-Language Arts

**Writing 6.2.2** Write expository compositions (e.g., description, explanation, comparison and contrast, problem and solution).

## Expository Composition
## Using Order of Importance

### ▶ Introduction

One effective way to organize expository writing is to present ideas in the order of their importance. This means building from the least important idea to the most important one. An essay that is organized this way should have the following characteristics:

- The subject should involve several related items.

- The thesis statement should identify the items and explain how they are related.

- Each item should be described clearly.

- The relative importance of each item should also be clear.

- The most important item should be discussed last.

**Assignment** On the following pages, you will learn how to organize an expository essay by using order of importance. Each step will include an example from a sample essay that discusses the results of the development of writing.

First, read the instructions and the examples. Then, follow each step to plan and write a 500–700 word essay on this topic:

**Discuss the effect of writing on world civilizations.**

> For a review of the steps in the writing process, see the **Historian's Toolkit,** *Write Like a Historian.*

### ▶ Prewriting

**Clarify the assignment.** You can use order of importance to organize almost any essay that discusses several related items. Make sure that you understand what items you need to discuss and how they are related.

**Gather information.** Think about the details that you are going to write about. How are they connected? Which one is most important?

**Create a working thesis.** Write a sentence that sums up the items you are discussing. This "working thesis" may change as you organize your paper, but it should guide your thinking.

> **Sample Assignment:** Discuss the effect of writing on world civilizations. Note that this assignment asks about the way that writing affected the world, not the kinds of letters that people used.

> How has writing affected world civilizations?

> **Sample working thesis:** The development of writing has had great consequences for the world.

## ▶ Drafting

**Organize by order of importance.** An essay organized by order of importance begins by discussing the least important of the items and then builds to the most important item. The details for each item may also be discussed in order of importance.

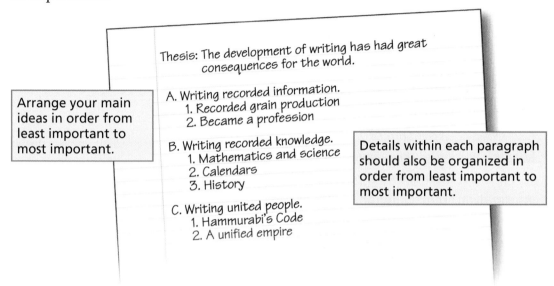

Arrange your main ideas in order from least important to most important.

Thesis: The development of writing has had great consequences for the world.

A. Writing recorded information.
   1. Recorded grain production
   2. Became a profession

B. Writing recorded knowledge.
   1. Mathematics and science
   2. Calendars
   3. History

C. Writing united people.
   1. Hammurabi's Code
   2. A unified empire

Details within each paragraph should also be organized in order from least important to most important.

**State your thesis.** Write an introductory paragraph that catches your audience's attention. Then, explain which items you are discussing, why you are discussing them, and which item is most important.

**Support your thesis with examples and details.** Now, write the body of your essay, providing enough facts, examples, reasons, and other information to discuss each item fully. As you are discussing each item, lead up to and end with the most important detail about each. When you are moving from one item to the next, build from the least important item to the most important item. Keep the relationships between your ideas clear with transitions such as *less, least, more,* and *most.*

**Write a strong conclusion.** In your final paragraph, give an overview of the items, indicate which is the most significant, and tell why.

# Writing Workshop *continued*

## ▶ Student Model

Read the following model of an essay that is organized by order of importance. Notice how it includes the characteristics you have learned.

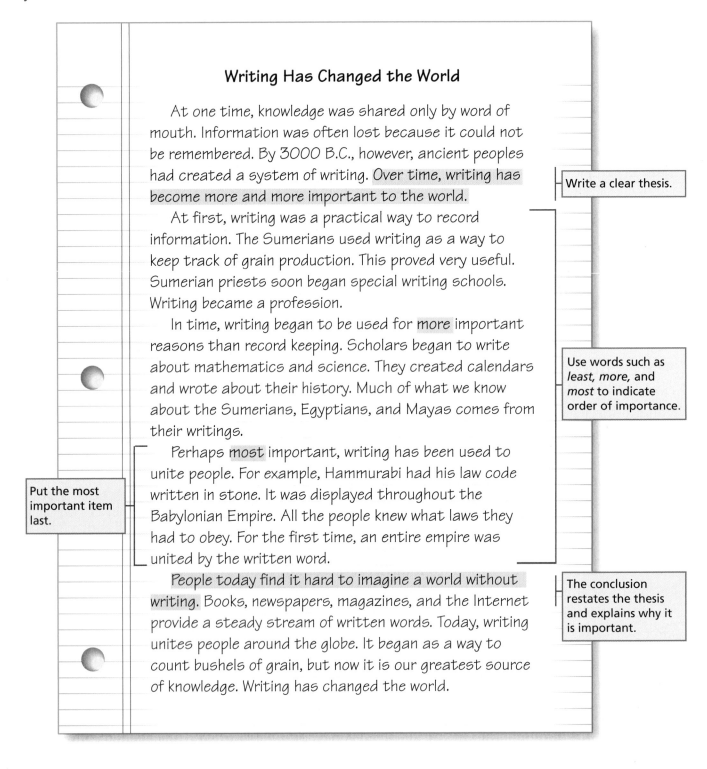

### Writing Has Changed the World

At one time, knowledge was shared only by word of mouth. Information was often lost because it could not be remembered. By 3000 B.C., however, ancient peoples had created a system of writing. Over time, writing has become more and more important to the world.

At first, writing was a practical way to record information. The Sumerians used writing as a way to keep track of grain production. This proved very useful. Sumerian priests soon began special writing schools. Writing became a profession.

In time, writing began to be used for more important reasons than record keeping. Scholars began to write about mathematics and science. They created calendars and wrote about their history. Much of what we know about the Sumerians, Egyptians, and Mayas comes from their writings.

Perhaps most important, writing has been used to unite people. For example, Hammurabi had his law code written in stone. It was displayed throughout the Babylonian Empire. All the people knew what laws they had to obey. For the first time, an entire empire was united by the written word.

People today find it hard to imagine a world without writing. Books, newspapers, magazines, and the Internet provide a steady stream of written words. Today, writing unites people around the globe. It began as a way to count bushels of grain, but now it is our greatest source of knowledge. Writing has changed the world.

Write a clear thesis.

Use words such as *least, more,* and *most* to indicate order of importance.

Put the most important item last.

The conclusion restates the thesis and explains why it is important.

## ▶ Revising

After completing your draft, read it again carefully to find ways to make your writing better. Here are some questions to ask yourself:

### Revise to increase interest
- Does the first paragraph capture the reader's attention?
- Can you describe the items in more vivid detail?
- Did you include any information that was less relevant than the other details?

### Revise to clarify the analysis
- As each item is discussed, are the least important items first? Are the most important items last?
- Did you leave out any information that would explain why you have put the items in this order?
- Are the relationships between the items clear? Can you add any transitions to make them clearer?

### Revise to meet Standard English conventions
- Are all sentences complete, with a subject and a verb?
- Are all words spelled correctly?
- Are all proper nouns capitalized?
- Did you use proper punctuation?

In time, writing *began* to be used for more important *a* resons than record keeping. Much of what we know about the ancient Sumerians and *E*gyptians comes from their writing.

## ▶ Rubric for Self-Assessment

*Use this rating scale to evaluate your expository essay.*

|  | Score 4 | Score 3 | Score 2 | Score 1 |
|---|---|---|---|---|
| **Organization** | Uses order of importance correctly and makes the relationships between the items and their relative importance clear | Uses order of importance and makes most of the reasons for their relative importance clear | Chooses an organization not suited to the topic | Shows lack of organizational strategy |
| **Presentation** | Develops ideas with relevant facts, details, or examples; links all information to the issue being analyzed | Develops most ideas with facts, details, or examples; links most information to the issue being analyzed | Does not develop most ideas in depth; some information is not linked to the issue being analyzed | Does not provide facts, details, or examples to support ideas |
| **Use of Language** | Varies sentence structure and vocabulary successfully; has no or very few mechanical errors | Uses some variety in sentence structure and vocabulary; has few mechanical errors | Uses the same types of sentences without varying them; does not vary vocabulary; has many mechanical errors | Writes incomplete sentences; uses language poorly; sounds confused; has many mechanical errors |

# Unit  3

 **Quick View** Video

**Discovery School Video** View *Ancient India* for a quick preview of the main ideas of this unit.

A Hindu temple in India

# Ancient India

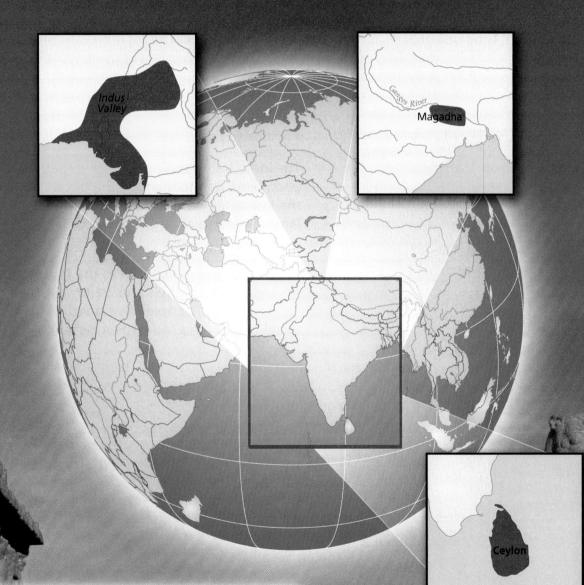

Indus Valley

Ganges River

Magadha

Ceylon

## *Think* like a historian

The map above shows the part of the world in which the civilization of ancient India developed. Several major religions also began in this area.

**As you read this unit, think about this question:**
*How do civilizations rise and fall?*

### Chapter 6

# The Early Civilizations of India (2500 B.C.–700 B.C.)

## Prepare to Read

### Chapter Standards

#### History-Social Science
6.5 Students analyze the geographic, political, economic, religious, and social structures of the early civilizations of India.

**Section 1,** pp. 166–169

✔ **What You Will Learn**

**The Geography of South Asia** | The landforms, river systems, and climate of the Indian subcontinent affected the growth of civilization in the area.

**Section 2,** pp. 170–175

**The Indus Valley Civilization** | The Indus Valley civilization developed as people learned to manage the floods of the Indus River. The civilization included large cities and an organized economy.

**Section 3,** pp. 178–183

**India's Vedic Age** | A group of people known as the Indo-Aryans arrived in the Indus Valley about 1500 B.C. These people developed a social structure called a caste system.

Indus Valley stone cubes

**2500 B.C.**
Mohenjo-Daro is a large city with 40,000 residents.

**1750 B.C.**
The Indus Valley people begin to abandon their cities.

**Chapter Events**

3250 B.C.

2500 B.C.

1750 B.C.

**Other Events**

**2540 B.C.** Construction of the Great Pyramid of Khufu takes place in Egypt.

**1800 B.C.** Early Shang culture begins in China's Huang He valley.

The Himalayas rise along the banks of the Indus River in present-day Pakistan.

**1500 B.C.**
Indo-Aryans begin to appear in the Indus Valley.

**700 B.C.**
Northern India is home to 16 Aryan kingdoms.

**1750**
**B.C.**

**1000**
**B.C.**

**250**
**B.C.**

**1500 B.C.** Conflict occurs among Hittites, Mitanni, and Egyptians in Mesopotamia.

**750 B.C.** Evidence suggests the Greek alphabet was first used.

The Early Civilizations of India **163**

# How to Read History

## History Reading Skill

*Previewing* **Explain Related Words**

When you read, you will encounter words with related, or similar, meanings. These words have "shades of meaning," just as a particular color may have many shades. Identifying related words will help you understand more fully the meaning of the text. Explaining shades of meaning further improves the accuracy of your understanding. Look at the examples below to learn more about words with related meanings.

**Chapter Standards**

**English-Language Arts**

**Reading 6.1.5** Understand and explain "shades of meaning" in related words.

---

**❶** Here, the two underlined words are synonyms, or words with very similar meanings. How are the word meanings different?

The river watered the <u>lush</u> landscape of the valley.
The <u>fertile</u> soil of the river valley drew many settlers.

> <u>Lush</u> might describe something rich and strong, while <u>fertile</u> might describe more specifically something's ability to produce.

---

**❷** Some related words have a difference of intensity, or degree. Here, one word has a stronger meaning than the other.

Questions like these inspired <u>debates</u> and <u>discussions</u> on the meaning of the laws.

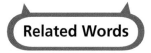

Related Words

Explain the shades of meaning you find as you read. Here is a sample explanation of the sentence above.

*Debates* are more like arguments than *discussions*, although both involve talking about issues.

# Vocabulary *Builder*

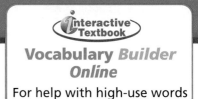

*interactive* Textbook
**Vocabulary** *Builder*
*Online*
For help with high-use words

## *Previewing* **High-Use Academic Words**

| High-Use Word | Definition | Sample Sentence About History |
|---|---|---|
| **consist** (kuhn SIHST) (Section 1, p. 167) | *v.* to be formed or made up of | The Nile River system consists of the Nile River and its various branches. |
| **fertile** (FERT uhl) (Section 1, p. 168) | *adj.* producing vegetation or crops abundantly | The region's fertile land made it a center of agriculture. |
| **rely** (rih LI) (Section 2, p. 171) | *v.* to depend on | The people came to rely on the area's rich natural resources for survival. |
| **collapse** (kuh LAPS) (Section 2, p. 174) | *n.* act of breaking down, failing, or giving way | Natural disasters and economic troubles led to the collapse of the civilization. |
| **similar** (SIHM uh luhr) (Section 3, p. 178) | *adj.* almost the same | The two groups spoke very similar languages. |
| **shift** (shihft) (Section 3, p. 180) | *v.* to replace by another or others; change or exchange | As the climate changed, the group had to shift its way of planting crops. |

## *Previewing* **Key Terms and People**

**Granary**

subcontinent, p. 166
natural barrier, p. 167
river system, p. 167
monsoon, p. 168
central planning, p. 172

granary, p. 172
import, p. 172
export, p. 172

caste, p. 181
caste system, p. 181
untouchable, p. 182

**Monsoon floods**

## Standards Preview

**H-SS 6.5.1** Locate and describe the major river system and discuss the physical setting that supported the rise of this civilization.

**E-LA Reading 6.1.5** Understand and explain "shades of meaning" in related words.

## Reading Preview

### Reading Skill

**Understand Shades of Meaning** Word meanings can have shades of intensity. For example, consider the words *old* and *ancient.* Both words describe times in the past, but *ancient* implies a time farther in the past than *old.* Relate the meanings of unfamiliar descriptive words to those of more familiar words, and find the shades of meaning between them.

### Vocabulary *Builder*

**High-Use Words**
consist (kuhn SIHST), p. 167
fertile (FERT uhl), p. 168

**Key Terms**
subcontinent (suhb KAHNT n uhnt), p. 166
natural barrier (NACH er uhl BEHR ee er), p. 167
river system (RIHV er SIHS tuhm), p. 167
monsoon (mahn SOON), p. 168

**Background Knowledge** Asia is a vast continent, covering about one third of the world's land area. Geographers have divided this enormous landmass into regions. The region located nearest the Mediterranean Sea is known as Southwest Asia. The ancient lands of Mesopotamia and Canaan were located in Southwest Asia. To the east of Mesopotamia lay South Asia. On a modern map, South Asia looks like a huge triangle jutting into the Indian Ocean. In this chapter, you will read about the land and climate of South Asia and how its physical setting affected life in the region.

**Main Idea**
South Asian civilization first arose in the Indus River valley. This region featured many natural barriers.

## The Indian Subcontinent

South Asia is also known as the Indian subcontinent. A subcontinent is a large landmass that is smaller than a continent. The Indian subcontinent stretches almost 2,000 miles from north to south. In some places, it is nearly as wide from east to west. Today this region is made up of India, Pakistan, Bangladesh, Sri Lanka, Nepal, Maldives, and Bhutan.

## Natural Barriers

The geography of South Asia had a strong impact on its civilization. For thousands of years, natural barriers limited contact between inhabitants of the region and other peoples. **Natural barriers are geographic features that make travel and communication difficult or dangerous.**

Mountain ranges form a natural barrier on the northern edge of the subcontinent. To the northeast stand the mighty Himalayas. Snow and ice cover many of these peaks year-round. In fact, the name *Himalaya* comes from an Indian word meaning "house of snow." A second range, the Hindu Kush, rises to the northwest. A few high mountain passes cut through this range. In ancient times, these rugged passes offered the best routes to South Asia from the north.

The rest of the subcontinent is mostly surrounded by ocean. To the west, the Arabian Sea separates South Asia from West Asia. The Indian Ocean lies to the south and the Bay of Bengal to the east.

## Major River Systems

As it had in Egypt, civilization in South Asia first arose in a river valley. The subcontinent has several large river systems. **A river system consists of a main river and all of its branches.** The Indus and Ganges river systems have played a major role in South Asian history. Both rivers flow from the Himalayas and drain large areas of the subcontinent.

**E-LA 6.1.5 Understand Shades of Meaning**
Reading Skill How does the meaning of the word *rugged* relate to that of the word *rough*?

**Vocabulary Builder**
**consist** (kuhn SIHST) *v.* to be formed or made up of

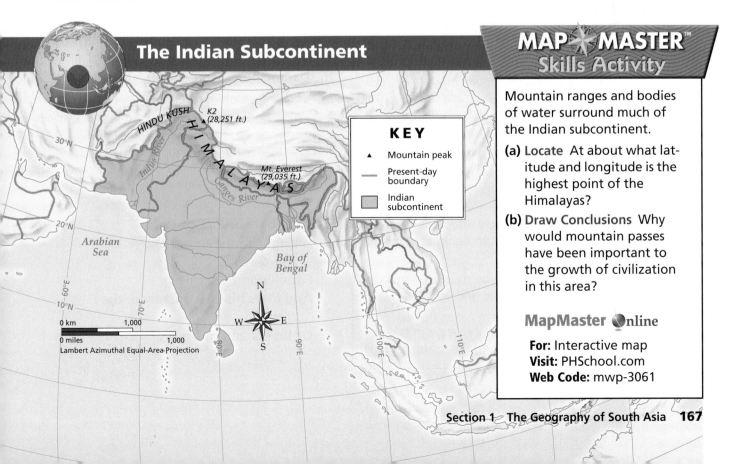

**The Indian Subcontinent**

**KEY**
▲ Mountain peak
— Present-day boundary
Indian subcontinent

HINDU KUSH
K2 (28,251 ft.)
HIMALAYAS
Mt. Everest (29,035 ft.)
Indus River
Ganges River
30°N
20°N
10°N
Arabian Sea
Bay of Bengal
60°E
70°E
80°E
90°E
100°E
110°E

0 km 1,000
0 miles 1,000
Lambert Azimuthal Equal-Area Projection

N W E S

## MAP MASTER™
### Skills Activity

Mountain ranges and bodies of water surround much of the Indian subcontinent.

**(a) Locate** At about what latitude and longitude is the highest point of the Himalayas?

**(b) Draw Conclusions** Why would mountain passes have been important to the growth of civilization in this area?

**MapMaster Online**

**For:** Interactive map
**Visit:** PHSchool.com
**Web Code:** mwp-3061

The Indus River flows down the western side of the sub-continent into the Arabian Sea. Near the end of its route, the Indus passes through a hot desert land. Civilization in South Asia first arose at this location. Today this region is part of the country of Pakistan.

The Ganges River flows across the northern edge of the subcontinent into the Bay of Bengal. Along the way it crosses a huge, <u>fertile</u> plain that also became a center of civilization in ancient times. Today the Ganges River valley is divided between the countries of India and Bangladesh.

**Vocabulary** *Builder*
<u>fertile</u> (FERT uhl) *adj.* producing vegetation or crops abundantly

✔**Checkpoint** What two major rivers played a key role in South Asian life?

**Main Idea**
The climate of South Asia affected the development of the region's early civilization.

# The South Asian Climate

Climate has also played an important role in the growth of civilization in South Asia. Most of the Indian subcontinent has a tropical climate. For much of the year, the land bakes under a high, hot sun.

**Impact of the Monsoon** A seasonal wind pattern known as the monsoon controls rainfall. In the winter, dry winds blow from the land to the sea. Little rain falls. In the summer, this pattern reverses, and wet winds from the oceans blow onto the land. The summer rains provide water for crops and bring relief from the baking heat. More than 1,500 years ago, an Indian poet wrote this poem about a summer monsoon storm.

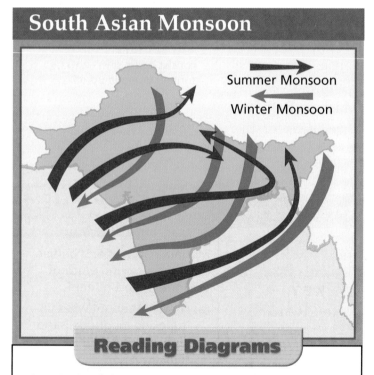

## South Asian Monsoon

Summer Monsoon

Winter Monsoon

### Reading Diagrams

The winds of the monsoon strongly affect the climate of South Asia. The summer rains can begin in May and last until October.

(a) **Read a Diagram** How would you describe the directions in which the summer and winter monsoon winds travel?

(b) **Apply Information** How might a change in these monsoon patterns have changed life in the region?

❝The rain advances like a king
　In artful majesty;
　Hear, dearest, how his thunder
　　rings
　Like royal drums and see
　His lightning-banners wave; a
　　cloud
　For elephant he rides,
　And finds his welcome from the
　　crowd
　Of lovers and of brides. . . .❞

—Kalidasa, "The Rains," from *The India Sourcebook*

From the time that farming began in South Asia, agriculture depended on the summer monsoon. If the rains came on time, all was well. If the rains came late or not at all, crops died and people starved. If the rains were too heavy, floods washed away farms and villages. Therefore, the monsoon had both positive and negative effects on daily life in South Asia.

The monsoon also influenced seagoing trade. Sailors from other lands used the winds of the summer monsoon to blow their ships to South Asian ports. Upon arrival the crews waited, sometimes for months, for the wind to change. When winter came, the monsoon blew the ships back out to sea and homeward. In this way, the monsoon winds connected South Asia with Western Asia, Europe, East Africa, and China and allowed an exchange of goods and cultures to occur.

 Checkpoint How have monsoons affected life in South Asia?

**Looking Back and Ahead** In this section, you have read about geographic factors that shaped life on the Indian subcontinent. In the next section, you will read about the rise of South Asia's first civilization in the Indus River valley.

**Monsoon Flooding**
This image shows flooding caused by the monsoon rains in India. **Critical Thinking: Draw Inferences** *Why do you think monsoon flood waters such as those shown here would be difficult to control?*

## Section 1 Check Your Progress

**Progress Monitoring** Online

**For:** Self-test with instant help
**Visit:** PHSchool.com
**Web Code:** mwa-3061

**Standards Review** H-SS: 6.5.1; E-LA: Reading 6.1.5

### Comprehension and Critical Thinking

**1. (a) List** What are two geographic factors that influenced the growth of early civilizations in India?
**(b) Evaluate Information** How might the large size of South Asia have affected the region's early civilizations?

**2. (a) Describe** Describe the climate of South Asia.
**(b) Draw Conclusions** How might early civilization in South Asia have been different if it had not been affected by monsoons?

### Reading Skill

**3. Understand Shades of Meaning** Read the sentence below. Then, explain whether and how its meaning would change if the word *hot* were replaced by *blistering*: For much of the year, South Asia bakes under a hot sun.

### Vocabulary *Builder*

**4.** Write two definitions for each word: river system, subcontinent. First, write a formal definition for your teacher. Second, write a definition in everyday English for a classmate.

### Writing

**5.** Make a list of details you could use to compare and contrast the land and climate of the Indian subcontinent with that of the area where you live.

 **Standards Preview**

**H-SS 6.5.1** Locate and describe the major river system and discuss the physical setting that supported the rise of this civilization.

**E-LA Reading 6.1.5** Understand and explain "shades of meaning" in related words.

## Reading Preview

 **Reading Skill**

**Understand and Explain Synonyms** Many words have meanings that are similar, but not exactly the same. These synonyms offer slightly different ways to present information. When you encounter words with similar definitions, ask yourself how the definitions are different. This will help you understand exactly what the text means.

### Vocabulary *Builder*

**High-Use Words**
rely (rih LI), p. 171
collapse (kuh LAPS), p. 174

**Key Terms**
central planning (SEHN truhl PLAN ihng), p. 172
granary (GRAN uh ree), p. 172
import (ihm PORT), p. 172
export (ehk SPORT), p. 172

**Background Knowledge** The first civilization on the Indian subcontinent appeared in the Indus River valley. At its peak, the Indus Valley civilization covered an area larger than those of either Egypt or Mesopotamia. In this section, you will study the rise and decline of the Indus Valley civilization.

**Main Idea**
The Indus Valley civilization arose around 2500 B.C. and featured organized cities and an efficient economy.

## Indus Valley Civilization: Lost and Found

The Indus Valley civilization arose around 2500 B.C. and deteriorated, or declined, about 1650 B.C. Little was known about the civilization until archaeologists uncovered two ancient cities in the 1920s. One ruined city was named Harappa, and the other Mohenjo-Daro. Because Harappa was the first site to be found, the Indus Valley civilization also became known as the Harappan civilization.

Since the 1920s, archaeologists have discovered some 1,400 Indus Valley cities and towns. About one third of those sites are in present-day Pakistan, and the rest are in India. These sites cover an astonishing 1.5 million square miles. This represents an area almost three times the size of Alaska.

**A River Valley Civilization**   Like those of Egypt and Mesopotamia, the Indus Valley civilization arose in a major river valley. The physical settings of the three civilizations were similar. All three developed in hot desert areas. Their people <u>relied</u> on a great river for water and fertile soil.

Like the Nile, the Indus River flooded every year. As you have read, these floods created a fertile plain, but they also washed away fields and farms. Over time, the people of the Indus Valley learned to manage these floods. They planted crops in the rich soil and raised a surplus of food.

**Vocabulary** *Builder*
<u>rely</u> (rih LI) *v.* to depend on

**Well-Planned Cities**   The Indus Valley people built large and well-organized cities. These cities were constructed on huge raised mounds of earth and rock. During times of flooding, these sites remained above water. Most cities had wide, straight streets arranged in a grid pattern. In contrast, the streets of Egyptian and Sumerian cities twisted and turned without any visible plan.

The people of the Indus Valley used hard, oven-fired brick to build the most important buildings in each city. These bricks were uniform, or the same in size, from one city to the next. The bricks lasted longer and had a much harder composition than the sun-dried bricks used in Egypt and Mesopotamia.

Indus Valley cities offered well-designed plumbing and sewage systems. Each house had a bathroom and toilet. Wastewater from houses flowed into brick-lined sewage channels. A trash chute in each house led to a rubbish bin in the street. You will learn more about these systems in the feature that follows this section.

**Mohenjo-Daro Site**
The Indus Valley city of Mohenjo-Daro was about three miles around and included a central mound that rose more than 20 feet high.
**Critical Thinking: Apply Information** *What clues does this photograph give about the importance of order in the city?*

All of these features reflected a surprising level of **central planning,** or planning carried out by a single strong government, yet scholars know almost nothing about Indus Valley government. Archaeologists have found no royal statues or tombs to suggest that kings ruled the Indus Valley cities. Instead, a few strong rulers may have governed the cities.

**The Indus Valley Economy**  The Indus Valley people developed an efficient economy. As in other early civilizations, most people practiced farming. Indus Valley farmers used irrigation to raise wheat and barley. They stored surplus crops in a **granary,** or special building used to hold grain. These farmers were the first to grow cotton for use in making cloth.

Indus Valley farmers domesticated a number of animals. They raised sheep, cattle, chickens, and ducks for food. They kept horses, camels, and donkeys for transportation. They may also have domesticated the Indian elephant. Animals seem to have been important to these people. They carved wooden animals and painted pictures of animals on pottery.

**Far-Reaching Trade**  Trade was another key economic activity. Traders imported precious metals, stones, and timber from distant lands. To **import** means to bring goods in from another land. Archaeologists have found gold from India, copper from present-day Afghanistan, and turquoise from present-day Iran at Indus Valley sites. They have also discovered pottery from Mesopotamia.

Indus Valley traders also exported jewelry, cotton cloth, and other goods to Egypt and Mesopotamia. To **export** means to send goods out to another land for sale. Most were shipped by boat from the port city of Lothal on the Arabian Sea. Archaeologists have found a 700-foot dock at Lothal. Granaries and factories for making trade beads stood next to the dock.

Indus Valley trade was well organized. Traders used stone seals to identify their goods. They stamped the seals on soft clay squares and attached these markers to the goods. Trade was also regulated, or controlled, by a system of uniform weights and measures. Under this system, every trader used the same units to weigh and measure goods. Traders used scales and stone cubes to weigh objects and measured objects by using a standard unit of length of just over one foot.

 Checkpoint  **Describe the economic organization of Indus Valley cities.**

**Regulating Trade**
Stone cubes such as these, which were chiseled from red stone, allowed Indus Valley traders to weigh the items they exchanged. **Critical Thinking: Explain Problem** *What problems do you think Indus Valley traders avoided by using blocks such as these?*

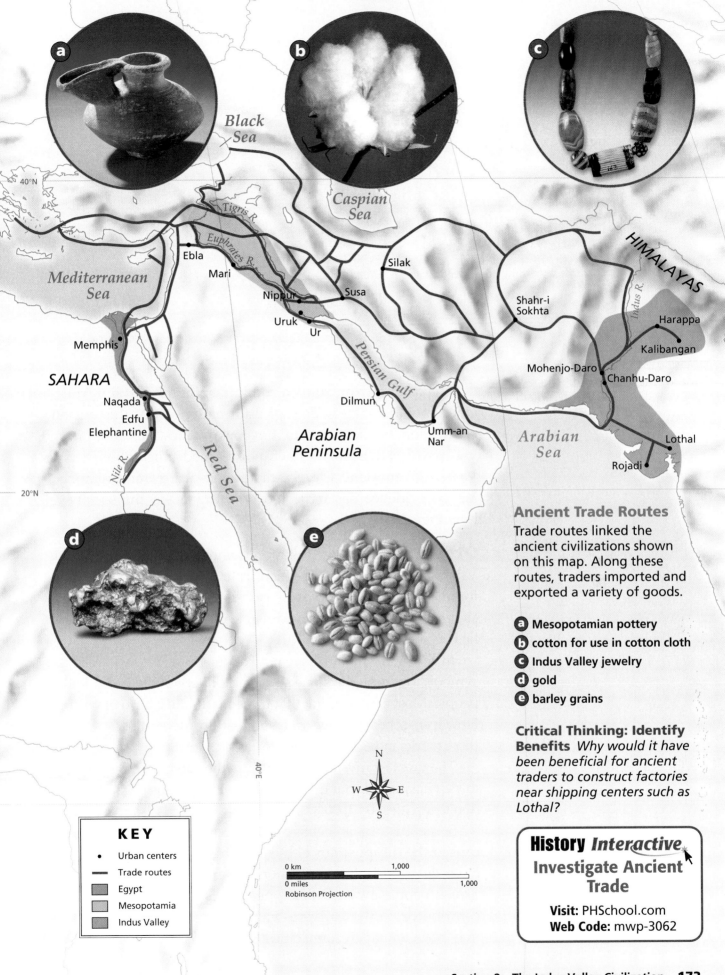

Black Sea

Caspian Sea

Mediterranean Sea

HIMALAYAS

Tigris R.

Euphrates R.

Ebla

Mari

Nippur

Uruk

Ur

Susa

Silak

Shahr-i Sokhta

Indus R.

Harappa

Kalibangan

Mohenjo-Daro

Chanhu-Daro

Memphis

SAHARA

Naqada

Edfu

Elephantine

Nile R.

Red Sea

Persian Gulf

Arabian Peninsula

Dilmun

Umm-an Nar

Arabian Sea

Lothal

Rojadi

20°N

40°N

40°E

## Ancient Trade Routes

Trade routes linked the ancient civilizations shown on this map. Along these routes, traders imported and exported a variety of goods.

**a** Mesopotamian pottery
**b** cotton for use in cotton cloth
**c** Indus Valley jewelry
**d** gold
**e** barley grains

**Critical Thinking: Identify Benefits** *Why would it have been beneficial for ancient traders to construct factories near shipping centers such as Lothal?*

**History** *Interactive.*
**Investigate Ancient Trade**

**Visit:** PHSchool.com
**Web Code:** mwp-3062

### KEY

- Urban centers
— Trade routes
Egypt
Mesopotamia
Indus Valley

0 km ————— 1,000
0 miles ————— 1,000
Robinson Projection

N W E S

**Indus Valley Seals**
Many Indus Valley stone seals had the square shape of the seals shown here. The seals were likely cut from soft stone using a saw.
**Critical Thinking: Apply Information** *How might scholars use these seals to learn more about Indus Valley trade?*

**Main Idea**
Many questions about the Indus Valley civilization remain unanswered.

# Indus Valley Mysteries

The artifacts and ruins of buildings found in Indus Valley cities provide a great deal of information about this ancient civilization, but scholars still have many questions about it. As you have read, scholars have not learned much about Indus Valley government. Clearly, the people were well organized. Yet no evidence has indicated who organized the society or how they did so.

**Other Mysteries** Religion is another aspect of the Indus Valley civilization about which little is known. Scholars have found no sign of temples or priests, although some artifacts suggest links with later Hinduism. Also, little evidence of war has been found in this region.

In addition, scholars have not yet determined how to read the symbols found on the stone seals and pottery of the Indus Valley people. Most experts think that these marks are a form of writing. However, scholars have not successfully determined whether these marks indicated names, stories, or something else.

The greatest mystery, however, is the cause of the decline of this civilization. Around 1750 B.C., the Harappans began to abandon their cities. By 1500 B.C., the civilization had disappeared.

Some historians believe that climate change may have caused the disappearance. In some areas, heavy flooding may have destroyed cities. In others, years of drought may have driven people away. Other types of disasters could also have contributed to the collapse. Earthquakes or foreign invaders may have damaged some cities.

**Vocabulary** *Builder*
collapse (kuh LAPS) *n.* act of breaking down, failing, or giving way

Some historians believe that economic problems led to the decline. After years of heavy farming, the Indus Valley soil may have lost its fertility. Smaller harvests would have harmed the economy.

Troubles in Mesopotamia would probably have hurt trade between the Indus Valley and Sumer. Such events may have resulted in hard times for both traders and artisans in the Indus Valley. Whatever the cause of the civilization's collapse, it would take another thousand years for a new civilization to take root on the Indian subcontinent.

**Checkpoint** Describe two mysteries surrounding the Indus Valley civilization.

**Looking Back and Ahead** In this section, you have read about the Indus Valley civilization that arose more than 4,000 years ago. You have learned that Indus Valley cities were built with central planning. You have also learned that many questions about this civilization, including the reasons for its decline, remain unanswered. In the next section, you will learn about the rise of a second civilization in ancient India and the development of a new social structure in the area.

**E-LA 6.1.5 Understand and Explain Synonyms** What shades of meaning distinguish the synonyms *harm* and *hurt* from each other?

---

## Section 2 Check Your Progress

**Progress Monitoring Online**
**For:** Self-test with instant help
**Visit:** PHSchool.com
**Web Code:** mwa-3062

**Standards Review** H-SS: 6.5.1; E-LA: Reading 6.1.5

**Comprehension and Critical Thinking**

1. **(a) List** List two important features of early Indus Valley cities.
   **(b) Evaluate Information** How do these features provide evidence of central planning?

2. **(a) Recall** What is the largest mystery surrounding the Indus Valley civilization?
   **(b) Draw Conclusions** How does writing play a key role in this mystery?

**Reading Skill**

3. **Understand and Explain Synonyms** Read the following sentence: In contrast, the streets of Egyptian and Sumerian cities twisted and turned without any visible plan. Which words are synonyms? How are their meanings related?

**Vocabulary Builder**

Complete each of the following sentences so that the second part further explains the first part and clearly shows your understanding of the highlighted word.

4. Indus Valley cities featured central planning; _____.

5. Farmers often used a granary; _____.

6. An important task of Indus Valley traders was to export goods; _____.

**Writing**

7. Make a Venn diagram that shows how the cities of the Indus Valley civilization and those of other early civilizations were alike and different.

# Clean Living in Mohenjo-Daro

*Mohenjo-Daro* means "Hill of the Dead." This name was given to the city hundreds of years after the civilization collapsed. But in about 2500 B.C., it was a thriving city of around 40,000 people. Mohenjo-Daro was carefully planned. There was an artificial hill on which public buildings stood, high and protected. The streets were laid out in a grid pattern. There were drains under the streets. Homes were comfortable and had indoor plumbing. Being clean, both in body and spirit, seems to have been very important to the people of the city.

**History-Social Science**

**Chronological and Spatial Thinking 3** Students use a variety of maps and documents to identify physical and cultural features of neighborhoods, cities, states, and countries and to explain the historical migration of people, expansion and disintegration of empires, and the growth of economic systems.

**Homes In Mohenjo-Daro**

Wealthy families lived in houses built around a courtyard. There were indoor wells for water. There were toilets, as well as bathrooms where people bathed by pouring pitchers of water over themselves.

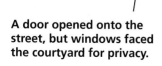

A door opened onto the street, but windows faced the courtyard for privacy.

Drains were laid under the streets. Workers could get into the drains through inspection holes.

The inner courtyard was the center of family life. A wooden balcony overlooked it.

### The Great Bath

Archaeologists think that the Great Bath was used for religious functions. The water may have been used to renew and purify the bathers. The pool measures 39 feet long, 23 feet wide, and 8 feet deep.

### Well

This well would have been set into the floor of a home. Here, it stands like a chimney because the surrounding earth has been removed during excavation.

### Toilet

Archaeologists think that this was a toilet. A wooden plank or a longer brick would have formed its seat.

The roof was used for drying crops for storage. In the heat of the summer, people often slept on the roof.

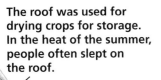

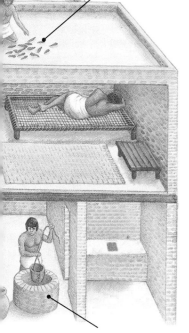

### Drains

Mohenjo-Daro had a complex drainage system for wastewater and sewage. Drains in homes and other buildings connected to drains under streets.

Homes had their own wells. Cool water was drawn up when needed.

### Analyze LIFE AT THE TIME

Many features at the ruins of Mohenjo-Daro suggest that the city's inhabitants valued cleanliness, both for individuals and the community as a whole. Why might this have been an important value in a large, growing city such as Mohenjo-Daro? For each image shown, write a brief explanation of its usefullness for preserving the cleanliness of individuals or the community.

**Standards Preview**

**H-SS 6.5.2** Discuss the significance of the Aryan invasions.

**6.5.4** Outline the social structure of the caste system.

**E-LA Reading 6.1.5** Understand and explain "shades of meaning" in related words.

## Reading Preview

### Reading Skill

**Explain Shades of Meaning** Sometimes you will find related words used within the same passage of text. At other times, you will recognize a word with a meaning related to another word that you know. In both cases, define the words in your mind (or use a dictionary) to make sure that you understand their meanings.

### Vocabulary *Builder*

**High-Use Words**
similar (SIHM uh luhr), p. 178
shift (shihft), p. 180

**Key Terms**
caste (kast), p. 181
caste system (kast SIHS tuhm), p. 181
untouchable (uhn TUHCH uh buhl), p. 182

**Background Knowledge** About 1500 B.C., a new group of people appeared in the Indus Valley. They called themselves Aryans, which meant "the noble ones" in their language. They brought with them beliefs about gods and goddesses. They used these beliefs to compose a collection of sacred hymns called Vedas. Because the Vedas were central to Aryan culture, this period of Indian history is called the Vedic age. In this section, you will read about the Indo-Aryans and their impact on ancient India.

**Main Idea**
The Indo-Aryans brought a new culture to the Indus Valley.

**Vocabulary** *Builder*
similar (SIHM uh luhr) *adj.* almost the same

## The Origins of the Aryans

The origins of Aryan language speakers are a mystery. In the past, historians believed that the Indo-Aryan people invaded India from the north. This Indo-Aryan invasion theory was originally based mainly on studies of languages. Sanskrit, the language spoken by the Indo-Aryans, is <u>similar</u> in many ways to some European languages, such as Latin and Greek. More recent studies of the traits passed among people of the region, as well as of languages, suggest that the Indo-Aryan invasion theory may not be accurate.

This theory suggests that the Indo-Aryans were related to the people who first settled Europe. Today, however, many historians believe that the Indo-Aryans were people who raised livestock and entered India over a long period of time. Some scholars even suggest that the Indo-Aryans did not migrate to India, but were its original inhabitants.

**The Vedas**  Like most nomads, the Indo-Aryans did not create a written language. However, after settling along the Indus River, they did compose a rich oral, or spoken, literature called the Vedas. The Vedas are poems that tell the story of the Indo-Aryan people and their gods. Religious leaders often recited these poems during ceremonies or rituals.

For centuries, Indo-Aryans passed down the Vedas by word of mouth. People later collected and wrote down the poems. The best known of these collections is the *Rig Veda.* This work includes more than 1,000 poems and was the primary collection from which poems were recited. Almost everything scholars know about early Aryan life in India comes from the Vedas.

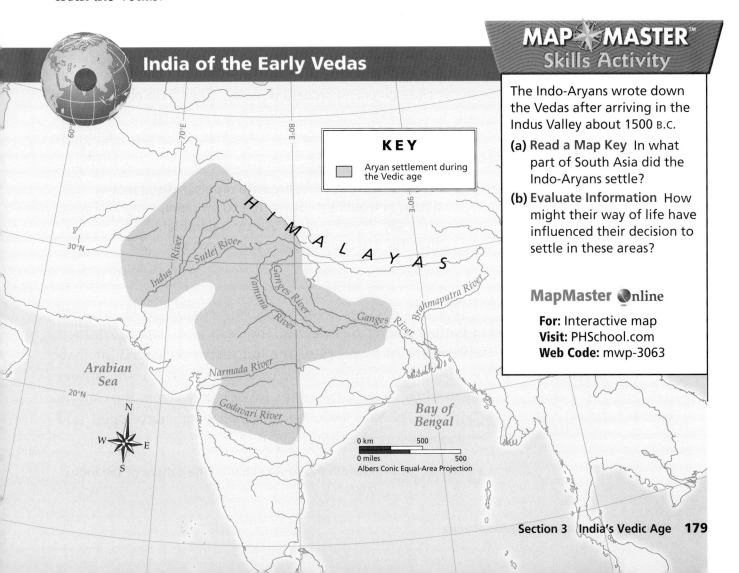

**India of the Early Vedas**

**KEY**

Aryan settlement during the Vedic age

Arabian Sea

Bay of Bengal

0 km 500
0 miles 500
Albers Conic Equal-Area Projection

# MAP★MASTER™
## Skills Activity

The Indo-Aryans wrote down the Vedas after arriving in the Indus Valley about 1500 B.C.

**(a) Read a Map Key**  In what part of South Asia did the Indo-Aryans settle?

**(b) Evaluate Information**  How might their way of life have influenced their decision to settle in these areas?

**MapMaster ⊙nline**

**For:** Interactive map
**Visit:** PHSchool.com
**Web Code:** mwp-3063

## The *Rig Veda*

This image shows a passage from the *Rig Veda* in Sanskrit. **Critical Thinking: Identify Benefits** *Why might scholars benefit from studying a text in its original language?*

२४२ ॥ ऋग्वेदः ॥ [अ॰ ८. अ॰ ४. व॰ १६.

॥ अथ षोडशी ॥

पुरूणि हि त्वा सवना जनानां ब्रह्माणि मंदन् गृणतामृषीणां ।
इमामाघोषन्नवसा सहूतिं तिरो विश्वाँ अर्चंतो याह्यर्वाङ् ॥१६॥

पुरूणि । हि । त्वा । सवना । जनानां । ब्रह्माणि । मंदन् । गृणतां । ऋषीणां ।
इमां । आ॰घोषन् । अवसा । स॰हूतिं । तिरः । विश्वान् । अर्चंतः । याहि । अर्वाङ्॥१६॥

हे इंद्र त्वा तां जनानां संबंधीनि पुरूणि बहूनि सवना सवनानि ब्रह्माणि
स्तोत्राणि च मंदन् । सुवंति मोदयंति वा । गृणतां सुवतामृषीणामिमां सहूतिं
सुतिं त्वमाघोषन् महती शब्दवती चेयं स्तुतिरिति वदन् अर्चंतः सुवतोऽन्यानि-
भ्यास्त्वदीयानपि तिरस्तिरस्कृत्यावसा रक्षणेन सहावाङ्॰सदभिमुखं याहि । गच्छ ॥

## Aryan Life

The Indo-Aryans who migrated to the Indus River valley lived as nomadic herders. They herded both horses and cattle, though cattle held special importance for them. The Indo-Aryans measured their wealth by the size of their cattle herds. These herds formed the basis of the Indo-Aryan economy. But over time, the Indo-Aryan way of life shifted from herding to farming.

The Vedas show that the Indo-Aryans liked to enjoy themselves. They loved music and dancing. They held chariot races and enjoyed gambling. The following passage from a poem in the Vedas describes one family's reaction to a man who gambled too much:

> **❝**Her mother hates me; my wife repels [resists] me—
> a man in trouble finds no one to pity him,
> They say, "I've no more use for a gambler,
> than for a worn-out horse put up for sale." **❞**
>
> —*Rig Veda*

The Indo-Aryans were also great warriors. They engaged in battles among themselves, and also took part in conflicts with other nearby peoples. The Indo-Aryans charged into battle in horse-drawn chariots. Around 1000 B.C., Aryan armies began to move from the Indus River valley across the Ganges Plain. By 700 B.C., 16 Aryan kingdoms had developed and spread across northern India.

 **Checkpoint** How did the Aryans change the culture of the Indus Valley?

# The Caste System

Aryan society developed a social structure based on caste. Over time, caste became a fixed social class into which a person is born. Often, the members of different castes remained separate for many important activities. A person's caste is inherited at birth and does not change over his or her lifetime. A social structure in which social class is inherited from one's parents is known as a **caste system.**

## Origins of Caste
When Indo-Aryans arrived in the Indus River valley, their society already had three social classes: priests, rulers, and common people. They soon added a fourth caste for the native peoples who already lived in the area.

**Levels of the Caste System**

As this chart shows, the levels of the Indo-Aryans' caste system were related to the jobs that their members performed. **Critical Thinking: Interpret Charts** *Which of these castes do you think would have included the greatest numbers of people?*

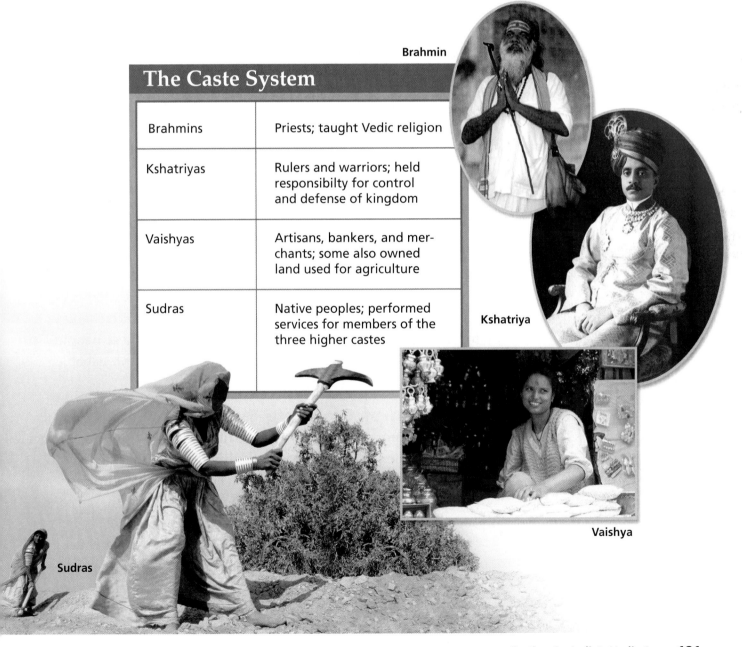

## The Caste System

| | |
|---|---|
| Brahmins | Priests; taught Vedic religion |
| Kshatriyas | Rulers and warriors; held responsibilty for control and defense of kingdom |
| Vaishyas | Artisans, bankers, and merchants; some also owned land used for agriculture |
| Sudras | Native peoples; performed services for members of the three higher castes |

Brahmin

Kshatriya

Vaishya

Sudras

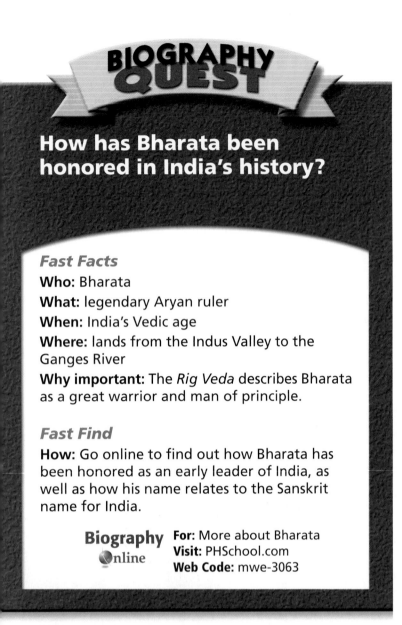

## BIOGRAPHY QUEST

## How has Bharata been honored in India's history?

**Fast Facts**

**Who:** Bharata

**What:** legendary Aryan ruler

**When:** India's Vedic age

**Where:** lands from the Indus Valley to the Ganges River

**Why important:** The *Rig Veda* describes Bharata as a great warrior and man of principle.

**Fast Find**

**How:** Go online to find out how Bharata has been honored as an early leader of India, as well as how his name relates to the Sanskrit name for India.

**Biography Online**

**For:** More about Bharata
**Visit:** PHSchool.com
**Web Code:** mwe-3063

**E-LA 6.1.5 Explain Shades of Meaning**
Do shades of meaning separate the words *class* and *caste* from each other?

For the first few hundred years after the arrival of the Indo-Aryans in India, the castes had not yet become hereditary. Once their society had merged with the local population, a late hymn of the *Rig Veda* described the four castes. The highest caste consisted of priests known as Brahmins. Next came the Kshatriyas, a caste made up of rulers and warriors. Below them were the Vaishyas, a caste of artisans, bankers, and merchants.

The members of these three highest castes were considered "twice-born." This meant that males from these castes could belong to the Vedic religion. They could study Sanskrit and the Vedas. "Twice-born" males also had the right to take part in particular religious ceremonies.

At the bottom of the caste system stood the native peoples known as Sudras. The higher castes looked down on the Sudras and made them work as farmers and menial workers.

Later Indo-Aryans identified a class of workers below the Sudras, and they called its members **untouchables.** The members of this group often did the dirty jobs that no one else would do. Members of the higher castes would not have contact with untouchables for fear of being made unclean. In modern India, these people are now called Dalits, and treating someone as an untouchable is a crime against the law.

**Evolution of the Caste System**  As Indian society developed more occupations and skills, the caste system grew more complex. The larger castes divided into hundreds of smaller castes. Most of these castes were based on occupation. People who did the same job belonged to the same caste. Today, the total number of castes in India may exceed 2,000.

Caste rules also became more rigid. People were born into a caste and could not leave it. They could marry only members of their own caste. They had to work and eat among their caste members. All social events took place within one's caste.

In time, the caste system became the most powerful force in Aryan society. The system brought both costs and benefits. For instance, the system limited people's individual freedom. They could not develop talents, interests, or friendships outside their caste. The patterns of their lives were fixed at birth.

However, the caste system also brought stability to Aryan society. It gave people a sense of belonging because every person had a place within a caste. Indian goods became famous because of the skills passed down through members of the castes. The system also allowed different groups to follow their own beliefs and customs within their caste while maintaining a place in the larger society.

 **Checkpoint** **What is the caste system?**

**Looking Back and Ahead** In this section, you have read about India's Vedic age. You have learned that nomads known as Aryans appeared in the Indus River valley around 1500 B.C. The Aryans established a social structure based on a caste system. In the next chapter, you will read about the development of India's first major religion, Hinduism.

---

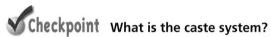

Section **3** **Check Your Progress**

**Progress Monitoring** ⏱nline
**For:** Self-test with instant help
**Visit:** PHSchool.com
**Web Code:** mwa-3063

**Standards Review** **H-SS:** 6.5.2, 6.5.4; **E-LA:** Reading 6.1.5

**Comprehension and Critical Thinking**

1. **(a) Recall** What are two possible explanations for the origins of the Indo-Aryans?
   **(b) Apply Information** Why might the Indo-Aryans have composed the Vedas after they settled in the Indus Valley?

2. **(a) Recall** On what idea was Aryan social structure based?
   **(b) Understand Sequence** How did this social structure change over time?

**Reading Skill**

3. **Explain Shades of Meaning** Use shades of meaning to explain how the words *occupation* and *job* are related.

**Vocabulary Builder**

Read each sentence below. If the sentence is true, write YES. If the sentence is not true, write NO and explain WHY.

4. Sanskrit was <u>similar</u> to some languages spoken in Europe.

5. The Indo-Aryans' way of life <u>shifted</u>, or stayed the same, as their civilization developed in the Indus River valley.

**Writing**

6. Write three or four sentences that explain the major similarities and differences between the lives of members of the three highest groups of the Indo-Aryan caste system and the members of the fourth group.

A *cause* is an event or a condition that makes something else happen. An *effect* is what happens as a result of a cause. Causes and their effects occur throughout history. By identifying the relationships between them, you can gain a better understanding of historical events.

 **Chapter Standards**

**History-Social Science**

**Historical Interpretation 2** Students understand and distinguish cause, effect, sequence, and correlation in historical events, including the long- and short-term causal relations.

Why did ancient South Asian civilizations grow in the way they did? There were many reasons. Some of the reasons had to do with geography. Vast mountain ranges presented natural barriers. Oceans and seas also created barriers.

However, geography also allowed civilization in South Asia to grow. India's river systems and monsoons supported agriculture. Farming produced food for the people of the area. As a result, unique civilizations developed in the Indus Valley.

**Learn the Skill** *Follow these steps to identify cause and effect.*

1. **Read a passage, and recognize important events.** Choose one event or condition as a starting point. Decide whether this item represents a cause or an effect.

2. **Identify earlier events or conditions as possible causes.** Ask, "Why did this happen?" or "What led to this?" You may also find such clue words as *because* and *reason* that suggest cause-and-effect relationships.

3. **Look at later events or conditions for possible effects.** Ask, "What did this lead to?" or "What was a result?" You may find such clue words as *brought about, led to, as a result,* and *therefore.*

4. **Summarize important cause-and-effect relationships.** You may choose to organize these relationships in a chart.

**Practice the Skill** *Answer the following questions about the passage above.*

1. **Read a passage, and recognize important events. (a)** What event is mentioned in the paragraph's first sentence? **(b)** Is this event a cause or an effect?

2. **Identify earlier events or conditions as possible causes.** Which events or conditions preceded the event in the first sentence?

3. **Look at later events or conditions for possible effects.** What clue words or phrases in the passage indicate an effect?

4. **Summarize important cause-and-effect relationships.** What cause-and-effect relationships did you identify in the passage?

**Apply the Skill**
*See page 187 of the Review and Assessment.*

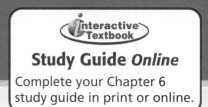

**Study Guide** *Online*
Complete your Chapter 6 study guide in print or online.

## Chapter Summary  H-SS: 6.5.1; 6.5.2; 6.5.4

### Section 1 The Geography of South Asia

- Natural barriers strongly influenced the development of civilization in South Asia.
- The Indus River valley supported the growth of early civilization on the Indian subcontinent.
- Early agriculture in South Asia depended on the rains of the summer monsoon.

### Section 2 The Indus Valley Civilization

- Studies of archaeological sites have provided information about the Indus Valley civilization.
- This civilization demonstrated central planning, as well as an extensive trade network.
- The reason for its decline is one of several mysteries surrounding the Indus Valley civilization.

### Section 3 India's Vedic age

- The emergence of the Indo-Aryans marked the beginning of India's Vedic age.
- The Indo-Aryans were a nomadic people who composed an oral literature called the Vedas.
- The caste system was a social structure that had a strong impact on Aryan society.

**Indus Valley seals**

## Standards Practice  H-SS: 6.5.1; 6.5.2; 6.5.4

## Vocabulary *Builder*

### High-Use Words

Read each sentence below. If the sentence is true, write YES. If the sentence is not true, write NO and explain WHY.

1. The **fertile** plain of the Ganges River valley caused people to avoid settling there.

2. The people of the Indus Valley civilization **relied** on the waters of the Indus River for raising crops.

3. The **collapse** of the Indus Valley civilization was caused by earthquakes.

4. Over time, the rules of the Indo-Aryans' caste system **shifted** to become less strict.

### Key Terms

Answer the following questions in complete sentences that show your understanding of the Key Terms.

1. How did the **monsoon** affect early trade in South Asia?

2. What types of **natural barriers** surround the Indian subcontinent?

3. What purpose did **granaries** serve in the Indus Valley civilization?

4. What was one good that Indus Valley traders **exported?**

5. Which groups of people became known as **untouchables** in Aryan society?

## Standards Practice
*(continued)*  **H-SS:** 6.5.1, 6.5.2, 6.5.4; **E-LA:** Reading 6.1.5; Writing: 6.2.2

## Apply Reading Skills

**Understand and Explain Shades of Meaning** Choose a word from Section 2, and then identify a word you know that has a related meaning. Explain how the words' shades of meaning relate.

## Comprehension and Critical Thinking

**1. (a) Identify** Which two rivers played key roles in the development of civilization in India?
**(b) Analyze Cause and Effect** How did India's physical setting influence the growth of civilization?
**(c) Identify Costs and Benefits** Why might India's location have had both positive and negative effects?

**2. (a) List** What were two important economic activities of the Indus Valley civilization?
**(b) Draw Conclusions** How did these activities link the civilization with other parts of the world?
**(c) Evaluate Information** In what ways did Indus Valley people organize their economic activities?

**3. (a) Link Past and Present** What items have provided scholars with information about the Indus Valley civilization?
**(b) Explain Problem** What might have prevented scholars from determining how to read symbols found on Indus Valley seals and pottery?

**4. (a) Explain** Why is the period of the Indo-Aryans called the Vedic age?
**(b) Contrast** How were the Indo-Aryans different from the people of the Indus Valley civilization?

## Researching

**The Ruins of Mohenjo-Daro** The archaeological site of the ruins of Mohenjo-Daro has provided a great deal of information to people seeking to learn more about the Indus Valley civilization. In this activity, you will use the Internet and the library media center to research and report on this site. Choose a task below to work on. Share your work with the class by displaying your completed project in the classroom.

**Artist Historian:** Create a poster that presents a work of art found at the Mohenjo-Daro site. You may choose to include photographs of the item, or illustrate it yourself.

**Government Officials:** Since its excavation began in 1922, environmental factors have caused the further decay of the ruins. Create an outline to show some of the important steps that officials from governments and other organizations are taking to protect this site.

> **Researching Online**
> **For:** Help in starting this activity
> **Visit:** PHSchool.com
> **Web Code:** mwe-3064

## Writing

**1. Write a paragraph on the following topic.** Explain how the ways in which scholars have learned about the people of the Indus Valley civilization and the Indo-Aryans are alike and different.
**Your paragraph should:**
• contain a clear topic sentence.
• use signal and transition words.
• organize supporting details clearly.

**2. Write a short narrative.** Imagine you are a trader in an ancient Indus Valley city. Write a brief narrative describing your work.

Progress Monitoring ●nline
For: Self-test with instant help
Visit: PHSchool.com
Web Code: mwa-3064

# Apply Analysis Skills

**Use the paragraph at right to answer these questions.**

1. What are three events or conditions listed in this paragraph?

2. What clue words might help you identify some of these events as causes?

3. What is the latest event or condition described in the paragraph?

4. Does this event or condition represent an effect?

5. How might you present cause-and-effect relationships from this passage in a chart?

> **❝**Why did ancient South Asian civilizations grow in the way they did? There were many reasons. Some of the reasons had to do with geography. Vast mountain ranges presented natural barriers. Oceans and seas also created barriers. However, geography also allowed civilization in South Asia to grow. India's river systems and monsoons supported agriculture. Farming produced food for the people of the area. As a result, unique civilizations developed in the Indus Valley.**❞**

# Test Yourself

1. **South Asia is a subcontinent with natural barriers such as**

   A a vast desert.

   B lush green valleys.

   C a large river system.

   D tall mountains.

2. **Which of the following statements is true?**

   A The Indus River flows from the Himalayas to the Arabian Sea.

   B The Ganges River flows from the Hindu Kush to the Arabian Sea.

   C Harappa is the only large Indus Valley city to be discovered.

   D Most Indus Valley towns developed in present-day Bhutan.

**Refer to the image below to answer question 3.**

3. **This artifact offers evidence that the Indus Valley civilization had**

   A an efficient economy.

   B temples run by priests.

   C indoor plumbing and a sewage system.

   D large tombs built for kings.

4. **Some historians believe the Indo-Aryans invaded South Asia from the north. Others believe the Indo-Aryans**

   A arrived from Sri Lanka.

   B invaded from east Asia through the Himalayas.

   C migrated to the area over a long period of time.

   D sailed across the sea from the Arabian Peninsula.

**Refer to the reading below to answer question 5.**

> *Her mother hates me; my wife repels [resists] me— a man in trouble finds no one to pity him, They say, "I've no more use for a gambler, Than for a worn-out horse put up for sale."*

5. **This quote from the Rig Veda reflects the Indo-Aryans'**

   A use of chariots in battle.

   B desire to enjoy themselves.

   C lives as nomadic herders.

   D development of farming.

## Chapter 7

# Hinduism

### (ABOUT 500 B.C.–A.D. 1800s)

## Prepare to Read

 **Chapter Standards**

### History-Social Science
**6.5** Students analyze the geographic, political, economic, religious, and social structures of the early civilizations of India.

**Section 1,** pp. 192–195

 **What You Will Learn**

### The Origins of Hinduism

Hinduism, which evolved from early Brahmanism, has been the major religion of India for more than 2,500 years. The religion continues to develop today.

**Section 2,** pp. 196–201

### The Beliefs of Hinduism

All Hindus share the same basic beliefs and want to achieve four main goals during their lifetimes. Hindus believe that there are three different paths to becoming one with God.

**Section 3,** pp. 204–209

### The Spread of Hinduism

Hinduism has spread to many places outside India. The religion is the third largest in the world today.

Shiva

**About 800 B.C.**
Ways of worship begin to change in India.

**About 500 B.C.**
Hinduism becomes a major religion in India.

**Chapter Events**

**Other Events**

**2000 B.C.**

**1000 B.C.**

**B.C./A.D.**

**About 1750 B.C.** Hammurabi becomes king of Babylon.

**700s B.C.** King Piye unites Egypt and Kush.

## Where and When?
For more than 2,500 years, Hinduism has been the major religion of India.

This image at a Hindu temple shows the Green Goddess, who symbolizes nature.

**A.D. First century**
Indian merchants establish trading posts in Southeast Asia.

**A.D. 1800s**
Indian Hindus migrate to the Caribbean islands.

B.C./A.D.

A.D. 1000

A.D. 2000

**A.D. 70** The Romans attack Jerusalem.

**A.D. 1920s** Harappa and Mohenjo-Daro are uncovered.

# How to Read History

## History Reading Skill

### Previewing Figurative Language

When you read, you may come across figurative language. This type of language refers to a word or phrase used in a way that differs from its actual meaning. The most common types of figurative language are used to make comparisons. Words with multiple meanings may have several unrelated meanings. Use context clues to find the correct meaning for the word.

**Chapter Standards**

**English-Language Arts**

**Reading 6.1.2** Identify and interpret figurative language and words with multiple meanings.

**1** The sentence below uses figurative language to connect two things to help the reader see an image.

"Overnight the snow fell on the roofs like pure moss."

> **Snow fell** like **pure moss**

In this sentence, figurative language lets the reader know the writer's feelings about the pharaoh.

"He is the god Re whose beams enable us to see."

> **Words that describe the power of the pharaoh**

**2** In this sentence, context helps you choose the correct meaning for the word *ruler,* which can be a measuring device or a person who rules others:

"Next came the Kshatriyas, a caste made up of rulers and warriors."

> **Clue that the word *rulers* refers to people**

# Vocabulary *Builder*

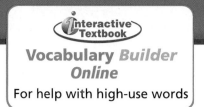

Vocabulary *Builder* Online
For help with high-use words

## Previewing **High-Use Academic Words**

| High-Use Word | Definition | Sample Sentence About History |
|---|---|---|
| **text** (tehkts) (Section 1, p. 192) | *n.* words in a piece of writing | The Vedas are India's oldest religious <u>texts</u>. |
| **involve** (inh VAWLV) (Section 1, p. 193) | *v.* to include by necessity; require | Offerings to the gods sometimes <u>involved</u> food and drink. |
| **tradition** (truh DIHSH uhn) (Section 2, p. 196) | *n.* long-established custom or practice | The <u>tradition</u> of offering gifts to the gods continues today. |
| **assign** (uh SĪN) (Section 2, p. 197) | *v.* to set apart or mark for a specific purpose | The ruler <u>assigned</u> his army to the northern part of the territory. |
| **achieve** (uh CHEEV) (Section 2, p. 200) | *v.* to do, or succeed in doing; accomplish | The army <u>achieved</u> its goal by destroying the enemy. |
| **absorb** (ab SORB) (Section 3, p. 204) | *v.* to take in and incorporate | Some cultures <u>absorb</u> characteristics of many other cultures. |
| **migrate** (MĪ grayt) (Section 3, p. 206) | *v.* to move from one place to another; to change location | People as well as ideas <u>migrated</u> from India to other parts of the world. |

**Hindu street shrine**

## Previewing **Key Terms and People**

Hinduism, p. 192
Brahmanism, p. 193
guru, p. 194
Brahman, p. 194
epic poem, p. 194

dharma, p. 197
moksha, p. 197
reincarnation, p. 198
karma, p. 199
ethnic group, p. 204

shrine, p. 205
sect, p. 205
pilgrim, p. 208

**The god Brahma**

**Standards Preview**

**H-SS** 6.5.3 Explain the major beliefs and practices of Brahmanism in India and how they evolved into early Hinduism.

**E-LA Reading 6.1.2** Identify and interpret figurative language and words with multiple meanings.

## Reading Preview

 **Reading Skill**

**Identify Figurative Language** Writers often use special language in descriptions. A Chinese poet writes that the towering mountains in his homeland "soar dizzily like a stack of cooking pots." The words "towering" and "soar dizzily" tell the reader the mountains are tall and magnificent.

**Vocabulary** *Builder*

**High-Use Words**
text (tehkst), p. 192
involve (inh VAWLV), p. 193

**Key Terms and People**
Hinduism (HIHN doo ihz uhm), p. 192
Brahmanism (BRAH muhn ihz uhm), p. 193
guru (GOO roo), p. 194
Brahman (BRAH muhn), p. 194
epic (EHP ihk) poem, p. 194

**Background Knowledge** Hinduism is one of the oldest religions in the world. It began in India during the Vedic age in a form known as Brahmanism. In this section, you will read about the origins of this ancient faith. You will also learn how Brahmanism evolved, or grew into Hinduism.

**Main Idea**
Hinduism evolved from Brahmanism into the major religion of India.

## The Roots of Hinduism

For more than 2,500 years, Hinduism has been the major religion of India. In fact, the word Hinduism means the religion of the peoples of India.

**Vocabulary** *Builder*

text (tehkst) *n.* words in a piece of writing

**E-LA 6.1.2 Identify Figurative Language** What figurative language appears in the last paragraph?

**Vedic Age Beliefs and Practices** As you have learned in Chapter 6, the Vedas are India's oldest religious texts. Priests in the Vedic age memorized these works and passed them on orally. Later, they were written down.

The Vedas contained hymns to many gods and rituals designed to keep the gods happy. These rituals often included sacrifices to the gods, such as Agni, the god of fire. Agni was seen in three ways: He was the fiery sun in the sky. He was lightning in the air. On Earth, Agni was the fire that "ate" the sacrifices offered to the gods.

**Brahmanism** Scholars call this Vedic age religion **Brahmanism.** The name comes from *brahman,* a word that refers to a single spiritual power that lives in everything. Later, this word would <u>involve</u> much larger meanings.

Brahmanism was a religion ruled by priests and rituals. Only Brahmins, or priests from the highest caste, could perform the rituals described in the Vedas. People believed that any mistake in pronouncing the ritual words from the texts would anger the gods. Their "sacred knowledge" gave the Brahmins great power and influence in Indian society.

✔ **Checkpoint** **How did Hinduism begin?**

# The Evolution of Hinduism

Beginning about 500 B.C., Indian ways of worship began to change. The old gods became less important. Some people began to doubt that carrying out precise rituals was as important as the priests claimed. Other people began asking questions such as: Why are we born? How should we live? What happens to us when we die? Hinduism evolved from Indians' efforts to answer these challenging questions.

**Vocabulary** *Builder*
<u>involve</u> (inh VAWLV) *v.* to include by necessity; require

**Main Idea**
Two beliefs forming the foundation for Hinduism come from the Hindu scriptures, the Upanishads.

**Hindu Temples**
Two of the many temples at Khajuraho, India, built between the ninth and eleventh centuries A.D. **Critical Thinking: Draw Inference** *Followers of Hinduism believe some Hindu gods live in mountains. Why do you think Hindu temples resemble mountains?*

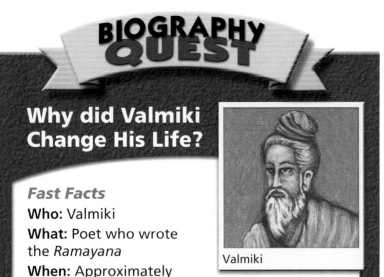

## Why did Valmiki Change His Life?

Valmiki

### Fast Facts

**Who:** Valmiki

**What:** Poet who wrote the *Ramayana*

**When:** Approximately 200 B.C.

**Where:** India

**Why important:** As a young man, Valmiki was a thief. However, Valmiki later became a wise and holy man.

### Fast Find

**How:** Go online to find out how Valmiki transformed his life.

**Biography** ⓞnline

**For:** More about Valmiki
**Visit:** PHSchool.com
**Web Code:** mwe-3071

**The Upanishads** To find those answers, thinkers and teachers known as gurus left their homes to live in nature. The gurus spent their days thinking and talking about religious ideas. Some of their conversations were written in sacred, or holy, Hindu scriptures known as the Upanishads (oo PAN ih shahdz). The word *Upanishad* means "sitting down near a teacher."

The Upanishads introduced two beliefs that lie at the heart of Hinduism. The first is the belief that there is one supreme God known as **Brahman.** The Upanishads describe Brahman as "He who constantly rules the world." Brahman is the creator and soul of all things. People might worship Brahman in the form of many different gods, but those gods are just aspects of "The One."

The second belief that lies at the heart of Hinduism is that every person is born with a soul that is part of Brahman. This soul, or inner self, is known as atman. According to the Upanishads:

> **This soul of mine within the heart is smaller than a grain of rice. . . . This soul of mine within the heart is greater than the earth, . . . greater than the sky. . . . This soul of mine within the heart, this is Brahman.**
>
> —*The Thirteen Principal Upanishads*

Although only priests were supposed to interpret the Vedas, Indians of all castes could read and study the Upanishads.

**The *Mahabharata* and the *Ramayana*** These new ideas also found their way into Hinduism's two great epic poems—the *Mahabharata* (muh HAH bahr AH tuh) and the *Ramayana* (rah mah YAH nuh). An **epic poem** is a long story of heroes and history told in verse. These stories helped explain Hindu religious ideas to all people. They also set standards for how people should live their lives as Hindus.

With 100,000 stanzas, or verses, the *Mahabharata* may be the world's longest poem. *Maha* means greatness; *barata* means victory or triumph. It tells the story of two related families at war. The best-loved section of the *Mahabharata* is the *Bhagavad-Gita* (BAH gah vahd GEET ah), or "Song of the Lord." It contains a conversation between the warrior Arjuna and the god Krishna. Arjuna tells Krishna that he cannot bring himself to spill the blood of his relatives. Krishna assures Arjuna that he cannot kill what never dies—a person's soul. The *Bhagavad-Gita* has played an important role in the lives of Hindus for many hundreds of years.

 **Checkpoint** **What beliefs from the Upanishads shaped the Hindu religion?**

**Looking Back and Ahead** In this section, you have read about the origins of one of the world's oldest religions. You also have learned how Brahmanism evolved into early Hinduism. You have read about the sacred texts, scriptures, and poems that helped shape Hindu ideas and practices. In the next section, you will read more about Hindu beliefs and ways of worship.

---

**Section 1 Check Your Progress**

**Progress Monitoring** Online
**For:** Self-test with instant help
**Visit:** PHSchool.com
**Web Code:** mwa-3071

 **Standards Review** H-SS: 6.5.3; E-LA: Reading 6.1.2

**Comprehension and Critical Thinking**

1. **(a) Recall** Describe the religion of ancient India.
   **(b) Apply Information** How were rituals important to the religion of ancient India?

2. **(a) Identify** What are the major Hindu religious texts?
   **(b) Link Past and Present** People in India today still enjoy the *Ramayana* and *Mahabharata*. What does this tell you about Hinduism?

**Reading Skill**

3. **Identify Figurative Language** Read the following sentence: These two beliefs lie at the heart of Hinduism. What is the figurative language in this sentence, and what does it mean?

**Vocabulary** *Builder*

4. Write two definitions for each of the following key terms: Brahman, guru, and epic poem. First, write a formal definition for your teacher. Second, write a definition in everyday English.

**Writing**

5. Create a Venn diagram that shows the similarities and differences between the two epic poems the *Mahabharata* and the *Ramayana*.

## Section 2 The Beliefs of Hinduism

**Standards Preview**

**H-SS 6.5.3** Explain the major beliefs and practices of Brahmanism in India and how they evolved into early Hinduism.

**E-LA Reading 6.1.2** Identify and interpret figurative language and words with multiple meanings.

### Reading Preview

 **Reading Skill**

**Interpret Figurative Language** Figurative language often suggests a comparison to help readers understand the writer's ideas. For example, the sentence "Hinduism is sometimes compared to a great river" compares a religion to a river. This means that Hinduism changes by absorbing ideas in the way that a river moves, *not* that Hinduism has fish in it or freezes in the winter.

**Vocabulary *Builder***

**High-Use Words**
**tradition** (truh DIHSH uhn), p. 196
**assign** (uh SīN), p. 197
**achieve** (uh CHEEV), p. 200

**Key Terms and People**
dharma (DAHR muh), p. 197
moksha (MAHK shuh), p. 197
reincarnation (ree ihn kahr NAY shuhn), p. 198
karma (KAHR muh), p. 199

**Vocabulary *Builder***
**tradition** (truh DIHSH uhn) *n.* a long-established custom or practice

**Main Idea**
For Hindus, the Four Goals of Life are pleasure, success, a moral life, and release from life.

**Background Knowledge** Hinduism is sometimes compared to a great river. Over thousands of years, many streams of beliefs, practices, and <u>traditions</u> have flowed into this great river. As a result, Indians may honor different gods and follow different rituals. But, as you will read, all Hindus share the same basic beliefs.

## The Four Goals of Life

Hindus believe that people are born wanting four basic things. All four goals are desirable, but not all people achieve all of these goals in a lifetime.

**Pleasure and Success** People begin their lives by wanting pleasure. This may be a simple pleasure such as eating, or it may be a deeper pleasure such as falling in love.

The second goal is success. Success may mean gaining fame, wealth, or power, or it may mean becoming important in the community in some way.

Hindus see nothing wrong with wanting these things. To desire pleasure and success is human nature. But as desirable as these goals are, over time, they may leave people feeling empty. By themselves, Hindus believe, pleasure and success do not bring true happiness.

**Dharma** The third goal is an ethical, moral life. Hindus call living a moral life **dharma.** What people must do to live such a life depends on their age and place in life. Dharma for a student will be different than dharma for a teacher. For a Hindu, dharma means fulfilling as well as possible the duties that are <u>assigned</u> to one's caste, or position in life.

These duties for Hindus are spelled out in great detail in a book called *The Laws of Manu.* The laws cover everything from what a person should eat or wear to how a person should conduct business. People who do not follow their proper *dharma* threaten the social order. In the *Bhagavad-Gita,* Krishna tells Arjuna that it is "better to do one's own duty imperfectly than to do another's well."

**Moksha** The last goal is **moksha,** or release from life. When this happens, a person's soul is united with the universal soul. Atman, one's soul, and Brahman become one.

For Hindus, to become one with God is the purpose of human life. A soul that has achieved moksha is free from want, fear, and pain. It lives forever in a state of joy.

E-LA 6.1.2 **Interpret Figurative Language**
Why is "leave people feeling empty" figurative language?

**Vocabulary** *Builder*
**assign** (uh SĪN) *v.* to set apart or mark for a specific purpose

**Krishna**
The painting *The Forest Fire* shows Krishna, in center, protecting the herdboys who raised him as a child. In Hindu legend, fire represents protection. **Critical Thinking: Distinguish Relevant Information** *What can you tell about Krishna from this painting? Explain.*

**Reincarnation** Hindus believe that few people can achieve moksha in one lifetime. Instead, they believe that when most people die, their souls live on to be reborn in another body. The rebirth of a soul in a new body is known as **reincarnation.**

Hinduism teaches that a person may be reborn as a human being of a higher or lower caste. The person may be reborn as an animal, or even as an insect. In the *Bhagavad-Gita*, Krishna explains reincarnation in this way:

> **❝As a man discards**
> **worn-out clothes**
> **to put on new**
> **and different ones,**
> **so the embodied self (soul)**
> **discards**
> **its worn-out bodies**
> **to take on other new ones.❞**
>
> —*Bhagavad-Gita*

**Chariot and Driver**

In this image from the *Bhagavad-Gita*, Krishna takes the form of a chariot driver for the warrior Arjuna, urging him to action during a battle. **Critical Thinking: Draw Inferences** *Why do you think Krisha is shown as a chariot driver in this and in many other Hindu illustrations?*

ⓐ **Driver** Krishna, symbolizing control of one's mind
ⓑ **Passenger** Arjuna the warrior
ⓒ **Horses** The horses symbolize the body's outer senses
ⓓ **Chariot** The chariot symbolizes one's body
ⓔ **Reins** The reins symbolize one's mind

**History** *Interactive*
Visit the Battlefield described in the *Bhagavad-Gita*
**Visit:** PHSchool.com
**Web Code:** mwp-3072

**The Law of Karma** How a person is reborn is determined by the law of karma. Karma is the sum of a person's actions and consequences, words, and thoughts. Hindus believe that bad karma—evil actions or thoughts—will bring rebirth in a lower form of life. Good karma brings rebirth in a higher caste or social class.

✔ **Checkpoint** Why are the four goals important for a Hindu?

## The Three Paths to God

Hinduism recognizes that people are different. The religion lays out three different paths to moksha, or becoming one with God. Hindus may try to follow just one or two of these paths, or they may try all three at once.

**The Way of Knowledge** Traditionally, the way of knowledge was chosen mainly by Brahmins. For one following the way of knowledge, moksha comes with a true understanding of atman and Brahman. Such understanding does not come easily. "Rare are the wise who shut their eyes to outside things," say the Upanishads, "and behold [see] the glory of the atman within."

**Main Idea**
For Hindus, the Three Paths to God are the way of knowledge, the way of works, and the way of devotion.

**Offerings to the Gods**
These Hindu women are offering flowers, food, and other gifts to their gods. The smaller image, above, is a floating shrine of flowers and candles. **Critical Thinking: Apply Information** *Why do Hindus offer items such as flowers and food to their gods?*

**Vocabulary** *Builder*
achieve (uh CHEEV) *v.* to do, or succeed in doing; accomplish

## The Way of Works

The way of works involves carrying out the religious rituals and duties that will improve one's karma. This has been the path chosen by most Hindus.

People who follow this path pay close attention to dharma, or the duties of their caste. They offer prayers and food to the gods at temple ceremonies or at informal ceremonies such as shown in the picture above. They do good deeds without expecting any reward. In the *Bhagavad-Gita,* Krishna praises "he who does the task dictated by duty, caring nothing for the fruit (reward) of the action."

## The Way of Devotion

The way of devotion is also known as the Path of Love. People on this path achieve moksha by devoting themselves to loving God. The *Bhagavad-Gita* suggests that the way of devotion is superior to the other ways. This is true partly because anyone, regardless of his or her position in life, can show devotion.

For most Hindus, loving God is easier when he is represented by one of India's many gods or goddesses. These lesser gods and goddesses have human forms and personalities. People can approach loving them much as they might love a parent, a child, or a friend.

The way of devotion takes many forms. People on this path may repeat their god's name all day long. They may present gifts to their god's temple. They may travel to sites sacred to their god. In all of these ways, Hindus try to move closer to God in their hearts.

 **Checkpoint** What are the three paths to God in Hinduism?

**Looking Back and Ahead** In this section, you have read about the basic beliefs of the Hindu religion. You have learned about the four goals of life for Hindus: pleasure, success, dharma, and moksha. You have also read about the three paths that Hindus can follow to become one with God: the way of knowledge, the way of works, and the way of devotion. In the next section, you will read about the spread and legacy of Hinduism.

# Section 2 Check Your Progress

**Progress Monitoring Online**
For: Self-test with instant help
Visit: PHSchool.com
Web Code: mwa-3072

**Standards Review** H-SS: 6.5.3; E-LA: Reading 6.1.2

## Comprehension and Critical Thinking

1. **(a) Explain** Discuss the Hindu belief in the cycle of life and rebirth.
   **(b) Analyze Cause and Effect** What determines a person's next reincarnation?

2. **(a) Explain** In the Hindu religion, what are the differences among the three paths to God?
   **(b) Evaluate Information** Explain Hinduism's four goals in life. How does each goal differ from the others?

## Reading Skill

3. **Interpret Figurative Language** Read the following sentence part: ". . . he who does the task dictated by duty, caring nothing for the fruit of the action." Explain the figurative use of the phrase *fruit of the action*. What is being compared

## Vocabulary *Builder*

Answer the following questions in complete sentences that show your understanding of the Key Terms.

4. How are dharma, moksha, and karma different from one another?

5. Explain the Hindu belief in reincarnation.

## Writing

6. Write three or four sentences explaining how Brahmanism is similar to Hinduism.

# How Ganesh Got His Elephant Head
retold by Madhur Jaffrey (1937–)

## Prepare to Read

### Standards Preview

**H-SS 6.5** Students analyze the geographic, political, economic, religious, and social structures of the early civilizations of India.

**Literary Response and Analysis 3.5** Identify the speaker and recognize the difference between first- and third-person narration (e.g. autobiography compared with biography).

### Reading Skill

**Narrator's Point of View** A narrator is the person who tells a story, either from a first-person or a third-person point of view. From a first-person point of view, the narrator uses the words *I* and *me* to refer to himself or herself. From a third-person point of view, the narrator uses *he, she, him, her, they,* and *them* to refer to the characters.

### Vocabulary *Builder*

As you read this literature selection, look for the following underlined words:

**pliable** (PLĪ uh buhl) *adj.* shapeable or moldable

**redeem** (rih DEEM) *v.* to make up for something or to make it less bad

> **BACKGROUND**
>
> The elephant-headed Hindu god Ganesh is known as the remover of obstacles and the god of knowledge. Parvati, his mother, is a goddess married to Shiva the Destroyer. One day, during one of Shiva's long absences, Parvati decides that she needs some company. She decides to make a baby boy.

**E-LA 3.5 Narrator's Point of View**

Is the narrator a character in this story?

. . . Parvati found some clay and water. She pounded the clay until it was soft and <u>pliable</u> and then she began to shape a baby. The first form she made looked too ordinary and not cuddly enough. So she began to add clay to its stomach until it was fat and round.

. . . She put the baby in the sun to dry. Soon it opened its eyes and began to smile. Parvati was overjoyed. She had found the perfect playmate.

Several years passed this way. One day, Parvati took her son for a long walk. They were both quite tired and when they came to a pool of water Parvati wanted to stop and bathe in it, but she felt shy about being seen by a passerby. So she said to her son, "Could you please be my guard? Don't let anyone come near the pool while I am bathing."

. . . Now, it so happened that Shiva had just finished dancing on a mountain top and was returning home. He heard some splashing in a pool and knew that it had to be his wife. He was about to walk towards the water when he found himself stopped by a fat little boy.

"Don't go any further," the boy ordered.

Shiva was not used to taking orders. He tried to brush the boy aside but the boy resisted and fought back. Shiva's anger began to mount. His throat became bluer and the veins in his forehead began to swell and throb. Suddenly, without warning, Shiva drew out a sword and cut off the boy's head.

Parvati, hearing a commotion, slipped into her clothes and rushed towards Ganesh. She let out a scream and fell sobbing to the ground.

Shiva watched in amazement. He realized that he had done something terrible but did not know what it was. He apologized, hoping that would calm his wife, and then asked her what he had done to upset her so. . . .

"You have murdered our child. . . ."

"Our child?" asked Shiva. This was the first he had heard of a child.

"You said that I had killed our child. But we have no child!"

"Of course we have," Parvati said. "We have a child because I made one. I made one because I was lonely. . . . Of course we have a child. I should say that . . . . we . . . . *had* . . . . a child."

The pieces in the puzzle suddenly locked into place. Shiva was so sorry that he begged his wife to tell him what he could do to <u>redeem</u> himself.

Parvati said, "Go out into the forest with your mighty sword. I want you to cut off the head of the first living creature you see and bring it back. Fit the head on our child and give it life. That is what I want. If you do not do this for me, I will never speak to you again."

Even though Shiva's work took him away for long periods, he did love his wife and did not want to lose her. So he did as he was told. He went into the forest with his mighty sword, looking for a living creature.

Well, the first living creature he saw was an elephant. Shiva cut off its head and dutifully brought it home. He fitted the head on to the child's body, breathing life into it as he did so, and waited for his wife's reaction.

To his surprise, Parvati was enchanted. She stroked the child's trunk and declared that this boy was even better than her first creation.

Shiva sighed with relief. By now, he was beginning to get very fond of the child himself. . . .

—From *Seasons of Splendour* by Madhur Jaffrey.
© Atheneum, New York, 1985.

The elephant-headed god Ganesh

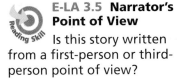

**E-LA 3.5 Narrator's Point of View**

Is this story written from a first-person or third-person point of view?

If you liked this story about Ganesh (also called Ganesha), you might want to read another book about the elephant-headed Hindu god: *The Broken Tusk: Stories of the Hindu God Ganesha,* by Uma Krishnaswami. *Linnet Books, 1996.*

## Analyze LITERATURE

Rewrite one or more paragraphs in the story from a first-person point of view. First, pick the story character you want to be. Then, choose the passage you want to rewrite. Remember to use the words *I* and *me* in your writing.

### Standards Preview

**H-SS 6.5.3** Explain the major beliefs and practices of Brahmanism in India and how they evolved into early Hinduism.

**H-SS 6.5.7** Discuss important aesthetic and intellectual traditions (e.g., Sanskrit literature, including the *Bhagavad-Gita;* medicine, metallurgy; and mathematics, including Hindu-Arabic numerals and the zero).

**E-LA Reading 6.1.2** Identify and interpret figurative language and words with multiple meanings.

## Reading Preview

 **Reading Skill**

**Interpret Words With Multiple Meanings** Some words have several unrelated meanings. Recognizing the correct meaning helps you read the text accurately. The words and sentences around words with multiple meanings can usually tell you which definition applies.

**Vocabulary *Builder***

**High-Use Words**
absorb (ab SOHRB), p. 204
migrate (MĪ grayt), p. 206

**Key Terms**
ethnic group (EHTH nihk GROOP), p. 204
shrine (SHRĪN), p. 205
sect (sehkt), p. 205
pilgrim (PIHL grihm), p. 208

**Background Knowledge** Hinduism is the major religion of India. Hindus now live and worship in many places outside India as well. In this section, you will read more about Hinduism's growth and its legacy to our world today.

**Main Idea**
Hinduism has spread to countries throughout the world.

## How Hinduism Spread

The Indian subcontinent is a vast region. Its people belong to many different ethnic groups. An **ethnic group** is a group of people who share a distinctive culture and a sense of identity. Long ago, each of these ethnic groups had its own language, rulers, and religion. Despite these differences, most Indians became Hindus.

**The Growth of Hinduism in India** Several factors aided the growth of Hinduism in India. One was Hinduism's flexibility, or ability to adapt. Hinduism did not ask people to give up their old gods or ways of worship. Instead, these gods and traditions simply were <u>absorbed</u> into Hinduism.

**Vocabulary *Builder***
<u>absorb</u> (ab SOHRB) *v.* to take in and incorporate

Hinduism was flexible in another way. Hindus did not form organized groups to worship together. They prayed and made offerings to the gods at shrines in their homes or at a local temple. A shrine is a place of worship that is often dedicated to a sacred object or person. So, no matter where Indians went, they could easily carry their religion with them.

**Hindu Sects** As Hinduism spread, different sects developed in India. A sect is a smaller religious group that has broken away from a larger established religion. Most sects centered around one special god.

Three Hindu sects attracted large numbers of followers. One was made up of those who worshiped the god Vishnu. A second popular sect grew up around the god Shiva. A third major sect was devoted to the goddess Shakti. She was worshiped as the Supreme Mother of the Universe.

**E-LA 6.1.2 Interpret Words With Multiple Meanings**

What are two meanings for the word *form*? Which applies here?

**Three Hindu Gods**
**Vishnu,** far left, is the Preserver, or Protector. **Shiva,** center, is the powerful Hindu god known as both the Destroyer and the Restorer. **Brahma,** far right, is the Creator. **Critical Thinking: Apply Information** *Why do you think these Hindu gods have many qualities that humans have?*

**Vocabulary** *Builder*

<u>migrate</u> (MĪ grayt) *v.* to move
from one place to another; to
change location

**Hinduism in Other Parts of Asia** Over time, Hinduism spread to other lands around the globe. In the first century A.D., Indian merchants set up trading posts throughout Southeast Asia. Wherever they settled, Hindu priests traveled with them. These traveling traders and priests introduced Hinduism to the present-day country of Vietnam and the island nations of present-day Borneo and Bali. Today, those islands are part of Indonesia.

<u>Migrating</u> people from northern India took Hinduism into the mountain kingdom of Nepal. Hindu kings have ruled Nepal for hundreds of years. Today, 90 percent of Nepal's population is Hindu, making Nepal the country with the world's second-largest Hindu population.

Sri Lanka, the island at the southern tip of India, also has a large Hindu community today. That island nation is home to more than two million Hindus. Wherever Hinduism spread in Asia, it took on traditions from the local culture. At the same time, the religion remained Indian in spirit.

**Worldwide Hindu Communities** In more recent times, Hinduism has continued to spread around the world. Today Hindus live in some 150 countries. In most cases, they or their ancestors originally came from India. In the 1800s, many Indians migrated to Caribbean islands to work. As a result, about one fourth of the people living on the Caribbean islands of Trinidad and Tobago practice the Hindu religion.

In the past 50 years, large numbers of Hindus have migrated to Great Britain, the United States, and Canada. More than a million Hindus now live in the United States. Today, Hinduism is the fifth-largest religion in the United States.

✔**Checkpoint** **Besides India, in what other countries do Hindus live?**

# The Legacy of Hinduism

**Main Idea**
Hinduism has influenced
India's religious, intellectual,
and artistic traditions.

Hinduism today is the world's third-largest religion. More than 800 million people worldwide follow this faith. However, India remains the spiritual and cultural center of Hinduism.

**Religious Traditions** Over thousands of years, Hinduism has shaped Indian life. Placing flowers or food at a shrine is a daily ritual in millions of Indian homes. The whole country takes part in Hindu religious festivals throughout the year.

# Hinduism in the World Today

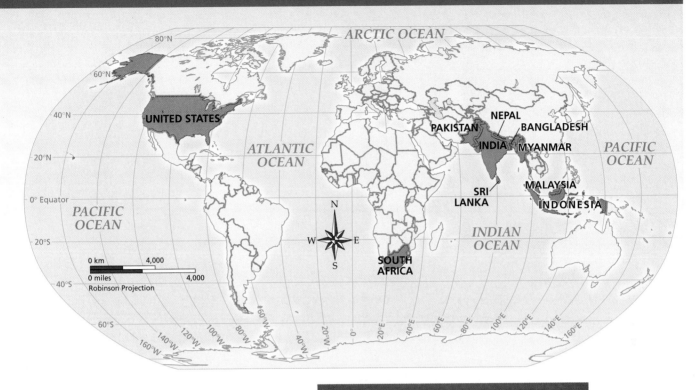

## Hindu Populations

The chart at right shows the estimated numbers of Hindus in countries with the largest Hindu populations today. These countries are also shown on the map above.

### World's Largest Hindu Populations

| Country | Estimated Population (2000) |
|---|---|
| India | 755,135,000 |
| Nepal | 18,354,000 |
| Bangladesh | 15,995,000 |
| Indonesia | 7,259,000 |
| Sri Lanka | 2,124,000 |
| Pakistan | 1,868,000 |
| Malaysia | 1,630,000 |
| United States | 1,032,000 |
| South Africa | 959,000 |
| Myanmar | 893,000 |

Source: David B. Barrett and Todd M. Johnson, *World Christian Trends*, William Carey Library, 2001

## MAP★MASTER
### Skills Activity

The Hindu religion began in India. Shown here are the ten countries in the world that have the largest numbers of Hindus.

**(a) Location** Which country in the southern hemisphere has one of the highest numbers of Hindus today?

**(b) Draw Inferences** Why do you think the countries with the largest Hindu populations are closest to India?

**MapMaster ⬤nline**

**For:** Interactive map
**Visit:** PHSchool.com
**Web Code:** mwp-3073

**The Ganges River**
Hindus from all over the world make a pilgrimage, or special trip for the purpose of devotion, to the Ganges River. The river's waters are sacred to the Hindu religion. **Critical Thinking: Draw Conclusions** *Why do you think Hindus feel the Ganges River is a sacred place?*

Most Indians believe that they live among holy places. Many rivers, mountains, rocks, and forests are connected with legends of gods and gurus. That may be one reason that Hinduism remains so closely connected to its Indian homeland.

The mighty Ganges River is one of India's holiest sites. Every year, hundreds of thousands of pilgrims flock to the banks of the Ganges to bathe in its waters. A pilgrim is someone who travels to a shrine or sacred place. Some pilgrims believe that the waters of the Ganges will wash away bad karma. Others come hoping that the river's waters will cure a disease or disability.

## Intellectual Traditions
Hinduism also shaped India's intellectual traditions. Thinkers in ancient India asked questions about life and death that still concern Hindus today.

Because the early Hindu texts were written in Sanskrit, that language became India's first language of learning. Long after Sanskrit ceased being used as a spoken language, Indian scholars continued to read and write in this ancient language.

**Aesthetic Traditions** Hinduism shaped India's aesthetic, or artistic, traditions as well. The religion inspired India's first great works of literature. Today, people all over the world still read the *Mahabharata* and the *Ramayana*. In India, stories from these epic poems are retold in comic books and movies.

In addition, Hinduism encouraged the development of the arts. Hindu temples are designed around religious ideas. Detailed carvings of gods and goddesses decorate temple walls. Hindu temples are centers of art, music, and dance as well as places of worship. For someone practicing the Hindu religion, the act of creating something beautiful is a form of worship.

 **Checkpoint** How has Hinduism influenced India's intellectual traditions?

**Looking Back and Ahead** In this section, you have read about the spread of Hinduism around the world and have learned which countries today have large Hindu populations. You have learned how Hinduism shaped life and culture in India. In the next chapter, you will learn about the second major religion to come out of India, Buddhism.

---

**Section 3 Check Your Progress**

**Progress Monitoring** Online
**For:** Self-test with instant help
**Visit:** PHSchool.com
**Web Code:** mwa-3073

 **Standards Review** H-SS: 6.5.3; 6.5.7; E-LA: Reading 6.1.2

**Comprehension and Critical Thinking**

**1. (a) Recall** Where in Asia did Hinduism spread from India?
**(b) Apply Information** Why has Hinduism remained centered in India?

**2. (a) Identify** Which three Hindu sects have attracted large numbers of followers?
**(b) Draw Conclusions** Why is it possible to have different sects in Hinduism?

**Reading Skill**

**3. Interpret Words With Multiple Meanings** Read the following sentence: "Many rivers, mountains, rocks, and forests are connected with legends. . . ." Which word has two meanings? Explain.

**Vocabulary** *Builder*
Read each sentence below. If the sentence is true, write YES. If the sentence is not true, write NO and explain WHY.

**4.** Ethnic groups are small religious groups that have branched off from a larger established religion.

**5.** A sect is a group of people who share a distinct culture and sense of identity.

**6.** A pilgrim is someone who travels to a shrine or sacred place.

**Writing**

**7.** Write three sentences about the influence that Hinduism has had on the life and culture of the people of India in the past compared with people in India today. Use signal and transition words such as *and, or, similarly, different, on the one hand, on the other hand, less,* or *more.*

# Analysis Skills

# Analyze Graphic Data: Circle Graphs

Graphs show numerical facts in picture form. Circle graphs show percentages, or parts of a whole. They show how different things compare with one another. Analyzing circle graphs helps you understand facts about the world and its people.

**Chapter Standards**

**History-Social Science**

**Research, Evidence, and Point of View 4** Students assess the credibility of primary and secondary sources and draw sound conclusions from them.

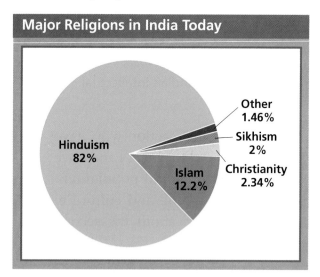

**Major Religions in India Today**

Hinduism 82%

Islam 12.2%

Christianity 2.34%

Sikhism 2%

Other 1.46%

**Learn the Skill** *Follow these steps to analyze circle graphs.*

1. **Read the title to see what type of information the graph provides.** This circle graph uses percentages to show the major religions practiced in India today.

2. **Read the labels.** Each section of the graph is sized and labeled to show the percentage of people who practice each religion.

3. **Look for similarities and differences.** Obviously, Hinduism is practiced by more people than any other religion in India.

4. **Draw a conclusion about what the graph shows.** This graph shows that most of India's people are Hindus. It shows that there are quite a few Muslims and that Christianity and Sikhism have smaller followings.

**Practice the Skill** *Use the circle graph on page 213 to practice the steps you have just learned.*

1. **Read the title to see what type of information the graph provides.** What is the graph's title? What time period does it cover?

2. **Read the labels.** What religions are included? What two groups does the "Other" category include?

3. **Look for similarities and differences.** What percentage of people are Christians? Islam? Hindus?

4. **Draw a conclusion about what the graph shows.** What conclusion can you make about the graph?

**Apply the Skill**

*See page 213 of the Review and Assessment.*

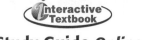
**Study Guide** *Online*
Complete your Chapter 7 study guide in print or online.

## Chapter Summary  H-SS: 6.5.3, 6.5.7

### Section 1 The Origins of Hinduism

- Hinduism evolved from Brahmanism into the major religion of India.
- The religion continues to change over time.

### Section 2 The Beliefs of Hinduism

- The four main goals that Hindus want to achieve during their lifetimes are pleasure, success, an ethical and moral life, and release from life.
- Hindus believe that there are three different paths to becoming one with God: the way of knowledge, the way of works, and the way of devotion.

### Section 3 The Spread of Hinduism

- Today, Hinduism is the third-largest religion in the world.
- Hinduism has spread to many places outside India, including the United States.

**An image from the *Bhagavad-Gita***

## Standards Practice  H-SS: 6.5.3; 6.5.7

## Vocabulary *Builder*

### High-Use Words

Read each sentence below. If the sentence is true, write YES. If the sentence is not true, write NO and explain WHY.

1. The Vedas are new Hindu **texts** that **involve** rituals to make the gods worry about life on Earth.

2. Many **traditions**, such as **assigning** animal characteristics to their gods, form the Hindu religion.

3. The Hindu religion **achieved** great growth around the world.

4. Hinduism did not spread to other countries because it did not **absorb** other ways of worship.

5. Hindu pilgrims **migrate** to the Ganges River to bathe in its sacred waters.

### Key Terms

Answer the following questions in complete sentences that show your understanding of the Key Terms.

1. How did Hinduism evolve from Brahmanism?

2. What does a guru do?

3. Did a Brahman write epic poems? Explain.

4. How can a person achieve dharma in his or her life?

5. How is the law of karma linked to reincarnation?

6. What would you expect to see at a Hindu shrine?

## Apply Reading Skills

**Figurative Language and Words With Multiple Meanings** Write a short paragraph. Use figurative language at least once. Include one of these words with multiple meanings: *rocks, banks, ruled, form.* Make sure that the word's meaning is clear from the context.

## Comprehension and Critical Thinking

**1. (a) Explain** In Hinduism, who or what is Brahman?
**(b) Understand Sequence** What changes in worship took place as Brahmanism became Hinduism?

**2. (a) Identify** Name three main Hindu gods.
**(b) Apply Information** How does the following statement describe the goal of Hindu beliefs? "God is one, but wise people know it by many names."

**3. (a) List** List the countries in which Hinduism spread.
**(b) Draw Conclusions** Although Hinduism spread, why is it still most associated with India?

## Researching

**Hindu Gods** The followers of Hinduism believe in and worship many different gods for many different reasons. Use the library, the Internet, or other research sources to report on one of the gods in the Hindu religion. Share your work with the class on "Hinduism" day. Make a list of the resources you used to go with your presentation.

**Historian:** Write several paragraphs about the role of a god in Hinduism. Focus your writing on the role the god has served to Hindus throughout history.

**Musician:** Compose a song in honor of one of the Hindu gods. Include the meaning that the god has for Hindus.

> **Researching Online**
> **For:** Help in starting this activity
> **Visit:** PHSchool.com
> **Web Code:** mwe-3074

## Writing

**1. Write a paragraph on the following topic.** At one time, Brahmanism and Hinduism were very closely related to each other. Explain how Hinduism evolved from early Brahmanism. Describe what has remained from the Brahmanism religion and what has changed.
**Your essay should:**
• use supporting details about both Brahmanism and Hinduism.
• include a strong conclusion stating the most significant similarities and differences as Hinduism evolved from Brahmanism.
• revise for style, grammar, and clarity.

**2. Write a short narrative.** Describe in a short narrative a conversation that may have taken place in the *Bhagavad-Gita* between Krishna and Arjuna.

## Apply Analysis Skills

Use the circle graph at right to answer these questions.

1. Which religion has the most followers today?

2. Which religion has the fewest followers today?

3. Which religion has more followers today than Judaism, but fewer than Buddhism?

4. What is the percentage of followers of Hinduism today compared with the other religions shown on the graph?

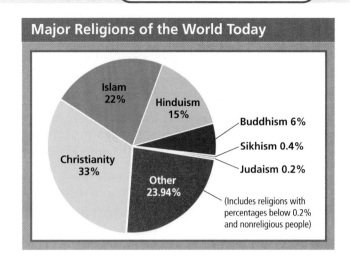

**Major Religions of the World Today**

Islam 22%
Hinduism 15%
Buddhism 6%
Sikhism 0.4%
Judaism 0.2%
Christianity 33%
Other 23.94%
(Includes religions with percentages below 0.2% and nonreligious people)

## Test Yourself

1. **Which idea originated in Brahmanism?**
   A Only Brahmins could be priests.
   B One can be reincarnated as an animal.
   C There is one God known as Brahma.
   D Every person is born with a soul.

2. **In Hinduism, living a moral and ethical life is called following one's**
   A karma.
   B dharma.
   C moksha.
   D pleasures.

**Refer to the image below to answer Question 3.**

3. **These Hindu women are expressing their religious devotion**

   A in temple.
   B in public.
   C at home.
   D at a private shrine.

4. **Identify Hinduism's two great epic poems.**
   A Torah and Talmud
   B Vedas and Upanishads
   C *Mahabharata* and *Ramayana*
   D *Bhagavad-Gita* and *The Laws of Manu*

5. **The Hindu scriptures are written in ancient**
   A Arabic.
   B Hebrew.
   C Sanskrit.
   D Sumerian.

**Refer to the chart below to answer Question 6.**

6. **Which two countries have the closest number of Hindus today?**

**World's Largest Hindu Populations**

| Country | Est. Population (2000) |
|---------|------------------------|
| India | 755,135,000 |
| Nepal | 18,354,000 |
| Bangladesh | 15,995,000 |
| Indonesia | 7,259,000 |
| Sri Lanka | 2,124,000 |

   A India and Nepal
   B Nepal and Bangladesh
   C Bangladesh and Indonesia
   D Indonesia and Sri Lanka

### Chapter 8

# The Development of Buddhism (563 B.C. – A.D. 200)

## Prepare to Read

### Chapter Standards

**History-Social Science**

**6.5** Students analyze the geographic, political, economic, religious, and social structures of the early civilizations of India.

**Section 1,** pp. 218–222

**What You Will Learn**

### The Origins of Buddhism

Siddhartha Gautama was a prince who was shocked by the suffering that people experience. His search for truth led to his enlightenment, and he became known as the Buddha.

**Section 2,** pp. 223–227

### The Beliefs of Buddhism

Through his teachings, the Buddha shared with others the understanding he had gained. His teachings formed the basis of the Buddhist religion.

**Section 3,** pp. 230–235

### The Spread of Buddhism

Missionaries carried the Buddha's teachings throughout Asia, and two groups developed that interpret the teachings differently. Buddhism has influenced teachings, literature, architecture, and art in many countries.

Prayer wheel

**About 563 B.C.**
Siddhartha Gautama, founder of Buddhism, is born.

**Chapter Events**

**Other Events**

| 600 B.C. | 400 B.C. | 200 B.C. |
|---|---|---|

**About 587 B.C.** Nebuchadnezzar destroys Jerusalem.

**221 B.C.** Qin forces unite north China.

## Where and When?
Buddhism arose in northern India about 2,500 years ago and later spread to other parts of the world.

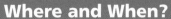

Traditionally, images of the Buddha lying down show his achievement of inner peace.

**About 43 B.C.**
The first Buddhist scriptures are collected in writing.

**A.D. 100s**
Mahayana Buddhism appears as a major school of Buddhism.

**200 B.C.**

**B.C./A.D.**

**A.D. 200**

**About 100 B.C.**
Ancient Romans adopt the Greek alphabet.

**A.D. 70** Romans destroy the Second Temple in Jerusalem.

## History Reading Skill

*Previewing* **Clarify, Connect, and Relate Main Ideas**

Social studies text often includes information and ideas from other sources. These may be included in the instructions or presented as an excerpt or a quotation. You can extend your understanding of key social studies ideas by looking at how the instruction text connects with the text from other sources. Then look at how the ideas work together with ideas from other chapters to build a big idea.

 **Chapter Standards**

**English-Language Arts**

**Reading 6.2.3** Connect and clarify main ideas by identifying their relationships to other sources and related topics.

> This is the main idea. You can connect this to earlier reading in Chapter 7 about Hinduism.

> Information related to the main idea

In truth, <u>all this universe is Brahman. All things come from Him, all things become Him, and all things are kept alive by Him</u>. . . . On Him should one meditate in peace. . . .

He, who enters the mind, . . . who is free from anxiety and eagerness, this Soul of mine within the heart is smaller than a grain of rice, or a barley corn, or a mustard seed, or a grain of millet, or the kernel of a grain of millet. This Soul of mine within the heart is greater than the earth, greater than the atmosphere, higher than the sky, surrounds all of heaven and earth. . . .

> How does the main idea of this paragraph connect to the main idea of the first paragraph?

<u>He is the Soul of mine</u> residing in my heart; <u>He is Brahman.</u> On leaving this place I shall achieve His being. Only one who is steady in this faith will achieve the result.

— *Chandogya Upanishad*, III, 14, 3-4

> In Chapter 7, you read about Hinduism, the first major religion to take root in ancient India. A second major religion known as Buddhism also started in India. As you read Chapter 8, look for other connections between Hinduism and Buddhism.

# Vocabulary *Builder*

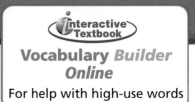

**i**nteractive
**T**extbook
**Vocabulary** *Builder*
*Online*
For help with high-use words

## *Previewing* High-Use Academic Words

| High-Use Word | Definition | Sample Sentence About History |
|---|---|---|
| **luxury** (LUHK shuh ree) (Section 1, p. 219) | *n.* something expensive that you want but do not need | Egyptian nobles could afford such luxuries as precious stones and perfumes. |
| **cycle** (SĪ kuhl) (Section 1, p. 220) | *n.* related events that happen again and again in the same order | Hinduism and Buddhism include a belief in a continuous cycle of birth, death, and rebirth. |
| **saint** (saynt) (Section 1, p. 221) | *n.* someone who is very good, kind, or patient | People regarded the religious leader as a saint. |
| **aware** (uh WEHR) (Section 2, p. 225) | *adj.* realizing that something is true, exists, or is happening | The Maya had no contact with China, so they were not aware of Chinese civilization. |
| **previous** (PREE vee uhs) (Section 2, p. 227) | *adj.* happening or existing before a particular event, time, or thing | Today, people use alphabets to write, but pictographs were a previous form of writing. |
| **welfare** (WEHL fair) (Section 3, p. 230) | *n.* health, comfort, or happiness | Jacob was concerned with his family's welfare, so he moved them to Egypt, where food was more plentiful. |
| **appealing** (uh PEEL ihng) (Section 3, p. 235) | *adj.* attractive or interesting | River valleys offered an appealing location for settlement because of plentiful water and rich soil. |

## *Previewing* Key Terms and People

**A Buddhist nun**

Buddhism, p. 218
Siddhartha Gautama, p. 218
salvation, p. 220
ascetic, p. 220

meditate, p. 220
enlightenment, p. 221
nirvana, p. 226
monastery, p. 226

monk, p. 226
nun, p. 226
Asoka, p. 231
missionary, p. 231

virtue, p. 232
compassion, p. 232
*bodhisattva*, p. 233

**Siddhartha Gautama**

# 1 The Origins of Buddhism

**Standards Preview**

**H-SS 6.5.5** Know the life and moral teachings of the Buddha and how Buddhism spread in India, Ceylon, and Central Asia.

**E-LA Reading 6.2.3** Connect and clarify main ideas by identifying their relationships to other sources and related topics.

## Reading Preview

 **Reading Skill**

**Clarify Main Ideas** This chapter includes many quotations from the texts of religions that it discusses. Connect those quotations to the chapter text to better understand the religious beliefs discussed. Ask yourself: How does this quotation relate to the beliefs discussed in the main text? Is it a description of the beliefs?

**Vocabulary** *Builder*

**High-Use Words**
**luxury** (LUHK shuh ree), p. 219
**cycle** (SĪ kuhl), p. 220
**saint** (saynt), p. 221

**Key Terms and People**
Buddhism (BOO dihz uhm), p. 218
Siddhartha Gautama (sihd DAHR tuh GOW tuh muh), p. 218
salvation (sal VAY shuhn), p. 220
ascetic (uh SEHT ihk), p. 220
meditate (MEHD uh tayt), p. 220
enlightenment (ehn LĪT n muhnt), p. 221

**Background Knowledge**   In Chapter 7, you read about Hinduism, the first major world religion to take root in ancient India. A second major religion known as Buddhism also has its roots in India. **Buddhism is a religion based on the teachings of Siddhartha Gautama, an Indian spiritual leader.** In this chapter, you will read about Siddhartha's life and learn about his founding of Buddhism.

**Main Idea**
The Buddha gives up a life of wealth to search for truth and gain spiritual wisdom.

## The Life of the Buddha

The story of the Buddha begins like a fairy tale. He was born a prince named Siddhartha Gautama around 563 B.C. His father ruled a kingdom in what is now Nepal, a country north of India. According to legend, a fortuneteller predicted two possible futures for the young prince. Siddhartha could become a mighty king who would unite all of India, or he could become a religious leader. Siddhartha's father tried to guide his son toward becoming a king.

**The Protected Prince**   Siddhartha was raised in wealth and <u>luxury</u>. "I wore garments of silk," he recalled. "Night and day a white parasol [umbrella] was held over me so that I might not be touched by heat or cold, dust, leaves or dew."

As Siddhartha grew up, his father protected him from everything unpleasant. The prince never saw anyone who was poor, sad, or sick. When the prince rode out of the palace in his chariot, guards traveled ahead of him. They made sure that there were no beggars or sick people on the streets.

As a young man, Siddhartha married, and the entire court celebrated. He and his wife had a son. It seemed that the prince had just about everything a person could want.

**The Four Passing Sights**   Legends say that one day when Siddhartha was about 29, he rode out of the palace without any guards. Only his chariot driver was with him. During that ride, Siddhartha came upon the first of "the Four Passing Sights." He saw an old man leaning on a stick. During a second ride, Siddhartha saw a man shrunken by disease. During a third, the prince saw a man who had died. The man's family stood nearby, and all of them were crying.

Siddhartha was shocked and horrified. He had never seen such suffering and sadness before. His servant explained that people grow old, get sick, and die. The prince thought about what he had seen and realized that he, too, faced these hardships. Later, when Siddhartha told people about that moment, he said, "All the joy of life which there is in life died within me."

**Vocabulary** *Builder*
<u>luxury</u> (LUHK shuh ree) *n.*
something expensive that you want but do not need

**E-LA 6.2.3 Clarify Main Ideas**
*Reading Skill*
What is the main idea of this paragraph? What other source supports that idea?

**The Third Passing Sight**
Outside the palace, Prince Siddhartha Gautama sees a man who has died. **Critical Thinking: Evaluate Information** *Based on the picture, how do you know that the prince is surprised and shocked?*

A few days later, Siddhartha rode out of the palace again. He came upon the fourth sight, a wandering holy man. Although the holy man was homeless and possessed nothing, he seemed content. Siddhartha decided to search for the same serenity, or calmness, that the holy man exhibited. That night, he secretly left the palace and went into the forest. He cut off his hair and traded his rich clothes for the simple yellow robe of a religious seeker.

**The Search for Truth** The once-protected prince searched for the truth about life, suffering, and death. Siddhartha lived on the food that strangers placed in his begging bowl, his only possession. At night he slept in the shelter of a tree or in a cave.

Siddhartha began his search by studying with Hindu gurus. They taught him that life was an endless <u>cycle</u> of birth, death, and rebirth. The suffering that had so upset Siddhartha, they said, was part of that cycle. The gurus also taught that there was a path to **salvation, or escape,** from this endless cycle. But their approach to salvation did not satisfy Siddhartha.

**The Path of Self-Denial** Siddhartha's next step was to join a band of religious ascetics. **Ascetics are people who practice extreme self-denial as part of their religious life.** For Siddhartha, living as an ascetic meant denying himself all physical comforts. He wore scratchy clothes. He ceased bathing for long periods. He sat for days in one position while meditating. In Hinduism and Buddhism, to **meditate means to calm or empty the mind, often by focusing on a single object.**

Siddhartha also ate less and less until he was living each day on "a single grain of rice" and "one jujube fruit." He lost a great deal of weight. Later he described the effects on his body by saying, "If I sought to feel my belly, it was my backbone which I found in my grasp."

**Vocabulary** *Builder*
**cycle** (sī kuhl) *n.* related events that happen again and again in the same order

# BIOGRAPHY QUEST

## What kind of life did Mahavira live?

Mahavira

### Fast Facts

**Who:** Mahavira
**What:** Spiritual leader of Jainism
**When:** about 599 B.C.–527 B.C.
**Where:** India
**Why important:** After gaining spiritual knowledge, Mahavira organized the beliefs of Jainism and set up rules for monks.

### Fast Find

**How:** Go online to find out about Mahavira's life and the changes he made to Jainism.

**Biography** **Online**
**For:** More about Mahavira
**Visit:** PHSchool.com
**Web Code:** mwe-3081

After five years of self-denial, Siddhartha's body was very weak. He fainted. When he awoke, it was clear to him that this was not the path to truth. When a milkmaid offered him a bowl of milk and rice, he ate it with great enjoyment. The ascetics he lived with were outraged at Siddhartha's rejection of self-denial. As a result, the ascetics abandoned him.

**The Great Enlightenment** As his strength returned, Siddhartha renewed his search. One day he sat under a fig tree to meditate. Later this tree would come to be known as the Bodhi Tree, or the Tree of Knowledge. "Even if my blood should run dry," Siddhartha told himself, "I will not leave this seat until truth has been realized!"

Siddhartha meditated there for 49 days. Legends say that he was visited by Mara, the god of desire and death. Mara tried to tempt him to give up his search by offering wealth and other desirable things. When that failed, Mara attacked Siddhartha with rains and showers of rocks.

Siddhartha went deeper into meditation and saw his past lives. He understood the cycle of birth, death, and rebirth. Then he became aware that he had escaped that which tied him to the world. He entered a new life free of desire and suffering. He had achieved **enlightenment**—a state of perfect wisdom, and become the Buddha, which means "the Enlightened One."

 **Checkpoint** How did Siddhartha give up his life of wealth?

# Awakening the World

The Buddha had freed himself from the cycle of rebirth and suffering. But instead of enjoying his own liberation, he chose to go back into the world to teach others what he had learned.

For the next 45 years, the Buddha traveled across India, preaching a message of truth and hope. As he traveled and taught, he answered the questions people asked. They often asked him what he was.

"Are you a god?" people asked.

"No," answered the Buddha.

"Are you an angel?"

The answer was "No."

"Are you a saint?"

Again the Buddha replied, "No."

"Then what are you?"

The Buddha answered, "I am awake."

**Under the Bodhi Tree**
Siddhartha Gautama sat under the Bodhi Tree until he gained enlightenment. **Critical Thinking: Distinguish Facts from Opinions** *Do you think that this is a factual representation of the event? Why or why not?*

**Main Idea**
The Buddha taught others how to achieve freedom from suffering and rebirth.

**Vocabulary** *Builder*
saint (saynt) *n.* someone who is very good, kind, or patient

The Buddha's purpose was to awaken the world to the true nature of life. Only with that understanding could people finally escape the endless cycle of suffering and rebirth. The Buddha continued to travel and teach. He attracted many followers, and he trained some of them to become teachers. He died at about age 80. His dying words to his followers were these:

> **This is my last advice to you. All . . . things in the world are changeable. They are not lasting. Work hard to gain your own salvation.**
>
> —Reverend Siridhamma, *Life of the Buddha*

**Prayer Wheel from Tibet**
This hand-held wheel contains a prayer that appears as the wheel is turned. The wheel symbolizes the Buddha's teachings, which are known as "the wheel of the dharma."
**Critical Thinking: Apply Information** *What are some other types of objects that people use to symbolize religious teachings?*

 **Checkpoint** How did the Buddha share what he had learned?

**Looking Back and Ahead** In this section, you have learned about the life of Siddhartha Gautama, the founder of Buddhism. You learned how he devoted his life to teaching others what he had learned about life. In the next section, you will read more about the basic teachings of the Buddha.

## Section 1 Check Your Progress

**Progress Monitoring** Online
**For:** Self-test with instant help
**Visit:** PHSchool.com
**Web Code:** mwa-3081

**Standards Review** H-SS: 6.5.5; E-LA: Reading 6.2.3

**Comprehension and Critical Thinking**

1. **(a) Recall** What four sights changed Siddhartha's life?
   **(b) Compare** How was his life as an ascetic different from his life as a prince?

2. **(a) Describe** What happened to Siddhartha under the Bodhi Tree?
   **(b) Draw Conclusions** Why would people from distant lands travel to hear the Buddha speak?

**Reading Skill**

3. **Clarify Main Ideas** Read the first paragraph of the text entitled The Great Enlightenment on page 221. How does Siddhartha's statement clarify the main idea of the paragraph?

**Vocabulary** *Builder*

4. Write two definitions for each word: luxury, cycle, saint. First, write a formal definition for your teacher. Second, write a definition in everyday English for a classmate.

**Writing**

5. Write a brief explanation of some of the similarities and differences that exist between the origins of Hinduism and Buddhism. You may choose to present this information in a Venn diagram.

# 2 The Beliefs of Buddhism

**H-SS 6.5.5** Know the life and moral teachings of the Buddha and how Buddhism spread in India, Ceylon, and Central Asia.

**E-LA Reading 6.2.3** Clarify and connect main ideas by identifying their relationships to other sources and related topics.

## Reading Preview

 **Reading Skill**

**Connect Main Ideas** Some passages have several ideas in them. You must determine which is the most important, or main, idea. For example, Section 2 of this chapter is divided into smaller sections and subsections. Each subsection has a main idea that relates to the section's main idea and to the larger main idea of Section 2.

**Vocabulary** *Builder*

**High-Use Words**
<u>aware</u> (uh WEHR), p. 225
<u>previous</u> (PREE vee uhs), p. 227

**Key Terms and People**
nirvana (nihr VAH nuh), p. 226
monastery (MAHN uh stehr ee), p. 226
monk (muhngk), p. 226
nun (nuhn), p. 226

**Background Knowledge** In his search for enlightenment, the Buddha studied the teachings of Hinduism. He accepted the ideas of reincarnation, the cycle of life, and the law of karma.

From there, however, the Buddha moved away from Hindu ideas. He did not believe in Brahman as the supreme God of the universe. He questioned the idea of atman, or that each person has a soul that survives death. He also rejected the caste system. In his view, the good and bad actions of people were more important than their caste. In this section, you will read about the teachings of the Buddha and the religion he founded. You will also learn about the people who chose to follow the Buddha and the development of early Buddhist texts.

## The Buddha's Teachings

When Siddhartha Gautama gained enlightenment, he had a flash of insight, or understanding. He understood why people suffer. He also saw how people could escape the endless cycle of death and rebirth. These insights formed the basis of his teachings.

**Main Idea**
The teachings of the Buddha, which include some ideas from Hinduism, form the basis of Buddhism.

**The Middle Way** The Buddha began his teaching with the ascetics who had abandoned him earlier. He met them in a deer park, or a hunting ground for deer, near the city of Benares. "Here comes the ascetic Gautama, he who eats rich food," they said on seeing the Buddha. "Let us show him no respect, nor rise to see him." But his face shone with such joy that they could not help but welcome him.

The Buddha then gave what is called the Deer Park Sermon. He told the ascetics that they should avoid two extremes in seeking wisdom. One extreme was "a life given to pleasures." The other was a life of painful self-denial. The Buddha explained that he had not gained understanding while living as a wealthy prince or while practicing self-denial. Instead, he advised them to follow a Middle Way. "To keep the body in good health is a duty," the Buddha said. "For otherwise we shall not be able to . . . keep our minds strong and clear."

**The Four Noble Truths** The Buddha continued his Deer Park Sermon by describing the Four Noble Truths that he had learned while sitting under the Bodhi Tree.

The First Noble Truth is that all life includes suffering. Birth, sickness, old age, and death bring suffering. People also suffer from being separated from the people they love.

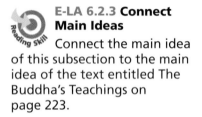

**E-LA 6.2.3 Connect Main Ideas** Connect the main idea of this subsection to the main idea of the text entitled The Buddha's Teachings on page 223.

**Deer Park Sermon**
Buddha teaches the ascetics in Deer Park.
**Critical Thinking: Detect Points of View** *Based on this picture, how do the ascetics feel about the Buddha?*

The Second Noble Truth is that suffering is caused by wanting or desiring things that one does not have. The Buddha did not preach that all desires were bad. For example, it is not wrong to desire the happiness of others, but selfish desires lead to suffering.

The Third Noble Truth is that suffering can be ended. Its cure is to overcome selfish desires and wants.

The Fourth Noble Truth is that the way to overcome selfish desires is to follow the Eightfold Path.

**The Eightfold Path**   The Eightfold Path describes a way of life that leads to the end of desire. The first steps on this path are not hard to carry out in everyday life. The later ones involve becoming <u>aware</u> of one's thoughts and feelings, and require more effort. The Buddha taught that this path was open to anyone, no matter what caste the person was born into.

**Vocabulary** *Builder*
<u>aware</u> (uh WEHR) *adj.* realizing that something is true, exists, or is happening

## The Eightfold Path

| The first two steps involve preparing one's mind for a new way of life. | |
|---|---|
| **1. Right Belief** | The first step is belief in and understanding of the Four Noble Truths. |
| **2. Right Purpose** | The second step is to make spiritual growth the purpose of one's life. |

| The next three steps involve taking charge of one's behavior. | |
|---|---|
| **3. Right Speech** | The third task is to become aware of what one says. This means avoiding lies or statements that hurt others. |
| **4. Right Conduct** | The next task is to understand one's behavior and work to improve it. Right conduct means not killing, stealing, lying, or hurting others. |
| **5. Right Livelihood** | This involves choosing a livelihood, or profession, that supports one's spiritual growth. A person should earn a living in a way that does not harm other living things. |

| The last three steps help train the mind to gain enlightenment. | |
|---|---|
| **6. Right Effort** | The sixth step involves making an effort to avoid bad thoughts and to hold only good thoughts in one's mind. |
| **7. Right Mindfulness** | Being mindful means becoming aware of what one thinks and feels. A person who has achieved right mindfulness controls his or her thoughts and emotions rather than being controlled by them. |
| **8. Right Meditation** | The last step is to practice the kind of meditation that can lead to enlightenment. Those who complete this step often feel as if they have awakened from a dream to experience a new reality. |

**The Temple of Borobudur in Indonesia**
This temple is believed to represent the path to enlightenment. **Critical Thinking: Draw Conclusions** *Why do you think the pathway rises upward?*

**Main Idea**
Buddhists may learn about the Buddha's teachings by living in religious communities or by studying Buddhist scriptures.

**Reaching Nirvana**  The final goal of a person who follows the Eightfold Path is to reach nirvana. **Nirvana is a state of blissful peace without desire or suffering.** Those who enter nirvana are liberated from the cycle of death and rebirth. They are no longer subject to the law of karma. However, this does not mean that death occurs.

Buddhist art often depicts the Buddha in a state of nirvana. In the picture on Page 221, for example, the Buddha appears calm and blissful with a shining circle around his head. Buddhists sometimes compare a person entering nirvana to "a dewdrop that slips into the shining sea."

✔ **Checkpoint**  **How did the Buddha's teachings outline a Buddhist way of life for his followers?**

## The Buddhist Religion

The Buddhist religion is based on the moral teachings of the Buddha. The majority of Buddhists use the Four Noble Truths and the Eightfold Path to guide their daily lives. The most committed Buddhists live in religious communities that offer them time for study and meditation.

**Buddhist Monasteries**  As the Buddha preached, he gained many followers. At first they followed him from place to place. As their number grew, the Buddha found places for them to rest during the rainy season. This was the beginning of Buddhist monasteries. **A monastery is the home of a religious community. The men who live in a monastery are called monks.**

Women soon joined Buddhist monasteries as well. The Buddha's aunt and several other family members, including his wife and son, joined. **Women who live in a religious community are known as nuns.**

The Buddha set up rules for monks and nuns to live by. Their duties were to meditate and to spread the Buddha's teachings. Monasteries became important centers of learning.

**Buddhist Texts** Buddhism has no single sacred book like the Bible. For hundreds of years, the Buddha's followers memorized his teachings. The first scriptures were not written down until about 43 b.c. Some of the earliest writings describe the Buddha's stories about his life. In them, he tells about his journey from a life of wealth to his enlightenment. Other scriptures include the Buddha's teachings, his rules for monks and nuns, and other statements he made.

The most popular Buddhist texts are the Jataka tales. These tales tell about 547 <u>previous</u> lives of the Buddha before he eventually achieved enlightenment. In some Jataka tales, the Buddha is a human being. In the rest, he is an animal or a plant. Besides being interesting to read, each tale teaches Buddhist ideas and values.

 **Checkpoint** **What are the main duties of Buddhist monks and nuns?**

**Looking Back and Ahead** In this section, you have read about the basic moral teachings of Buddhism, Buddhist monasteries, and religious texts. In the next section, you will find out how Buddhism spread to other parts of the world.

**Vocabulary** *Builder*
<u>previous</u> (PREE vee uhs) *adj.*
happening or existing before a particular event, time, or thing

---

# Section 2 Check Your Progress

**Progress Monitoring** Online
**For:** Self-test with instant help
**Visit:** PHSchool.com
**Web Code:** mwa-3082

**Standards Review** H-SS: 6.5.5; E-LA: Reading 6.2.3

**Comprehension and Critical Thinking**

**1. (a) Explain** What are the Four Noble Truths of Buddhism?
**(b) Draw Conclusions** How did these teachings make Buddhism appealing to people of all castes?

**2. (a) Recall** What kinds of works are found in Buddhist scriptures?
**(b) Compare** Devout Hindus believe that the Vedas were given to people by the gods. How does that make the Vedas different from the Buddhist scriptures?

**Reading Skill**

**3. Connect Main Ideas** Look at the different sections within Section 2. How do the ideas in these smaller sections connect to build the larger main idea of Section 2 regarding the founding and beliefs of Buddhism?

**Vocabulary** *Builder*
Answer the following questions in complete sentences that show your understanding of the Key Terms.
**4.** How did the Buddha suggest people could reach nirvana?

**5.** What led to the establishment of the first Buddhist monasteries?

**6.** In what sources might you read the Buddha's rules for monks?

**7.** Who was one member of the Buddha's family that became a nun?

**Writing**
**8.** Write a topic sentence that identifies the general similarities and differences between the major beliefs of Hinduism and Buddhism.

# The Lives of Buddhist Monks and Nuns

After attaining enlightenment, the Buddha formed a community of monks. Since then, monks and nuns have been central to Buddhism. Today, in many Buddhist countries, young men or women may enter a monastery. They may stay for only a month, or they may stay for many years. While there, they learn to follow the Eightfold Path.

**History-Social Science**

**6.5.5** Know the life and moral teachings of the Buddha and how Buddhism spread in India, Ceylon, and Central Asia.

**Historical Interpretation 3** Students explain the sources of historical continuity and how the combination of ideas and events explains the emergence of new patterns.

▼ **A Buddhist Temple**

Buddhist temples may look very different from one another. Wat Phra Singh is a temple complex in Thailand built in 1345. Wherever they are located, temples often include a monastery, schoolrooms, and shrines, such as the small building at the left of the temple. Inside this shrine is a statue of the Buddha.

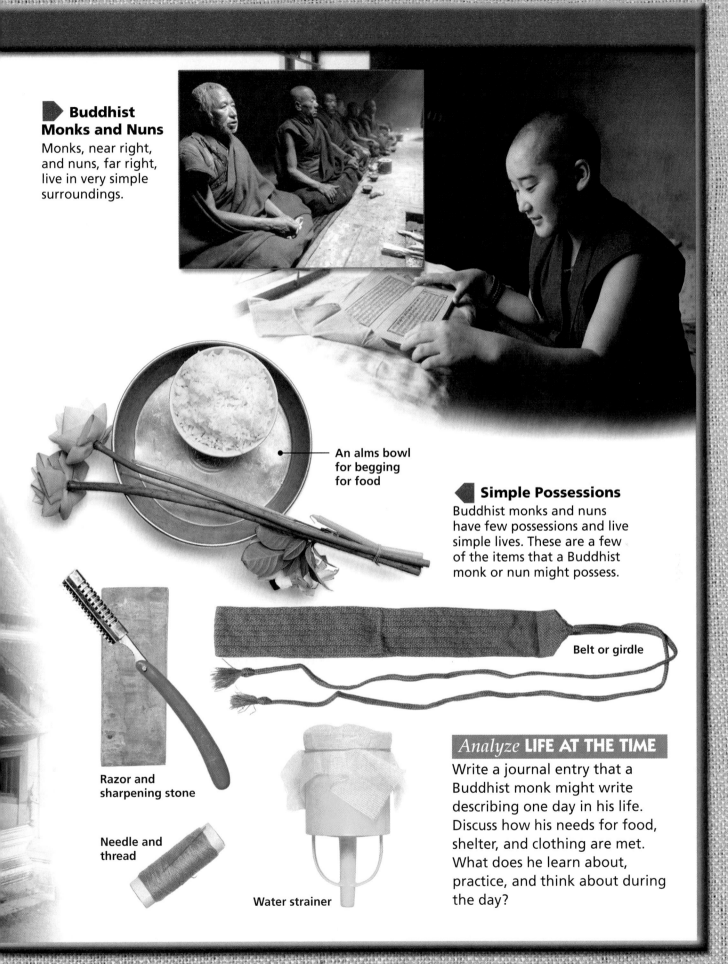

## ▶ Buddhist Monks and Nuns

Monks, near right, and nuns, far right, live in very simple surroundings.

An alms bowl for begging for food

## ◀ Simple Possessions

Buddhist monks and nuns have few possessions and live simple lives. These are a few of the items that a Buddhist monk or nun might possess.

Belt or girdle

Razor and sharpening stone

Needle and thread

Water strainer

### Analyze LIFE AT THE TIME

Write a journal entry that a Buddhist monk might write describing one day in his life. Discuss how his needs for food, shelter, and clothing are met. What does he learn about, practice, and think about during the day?

**H-SS 6.5.5** Know the life and moral teachings of the Buddha and how Buddhism spread in India, Ceylon, and Central Asia.

**E-LA Reading 6.2.3** Connect and clarify main ideas by identifying their relationships to other sources and related topics.

## Reading Preview

 **Reading Skill**

**Connect to Related Topics** This chapter discusses Buddhism. In Chapter 7 you learned about Hinduism, and in Chapter 5 you learned about Judaism. You can clarify your understanding of these important chapters by looking at how their main ideas relate or connect. For example, you can see that each of the chapters discusses a different religion. Connections could also include comparing and contrasting ideas or making cause-and-effect links.

**Vocabulary** *Builder*

**High-Use Words**
**welfare** (WEHL fair), p. 230
**appealing** (uh PEEL ihng), p. 235

**Key Terms and People**
Asoka (uh SOHK), p. 231
missionary (MIHSH uhn ehr ee), p. 231
virtue (VER choo), p. 232
compassion (kuhm PASH uhn), p. 232
*bodhisattva* (boh dih SUHT vuh), p. 233

**Background Knowledge** Religions spread in different ways. As you read earlier, events prompted Jews to move to many different places. Hinduism remained centered in India. Buddhism's followers carried its teachings throughout most of Asia. In this section, you will read about the spread of Buddhist teachings and Buddhism's influence in the world.

**Main Idea**
Buddhism spread throughout India and, after the Buddha's death, to many parts of Asia.

**Vocabulary** *Builder*
**welfare** (WEHL fair) *n.* health, comfort, or happiness

## The Growth of Buddhism

For a time, Buddhism spread rapidly in India. Before his death, the Buddha urged his followers to spread his teachings to all corners of Earth, saying:

**❝Go forth for the gain of many, for the welfare of many, in compassion for the world. Preach the glorious doctrine. Proclaim the life of holiness.❞**

—Siddhartha Gautama, quoted in *Buddhism* by Madhu Bazaz Wangu

Some Indian rulers encouraged the growth of the new religion. In the next chapter, you will meet **Asoka,** a ruler of India. Asoka sent Buddist missionaries out in all directions. A **missionary** is a person who goes to another place to teach about his or her religion.

**Buddhist Missionaries**   In the centuries after the Buddha's death, missionaries carried his teachings throughout Asia. Asoka's son took Buddhism south to Ceylon, or present-day Sri Lanka. Other monks took Buddhism into Southeast Asia.

Missionaries also traveled north across the Himalayas into Central Asia. Once there, they followed trade routes east into China. From China, Buddhism spread to Korea and Japan.

Buddhism came later to the mountain kingdom of Tibet, where it became central to the Tibetan way of life. Over time, Buddhist religious teachers called *lamas* gained much influence. Today Tibet is ruled by China. But the Dalai Lama, or "great teacher," of Tibet is still viewed as the spiritual leader of the Tibetan people.

**E-LA 6.2.3 Connect to Related Topics**
Connect the spread of Buddhism to the ways in which followers of Hinduism and Judaism spread their beliefs during the same period of time.

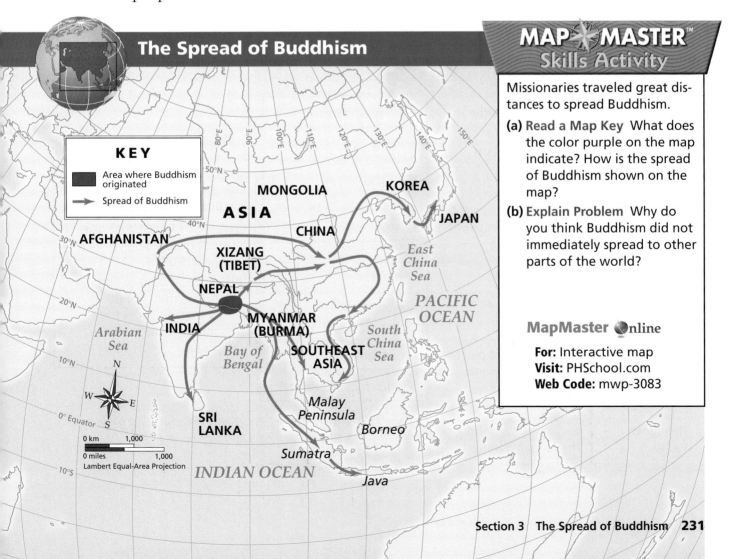

**The Spread of Buddhism**

**KEY**

■ Area where Buddhism originated

→ Spread of Buddhism

**MAP★MASTER™**
**Skills Activity**

Missionaries traveled great distances to spread Buddhism.

**(a) Read a Map Key**  What does the color purple on the map indicate? How is the spread of Buddhism shown on the map?

**(b) Explain Problem**  Why do you think Buddhism did not immediately spread to other parts of the world?

**MapMaster ●nline**

**For:** Interactive map
**Visit:** PHSchool.com
**Web Code:** mwp-3083

**Two Schools of Buddhism** As Buddhism spread, its followers split into two major schools, or sects. The two schools share the same basic beliefs, but they interpret the Buddha's life and teachings in different ways. One group believes that his greatest **virtue,** *or good quality,* was his wisdom. The other believes that his greatest virtue was his **compassion,** *or loving concern for others.*

The oldest school is Theravada Buddhism. This group believes that wisdom was the Buddha's greatest virtue. Followers of Theravada Buddhism also think that the most important aspect of the Buddha's life was his enlightenment and entry into nirvana. They try to follow his teachings strictly in order to achieve enlightenment. Most spend some part of their lives in a monastery, practicing meditation.

The other major school is Mahayana Buddhism. Its name comes from the Buddha's description of his teachings as a raft that could carry people across the sea of life to enlightenment. *Mahayana* means "big raft." As this name caught on, the Theravada school became known as *Hinayana,* or "little raft." A majority of Buddhists today are Mahayanas.

## Two Schools of Buddhism

| | Theravada "Little Raft" Buddhism | Mahayana "Big Raft" Buddhism |
|---|---|---|
| **View of the Buddha** | A supreme teacher | A godlike savior |
| **The way to enlightenment** | Through the efforts of each person | Through the help of *bodhisattvas* |
| **Key virtue** | Wisdom | Compassion |
| **Main religious practice** | Meditation | Prayer |
| **Ideal person** | An enlightened person who enters nirvana after death | An enlightened person who becomes a *bodhisattva* after death |
| **Where strongest today** | Southeast Asia (Sri Lanka, Cambodia, Thailand, Myanmar) | East Asia (China, Korea, Japan) |

### Reading Charts

The two schools of Buddhism interpreted the teachings of the Buddha differently.

(a) **Read a Chart** What does each group believe is the key virtue?

(b) **Critical Thinking: Organize Information** Create a Venn diagram to show the similarities of the two groups.

For Mahayana Buddhists, the most important aspect of the Buddha's life was his decision not to remain in nirvana after his enlightenment. He showed compassion by choosing to remain on Earth to help all who suffered. Mahayanas believe that there are others who have made that same choice. Enlightened ones who return to Earth after death to help others are called *bodhisattvas.* Mahayanas pray to *bodhisattvas* and look to them for help in achieving enlightenment.

**The Decline of Buddhism** While Buddhism was spreading across much of Asia, it almost died out in India. Missionaries traveled long distances to spread the Buddha's teachings. Theravada Buddhism extended into Sri Lanka and countries in Southeast Asia. Mahayana Buddhism spread across Central Asia into China and several other east Asian countries.

Buddhism's decline in India occurred partly as a result of wars. But the most important factor may have been that Hinduism absorbed many of the Buddha's teachings. Many Hindus came to believe that the god Vishnu came to Earth as the Buddha to help people overcome suffering.

**Buddhism and Hinduism**
In Hinduism, Vishnu is said to have returned to Earth as the Buddha. In this carving, the Indian gods Brahma and Indra invite the Buddha to teach. **Critical Thinking: Detect Bias** *Why do you think the image of the Buddha is larger?*

 Checkpoint  **How did Buddhism spread into Central Asia?**

# The Legacy of Buddhism

Today, nearly 360 million people call themselves Buddhists. In fact, about one of every eight people in the world practice Buddhism. Most of these people are in Asia, although about 2.7 million Buddhists live in North America.

**Moral Teachings**  The moral teachings, or lessons that teach what is right and wrong by society's standards, of Buddhism appeal not only to Buddhists but also to people of other faiths. Many people appreciate the Buddhist teachings of respect for all living things and compassion for others.

**Main Idea**
Throughout the world, Buddhism has influenced literature and the arts as well as moral teachings.

The temple reaches 170 feet high.

Nuns sing songs of praise to the Buddha. Other offerings include hundreds of devotional candles.

The temple was built as a monument, not a shrine.

A giant image of the Buddha can be seen inside the temple.

## Mahabodhi Temple

This temple was built on the site of the Bodhi Tree, where the Buddha gained enlightenment. **Critical Thinking: Draw Conclusions** *What does the picture tell you about the importance of this site to Buddhists?*

**History** *Interactive*
**Tour a temple**

**Visit:** PHSchool.com
**Web Code:** mwp-3084

**Literature and the Arts**   Buddhism has left the world a large number of religious writings as well as the appealing Jataka tales. It has also inspired the building of beautiful temples and monasteries. In India, Buddhist temples were rounded structures called *stupas*. In China, most temples were many-storied buildings with curved roofs called pagodas. The multiple stories of these buildings usually had the same shape, with each higher story decreasing in size from the story below it.

Buddhist artists have decorated temples with colorful scenes from the life of the Buddha. Statues of a gently smiling Buddha are a common sight across much of Asia. In some countries today, Buddhist statues and temples are viewed as national treasures.

**Vocabulary Builder**
appealing (uh PEEL ihng) *adj.*
attractive or interesting

**Checkpoint**   How has Buddhism influenced the arts?

**Looking Back and Ahead**   In this section, you have learned how Buddhism spread from India to other parts of Asia. You have read about the rich legacy of this religion. In the next chapter, you will read about some of India's great rulers and how Buddhism affected their lives.

## Section 3 Check Your Progress

**Progress Monitoring Online**
For: Self-test with instant help
Visit: PHSchool.com
Web Code: mwa-3083

**Standards Review**   H-SS: 6.5.5; E-LA: Reading 6.2.3

**Comprehension and Critical Thinking**

1. **(a) Identify** What are the two major schools of Buddhism?
   **(b) Compare and Contrast** Describe one way in which the two schools are the same and one way in which they are different.

2. **(a) Recall** What is the most common subject of Buddhist sculpture?
   **(b) Apply Information** What aspects of Buddhism appeal to people who do not actually practice the religion?

**Reading Skill**

3. **Connect to Related Topics** Summarize the connections between the discussions of major religions in Chapters 5, 7, and 8.

**Vocabulary Builder**
Complete each of the following sentences so that the second part further explains the first part and clearly shows your understanding of the highlighted word.

4. The growth of Buddhism was encouraged by Asoka, _____.

5. The two schools of Buddhism disagreed on what was the Buddha's greatest virtue, _____.

**Writing**

6. Prepare an outline for a short essay that compares and contrasts the spread of Hinduism with that of Buddhism. For example, you may want to present details about the spread of one religion, followed by details about the spread of the other.

When you compare, you look for the ways in which things are similar. When you contrast, you look for differences between things. Comparing and contrasting ideas, beliefs, and situations can help you understand history.

 **Chapter Standards**

**English-Language Arts**

**Writing 6.2.2** Analyze text that uses the compare-and-contrast organizational pattern.

|  | Buddhism | Hinduism |
|---|---|---|
| **Spiritual leaders or teachers** | Siddhartha Gautama (the Buddha) | Gurus |
| **Religious texts** | The Buddha's teachings, Jataka tales | The Vedas, Upanishads, the Mahabharata, and the Ramayana |
| **The afterlife** | Either nirvana or reincarnation | Either moksha or reincarnation |
| **Beliefs and practices** | Middle Way, Four Noble Truths, Eightfold Path, karma, meditation | Atman, Four Goals of Life, Three Paths to God, karma, meditation, caste system |

**Learn the Skill** *Follow these steps to learn how to compare and contrast.*

1. **Identify the topic and your purpose.** What are you comparing and contrasting?

2. **Identify characteristics to compare and contrast.** You might want to compare how Buddhists and Hindus view the afterlife.

3. **Identify what you know about each characteristic.** Use what you know to fill in the chart. For example, you learned that Siddhartha Gautama is the spiritual leader of Buddhism. In Chapter 7, you learned that gurus were Hindu spiritual teachers.

4. **Identify similarities and differences.** Mark each similarity with an "s" and each difference with a "d." For example, you could write an "s" beside *reincarnation* in the chart above.

5. **Draw conclusions.** Use the information you have gathered to draw conclusions.

**Practice the Skill** *Draw the chart above, and add a column for Judaism. Use information about Judaism in Chapter 5 to answer the questions.*

1. **Identify the topic and your purpose.** What will you learn by completing this chart?

2. **Identify characteristics to compare and contrast.** What other characteristics could be added to the chart?

3. **Identify what you know about each characteristic.** Use what you know to complete the rest of the chart.

4. **Identify similarities and differences.** Name one similarity and one difference between Judaism and Buddhism.

5. **Draw conclusions.** How are the three religions similar? How are they different?

**Apply the Skill**

*See page 239 of the Review and Assessment.*

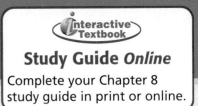

## Chapter Summary  H-SS: 6.5; 6.5.5

### Section 1 The Origins of Buddhism

- When Siddhartha Gautama saw people's suffering and sadness, he began to search for truth.
- Siddhartha studied with Hindu gurus and later joined a group of ascetics in his search for enlightenment.
- After achieving enlightenment, the Buddha spent his life teaching others what he had learned.

### Section 2 The Beliefs of Buddhism

- The teachings of the Buddha formed the basis of Buddhism. He advised following a Middle Way between pleasure and self-denial.
- The Buddha described the Four Noble Truths and the Eightfold Path that leads to nirvana.
- Some Buddhists join religious communities and become monks or nuns, but anyone may study Buddhist texts.

### Section 3 The Spread of Buddhism

- After the Buddha's death, missionaries spread his teachings from India to many parts of Asia.
- Two major schools of Buddhism developed, Theravada and Mahayana. But as Buddhism reached other countries, it declined in India.
- Today, many people besides Buddhists respect the Buddha's moral teachings. Buddhism has also influenced art and literature throughout the world.

**Brahma and Indra beside the Buddha**

## Standards Practice  H-SS: 6.5; 6.5.5

## Vocabulary *Builder*

### High-Use Words

Decide whether each underlined word is used correctly. If it is, explain why. If not, rewrite the rest of the sentence to make it logical.

1. Siddhartha Gautama was born into a life of riches and **luxury**.

2. When you are **aware** of your thoughts and feelings, they are unknown to you.

3. The Jataka tales tell about the hundreds of **previous** lives that the Buddha lived after he was reborn.

### Key Terms

Answer the following questions in complete sentences that show your understanding of the Key Terms.

1. What did Hindu gurus teach Siddhartha about salvation?

2. How did Siddhartha's life change when he became an ascetic?

3. What does it mean for a Hindu or Buddhist to meditate?

4. Why is compassion important to Mahayana Buddhists?

**Apply Reading Skills**

**Clarify, Connect, and Relate Main Ideas** Choose two main ideas from Chapter 8. One choice may be a quotation. Connect them to each other and then to a main idea from Chapter 5 or Chapter 7.

## Comprehension and Critical Thinking

**1. (a) Identify** Who was Siddhartha Gautama?
**(b) Understand Sequence** What events occurred between Siddhartha's leaving the palace and his sermon in the Deer Park?

**2. (a) Explain** What is the Middle Way?
**(b) Draw Conclusions** Why do you think the Buddha's First Noble Truth might have drawn people to learn more about his teachings?
**(c) Apply Information** How do the steps of the Eightfold Path change as they go higher?

**3. (a) Discuss** What is the Mahayama school of Buddhism?
**(b) Draw Conclusions** Why are fewer people followers of Theravada Buddhism?
**(c) Detect Points of View** Which event is most important to Mahayana Buddhists, the Buddha's enlightenment or his decision to remain on Earth after enlightenment? Why?

## Researching

**The Spread of Buddhism** It is said that someone once asked the Buddha how to prevent a drop of water from drying up. He answered, "By throwing it into the sea." In this activity, you will use the Internet and library media to research and report on the influences of Buddhism as it spread throughout the world. Choose a task below to work on. Share your completed project with the class by making a brief oral presentation in which you explain your findings.

**Historians:** Create a chart that lists several countries to which Buddhism has spread. Include information in the chart about the effects of Buddhism on culture and historical events in each country.

**Artists:** Choose one type of art, such as painting, sculpture, or architecture. Research the ways in which Buddhism has influenced the chosen art form in one of the countries to which Buddhism spread.

> **Researching Online**
> **For:** Help in starting this activity
> **Visit:** PHSchool.com
> **Web Code:** mwe-3084

## Writing

**1. Write an essay on the following topic.** As followers of both Buddhism and Hinduism spread their beliefs, different sects emerged within the religions. Explain how the ways in which the development of sects affected these religions were similar and different.
**Your essay should:**
- State a thesis or purpose for writing.
- Offer evidence to support your comparisons and contrasts.
- Include a strong conclusion that states your key points.

**2. Write a short narrative.** Suppose you are an early Buddhist missionary traveling from India to spread your beliefs. Write a short narrative that explains the work you perform and identifies the places to which you travel.

**Progress Monitoring Online**
**For:** Self-test with instant help
**Visit:** PHSchool.com
**Web Code:** mwa-3084

# Apply Analysis Skills

Use a Venn diagram and the following questions to compare and contrast the practices of the ascetics and those of the Buddha.

1. What goal did the ascetics and the Buddha share?

2. What was the main practice of the ascetics?

3. What are two examples of that practice?

4. What activity did the ascetics and the Buddha practice?

5. What is the main idea of the Middle Way?

## Comparisons and Contrasts of Ascetics and the Buddha

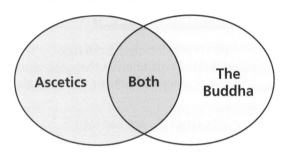

Ascetics    Both    The Buddha

# Test Yourself

1. **Siddhartha Gautama began his personal religious transformation when he**
   A got married.
   B became a father.
   C became known as the Buddha.
   D experienced the Four Passing Sights.

2. **Siddhartha Gautama achieved enlightenment through many years of**
   A meditation.
   B going hungry.
   C walking barefoot.
   D religious education.

**Refer to the image below to answer Question 3.**

3. **In this image, the Buddha's success at reaching nirvana is represented by his**

   A crossed legs.
   B folded hands.
   C calm expression.
   D robe of gold.

4. **According to the Buddha, what must people follow to end selfish desires?**
   A Nirvana
   B Eightfold Path
   C Four Noble Truths
   D Four Passing Sights

**Refer to the quotation below to answer question 5.**

5. **With this statement, the Buddha asked his followers to**

*"Go forth for the gain of many, for the welfare of many, in compassion for the world. Preach the glorious doctrine. Proclaim the life of holiness."*

   A split into different sects.
   B reject physical comforts.
   C spread Buddhist teachings.
   D follow the Eightfold Path.

6. **Which Hindu concept did the Buddha reject?**
   A caste
   B karma
   C moksha
   D reincarnation

# Chapter 9

# India's Empires and Achievements (321 B.C.–A.D. 540)

## Prepare to Read

### Chapter Standards

**History-Social Science**
**6.5** Students analyze the geographic, political, economic, religious, and social structures of the early civilizations of India.

**Section 1,** pp. 244–248

**What You Will Learn**

**The Maurya Empire**

The first Indian emperor used new methods to win power. He established a complex government to hold that power.

**Section 2,** pp. 249–252

**Asoka's Rule of Tolerance**

Emperor Asoka attempted to make life better for all of his people. He also encouraged the growth of Buddhism.

**Section 3,** pp. 254–259

**India's Classical Age**

During the Classical Age, many kinds of art and learning developed that still affect India's culture today.

Asoka's Pillar

**Chapter Events**

**321 B.C.**
Chandragupta overthrows the King of Magadha and begins his wars of conquest.

**185 B.C.**
Mauryan Empire comes to an end.

**Other Events**

**500 B.C.**

**326 B.C.** Alexander the Great leads his army to the Indus River.

**250 B.C.**

**221 B.C.** Qin forces unite North China.

**B.C./A.D.**

## Where and When?

Two great empires arose in India between 350 B.C. and A.D. 450.

This dome-shaped shrine was built to provide a place for Buddhists to worship.

**A.D. 330**
Samudra Gupta extends his father's empire.

**A.D. 499**
Aryabhatta writes a book on advanced mathematics.

B.C./A.D.

A.D. 250

A.D. 500

**A.D. 70** The Romans destroy Jerusalem.

**A.D. 313** Constantine ends persecution of Christians.

# How to Read History

### *Previewing* Use Clues to Determine Meaning

Archaeologists trying to read ancient writing frequently come across words they do not understand. They must study the writing for clues to the meaning of the words. When you come across unfamiliar words in your reading, use clues in the words and in other sentences of a paragraph to understand the meanings. The strategies and suggestions below can help you use clues to determine meaning.

**Chapter Standards**

**English-Language Arts**

**Reading 6.1.4** Monitor expository text for unknown words or words with novel meanings by using word, sentence, and paragraph clues to determine meaning.

**1** In this sentence, an unfamiliar word is built from two words. Define each separate word, then combine their meanings.

After five years of **self-denial,** Siddhartha's body was severely weakened.

> Two words combined into one

**2** In this example, an unfamiliar word is defined in another part of the sentence.

> Unfamiliar word

> Word is defined

As a **missionary** or a person who goes to another place to teach about his or her religion, the teacher traveled far from her home.

**3** Here, you must use other sentences in the paragraph for clues to the meaning of the unfamiliar word.

> Unfamiliar word

> Clues to the meaning of *sects*

> Unfamiliar word

As Buddhism spread, its followers split into two major schools, or sects. *Both share the same basic beliefs. But they* interpret *Buddha's life and teachings in different ways.* One group believes *that his greatest virtue, or good quality, was his wisdom.* The other believes *that it was his compassion, or loving concern for others.*

> Clues to the meaning of *interpret*

# Vocabulary *Builder*

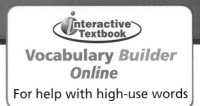
## *Previewing* High-Use Academic Words

| High-Use Word | Definition | Sample Sentence About History |
|---|---|---|
| **terrify** (TEHR uh fī) (Section 1, p. 245) | *v.* to frighten greatly | Armies of ancient India sometimes used elephants to terrify their enemies. |
| **efficient** (eh FIHSH uhnt) (Section 1, p. 246) | *adj.* working well | By learning to manage the waters of the Indus River, Indian farmers created efficient farms that produced a food surplus. |
| **conflict** (KAHN flihkt) (Section 2, p. 250) | *n.* fight or disagreement | The Aryan kings occasionally came into conflict with other kingdoms. |
| **maintain** (mayn TAYN) (Section 2, p. 251) | *v.* to keep in good condition | The people of Mohenjo-Daro maintained working plumbing and sewer systems. |
| **circumstances** (SER kuhm stan sehz) (Section 3, p. 255) | *n.* the facts or conditions that affect a situation | According to Buddhists, Siddhartha Gautama was raised in unusual circumstances, which kept him from seeing any unpleasant sights. |
| **medical** (MEHD ih kuhl) (Section 3, p. 258) | *adj.* relating to the treatment of disease or injury | Some medical treatments from ancient India are still used to treat sickness today. |

## *Previewing* Key Terms and People

Asoka

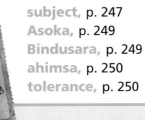

**Chandragupta Maurya**

**Standards Preview**

**H-SS** 6.5.6 Describe the growth of the Maurya empire and the political and moral achievements of the emperor Asoka.

**E-LA** Reading 6.1.4 Monitor expository text for unknown words or words with novel meanings by using word, sentence, and paragraph clues to determine meaning.

## Reading Preview

### Reading Skill

**Use Word Clues to Determine Meaning** Look for several kinds of clues within an unfamiliar word. First, look at the word's part of speech. Knowing whether it is a noun, a verb, or an adjective can help you determine its meaning. Second, look at suffixes such as *-less* or prefixes such as *un-* that you can combine with a familiar base word. Third, look for smaller, familiar words or word parts within the larger unfamiliar word.

### Vocabulary *Builder*

**High-Use Words**
terrify (TEHR uh fī), p. 245
efficient (eh FIHSH uhnt), p. 246

**Key Terms and People**
Chandragupta Maurya (chuhn druh GUP tuh MOWR yuh), p. 244
Kautilya (kow TIHL yuh), p. 245
strategy (STRA tuh jee), p. 245
bureaucracy (byu RAH kruh see), p. 246
province (PRAHV ihns), p. 247
subject (SUHB jihkt), p. 247

**Background Knowledge** In Chapter 6, you read about the growth of Aryan kingdoms in northern India during the Vedic age. The strongest of these kingdoms was known as Magadha. Around 321 B.C., a rebel army overthrew the king of Magadha. The leader of the rebels was a young man named **Chandragupta Maurya.** In this chapter, you will learn how Chandragupta built India's first empire. You will also read about his methods of ruling the Maurya Empire.

**Main Idea**
The first empire in India was formed by a military conqueror before 305 B.C.

## Chandragupta Unites India

Many tales are told about Chandragupta's early life. Most accounts say that he came from a poor family. His last name, Maurya, comes from the word for peacock. This may mean that he came from a caste that raised peacocks. Other accounts say that he was born into the warrior caste. Historians may never know for sure.

Ancient accounts and legends tell us that Chandragupta did not succeed on his own. As a young man, he teamed up with a Brahmin named **Kautilya.** According to tradition, Kautilya had been insulted by the king of Magadha. In Chandragupta, he found a means of revenge. Kautilya helped Chandragupta raise a rebel army and develop a strategy for conquering Magadha. A **strategy** is a long-term plan for achieving a goal.

**Military Success** Kautilya had chosen well. Chandragupta was a brilliant military leader. He armed his men with powerful weapons, including the enormous Indian bow. This bow, which was as tall as a man, could shoot a nine-foot arrow. An arrow shot from this bow could pierce a strong shield.

Another impressive weapon used by Chandragupta was the war elephant. The animals were painted bright colors and trained to carry warriors into battle. Because of their great size and startling appearance, the war elephants <u>terrified</u> even the best-trained enemy troops.

After conquering Magadha, Chandragupta moved on to other kingdoms. By 305 B.C., he controlled most of the Indian subcontinent. His empire stretched from the Bay of Bengal to present-day Afghanistan.

 **Checkpoint** How did Chandragupta establish the first Indian empire?

 **E-LA 6.1.4 Use Word Clues to Determine Meaning**
What does *enormous* mean? How does its part of speech help you define it?

**Vocabulary** *Builder*
**terrify** (TEHR uh fī) *v.* to frighten greatly

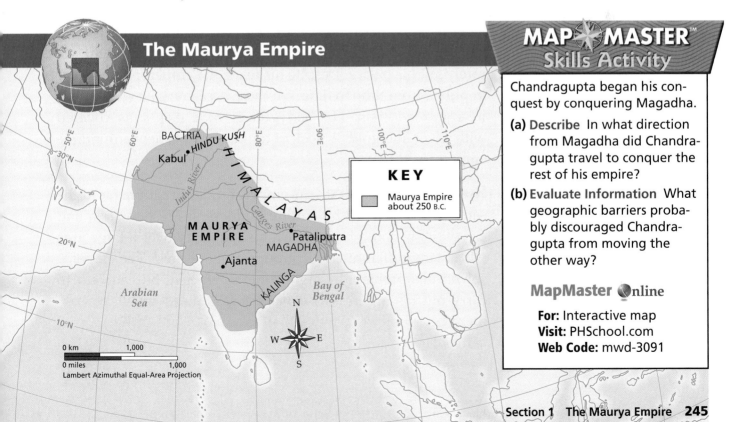

**The Maurya Empire**

**KEY**

Maurya Empire about 250 B.C.

BACTRIA
Kabul • HINDU KUSH
HIMALAYAS
Indus River
Ganges River
MAURYA EMPIRE
Pataliputra
MAGADHA
Ajanta
KALINGA
Arabian Sea
Bay of Bengal

0 km 1,000
0 miles 1,000
Lambert Azimuthal Equal-Area Projection

N W E S

**MAP MASTER**
**Skills Activity**

Chandragupta began his conquest by conquering Magadha.

**(a) Describe** In what direction from Magadha did Chandragupta travel to conquer the rest of his empire?

**(b) Evaluate Information** What geographic barriers probably discouraged Chandragupta from moving the other way?

**MapMaster** Online

**For:** Interactive map
**Visit:** PHSchool.com
**Web Code:** mwd-3091

The Maurya emperors used elephants in combat. Although this painting shows a single rider, war elephants often carried as many as five warriors, armed with spears and bows, and riding in a large shelter. **Critical Thinking: Compare** *How are army tanks used in modern warfare similar to the use of elephants by Chandragupta?*

## Explore More Video

**Discovery School Video**
View *The Maurya Elephant Army* to learn more about the ways elephants were used to conquer India.

**Main Idea**
Chandragupta used big government and many spies to control his empire.

**Vocabulary** *Builder*
**efficient** (eh FIHSH uhnt) *adj.* working well

# The Emperor's Iron Rule

Chandragupta had conquered a vast empire. Nevertheless, he lived in constant fear of his enemies. He had servants taste his food for poison. He slept in a different bed every night. He rarely left his palace. Despite his fears, the emperor did appear in public from time to time. On these occasions, he was carried in a jeweled chair. His bodyguards rode elephants covered with silver and gold. A flock of trained parrots flew around the emperor's head.

**Ruling an Empire**   As emperor, Chandragupta faced the same problem faced by empire builders in Mesopotamia and Egypt. How could he establish his authority over a large area with many different ethnic groups and cultures? The emperor solved this problem by organizing an efficient bureaucracy to carry out his orders. A **bureaucracy** is a system of government based on fixed rules that are carried out by appointed officials.

Chandragupta divided his empire into four regions. A trusted official in each region carried out the emperor's orders. Each region was divided into smaller provinces that were run by officials loyal to the emperor. A **province** is a district or region of a country with its own government bureaucracy. The provinces were further divided into groups of villages, each run by an appointed official. In this way, the emperor's authority reached down to every village in his empire.

Chandragupta also divided the work of his central government among six committees. Each committee managed one key activity, such as agriculture, trade, or tax collection. Tax officials claimed a quarter of the crops raised by farmers as taxes. They also collected a sales tax of ten percent on traded goods. The money collected in taxes was used to pay government officials and support a large army.

**Subjects and Spies** Chandragupta received many of his ideas for government from his capable advisor Kautilya. These ideas were later collected in a book called the *Arthashastra*. The book provides detailed advice on how a ruler should deal with his **subjects,** or people under his control. "The primary duty of a king," the *Arthashastra* says, "is the protection of his subjects." It goes on to say:

> **❝In the happiness of his subjects lies the king's happiness,**
> **In the welfare of his subjects, his welfare.**
> **A king's good is not that which pleases him,**
> **But that which pleases his subjects.❞**
>
> —Kautilya, *Arthashastra*

The book also advises the ruler to do whatever is necessary to stay in power. People, it warns, cannot be trusted. They need to be closely watched. The *Arthashastra* also urges severe punishments for crimes. In fact, it describes government as "the science of punishment."

# BIOGRAPHY QUEST

## Which great leader may Chandragupta have met?

Coin of Chandragupta

### Fast Facts
**Who:** Chandragupta
**What:** Maurya Emperor
**When:** c. 321 B.C.–298 B.C.
**Where:** India
**Why Important:** Chandragupta founded the first empire on the Indian subcontinent.

### Fast Find
**How:** Go online to find out the name of the leader in ancient Greece who invaded India shortly before Chandragupta rose to power. Some legends say that Chandragupta and this leader actually met.

**Biography Online**
For: More about Chandragupta
Visit: PHSchool.com
Web Code: mwd-3094

**Chandragupta Stamp**
This postage stamp, issued in 2001, honors the first emperor of India. **Critical Thinking: Draw Conclusions** *What qualities of Chandragupta might the people of India admire?*

Following Kautilya's advice, Chandragupta set up a huge spy network to check up on his subjects. He even hired spies to check up on other spies. There were even specially trained female warriors to guard his palace. The emperor set aside a time twice each day to receive reports from his spies.

Kautilya's influence led Chandragupta to create an orderly but powerful government. The government controlled most large businesses and most of the empire's resources, such as mines and forests. For the first time in history, most of the Indian subcontinent was politically and economically united.

Chandragupta's empire became known in the Middle East and Europe when a Greek ambassador wrote about India. Egypt and Syria also sent ambassadors to the Maurya Empire.

✓**Checkpoint** How did Chandragupta support his empire?

**Looking Back and Ahead** In this section, you have read about the beginnings of the Maurya Empire. You learned how Chandragupta organized an efficient bureaucracy to rule his empire. In the next section, you will read about the remarkable rule of Chandragupta's grandson Asoka.

---

## Section 1 Check Your Progress

**Progress Monitoring** ⬤nline
**For:** Self-test with instant help
**Visit:** PHSchool.com
**Web Code:** mwa-3091

 **Standards Review** H-SS: 6.5.6; E-LA: Reading 6.1.4

**Comprehension and Critical Thinking**

**1. (a) Recall** How did the Maurya Empire begin?
**(b) Evaluate Information** According to the *Arthashastra*, the primary duty of a king is to please his subjects. How successful was Chandragupta in fulfilling this role? Explain.

**2. (a) Explain** How was Maurya government organized?
**(b) Analyze Cause and Effect** What made Maurya rule so effective?

**Reading Skill**
**3. Use Word Clues to Determine Meaning** Read the following sentence, and then use word clues to determine what *impressive* means: Another *impressive* weapon used by Chandragupta was the war elephant.

**Vocabulary Builder**
Complete each of the following sentences so that the second part further explains the first part and clearly shows your understanding of the highlighted word.

**4.** Chandragupta and Kautilya developed a strategy for conquering India; _____.

**5.** A bureaucracy helped Chadragupta govern his empire; _____.

**6.** Kautilya told Chandragupta how to deal with his subjects; _____.

**Writing**
**7.** Write three sentences about the rule of Chandragupta.

# 2 Asoka's Rule of Tolerance

## Standards Preview

**H-SS 6.5.6** Describe the growth of the Maurya empire and the political and moral achievements of the emperor Asoka.

**E-LA Reading 6.1.4** Monitor expository text for unknown words or words with novel meanings by using word, sentence, and paragraph clues to determine meaning.

## Reading Preview

 **Reading Skill**

**Use Sentence Clues** You may find clues to an unfamiliar word in the surrounding sentence. The sentence may contain definition or a restatement of the word that suggests its meaning. Look at this example: A province *is* a district or region of a country with its own government bureaucracy. The word *is* alerts you that a definition will follow in the sentence.

## Vocabulary *Builder*

**High-Use Words**
conflict (KAHN flihkt), p. 250
maintain (mayn TAYN), p. 251

**Key Terms and People**
Asoka (uh SOHK), p. 249
Bindusara (bihn du SAHR uh), p. 249
*ahimsa* (uh HIHM sah), p. 250
tolerance (TAHL er uhns), p. 251

**Background Knowledge** As Chandragupta grew older, he became interested in religion. According to legend, he gave up being emperor to enter a monastery. Power passed first to Chandragupta's son and then to his grandson **Asoka.** In this section, you will learn how Asoka rose to become emperor. You will also read about Asoka's political and moral achievements as ruler of the Maurya Empire.

## Asoka's Rise to Power

When Chandragupta gave up power, he turned his empire over to his son **Bindusara.** For 26 years, Bindusara expanded the Maurya Empire until most of India was under his control. Only the kingdom of Kalinga remained independent of Maurya rule.

Asoka was one of seven sons born to Bindusara. Legends say that he was a homely, or plain, child who was not liked by his father. As soon as Asoka was old enough to hold a government job, his father made Asoka the ruler of a distant province.

**Main Idea**
Emperor Asoka conquered the last remaining independent kingdom in India.

**Vocabulary** *Builder*
conflict (KAHN flihkt) *n.* fight or disagreement

When Bindusara died, there was political <u>conflict</u> and a struggle for the throne. One legend even states that Asoka killed his own brothers in order to become emperor. In 269 B.C., after four years of conflict, Asoka became the third Maurya emperor.

✔**Checkpoint**  **How did Asoka become emperor?**

**Main Idea**
Asoka turned from war to making improvements for the people of the empire.

# The Empire Under Asoka

According to ancient writings, Asoka spent the next eight years strengthening his hold on power. Then, he went to war again. His target was Kalinga, the last major independent kingdom in India. The war was long and terrible. Approximately 100,000 soldiers died. Another 150,000 people were captured and sent to other parts of the empire. Kalinga became part of the Maurya Empire, but at a terrible cost.

As he witnessed the results of his conquest, Asoka was shocked by the suffering. "The slaughter, death, and carrying away of captive people," he later wrote, "is a matter of profound sorrow and regret to His Sacred Majesty."

**Primary** Sources

See Asoka's Speech in the Reference Section at the back of this book.

**New Rules for the Empire**  According to ancient writings, the suffering that Asoka saw made him think hard about what kind of ruler he wanted to be. Asoka began attempting to rule by many principles of the Buddhist religion. He turned away from violence. He also turned away from some of the harsher teachings of the *Arthashastra.* Whenever possible, he replaced rule by force with rule based on "moral law."

Asoka's rule of moral law was based on three principles. The first was the principle of *ahimsa,* or the belief that one should not injure any living thing. *Ahimsa* is based on the view that all living creatures should be treated with love and compassion. Following this ideal, Asoka gave up hunting. He banned the killing of wild animals and urged people not to eat meat.

**Temple Carving**
This carving of people praying is from a temple built during Asoka's reign. **Critical Thinking: Apply Information** *Does this carving show principles of the Arthashastra or principles of Buddhism? Explain.*

## Principles of Asoka's Rule

| Principle | Example |
|---|---|
| Ahimsa | Asoka outlawed the hunting of wild animals and encouraged people not to eat meat. |
| Tolerance | Asoka supported Buddhism, but he respected other religions. |
| Welfare of the common people | During Asoka's reign, the Indian government built hospitals, wells for drinking water, and an excellent road system. |

**Reading Charts**

Once Asoka had finished his wars of conquest, he attempted to govern according to the principles in this chart.

(a) **Read a Chart** Which principles affected animals as well as people?

(b) **Apply Information** List one example of how you might demonstrate each principle today.

The second principle was tolerance. **Tolerance is a willingness to respect different beliefs and customs.** Although Asoka promoted Buddhism, he respected other religions. He wrote that "contact [between religions] is good. One should listen to and respect the doctrines [teachings] professed by others."

The third principle was the welfare of the people. Asoka expanded the idea of dharma beyond the idea of personal duties. He believed that the dharma of a ruler meant that he must be careful to rule his people well. As a result, Asoka made many decisions that helped make his empire a better place to live.

**Rest Houses and Roads** Asoka ruled India for nearly forty years. During that time, he did much to improve life for his people. He set up hospitals and dug wells. He built and maintained an excellent road system. Asoka's Royal Road stretched for more than a thousand miles across northern India. Trees planted along the road provided shade for travelers. Rest houses provided travelers with food and shelter.

As a result of Asoka's efforts, India prospered. The country was at peace. There was little crime. People could leave their homes unguarded and travel the country without fear.

**Asoka's Stone Pillars** Asoka also had stone pillars, or columns, set up across his empire. The pillars rose 40 feet into the air, and each weighed 50 tons. They were so highly polished that some travelers were convinced that they were made of metal. Some of Asoka's stone pillars are still standing today.

**Vocabulary** *Builder*
**maintain** (mayn TAYN) *v.* to keep in good condition

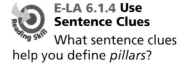
**E-LA 6.1.4 Use Sentence Clues** What sentence clues help you define *pillars*?

Asoka had messages carved into the polished pillars. In these messages, he assured his subjects of his devotion to their welfare. He apologized for making war on Kalinga. He wrote about his government reforms. He wrote about respecting one's parents and about being generous to other people. He urged respect for all religions. Most of all, he encouraged people to live moral lives.

Asoka died in 232 B.C. After his death, the Maurya empire began struggling. In 185 B.C., the last Maurya king was murdered by one of his own generals. After 140 years, the Maurya empire—and with it Asoka's vision of government—came to an end.

 **Checkpoint** **What were some of the changes Asoka made to improve the lives of his subjects?**

**Looking Back and Ahead** In this section, you have read about the achievements of the emperor Asoka. You have learned how Asoka worked to govern his empire according to Buddhist ideals. You have also learned that within fifty years of Asoka's death, the Maurya empire collapsed. In the next section, you will read about the rise of a new empire in India.

**Asoka's Pillar**
Pillars such as this one reminded people of the principles that were important to Asoka. **Critical Thinking: Identify Alternatives** *How else might Asoka have shared the messages that were important to him?*

---

## Section 2 Check Your Progress

**Progress Monitoring Online**
**For:** Self-test with instant help
**Visit:** PHSchool.com
**Web Code:** mwa-3092

 **Standards Review** H-SS: 6.5.6; E-LA: Reading 6.1.4

### Comprehension and Critical Thinking
1. (a) **Describe** How did Asoka become emperor?
   (b) **Apply Information** What did he do to expand and strengthen the empire?
2. (a) **Recall** Identify the main principles guiding Asoka's rule.
   (b) **Draw Conclusions** Were these ideas a useful basis for government? Explain.

### Reading Skill
3. **Use Sentence Clues to Determine Meaning** What does *tolerance* mean in the following sentence? Tolerance is a willingness to respect different beliefs and customs. What clue tells you to expect a definition?

### Vocabulary *Builder*
4. Write two definitions for each word: <u>conflict</u>, <u>welfare</u>, <u>maintain</u>. First, write a formal definition for your teacher. Second, write a definition in everyday English for a classmate.

### Writing
5. Create a chart to compare the rule of Chandragupta and Asoka.

# Citizen Heroes

**History-Social Science** 6.5.6 Describe the growth of the Maurya empire and the political and moral achievements of the emperor Asoka.

| Respect | Caring | Responsibility | Fairness | Honesty | Civic Virtue |
| --- | --- | --- | --- | --- | --- |

# Asoka Emperor of India

**One mark of a good citizen is respecting the rights and feelings of others. In India, the Maurya emperor Asoka encouraged this kind of respect for others.**

**Asoka** had stone pillars set up across India. They announced laws and promised fairness to the people. Asoka tried to be a moral example to his subjects.

Although he was a Buddhist, Asoka favored respect for people of all religions. One pillar said, "All people are my children. And just as I desire for my children that they should be well and happy, so do I wish the same for all people."

## Connect to Today

**Cesar Chavez** (SAY sahr CHAH vays) was a Mexican American leader. His motto was "Sí se puede!" or "It can be done!" He worked to improve the terrible working conditions of migrant farmworkers (people who move from place to place to find work).

Like Asoka, Cesar Chavez believed in respect for all people. As he said, "What is at stake is human dignity. If a man is not accorded respect, he cannot respect himself, and if he does not respect himself, he cannot demand it."

## Analyze CITIZEN HEROES

Suppose that you could set up a stone pillar that told everyone your views about respect. What would the pillar say? Write six "laws" that tell how to be respectful. Your laws can include both "do's" and "don'ts." Some examples include "Be polite to others" and "Don't make fun of differences."

## Section 3 India's Classical Age

**Standards Preview**

**H-SS** 6.5.7 Discuss important aesthetic and intellectual traditions (e.g., Sanskrit literature, including the *Bhagavad Gita;* medicine; metallurgy; and mathematics, including Hindu-Arabic numerals and the zero).

**E-LA** Reading 6.1.4 Monitor expository text for unknown words or words with novel meanings by using word, sentence, and paragraph clues to determine meaning.

### Reading Preview

#### Reading Skill

**Use Paragraph Clues to Determine Meaning**
Sometimes you will have to look beyond the sentence to find clues about the meaning of a word. Paragraphs will often have clues that can help you build meaning. They may provide examples that can help you understand an unfamiliar word. Another clue in a paragraph might include a description that suggests a meaning.

#### Vocabulary *Builder*

**High-Use Words**
**circumstances** (SER kuhm stan sehz), p. 255
**medical** (MEHD ih kuhl), p. 258

**Key Terms and People**
classical age (KLAS ih kuhl AYJ), p. 254
Samudra Gupta (suh MU druh GUP tuh), p. 255
Chandra Gupta II (CHUHN druh GUP tuh), p. 255
decimal system (DEHS uh muhl SIHS tuhm), p. 258

**Background Knowledge** After the collapse of the Maurya empire, India broke apart into many small kingdoms. However, the country continued to see advances in art, literature, math, and science. This time of great advances that affected the culture for centuries to come is sometimes called the classical age of India. During this time, a second great empire arose on the subcontinent. In this section, you will read about some of the achievements of this age.

**Main Idea**
The Gupta Dynasty created another Indian empire, starting in A.D. 335.

## The Gupta Empire

Chandra Gupta, the first Gupta ruler, was named after the founder of the Maurya Empire. Like the first Maurya emperor, he dreamed of building an empire, and he began his rule in the region of Magadha. He expanded his territory by war and by peaceful means. By the time Chandra Gupta died in A.D. 330, he had conquered several kingdoms in northern India. On his deathbed, he told his son to "rule the world."

**Samudra Gupta** did his best to follow his father's order. Calling himself the "Exterminator of Kings," he conquered most of northern India.

The Gupta Empire reached its greatest size under **Chandra Gupta II.** Chandra Gupta II used force to expand his power. Then, like Asoka, he worked to bring peace and prosperity to India. A Buddhist monk from China named Fa Hsien visited India during this time. He wrote:

> **❝The people are numerous and happy. . . . If they want to go, they go. If they want to stay, they stay. The king governs without . . . corporal [physical] punishments. . . . criminals are simply fined . . . according to the <u>circumstances</u> (of each case). . . . Throughout the whole country the people do not kill any living creature. . . .❞**

—Fa Hsien, *A Record of the Buddhistic Kingdoms*

**E-LA 6.1.4 Use Paragraph Clues to Determine Meaning**

What do you think *reign* means? What paragraph clues did you use?

**Vocabulary *Builder***

<u>circumstances</u> (SER kuhm stan sehz) *n.* surrounding conditions

✔**Checkpoint** How did the rule of Chandra Gupta II differ from that of his father?

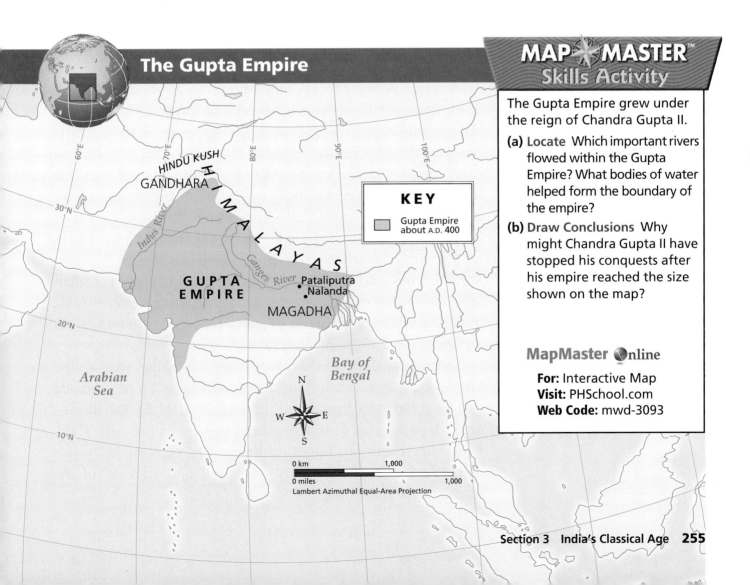

**The Gupta Empire**

KEY

Gupta Empire about A.D. 400

HINDU KUSH
GANDHARA
Indus River
HIMALAYAS
Ganges River
GUPTA EMPIRE
Pataliputra
Nalanda
MAGADHA
Arabian Sea
Bay of Bengal

0 km 1,000
0 miles 1,000
Lambert Azimuthal Equal-Area Projection

**MAP✦MASTER™ Skills Activity**

The Gupta Empire grew under the reign of Chandra Gupta II.

**(a) Locate** Which important rivers flowed within the Gupta Empire? What bodies of water helped form the boundary of the empire?

**(b) Draw Conclusions** Why might Chandra Gupta II have stopped his conquests after his empire reached the size shown on the map?

**MapMaster ◗nline**

**For:** Interactive Map
**Visit:** PHSchool.com
**Web Code:** mwd-3093

# Achievements of the Classical Age

Like many of the other leaders in India, Chandra Gupta II used his wealth to encourage artists and scholars. Across India, there was a burst of learning and creative activity.

**A Flowering of Literature**   Before and during Gupta rule, many kinds of literature flourished. The greatest writer of the time was the poet Kalidasa. You have read one of his poems in Chapter 6. Kalidasa wrote plays and poetry in the ancient language of Sanskrit. In this poem, he compares the court of a Gupta ruler to a monsoon storm:

> **❝Its mansions are your equals—
> they have for your lightning
> the flash of dazzling women,
> for your rainbow
> arrays of paintings,
> for your deep and soothing thunder
> drums beating for dance and song,
> for your core waters
> floors inset with gems,
> and roofs that graze the sky for your loftiness.❞**
>
> —Kalidasa, "The Gupta Court"

Another popular form of literature was the fable. A fable is a short story with a moral, or lesson, at the end. Often fables use animals to tell something about how people behave. One Indian fable describes two frogs that fall into a pail of milk and cannot jump out. They swim for a long time. Then, one of the frogs gives up hope and drowns. The other frog keeps swimming. Finally, the milk turns into butter. The frog that kept swimming can now jump out easily. This fable's lesson is to keep trying even when things look hopeless.

Folk tales and fairy tales were also widely read. Indian fairy tales often include great journeys and magical creatures. Indian folk tales often involve common people who win out in difficult situations by being clever.

One Indian folk tale involves a farmer whose well is dry. Worse yet, thieves are lurking around his farm. So he pretends that he is hiding a treasure in the well. That night, the thieves dig so hard looking for the treasure that they fix the well. Then, when they climb out they find themselves surounded by soldiers. So the farmer gets his well fixed and gets rid of the thieves at the same time.

Lotus in bloom

Crown or flag

Picking a flower

**Arts and Entertainment**   Other arts flourished under Chandra Gupta II as well. For example, sculptors made statues from stone and bronze. Most of these sculptures were used to decorate Hindu and Buddhist temples.

Many temples and monasteries were built during this time. In some areas, stonecutters carved groups of temple buildings from one huge rock. Today, tourists from all over the world travel to India to visit these rock-cut shrines.

Music and dance also thrived during the Gupta period. Dancers created works based on Hindu literature. Musicians composed songs for Indian instruments such as the *veena*, a stringed instrument, and the *mridangam,* a drum that was held sideways and played with both hands.

The game of chess was invented in India. The pieces of an early chess set represented an ancient Indian army. They included a king, war chariots, horse soldiers, elephants, and foot soldiers. The game first appeared in northern India. From India, chess moved along trade routes both east, into other parts of Asia, and west, into the Middle East and Europe.

**Math and Astronomy**  One advance under Gupta rule was the development of Hindu-Arabic numerals and the concept of zero as a number. The Hindu-Arabic numerals, which are the numerals 0 through 9, can be used to write any number.

Another advance was the development of the *decimal system.* This is a counting system based on units of ten. Together these advances created a number system that was later adopted by Arabs and spread to Europe. Today, Hindu-Arabic numerals and the decimal system are used worldwide.

An important scientist of the time was an astronomer and mathematician named Aryabhatta. In A.D. 499, Aryabhatta wrote an important book on Hindu mathematics. It covered arithmetic, algebra, and trigonometry. Hundreds of years later, mathematicians in Europe used Aryabhatta's writings to learn how to calculate the area of triangles and the volume of spheres.

Aryabhatta was the first astronomer to understand that the Earth is round and that it rotates on its own axis to create day and night. He realized that the moon shines only because of reflected sunlight. He also realized that eclipses of the sun and moon are caused by movements of Earth and its moon, not by angry gods, as was widely believed at that time.

**Vocabulary** *Builder*
**medical** (MEHD ih kuhl) *adj.* relating to medicine and the treatment of disease or injury

**Medicine**  Indian doctors made progress in medical science as well. A system of medicine that evolved from the early medicine of Vedic times is known as *Ayurveda*, which means "the science of life."

Ancient Ayurvedic medical textbooks describe more than a thousand diseases and hundreds of medicines made from plants, animal parts, and minerals. The texts also explain how to treat problems from broken bones to blindness.

**Medical Herbs**
Some of the herbs which were used for medical purposes in ancient India are still used today. **Critical Thinking: Apply Information** *Why do you think herbal medicine is still practiced today?*

**Metallurgy**   Gupta artisans also made progress in metallurgy, the science that deals with extracting metal from ore and using it to create useful objects. Gupta artisans produced metal of great purity. The Iron Pillar of Delhi is a famous example of that skill. This 23-foot-high column was made from a single piece of iron. It has stood outside for more than 1,500 years without showing any sign of rust.

**The End of Gupta Rule**   Many achievements in art and science continued after the death of Chandra Gupta II. Eventually, though, the Gupta Empire grew weak. By 540 A.D., Gupta rule had ended. However, the great achievements of India's classical age continued to influence Indian life and culture.

 **Checkpoint**   **What were two key advances in mathematics during the Gupta age?**

**Looking Back and Ahead**   In this section, you have read about the rise of the Gupta Empire. You have also learned about some of the achievements of India's classical age. In the next unit, you will read about the rise of another great Asian civilization in ancient China.

**Iron Pillar of Delhi**
This monument from the Gupta age of India shows the great skill of ancient metalworkers. **Critical Thinking: Link Past and Present** *What are monuments in America today usually made of? What is iron used for today?*

---

## Section 3   Check Your Progress

**Progress Monitoring** Online
**For:** Self-test with instant help
**Visit:** PHSchool.com
**Web Code:** mwa-3093

 **Standards Review**   H-SS: 6.5.7; E-LA: Reading 6.1.4

**Comprehension and Critical Thinking**

**1. (a) Explain** How was the Gupta Empire created?
**(b) Apply Information** How did the Gupta kings rule their empire?

**2. (a) List** What were the important cultural achievements of the Gupta age?
**(b) Draw Inferences** What factors helped inspire the arts in Gupta India?

**Reading Skill**

**3. Use Paragraph Clues to Determine Meaning** Read the first paragraph under **Medicine** on page 258. What is medical science? Explain the clues you used.

**Vocabulary** *Builder*

On a separate piece of paper, finish the following sentences in a way that shows that you understand the underlined word.

**4.** Examples of <u>medical</u> advances during India's classical age include _____.

**5.** Many <u>circumstances</u> surrounded Asoka's decision to change the way he led his empire, including _____.

**Writing**

**6.** You are assigned to write a paragraph about the most important development of the classical age. Write a sentence you could use as a topic sentence. Then write a sentence that you could use as a concluding sentence.

# Analysis Skills

# Distinguish Primary and Secondary Sources

A *primary source* is information from someone who saw or was a part of what is being described. A *secondary source* is information recorded later by someone who was not a part of it. Knowing which is which will help you understand history.

**Chapter Standards**

**History-Social Science**

**Research, Evidence, and Point of View 4**
Students assess the credibility of primary and secondary sources and draw sound conclusions from them.

**❝**The king shall ever be wakeful. He shall divide both the day and the night into eight nalikas [1.5 hours]. During the first one-eighth part of the day, he shall post watchmen and attend to the accounts. During the second part, he shall look to the affairs of both citizens and country people. During the third, he shall receive revenue in gold and attend to the appointments of superintendents. During the fifth, he shall correspond with his ministers, and receive the secret information gathered by his spies. During the sixth, he may engage himself in his favorite amusements. During the seventh, he shall superintend elephants, horses, chariots, and infantry. During the eighth part, he shall consider plans of military operations with his commander-in-chief. At the close of the day he shall observe the evening prayer.**❞**

—Kautilya, The Arthashastra, c. 250 B.C

**❝**Chandragupta got many of his ideas for government from his capable advisor Kautilya. These ideas were later collected in a book called the Arthashastra. The book provides detailed advice on how a ruler should deal with his subjects, or people under his control. "The primary duty of a king," the Arthashastra says, "is the protection of his subjects.**❞**

—Ancient History by Diane Hart. Copyright © 2006, Prentice Hall

**Learn the Skill** *Follow these steps to distinguish primary and secondary sources.*

1. **Identify the source of the information.** Who wrote the information? Was it created at the time of the event or much later?

2. **Identify the form of the information.** Examples of primary sources include letters, photographs, and speeches. Examples of secondary sources include biographies, textbooks, and encyclopedia entries. Sometimes a secondary source will include pieces of primary sources.

3. **Decide whether the source is primary or secondary.** Use the information you have gathered to decide.

**Practice the Skill** *Answer the following questions for each passage above.*

1. **Identify the source.** (a) Who wrote the first passage? When was it written? (b) Who wrote the second passage? When?

2. **Identify the form.** (a) Is the first passage a written record or a speech? (b) Is the second passage a textbook entry or a biography?

3. **Decide whether the source is primary or secondary.** (a) Is the first passage a primary or a secondary source? (b) Is the second passage a primary or a secondary source?

**Apply the Skill**
*See page 263 of the Review and Assessment.*

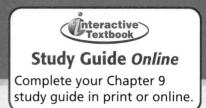

## Chapter Summary  H-SS: 6.5.6, 6.5.7

### Section 1 The Maurya Empire

- Chandragupta conquered many kingdoms to create India's first empire.
- Chandragupta established a bureaucracy to govern the regions and provinces of his empire.
- A spy network kept the emperor informed of dangers.

### Section 2 Asoka's Rule of Tolerance

- Chandragupta's grandson Asoka came to power during a time of conflict.
- After he had conquered Kalinga, Asoka converted to Buddhism.
- During the rest of his reign, Asoka practiced tolerance and worked for the welfare of his people.

### Section 3 India's Classical Age

- The Gupta Empire was founded by Chandra Gupta. It arose during a time of increased learning and culture.
- The classical age saw growth in arts, entertainment, and science.

**Coin of Chandragupta**

## Standards Practice  H-SS: 6.5.6, 6.5.7

# Vocabulary *Builder*

### High-Use Words

Decide whether each underlined word is used correctly. If it is, explain why. If not, rewrite the rest of the sentence to make it logical.

1. Because Chandragupta's government was **efficient**, it collapsed during his lifetime.

2. After Asoka completed his conquest of Kalinga, his reign was noted for great **conflict**.

3. Asoka believed that he had a duty to **maintain** roads and other facilities for the good of his people.

4. **Medical** science grew during the classical age.

5. War elephants could **terrify** the enemy.

### Key Terms

Answer the following questions in complete sentences that show your understanding of the Key Terms.

1. How did Asoka show tolerance toward his people?

2. What are some examples of Chandragupta's military strategy?

3. How did dividing his empire into provinces help Chandragupta govern?

4. How did Chandragupta's bureaucracy help him govern his empire?

5. How did the principle of *ahimsa* affect the way Asoka treated animals?

## Apply Reading Skills

**Use Clues to Determine Meaning** Find an unfamiliar word in Chapter 9. Use word, sentence, or paragraph clues to determine its meaning. Write the definition and the clues you used to find it.

## Comprehension and Critical Thinking

1. (a) **Recall** When was India first united into a single empire?
   (b) **Apply Information** What methods did Chandragupta use to create his empire?
   (c) **Analyze Cause and Effect** How did the ruling system reflect those methods?

2. (a) **Explain** How did Asoka rule India?
   (b) **Contrast** How did his rule differ from those of previous Maurya kings?
   (c) **Identify Benefits** Which style of rule is more effective? Why?

3. (a) **Describe** Discuss the Gupta Empire.
   (b) **Compare** How did it compare with the Maurya Empire?

4. (a) **Recall** Why is the Gupta period called a Classical Age?
   (b) **Distinguish Facts from Opinions** Read the following sentence and decide if it contains a fact or an opinion. Defend your decision with supporting details. "The best stories and the best art that India ever produced were created during the Gupta period."

5. (a) **Recall** What are some of India's important advances in mathematics?
   (b) **Draw Inferences** How might understanding mathematics have helped Aryabhatta understand the movement of the earth and the moon?

## Researching

**Advances During the Classical Age**
Before, during, and after Gupta rule came many advances in learning and culture. Use library resources and the Internet to learn more about Indian advances in an area of learning or culture that is important to you. Choose a task below to work on. Share your work with the class in an oral presentation.

**Musicians:** Listen to a recording of Indian classical music. Then write a review of the recording. Provide the name of the tune, and list the instruments used. Then describe how the different parts of the recording make you feel.

**Scientists:** Write a paragraph describing one or more important contributions made by Indian scientists or mathematicians during the classical age.

**Researching Online**
**For:** Help in starting this activity
**Visit:** PHSchool.com
**Web Code:** mwe-3093

## Writing

1. **Write a paragraph on the following topic.** Two great ancient empires arose in India, the Maurya Empire and the Gupta Empire. Write a paragraph telling how these empires were alike and how they were different.
   **Your paragraph should:**
   • state a thesis or purpose for writing.
   • offer details of how the empires were alike.
   • offer details of how the empires were different.
   • conclude with a two- or three-sentence summary.

2. **Write a Short Narrative.** Imagine you are a foreigner in India seeing war elephants for the first time. Write a short paragraph describing what happened.

# Apply Analysis Skills

**Use the quote at the right to answer these questions.**

1. Who wrote the information?

2. Was it created at the time of the event or much later?

3. What is the form of the information?

4. Is this a primary or secondary source of information?

> **"**Wherever medical roots or fruits are not available I have had them imported and grown. Along roads I have had wells dug and trees planted for the benefit of humans and animals.**"**
>
> —Pillar of Asoka, 3rd Century B.C.

# Test Yourself

1. **Chandragupta united India through military conquest and by**
   A using Hindu priests.
   B following the Eightfold Path.
   C establishing a strong government.
   D allowing local leaders to rule their villages.

2. **Which empire did Chandragupta establish?**
   A Magadha
   B Maurya
   C Kalinga
   D Gupta

**Refer to the image below to answer Question 3.**

3. **Asoka built shrines such as the one shown below as part of his commitment to**

   A Hinduism.
   B Buddhism.
   C the *Arthrashasta.*
   D none of the above

**Refer to the quotation below to answer Question 4.**

*"Respect for mother and father is good. Generosity to friends, acquaintances, relatives, Brahmans and ascetics is good. Not killing living beings is good. Moderation in spending and moderation in saving is good."*

4. **This quote is from one of Asoka's pillars, which describe the moral law under which Asoka attempted to rule. Which of the following is NOT a principle of Asoka's moral law?**
   A welfare of the people
   B tolerance
   C reincarnation
   D *ahimsa*

5. **Asoka's ruthless takeover of the Maurya Empire was based on his acceptance of the ideas of**
   A the *Arthashastra.*
   B Buddhism.
   C both (A) and (B).
   D none of the above

# Writing Workshop

## Expository Composition
## Comparison and Contrast

### ▶ Introduction

In a comparison-and-contrast essay, you analyze the similarities and differences between two or more people, places, things, events, or ideas. A comparison-and-contrast essay should have the following characteristics:

- The subject should involve at least two subjects that are similar in some ways and different in others.

- The thesis statement should clearly state in general terms the main point you want to make.

- The organizational pattern should show how your subjects are alike and different.

**Assignment** On the following pages, you will learn how to write a comparison-and-contrast essay. You will get step-by-step instructions. Each step will include an example from a sample essay comparing and contrasting the Maurya rulers Chandragupta and Asoka.

Read the instructions and the examples. Then, follow each step to plan and write a 500–700 word essay on this topic:

**Compare and contrast the Maurya rulers Chandragupta and Asoka.**

### ▶ Prewriting

**Clarify the assignment.** Before you begin, identify the items that you are supposed to write about.

**Gather details.** Look for facts, descriptions, and examples that show how your subjects are similar and different. One way to organize these details is by using a Venn diagram.

**Create a working thesis.** After you review your notes, write a sentence that states your main point about the overall similarities and differences between your subjects. This "working thesis" may change, but it should guide your drafting.

> **Sample working thesis:** Both Chandragupta and Asoka waged war and ruled empires on the Indian subcontinent, but their ways of ruling were very different.

**History-Social Science**

**6.5** Students analyze the geographic, political, economic, religious, and social structures of the early civilizations of India.

**English-Language Arts**

**Writing 6.2.2** Write expository compositions (e.g., description, explanation, comparison and contrast, problem and solution).

> For a review of the steps in the writing process, see the **Historian's Toolkit,** *Write Like a Historian.*

> **Sample assignment:** Compare and contrast the Maurya rulers Chandragupta and Asoka. Note that this assignment asks you to show how two rulers were similar and different.

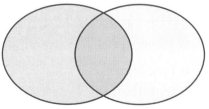

Chandragupta          Asoka

## ▶ Drafting

**Decide how to organize your writing.** There are two main ways to organize a comparison-and-contrast essay: the block method and the point-by-point method. Choose the one that best fits your topic and thesis.

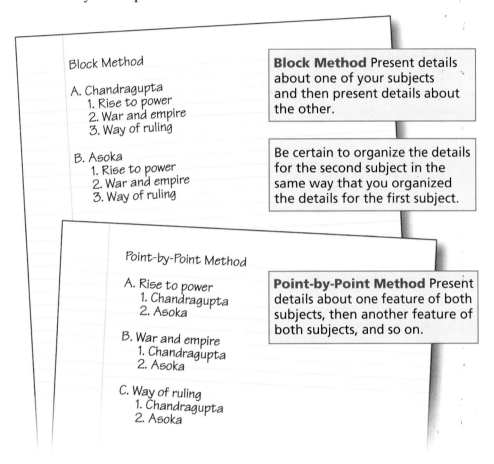

Block Method

A. Chandragupta
   1. Rise to power
   2. War and empire
   3. Way of ruling

B. Asoka
   1. Rise to power
   2. War and empire
   3. Way of ruling

**Block Method** Present details about one of your subjects and then present details about the other.

Be certain to organize the details for the second subject in the same way that you organized the details for the first subject.

Point-by-Point Method

A. Rise to power
   1. Chandragupta
   2. Asoka

B. War and empire
   1. Chandragupta
   2. Asoka

C. Way of ruling
   1. Chandragupta
   2. Asoka

**Point-by-Point Method** Present details about one feature of both subjects, then another feature of both subjects, and so on.

**State your thesis.** Write an introductory paragraph that clearly states your thesis, or main point.

**Support your thesis with examples and details.** The more specific and concrete your supporting details are, the better the reader will understand how they relate to your thesis. Use comparison-and-contrast transitions such as *like, similarly, different from, in contrast, on the one hand,* and *on the other hand.*

**Write a strong conclusion.** In your final paragraph, show the reader how the evidence you present supports your thesis.

# Writing Workshop *continued*

## ▶ Student Model

Read the following model of a comparison-and-contrast essay. Notice how it includes the characteristics you have learned.

### Chandragupta and Asoka

India's Maurya Empire had two outstanding leaders. Although Chandragupta and his grandson Asoka both defeated enemies and ruled India, the ways they came to power and the ways they ruled were very different.

> The opening paragraph contains the thesis statement.

Each became ruler of India but in different ways. Chandragupta was not born into a royal family. He may have been born into a family that was poor or in the warrior caste. He rose to power by waging war. As the grandson of Chandragupta, however, Asoka was in line to rule. Both rulers used war to increase their power. Chandragupta conquered India's many independent kingdoms. He had his army use the Indian long bow and fierce war elephants. These methods helped defeat enemy soldiers. By 305 B.C., he had created an empire. Asoka also waged war. His army crushed Kalinga, India's last important independent kingdom.

> Is this composition organized using the block method or the point-by-point method?

> Each paragraph begins with a topic sentence. The sentences that follow contain supporting details.

After they had defeated their enemies, however, Asoka and Chandragupta ruled their empires in entirely different ways. Chandragupta did not trust his people. His spies were everywhere. He used fear of punishment to control his empire. In contrast, Asoka tried to govern by the Buddhist principle of nonviolence. Under Asoka's rule, the government built roads and hospitals. The people lived in peace and without fear. India prospered.

In conclusion, there were as many differences between these two emperors as there were similarities. Chandragupta and Asoka were both strong rulers who governed a large empire. However, Chandragupta ruled through force and fear. Asoka tried to make life better for his subjects.

> The last paragraph restates the thesis and summarizes the key information.

## ▶ Revising

After completing your draft, read it again carefully to find ways to improve your writing. Here are some questions to ask yourself:

### Revise to strengthen your thesis
- Is the thesis statement strong and clear?
- Do all of the details support your main point?
- Are the similarities and differences between your subjects clear throughout your essay?
- What other details could you add?

### Revise to heighten interest
- Does the first paragraph capture the reader's attention?
- Can you describe the details in more specific or colorful language?
- Is there any repeated information that you could cut?

### Revise to meet Standard English conventions
- Are all the sentences complete, with a subject and a verb?
- Are all the words spelled correctly? Use a spell-checker or a dictionary to make sure.
- Are all the proper nouns capitalized, including names of people and places?
- Did you use proper punctuation? Check punctuation within sentences as well as at the ends of sentences.

*Like his grandfather, Asoka waged war. First, he battled his brothers in order to rule the empire. He was the third maurya emperor Next, he sent his soldiers to conquer Kalinga.*

## ▶ Rubric for Self-Assessment

*Evaluate your comparison-and-contrast essay using this rating scale.*

|  | Score 4 | Score 3 | Score 2 | Score 1 |
|---|---|---|---|---|
| **Organization** | Uses either block method or point-by-point method and presents information clearly | Uses either block method or point-by-point method and presents most information clearly | Chooses an organization not suited to a comparison-and-contrast essay | Shows lack of organizational strategy |
| **Presentation** | Develops ideas with relevant facts, details, or examples; links all information to comparison and contrast | Develops most ideas with facts, details, or examples; links most information to comparison and contrast | Does not develop most ideas in depth; some information is not linked to comparison and contrast | Does not provide facts, details, or examples to support ideas |
| **Use of Language** | Varies sentence structure and vocabulary successfully; has very few mechanical errors | Uses some variety in sentence structure and vocabulary; has few mechanical errors | Uses repetitive sentence structure and vocabulary; has many mechanical errors | Shows poor use of language; generates confusion; has many mechanical errors |

# Unit 4

 **Chapter Standards**

## History-Social Science

**6.6** Students analyze the geographic, political, economic, religious, and social structures of the early civilizations of China.

## ✓ What You Will Learn

**CHAPTER 10,** pp. 270–295

### The Rise of Civilization in China

Civilization in China began in the Huang He valley. Dynasties such as the Shang and the Zhou came to power.

**CHAPTER 11,** pp. 296–321

### Chinese Society and Thought

Family relationships and religious beliefs were important to the people of ancient China. The teachings of Confucius, a Chinese scholar, significantly affected Chinese society.

**CHAPTER 12,** pp. 322–349

### Growth of the Chinese Empire

After many years of conflict, the Qin Dynasty united China under one rule. Under the Han Dynasty, China experienced expansion and cultural growth.

##  Quick View Video

**Discovery School Video** View Ancient China for a quick preview of the main ideas of this unit.

The Great **Wall** of China

# Ancient China

Shang territory
1700 B.C.

Qin China
221 B.C.

Lu
551 B.C.

Huang He
Yangtze (Chang) R.

## *Think* like a historian

This map shows the part of the world in which the civilization of ancient China developed. Over time, several different ruling families came to power.

**As you read this unit, think about this question:**
*In what ways do earlier civilizations help to shape how people live today?*

# The Rise of Civilization in China (3500 B.C.–481 B.C.)

## Prepare to Read

### Chapter Standards

**History-Social Science**
**6.6** Students analyze the geographic, political, economic, religious, and social structures of the early civilizations of China.

**Section 1,** pp. 274–277

**The Middle Kingdom**

**Section 2,** pp. 280–285

**China's First Dynasties**

**Section 3,** pp. 286–291

**China Under the Zhou Dynasty**

### ✔ What You Will Learn

Geographic features of China, such as its location and landforms, caused civilization there to develop in isolation.

China's first historical dynasty, the Shang, developed in the Huang He valley. The Shang developed a strong government, built large cities, and created many works of art.

The Zhou Dynasty seized control of China from the Shang Dynasty around 1050 B.C. Zhou leaders established a government tradition known as the Mandate of Heaven.

Shang bronze elephant

**Chapter Events**

**3500 B.C.**
Farming villages form in the Huang He valley.

**2200 B.C.**
A strong ruler appears in the Huang He valley region.

**Other Events**

**4000 B.C.**

**3000 B.C.**

**2000 B.C.**

**3700 B.C.** Mesopotamians begin to use the plow.

**2150 B.C.** Floods affect civilization in Egypt.

## Where and When?
The farming culture that began in China's Huang He valley about 6,000 years ago developed into one of the ancient world's great civilizations.

The Gobi Desert was an important geographic feature that separated ancient China from other parts of the world.

**1760 B.C.**
The Shang Dynasty comes to power in China.

**481 B.C.**
The Era of the Warring States begins.

**2000 B.C.**

**1000 B.C.**

**B.C./A.D.**

**1650 B.C.** The Hittite Empire is established.

**490 B.C.** Greek forces win victory at Marathon.

The Rise of Civilization in China    **271**

# How to Read History

 ## History Reading Skill

### *Previewing* Clarify Texts

Taking notes is an important reading skill that you will use in many subject areas. It can prove especially useful when you need to keep track of dates, people, and events. In addition, note taking helps you clarify your understanding of events by drawing key connections between them. Look at the example below for some note-taking strategies.

 **Chapter Standards**

**English-Language Arts**

**Reading 6.2.4** Clarify an understanding of texts by creating outlines, logical notes, summaries, or reports.

**1** Review the text under the heading Asoka's Rise to Power in Chapter 9. Create a two-column note-taking organizer. Label the left side "Main Ideas" and the right side "Important Facts."

**2** Next, list main ideas. Here, one main idea can be taken from the heading. The other main idea links several related people in the text.

**3** This excerpt notes important facts about Asoka's rise to power. It includes the dates and a brief description of events. Listing the three emperors in order helps you remember who they were and when they ruled. You can also use arrows and numbers to indicate links between information.

**Main idea taken from the text heading**

**Key date**

| Main Ideas | Important Facts |
|---|---|
| Asoka rose to power | Fought brothers to take throne—269 B.C. |
| Mauryan emperors | Chandragupta ➡ Bindusara ➡ Asoka |

**Main idea grouping key people**

**Symbols show links between facts**

# Vocabulary *Builder*

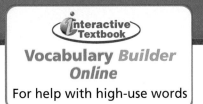
**Interactive Textbook**

**Vocabulary *Builder* Online**

For help with high-use words

## *Previewing* **High-Use Academic Words**

| High-Use Word | Definition | Sample Sentence About History |
|---|---|---|
| **varied** (VEHR eed) (Section 1, p. 274) | *adj.* consisting of or including many different types of things or people | The <u>varied</u> landscape affected the types of civilizations that developed in the area. |
| **drain** (drayn) (Section 1, p. 275) | *v.* to empty its waters | The waters of the river system <u>drain</u> the lands of the surrounding valley. |
| **channel** (CHAN uhl) (Section 2, p. 281) | *n.* long passage dug into the ground that water or other liquids can flow along | The excess water was directed through a <u>channel</u> to prevent flooding. |
| **interpret** (ihn TER pruht) (Section 2, p. 284) | *v.* to explain the meaning of; make understandable | Scholars have learned to <u>interpret</u> the ancient text in order to gain knowledge about the civilization. |
| **demonstrate** (DEHM uhn strayt) (Section 3, p. 287) | *v.* to show that you have a particular skill, quality, or ability | The king <u>demonstrated</u> many qualities of a good ruler. |
| **capable** (KAY puh buhl) (Section 3, p. 291) | *adj.* having the skill, power, or intelligence to do something | The army proved <u>capable</u> of defending the region. |

## *Previewing* **Key Terms and People**

ideograph

**oracle bones**

loess, p. 275
cultivation, p. 275
steppe, p. 276
tributary, p. 276

dike, p. 281
dynasty, p. 281
oracle bones, p. 284
ideograph, p. 284

Mandate of Heaven, p. 287
warlord, p. 289
chaos, p. 289
cavalry, p. 291

# 1 The Middle Kingdom

**Standards Preview**

**H-SS 6.6.2** Explain the geographic features of China that made governance and the spread of ideas and goods difficult and served to isolate the country from the rest of the world.

**E-LA Reading 6.2.4** Clarify an understanding of texts by creating outlines, logical notes, summaries, or reports.

## Reading Preview

 **Reading Skill**

**Clarify Main Points** You will notice that this text includes headings of different sizes. Smaller headings give information related to the topic of the larger headings. Use both types of headings when organizing your notes. Start by listing main ideas linked to larger headings. Then, add details linked to smaller headings.

**Vocabulary** *Builder*

**High-Use Words**
varied (VEHR eed), p. 274
drain (drayn), p. 275

**Key Terms**
loess (LOH ehs), p. 275
cultivation (kuhl tuh VAY shuhn), p. 275
steppe (stehp), p. 276
tributary (TRIHB yoo ter ee), p. 276

**Vocabulary** *Builder*
varied (VEHR eed) *adj.* consisting of or including many different types of things or people

**Main Idea**
Geographic features, such as mountains and deserts, isolated ancient China from other early civilizations.

**Background Knowledge** The geographic features of a country include its borders, climate, and landforms, such as mountains and deserts. China is a large country with a highly varied geography. In this section, you will read about some of the geographic features of China. You will learn how these features influenced the development of China and isolated it from the rest of the world.

## Key Geographic Features

China is an enormous land. It covers an area one-third larger than that of the United States. As you can see from the map on the next page, China also has many different geographic features, such as rugged mountains, vast deserts, and dense forests. These geographic features played a key role in Chinese history. They divided the land into separate regions and made travel difficult. This limited the spread of goods and ideas in China. The country's geography also made governance, or the act of governing, more difficult for its people. Despite these challenges, however, China gave rise to a great civilization.

**River Systems** Rivers contributed to China's development, just as they did in Mesopotamia, Egypt, and India. China has two main river systems. The Huang He, or Yellow River, flows through northern China. The Chang, China's longest river, <u>drains</u> south-central China. These rivers provided water for farming and helped move people and goods.

Chinese civilization began in the Huang He valley. The Huang He begins in the high mountains of western China and flows east to the Yellow Sea. Before entering the sea, it crosses a low, flat area called the North China Plain. A fine yellow dust called **loess** covers this plain. This dust blows in from the deserts to the north. Loess is very fertile and makes perfect soil for the **cultivation,** or growing, of grain and other crops. This plain remains an important agricultural region in which crops such as wheat, cotton, and corn are grown.

The Huang He carries huge amounts of loess as it flows toward the sea. In fact, the name Yellow River comes from the color of this soil in the water. The river deposits loess on its banks and in its riverbed. Over time, the riverbed fills with soil, causing the water level to rise. Eventually, the river overflows its banks and floods the surrounding plain. In years past, hundreds of thousands of people died in these floods. Thus, while the Huang He has brought great benefits to China, it has also caused great harm. For that reason, it is often called "China's Sorrow."

**Vocabulary Builder**
<u>drain</u> (drayn) v. to empty its waters

**E-LA 6.2.4 Clarify Main Points**
What important details might you list in your notes for the text below the smaller heading, "River Systems"?

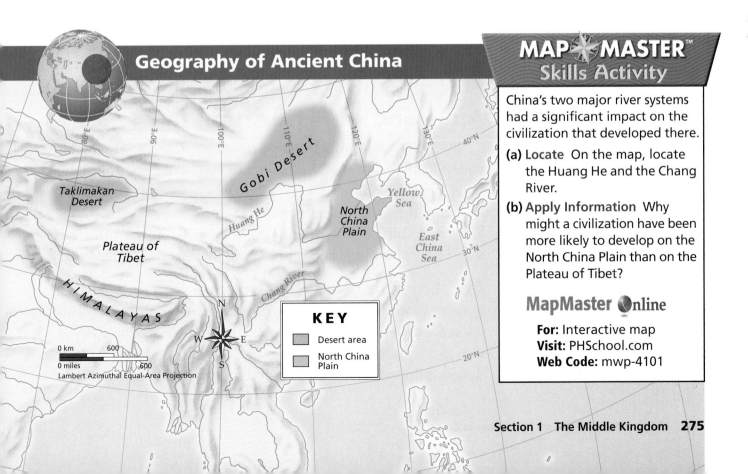

**Geography of Ancient China**

**MAP MASTER™ Skills Activity**

China's two major river systems had a significant impact on the civilization that developed there.

**(a) Locate** On the map, locate the Huang He and the Chang River.

**(b) Apply Information** Why might a civilization have been more likely to develop on the North China Plain than on the Plateau of Tibet?

**MapMaster Online**

**For:** Interactive map
**Visit:** PHSchool.com
**Web Code:** mwp-4101

KEY
Desert area
North China Plain

Taklimakan Desert
Gobi Desert
Plateau of Tibet
HIMALAYAS
Huang He
North China Plain
Yellow Sea
East China Sea
Chang River

0 km 600
0 miles 600
Lambert Azimuthal Equal-Area Projection

**Natural Barriers**

This photograph shows the landscape of the Plateau of Tibet. **Critical Thinking: Link Past and Present** *Explain why natural features such as the Plateau of Tibet may no longer present as great an obstacle to travel and communication.*

**China's Isolation** Two other geographic factors also influenced Chinese history by isolating the country from other civilizations. One factor was China's location in east Asia, thousands of miles from the ancient cultures of the Middle East, Africa, and South Asia. This made it difficult for ideas and customs to travel between China and those areas.

Natural barriers also worked to isolate China. The country is nearly surrounded by mountains, deserts, and seas. Two great deserts, the Taklimaken and the Gobi, create a barrier to the northwest. To the southwest lie towering mountains, including the Himalayas and the high Plateau of Tibet. To the south lie more mountain ranges, and to the east stretches the vast Pacific Ocean. The easiest route to China crosses the Mongolian **steppe, a dry, grass-covered plain,** that extends northward into Central Asia. This was a key route for the nomadic invaders who entered China in ancient times.

The isolation in which Chinese civilization developed helped produce a unique culture. Largely cut off from other civilizations, China developed its own customs and way of life.

**Checkpoint** **What two factors isolated China from other cultures?**

**Main Idea**

The development of farming villages in the Huang He valley marks the beginning of civilization in ancient China.

# An Island of Civilization

By 3500 B.C., farming villages had formed in the Huang He valley, just west of the North China Plain. Villagers built their houses on low hills above the plain, where flooding presented less of a threat. This early farming culture is known as the Yangshao culture. The people planted grains in the soft loess soil. They raised pigs and dogs, and they hunted and fished.

**An Emerging Civilization** Some of the oldest remains from this time come from the village of Banpo. This village was set on a tributary of the Huang He. **A tributary is a river or stream that flows into a larger river.** The people of Banpo fashioned tools, crafted pottery, and made silk cloth.

Over thousands of years, the culture of the Huang He valley and North China Plain developed into China's first civilization. Villages grew larger. Social classes began to emerge. Trade developed. However, it would take many years for China to unite because of its vast size and rugged terrain.

Because other civilizations were so far away, the people of ancient China knew little about advances in the rest of the world. Their main outside contact occurred with the nomadic groups that lived along China's borders. In the view of the Chinese, China represented an island of civilization in a sea of barbarians. They called China the Middle Kingdom. This meant that, to the Chinese people, China was the center of the world.

 **Checkpoint** How did civilization begin to develop in ancient China?

**Looking Back and Ahead** In this section, you have read about geographic features that influenced early Chinese history and culture. You have also learned that China's location and natural barriers helped isolate the country from the rest of the world. In the next section, you will read about the growth of Chinese civilization and the first Chinese kingdoms.

# Section 1 Check Your Progress

**Progress Monitoring** Online
**For:** Self-test with instant help
**Visit:** PHSchool.com
**Web Code:** mwa-4101

 **Standards Review** H-SS: 6.6.2; E-LA Reading 6.2.4

## Comprehension and Critical Thinking

**1. (a) List** What are the two main river systems of China?
**(b) Evaluate Information** How did such geographic features contribute to the development of China's earliest civilization?

**2. (a) Explain** In what kind of location did the earliest farming villages in northern China arise?
**(b) Identify Cause and Effect** Why did the civilization that grew from these villages become known as the Middle Kingdom?

## Reading Skill

**3. Clarify Main Points** After you have finished reading Section 1, complete your notes for this section. What main ideas and important details did you list for the heading An Emerging Civilization?

## Vocabulary *Builder*

**4.** Write two definitions for each word: loess, cultivation, steppe, and tributary. First, write a formal definition for your teacher. Second, write a definition in everyday English for a classmate.

## Writing

**5.** Write a short description of a topic from this section on which you might choose to write a research paper. Identify the topic and briefly explain some potential main ideas that would relate to your topic.

# The Bird and the Sea
by Tao Tao Liu Sanders

## Prepare to Read

### Reading Skill

**Analyze Setting** The setting of a story is the time and place in which it takes place. Often, a story's plot depends heavily on the setting, giving this element a great deal of importance. As you read the tale below, look for ways in which the setting causes a problem. Then, decide whether the problem is resolved.

### Vocabulary *Builder*

As you read this literature selection, look for the following underlined words:

**mourn** (morn) *v.* to be sad or show sorrow

**burden** (BERD uhn) *n.* anything that a person has to carry or endure, such as sorrow

**foaming** (FOHM eeng) *adj.* forming or gathering a mass of bubbles

**cruelty** (KROO uhl tee) *n.* quality of causing suffering

> **BACKGROUND**
> The earliest Chinese cultures had a religion based on many gods. Gods often represented different aspects of nature. The mysteries of nature were explained in human terms, as shown in this ancient tale.

The Sun God had a daughter whom he loved dearly, more than all his other children. One day, to amuse herself, the little girl took a boat out on the Eastern Sea. Unfortunately a storm blew up while she was quite out of sight of land and waves the size of mountains overwhelmed the boat and drowned her. The Sun God grieved for his favourite daughter but even his powerful rays could not call her back to life and he took his grief away with him to <u>mourn</u> in private.

The dead girl resented her early death and her soul became a small bird called Jingwei. Jingwei had a speckled head, a white beak and red claws, and she hated the sea for depriving her of her life and for robbing her father of his child. Every day she picked up a small stone or twig in her beak and, spreading her wings, flew from the land out over the Eastern Sea. Hovering over the waves she dropped her <u>burden</u> into the water, hoping that one day the sea would be filled with stones and twigs.

For a long time the sea took no notice of the small bird. Then one day he laughed aloud at her, showing his <u>foaming</u> white teeth and taunting, "Tiny bird, tiny bird, cease your labour. Your work will never be done, not in a million years. How can you think that you can ever fill the sea up with stones and twigs?"

The bird beat her wings and cried, "What if I drop stones and twigs for a million years, for a million times a million years, until the end of the world? I shall never stop and one day I shall fill you right up."

"Why do you hate me so much?"

"Because you took away my young life and the lives of countless, countless others who have died from your <u>cruelty</u>."

"Stupid bird," jeered the sea again. "You will never succeed."

"I will, I will," came the mournful cry of the bird as she hovered over the sea. "One day I will succeed."

The small bird flew back to land, only to return again, time after time, to drop her small stones and twigs into the waves. And so she continues to this day.

—From *Dragons, Gods & Spirits from Chinese Mythology,* by Tao Tao Liu Sanders ©1995, Peter Bedrick Books

✓ **Checkpoint** **What was Jingwei trying to do, and why?**

*Analyze* **LITERATURE**

In this tale, the sun, the sea, and the bird think and act like humans. For example, the sun mourns a death, the sea has teeth, and the bird hates the sea. Imagine that you are one of these three characters. Write a letter to one of the other characters. The letter should show your feelings about the story's events.

**E-LA 6.3.3 Analyze Setting**
The setting of a story is its time and place. In this story's plot, the place is much more important than the time. Where does the story take place? What terrible event takes place because of the setting? What is the result of this tragic event?

If you liked this story about the bird and the sea, you might want to read about other ancient Chinese beliefs in *The Gods and Goddesses of Ancient China* by Leonard Everett Fisher.
*Holiday House, 2003*

THE GODS AND GODDESSES OF ANCIENT CHINA
LEONARD EVERETT FISHER

# 2 China's First Dynasties

**H-SS 6.6.1** Locate and describe the origins of Chinese civilization in the Huang-He Valley during the Shang Dynasty.

**E-LA Reading 6.2.4** Clarify an understanding of texts by creating outlines, logical notes, summaries, or reports.

## Reading Preview

### Reading Skill

**Create Logical Notes** As you take notes, you will list important dates. However, do not record *all* dates—only those that relate in a significant way. Always explain in your notes the significance of any dates listed. Doing so will help you remember the dates and clarify your understanding of their meanings in history.

### Vocabulary *Builder*

**High-Use Words**
channel (CHAN uhl), p. 281
interpret (ihn TER pruht), p. 284

**Key Terms**
dike (dik), p. 281
dynasty (DI nuhs tee), p. 281
oracle bones (AWR uh kuhl bohnz), p. 284
ideograph (ihd ee oh GRAF), p. 284

**Background Knowledge** Civilizations arose in just a few parts of the ancient world. In China, the farming culture that began in the Huang He valley grew into one of the world's great civilizations. In this section, you will read about early Chinese civilization. You will learn about the powerful Shang rulers who laid the foundations of Chinese culture, as well as important cultural and artistic advancements that took place during their rule.

**Main Idea**
Archaeologists believe that a strong ruler controlled the civilization of the Huang He valley more than 4,000 years ago.

## The First Ruling Family

Experts are uncertain about when Chinese civilization first began. Ancient Chinese texts describe legendary, or mythical, kings with magical powers, who ruled China long ago. Most historians doubt these accounts. Many do believe, however, that a real king rose to power in northern China about four thousand years ago. This king was known as Yu the Great.

**King Yu's Rise** Although much of King Yu's story appears to be legend, some facts have emerged to support the story. Archaeological finds in the Huang He valley suggest that a strong ruler began to govern in the region around 2200 B.C.

According to legend, Yu worked as an engineer and saved the people from a series of terrible floods. He organized workers and built a flood-control system. The system consisted of drainage <u>channels</u> and dikes, or walls to hold back water. Yu's system ended years of flooding and allowed settlement on the North China Plain. The people were grateful. As one saying goes, "We would have been fish, except for Yu."

For his success, Yu was crowned king. The crown later passed down through Yu's family. For this reason, he is considered the founder of the first Chinese dynasty, or ruling family. Yu's dynasty became known as the Xia [SHEE ah] Dynasty.

## Xia Rule
A total of seventeen kings ruled during the Xia dynasty. They built cities and palaces and also formed large armies. Xia warriors fought with bronze weapons. Bronze is a substance made mostly from copper and tin. Xia artisans, or craft workers, carved beautiful objects from jade.

The Xia kings ruled with a heavy hand. They used armed force to maintain control of China. They also practiced human sacrifice. Remains of human victims have been found at the Xia capital of Erlitou. Xia rule lasted for about 400 years, before the dynasty fell to an invading army.

✔ Checkpoint **According to legend, how did Yu become the ruler of ancient China?**

**Vocabulary *Builder***
<u>channel</u> (CHAN uhl) *n.* long passage dug into the ground that water or other liquids can flow along

**Flood Control**
Dams such as this one continue to provide flood control along the Huang He. **Critical Thinking: Explain Problem** *Why might it be necessary to improve flood-control systems over time?*

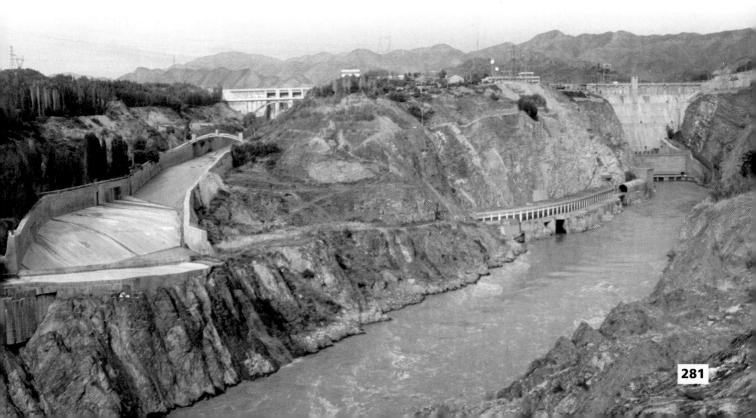

**Shang Rulers**
This image shows a ruler from the Shang Dynasty of ancient China. **Critical Thinking: Distinguish Facts from Opinions** *What is one fact that you might state about Shang Dynasty rulers based on this image? What is one opinion?*

# The Shang Dynasty

Around 1760 B.C., a people called the Shang conquered the Xia kingdom and founded the Shang Dynasty. They came from a neighboring region of China. Many artifacts survive from this period, including written records. Because such records exist, some historians view the Shang as China's first historical dynasty.

**Shang Culture**   The Shang adopted many of the customs of the Xia rulers, however, Chinese culture continued to advance. Shang rulers remained in power for approximately 600 years, during which time China developed into a true civilization.

The Shang kingdom centered on the North China Plain. Using flood-control methods learned from the Xia, the Shang brought much of this land under cultivation. They grew several different types of grains, including millet and wheat. Even though Shang farmers had only simple farming tools, they were able to produce large harvests from the rich loess soil. As a result, the Shang managed to create a food surplus.

The Shang also created a strong government that carried out great building projects. Shang rulers built a number of large walled cities. In the center of each city stood the palaces and great houses of the upper classes. The homes of artisans and traders surrounded these buildings. Shang Dynasty homes were constructed using timber, as well as rods and twigs woven together. Peasant farmers lived in simple huts outside the city walls. These walls were made of soil, pounded down until it became as hard as concrete.

The wall at Zhengzhou, one of several Shang capitals, was 4 miles around and 27 feet tall. Building such a massive wall required a significant amount of labor. The ability to organize labor revealed the power of Shang rulers.

The construction of these walls also shows the importance placed on defending Shang cities. Warfare was common during the Shang Dynasty. Shang kings established large, well-organized armies. They attacked neighboring lands to expand the kingdom's territory. Some soldiers rode into battle in horse-drawn chariots. Others marched in great columns, carrying flags and ringing bronze bells. Soldiers fought with bows, lances, and bronze axes. Many people lost their lives during these battles.

**Arts of the Shang Dynasty** The Shang were not only warriors, but also skilled artists and craftworkers. Shang artists produced pottery and jade carvings. The greatest art of the Shang Dynasty was bronze metalworking. Bronze artists made a variety of objects—including pots, jars, and ornaments—using a special metal-casting method. These works, which feature rich decoration, rank among the world's great artistic achievements.

Many bronze objects were found in the tombs of Shang rulers. The most famous tombs are at Anyang, another Shang capital. These tombs consisted of large pits dug deep in the ground and covered with a wooden roof. They were filled with goods, including jewelry, food, weapons, and even whole chariots, as well as the rulers' remains. Often, prisoners of war were sacrificed and buried with the king. At other times, a king's servants and aides were also sent with him to the grave. The artifacts and remains in these tombs provide a wealth of information about Shang life and customs.

**Shang Tombs and Arts**
A chariot from a Shang tomb is pictured at left. The elephant to the right is an example of a bronze work of art from the Shang Dynasty. **Critical Thinking: Apply Information** *Why do you think people of the Shang Dynasty would have chosen to place bronze objects in the tombs of their rulers?*

## Chinese Writing

| Pictograph | Modern Chinese character | Meaning |
|:---:|:---:|:---:|
| 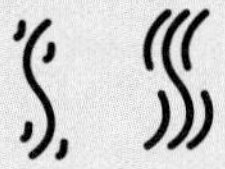 氵 巛 | 水 | river, water |
|  雨 | 雨 | rain |
|  木 | 木 | tree |
|  羊 | 羊 | goat, sheep |
|  ⊃ | 月 | moon |
|  天 | 天 | heaven |

**Reading Diagrams**

Chinese writing developed from a series of pictographs into a system that uses many symbols to represent words or ideas.

**(a) Read a Diagram** What modern Chinese character represents the word *moon?*

**(b) Link Past and Present** How are pictures used as symbols today?

**Vocabulary** *Builder*

interpret (ihn TER pruht) *v.* to explain the meaning of; make understandable

**Chinese Writing** Perhaps the most important artifacts of Shang history, however, were written records known as **oracle bones.** These were animal bones carved with written characters that were used to tell the future. A king or scribe would write a question on the bone and heat the bone until it cracked. Then he would <u>interpret</u> the cracks to answer the question. A typical question might be "Will we win the battle?" or "Will floods occur in the next few days?" Shang rulers used oracle bones to make important decisions. They believed that the answers to their questions came from the spirits of great rulers of the past. At times, the people of ancient China also used oracle bones to record important events related to their questions. The writings on oracle bones have provided scholars with information on ancient China and its rulers.

The first writing on the oracle bones used pictographs. But this picture writing soon developed into **ideographs,** or symbols for words. Scholars do not know for certain when Chinese writing started, but the first examples appear during the Shang Dynasty. By 1300 B.C., China had a fully developed writing system.

Chinese writing differs from our alphabet system. The characters represent words or ideas rather than sounds. For this reason, written Chinese has many characters, making it difficult to learn. A person needs to know nearly 10,000 characters just to read a newspaper. At the same time, this system proves useful in a country with many different spoken languages. No matter which language the Chinese speak, they can still read written Chinese. In this sense, Chinese characters are like our numerals, which have the same meaning in several languages.

Over time, the Chinese have added new symbols to their writing system. Today, written Chinese includes more than 50,000 characters. Nevertheless, modern Chinese remains based on the same principles used in the Shang writing system.

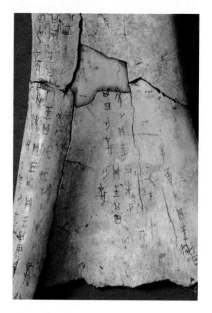

**Oracle Bones**
People of the Shang Dynasty typically used ox bones and turtle shells to craft oracle bones. **Critical Thinking: Evaluate Information** *How can the questions written on oracle bones help us understand the values of the Shang culture?*

 Checkpoint **How did scholars learn about Chinese culture under Shang rule?**

**Looking Back and Ahead** In this section, you have read about China's first ruling families. You have learned about the Xia Dynasty and about the growth of Chinese civilization under the Shang. In the next section, you will read about China's third dynasty, the Zhou.

---

## Section 2 Check Your Progress

**Progress Monitoring** Online
**For:** Self-test with instant help
**Visit:** PHSchool.com
**Web Code:** mwa-4102

 **Standards Review** H-SS: 6.6.1; E-LA Reading 6.2.4

### Comprehension and Critical Thinking

**1. (a) Recall** When did the Xia Dynasty rule China?
**(b) Identify Alternatives** What might have resulted had the rulers of the Xia Dynasty not come to power?

**2. (a) Recall** When did the Shang Dynasty begin?
**(b) Evaluate Information** What characteristics of the Shang Dynasty cause historians to consider it China's first historical dynasty?

### Reading Skill

**3. Create Logical Notes** Review your notes for this section. What dates did you include in these notes? Explain the significance of these dates.

### Vocabulary Builder

Read each sentence below. If the sentence is true, write YES. If the sentence is not true, write NO and explain WHY.

**4.** Legend states that Yu helped build channels that improved travel to and from China.

**5.** Shang rulers often interpreted oracle bones when making important decisions.

### Writing

**6.** Brainstorm a list of key concepts you might include in a research paper on achievements of the Shang Dynasty. Explain how making this list might help you narrow the focus of such a paper.

**H-SS 6.6.4** Identify the political and cultural problems prevalent in the time of Confucius and how he sought to solve them.

**E-LA Reading 6.2.4** Clarify an understanding of texts by creating outlines, logical notes, summaries, or reports.

## Reading Preview

 **Reading Skill**

**Clarify Historical Importance** People and events appear throughout historical readings. To take useful notes, you must determine which people and events are most important. Briefly summarize connections between people and events in your notes. As you did with dates, be sure to describe why the listed people and events are important. Doing so will help you understand the text.

## Vocabulary *Builder*

**High-Use Words**
**demonstrate** (DEHM uhn strayt), p. 287
**capable** (KAY puh buhl), p. 291

**Key Terms**
Mandate of Heaven (MAN dayt uhv HEHV uhn), p. 287
warlord (WAWR lawrd), p. 289
chaos (KAY ahs), p. 289
cavalry (KAV uhl ree), p. 291

**Background Knowledge** Political and cultural problems can weaken civilizations or governments and cause them to fall. In this section, you will read about the fall of the Shang Dynasty and the rise of Zhou rule. You will also learn about the reasons for the collapse of the Zhou Dynasty.

## A New Dynasty

**Main Idea**
The Zhou Dynasty replaced the Shang rulers of China about 1050 B.C.

Around 1050 B.C., a group of invaders called the Zhou attacked the Shang kingdom from the west. They overthrew the last Shang ruler and established a new dynasty. The first ruler of the Zhou Dynasty was King Wen.

**The Right to Rule** The Zhou gained power, in part, because the Shang kings had grown corrupt. The last Shang king, Di Xin, was a poor ruler. He raised taxes and spent the money on lavish parties. He was also cruel. When the Zhou attacked the Shang kingdom, many Shang warriors refused to fight. They surrendered to the Zhou and accepted King Wen as their new ruler.

After taking power, the Zhou leaders said that their success was proof of heaven's support. They believed that heaven was a supreme force of nature that gave dynasties the right to rule. They called this right to rule the **Mandate of Heaven.** If a dynasty failed to act properly, it lost this right. This mandate would then fall to a new dynasty that had earned the right to rule. The mandate permitted such new dynasties to seize control from a ruling dynasty by force, if necessary. Success at doing so was viewed as proof of heaven's support for the new rulers. According to these beliefs, proper behavior for rulers of the dynasty involved <u>demonstrating</u> righteousness and kindness in their actions. The concept of the Mandate of Heaven became a tradition of Chinese government. Under this tradition, the ruler was called the Son of Heaven.

**E-LA 6.2.4 Clarify Historical Importance**
How would you explain the significance of the Mandate of Heaven in your notes?

**Vocabulary** *Builder*

**demonstrate** (DEHM uhn strayt) *v.* to show that you have a particular skill, quality, or ability

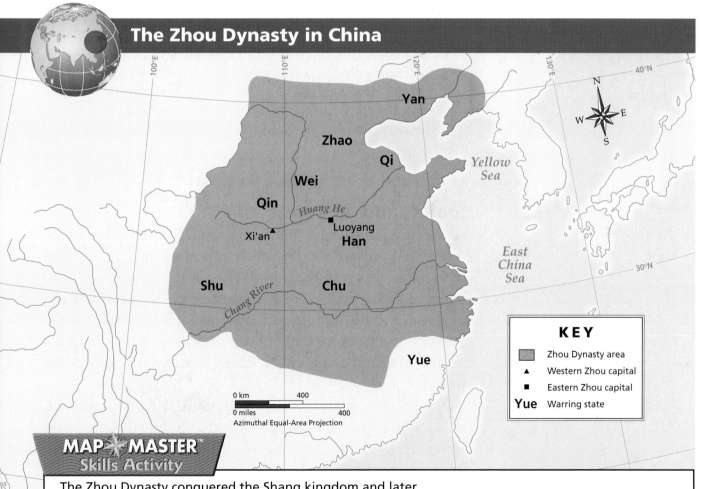

## The Zhou Dynasty in China

**KEY**
- Zhou Dynasty area
- ▲ Western Zhou capital
- ■ Eastern Zhou capital
- **Yue** Warring state

0 km 400
0 miles 400
Azimuthal Equal-Area Projection

**MAP MASTER**
*Skills Activity*

The Zhou Dynasty conquered the Shang kingdom and later expanded its territory beyond the Huang He valley.

**(a) Locate** What was the capital of the Western Zhou? What state was north of the capital city?

**(b) Evaluate Information** Why might states such as those shown above have become important during the Zhou Dynasty?

**MapMaster ⊙nline**

**For:** Interactive map
**Visit:** PHSchool.com
**Web Code:** mwp-4103

One ancient Chinese book, the *Book of History*, explains why the Zhou received the Mandate of Heaven:

> **The kings of Zhou treated the people well, brought good government, and carried out all the proper rituals to spirits and to Heaven. Heaven therefore instructed them, increased their excellence, and chose them to rule over China's many regions.**
>
> —Shu Jing, *Book of History*

**Nobles and Peasants** The Zhou maintained many customs established by the Shang and Xia dynasties. Like these earlier dynasties, the Zhou produced bronze art and wrote messages on oracle bones. They also built walled cities, including a new capital at Xi'an, west of the Shang heartland. Some major Zhou cities included large buildings made of soil, as well as tall observation towers. Because of the capital's location, this first stage of the Zhou Dynasty was called the Western Zhou.

Zhou society included two main classes. At the top were nobles, who owned the land and lived in comfortable wooden houses. At the bottom were peasants, who owned very little and lived in pit houses dug into the ground. The nobles were expected to serve the king and raise armies to support him. Peasants had duties such as farming the land of the nobles and serving as soldiers in battle.

 **Checkpoint** How did the Zhou Dynasty establish their right to rule China?

# Political and Cultural Problems

When the Zhou conquered the Shang, they took over a kingdom centered on the North China Plain. Over the next several hundred years, the Zhou expanded their kingdom to include lands far from the Huang He valley. At its height, the Zhou Dynasty ruled a territory stretching from the Mongolian steppe in the north to the Chang River in the south.

**Governing Challenges** The Zhou kingdom was large and diverse. It included many cultures and peoples. This expanded kingdom proved difficult for a single ruler to govern. As a result, the Zhou king placed family members in charge of individual regions or states. In this way, the king hoped to ensure that different parts of the kingdom would remain loyal.

Over time, however, this loyalty broke down. Ties between the king and local rulers weakened. In 771 B.C., a group of nobles joined with nomadic invaders to overthrow the king. The king was killed, and his son took the throne. The capital was moved east, to the city of Luoyang. This second stage of the Zhou Dynasty became known as the Eastern Zhou.

Although the dynasty continued, the kingdom of the Eastern Zhou was smaller and less powerful. The king was dependent on the nobles who had placed him on the throne. The states that had once been tied to the kingdom grew more independent. Fighting broke out between rival warlords, or military rulers of small states. Although these warlords claimed loyalty to the king, they often really hoped to gain power for themselves.

**The Warring States** Eventually, minor battles escalated into full-scale warfare. China entered a long period of chaos, or total disorder and confusion. This period, about 481 B.C. to 221 B.C., became known as the Era of the Warring States.

**Main Idea**
The large Zhou kingdom proved difficult to rule, and China eventually became divided into smaller states.

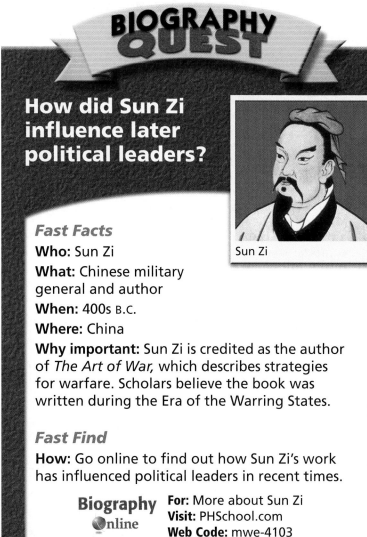

# BIOGRAPHY QUEST

## How did Sun Zi influence later political leaders?

Sun Zi

### Fast Facts

**Who:** Sun Zi
**What:** Chinese military general and author
**When:** 400s B.C.
**Where:** China
**Why important:** Sun Zi is credited as the author of *The Art of War*, which describes strategies for warfare. Scholars believe the book was written during the Era of the Warring States.

### Fast Find

**How:** Go online to find out how Sun Zi's work has influenced political leaders in recent times.

**Biography Online**

**For:** More about Sun Zi
**Visit:** PHSchool.com
**Web Code:** mwe-4103

This mural from a tomb in China suggests that the use of cavalry continued well beyond the Era of Warring States.

This bronze sword from China may have been used by warriors during the Era of the Warring States.

## Military Developments

As small states battled one another during the Era of the Warring States, new weapons and strategies played an important role in these conflicts. The emergence of the crossbow and cavalry represented two such developments which remained important in China for several centuries. **Critical Thinking: Draw Inferences** *How might a period of change and disorder like the Era of the Warring States encourage the development of new ideas and inventions?*

**History** *Interactive*

**Learn More about Military Technology in China**
**Visit:** PHSchool.com
**Web Code:** mwp-4104

This carving from around the time of the Era of Warring States shows a horseback figure.

In later eras Chinese soldiers carried devices that could propel arrows using gunpowder.

During this period, stronger states conquered weaker ones. Over time, a few large states emerged. These states had huge armies equipped with new weapons. One weapon was the crossbow, which was <u>capable</u> of shooting arrows with great power over a long distance. The use of cavalry, or soldiers on horseback, represented another key development.

The fighting during the Warring States period was brutal and destructive. Millions of people died. Battles ravaged the countryside. Eventually, this warfare brought down the Zhou Dynasty. In 256 B.C., the last Zhou ruler was overthrown. Fighting continued for years, however, before a new dynasty managed to unite China.

**Checkpoint** Explain why the Zhou kingdom proved difficult to rule.

**Looking Back and Ahead** This section described the rise and fall of the Zhou Dynasty. You have learned that the Zhou kings claimed the right to rule through the Mandate of Heaven. You have also learned how power struggles finally ended Zhou rule. In the next chapter, you will read about how China was united under new rulers.

**Vocabulary** *Builder*
<u>capable</u> (KAY puh buhl) *adj.*
having the skill, power, or intelligence to do something

## Section 3 Check Your Progress

**Progress Monitoring** Online
**For:** Self-test with instant help
**Visit:** PHSchool.com
**Web Code:** mwa-4103

**Standards Review** H-SS: 6.6.4; E-LA Reading 6.2.4

### Comprehension and Critical Thinking

1. **(a) Describe** What was the Mandate of Heaven?
   **(b) Draw Conclusions** How did this idea set moral standards for Chinese rulers?

2. **(a) Explain** What steps did Zhou rulers take to better manage their large kingdom?
   **(b) Analyze Cause and Effect** Why did these actions eventually cause the Zhou Dynasty to decline?

### Reading Skill

3. **Clarify Historical Importance** Examine the notes you took for this section. What clues do your notes provide about the historical importance of the Zhou dynasty?

### Vocabulary *Builder*

Complete each of the following sentences so that the second part further explains the first part and clearly shows your understanding of the highlighted word.

4. Zhou rulers believed in the Mandate of Heaven; _____.

5. Conflict began among Eastern Zhou warlords; _____.

6. The Era of the Warring States was a period of chaos; _____.

7. During the Era of the Warring States, armies began using cavalry; _____.

### Writing

8. What types of information would you need to find to write a research paper on the Zhou Dynasty? What sources might you use?

# Distinguish Fact and Opinion

In order to understand the past, historians study written sources left by people who lived long ago. Many of these sources mix fact and opinion. This makes it necessary for historians to distinguish between fact and opinion.

**Chapter Standards**

**History-Social Science**

**Research, Evidence, and Point of View**
**2** Students distinguish fact from opinion in historical narratives and stories.

> **"** He arranged the orders of nobility into five. . . . He gave offices only to the worthy, and jobs only to the able. He attached great importance to the people being taught the duties of the five relations of society. . . . He showed that he was truthful, and proved that he was righteous. He honored virtue, and rewarded merit. Then he had only to let his robes fall down, fold his hands, and the kingdom was orderly ruled. **"**

—*Shu ching (Book of History)*

**Learn the Skill** *Follow these steps to learn how to distinguish fact from opinion.*

1. **Identify the facts.** A fact is something that can be proved to be true. A fact usually provides information such as *who, what, where,* or *how much.*

2. **Determine whether each fact can be verified.** Consult reliable sources, such as an encyclopedia, in order to prove facts true. Primary sources or artifacts might also contain facts.

3. **Identify the opinions.** An opinion is a personal belief or a judgment. To help decide whether a sentence contains an opinion, look for words such as *think, feel,* or *believe.*

4. **Decide whether each opinion is supported by facts.** Although opinions cannot be proved true, they can be supported with facts.

**Practice the Skill** *Answer the following questions for the passage above.*

1. **Identify the facts. (a)** What is one fact included in the passage? **(b)** What type of information does it provide?

2. **Determine whether each fact can be verified. (a)** In which type of reference book might you find information to verify this fact? **(b)** Would primary sources or artifacts be useful in proving this fact?

3. **Identify the opinions. (a)** What is one opinion included in the passage? **(b)** Which words provide clues that the statement is an opinion?

4. **Decide whether each opinion is supported by facts. (a)** Could this opinion be supported by facts? **(b)** If so, what information would provide this support?

**Apply the Skill**
*See page 295 of the Review and Assessment.*

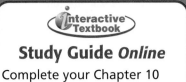

**interactive Textbook**

**Study Guide** *Online*
Complete your Chapter 10 study guide in print or online.

## Chapter Summary  H-SS: 6.6.1; 6.6.2; 6.6.4

### Section 1  The Middle Kingdom

- Geographic features such as mountains, deserts, and forests made the transport of goods and ideas difficult in ancient China.
- China's earliest civilization arose in the Huang He valley.
- China's location and natural barriers isolated the area from other early civilizations.

### Section 2  China's First Dynasties

- The ruler Yu became the founder of China's first dynasty, the Xia.
- China's first historical dynasty, the Shang, lasted about 600 years.
- During the Shang Dynasty, China expanded its territory and developed a system of writing.

### Section 3  China Under the Zhou Dynasty

- A group known as the Zhou gained control of China from the Shang about 1050 B.C.
- The Zhou kingdom grew very large and became difficult for one ruler to control. Zhou kings asked family members to rule different parts of the kingdom.
- Conflicts between rulers of individual states marked the end of the Zhou Dynasty.

**Chariot of Zhou ruler**

## Standards Practice  H-SS: 6.6.1; 6.6.2; 6.6.4

## Vocabulary *Builder*

### High-Use Words

Read each sentence below. If the sentence is true, write YES. If the sentence is not true, write NO and explain WHY.

1. China's <u>varied</u> geography includes very few different types of physical features.

2. The waters of the Huang He <u>drain</u> the surrounding valley of its fertile soil.

3. Rulers under the Mandate of Heaven were expected to <u>demonstrate</u> kindness.

4. During the Era of the Warring States, the crossbow was <u>capable</u> of shooting arrows a great distance.

### Key Terms

Answer the following questions in complete sentences that show your understanding of the Key Terms.

1. How did loess aid the development of civilization in the Huang He valley?

2. Why is the use of ideographs useful in a country such as China?

3. Why was the period following the Zhou Dynasty considered a time of chaos?

4. How might the use of cavalry have been important during the Era of the Warring States?

## Apply Reading Skills

**Clarify Texts** Choose a passage from Chapter 10 for which you have not yet taken notes. Using headings, dates, and people or events, create logical notes for the section.

## Comprehension and Critical Thinking

**1. (a) Describe** What types of geographic features isolated China from other early civilizations?
**(b) Analyze Cause and Effect** What effect did this isolation have on the development of civilization in China?
**(c) Evaluate Information** How might China's development have differed if the area had been less isolated?

**2. (a) List** What were China's first two dynasties?
**(b) Distinguish Verifiable Information** How does archaeological evidence support ancient Chinese legends of King Yu?
**(c) Draw Conclusions** In which aspects of Chinese culture did the Shang Dynasty show important advancements?

**3. (a) Explain** What was the tradition known as the Mandate of Heaven?
**(b) Clarify Problems** How did the expansion of the Zhou kingdom contribute to its eventual downfall?
**(c) Evaluate Information** Do you think the Mandate of Heaven helped Zhou rulers remain in power in spite of the problems facing the kingdom? Explain.

## Researching

**Ruling the Zhou Dynasty** More than 3,000 years ago, the Zhou Dynasty came to power in China, bringing new traditions and ideas to Chinese government and society. In this activity, you will use the Internet and the library media center to research and report on some of the important aspects of Zhou rule. Choose a task below to research. Share your work with the class by posting it on a "Ruling the Zhou Dynasty" bulletin board.

**Journalists:** Write a short article about the events that led to the end of the Western Zhou. Include a headline for your article, and make sure that the article answers important questions such as *who, what, where, when, why,* and *how.*

**Historians:** The Zhou kingdom presented several governing challenges to its rulers, which affected the organization of their government. Create a chart that compares the structure of the Zhou government with another historic or contemporary government. Briefly explain why you think the Zhou rulers chose to organize their government the way they did.

> **Researching Online**
> **For:** Help in starting this activity
> **Visit:** PHSchool.com
> **Web Code:** mwe-4104

## Writing

**1. Write a paragraph on the following topic.** Each early dynasty discussed in this chapter eventually lost its control of ancient China. Explain one way in which the conditions that caused these dynasties to fall were similar.
**Your paragraph should:**
- contain a clear topic sentence.
- use evidence to support your argument.
- end with a summary that restates your main points.

**2. Write a short narrative.** Suppose you were a scribe during the Shang Dynasty who interpreted the cracks and writing on oracle bones. Write a brief description of your experience seeking an answer to an important question.

# Apply Analysis Skills

**Use the paragraph at right to answer these questions.**

1. What is one fact presented in this paragraph?

2. What types of sources could you use to verify this fact?

3. What opinion does the writer include in this paragraph?

4. What word or words provide clues that this statement is an opinion?

> ❝The Shang conquered the Xia kingdom about 1700 B.C. This dynasty harvested crops, established a strong government, and produced works of art. I believe the Shang Dynasty's greatest achievement was the construction of walled cities. This construction required a great deal of planning as well as hard work.❞

# Test Yourself

1. **China was isolated from the rest of the ancient world by mountains, deserts, and the**

   A Indian Ocean.

   B Pacific Ocean.

   C Atlantic Ocean.

   D South China Sea.

2. **Chinese civilization developed in the Huang He Valley because the river**

   A was good for boat travel.

   B made trade with India easier.

   C deposited loess when it flooded.

   D was a barrier to invading nomads.

**Refer to the image below to answer Question 3.**

3. **Ancient Chinese writing used symbols such as this to represent**

   A ideas.

   B words.

   C names.

   D dates.

天

**Refer to the reading below to answer Question 4.**

4. **During what activity would a person of ancient China have spoken these words?**

   *"Will there be a disaster in the next ten days? . . . The king . . . said, 'There will be no harm; there will perhaps be the coming of alarming news."*

   A making a bronze ornament

   B constructing a wall from soil

   C interpreting oracle bones

   D building a pit house

5. **What was the main problem facing Chinese society following the Zhou dynasty?**

   A war

   B famine

   C drought

   D flooding

6. **Scholars have learned the most about the Shang Dynasty from**

   A artifacts found in burial tombs.

   B the writings of Sun Zi.

   C remains of palaces.

   D oral history.

# Chapter 11 Chinese Society and Thought (551 B.C.–A.D. 300s)

## Prepare to Read

### Chapter Standards

**History-Social Science**

**6.6** Students analyze the geographic, political, economic, religious, and social structures of the early civilizations of China.

| | ✓ Reading Check |
|---|---|
| **Section 1,** pp. 300–304 | |
| **Family and Religion** | Family and religion were important parts of China's social structure during the Era of the Warring States. Some important religious practices centered on ancestor worship. |
| **Section 2,** pp. 305–310 | |
| **The Teachings of Confucius** | Scholars such as Confucius proposed solutions to political and social problems in ancient China. The ideas of Confucius greatly influenced Chinese society and government. |
| **Section 3,** pp. 312–317 | |
| **Daoism and Buddhism in China** | Daoism and Buddhism were two systems of beliefs that also became important in ancient China. Along with Confucianism, these systems became known as the "Three Ways." |

Chinese dragon

**551 B.C.**
Confucius is born in Lu.

**479 B.C.**
Confucius, philosopher and teacher, dies in Lu.

Chapter Events

Other Events

**600 B.C.**

**300 B.C.**

**B.C./A.D.**

**About 534 B.C.** Siddhartha Gautama witnesses "the Four Passing Sights."

**About 322 B.C.** The Mauryan Empire begins in India.

## Where and When?

About 2,500 years ago, the teachings of Confucius, Laozi, and beliefs of Buddhism began to influence Chinese society and thought.

The Hanging Monastery was built into the cliffs of the Heng Shan Mountain about 1,400 years ago.

**A.D. First century**
Missionaries from India bring Buddhism to China.

**A.D. 300s**
Pure Land Buddhism is introduced in China.

**B.C./A.D.**

**A.D. 300**

**A.D. 600**

**A.D. First century** Indian merchants spread Hinduism to Southeast Asia.

**About A.D. 250** Mayan culture begins to flourish in Mesoamerica.

# How to Read History

## History Reading Skill

### Previewing Analyze Comparisons and Contrasts in Text

Writers often organize information in a compare-and-contrast pattern. When you read, look for places where there are comparisons and contrasts. Finding how events are similar or different will help you more fully understand history. Look at the examples below to learn how to find compare-and-contrast patterns.

**Chapter Standards**

**English-Language Arts**

Reading 6.2.2 Analyze text that uses the compare-and-contrast organizational pattern.

**1** In these sentences, China's size in the past is contrasted with its current size. The word **but** signals the contrast.

China today is one of the world's largest countries. **But** it was not always so large or so united.

> This word signals a contrast.

**2** In this example, written Chinese is compared to Hindu-Arabic numbers to show how they are similar.

> This word signals a comparison.

In this sense, Chinese characters are **like** our numerals, which have the same meaning in several languages.

**3** Some comparisons or contrasts are not as clearly marked. Here, the writer organizes information about two groups in a contrast pattern.

> This phrase is a clue that two items will be discussed.

Zhou society was divided into **two main classes**.

> These phrases are clues to contrast.

**At the top** were nobles, who owned the land and lived in comfortable wooden houses.

**At the bottom** were peasants, who owned very little and lived in pit houses dug into the ground.

# Vocabulary *Builder*

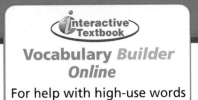
## *Previewing* High-Use Academic Words

| High-Use Word | Definition | Sample Sentence About History |
|---|---|---|
| **traditional** (truh DIHSH uh nuhl) (Section 1, p. 300) | *adj.* of, handed down by, or following tradition | <u>Traditional</u> beliefs often structured life in the ancient society. |
| **bond** (bahnd) (Section 1, p. 303) | *n.* uniting or binding force; tie | The <u>bonds</u> between family members were important to the culture. |
| **capable** (KAY puh buhl) (Section 2, p. 306) | *adj.* having ability; able to do things well; skilled | The ruler proved <u>capable</u> of governing a great number of people. |
| **principle** (PRIHN suh puhl) (Section 2, p. 310) | *n.* rule of conduct | Children behaved according to the <u>principle</u> of devotion to family. |
| **conclude** (kuhn KLOOD) (Section 3, p. 313) | *v.* to decide by reasoning | Scholars were able to <u>conclude</u> that the society held religious beliefs. |
| **conduct** (KAHN duhkt) (Section 3, p. 315) | *n.* way that one acts; behavior | The belief system set forth a series of rules for proper <u>conduct</u>. |

## *Previewing* Key Terms and People

**Laozi**

**Confucius**

**H-SS 6.6** Students analyze the geographic, political, economic, religious, and social structures of the early civilizations of China.

**E-LA Reading 6.2.2** Analyze text that uses the compare-and-contrast organizational pattern.

## Reading Preview

 **Reading Skill**

**Identify Contrasts in Text** Contrasts show ways that things are different. Signal words such as *but, unlike,* and *instead* can help you find contrasts. Comparative adjectives such as *stronger* or *wiser* also signal contrasts. Here, the words *some* and *others* identify two groups that behaved differently: "Some Shang soldiers rode on horse-drawn chariots. Others marched in great columns."

**Vocabulary *Builder***

**High-Use Words**
traditional (truh DIHSH uh nuhl), p. 300
bond (bahnd), p. 303

**Key Terms and People**
value (VAL yoo), p. 300
generation (jehn uhr AY shuhn), p. 300
extended family (ehk STEHN dihd FAM uh lee), p. 301
ancestor worship (AN sehs tuhr WER shihp), p. 304

**Background Knowledge** The Era of the Warring States was a dark period in China's history. During this time, family and religion helped hold China's social structure together. In this section, you will read about the Chinese family, and how it was supported by traditional Chinese religious beliefs.

**Main Idea**
Family relationships strongly influenced the social structure of early Chinese civilizations.

## The Chinese Family

Families are important in most cultures. They help ensure that children are protected as they grow up. But in China, loyalty to one's family was more important than almost any other value. A **value** is an ideal thought to be worthwhile by a person or group.

**Vocabulary *Builder***
traditional (truh DIHSH uh nuhl) *adj.* of, handed down by, or following tradition

**The Family Unit** The traditional family in China included many generations. A **generation** is a group of family members born and living at about the same time. Your grandparents are part of an older generation. Your parents, aunts and uncles belong to the next generation. You, your siblings, and your cousins belong to a younger generation.

The Chinese family usually consisted of children, parents, grandparents, aunts, uncles, and cousins. Often a family occupied rooms or houses around a common courtyard. A family with several generations living together is called an extended family.

**Family Relationships** Within this extended family, each person's position was based mainly on age and sex. Older family members had more power and privileges than younger ones. Men were considered more important than women.

Strict rules governed relationships between family members. A father was the absolute head of his family. His wife and children were expected to obey him in all things.

The welfare of the family was more important than that of any individual member. Marriages were arranged by parents to strengthen the family, not to please their children. Often the young couple to be married did not meet until their wedding day. Still, as this Zhou era poem suggests, young people did fall in love, despite fears of their parents' disapproval.

**Marriage in Ancient China**
Families often used marriage to increase their wealth and social status. Expert matchmakers were hired to ensure that marriages benefited both families.
**Critical Thinking: Link Past and Present** *Based on the picture, how is the ancient Chinese wedding similar to weddings today?*

> **❝I beg of you, Chung Tzu,
> Do not climb into our homestead,
> Do not break the willows we have planted.
> Not that I mind about the willows,
> But I am afraid of my father and mother.
> Chung Tzu I dearly love.
> But of what my father and mother say
> Indeed I am afraid.❞**
>
> —Shijing (Book of Poetry)

**The Role of Women** Chinese women had little power in the traditional family. Their job was to serve other family members. An ancient scholar described a woman's role in these words:

> **A woman's duty is not to control or to take charge. . . . When she is young, she must submit to her parents. After her marriage, she must submit to her husband. When she is widowed [loses her husband], she must submit to her son. These are the rules of propriety [correct behavior].**
>
> —Liu Hsiang, Biographies of Admirable Women

Of course, not every Chinese family followed this pattern exactly. Still, it was the ideal. Centuries of tradition supported it. So did Chinese religious beliefs.

 **Checkpoint** What role did family relationships play in determining an individual's status in ancient China?

## Traditional Religious Beliefs

The ancient Chinese viewed Earth as a flat disk. At the center of this disk lay the Middle Kingdom. Above Earth stretched the sky. This was the location of Heaven, the supreme force in nature. Heaven gave Chinese leaders their right to rule. But for ordinary people, Heaven was far away. They were more concerned with the spirits that they believed surrounded them every day.

**A World of Spirits** The Chinese believed that the world was alive with spirits. Heaven was home to the spirits of the sun, moon, stars, and storms. On Earth, spirits lived in hills, rivers, rocks, and seas. These spirits ruled the daily lives of people.

Many spirits were good. They made the rains fall and crops grow. The Chinese dragon was a symbol of these kindly forces of nature. The people of ancient China believed that dragons could bring rain, as well as help sailors travel safely on the ocean. Not all spirits were so kind. Demons and devils haunted dark and lonely places. These evil spirits made it unsafe to walk the roads at night. Demons also hid in homes, bringing bad luck to all who lived there. During festivals, the people used bonfires, loud sounds, and paper dragons to frighten evil spirits away.

**Main Idea**
Religious beliefs in China focused on the worship of spirits, particularly those of people's ancestors.

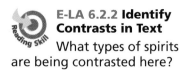

**E-LA 6.2.2 Identify Contrasts in Text**
What types of spirits are being contrasted here?

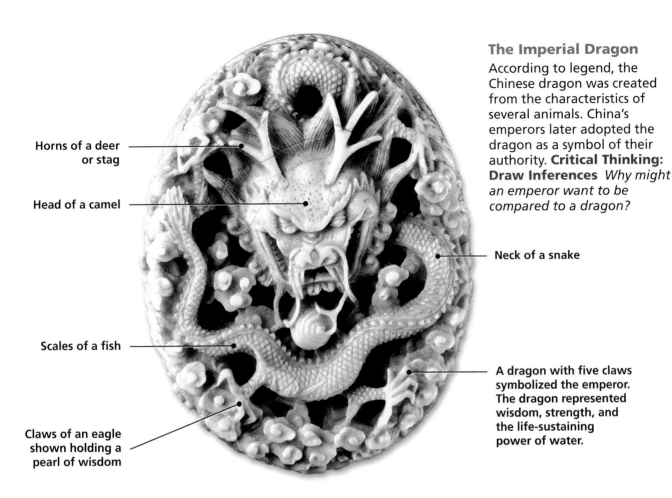

Horns of a deer or stag

Head of a camel

Scales of a fish

Claws of an eagle shown holding a pearl of wisdom

**The Imperial Dragon**
According to legend, the Chinese dragon was created from the characteristics of several animals. China's emperors later adopted the dragon as a symbol of their authority. **Critical Thinking: Draw Inferences** *Why might an emperor want to be compared to a dragon?*

Neck of a snake

A dragon with five claws symbolized the emperor. The dragon represented wisdom, strength, and the life-sustaining power of water.

**The Spirits of Ancestors** The most important spirits to most Chinese were those of their ancestors. They believed that family members lived on after death in the spirit world. When Chinese spoke of their family, they meant not only its living members. The spirits of ancestors were viewed as part of the family as well.

The living and dead were tied by powerful <u>bonds</u>. The dead looked to the living to keep their memory alive. Ancestors were remembered in family celebrations. They were honored with prayers and gifts. Living family members were happy to do this, because they believed that the more honor they paid to their ancestors, the more likely the dead would become kindly spirits. Ancestors who were ignored might turn into demons. Many people believed that the angered spirits of these ancestors could bring hardships to living family members.

In turn, the living looked to the dead for help in their ongoing affairs. People believed that the spirits of the dead were more powerful than living beings. The spirits of ancestors could protect and guide living family members. People often sought the approval of ancestors when making decisions. A family that honored its ancestors could expect to prosper.

**Vocabulary** *Builder*
**bond** (bahnd) *n.* uniting or binding force; tie

**Ancestral Tablet**
The ancestral tablet displays the name, birth date, and date on which a person died.
**Critical Thinking: Draw Inferences** *Why do you think older family members often performed the ceremonies for honoring ancestors?*

**Ancestor Worship**   The Chinese found many ways to honor their ancestors. Every home had a family shrine known as the "red table." It held tablets with the names of family ancestors. People burned incense at this shrine to honor the dead. They also set out food for the dead. In the spring and fall, families visited family graves to leave offerings to the dead. This practice of honoring the spirits of the dead is known as **ancestor worship.**

Historians are not sure how widespread ancestor worship was in ancient China. In early times, only powerful noble families may have honored their dead. Poor peasants may not have had the time or money for elaborate rituals. Over time, however, ancestor worship, like the extended family, became deeply rooted in Chinese culture.

 **Checkpoint**   Through which religious practices did Chinese families honor their ancestors?

**Looking Back and Ahead**   In this section you have learned about the importance of the family in the social structure of ancient China. In the next section, you will see how the extended family came to be a model for all of Chinese society.

---

**Section 1 Check Your Progress**

**Progress Monitoring Online**
**For:** Self-test with instant help
**Visit:** PHSchool.com
**Web Code:** mwa-4111

 **Standards Review**   H-SS: 6.6; E-LA Reading 6.2.2

**Comprehension and Critical Thinking**

1. (a) **Describe** Describe the structure of the traditional Chinese family.
   (b) **Draw Inferences** Why might the rules governing people's roles in Chinese families have become very strict?

2. (a) **Explain** In what ways did the ancient Chinese believe spirits affected their daily lives?
   (b) **Draw Conclusions** How did ancestor worship help keep Chinese family structures strong?

**Reading Skill**

3. **Identify Contrasts in Text** Read this sentence: People believed that the ancestors, or spirits, were more powerful than living beings. What two items are being contrasted?

**Vocabulary Builder**
Complete each of the following sentences so that the second part further explains the first part and clearly shows your understanding of the highlighted word.

4. Family loyalty was an important Chinese value; _____.

5. Your parents, aunts, and uncles belong to an older generation; _____.

6. People of ancient China often lived with their extended families; _____.

7. An important part of ancient Chinese religion was ancestor worship; _____.

**Writing**

8. Write one or two sentences describing a topic from this section on which you might write a research paper, such as traditional families in China or the role of women in ancient China.

## Section 2 The Teachings of Confucius

# The Teachings of Confucius

**Standards Preview**

**H-SS 6.6.3** Know about the life of Confucius and the fundamental teachings of Confucianism and Daoism.

**H-SS 6.6.4** Identify the political and cultural problems prevalent in the time of Confucius and how he sought to solve them.

**E-LA Reading 6.2.2** Analyze text that uses the compare-and-contrast organizational pattern.

## Reading Preview

 **Reading Skill**

**Identify Comparisons in Text** Comparisons show ways that events, people, or ideas are similar. Signal words such as *like*, *also*, and *similarly* can help you find comparisons. Read this example: An armed man on horseback had a great advantage over a similarly armed foot soldier. Here, the word *similarly* tells you that the man on horseback and the foot soldier were armed in the same way.

**Vocabulary** *Builder*

**High-Use Words**
capable (KAY puh buhl), p. 306
principle (PRIHN suh puhl), p. 310

**Key Terms and People**
anarchy (AN uhr kee), p. 305
Hanfeizi (HAN FAY DZEE), p. 305
Legalism (LEE guhl ihz uhm), p. 305
Confucius (kuhn FYOO shuhs), p. 306
Confucianism (kuhn FYOO shuhn ihz uhm), p. 307
filial piety (FIHL ee uhl PI uh tee), p. 309

**Background Knowledge** During the Era of the Warring States, China was in a state of anarchy, or disorder and confusion. The social order was collapsing. In this section you will learn about the ways in which Chinese thinkers began looking for solutions to the problems of this era.

## The "Law and Order" Solution of the Legalists

A teacher named Hanfeizi promoted a tough "law and order" solution to China's problems. Hanfeizi believed that "the nature of man is evil." People had to be made to be good. This could best be done by establishing a code and making sure that its laws were enforced. Those who obeyed the law should be rewarded. Those who did not should be punished severely. The belief that a strong legal system, not moral values, was the key to social order became known as Legalism.

**Main Idea**
Chinese thinkers such as Hanfeizi and Mo-zi proposed solutions to political and cultural problems that arose during the Era of the Warring States.

**Vocabulary** *Builder*

<u>capable</u> (KAY puh buhl) *adj.*
having ability; able to do things
well; skilled

To Legalists, the most important quality in a ruler was not kindness, but strength. "The reason why . . . subjects do not dare deceive their ruler is not because they love him," wrote a Legalist, "but because they fear his awe-inspiring power." Only a strong ruler, they believed, would be <u>capable</u> of bringing order to China.

**The Solution of Mo-zi** A government official named Mo-zi came up with a different solution. He believed that order would be restored if people learned to love one another.

Under Mo-zi's ideal government, everyone would work for the common good. This would not only bring peace to China, but also would be doing the will of Heaven. "I know Heaven loves men dearly," he wrote. "Everything is prepared for the good of man." People needed only to turn from hate to love.

 **Checkpoint** What solutions did Hanfeizi and Mo-zi propose for the problems facing Chinese society?

**Main Idea**
Confucius sought to solve political and cultural problems by encouraging a return to traditional values.

## The "Traditional Values" Solution of Confucius

A third solution was proposed by the great teacher Confucius. Of all those who tried to bring order to China, Confucius had the greatest impact. In China, he is known as the "First Teacher." There were other teachers before him, but he is honored above all others for his great wisdom.

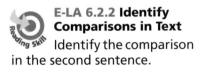 **E-LA 6.2.2 Identify Comparisons in Text** Identify the comparison in the second sentence.

**The Early Life of Confucius** Born in the small state of Lu in 551 B.C., Confucius lived at about the same time as the Buddha in India. Unlike Buddha who was born a prince, Confucius came from a poor but respected family. Despite his poverty, Confucius received a good education. He studied poetry and history. He learned archery and music.

As a young man, Confucius took a job collecting taxes from farmers for the ruler of Lu. Soon he saw for himself some of the problems of his time. Laws were not enforced. Dishonest officials took bribes, or illegal payments, to do favors for the rich. Peasants starved while rulers taxed them to pay for wars.

Confucius believed that the cause of the anarchy he saw around him was simple. The Chinese had turned away from the values and virtues of their ancestors. Only a return to those traditional values could bring order to China. Confucius made teaching the wise ways of the ancestors his life's work.

**Teacher and Scholar**   To carry out this work, Confucius started his own school. He did not teach about religion, gods, or an afterlife. He was interested in practical questions of moral and ethical behavior. His goal was to instruct young men on how to become *junzi,* or "true gentlemen." "A gentleman takes as much trouble to discover what is right," Confucius told his students, "as lesser men take to discover what will pay."

Confucius was an excellent teacher. He attracted many students. Over time, some wrote down their teacher's lectures and sayings. These teachings were collected in a book called the *Analects.* Here are a few of his sayings from the *Analects.*

**❝Forget injuries, never forget kindnesses.**
   **Ignorance is the night of the mind, but a night**
      **without moon and star.**
   **What you do not want done to yourself, do not do**
      **to others.❞**

—Confucius, *The Analects*

The teachings of Confucius became known as **Confucianism.**

**Primary** Sources

See "Confucius and Good Government" in the Reference Section at the back of this book.

**Confucius as Leader**
When he was 50 years old, Confucius (left) served as Lu's minister of crime. Under his leadership, crime in Lu was greatly reduced. **Critical Thinking: Draw Conclusions** *How does the artist show the importance of Confucius?*

Late in his life, Confucius hoped to find a ruler who would follow his teachings. For 13 years, he traveled from state to state urging rulers to lead by setting a good example. "If you govern with the power of your virtue," he told one ruler, "you will be like the North Star. It just stays in its place while all the other stars position themselves around it." He also argued against Legalist ideas about government.

> **If the people are governed by laws and punishment is used to maintain order, they will try to avoid the punishment but have no sense of shame. If they are governed by virtue and rules of propriety [proper ritual] are used to maintain order, they will have a sense of shame and will become good as well.**
>
> —Confucius, *The Analects*

## Symmetry at the Confucian Temple and Mansion

The home of Confucius became a temple, which his descendants cared for from the nearby Kong Family Mansion. Confucius' plan for an orderly society extended to a belief in showing symmetry and order in things such as buildings and works of art.

**Critical Thinking: Analyze Information** *How are the Confucian principles of order and symmetry apparent at the Temple of Confucius and the Kong Family Mansion?*

**History** *Interactive*
**Tour the Temple of Confucius**
**Visit:** PHSchool.com
**Web Code:** mwp-4112

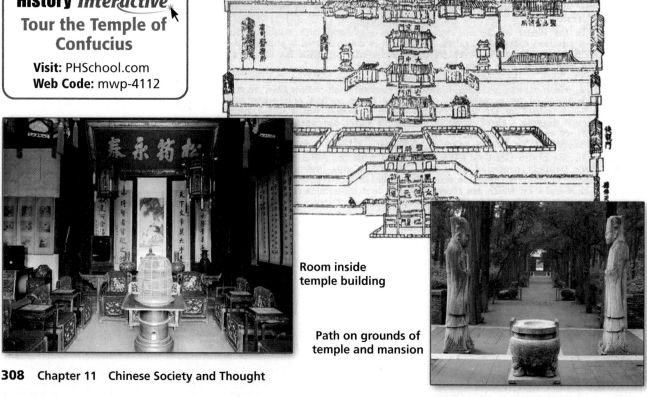

1912 map of the Temple of Confucius

Room inside temple building

Path on grounds of temple and mansion

Few rulers took such ideas seriously. Confucius died in Lu in about 479 B.C., thinking of himself as a failure. He could not know that his teachings would influence Chinese society and government up to the present day.

**The Five Key Relationships** The heart of Confucianism lay in a vision of a stable society based on five relationships. The chart below lists these relationships. The first was the relationship between ruler and subject. The other four were between father and son, husband and wife, older and younger brothers, and older and younger friends.

Confucius taught that these five relationships should be the foundation of China's social order. In each one, the superior or older person should expect respect and obedience from the junior person. In return, the superior person should set a good example of proper behavior. If rulers or fathers set a bad example, then it was their fault if their subjects or children also behaved badly.

Each relationship was based on traditional virtues. In the relationship between rulers and subjects, an important virtue for the ruler was kindness toward his subjects. For the subjects, it was loyalty to the ruler. In the relationship between husband and wife, the key virtue of the wife was demonstrating obedience.

The most important virtue in Confucianism, however, was **filial piety.** For Confucius, this meant the unending devotion of children, especially sons, to their parents and family. He believed that establishing the proper relationship with one's parents and others was of even greater importance than getting a good education.

> **❝A young man should serve his parents at home and be respectful to elders outside his home. He should be earnest and truthful, loving all. . . . After doing this, if he has energy to spare, he can study literature and the arts.❞**
>
> —Confucius, *The Analects*

## Five Key Relationships

| Superior or Older Person (Duty to set a good example of proper behavior) | Junior or Younger Person (Duty to offer respect and obedience) |
| --- | --- |
| Ruler | Subject |
| Father | Son |
| Husband | Wife |
| Older brother | Younger brother |
| Older friend | Younger friend |

### Reading Charts

The five key relationships suggested by Confucius formed the basis of his plan for a stable social order in China.

**(a) Read a Chart** What was the duty of a son according to the five key relationships?

**(b) Apply Information** Why do you think people in China might continue to follow these values today?

Confucius viewed the practice of filial piety as the primary step toward becoming a moral human being. He believed that if people were to act with filial piety within their families, the entire society would benefit as a result.

However, such devotion went beyond respecting and caring for one's parents. It also meant respecting the spirits of one's ancestors. This devotion even extended to the ruler, who was viewed as the father of his family of subjects. "By the <u>principle</u> of filial piety the whole world can be made happy," wrote a Confucian scholar. No wonder Confucians called filial piety "the source of all virtues."

**Checkpoint** What traditional values did Confucius encourage?

**Looking Back and Ahead** In this section, you have read about solutions proposed by Chinese thinkers to the anarchy of the Era of the Warring States. You have learned that one solution—Confucianism—would have a lasting impact on Chinese society. You have also learned about the life of its founder, Confucius. In the next section, you will read about other ways of thinking that took root in ancient China.

**Vocabulary** *Builder*

<u>principle</u> (PRIHN suh puhl) *n.* rule of conduct

---

## Section 2 Check Your Progress

**Progress Monitoring** Online

**For:** Self-test with instant help
**Visit:** PHSchool.com
**Web Code:** mwa-4112

**Standards Review** H-SS: 6.6.3; 6.6.4; E-LA Reading 6.2.2

**Comprehension and Critical Thinking**

1. **(a) Recall** What was Confucius' goal for his life?
   **(b) Draw Conclusions** In what ways did he both succeed and fail in achieving this goal?

2. **(a) Identify** What were the five key relationships in Confucian philosophy?
   **(b) Evaluate Information** How did Confucius' vision of Chinese society compare with the traditional Chinese family structure?

**Reading Skill**

3. **Identify Comparisons in Text** Read this sentence: Confucius emphasized that respect for elders was as important as food and shelter. What comparison does it make?

**Vocabulary** *Builder*
Read each sentence below. If the sentence is true, write YES. If the sentence is not true, write NO and explain WHY.

4. Legalists believed that only a strong ruler would be capable of restoring order in China.

5. Principles such as filial piety did not influence the conduct of students of Confucianism.

**Writing**

6. Briefly explain how you might gather information to write a research paper on Confucianism. Identify any sources that you would use.

# Citizen Heroes

**History-Social Science** 6.6.3 Know about the life of Confucius and the fundamental teachings of Confucianism and Daoism.

| Respect | Caring | Responsibility | Fairness | Honesty | Civic Virtue |

# CONFUCIUS
## "The First Teacher"

**Good citizens and leaders are responsible. They have a sense of duty to others. In ancient China, Confucius spoke about leaders and how they should rule.**

**Confucius** believed that the relationship between a ruler and his people was important. He taught that rulers should govern by moral example. As he said, "To govern is to correct. If you set an example by being correct, who would dare remain incorrect?"

Confucius thought that rulers had a responsibility to work very hard. A saying from the *Analects* that illustrates this is "To demand much from oneself and little from others is the way (for a ruler) to banish discontent."

## Connect to Today

**Wilma Mankiller** served as the Principal Chief of the Cherokee Nation from 1985 until 1995. She was the leader of more than 140,000 tribal members.

Like Confucius, Wilma Mankiller believes that leaders have a responsibility to work hard. She thinks that people have the same responsibility. She once said, "If you look to the people in a community themselves and ask them where they want to go and what they want to do, they know. Sometimes all they need is some outside help to figure out how to get there."

### Analyze CITIZEN HEROES

A responsibility is a duty or obligation. Everyone has responsibilities. People have responsibilities at home, at school, and at work. They have responsibilities to their families and to their country. List at least ten responsibilities that you have. They might include things you do (such as taking out the trash) and ways you behave (such as treating people with respect).

**H-SS 6.6.3** Know about the life of Confucius and the fundamental teachings of Confucianism and Daoism.

**H-SS 6.6.8** Describe the diffusion of Buddhism northward to China during the Han Dynasty.

**E-LA Reading 6.2.2** Analyze text that uses the compare-and-contrast organizational pattern.

## Reading Preview

 **Reading Skill**

**Analyze Comparisons and Contrasts in Text** Sometimes writers will organize an entire section to compare and contrast ideas. For example, this section compares and contrasts different philosophies or religions in China. The text moves back and forth between the belief systems. Look at headings to identify which philosophy is being described.

**Vocabulary** *Builder*

**High-Use Words**
<u>conclude</u> (kuhn KLOOD), p. 313
<u>conduct</u> (KAHN duhkt), p. 315

**Key Terms and People**
philosophy (fih LAHS uh fee), p. 312
Daoism (DOW ihz uhm), p. 312
Laozi (LOWD ZEE), p. 312
yin and yang (yihn and yahng), p. 313
Dao (dow), p. 314
Amitabha (ah mee TAH bah), p. 316

**Background Knowledge** Confucianism was a practical **philosophy,** or set of beliefs about how to live. Its goal was the creation of an orderly society. As you will read, other Chinese thinkers of Confucius's time had different interests. So did Buddhist missionaries from India.

**Main Idea**
The fundamental teachings of Daoism directed people to live simple lives in harmony with the natural world.

## The Teachings of Daoism

While Confucius was trying to solve China's political and social problems, other thinkers were trying to grasp the mysteries of the universe. Their search led to the development of Daoism. **Daoism** is an ancient Chinese philosophy that emphasizes a simple and natural life.

**The Legend of Laozi** According to legend, Daoism was founded by a scholar named **Laozi.** The name Laozi means "The Old Master." Laozi worked for one of the rulers of the Zhou dynasty. Late in life, he grew tired of the ruler's dishonest ways and quit his job. Then he decided to leave China altogether for the unknown land of Tibet.

Riding west on a water buffalo, Laozi came to a gatehouse near the Chinese border. There a gatekeeper recognized the scholar and tried to persuade him to turn back. When this failed, the gatekeeper begged Laozi to stay long enough to write down his beliefs. Three days later, Laozi handed the gatekeeper a book called the *Tao Te Ching*. The title may be translated as *The Way and Its Power.* Then he climbed onto his water buffalo and rode away, never to be seen again.

Historians do not know whether Laozi was a real person. They do believe that the *Tao Te Ching* was probably written by many people. It is a small book, made up mostly of poems. Although its ideas are often puzzling, people throughout the world still read the *Tao Te Ching* for its wisdom and quiet beauty. The *Tao Te Ching* has been translated into English more often than any other book except the Bible.

## Who was the real Laozi?

Laozi

### *Fast Facts*

**Who:** Laozi
**What:** Founder of Daoism
**When:** 500s B.C.
**Where:** China
**Why important:** Legend credits Laozi as the founder of Daoism. Though historians question the facts of his life, Laozi remains an important figure among Chinese thinkers.

### *Fast Find*

**How:** Go online to find out about Laozi's life and what various ancient legends suggest about his identity.

**Biography**
**Online**

**For:** More about Laozi
**Visit:** PHSchool.com
**Web Code:** mwe-4113

**Yin, Yang, and the Dao** Daoism is based on ancient Chinese beliefs about how the world works. In ancient times, the Chinese lived close to the natural world. They saw the quiet order of nature in the cycle of day and night, the movement of the stars, and the changing of the seasons. They also saw the violence of nature in floods and storms.

These observations led the Chinese to <u>conclude</u> that two great forces are at work in the universe, called *yin* and *yang*. *Yin* represents the female force in nature. It is dark, cool, and quiet. Earth is mostly *yin*. *Yang* represents the male force. It is bright, warm, and active. Heaven is mostly *yang*. An ancient Chinese book on medicine wrote that:

> **❝The principle of Yin and Yang is the foundation of the entire universe. . . . Yang stands for peace and serenity [calm]. Yin stands for confusion and turmoil [chaos]. Yang stands for destruction. . . . Yin gives shape to things.❞**

—The Yellow Emperor's Classic of Medicine

**Vocabulary *Builder***
<u>conclude</u> (kuhn KLOOD) *v.* to decide by reasoning

**E-LA 6.2.2 Analyze Comparisons and Contrasts**
What concepts are compared and contrasted in the text below the heading Yin, Yang, and the Dao?

**Practicing Daoism**
The worshipers above are shown making offerings at a Daoist temple. The circular symbol above came to represent the harmony of *yin* and *yang* in the universe.
**Critical Thinking: Apply Information** *Based on the picture, what types of items are given as offerings by modern followers of Daoism?*

The people of ancient China believed that when *yin* and *yang* worked together in harmony, there was order in the universe. But what made these forces work together? Their answer was the *Dao*. The word ***Dao*** can mean "a way," "a road," or "the way of nature."

**Following the Dao** The most fundamental teaching of Daoism is that all things in the universe—Earth, Heaven, and people—should follow the Dao. If this happened, then all would be well in the world. No one would be greedy for power or wealth. Everyone would live together in love and peace. There would be no more war.

Followers of Daoism were content to live simple lives in harmony with the Dao. They disliked the Confucians' talk of relationships between "superior" and junior people. Daoists saw everyone as basically good and equal. They also had little use for laws and government. In their view, government should leave people alone to follow their own nature.

✓ Checkpoint  **What is the importance of the forces *yin* and *yang* in the teachings of Daoism?**

# Buddhism Spreads to China

Missionaries from India brought Buddhism to China in the first century A.D. They were followers of the Mahayana, or "big raft" school of Buddhism. They believed that ordinary people could gain release from the cycle of rebirth to enter the blissful peace of nirvana. They also believed in a kind of earthly saint called a *bodhisattva.* The *bodhisattvas* were people who had achieved enlightenment. But after death, they chose to remain on Earth to help others reach nirvana. Followers of the Mahayana school of Buddhism viewed such a decision as an admirable act of compassion.

**Pure Land Buddhism** The missionaries introduced surprising new ideas to China. These included beliefs about reincarnation, karma, enlightenment, and salvation. Such ideas appealed to many Chinese. Confucianism had laid down rules for <u>conduct</u>, but it did not say anything about what happens to people after death. Buddhism's promise of an afterlife in nirvana represented a type of life without death for the people of ancient China. This promise gave them hope that they too might escape the suffering of this world.

**Main Idea**
Missionaries from India introduced Buddhism to the Chinese, some of whom adapted the religion's ideas into their own sects.

**Vocabulary** *Builder*
<u>conduct</u> (KAHN duhkt) *n.* way that one acts; behavior

**A Buddhist Statue**
This statue shows the bodhisattva Avalokitesvara, who is commonly worshipped in China. **Critical Thinking: Apply Information** *Why might the worship of bodhisattvas vary in different parts of the world?*

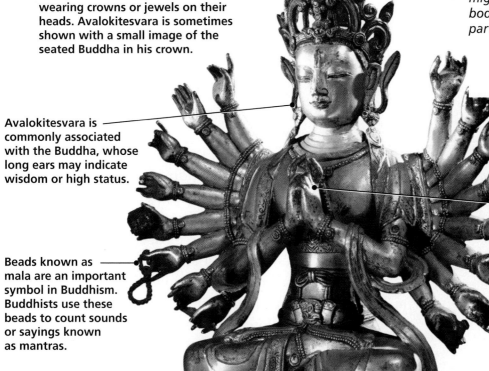

Bodhisattvas are often shown wearing crowns or jewels on their heads. Avalokitesvara is sometimes shown with a small image of the seated Buddha in his crown.

Avalokitesvara is commonly associated with the Buddha, whose long ears may indicate wisdom or high status.

Beads known as mala are an important symbol in Buddhism. Buddhists use these beads to count sounds or sayings known as mantras.

This symbolic hand gesture, or mudra, represents supreme enlightenment in the bodhisattva.

Chinese thinkers shaped these ideas into their own Buddhist sects. The most popular was known as Pure Land Buddhism, which some scholars believe was introduced during the A.D. 300s. The sect was based on worship of a *bodhisattva* named Amitabha. Buddhist writings say that Amitabha promised to save people from reincarnation by granting them rebirth in his own pure land known as the Western Paradise. From this pure land, people can easily find their way to nirvana.

Followers of Pure Land Buddhism tried to live good lives. But what mattered most in gaining entrance to the Western Paradise was a sincere belief in Amitabha. Pure Land Buddhists believed that uttering his name throughout the day—or even thinking his name at the moment of death—was enough to bring about their rebirth in his pure land. Depictions of Amitabha also became a popular theme in the works of art produced by Pure Land Buddhists.

**Three Great Teachers**

In this fourteenth century painting, Confucius and Laozi are shown caring for the infant Buddha. **Critical Thinking: Draw Inferences** *Why do you think Buddha is portrayed as an infant in this picture?*

**The "Three Ways"** As the new religion spread, China became the land of the "Three Ways"—Confucianism, Daoism, and Buddhism. Each offered the Chinese something different. Confucianism helped bring order to Chinese society. Daoism encouraged people to live in harmony with nature. Buddhism offered hope for an afterlife. The three ways mixed and borrowed ideas from each other. They also absorbed older Chinese beliefs and practices, such as ancestor worship.

At first, some rulers tried to stop the spread of Buddhism. Some even argued that Buddhism could not be a true faith because it had not begun in China. Over time, however, most rulers came to accept and support all three ways. For example, a ruler might apply Confucian principles in his government. In private, he might follow the Dao. And, if many of his subjects were Buddhists, he might fund the construction of Buddhist temples and monasteries.

Daoism and Buddhism both offered women more opportunities than did Confucianism. In a society organized around the five relationships of Confucianism, women were clearly inferior. Women were not seen as individuals. They were seen as wives, mothers, or daughters. In Daoism, on the other hand, femininity was valued and women could be teachers of the Dao. Daoism also permitted women to conduct religious ceremonies. Buddhism allowed women to become nuns, though they had stricter rules than monks did. As a result, these two beliefs attracted many Chinese women.

 **Checkpoint** How did Buddhism spread through China and mix with other systems of belief?

**Looking Back and Ahead** In this section, you have read about the development of Daoism and Buddhism in China, as well as the important ideas of each. You also have learned how China became a land of the "Three Ways," as the ideas of Daoism and Buddhism mixed with those of Confucianism. In the next chapter, you will learn how China was reunited under a single ruling group following the Era of the Warring States.

## Section 3 Check Your Progress

**Progress Monitoring** Online
**For:** Self-test with instant help
**Visit:** PHSchool.com
**Web Code:** mwa-4113

 **Standards Review** H-SS: 6.6.3, 6.6.8; E-LA Reading 6.2.2

### Comprehension and Critical Thinking

**1. (a) Recall** What is the meaning of the term *Dao?*
**(b) Draw Conclusions** How does this concept relate to the goals of Daoism for society and individuals?

**2. (a) Explain** How did Buddhism reach China?
**(b) Detect Points of View** Why did some Chinese rulers oppose the spread of Buddhism at first?

### Reading Skill

**3. Analyze Comparisons and Contrasts in Text** Read the section entitled The Three Ways on pages 316–317. Describe the organizational pattern of this section. What is being compared and contrasted?

### Vocabulary *Builder*

**4.** Write two definitions for each term: philosophy, Daoism, yin and yang, Dao. First, write a formal definition for your teacher. Second, write a definition in everyday English for a classmate.

### Writing

**5.** Review the text from this section on the life and ideas of Laozi. Take notes on the important ideas. Then, use your notes to write a short summary of what you have learned about Laozi.

A *point of view* is an opinion on a topic or issue. An individual's point of view is influenced by the time and place in which he or she lives, as well as by his or her personal background. The ability to recognize an author's or speaker's point of view will help you better understand history.

 **Chapter Standards**

**History-Social Science**

**Research, Evidence, and Point of View 5** Students detect the different historical points of view on historical events and determine the context in which the historical statements were made (the questions asked, sources used, author's opinion).

> **❝**When you serve your mother and father it is okay to try to correct them once in awhile. But if you see that they are not going to listen to you, keep your respect for them and don't distance yourself from them. Work without complaining.
>
> When your parents are alive, serve them with propriety; when they die, bury them with propriety, and then worship them with propriety.

> If good men were to govern a country for a hundred years, they could overcome cruelty and do away with killing. How true this saying is!
>
> In doing government, what is the need of killing? If you desire good, the people will be good. The nature of the Superior Man is like the wind, the nature of the inferior man is like the grass. When the wind blows over the grass, it always bends.**❞**
>
> —Confucian teachings from *The Analects*

**Learn the Skill** *Follow these steps to recognize Confucius's point of view in the passages above.*

1. **Identify the topic or issue.** What is the author writing about? What is the main idea of the passage?

2. **Determine the author's position on the topic or issue.** What is the author's opinion on the subject? An author may state his or her overall point of view in a topic sentence.

3. **Identify important background information about the passage.** Identifying facts such as the author's background and the time and place in which the author lived can prove valuable when analyzing point of view.

4. **Ask how this background information might influence the author's beliefs.** People's beliefs and opinions may be influenced by what is happening in their world. Understanding the context of a passage will help you better analyze the author's point of view.

**Practice the Skill** *Answer the following questions about the passages above.*

1. **Identify the topic or issue. (a)** What is the topic of the quotes on the left? **(b)** What is the topic of the quotes on the right?

2. **Determine the author's position on the topic or issue.** What were Confucius's positions on these topics?

3. **Identify important background information about the passage. (a)** What types of work did Confucius perform during his life? **(b)** How would you describe Chinese government and society at this time?

4. **Ask how this background information might influence the author's beliefs.** How might this background information have influenced Confucius's point of view on these topics?

**Apply the Skill**
*See page 321 of the Review and Assessment.*

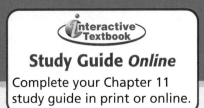

**Study Guide** *Online*
Complete your Chapter 11 study guide in print or online.

## Chapter Summary  H-SS: 6.6; 6.6.3; 6.6.4; 6.6.8

### Section 1 Family and Religion

- Loyalty to one's family was one of the most important values in ancient China.
- A person's age and sex often determined their status in a family in ancient China.
- Religious views in ancient China focused on a belief in spirits. The worship of the spirits of ancestors was important in Chinese religion.

### Section 2 The Teachings of Confucius

- Chinese thinkers such as Hanfeizi and Mo-zi proposed solutions to the state of anarchy in China during the Era of the Warring States.
- A Chinese thinker named Confucius suggested that China could restore order by returning to traditional values.
- Important Confucian ideas, such as the five key relationships, had a strong impact on Chinese society.

### Section 3 Daoism and Buddhism in China

- The philosophy of Daoism encouraged people of ancient China to lead simple lives that worked in harmony with the way of nature.
- After Buddhism spread from India to China in the first century A.D., the Chinese shaped these ideas into their own sects.
- Important ideas of Confucianism, Daoism, and Buddhism were mixed and borrowed in China.

**Confucius and followers**

## Standards Practice  H-SS: 6.6; 6.6.3; 6.6.4; 6.6.8

## Vocabulary *Builder*

### High-Use Words

Read each sentence below. If the sentence is true, write YES. If the sentence is not true, write NO and explain WHY.

1. A **traditional** Chinese family included only parents and their children.

2. The people of ancient China believed that **bonds** protected them from evil spirits.

3. Historians **concluded** that Laozi was the only author of the *Tao Te Ching.*

4. Confucius explained the type of **conduct** that rulers should demonstrate.

### Key Terms

Answer the following questions in complete sentences that show your understanding of the Key Terms.

1. Why was the Era of the Warring States considered a time of anarchy?

2. How did Legalism propose to solve the problems facing China?

3. What led to the development of Confucianism?

4. How might a child show filial piety toward a parent?

## Apply Reading Skills

**Analyze Comparisons and Contrasts in Text** Read the text under the heading Following the Dao on page 314. Explain the comparisons and contrasts that this text makes between Daoism and other systems of belief, such as Confucianism and Legalism.

## Comprehension and Critical Thinking

1. **(a) Explain** What was the structure of a traditional Chinese family?
   **(b) Draw Conclusions** How was the importance of families tied to ancient Chinese religious beliefs?
   **(c) Link Past and Present** How are traditional Chinese family structures similar to and different from family structures of today?

2. **(a) Recall** What fundamental ideas did Confucius teach his students?
   **(b) Organize Information** How did Confucius suggest that the five key relationships would bring order to Chinese society?
   **(c) Apply Information** Explain how the principle of filial piety was applied beyond the living members of one's family.

3. **(a) Identify** According to legend, who is the founder of Daoism?
   **(b) Understand Sequence** When was Buddhism introduced to China in relation to the development of Confucianism?
   **(c) Identify Alternatives** How did each of China's "Three Ways" of belief satisfy different needs of the people?

## Researching

**Chinese Families** In ancient China, social structures were often defined by family relationships. In this activity, you will use the Internet and the library media center to research and report on these relationships. Choose a task below to work on. Share your work with the class on Chinese Families Day. Make a list of the resources you used to go with your presentation.

**Historians:** Create a diagram that shows the various members and generations of a typical traditional Chinese family. You may choose to organize your diagram as a family tree.

**Journalists:** Write a newspaper feature that describes some of the ways in which traditional Chinese families worshipped their ancestors. You may wish to include images or graphics to help explain these practices for your reader.

> **Researching Online**
> **For:** Help in starting this activity
> **Visit:** PHSchool.com
> **Web Code:** mwe-4114

## Writing

1. **Write a paragraph on the following topic.** In the later years of his life, Confucius traveled in search of a ruler who would govern according to Confucian teachings. Why do you think many rulers would have chosen not to accept these principles?
   **Your paragraph should:**
   • contain a clear topic sentence.
   • offer evidence to support your ideas.
   • conclude with a sentence summarizing your main points.

2. **Write a short narrative.** Suppose you were living in ancient China as Buddhism spread into the area. Describe how the ideas of Confucianism, Daoism, and Buddhism mixed together to affect your life.

**Progress Monitoring ⚫nline**
**For:** Self-test with instant help
**Visit:** PHSchool.com
**Web Code:** mwa-4114

# Apply Analysis Skills

**Use the quote at right to answer these questions.**

1. What is the topic of the quote?

2. How would you describe the author's position on the topic?

3. What do you think you can learn about the author's background from this quote?

4. How might this information help you interpret the author's point of view?

> ❝The reason why. . . . subjects do not dare deceive their ruler is not because they love him, but because they fear his awe-inspiring power.❞
>
> —Legalist author

# Test Yourself

1. **The welfare of the traditional Chinese family was**

    A more important than that of individual family members.

    B less important than honoring one's ancestors.

    C the responsibility of the grandparents.

    D determined by a family council.

2. **Which spirits were the most important in traditional Chinese religion?**

    A storms

    B demons

    C dragons

    D ancestors

**Refer to the quote below to answer Question 3.**

3. **Which of the following statements is supported by this quote?**

    *"What you do not want done to yourself, do not do to others."*

    A Laozi believed that law and order would save Chinese society.

    B Hanfeizi believed that peace would come if people loved one another.

    C Confucius believed that superiors should rule by setting a good example.

    D Mo-zi believed that everyone should follow the principles of *yin* and *yang*.

4. **Confucius thought that anarchy would end if everyone respected the**

    A rule of law.

    B Mandate of Heaven.

    C teachings of Buddha.

    D five key relationships.

**Refer to the image below to answer Question 5.**

5. **This symbol represents the Daoist belief that**

    A men were superior to women.

    B two great forces were at work in the universe.

    C rulers should have power over citizens.

    D Amithaba would save them from the cycle of reincarnation.

6. **Which school of Buddhism did missionaries from India bring to China?**

    A Theravada

    B Mahayana

    C Pure Land

    D Western Paradise

# Chapter 12 Growth of the Chinese Empire (ABOUT 221 B.C.–100 B.C.)

## Prepare to Read

### Chapter Standards

**History-Social Science**

**6.6** Students analyze the geographic, political, economic, religious, and social structures of the early civilizations of China.

**Section 1,** pp. 326–332

**Shi Huangdi Unites China**

**What You Will Learn**

Qin armies united China and founded a new dynasty. The powerful Qin ruler Shi Huangdi expanded and unified China into one people under one government.

**Section 2,** pp. 333–337

**Expansion Under the Han Dynasty**

The Han Dynasty built on Shi Huangdi's success to create one of the most successful dynasties in Chinese history.

**Section 3,** pp. 340–345

**Han Society and Achievements**

The Han Dynasty made aspects of life more uniform in China. This fact, plus Confucian values were important contributions to the expansion and success of the Han Dynasty.

A Chinese chariot

**221 B.C.**
Qin forces unite north China.

**Chapter Events**

**Other Events**

**300s B.C.**

**250 B.C.**

**200 B.C.**

**300s B.C.**
Egypt prospers.

**273 B.C.** Asoka becomes India's third Mauryan emperor.

An army of life-size clay soldiers, horses, and chariots guarded the First Emperor's tomb. Each figure represented a soldier from the Qin army.

**140 B.C.**
Wudi becomes the sixth Han emperor.

**About 100 B.C.**
The wheelbarrow is invented in China.

**200 B.C.**

**150 B.C.**

**100 B.C.**

**About 185 B.C.**
Mauryan Empire ends.

**First century B.C.** Meroë becomes a major producer of iron.

## History Reading Skill

### *Previewing* Words with Multiple Meanings

Not all words have only one meaning. Sometimes you will come across words that have more than one meaning. There are several ways to determine which meaning is used. Use context clues to choose the correct meaning for the word. Determining the part of speech is also a useful strategy. Sometimes using figurative language will change the meaning of words.

 **Chapter Standards**

**English-Language Arts**

**Reading 6.1.2** Identify and interpret figurative language and words with multiple meanings.

"According to legend, the Chinese philosopher Laozi was so upset with the behavior of his countrymen that he decided to ride a water buffalo to Tibet. However, before he crossed the border, Laozi was persuaded by a guard to record his beliefs.

The *Tao Te Ching* is a collection of short puzzle-like poems credited to Laozi, which illustrate the right "way," or path. In general, the *Tao Te Ching* says people should abandon worldly knowledge and listen to their instincts for wisdom. In addition, the poems suggest surrendering to one's role in life, rather than harboring ambition. Laozi argues that when one does not desire, he or she will finally have peace. The *Tao Te Ching* further states that when a person has peace, he or she can finally think and see clearly."

—*Benjamin James Smith*

> **Examples of figurative language**

> One cannot literally surrender, as an army in battle, to one's role in life. This figurative language instead suggests that a person should accept his or her circumstances in life. Harboring also has a figurative meaning of "to hold onto."

Ask these questions as you interpret figurative language:

- Why do writers use figurative language?
- What are some potential problems in using figurative language?
- What is another example of figurative language found in this passage?

# Vocabulary *Builder*

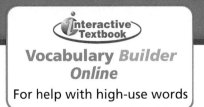
## *Previewing* **High-Use Academic Words**

| High-Use Word | Definition | Sample Sentence About History |
|---|---|---|
| **policy** (PAHL uh see) (Section 1, p. 329) | *n.* principle, plan, or course of action as pursued by a government or organization | The emperor's <u>policy</u> was to unify all the lands under his control. |
| **accomplish** (uh KAHM plish) (Section 1, p. 330) | *v.* to do; succeed in doing; complete | The ruler <u>accomplished</u> much during his reign. |
| **contribution** (kahn trih BYOO shuhn) (Section 2, p. 334) | *n.* something given or provided | The scientific <u>contributions</u> of the Egyptians had a lasting impact on society. |
| **establishment** (eh STAB lish mehnt) (Section 2, p. 336) | *n.* the setting up of something, such as a business or government | The <u>establishment</u> of the nation's first government took place in 330 B.C. |
| **occupy** (AH kyoo pī) (Section 3, p. 341) | *v.* to live, exist, or stay in a particular place | Invaders <u>occupied</u> the northern territories for two years. |
| **foundation** (fown DAY shuhn) (Section 3, p. 342) | *n.* basic idea; principle; situation | The group's religious beliefs also were the <u>foundation</u> for its government. |

## *Previewing* **Key Terms and People**

**Shi Huangdi**, p. 327
**Chen Sheng**, p. 332
**Liu Bang**, p. 333

**Wudi**, p. 334
**Zhang Qian**, p. 335

**Ban Zhao**, p. 342
**traditional arts**, p. 343

**Shi Huangdi**

**Example of traditional art of China, lacquerware**

## Standards Preview

**H-SS 6.6.5** List the policies and achievements of the emperor Shi Huangdi in unifying northern China under the Qin Dynasty.

**E-LA Reading 6.1.2** Identify and interpret figurative language and words with multiple meanings.

## Reading Preview

### Reading Skill

**Identify Figurative Language** Two important kinds of figurative language are similes and metaphors. Similes use the words *like* or *as* to make comparisons. Metaphors describe one thing as if it were another. For example, the statement "The emperor roars at his subjects" means that the emperor acts the way that an angry lion would.

### Vocabulary *Builder*

**High-Use Words**
**policy** (PAHL uh see), p. 329
**accomplish** (uh KAHM plish), p. 330

**Key Terms and People**
Shi Huangdi (shee hwahng DEE), p. 327
Chen Sheng (CHEHN shehng), p. 332

**Background Knowledge** During the Era of the Warring States, many leaders tried to unify China. But geography and opposition from rival warlords made it difficult to unite the country under one rule. Despite these challenges, one kingdom did finally succeed in uniting China. Its leader founded the ruling family known as the Qin Dynasty.

**Main Idea**
Qin armies united China and founded a powerful new dynasty.

## The Rise of the Qin

Conflicts between the Warring States divided China for more than 200 years. By the end of this period, several powerful kingdoms had emerged in China. The most powerful was the kingdom known as Qin.

**The Qin Kingdom** Qin, pronounced "Chin," was a mountain kingdom located in northwestern China. Beyond Qin lay the barbarian lands of Central Asia. To most Chinese, the Qin also seemed to be barbarians. But the Qin rulers built a strong kingdom with an efficient government.

The Qin were also great warriors who fought with swords and crossbows. They were skilled on horseback and ruthless in battle. After one victory, the Qin were reported to have killed an entire army of 400,000 men.

**The Qin Unite China** One by one, the Qin brought down rival kingdoms. An observer wrote that the Qin "ate up its neighbors as a silkworm devours a leaf." In 221 B.C., Qin forces finally united northern China under their rule.

The Qin ruler decided that "king" was too small a title for the leader of such a vast empire. He thus declared himself to be Shi Huangdi, or "First Emperor," a title given to gods and legendary rulers. The first Qin emperor hoped that the dynasty he had founded would rule China forever. The name Qin gave rise to the name we use today for the Middle Kingdom—China.

✔ **Checkpoint** How did the Qin unite Chinese territory?

**E-LA 6.1.2 Identify Figurative Language** What does the figurative language in the second sentence of this paragraph mean?

# Qin Policies and Achievements

Once in power, Shi Huangdi faced many challenges. His empire was divided into distinct regions. Languages and customs varied from place to place. Rebellion was always a danger, as was invasion by barbarians from Central Asia. Shi Huangdi needed to do what no ruler had done before—unify China into one people under one government.

**Main Idea**
The Qin Emperor Shi Huangdi unified China's people under his rule.

**First Emperor**
China's First Emperor, Shi Huangdi, is shown using sand to plan and map the Great Wall. He ruled his subjects harshly, but he had a lasting impact on Chinese society.
**Critical Thinking: Explain Problems** *Why might it have been difficult for Shi Huangdi to unite China?*

# The Great Wall of China

In 214 B.C., China's First Emperor ordered a series of great protective walls to be built and joined together. Today it is still the longest structure ever built. **Critical Thinking: Analyze Cause and Effect** *What effect did the Great Wall have on China?*

## Explore More Video

**Discovery School Video** View *The Great Wall* to learn more about the importance of China's Great Wall.

The Great Wall was constructed of hard-baked bricks with clay filling between layers.

The First Emperor used forced labor to build the Great Wall.

**The Great Wall** Shi Huangdi continued to expand his empire. He also began work on what may be the largest public-works project in history—the Great Wall of China. The wall's purpose was to defend the empire from attack by nomads living on China's northern borders.

The wall went up quickly. In just seven years, Chinese workers built a 2,600-mile stone barrier. Each section was dotted with watchtowers. This amazing engineering achievement came at a high cost, however. One million workers were reported to have died while building the wall.

Troops were stationed along the wall as a first line of defense against invaders. These soldiers used signal fires to warn nearby towns of an attack. Impressive as these defenses were, the Great Wall never really worked as Shi Huangdi had hoped. Determined invaders were still able to find a way around or through this stone barrier.

Watchtowers were stationed along the wall to provide lookout posts as well as shelter for soldiers during an attack.

The wall was 30 feet tall and wide enough for a chariot to use.

**A Legalist Government** Shi Huangdi based his empire's government on Legalist ideas which were developed during the Era of the Warring States. Legalists believed in strict laws and a strong government to enforce those laws.

Shi Huangdi set out to create such a government. He introduced the concept of centralization, or a central governing system. Shi Huangdi organized China into 36 provinces, each of which was divided into counties. County leaders were responsible to the heads of provinces. Province heads reported to the central government. Officials of the central government were responsible to the emperor. Any official who failed to carry out the emperor's <u>policies</u> was dismissed.

To prevent rebellion, Shi Huangdi forced thousands of noble families to relocate to the capital city. There government spies could watch over them. Warlords' weapons were seized and melted down into statues for the imperial palace.

**Vocabulary** *Builder*
<u>policy</u> (PAHL uh see) *n.* principle, plan, or course of action as pursued by a government or organization

## Harsh Laws

The emperor established a uniform legal code across his empire. The laws applied equally to nobles and commoners. Penalties for breaking a law were severe. For example, anyone caught in the act of hiding a criminal risked being cut in half. Other punishments included cutting off feet and noses or being buried alive. An official named Shang Yang explained the reason for such punishments:

> **Punish severely light crimes. People do not easily commit serious crimes. But light offenses (crimes) are easily abandoned by people. . . . Now, if small offenses do not arise, big crimes will not come. And thus people will commit no crimes and disorder will not arise.**
>
> —*The Book of Lord Shang*

**Vocabulary** *Builder*

<u>accomplish</u> (uh KAHM plish) *v.* to do; succeed in doing; complete

## Uniform Standards

Shi Huangdi's policies also unified China's economy and culture. He <u>accomplished</u> this by standardizing many aspects of daily life.

The Qin government established a single written language with standard characters. It created a uniform set of weights and measures for use in commerce. It produced uniform coins, called *cash,* to be used as currency across China. Anyone who did not adopt these standards could be accused of treason.

Transportation was standardized as well. The government established a standard length for the axles of all vehicles. As a result, all ruts made in Chinese roads by the wheels of carts would be the same distance apart. This made moving goods for long distances easier because all carts and wagons could travel in the same ruts.

**Road Travel**

Carts and chariots could more easily travel on early Chinese roads after the government established a standard axle length for vehicles. **Critical Thinking: Clarify Problems** *Why would it be difficult for vehicles with different axle lengths to travel on Chinese roads?*

**The Burning of the Books**
The First Emperor ordered that books written by scholars who disagreed with him be burned. Anyone who spoke against this policy was executed. Books about medicine and agriculture were spared, however. **Critical Thinking: Analyze Cause and Effect** *What effect do you think that the burning of books had on the people under the First Emperor's rule? Explain.*

**Thought Control**  The First Emperor even tried to control Chinese thought by adopting a policy of censorship, or banning ideas he found dangerous or offensive. Censorship took many forms. Debate about the government was banned. People were not allowed to praise past rulers or criticize the present one. The emperor ordered the burning of all books that did not support his policies. The emperor also had 460 scholars executed for criticizing his policies. These policies were not popular. But they did help create a single nation from China's diverse regions. As a stone carving said at the time, the emperor "made the world a single family."

**The Fall of the Qin Dynasty**  In 210 B.C., Emperor Shi Huangdi died. He was buried in a magnificent tomb with an army of clay soldiers to serve him in death. The First Emperor believed that his dynasty would live forever, but it collapsed in three brief years.

**Primary** Sources

See "Qin Dynasty: Achievements of Shi Huangdi" in the Reference Section at the back of this book.

**A Qin Soldier**
This statue of a Qin Dynasty soldier shows the warrior in a typical fighting position.
**Critical Thinking: Draw Conclusions** *What might this soldier have been holding when the statue was made?*

The Qin dynasty was undone by the harshness of its laws. A rebellion was sparked by a soldier named Chen Sheng, who led a band of men north to guard China's border. Along the way, heavy rains delayed the band. Chen knew that the penalty for arriving late would be severe. So he and his men decided that they had nothing to lose by rebelling.

As word of Chen's uprising spread, thousands rose up to support him. Qin generals tried to put down the uprisings, but the rebellions spread rapidly. Knowing the harsh punishments for failure, many generals joined the rebellions.

The rebels joined together long enough to overthrow the Qin dynasty. But then the rebels began fighting among themselves. Once again, China slid into chaos.

 **Checkpoint** How did Shi Huangdi succeed in uniting China under one government?

**Looking Back and Ahead** In this section, you have read how Qin armies united China and founded a new dynasty. You have learned about the efforts of Shi Huangdi to expand and unify China. In the next section, you will read about the Han dynasty and its impact on China's history and government.

## Section 1 Check Your Progress

**Progress Monitoring Online**
For: Self-test with instant help
Visit: PHSchool.com
Web Code: mwa-4121

 **Standards Review** H-SS: 6.6.5; E-LA: Reading 6.1.2

**Comprehension and Critical Thinking**

1. **(a) Identify** Who founded the first Chinese empire?
**(b) Draw Inferences** What was the secret of his success?

2. **(a) Explain** What type of government did the Qin establish?
**(b) Apply Information** What were the costs and benefits of policies established by the Qin government?

**Reading Skill**

3. **Identify Figurative Language** Read this sentence: The Qin crushed their enemies as an elephant steps on an ant. What two unlike things are being compared?

**Vocabulary Builder**

4. Answer the following questions in complete sentences that show your understanding of the Key People.
**(a)** Who was Shi Huangdi and what was his greatest accomplishment? **(b)** How did Chen Sheng contribute to the fall of the Qin dynasty?

**Writing**

5. Write three or four sentences that summarize how Shi Huangdi united China. In one of the sentences, write what you believe to be his greatest accomplishments as First Emperor.

**Standards Preview**

**H-SS 6.6.6** Detail the political contributions of the Han Dynasty to the development of the imperial bureaucratic state and the expansion of the empire.

**H-SS 6.6.7** Cite the significance of the trans-Eurasian "silk roads" in the period of the Han Dynasty and Roman Empire and their locations.

**E-LA Reading 6.1.2** Identify and interpret figurative language and words with multiple meanings.

## Reading Preview

 **Reading Skill**

**Interpret Words With Multiple Meanings**
Sometimes you may be confused by words that have more than one meaning. For example, you might read the word *type* in the sentence "This is a type of government." *Type* can mean "a variety of something," or it can mean "to enter letters on a keyboard." The first meaning is a noun; the second is a verb. Use the word's place in the sentence to choose the correct meaning.

## Vocabulary *Builder*

**High-Use Words**
<u>contribution</u> (kahn trih BYOO shuhn), p. 334
<u>establishment</u> (eh STAB lish mehnt), p. 336

**Key Terms**
Liu Bang (lee OO bahng), p. 333
Wudi (WOO dee), p. 334
Zhang Qian (JAHNG chī ehn), p. 335

**Background Knowledge** Besides founding China's first empire, Shi Huangdi also laid the foundation for a government. In this section, you will read about China's next ruling family, the Han. Han emperors built on the Qin foundations to create one of the most successful dynasties in Chinese history.

## The Rise of the Han

The fighting that toppled the Qin Dynasty lasted for several years. Finally, a rebel general named Liu Bang gained control of China. In 206 B.C., he founded the Han Dynasty. The Han ruled China for 400 years. Today, the Chinese still call themselves "the people of Han."

**The First Han Emperor** Unlike most Chinese rulers, the first Han emperor came from a poor family. Liu Bang's aides persuaded him to study with Confucian scholars to learn how to govern. They pointed out that the Qin had lost power because their policies were so unpopular.

**Main Idea**
The Han Dynasty built upon Shi Huangdi's foundations to create one of the most successful dynasties in Chinese history.

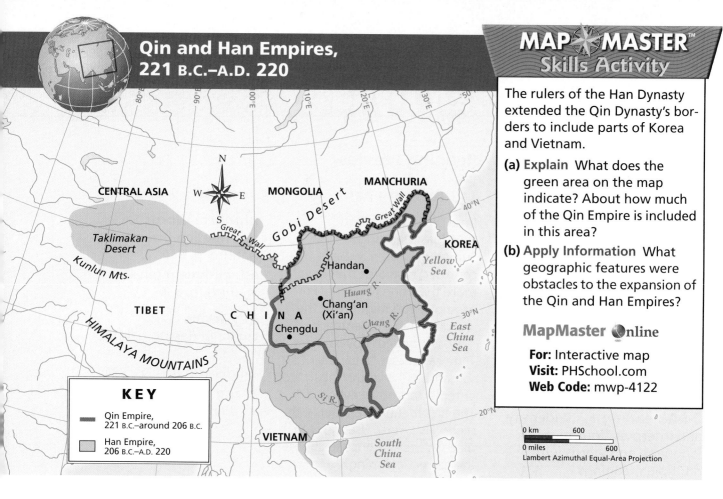

## Qin and Han Empires, 221 B.C.–A.D. 220

**MAP MASTER™**
**Skills Activity**

CENTRAL ASIA

MONGOLIA

MANCHURIA

Taklimakan Desert

Gobi Desert

Great Wall

Great Wall

Kunlun Mts.

KOREA

Handan

Yellow Sea

TIBET

Huang R.

CHINA

Chang'an (Xi'an)

Chengdu

Chang R.

30°N

East China Sea

HIMALAYA MOUNTAINS

Si R.

VIETNAM

South China Sea

20°N

### KEY

— Qin Empire, 221 B.C.–around 206 B.C.

▢ Han Empire, 206 B.C.–A.D. 220

The rulers of the Han Dynasty extended the Qin Dynasty's borders to include parts of Korea and Vietnam.

**(a) Explain** What does the green area on the map indicate? About how much of the Qin Empire is included in this area?

**(b) Apply Information** What geographic features were obstacles to the expansion of the Qin and Han Empires?

**MapMaster** ●nline

**For:** Interactive map
**Visit:** PHSchool.com
**Web Code:** mwp-4122

0 km 600
0 miles 600
Lambert Azimuthal Equal-Area Projection

**E-LA 6.1.2 Interpret Words With Multiple Meanings**

Define the word *order* as it is used in the third sentence.

**Vocabulary** *Builder*

**contribution** (kahn trih BYOO shuhn) *n.* something given or provided

The result was a government that continued its efforts to standardize Chinese life, but also followed Confucian teachings. The emperor encouraged learning, lowered taxes, reduced punishments for crimes, and ended censorship. These policies did much to restore order to China. The population grew rapidly. So did the economy. The country was peaceful and prosperous.

**The Emperor Wudi** In 140 B.C., a 16-year-old boy named Liu Che became the sixth Han emperor. Later known as Wudi, he ruled for more than 50 years. Wudi made important contributions to Han society and is known as one of the greatest emperors in Chinese history. During his long reign, Wudi sent an army south into what is now Vietnam. The Vietnamese adopted many elements of Chinese culture. However, they never lost their own identity or their desire to be free of Chinese rule. Another army marched north into Manchuria and the Korean Peninsula. The Han ruled most of Korea as well. Like the Vietnamese, the Koreans borrowed aspects of Chinese culture. However, they remained determined to free themselves from Chinese control.

✔**Checkpoint** How did the first Han emperor bring peace to China?

# War Against the Xiongnu

**Main Idea**
The Silk Road was started in part as the result of Zhang Quian's journeys to Central Asia.

Wudi's most important military goal was to destroy the nomads known as the Xiongnu, or Huns. The Great Wall was built to stop the Xiongnu's raids, but it failed to keep the nomadic warriors from the region.

Liu Bang tried to end the Xiongnu threat through diplomacy. Diplomacy is the art of reaching agreements between peoples and nations. Liu Bang agreed to give the nomads goods in exchange for their promise of peace, but the agreement did not work. The Xiongnu continued to attack Chinese territory.

Wudi declared war against the Xiongnu, but fighting them was not easy. They "move on swift horses," his generals said. "They shift from place to place like a flock of birds. Thus, it is difficult to corner them and bring them under control."

**Zhang Qian's Long Journey**  During this conflict, the emperor questioned captured nomads. "They all reported that the Xiongnu had defeated the king of the Yuezhi people and had made his skull into a drinking vessel," wrote Sima Qian, the emperor's historian. "As a result, the Yuezhi had fled and bore a constant grudge, or bad feeling, against the Xiongnu."

Wudi sent an official named Zhang Qian to seek out the Yuezhi. Zhang's search took him deep into Central Asia. There, he was captured by the Xiongnu and held prisoner for ten years. Zhang finally escaped and found the Yuezhi. However, he was not able to persuade them to attack the Xiongnu.

On his return to China, Zhang reported on all he had seen. Of great interest to Wudi was Zhang's description of Central Asia's "blood-sweating horses." If Chinese troops had such horses, Wudi reasoned, they might be better able to fight the Xiongnu. The emperor was also interested in what Zhang had learned about even more distant lands, including India, Persia, and Mesopotamia.

> **❝All these states, he was told, were militarily weak and prized Han goods and wealth. . . If it were only possible to win over these states by peaceful means, the emperor thought, he could then extend his domain ten thousand li (about 3,300 miles). . . . and his might would become known to all the lands within the four seas.❞**
>
> —Sima Qian, *Records of the Grand Historian*

**Vocabulary** *Builder*

**establishment** (eh STAB lish mehnt) *n.* the setting up of something, such as a business or government

**The "Silk Roads"** Zhang's travels into Central Asia took him as far as present-day Kazakhstan and Afghanistan. His report led to the <u>establishment</u> of China's first trade routes to the West—the famous "silk roads" that ran across Central Asia. From there, they connected with trade routes leading south into India and west to the Mediterranean Sea. The map on page 339 shows the extent of the Silk Road.

✔ **Checkpoint** **How did Zhang's report contribute to the establishment of the Silk Road?**

**Main Idea**
The Han Dynasty expanded China and established an imperial bureaucratic state.

# The Imperial Bureaucratic State

Wudi not only expanded the Chinese Empire. He also helped build an imperial bureaucracy to govern the vast lands of China.

## The Structure of Government
Han government was organized like a pyramid. The broad base of the pyramid was made up of China's many small towns and villages. Above that base came districts. The districts were topped by counties and provinces. At the top of the governmental pyramid were the emperor and his chief advisers. Officials at each level of the pyramid took orders from those above them and gave orders to those below them.

**Civil Service** The strength of the Han government lay in its educated civil service. A civil service consists of the people who work for the government. The Han civil service was large. It included more than 130,000 officials.

To find the best people for the jobs in his civil service, Emperor Wudi created exams based on the teachings of Confucius. To prepare, students spent many years memorizing thousands of words from books of Confucian thought. Only a small number of those who took the exams passed the test each year.

## What was Zhang Qian's contribution to China?

Zhang Qian

### Fast Facts

**Who:** Zhang Qian
**What:** Explorer, diplomat
**When:** 100s B.C.
**Where:** Central Asia, China
**Why important:** Zhang Qian set out in 138 B.C. on a diplomatic mission for Emperor Wudi. Zhang's discoveries helped start the Silk Road trade.

### Fast Find

**How:** Go online to find out how China's historic isolation makes Zhang Qian's story even more remarkable.

**Biography** ⬤nline

**For:** More about Zhang Qian
**Visit:** PHSchool.com
**Web Code:** mwe-4122

For those who succeeded, the rewards were great. Han officials enjoyed high salaries and a life of comfort and influence. They wore special clothes that indicated their rank in the civil service.

Officials had great power. They collected taxes, organized labor, and enforced laws. They could even force people to move. If there were too many people in a village or district, officials could relocate them to lands with fewer people. But the officials' power was limited. Han officials were not allowed to serve in their home districts. This rule helped keep officials from favoring their family and friends.

 **Checkpoint** **What is the main strength of Han government?**

**Looking Back and Ahead** In this section, you have read about the expansion of China under the Han Dynasty. You have also learned about Han contributions to the growth of the imperial bureaucratic state. These contributions include an organized government and an educated civil service. In the next section, you will read about Han society and its many achievements.

**A Chinese Civil Servant**
Civil servants held a high place in Chinese society. **Critical Thinking: Compare** *How are civil servants in the U.S. government similar to civil servants in ancient China?*

## Section 2 Check Your Progress

**Progress Monitoring** Online
**For:** Self-test with instant help
**Visit:** PHSchool.com
**Web Code:** mwa-4122

**Standards Review** H-SS: 6.6.6, 6.6.7; E-LA: Reading 6.1.2

**Comprehension and Critical Thinking**

1. **(a) Identify** Why is Wudi considered to be a great ruler?
   **(b) Draw Conclusions** How did Liu Bang's policies make it possible for Wudi to rule successfully?

2. **(a) Explain** What was the basis for the civil service exams?
   **(b) Evaluate Information** Why were the exams important?

**Reading Skill**

3. **Interpret Words With Multiple Meanings** Read this sentence: "He points out that the Qin had lost power." What does the word *points* mean in this sentence?

**Vocabulary** *Builder*

Read each sentence below. If the sentence is true, write YES. If the sentence is not true, write NO and explain WHY.

4. A rebel general named Liu Bang founded the Chin Dynasty in 206 B.C.

5. Wudi ruled China for more than 50 years.

6. Zhang Qian had no part in establishing what became known as the Silk Road.

**Writing**

7. You have just read a letter that Zhang Qian wrote to the emperor on his journey through Central Asia, describing what he saw. Write three sentences containing Zhang's thoughts about his discoveries.

# The Silk Road

The Silk Road was not always called the Silk Road. A German geographer gave it that name in the 1800s in honor of its most successful export. But no matter what the name, these important trade routes were used for more than 1,000 years. Information and ideas also traveled along this trade route. Buddhism was just one import that came to China on the Silk Road during the Han Dynasty. For the first time, the Chinese began to have contact with civilized people living far beyond the Great Wall.

**History-Social Science**

**6.6.7** Cite the significance of the trans-Eurasian "silk roads" in the period of the Han Dynasty and Roman Empire and their locations.

Silk cloth was highly valued. Bolts of it were used as money in the Silk Road trade.

Silk cocoons

### The Secret of Silk

About 5,000 years ago, the Chinese learned to make silk from the cocoons of worms that fed on mulberry trees. The Chinese carefully guarded the secret of silk making. During the Han Dynasty, a person could be put to death for exporting silkworms or telling outsiders how to make silk.

### Military Control Posts

The Silk Road was not always safe for travelers. Military troops were stationed at control posts along the way. This beacon tower was one of many built during the Han Dynasty. Signals were sent between the towers by using colored flags, smoke, and fire.

## Camel Caravans

Merchants used camels to carry their goods along the Silk Road. Camels were easy to handle and carried huge loads across high mountains and dry deserts. Because transport by camel was expensive, camels were used to carry luxury goods, such as precious stones, wine, and, of course, silk.

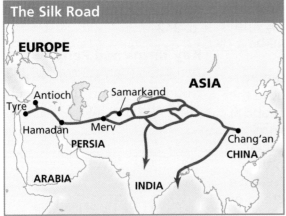

**The Silk Road**

EUROPE

ASIA

Antioch     Samarkand

Tyre

Hamadan     Merv

PERSIA                    Chang'an

CHINA

ARABIA

INDIA

**This map shows the extent of the Silk Road.**

Ceramic camel made during the Silk Road years

## Money

In ancient times, traveling merchants used money shaped like knives, fish, and other objects. The First Emperor introduced round bronze coins, known as *cash.* These remained in use for more than 2,000 years.

**A standard round coin used during the Han Dynasty**

**The hole allowed coins to be threaded on a string.**

### *Analyze* LIFE AT THE TIME

You are a Chinese merchant traveling on the Silk Road. Write a description of one day of your journey. Your description should answer the following questions:

- What trade goods are packed on your camel?
- What trade goods do you hope to get in return?
- What is the land like? The weather? The journey?

Section

# 3 Han Society and Achievements

 **Standards Preview**

**H-SS 6.6.6** Detail the political contributions of the Han Dynasty to the development of the imperial bureaucratic state and the expansion of the empire.

**E-LA Reading 6.1.2** Identify and interpret figurative language and words with multiple meanings.

## Reading Preview

 **Reading Skill**

**Interpret Words with Multiple Meanings** Even though many words have multiple meanings, only one meaning of a word will be used at any time in a sentence. Try each meaning of the word. Then choose the one that makes sense. Look at this example: "They wore badges that indicated their rank in the service." In this context, *rank* means "relative position to others" instead of "unpleasant in odor."

## Vocabulary *Builder*

**High-Use Words**
occupy (AH kyoo pī), p. 341
foundation (fown DAY shuhn), p. 342

**Key Terms and People**
Ban Zhao (bahn ZHOW), p. 342
traditional arts (truh DIHSH uh nuhl ahrts), p. 343

---

 **E-LA 6.1.2 Interpret Words With Multiple Meanings**

The words *stable* and *civil* each have two meanings. Which meanings are used here?

**Background Knowledge** During the Han Dynasty, China's population grew to about 60 million people. Ruling such a large and diverse population was not easy—even with an efficient civil service. It would have been impossible without a stable society. This section examines Han society and its achievements.

## Han Society

**Main Idea**
Han society was based on order and Confucian teachings, creating a strong economy.

Han society was a mixture of peoples and cultures. Two forces bound these groups together. One was the imperial bureaucratic state and its efforts to standardize life in China. To standardize means to make things of the same type all have the same basic features. The other was Confucian values and virtues.

**The Social Order** Han society was divided into two main groups: nobles and commoners. The nobles included the emperor and his family, along with the ruling families of China's old kingdoms. The commoners included everyone else.

China's social order was based on Confucian values. In the Confucian system, mental work was valued more than physical labor. Scholars stood at the top of the social order. Physical work was valued more than making money, so farmers and artisans <u>occupied</u> the center of the social order. Merchants did not produce anything; therefore, they were at the bottom.

The government placed many restrictions on merchants. They were not allowed to wear fine clothing or own land. Their children could not become civil servants. Despite these limits on their lives, many merchants became wealthy and powerful.

**Family Life**  The family stood at the center of Chinese society. As you learned in Chapter 11, Confucian teachings about family loyalty and respect for elders were key values. Confucian beliefs about proper conduct in all areas of life remained important as well.

Most families lived in wooden houses surrounded by high walls. Wealthy families lived in large homes with fine furniture and gardens. They usually dressed in silk robes and ate rich foods. Peasant farmers lived in basic homes with few possessions. They ate simple foods. They wore rough clothing and straw sandals. Their lives were difficult.

**Vocabulary** *Builder*
<u>occupy</u> (AH kyoo pī) *v.* to live, exist, or stay in a particular place

**Working on the River**
Many Chinese families made their living by working on and near rivers. This picture shows an ancient bridge in China and people transporting goods to and from marketplaces.
**Critical Thinking: Apply Information** *What kinds of jobs could people have who lived near rivers?*

## The Role of Women

Although women had some rights in Han society, they played a subordinate, or lower, role to men. A woman was expected to obey her husband and take care of her home.

One woman who took a different path was **Ban Zhao.** Unlike most women of her time, she received a good education. Ban later became a teacher and historian in the royal court. In her most famous book, *Lessons for Women,* she wrote that young women deserved an education. But she also accepted many traditional roles for women. For example, she wrote that women should not challenge the authority of men:

> **If a husband does not control his wife, then the rules of conduct . . . are abandoned and broken. If a wife does not serve her husband, then the proper relationship between men and women and the natural order of things are neglected and destroyed.**
>
> —Ban Zhao, *Lessons for Women*

## Economic Life

**Vocabulary** *Builder*
**foundation** (fown DAY shuhn) *n.* basic idea, principle, situation

Farmers were the backbone of China's economy. They made up about 90 percent of the population. As one Han emperor wrote, "Agriculture is the <u>foundation</u> of the world. No duty is greater." Most farms in Han China were small. Farmers grew wheat, millet, barley, beans, and rice. Farmers with more land might also grow fruit or bamboo. Some nobles owned large estates on which they raised livestock and silkworms. Silk production became an important industry during the Han period.

Other industries, such as iron production, also became important. Iron was especially useful for making tools and weapons. Salt mining was another key industry. These industries became so important that Wudi turned them into state monopolies. Profits from the sale of iron and salt helped support Wudi's military adventures.

The strength of the Han economy could be seen in the size and splendor of Chang 'an, the Han capital. Chang 'an, one of the largest cities in the world, was surrounded by high walls. Inside the walls were broad avenues, parks, and great palaces. Marketplaces around the city were filled with merchants selling a wide variety of goods.

 **Checkpoint** How did Confucian values contribute to the structure of Han society?

# Han Achievements

The prosperity of Han China helped support many cultural achievements. Artists, writers, and musicians created works of beauty. Scientists and inventors also made important advances.

**China's Traditional Arts** The traditional arts of China include painting, sculpture, and poetry. Han artists painted colorful murals. Sculptors created beautiful works in stone, clay, and bronze. Poets wrote about the Chinese countryside.

Because Confucius believed that music was good for the spirit, Han rulers created an official Bureau of Music. Musicians played drums, bells, flutes, and harps. Music and dancing were common at public festivals and ceremonies.

Two other traditional arts were garden design and calligraphy. Garden designers carefully arranged plants, rocks, and water to resemble scenes in nature. Calligraphers expressed emotions in their paintings of Chinese characters.

Perhaps the greatest craft of the Han period was lacquerware. Lacquer is a liquid made from the sap of a special tree. Han artists brushed it on wood or metal objects to create a hard finish. The process required many layers of lacquer and many hours of work. When color was added, the lacquerware seemed to glow.

**Traditional Arts**
Many of China's traditional arts are still being created and enjoyed today. **Critical Thinking: Link Past and Present** *What are some similarities between China's traditional arts and those we enjoy today?*

**Lacquerware**

**Traditional musical instruments**

**Painting and calligraphy**

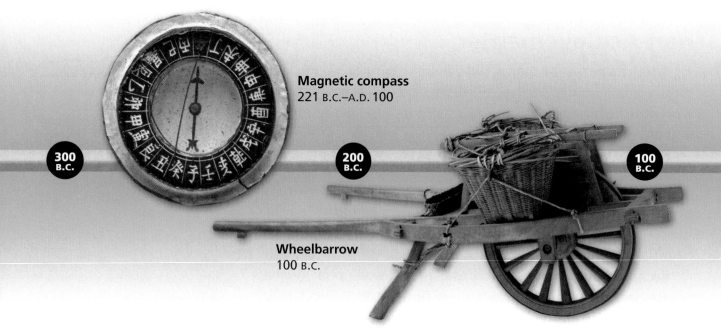

**Magnetic compass**
221 B.C.–A.D. 100

**300 B.C.**

**200 B.C.**

**100 B.C.**

**Wheelbarrow**
100 B.C.

**Technology in Han China**
Scientists and inventors in Han China made some of the most important advances in technology. The inventions shown here have close connections to many of today's technologies. **Critical Thinking: Identify Benefits** *Which inventions changed the way goods were transported? How did this help the economy?*

**History** *Interactive*
**Learn about Technology in Han China**

**Visit:** PHSchool.com
**Web Code:** mwp-4123

**Advances in Science**   Han China was also known for scientific advances. "It was in science and technology," one historian wrote, "that this brilliant civilization's achievements were most dazzling."

Han astronomers studied the sky and made important discoveries. They calculated the length of the solar year. They recorded eclipses of the sun and moon. Other scholars studied magnetism in nature. Their discoveries later led to the development of the magnetic compass.

Han doctors made progress in medicine. They explored the medical uses of herbs and understood the link between nutrition and health. Han doctors also developed the medical treatment known as acupuncture.

**Chinese Inventions**   Han inventors produced important new tools. One was the seismograph. The Chinese seismograph was a metal jar that dropped small balls when a tremor from an earthquake was first detected.

Another invention was the wheelbarrow. This human-powered cart appeared in China about 100 B.C. It was so useful for moving heavy loads that it was called the "wooden ox."

Perhaps the most important innovation of Han China was paper. The first paper was made from rags, bark, and leaves. At first paper was used to wrap items. Later, it was used for writing. The Han government soon was producing large amounts of paper for its official documents.

✔ Checkpoint   **What scientific achievements occurred during the Han period?**

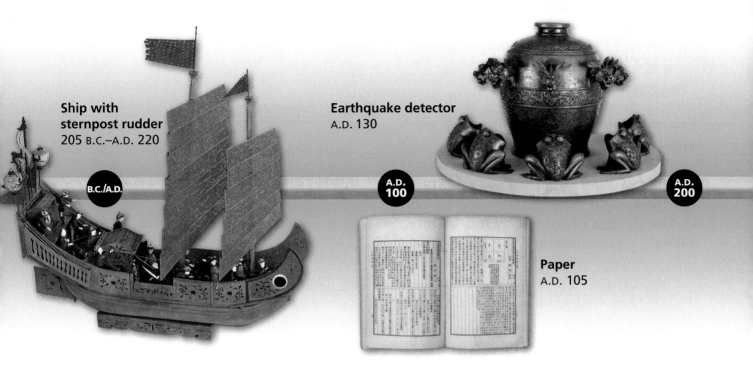

**Ship with sternpost rudder**
205 B.C.–A.D. 220

**Earthquake detector**
A.D. 130

B.C./A.D.

A.D. 100

A.D. 200

**Paper**
A.D. 105

**Looking Back and Ahead**  In this section, you have read about Han society and its achievements. You learned that the Han social order was based on Confucian values. You have also read that the Han developed a strong economy based on farming, industry, and trade. This prosperity helped produce many notable achievements in the arts and sciences.

## Section 3 Check Your Progress

**Progress Monitoring** Online
**For:** Self-test with instant help
**Visit:** PHSchool.com
**Web Code:** mwa-4123

 **Standards Review**  H-SS: 6.6.6; E-LA: Reading 6.1.2

**Comprehension and Critical Thinking**

1. **(a) Recall** What values influenced the Han social order?
   **(b) Evaluate Information** What does the position of scholars in Chinese society tell you about Chinese culture?

2. **(a) List** Identify some traditional arts of China.
   **(b) Analyze Cause and Effect** What factors might account for the great achievements of Han culture?

**Reading Skill**

3. **Interpret Words With Multiple Meanings** Read this sentence: All these traditional arts have roots in the Han period. Which word in the sentence has two meanings? Explain how it is used here.

**Vocabulary** *Builder*

Complete each of the following sentences so that the second part further explains the first part and clearly shows your understanding of the highlighted word.

4. Ban Zhao was unlike many Chinese women because ____.

5. We know that Confucianism influenced Chinese traditional arts by the fact that ____.

**Writing**

6. Prepare an outline for an essay about one of the traditional arts of China. Use the Internet or the school library to gather information. Make a list of the sources you used.

Why do some societies survive for thousands of years and others die out or disappear? One answer has to do with continuity. Things that have continuity stay the same over time. Learning to identify the sources of continuity in a society will help you understand history.

 **Chapter Standards**

**History-Social Science**

**Historical Interpretation 3** Students explain the sources of historical continuity and how the combination of ideas and events explains the emergence of new patterns.

When historians study a society, they look at the following possible sources of continuity:

- **Government**
  Does the society have a stable government? Are there things about it that stay the same over time, even when the people who govern change?
- **Values**
  Do the people within the society share the same ideas about what is important?
- **Family**
  Is the family unit valued as a source of stability?

- **Economy**
  Is the economy stable? Are there things that stay the same, such as how most people make a living?
- **Religion and Philosophy**
  Do most people in the society follow a traditional religion or philosophy of life?
- **Language and Culture**
  Do the people share a common language and way of life?

The more sources of continuity a society has, the more likely it is to endure, as China has, for thousands of years.

**Learn the Skill** *Follow these steps to learn to identify the sources of continuity in a society.*

1. **Gather information about the society.** Look at a variety of resources to learn about life in the society that you are studying.

2. **Identify possible sources of continuity in the society.** Look for information about the society's government, values, family life, economy, religion, philosophy, language, and culture.

3. **Determine which sources of continuity are important in the society.** You may want to list the sources of continuity shown above and take notes about each one.

4. **Summarize what you discover.** Use the information you have learned to make a general statement.

**Practice the Skill** *Use the information in Unit 4 of your text to answer the following questions.*

1. **Gather information about the society.** **(a)** Which chapters in this unit tell you about ancient China? **(b)** Where else could you find information about ancient China?

2. **Identify possible sources of continuity in the society. (a)** What role did the family play in ancient China? **(b)** What kind of government brought order to China? **(c)** How did most people make their living in ancient China?

3. **Determine which sources of continuity are important in the society.** What held the Chinese society together over time?

4. **Summarize what you discover.** Why did Chinese society survive for thousands of years?

**Apply the Skill**
*See page 349 of the Review and Assessment.*

**Study Guide Online**
Complete your Chapter 12 study guide in print or online.

**Chapter Summary**  H-SS: 6.6.5, 6.6.6, 6.6.7

### Section 1 Shi Huangdi Unites China

- Qin armies united China and founded a new dynasty.
- The powerful Qin ruler Shi Huangdi succeeded in expanding and unifying China into one people under one government.

### Section 2 Expansion Under the Han Dynasty

- The Han Dynasty built upon Shi Huangdi's foundations to create one of the most successful dynasties in Chinese history.
- An imperial bureaucratic state and expansion of the empire were important contributions of the Han Dynasty.

### Section 3 Han Society and Achievements

- Confucian teachings helped create a strong economy in Han society.
- Many achievements in technology, arts, and science resulted from a prosperous Han society.

**A ceramic camel made during the time of the Silk Road**

## Standards Practice H-SS: 6.6.5, 6.6.6, 6.6.7

## Vocabulary *Builder*

### High-Use Words

Decide whether each underlined word is used correctly. If it is, explain why. If not, rewrite the rest of the sentence to make it logical.

1. One of Shi Huangdi's **policies** was to unify China into one people and one government.

2. Shi Huangdi **accomplished** a great deal as emperor.

3. The **contribution** of Han society to the rest of the world was what it took from other cultures.

4. The Emperor's troops **occupied**, or retreated from, the northern territories.

### Key Terms and People

Answer the following questions in complete sentences that show your understanding of the Key Terms and People.

1. Who overthrew the Qin Dynasty, Chen Sheng or Shi Huangdi?

2. Which dynasty did Liu Bang found?

3. Describe what Wudi achieved during his reign.

4. Where did Zhang Qian travel, and what did he find?

5. Describe Ban Zhao's accomplishments.

6. What are some of China's traditional arts?

 ## Apply Reading Skills

**Words With Multiple Meanings** Read these sentences: "People in ancient China called the wheelbarrow a 'wooden ox.' The first paper was made from rags, hemp, bark, and leaves." Find and explain the figurative language. Then, tell what *bark* and *leaves* mean in this context.

## Comprehension and Critical Thinking

1. **(a) Explain** What kind of rulers were the Qin?
   **(b) Analyze Cause and Effect** How did their policies reflect Legalist ideas?
   **(c) Draw Conclusions** What consequences did Qin rule have for China?

2. **(a) Recall** How long did the Han Dynasty last?
   **(b) Evaluate Information** What were the two main accomplishments of Han rule?
   **(c) Draw Conclusions** Why was the Han Dynasty so successful?

3. **(a) Identify** What were the two main groups in Han society?
   **(b) Apply Information** Why were workers placed above merchants in the Han social order?
   **(c) Evaluate Information** Were Confucian values a good basis for organizing society? Explain.

## Researching

**The Great Wall** China's Great Wall was an important structural achievement as well as a military defense. In this activity, you will use the Internet, the school library, and other resources to report on some aspect of the Great Wall. Share your work with the class on Great Wall of China Day. Make a list of the resources you used to go with your presentation.

**Historians:** Write several paragraphs about the wall's symbolic meaning to the Chinese. Focus your writing on the role the wall has served throughout Chinese history.

**Geographer:** Create a map showing the extent of China's Great Wall. Include some geographic features on your map, such as mountains or rivers. Include political features too, such as cities.

> ### Researching Online
> **For:** Help in starting this activity
> **Visit:** PHSchool.com
> **Web Code:** mwe-4124

## Writing

1. **Write two paragraphs on the following topic.** Compare the achievements of Shi Huangdi with the achievements of Emperor Wudi. Narrow your point of comparison to the two individuals. Take notes as you review and organize material.
   **Your essay should:**
   • explain the subject you are writing about.
   • offer evidence, or details to support your topic sentences.
   • conclude with a short summary.

2. **Write a short narrative.** Imagine you were helping construct the Great Wall of China. Write a short narrative describing the experience.

# Apply Analysis Skills

**Use information from this chapter and the quotation at right to answer these questions.**

1. Which scientific achievements helped China's society survive?

2. Which technological achievements helped China's society survive?

3. What were some of ancient China's achievements with regard to government and family? Do you think these achievements were as important as those in science and technology? Explain.

4. Which achievements do you think had the most impact on the entire world? Explain.

**❝It was in science and technology that this brilliant civilization's achievements were most dazzling.❞**

# Test Yourself

1. **Shi Huangdi united the Qin Empire by**
   A winning the support of the warlords.
   B using Confucian principles to govern.
   C bringing northern and southern China together under one rule.
   D establishing a uniform currency, written language, and legal code.

2. **How did the Han use Legalist and Confucian ideas to govern?**
   A bureaucratic state and civil service exams
   B caravans and colonization
   C censorship and high taxes
   D diplomacy and trade

**Refer to the map below to answer Question 3.**

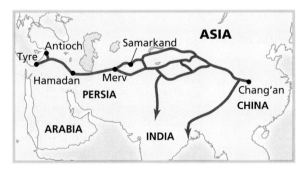

3. **Why were the Silk Roads important?**
   A They opened up trade with Central Asia.
   B They connected silk producers in China.
   C They prevented invasions of China.
   D They connected Europe with China.

4. **The Han government controlled the**
   A production of silk.
   B production of paper.
   C iron and salt industries.
   D traditional arts and sciences.

**Refer to the image below to answer Question 5.**

5. **Calligraphy and lacquerware are examples of Chinese**
   A inventions.
   B traditional arts.
   C garden designs.
   D styles of clothing.

# Writing Workshop

## Research Paper, Part 1

### ▶ Introduction

In a research paper, you gather information about a subject from several different sources and present this information to your readers. There are two things to consider as you start work on your research paper.

**You narrow your topic as you research.** At first, you may have only a general idea of a subject. But as you research, you may find a topic that is especially interesting. Then start looking for information that you need.

**You keep careful record of your sources.** At the same time you are researching, carefully record information about all of your sources. In an ideal research paper:

• You should have at least one source for every fact you state.

• Provide enough information about your sources so that a reader can easily find additional information about a subject.

**Assignment** On the following pages, you will learn how to plan a research paper and gather information for it. Each step will include an example from research about Confucius.

Read the instructions and the examples. Then, follow each step to plan a research paper on this topic:

**Cultural developments during China's Han Dynasty**

In Research Paper, Part 2, page 470, you will learn how to write a research paper.

### ▶ Prewriting

**Find a research subject.** A research paper presents information about a particular topic from several sources. Review what you already know about a topic to help narrow your focus.

**Narrow your topic.** In writing a research paper, you must narrow your topic down to something you can cover in the space you have. For instance, suppose that you are writing a research paper about Confucius. There is too much information about Confucius to  fit into one paper. So you need to narrow down to a more focused topic. Then research details that support your topic.

**History-Social Science**

**6.6** Students analyze the geographic, political, economic, religious, and social structures of the early civilizations of China.

**English-Language Arts**

**Writing 6.2.3** Write research reports.

For a review of the steps in the writing process, see the **Historian's Toolkit,** *Write Like a Historian*

**Sample assignment:** "Write a paper discussing one or more cultural developments during China's Han Dynasty." An assignment such as this one requires you to find information from more than source.

## ▶ Doing Your Research

**Find your sources.** You need to find outside sources about your topic. Visit your local library, and use the catalogue. For nonfiction books, use the table of contents and index to find the pages relating to your topic. For the Internet, try different key words and search engines to find material about your topic.

**Use primary and secondary sources.** A primary source comes directly from your subject. For example, a primary source for a paper about Confucius, teachings would be his *Analects*. A secondary source is one written about the subject, such as Patricia Buckley Ebrey's book *The Cambridge Illustrated History of China*.

**Take notes from your sources.** As you read a source, take notes on the information it presents. Write down key terms, and define them. Write down important ideas. Summarize longer sections. If you find a quotation that you want to use, copy it exactly, word for word. Identify the person who said or wrote it. Never use someone else's words without identifying the source. Using someone else's words without giving credit is called *plagiarism*.

Read this set of notes that a student took in reading a source about the times in which Confucius lived. Notice how the notes include a summary of information from the book as well as a quotation.

> Confucius lived during a time when several Chinese states were in constant war.
> —Ebrey, pp. 41–43.
>
> "Rulers searching for ways to survive or prevail were more than willing to patronize men of ideas."
> —Ebrey, p. 42.

**Keep track of your sources.** You need to identify each source that you consult.

You should have at least one source for each fact you discuss in your paper. You must also write down enough information so that a reader who wants to learn more can find each source that you used. You should always include the name of the author or editor, as well as the name of any article or book. But some of the other information you record will vary from source to source.

> Book
> Ebrey, Patricia Buckley. The Cambridge Illustrated History of China. Cambridge, United Kingdom: Cambridge University Press, 2003.
>
> Magazine article
> Robinson, Robert. "The Five Great Chinese Classics." History Now May 2002: 44-45.
>
> Internet source
> Hooker, Richard. "Chinese Philosophy: Confucius." World Civilizations. June 6, 1999. Washington State University. October 19, 2004
> <http://www.wsu.edu:8080/~dee/CHPHIL/CONF.HTM>

# Unit 5

##  Quick View Video

**Discovery School Video** View *Ancient Greece* for a quick preview of the main ideas of this unit.

The Parthenon in Athens, Greece

# Ancient Greece

Macedonia, 350 B.C.

Peloponnesian Peninsula, 1500 B.C.

Mycenae

Crete, 1600 B.C.

Knossos

Ionia, 750 B.C.

## *Think* like a historian

The map above shows a Mediterranean region that became home to a great empire.

**As you read this unit, think about this question:**
*How might geography affect how a civilization develops?*

## Prepare to Read

### Chapter Standards

**6.4.1** Discuss the connections between geography and the development of city-states in the region of the Aegean Sea, including patterns of trade and commerce among Greek city-states and within the wider Mediterranean region.

Shield showing Greek ship

**About 2000 B.C.**
People begin to migrate to the Greek Peninsula.

**About 1600 B.C.**
The Mycenaean civilization appears on the Greek Peninsula.

Chapter Events

**2000 B.C.**

**1500 B.C.**

**1000 B.C.**

Other Events

**About 1792 B.C.** Hammurabi becomes King of Babylon.

**1650 B.C.** Shang dynasty in Asia.

The early Minoan civilization was noted for trade and beautiful works of art, such as this painting.

**750 B.C.**
New city-states appear in Greece

**mid–500s B.C.**
Sparta controls most of the Peloponnesian Peninsula.

1000
B.C.

500
B.C.

B.C./A.D.

About 928 B.C. Israel splits into two kingdoms.

559 B.C. Cyrus the Great begins his reign of Persia.

# How to Read History

### *Previewing* Recognize and Analyze Greek Word Origins

Many English words are based on Greek words or word parts. You can use an understanding of these words and word parts to define unfamiliar English words. Read below to learn some ways to use Greek word origins to build meaning for unfamiliar English words.

**Chapter Standards**

**English-Language Arts**

**Reading 6.1.3** Recognize the origins and meanings of frequently used foreign words in English and use these words accurately in speaking and writing.

**1** This sentence contains the word *astronomy,* which comes from the Greek root *ast,* meaning "star." If you know that the suffix *-nomy* means "a sum of knowledge about" you can determine that *astronomy* is "the study of the stars."

<u>Astronomy</u> and medicine were two sciences that advanced during this time.

> The root *ast* offers a clue to meaning

**2** In this sentence, you can use both a Greek prefix *mono-* and the Greek root *polein* to help you define the word *monopoly.*

> *mono* means "one"

The government took control of these industries and established a **mono**poly.

> *poly* means "sell"

**3** This word web shows how to find new words and expand vocabulary, using Greek word origins.

To confirm that you understand a word with Greek origins, use it in a sentence. This sentence uses the word *biography.*

```
              telegraph
                  |
photograph — graph = write — autograph
                  |
              biography
```

A *biography* writes the story of a person's life.

# Vocabulary *Builder*

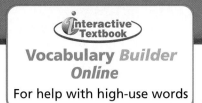

**Vocabulary *Builder* Online**
For help with high-use words

## *Previewing* **High-Use Academic Words**

| High-Use Word | Definition | Sample Sentence About History |
|---|---|---|
| **location** (loh KAY shuhn) (Section 1, p. 359) | *n.* a particular place or position | Jerusalem's <u>location</u> between Egypt and Mesopotamia meant that it was often caught between warring empires. |
| **enable** (ehn AY buhl) (Section 1, p. 361) | *v.* to make possible | Sailboats <u>enabled</u> Sumerian traders to bring goods to other countries. |
| **migration** (mī GRAY shuhn) (Section 2, p. 364) | *n.* the movement of a large group from one area to another | The Aryan <u>migration</u> into northern India probably took many centuries. |
| **exclude** (ehks KLOOD) (Section 2, p. 369) | *v.* to refuse to admit | Indian society used to <u>exclude</u> people of certain castes from many activities. |
| **contribute** (kuhn TRIH byoot) (Section 3, p. 370) | *v.* to help or give to an important cause | Sumerian scribes kept records of food that was <u>contributed</u> to the temple. |
| **capacity** (kuh PAS ih tee) (Section 3, p. 373) | *n.* the ability to do something | Plowing increased each farmer's <u>capacity</u> to grow grain. |
| **economy** (ih KAHN uh mee) (Section 4, p. 376) | *n.* the way money and business are organized in a particular area | The <u>economy</u> of Sumer depended on trading lumber for other goods. |
| **site** (sīt) (Section 4, p., 378) | *n.* location for building | The Indus Valley included many good <u>sites</u> on which to build cities. |

## *Previewing* **Key Terms and People**

peninsula, p. 359  monarchy, p. 364  aristocrat, p. 368  slavery, p. 371  helot, p. 377
mainland, p. 360  Agamemnon, p. 364  estate, p. 370  Aesop, p. 371  trading post, p. 378
isthmus, p. 360  Homer, p. 365  tenant farmer, p. 370  Xenophon, p. 371
Mediterranean climate, p. 361  politics, p. 367  status, p. 370  annex, p. 377  fleet, p. 379
acropolis, p. 367

## Standards Preview

**H-SS 6.4.1** Discuss the connections between geography and the development of city-states in the region of the Aegean Sea, including patterns of trade and commerce among Greek city-states and within the wider Mediterranean region.

**E-LA Reading 6.1.3** Recognize the origins and meanings of frequently used foreign words in English and use these words accurately in speaking and writing.

## Reading Preview

### Reading Skill

**Recognize Greek Roots** When you are familiar with common Greek roots, you will notice them in many English words. A word may contain one Greek root or several. The spelling, however, may have changed from the Greek to the English. Say each root aloud to hear its sound. Here are some roots with their meanings: *graph*—write; *arch*—chief; *geo*—earth; *photo*—light.

### Vocabulary *Builder*

**High-Use Words**
location (loh KAY shuhn), p. 359
enable (ehn AY buhl), p. 361

**Key Terms and People**
peninsula (puh NIHN suh luh), p. 359
mainland (MAYN land), p. 360
isthmus (IHS muhs), p. 360
Mediterranean climate (mehd uh tuh RAY nee uhn CLI muht), p. 361

**Background Knowledge** In much of the ancient world, civilizations developed in great river valleys. But there were no large rivers in Greece. Instead, Greek civilization developed on the dry, rocky lands surrounding the Aegean Sea. In this section, you will learn how geography helped shape Greek civilization.

## The Geography of Greece

**Main Idea**
The lands settled by early Greek-speaking peoples were noted for steep hills and many coastlines.

The land of Greece is small. But it has produced kings who conquered many lands and ideas that reached around the world. In fact, ancient Greek culture played a major part in the growth of western civilization. Western civilization is the civilization that began around the eastern Mediterranean in ancient times and grew to include the modern cultures of Europe and the Americas. Many words and ideas we use today can be traced to ancient Greek-speaking peoples.

Ancient Greece was not a single country. It was a region where people who spoke an early form of the Greek language settled about 2000 B.C. Greece's geography had important effects on how those people lived.

Most of Greece consists of a large peninsula that juts into the Mediterranean Sea. A peninsula is a body of land surrounded on three sides by water. The Greek Peninsula sits between Europe, Africa, and Asia. This <u>location</u> has made it a crossroads for people and commerce since ancient times. For centuries, travelers and traders passing through or near Greece have exchanged goods, ideas, and customs.

**Surrounded by Seas** Greece is bordered by three bodies of water. To the east lies an arm of the Mediterranean known as the Aegean Sea. Beyond the Aegean Sea is western Asia. In ancient times, the empire of Persia controlled much of the land across the Aegean Sea from Greece.

To the west of Greece is the Ionian Sea. This arm of the Mediterranean lies between Greece and the Italian Peninsula. To the south lie the open waters of the Mediterranean Sea and the coast of North Africa.

The seas surrounding Greece contain hundreds of small islands. Seagoing peoples have occupied these islands for thousands of years. The largest Greek island, Crete, lies off the southern tip of the Greek Peninsula.

**E-LA 6.1.3 Recognize Greek Roots**

*Reading Skill* What word in the last sentence of this paragraph comes from the Greek root *geo*?

**Vocabulary *Builder***
<u>location</u> (loh KAY shuhn) *n.* a particular place or position

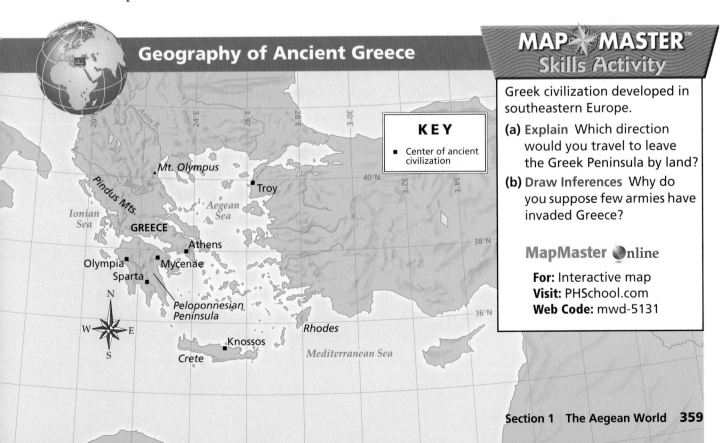

**Geography of Ancient Greece**

**KEY**
■ Center of ancient civilization

*Arios R.*
Mt. Olympus
*Pindus Mts.*
Troy
*Aegean Sea*
*Ionian Sea*
GREECE
Athens
Olympia
Mycenae
Sparta
Peloponnesian Peninsula
Rhodes
Knossos
Crete
*Mediterranean Sea*

N W E S

40°N
38°N
36°N
20°E 24°E 26°E 28°E 30°E 32°E 34°E

**MAP MASTER**
**Skills Activity**

Greek civilization developed in southeastern Europe.

**(a) Explain** Which direction would you travel to leave the Greek Peninsula by land?

**(b) Draw Inferences** Why do you suppose few armies have invaded Greece?

**MapMaster ●nline**

**For:** Interactive map
**Visit:** PHSchool.com
**Web Code:** mwd-5131

**The Palace at Knossos**
The Minoans created beautiful art and great palaces, such as this palace on Crete. **Critical Thinking: Frame Questions** *What questions might a historian ask about this palace or the Minoans?*

**Main Idea**
Greece's mountains and seas helped shape its way of life.

The first civilization to appear in Europe emerged on the island of Crete. It is known as the Minoan civilization, named after King Minos, described in later Greek legends. The Minoans built great stone palaces on Crete. They traded goods with people on the Greek Peninsula, with Egypt, and with other Mediterranean lands. Although the Minoans did not speak Greek, they influenced the culture and legends of early Greece. Then, in the early 1400s B.C., their palaces were destroyed and their civilization vanished. No one is quite sure why. Natural disasters such as earthquakes or a volcano may have played a part.

**A Rugged Land** The Greek Peninsula has a rugged or rough and rocky coastline. Many large bays cut into the Greek mainland. The **mainland** is the part of a country that is attached to a continent, as compared to its offshore islands.

A number of peninsulas also extend from the Greek mainland. The largest of these is the Peloponnesian Peninsula in southern Greece. This mountainous block of land is linked to the main part of Greece by an isthmus. An **isthmus** is a narrow strip of land that connects two larger bodies of land.

In ancient times, Greece also included the coastline along the eastern edge of the Aegean Sea, in what is now Turkey. This coastal region of Southwest Asia was called Ionia.

The Greek landscape is rugged. Most of the land is covered with mountains. The people of ancient Greece believed that the highest one, Mount Olympus, was the home of their gods. The rest of Greece is made up of narrow valleys and small plains.

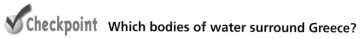

**Checkpoint** **Which bodies of water surround Greece?**

# The Effects of Geography

The geographic features of Greece played an important role in the development of Greek culture. Mountains, seas, and climate were factors that shaped the way ancient Greeks lived.

**The Influence of Landscape** The landscape of Greece had a major effect on agriculture. The mountains were good for grazing sheep and goats, but they were too steep and rocky for farming. Fertile land was limited to lowland valleys and plains. Less than one quarter of the land could be used for farming.

The lack of level farmland in Greece meant that the people of ancient Greece could not produce large amounts of grain. As you will recall from your study of other ancient civilizations, grain was the most important food crop. But Greece could not grow much grain.

The mountains also had another important effect—they separated Greek settlements from one another. Most Greek towns were isolated in deep valleys. Narrow paths crossed the mountains. But it might take days to travel between towns. This made it difficult to unite Greece into a single country.

Although food production in Greece was limited by the lack of farmland, Greece did have another key resource: the sea. Most towns in Greece were less than 60 miles from the sea. Many were much closer. This access to the sea <u>enabled</u> the Greeks to engage in fishing and trade. The sea provided an important food source. It also served as a highway for trade and transportation.

Vocabulary *Builder*
<u>enable</u> (ehn AY buhl) *v.* to make possible

Geographic barriers, along with small grain crops, kept the Greeks from building one unified country. Instead, they remained in small, independent communities.

**A Mild Climate** The climate of the Greek Peninsula was another factor in its development. Greece has a **Mediterranean climate. This is a climate that features mild, wet winters and hot, dry summers.** Greek farmers faced the risk of too much rain or flooding in the winter. They also had to cope with long, hot summers with little or no rain.

**Greece's Rocky Coastline**
Although much of the Greek shoreline is rocky, many people of ancient Greece made a living from the sea. **Critical Thinking: Identify Benefits** *How would having so much coastline help people who lived in Greece to develop trading businesses?*

**Harvesting Olives**

The markings on this ancient Greek jug show people harvesting olives. Olive oil was used as fuel for lamps as well as for cooking. **Critical Thinking: Identify Benefits** *Why do you think one Greek poet called olive oil "liquid gold"?*

Greece's Mediterranean climate made it difficult for Greek farmers to grow shallow-rooted crops such as grains, which need frequent watering. However, it was ideal for growing deep-rooted plants such as olive trees and grape vines. Olive oil and wine became important trade goods.

The Greeks believed that their mild, dry climate made them superior to other peoples. One Greek philosopher wrote that: "The Greeks occupy a middle position [between hot and cold climates] and . . . enjoy both energy and intelligence." Whether their climate made the Greeks smarter than other peoples is doubtful. However, they did succeed in building a great civilization in a land with limited resources.

✔**Checkpoint** **How did the Greek landscape affect farming?**

**Looking Back and Ahead** In this section, you have read about the geography of ancient Greece. Although Greece has limited farmland, the seas provide other economic opportunities. In the next section, you will learn how ancient Greek-speaking peoples used their land's resources to build a unique civilization.

## Section 1 Check Your Progress

**Progress Monitoring** ●nline
**For:** Self-test with instant help
**Visit:** PHSchool.com
**Web Code:** mwa-5131

**Standards Review** H-SS: 6.4.1; E-LA: Reading, 6.1.3

**Comprehension and Critical Thinking**

**1. (a) Identify** What seas border Greece?
**(b) Apply Information** Why would these seas be important to Greece?

**2. (a) Explain** Why were Greek villages isolated?
**(b) Evaluate Information** How did geography encourage the development of several independent communities in Greece?

**Reading Skill**
**3. Recognize Greek Roots** Read this sentence: "Visitors to Greece take photographs of Mount Olympus." Find a word in this sentence that has Greek roots. Write the word and its roots.

**Vocabulary** *Builder*
Read each sentence below. If the sentence is true, write YES. If the sentence is not true, write NO and explain why.
**4.** The location of Greece made it an important transportation center.

**5.** The hilly countryside of Greece enabled farmers to grow huge crops of grain.

**Writing**
**6.** Choose a subject that was discussed in Section 1 such as the geography or climate of Greece. Use the Internet or a library book to research the subject. Make a list of at least three topics that you could write about, based on what you have learned from your research.

# Section 2 The Rise of City-States

**Standards Preview**

**H-SS 6.4.1** Discuss the connections between geography and the development of city-states in the region of the Aegean Sea, including patterns of trade and commerce among Greek city-states and within the wider Mediterranean region.

**E-LA Reading 6.1.3** Recognize the origins and meanings of frequently used foreign words in English and use these words accurately in speaking and writing.

## Reading Preview

 **Reading Skill**

**Analyze Greek Word Origins** You can build meaning for unfamiliar words by defining their Greek word parts—such as roots and prefixes. Combine the meaning of these word parts with the rest of the word. For example, the place name *Mesopotamia* contains the Greek root *meso,* meaning "middle," and *potamos,* meaning "river." So, *Mesopotamia* literally means "between rivers."

## Vocabulary *Builder*

**High-Use Words**
migration (mi GRAY shuhn), p. 364
code (KOHD), p. 367

**Key Terms and People**
monarchy (MAHN ahr kee), p. 364
Agamemnon (ag uh MEHM nahn), p. 364
Homer (HOH muhr), p. 365
politics (PAL uh tihks), p. 367
acropolis (uh KRAHP uh lihs), p. 367
aristocrat (uh RIHS tuh krat), p. 368

**Background Knowledge** City-states first arose in Mesopotamia. These were cities that controlled surrounding lands. City-states also arose in Greece, where they had their own distinct features. In this section, you will read about the early history of Greece and the development of the Greek city-state.

## Early History of Greece

About 2000 B.C., Greek-speaking peoples began to migrate into the Greek Peninsula from lands to the north. Over time, they formed small kingdoms across Greece. They also developed a written language. The early writing, however, is very different from the writing of the later Greek-speaking peoples. The most important of the new kingdoms was Mycenae on the Peloponnesian Peninsula. It gave its name to the first civilization of mainland Greece.

**Main Idea**
The earliest Greek kingdoms were small and often at war with one another.

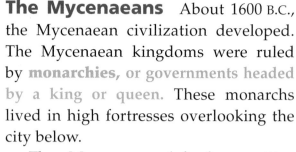

Agamemnon

## Did Agamemnon return from Troy?

### Fast Facts

**Who:** Agamemnon

**What:** Legendary leader of the Mycenaeans

**When:** c. 1194 B.C.–1184 B.C.

**Where:** Ionia

**Why important:** Agamemnon is an important king in legends of early Greek civilization. He is said to have led a successful war against Troy.

### Fast Find

**How:** Go online to find out about Agamemnon's journey home from Troy.

**Biography Online**

**For:** More about Agamemnon
**Visit:** PHSchool.com
**Web Code:** mwe-5132

**Vocabulary** *Builder*

**migration** (mi GRAY shuhn) *n.* the movement of a large group from one area to another

**The Mycenaeans** About 1600 B.C., the Mycenaean civilization developed. The Mycenaean kingdoms were ruled by **monarchies, or governments headed by a king or queen.** These monarchs lived in high fortresses overlooking the city below.

The Mycenaeans left few written records. But later Greeks preserved many legends about their leaders. One of those leaders was **Agamemnon,** a great Mycenaean king.

The Mycenaeans lived mainly by trade. They made fine bronze weapons and painted pottery. These goods were traded around the Mediterranean for copper, ivory, and luxury goods from Egypt. Mycenaeans also raided other lands to obtain gold and other goods. Eventually, however, the kingdoms grew weak.

Many historians believe that invaders from the north took advantage of that weakness around 1100 B.C. Known as Dorians, these invaders destroyed much of the Mycenaean civilization.

**The Dark Age** Like the Mycenaeans, the Dorians also spoke Greek. However, their culture was less advanced. Under the Dorians, Greece entered a period known as the Dark Age. During this time, even knowledge of writing disappeared. The Greeks were left without a strong government.

Not all of Mycenaean culture was lost. Some Mycenaeans fled Greece to settle on the eastern shore of the Aegean Sea, an area they called Ionia. Others settled on nearby islands. The effect of this migration was to turn the Aegean Sea into a transportation system for Greek knowledge and culture.

**The Trojan War** The Greeks at Ionia preserved many stories about the Mycenaeans. The most famous legends concerned the Trojan War. In these tales, the war began with a prince named Paris from the Ionian city of Troy. Paris kidnapped a beautiful queen from Sparta, known as Helen of Troy. This act so angered the Greeks that Agamemnon led a ten-year war against Troy.

Legends of the Trojan War were kept alive by Homer, a blind poet who probably lived in Ionia around 750 B.C. He traveled from town to town, singing ancient stories. These tales were written down in two poems, the *Iliad* and the *Odyssey*.

**Tales of Troy**  Homer's *Iliad* tells the story of Achilles. He was a Greek hero who almost destroyed the Greek cause when he was treated unfairly and refused to fight. Other poets tell about the Trojan horse. This was a huge wooden horse built by the Greeks to trick the Trojans. The Greeks pretended to sail away from Troy, leaving the horse behind as a gift. Celebrating, the Trojans brought the horse into their city.

Unknown to the Trojans, Greek soldiers were hidden in the horse. While Troy slept, the soldiers crept out and opened the city's gates to the returning Greeks. Troy was destroyed.

Homer's *Odyssey* describes the adventures of the hero Odysseus on his journey home after the war.

**The Impact of Homer**  The *Iliad* and the *Odyssey* had a huge impact on Greek culture. The values expressed in the poems became part of the Greek identity. One of those values was courage. In the *Iliad,* Achilles speaks to his troops before battle:

**❝Every man make up his mind to fight**
**And move on his enemy! Strong as I am,**
**It's hard for me to face so many men**
**And fight with all at once. . . .**
**And yet I will! ❞**

—Homer, the *Iliad*

**Greek Ships at Troy**
This ancient illustration shows Greek warriors protecting a ship from Trojan warriors.
**Critical Thinking: Draw Conclusions** *Why are the Trojans attacking the Greek ship with torches instead of swords?*

Both the Greeks and the Trojans showed values that included honor, family loyalty, cleverness, and ambition. The historian William McNeill describes Homer's impact in this passage:

**❝Homer's poems . . . have been called the Greek 'Bible,' and with good reason. Boys memorized the poems in school. Everyone knew about Homer's heroes. Even today, references to Homer remain familiar in all Western lands.❞**

—William McNeill, *A History of the Human Community*

The ancient Greeks tried to live up to the ideals of bravery, strength, and honor expressed in Homer's work.

✔**Checkpoint** How did Homer help preserve the memory of the Mycenaean and Trojan civilizations?

**Main Idea**
As Greek culture developed, each kingdom was noted for a central city that ruled the surrounding lands.

# The Greek City-States

By the time Homer's poems were written down, Greece was emerging from its Dark Age. The rediscovery of writing helped in its change. But equally important was the creation of a new form of government—the Greek city-state.

**New Cities Arise** By 750 B.C., new city-states were appearing in Greece. Their origins lay in the early Greek settlements of Ionia.

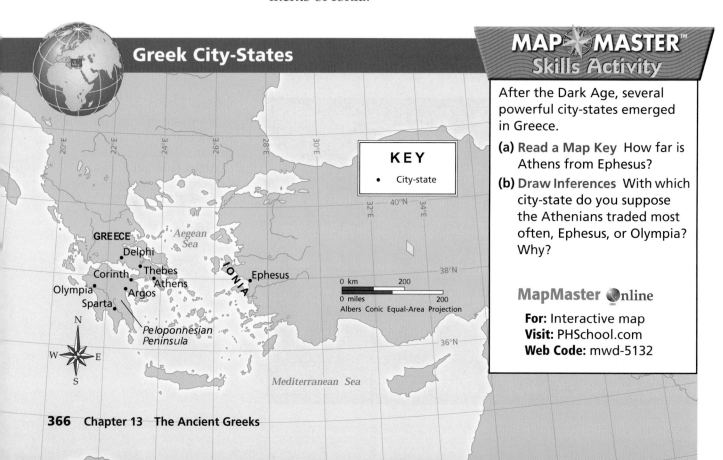

**Greek City-States**

**KEY**
• City-state

GREECE
Delphi
Corinth  •Thebes
Olympia•  •Athens
•Argos
Sparta•
Aegean Sea
IONIA
Ephesus
Peloponnesian Peninsula
Mediterranean Sea

0 km 200
0 miles 200
Albers Conic Equal-Area Projection

**MAP★MASTER™**
*Skills Activity*

After the Dark Age, several powerful city-states emerged in Greece.

**(a) Read a Map Key** How far is Athens from Ephesus?

**(b) Draw Inferences** With which city-state do you suppose the Athenians traded most often, Ephesus, or Olympia? Why?

**MapMaster ●nline**

**For:** Interactive map
**Visit:** PHSchool.com
**Web Code:** mwd-5132

The Greeks who migrated to Ionia had lost their kings, so they created new ways of ruling themselves. They formed independent cities run by ordinary citizens. From Ionia, the idea of citizen-led government spread to the rest of Greece.

The Greek city-state was called a *polis*. This word gave rise to the term *politics*. **Politics is the art and practice of government.** It is based on the Greek notion that the people who live in a place can work together and make decisions on key issues that affect them. This participation by citizens made the Greek city-state unique. Earlier city-states, such as those of Mesopotamia, were ruled by priests and kings. In Greece, the polis was governed by its citizens.

**The Ruins at Delphi**
In the Greek city at Delphi, the temples stood at the highest point in the city. **Critical Thinking: Draw Inferences** *Why might the ancient Greeks have built their temples in such places?*

## Features of the Polis

The polis physically consisted of a main city and its surrounding villages and countryside. The area and population of a polis were generally small. That small size made group decision making possible. It allowed citizens to easily assemble, or come together, to make decisions.

The polis was usually built on two levels. On a high hill stood the **acropolis, or upper part of the city.** Public buildings and marble temples were located on the acropolis. There people gathered to discuss public affairs. They also came together there for protection during an attack. On flatter ground beneath the hill lay homes, shops, public buildings, and fields.

The government of the polis was based on a <u>code</u> of laws. Unlike the laws of Hammurabi or Moses, the laws of the polis came from the community. Not everyone participated in making the laws, however. Women, slaves, and foreigners were all excluded from decision making.

Although citizen participation was a key feature of the polis, wealthy aristocrats held most of the power. At first, the ruler of the polis was a king. However, power began to move into the hands of the aristocrats. In Greek, the term aristocracy meant "rule by the best people." In theory, the best people might be people with superior talents or experience. In practice,

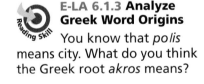

**E-LA 6.1.3 Analyze Greek Word Origins**
You know that *polis* means city. What do you think the Greek root *akros* means?

**Vocabulary** *Builder*
<u>code</u> (KOHD) *n.* a set of written rules

the **aristocrats** who ran the city-states were mostly upper-class, wealthy landowners.

**Pride in the Polis**   Another key feature of the polis was the pride and loyalty that citizens felt toward their city. This reflected the values of honor and manhood that were part of the Greek identity. Greeks believed that a "good" man should be willing to sacrifice for his city. He should be prepared to defend its interests. He should even die for his polis, if necessary.

In this sense, the polis was much more than a city-state. As one historian wrote, "The polis was the framework of Greek life." Greeks identified themselves with their city. If their city was a success, then so were they. Throughout the history of ancient Greece, the polis played a key role in Greek life.

 **Checkpoint**   **How did the rise of Greek city-states affect the way people felt about their cities?**

**Looking Back and Ahead**   In this section, you have read about the early history of Greece. You also learned about the development of the Greek city-state. In the next section, you will learn about the society of ancient Greece.

**Greek Warrior**
The ancient Greeks used helmets and shields to protect themselves from front or side attacks. **Critical Thinking: Draw Inferences** *Why might an army's leader allow his warriors to fight without any armor protecting their backs?*

---

## Section 2  Check Your Progress

**Progress Monitoring** Online
**For:** Self-test with instant help
**Visit:** PHSchool.com
**Web Code:** mwa-5132

 **Standards Review**   H-SS: 6.4.1; E-LA: Reading 6.1.3

**Comprehension and Critical Thinking**

1. **(a) Identify** Who was Homer?
   **(b) Draw Conclusions** Why was Homer important in Greek history?

2. **(a) Describe** Discuss the ways in which geography affected the settlement of the city-states.
   **(b) Apply Information** How did geography affect the loyalty of Greek citizens?

**Reading Skill**

3. **Analyze Greek Word Origins** Read this sentence: "The male *aristocracy* held most of the power." Use your understanding of Greek roots to define *aristocracy* in this context. How does it compare with the context used on page 369?

**Vocabulary** *Builder*

4. Write two definitions for each word: <u>migration</u> and <u>code</u>. First, write a formal definition for your teacher. Second, write a definition in everyday English.

**Writing**

5. Look up information about the growth of one ancient Greek city-state in the library, an encyclopedia, or on the Internet. Write one sentence that explains why the city-state emerged where it did. Using this sentence as a working thesis, list two facts from your research that support that sentence.

# 3 Daily Life in Ancient Greece

## Standards Preview

**H-SS 6.4.1** Discuss the connections between geography and the development of city-states in the region of the Aegean Sea, including patterns of trade and commerce among Greek city-states and within the wider Mediterranean region.

**E-LA Reading 6.1.3** Recognize the origins and meanings of frequently used foreign words in English and use these words accurately in speaking and writing.

## Reading Preview

### Reading Skill

**Recognize and Use Greek Word Origins** You can use your knowledge of Greek word origins in many ways. As you find words with Greek origins, you can define them. You can also connect groups of related words in the reading. Finally, you can expand your vocabulary by listing other words that come from the same root. These strategies will help you use words of Greek origin accurately in speaking and writing.

### Vocabulary *Builder*

**High-Use Words**
**contribute** (kuhn TRIHB yoot), p. 370
**capacity** (kuh PAS ih tee), p. 371

**Key Terms and People**
estate (uh STAYT), p. 370
tenant farmer (TEHN uhnt fahr muhr), p. 370
status (STAT uhs), p. 370
artisan (AHRT uh zaan), p. 370
slavery (SLAY vuhr ee), p. 371
Aesop (EE suhp), p. 371
Xenophon (ZEHN nuh fuhn), p. 371

**Background Knowledge** One of the features of early civilizations was the division of society into social classes. Like those civilizations, ancient Greece also had a social structure based on class distinctions. In this section, you will read about key features of Greek society.

## Greek Society

In general, early Greek society did not have great extremes of wealth and poverty. Because Greece had limited resources, it was hard for one person to acquire great wealth. Although there was a division between rich and poor, it was not as great as that in other ancient civilizations.

**Social Structure** Greek society consisted of four main social classes. The top class was made up of wealthy aristocrats. The lower classes consisted of small farmers, merchants and artisans, and slaves.

**Main Idea**
The society of ancient Greece included wealthy leaders, farmers, and many kinds of workers, including slaves.

# Greece's Social Structure

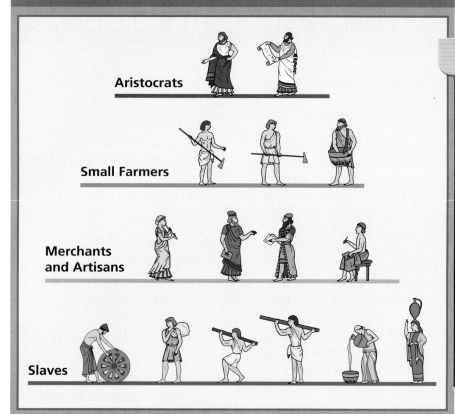

Aristocrats

Small Farmers

Merchants and Artisans

Slaves

## Reading Diagrams

In ancient Greek city-states such as Athens, most decisions were made by wealthy landowners, called aristocrats. But anyone who owned land was considered more important than people who did not.

(a) **Read a Diagram** What free people were considered less important than farmers?

(b) **Apply Information** How would you change the top line of this chart if you were trying to show the social structure of a Mycenaean city-state?

**E-LA 6.1.3 Recognize and Use Greek Word Origins**

Find two words in these paragraphs that have Greek roots.

**Vocabulary** *Builder*

**contribute** (kuhn TRIHB yoot) *v.* to help or give to an important cause

As you have read, wealthy aristocrats dominated the government in most Greek city-states. Their wealth came from owning large **estates,** or plots of land, where they raised crops and livestock. Slaves did most of the work on these estates. This left aristocrats with free time for politics and leisure activities, such as reading poetry or listening to music.

The second class in Greek society was made up of small farmers. Some small farmers owned their own land. Others were **tenant farmers.** These are people who pay rent, either in money or crops, to farm another person's land.

Small farmers rarely had enough land to raise livestock or produce a food surplus. Even so, as landowners they enjoyed a relatively high status in their polis. **Status** is a person's rank or position in a society. These farmers had the right to vote and <u>contribute</u> to the political life of the city.

Merchants and **artisans,** or tradesman and craft workers, stood below farmers in the social structure. Many of the merchants and artisans in Greek city-states were foreigners, or *metics.* A metic might be a Greek from another city-state or someone from another land. Metics had few rights.

**The Role of Slavery**  The lowest class in Greek society was made up of slaves. **Slavery is the ownership and control of other people as property.** The Greek philosopher Aristotle wrote that slavery was a natural condition of some people. "From the hour of their birth," he wrote, "some are marked out for slavery, others for rule."

Slaves were acquired in various ways. Most were prisoners of war. Others were bought from slave traders or were sold into slavery by their families. Sometimes parents who could not care for their children abandoned them. These children often become slaves. Many slaves in Greek city-states came from other lands. But some were Greeks from other city-states.

By the 500s B.C., slavery was widespread in Greece. In some city-states, slaves made up one third of the population.

Slaves did many jobs in Greek society. Household slaves cooked, cleaned, and took care of children. Others worked in small factories, on farms, as part of ship crews and in mines. Some worked as teachers. All together, their labor helped the Greek economy grow.

Slaves had no legal rights and could be punished freely by their owners. But some slaves were treated kindly. A few were freed. One former slave became a banker. According to Greek legends, a slave named **Aesop** became a famous author and storyteller. You will read more about Aesop and his fables in a later chapter.

**Checkpoint**  **What were the four main social classes in ancient Greece?**

**Greek Slavery**
This statue shows a female slave in ancient Greece.
**Critical Thinking: Draw Inferences** *Why do you think it was left to the women to manage the slaves?*

# The Greek Family

The typical Greek family consisted of husband, wife, and children. The man was the head of the house and had great control over his family. Women were expected to stay at home while the men took part in the public life of the polis. The Greek philosopher **Xenophon** wrote of the Greek family:

**Main Idea**
Greek society emphasized family life and education.

❝The gods have ordered and the law approves that men and women should each follow their own <u>capacity</u>. It is not so good for a woman to be out of doors as in. And it is more dishonorable for a man to stay indoors than to attend to his affairs outside.❞

—Xenophon, *Economics*

**Vocabulary *Builder***
<u>capacity</u> (kuh PAS ih tee) *n.* the ability to do something

Teacher · Scribe pouch · Lyre · Student · Slave supervising the student · Shield

**E-LA 6.1.3 Recognize and Use Greek Word Origins**

*Gymnasia* comes from the Greek root *gymnos*. What other English words build on this root?

**Greek Education** In ancient Greek society, children were considered important. In early childhood, youngsters received much attention. They had toys, games, and other amusements. At the age of six, however, boys and girls were separated. Girls stayed at home, and boys went off to school. Sons in rich families were often accompanied to school by slaves. The slaves made certain the students behaved and learned.

Education for boys lasted until the age of 18. They often went to school in an outdoor *gymnasia*, or training grounds. There, they studied reading, writing, arithmetic, poetry, music, and athletics. Instead of classroom instruction, students were often tutored one at a time by a master of each skill to be learned.

Students were expected to apply themselves faithfully to their studies. If not, they might be punished. As one Greek writer of the time put it, "If [the student] obeys, well and good; if not, he is straightened by threats and blows, like a piece of bent or warped wood."

Many boys attended school under the watchful eyes of a household slave. Despite the strict nature of Greek schools, they were among the best in the ancient world.

**The Role of Women** In the earliest Greek societies, women occasionally held political power and had a say in government decisions. By the rise of the Greek city-states, however, the role of women in government was reduced. Still, many women played important roles in the community. They took part in festivals and some women led religious activities.

In the home, Greek women had a great deal of responsibility. They ran the household, raised the children, kept track of money and spending, and managed the slaves. In addition, many Greek women made most or all of the clothing for their families. This could include spinning wool or flax into yarn, weaving fabric, and sewing or knitting the clothes.

Greek women also supervised the preparation of meals. A typical meal consisted of olives and olive oil, cheese, bread, wine, and maybe some fish and vegetables.

 **Checkpoint** Why did the Greeks value family life and education?

**Looking Back and Ahead** In this section, you learned about several features of Greek society. In the next section, you will learn about trade and expansion in the Greek world.

---

Section **3** **Check Your Progress**

**Progress Monitoring** ⏺nline
**For:** Self-test with instant help
**Visit:** PHSchool.com
**Web Code:** mwa-5133

**Standards Review** H-SS: 6.4.1; E-LA: Reading 6.1.3

**Comprehension and Critical Thinking**

1. (a) **Explain** How were small farmers regarded in Greek society?
   (b) **Draw Inferences** Why did owning land improve a person's status in ancient Greece?

2. (a) **Recall** What place did children have in ancient Greece?
   (b) **Apply Information** The Greeks placed great importance on healthy bodies and strong minds. How did Greek education teach these values?

**⊚ Reading Skill**

3. **Recognize and Use Greek Word Origins** Read this sentence: "They learned reading, writing, *arithmetic*, . . . and music." The Greek root *arithmos* means "number." Define *arithmetic*.

**Vocabulary *Builder***

Read each sentence below. If the sentence is true, write YES. If the sentence is not true, write NO and explain WHY.

4. Women in the Greek city-states often <u>contributed</u> to political decisions.

5. Few Greek men had the <u>capacity</u> to work outside.

**Writing**

6. Many great plays, works of art, and philosophical writing came from the ancient Greek city-states. Using the library or the Internet, look up a well-known Greek artist or writer from this period in Greek history. Then write a sentence that you could use as a "working thesis" for writing a paper about that person. Write two main points that would support your thesis.

# Women's World in Ancient Greece

Women in ancient Greece had fairly little freedom. They rarely took part in politics or public life. In most places, they could not inherit property. Although women had little freedom, they had much responsibility. They ran the household and made important decisions about home life, especially in times of war.

**History-Social Science**

**6.4** Students analyze the geographic, political, economic, religious, and social structures of the early civilizations of Ancient Greece.

Spindles were twirled around to spin wool fiber into thread.

 **A Daily Gathering**

Few houses had their own private wells. In Athens, women went to public fountains to fill water pots. This was a good opportunity to meet with friends and chat.

On this jug, a woman holds a spool of wool in her left hand, using her right hand to twist thread. A spindle weighs down the thread.

**Spinning and Weaving**

The women of ancient Greece turned raw materials like wool and flax into cloth and clothing for their families. Turning a basket of wool into a single item of clothing required countless hours of work, so this was a valuable economic contribution to the home. In addition to making clothing, Greek women made drapes, furniture fabrics, and beautiful wall hangings.

knucklebones

The mirror would have been highly polished so that its owner could see her reflection.

## Leisure Activities

Wealthy women had some time to relax and visit. A favorite game was knucklebones, which was similar to jacks. The knucklebones were made from ankle joints of cloven-footed animals such as sheep.

## Luxury Goods

Although the wealthy women of ancient Greece often made purchases for their household, they also sometimes bought items for themselves. They purchased many beauty aids, including combs, perfume, and mirrors such as this one.

### Analyze LIFE AT THE TIME

Write a list of five questions you would have liked to ask a woman who lived in Ancient Greece. Then choose one of the questions, and answer it as you think the woman might have answered it.

Section

# 4 Trade and Expansion

**Standards Preview**

**H-SS 6.4.1** Discuss the connections between geography and the development of city-states in the region of the Aegean Sea, including patterns of trade and commerce among Greek city-states and within the wider Mediterranean region.

**E-LA Reading 6.1.3** Recognize the origins and meanings of frequently used foreign words in English and use these words accurately in speaking and writing.

## Reading Preview

 **Reading Skill**

**Use Greek Word Origins in Speaking and Writing** When you fully understand words, you can use them correctly in speaking and writing. Remember that the literal meaning of the Greek word part may apply only generally to the modern English usage. For example, *theatron* means "viewing place," but our word *theater* refers specifically to a place where people go to view entertainment.

**Vocabulary** *Builder*

**High-Use Words**
**economy** (ih KAHN uh mee), p. 376
**site** (sīt), p. 378

**Key Terms and People**
annex (uh NEHKS), p. 377
helot (HEHL uht), p. 377
trading post (TRAYD ihng POHST), p. 378
fleet (fleet), p. 379

---

**Vocabulary** *Builder*
**economy** (ih KAHN uh mee) *n.* the way money and business are organized in a particular area

**Main Idea**
When Greek city-states no longer had enough resources to supply their people's needs, some of city-states began wars of conquest.

**Background Knowledge** Greece's location at the crossroads of three continents was important for the Greek economy. The ancient Greeks could travel the seas to trade with other lands. In this section, you will read about the expansion of the Greek civilization.

## A Changing Economy

You have read about the shortage of land and resources in Greece. As the Greek city-states grew over time, the Greeks had to find new ways to feed their people.

**Conquest** One way to solve the population problem was by conquest. A city-state could obtain more land and resources by conquering its neighbors. This was the approach taken by Sparta, a city-state located on the Peloponnesian Peninsula. Sparta did not have a port. So it could not depend on trade and travel as much as some of its neighbors.

## Spartan Warriors

The warriors of ancient Sparta worked very hard to stay physically fit and ready for battle. Once battle started, they were fierce fighters. **Critical Thinking: Identify Alternatives** *How might Sparta have expanded its economy in more peaceful ways?*

## Explore More Video

**Discovery School Video** View *Spartan Warriors* to learn more about Sparta's culture and military life.

As its population grew, Sparta built up its army. Spartan troops then conquered neighboring regions and **annexed,** or added, them to Sparta. Sparta called the conquered people **helots** and used them as slaves. With the helots' labor, Sparta grew stronger. By the mid-500s B.C., Sparta controlled most of the Peloponnesian Peninsula.

**Trade and Commerce**   Most city-states turned to commerce to provide for their growing populations.

Unlike Sparta, the city-state of Athens had an excellent port and grew through trade. Athens had been an important settlement since Mycenaean days. However, it had very little farmland. For that reason, the Athenians turned to commerce to meet their needs for food and other resources.

The streets and markets of Athens bustled with activity. Small factories produced pottery, jewelry, and other trade goods. These products, along with olive oil and wine, were exported by ship to other lands. Ships returned to Athens with imports of grain, timber, minerals, and other needed goods. Athens also imported luxury goods like ivory, glass, and perfume.

**E-LA 6.1.3 Use Greek Word Origins in Speaking and Writing**

Use the words *economy, geography,* and *olive,* in one or two sentences about Greek trade and commerce.

By the 800s B.C., Greek merchants were traveling widely in search of trading opportunities. They established **trading posts,** or trade centers, in distant lands. One important trading post was Naukratis, on the Nile delta. There, Greek merchants bartered for goods from Egypt and the African interior.

Checkpoint How did Greek city-states gain new lands and resources?

**Main Idea**
Some Greek cultures expanded by building colonies in new lands.

## Greek Expansion

Migration was another solution to Greece's population problem. Beginning in the 700s B.C., thousands of Greeks set out by sea to find new places to settle. This was not an easy decision, however. As a modern historian points out:

**❝The Greeks did not lightly leave home to join a colony. The voyage by sea was dangerous and uncomfortable, and at the end of it were uncertainty and danger. Only powerful pressures like overpopulation and land hunger drove thousands of Greeks to found new *poleis* [city-states].❞**

—Donald Kagan, *The Heritage of World Civilizations*

**Vocabulary Builder**
site (sīt) *n.* location for building

**Greek Colonies** Colonists settled in many different areas. The ideal site was on the sea, where they could anchor their ships. It had good land nearby for farming. It was also located near an important resource such as timber or minerals. In the *Odyssey*, Homer described the founding of a fictional colony:

**❝So [the founder] led them away, settling them in [a place called] Scheria, far from the bustle of men. He had a wall constructed around the town center, built houses, erected temples for the gods, and divided the land.❞**

—Homer, *Odyssey*

**E-LA 6.1.3 Use Greek Word Origins in Speaking and Writing**

Explain the relationship between colonists and their home city. Use the word *political.*

Greek colonists remained loyal to their home city. They brought a flame from home to light fires in the new colony. This flame symbolized their ties to their old city-state. They often traded with the home city. But aside from traders, most colonists never returned home. They made new lives in the new city-state.

By the 500s B.C., there were hundreds of Greek colonies spread around the Mediterranean Sea. These colonies stretched from the shores of the Black Sea to distant Spain.

**The Impact of Expansion** The establishment of colonies had a huge impact on Greece. Many of the colonies became prosperous, or successful. The colonies carried on an active trade with Greece. They also introduced the Greeks to new goods from foreign lands.

Colonization resulted in a new group of wealthy individuals. Greek merchants grew rich from the increased trade. They built large merchant *fleets, or groups of ships,* that crossed the Mediterranean. As their wealth increased, merchants began to play a greater role in the life of the Greek city-state.

Colonization also affected the rest of the Mediterranean world. Colonists brought Greek culture and goods to distant lands. They also carried new customs and ideas back to Greece. As a result, cultural borrowing increased throughout the Mediterranean region.

Checkpoint **Where were Greek colonies founded?**

**Looking Back and Ahead** In this section, you have read about trade and expansion in the Greek world. You learned that the Greeks founded overseas colonies to relieve population pressures. In the next chapter, you will read more about the two greatest Greek city-states: Athens and Sparta.

**Greek Shipping**
The Athenian trireme was a fast ship that could easily sink attackers. **Critical Thinking: Apply Information** *The fresco on p. 355 was painted almost a thousand years before this shield was decorated. What do the images have in common? What do they tell you about the importance of the sea to the people of ancient Greece?*

## Section 4 Check Your Progress

**Progress Monitoring** Online
**For:** Self-test with instant help
**Visit:** PHSchool.com
**Web Code:** mwa-5134

**Standards Review** H-SS: 6.4.1; E-LA: Reading 6.1.3

**Comprehension and Critical Thinking**

1. **(a) Explain** Why was population growth a problem for Greek city-states?
   **(b) Apply Information** Why did different Greek city-states use different methods to solve this problem?

2. **(a) List** What were two effects of Greek colonization?
   **(b) Draw Inferences** How do you think the aristocrats felt about the newly rich Greek merchants?

**Reading Skill**

3. **Use Greek Word Origins in Speaking and Writing** Use the word *geography* to explain how Greek colonists chose where to settle.

**Vocabulary** *Builder*

4. Write two definitions for each word: economy, resource. First, write a formal definition for your teacher. Second, write a definition in everyday English for a classmate.

**Writing**

5. Use the library or the Internet to find out more information about a colony founded by an ancient Greek city-state. Write a sentence about the colony that you could use as a working thesis for a paper about the colony.

When authors write about history, they draw conclusions about things. To make sure that an author's conclusions are correct, you should check the evidence the author provides.

 **Chapter Standards**

**English-Language Arts**

Reading 6.2.6 Determine the adequacy and appropriateness of the evidence for an author's conclusions.

Do you believe everything you read? You shouldn't. You should decide for yourself if an author's conclusions make sense. Here are some kinds of evidence to look for:

- **Facts** Has the author provided facts that support the conclusion? Remember, facts can be proved to be true.

- **Quotes** Look for quotes from people who lived at the time, and quotes from experts in the field.

- **Citations** Citations are notes that tell the source of information or quotes used.

- **Details** Does the author give details that show an understanding of what life was like at the time?

- **Examples** Does the author give examples that support the conclusion?

Authors do not always provide every kind of evidence listed above. But the more evidence they provide, the more likely it is that they've made sound conclusions.

**Learn the Skill** *Follow these steps to learn how to evaluate the evidence an author provides.*

1. **Read the information.** What is the information about?

2. **Identify the conclusion that the author draws.** A conclusion is an opinion or a judgment. It is often a summarizing statement, such as, "The establishment of colonies had a huge impact on Greece."

3. **Identify the evidence that the author gives.** Look for facts, quotes, citations, details, and examples.

4. **Decide whether the evidence supports the conclusion.** Has the author convinced you that the conclusion was a good one?

**Practice the Skill** *Read the section The Impact of Homer, on pages 365–366.*

1. **Read the information.** Read the section The Impact of Homer. What is the section about?

2. **Identify the conclusion that the author draws.** What is the author's conclusion?

3. **Identify the evidence that the author gives.** **(a)** Which writers are quoted? **(b)** What examples of Greek values are given?

4. **Decide whether the evidence supports the conclusion.** Does the author's conclusion make sense? Why or why not?

**Apply the Skill**
*See page 383 of the Review and Assessment.*

**Chapter 13** **Standards Review and Assessment**

**Study Guide** *Online*
Complete your Chapter 13 study guide in print or online.

## Chapter Summary  H-SS: 6.4.1

### Section 1  The Aegean World

- The Peloponnesian peninsula and surrounding islands became home to early Greek-speaking people.
- The earliest people of Greece developed independent settlements that were often known for trade and sea travel.

### Section 2  The Rise of City-States

- Because Greece's steep hillsides made travel by land difficult, ancient Greece was politically divided into city-states.
- The Greek city-states shared much culture but had differences in the way they were governed.

### Section 3  Daily Life in Greece

- City-states of ancient Greece were often governed by wealthy landowners called aristocrats.
- Although they had little direct say in government, Greek women contributed to the culture and economy of their family and community in many ways.
- Culture, the arts, and learning flourished.

### Section 4  Trade and Expansion

- The population of many Greek city-states eventually grew so great that the land could not support them.
- Some city-states began wars of conquest, while others became more dependent on trade or founded colonies in other regions.

## Standards Practice  H-SS: 6.4.1

# Vocabulary *Builder*

## High-Use Words

Look at the following words to see if you understand the meaning: **enable**, **contribute**, **site**, **economy**. Then use one of those words in each of the following sentences to complete the sentence.

1. Ionia made a good _____ for colonists of ancient Greece.

2. The aristocrats were expected to _____ to Greek politics and society.

3. The _____ of many Greek city-states came to depend on trade.

4. Greece lacked the kind of large, fertile plains that would _____ grain farming in other regions.

## Key Terms

Answer the following questions in complete sentences that show your understanding of the Key Terms.

1. How did Greece's location on a rocky peninsula encourage its people to become traders and explorers?

2. Why did owning large estates make aristocrats important in Greek politics?

3. How did Sparta acquire its force of Helots?

4. Why did a fleet of ships depart from Mycenaea for Troy?

5. Why was the location of the acropolis in each city significant?

6. How did the monarchy of the Mycenaeans differ from the aristocratic government of the later city-states?

## Apply Reading Skills

**Recognize and Analyze Words With Greek Origins** Define the following words, using their Greek word origins: *aristocracy, political, acropolis, economy, arithmetic, geography.* Then, use them in a paragraph about the chapter content.

## Comprehension and Critical Thinking

**1. (a) Explain** What made Greece a crossroads of the ancient world?
**(b) Evaluate Information** What kind of land and resources did Greece have?
**(c) Analyze Information** How did Greece's resources and location affect the growth of its civilization?

**2. (a) List** List three facts about the Mycenaean civilization.
**(b) Contrast** How did the government of the Greek city-state differ from Mycenaean rule?
**(c) Compare** How is the U.S. government similar to the Greek city-state?

**3. (a) Identify** Which group held the most power in the Greek city-state?
**(b) Make Predictions** How might Greek society and politics change with increased population and trade?

**4. (a) Explain** Why did Greek city-states turn to conquest or to trade and commerce?
**(b) Draw Conclusions** How did the Greek economy change as a result?
**(c) Analyze Cause and Effect** Explain how increased trade was both a cause and an effect of colonization.

## Researching

**The War on Troy** For many centuries, historians believed that the Trojan war was a myth. Then an archaeologist decided to look for the ancient city of Troy. His results surprised the world. In this activity you will use the Internet and library media center to research and report on what we now know about Troy and the Trojan war. When you have completed the assignment, put your work on display so your classmates can read it.

**Historians:** Write a one-page report on the archaeologists who have searched for information about Troy and what they have discovered. Attach a list of important discoveries.

**Geographers:** Research the *Iliad* to find the names of Greek city-states which, according to the legend, went to war against Troy. Create a map of ancient Greece showing the location of those city-states and the possible route that the Greek warriors took.

> **Researching Online**
> **For:** Help in starting this activity
> **Visit:** PHSchool.com
> **Web Code:** mwd-5135

## Writing

**1. Write a paragraph about a subject that you research.** Find a topic from this chapter about which you would like to learn more. Research that topic in the library or on the Internet until you have found a specific area about which you would like to write. Prepare a working thesis and look for details that support your thesis. Finally, organize and write your paragraph.
**Your paragraph should:**
• contain a clear topic sentence
• use details from your research
• demonstrate good organization and writing

**2. Write a short narrative.** Imagine you were inside the wooden horse when the Trojans led it into Troy. Write a short narrative describing how it felt to be inside the horse, and what happened when you got out.

**Progress Monitoring** ⊙nline
**For:** Self-test with instant help
**Visit:** PHSchool.com
**Web Code:** mwa-5135

# Apply Analysis Skills

Read the section on Greek Expansion, on pages 378–379 to answer these questions.

1. What is the information about?

2. What conclusion does the author draw?

3. Which modern historian is quoted?

4. What primary source is included?

5. Name a fact that supports the conclusion.

6. Name a detail that supports the conclusion.

**Judge Evidence**

Check facts.
Look for quotes.
Check citations.
Note details.
Note examples.

# Test Yourself

1. **The Greek Peninsula lies between**

    A Africa, Asia, and Europe.

    B the Aegean, Ionian, and Mediterranean seas.

    C both A and B

    D none of the above

2. **Why was ancient Greece a group of independent city-states?**

    A because each one grew different crops to trade with one another

    B because they had different religions

    C because they developed near rivers

    D because they were divided by mountains

**Refer to the image below to answer question 3.**

3. **Choose the statement that is false.**

    A Each polis was built in a valley.

    B The temples and government buildings were built on the higher parts of the hill.

    C The word acropolis refers to the location on which Greek cities were built.

    D The countryside of Greece was very hilly.

**Refer to the text below to answer question 4.**

*"Every man make up his mind to fight
And move on his enemy! Strong as I am,
It's hard for me to face so many men
And fight with all at once . . . .
And yet I will!"*

4. **Identify the speaker of these words and the situation being discussed.**

    A Dorian preparing to invade Mycenae

    B Agamemnon preparing to attack Sparta

    C Xenophon debating other philosophers

    D Achilles preparing to attack Troy

5. **Choose the correct definition of a Greek colony.**

    A temporary trading center

    B new land settled by Greek immigrants

    C foreign land conquered by Greek armies

    D body of land surrounded on three sides by water

6. **To be eligible to vote in Greek city-state elections, one had to be a**

    A male citizen.

    B merchant.

    C scholar.

    D priest.

## Chapter 14

# Athens and Sparta

## (950 B.C.–461 B.C.)

## Prepare to Read

**Chapter Standards**

### History-Social Science

**6.4** Students analyze the geographic, political, economic, religious, and social structures of the early civilizations of Ancient Greece.

**Section 1,** pp. 388–392

 **What You Will Learn**

### Political Changes in Greece

The governments of some ancient Greek city-states began to shift from rule by one person, or a few people, to rule by many people during the 600s B.C.

**Section 2,** pp. 393–398

### Democracy in Athens

The city-state of Athens developed a system of democracy in which citizens represented themselves directly in government affairs.

**Section 3,** pp. 400–405

### Oligarchy in Sparta

Sparta developed an oligarchy form of government and a society based on military discipline. Despite its military strength, the city-state's society remained rigid and resistant to change.

Spartan soldier

**Chapter Events**

**Other Events**

**950 B.C.**
Dorian invaders found Sparta on the Peloponnesian Peninsula.

**670 B.C.**
The phalanx becomes an important military formation in ancient Greece.

**1000 B.C.**

**800 B.C.**

**600 B.C.**

**945 B.C.** Civil war breaks out in Egypt.

**650 B.C.** Ironworking begins in China.

## Where and When?

More than 2,000 years ago, the ancient Greek city-states of Athens and Sparta developed different types of governments and societies.

The agora in Athens was an open area where people could gather for political or commercial activities.

**508 B.C.**
Cleisthenes' reforms reduce power of wealthy Athenians.

**461 B.C.**
Athens establishes a court system based on the authority of citizen juries.

 **600 B.C.**

**525 B.C.** Persia conquers Egypt.

 **400 B.C.**

**221 B.C.** China's Qin Dynasty begins.

 **200 B.C.**

# How to Read History

## History Reading Skill

### *Previewing* Compare and Contrast Patterns

When you read, you will often encounter text that organizes ideas in a compare-and-contrast pattern. Ideas and topics are examined for their similarities and differences. Use clues in the text to help you identify and analyze the comparisons and contrasts.

**Chapter Standards**

**English-Language Arts**

**Reading 6.2.2** Analyze text that uses the compare-and-contrast organizational pattern.

---

**1** The overall structure of a text will often suggest a compare-and-contrast pattern. Here, a heading indicates that several groups from early Greece will be discussed. The subheads about each group suggest that comparisons and contrasts will be drawn between the different groups.

### Peoples of Early Greece  ⟵ Heading

**The Mycenaeans     The Dorians     The Ionians**

⤷ Subhead for each group of people

---

**2** In the sentences below, you can use clue words to help you recognize the subjects being contrasted.

> Clue to contrast between boys and girls.

At the age of six, **however**, boys and girls were separated. Girls stayed at home, **while** boys went off to school.

> Clue to contrast between boys and girls.

---

**3** Here, two entirely different societies are contrasted. Headings again structure the contrast. Comparative description such as *not as strong* offers another clue.

### Conquest

Sparta built a strong army and used its troops to conquer neighboring regions.

### Trade and Commerce

Most city-states were not as strong as Sparta. So instead of conquest, these cities turned to trade and commerce. Athens was a good · example of a city-state that relied on trade.

# Vocabulary *Builder*

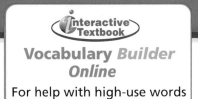
## *Previewing* **High-Use Academic Words**

| High-Use Word | Definition | Sample Sentence About History |
|---|---|---|
| **eventually** (ee VEHN choo uhl ee) (Section 1, p. 390) | *adv.* after a very long time; finally | The many separate groups <u>eventually</u> formed an organized government. |
| **grant** (grant) (Section 1, p. 391) | *v.* to give formally or according to legal procedure | The constitution <u>granted</u> important rights to the nation's citizens. |
| **major** (MAY jer) (Section 2, p. 394) | *adj.* greater in importance or rank | Several <u>major</u> events changed the outcome of the conflict. |
| **leisure** (LEE zher) (Section 2, p. 395) | *adj.* free and unoccupied; spare | New inventions allowed people to enjoy more <u>leisure</u> time. |
| **abandon** (uh BAN duhn) (Section 3, p. 404) | *v.* to leave, as in danger, out of necessity; desert | The military forces had to <u>abandon</u> their position due to the dangerous conditions. |
| **oblige** (uh BLĪJ) (Section 3, p. 404) | *v.* to compel by moral, legal, or physical force; constrain | The government <u>obliged</u> the citizens to meet its demands. |

## *Previewing* **Key Terms and People**

**jury**

oligarchy, p. 388
Plutarch, p. 389
phalanx, p. 389
citizen, p. 390
tyranny, p. 390
democracy, p. 390
Solon, p. 391
citizenship, p. 391

Pericles, p. 392
assembly, p. 393
jury, p. 394
Aristotle, p. 396
direct democracy, p. 397
representative
  democracy, p. 398
ephor, p. 401

military state, p. 402
barracks, p. 403
Thucydides, p. 405

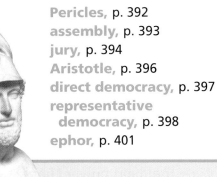

**Pericles**

**H-SS 6.4.2** Trace the transition from tyranny and oligarchy to early democratic forms of government and back to dictatorship in ancient Greece, including the significance of the invention of the idea of citizenship.

**E-LA Reading 6.2.2** Analyze text that uses the compare-and-contrast organizational pattern.

## Reading Preview

### Reading Skill

**Compare-and-Contrast Structures** Writers often use headings and text structure to highlight compare-and-contrast relationships in the text. Look at the headings and subheadings of this section, and identify topics that could be compared and contrasted.

### Vocabulary *Builder*

**High-Use Words**
eventually (ee VEHN choo uhl ee), p. 390
grant (grant), p. 391

**Key Terms and People**
oligarchy (AHL ih gahr kee), p. 388
Plutarch (PLOO tahrk), p. 389
phalanx (FAY langks), p. 389
citizen (SIHT uh zuhn), p. 390
tyranny (TIHR uh nee), p. 390
democracy (dih MAHK ruh see), p. 390
Solon (SOH luhn), p. 391
citizenship (SIHT uh zuhn shihp), p. 391
Pericles (PEHR uh kleez), p. 392

**Background Knowledge** In Chapter 13, you learned that Greece was once divided into small kingdoms headed by monarchs. With the rise of city-states, power shifted to groups of aristocrats. In this section, you will read about the different ways city-states organized their governments.

**Main Idea**
Many early city-states had governments controlled by a few powerful individuals.

## Rule by the Few

In the early city-states, small groups of powerful aristocrats usually controlled the government. The Greeks called this type of government an oligarchy. An **oligarchy** is a government in which most political power is held by a small segment of society. A wealthy upper class often makes up this segment. However, groups might also gain power through other means, such as the military.

**Oligarchies** In the Greek city-states, the small segment of society that held power changed over time. At first, it included large landowners. As trade and commerce increased, wealthy merchants and artisans also joined this class.

Oligarchies were usually headed by a council of leaders chosen by the upper class. These councils made laws that often benefitted wealthy Greeks. In Athens, for example, a law code drawn up by an official named Draco ordered harsh punishments for the poor. A learned Greek named Plutarch later wrote of Draco's laws that

**"** Death was appointed [chosen] for almost all offenses. . . . those that were convicted of idleness were to die, and those that stole a cabbage or an apple to suffer even as villains that committed . . . murder. . . . Draco's laws were written not with ink but blood.**"**

—Plutarch, *The Lives of the Noble Greeks and Romans*

Today people use the word draconian to describe a law that seems unnecessarily severe.

### The Rise of the Phalanx

Around 670 B.C., a new military formation called the phalanx began to change the ways the Greeks fought wars. In the past, Greek wars had been fought by aristocrats on horseback. Only the wealthy could afford the horse and armor needed to become a Greek warrior.

The **phalanx** was a formation of heavily armed soldiers who moved together as a unit. In battle, the soldiers lined up so close to one another that each man's shield helped protect his neighbor. Very little could stand in the way of a well-trained phalanx, which quickly became ancient Greece's most powerful fighting force.

**The Phalanx Formation**
This image shows a later phalanx similar to those developed by the ancient Greeks. A typical phalanx featured soldiers lined up in eight rows. **Critical Thinking: Explain Problem** *What challenges do you think soldiers in a phalanx might have faced during battle?*

**Tyranny in Athens**
The art on this vase shows the assassination of an Athenian tyrant. **Critical Thinking: Explain Problem** *How might an event such as this lead a state to adopt a different form of government?*

Unlike earlier warriors, soldiers in a phalanx did not have to buy a horse and armor. Most farmers and artisans could afford the necessary sword and shield. As city-states came to depend on the phalanx for defense, their leaders had to consider the interests of the lower classes, or risk losing the support of their army.

At the same time, ordinary citizens, or members of a state, became more aware of their importance in society. Some even began to insist that they receive a greater voice in government. As unrest grew, new types of government appeared in the city-states.

**Tyranny** One new type of government was based on strong rulers called tyrants. Tyrants usually belonged to the aristocracy. But they won popular support by promising land and other benefits to the poor. With that support, they set up tyrannies, or governments run by a single strong ruler.

Tyrants usually ruled with what is sometimes called an iron hand. They did not allow others to play significant roles in government. Nevertheless, tyrants were not always bad rulers. In some city-states, they governed fairly and worked to make life better for ordinary people.

Many tyrants tried to set up family dynasties so that their sons could continue in power after them. This seldom worked, because most tyrannies did not last long enough for power to be passed to new rulers. After taking power, many tyrants found that they could not fulfill their promises. Eventually, other forms of government replaced tyrannies.

**Vocabulary** *Builder*
**eventually** (ee VEHN choo uhl ee) *adv.* after a long time; finally

 **Checkpoint** **What were two common types of governments in early Greek city-states?**

**Main Idea**
Some city-states set up governments that allowed ordinary citizens to take part in civic matters, or those relating to citizens.

## Rule by the Many

While some city-states turned to tyranny, others moved toward rule by the many. The Greeks called this form of government democracy, which means "rule by the people". Under a democratic government, large numbers of people began to participate in civic affairs.

**The Beginnings of Democracy in Athens** The city-state of Athens was among the first to experiment with rule by the many. In the 600s B.C., Athens suffered from the same problems as other city-states. After years of unrest, Athenians found themselves on the brink of war.

In 594 B.C., the aristocrats who ruled Athens appointed a leader named Solon to make changes. Solon revised the city's law code to reduce punishments for crimes. He ended the practice of selling into slavery poor people who could not pay their debts. He also <u>granted</u> all male citizens the right to vote for government officials. These measures set Athens on the path to stable government and democracy.

This proved to be an indirect path, however. After Solon left office, a tyrant took control of Athens for many years. In general, though, Athens continued toward democratic rule.

**The Development of Citizenship** One of the factors that made rule by the many successful was the idea of citizenship. Citizenship is membership in a political community. Citizenship carries with it both rights and responsibilities.

The idea that people were citizens with rights and responsibilities set Greece apart from other parts of the world. In Egypt, India, and China, people lived as subjects of a ruler. They were expected to obey their rulers without question. They certainly did not take part in civic affairs.

**E-LA 6.2.2**
**Comparison-and-Contrast Structures**
What comparison-and-contrast relationship is described in the paragraphs below this heading?

**Vocabulary** *Builder*
<u>grant</u> (grant) *v.* to give formally or according to legal procedure

## Governments in Ancient Greece

| Type | Definition | Example from Ancient Greece |
|------|------------|------------------------------|
| Oligarchy | Political power held by a small segment of society; Oligarchy was an early form of government in many Greek city-states. | Corinth (around 550 B.C.) |
| Tyranny | Government run by a single strong ruler; Tyrannies arose in response to unrest in many oligarchies. | Samos (around 500s B.C.) |
| Democracy | Rule by the people; Democracy in Athens evolved over time in response to citizens' unrest. | Athens (gradual democratic reforms began as early as 594 B.C.) |

**Reading Tables**

Though the governments of many early Greek city-states were oligarchies, new forms of government also began to appear.

(a) **Read a Table** What type of government did Samos have during the 500s B.C.?

(b) **Draw Inferences** Which two of these types of government do you think were most alike? Why?

In contrast, the Greeks gave ordinary people the right to take part in government affairs. They also made such participation a responsibility. A leader named **Pericles** described the role of citizens in Athens:

**❝**Here each individual is interested not only in his own affairs but in the affairs of the state as well. Even those who are mostly occupied with their own business are extremely well informed on general politics. . . . We do not say that a man who takes no interest in politics is a man who minds his own business. We say he has no business here at all.**❞**

—from "Pericles' Funeral Oration"

**Voting Tablets**
People in ancient Greece often used fragments of pottery such as this one to voice their opinions on government affairs. At times, citizens used such fragments to identify people who had become too powerful to participate in the Athenian democracy. **Critical Thinking: Frame Questions** *What questions might a citizen ask before voting?*

 **Checkpoint** How did some city-states allow ordinary citizens to participate in government?

**Looking Back and Ahead** In this section, you have read about different types of rule in ancient Greece, such as oligarchy, tyranny, and democracy. You have also read about the importance of the idea of citizenship. In the next section, you will read more about Athens and the development of democracy.

## Section 1 Check Your Progress

**Progress Monitoring ●nline**
**For:** Self-test with instant help
**Visit:** PHSchool.com
**Web Code:** mwa-5141

 **Standards Review** H-SS: 6.4.2; E-LA: Reading 6.2.2

**Comprehension and Critical Thinking**

1. **(a) Identify** Who usually headed the oligarchies of ancient Greek city-states?
   **(b) Apply Information** How did the development of the phalanx threaten the power of the oligarchies?

2. **(a) Explain** Why was Solon appointed to make changes to the government of Athens?
   **(b) Analyze Cause and Effect** What effects did these changes have on Athens' government?

**⊙ Reading Skill**

3. **Compare-and-Contrast Structures** Review the passages from this section that describe oligarchies and tyrannies. How does the text structure the comparisons and contrasts made between these types of government?

**Vocabulary *Builder***
Complete each of the following sentences so that the second part further explains the first part and clearly shows your understanding of the highlighted word.

4. An important military development in ancient Greece was the phalanx; _____.

5. Strong rulers established tyrannies; _____.

6. Athenians enjoyed the benefits of citizenship; _____.

**Writing**

7. Make a simple outline that organizes important information from the section about changes to politics and government in ancient Greece.

## Section

# 2 Democracy in Athens

 **Standards Preview**

**H-SS 6.4.3** State the key differences between Athenian, or direct, democracy and representative democracy.

**E-LA Reading 6.2.2** Analyze text that uses the compare-and-contrast organizational pattern.

## Reading Preview

### Reading Skill

**Identify Comparison and Contrast** Clue words often point to comparisons and contrasts. These include contrast words, such as *unlike* or *instead*, and comparison words, such as *also* or *like*. Words can also indicate change or contrast through their meaning. Look for clue words as you read this section.

### Vocabulary *Builder*

**High-Use Words**
major (MAY jer), p. 394
leisure (LEE zher), p. 395

**Key Terms and People**
assembly (uh SEHM blee), p. 393
jury (JOOR ee), p. 394
Aristotle (AR ihs taht uhl), p. 396
direct democracy (duh REHKT dih MAHK ruh see), p. 397
representative democracy (rehp ruh ZEHN tuh tihv dih MAHK ruh see), p. 398

**Background Knowledge**   Democracy began in Athens during the late 500s B.C. Even then, however, powerful aristocrats kept control of the government. In this section, you will learn more about the growth of democratic government in Athens.

## The Path to Democracy

As you have read, Solon took the first steps toward democracy in Athens. Later, other leaders continued to make reforms. They helped create a more democratic system of government.

**The Reforms of Cleisthenes** In 508 B.C., a leader named Cleisthenes gained power in Athens. Cleisthenes carried out several reforms that reduced the power of the rich. For instance, he almost doubled the number of citizens who could vote. Most new voters represented the lower classes. Cleisthenes also increased the power of the assembly, which included all male citizens. An **assembly** is a group of persons who gather together for a common purpose. The assembly met to discuss political issues and make decisions for the city-state.

**Main Idea**
A series of reforms, as well as social and economic changes, contributed to the growth of democracy in Athens.

These reforms gave more citizens a voice in the government of Athens. For this reason, Cleisthenes is still remembered as the Father of Athenian Democracy.

**Later Democratic Reforms** The next major reform took place in 461 B.C. In that year, Athens established a new court system based on the authority of citizen juries. A jury is a group of people who hear evidence and decide a court case. Before, upper-class judges had controlled the courts. The new system put most legal decisions in the hands of ordinary citizens.

The leader Pericles carried out still more reforms in the 450s B.C. His first major reform was to pay citizens for jury service and other civic duties. Payment for public service helped poor people to take part in government. A second reform recognized women as citizens. Although women still could not vote or hold office, they were given legal rights.

**Democratic Values** Taken together, these reforms created the world's first democracy in Athens. Athenians were proud of what they had created. In 431 B.C., during a time of war, Pericles gave a speech honoring those who had died in battle. In that speech, he talked about the democratic values that made Athens special:

**❝**Our constitution is called a democracy because power is in the hands not of a small minority but of the whole people. When it is a question of settling private disputes, everyone is equal before the law. When it is a question of putting one person before another in positions of public responsibility, what counts is not membership in a particular class, but the actual ability which the man possesses. . . . We are free and tolerant in our private lives. But in public affairs we keep to the law. This is because it commands our deep respect.**❞**

—from "Pericles' Funeral Oration"

**Vocabulary** *Builder*

<u>major</u> (MAY jer) *adj.* greater in importance or rank

# BIOGRAPHY QUEST

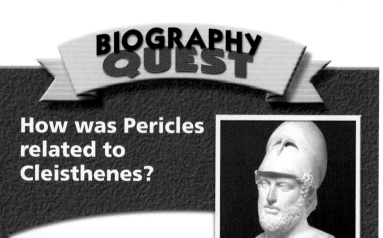

Pericles

## How was Pericles related to Cleisthenes?

*Fast Facts*

**Who:** Pericles
**What:** Athenian military and political leader
**When:** ca. 495 B.C.–429 B.C.
**Where:** Athens
**Why important:** Pericles carried out a series of reforms that contributed to the development of democracy in Athens.

*Fast Find*

**How:** Go online to find out how Pericles was related to Cleisthenes, the Father of Athenian Democracy.

**Biography**
**◑nline**

**For:** More about Pericles
**Visit:** PHSchool.com
**Web Code:** mwe-5142

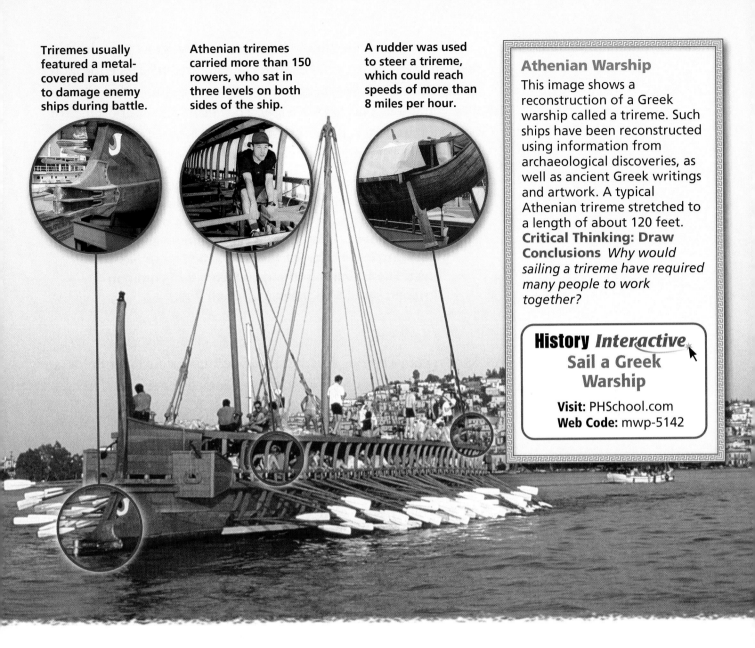

Triremes usually featured a metal-covered ram used to damage enemy ships during battle.

Athenian triremes carried more than 150 rowers, who sat in three levels on both sides of the ship.

A rudder was used to steer a trireme, which could reach speeds of more than 8 miles per hour.

**Athenian Warship**

This image shows a reconstruction of a Greek warship called a trireme. Such ships have been reconstructed using information from archaeological discoveries, as well as ancient Greek writings and artwork. A typical Athenian trireme stretched to a length of about 120 feet. **Critical Thinking: Draw Conclusions** *Why would sailing a trireme have required many people to work together?*

**History** *Interactive*
**Sail a Greek Warship**

**Visit:** PHSchool.com
**Web Code:** mwp-5142

**Social and Economic Factors** Other factors also helped the development of democracy in Athens. One was the growth of the Athenian navy.

In the late 400s B.C., Athens built a fleet of warships to increase Athenian influence. A team of rowers powered each ship. Most rowers came from the ranks of the poor. Like the members of the phalanx, rowers became an important force. By demanding a greater role in government, they helped open politics to the lower classes.

The increased prosperity of Athens was another factor in the growth of democracy. As you have read, trade and commerce helped make Athens a wealthy city-state. Many people could afford to buy slaves to do much of their work. This left citizens with more <u>leisure</u> time to devote to civic affairs.

**Vocabulary** *Builder*
<u>leisure</u> (LEE zher) *adj.* free and unoccupied; spare

Education represented a third factor in the growth of democracy. At the time, schools in Athens were private. The education students received was designed to produce well-rounded citizens who could take part in public life. The belief in the importance of education to citizenship led some Athenians to support free public education. The philosopher **Aristotle** wrote:

> **It is [clear] that education should be one and the same for all, and that it should be public, and not private—not as at present, when every one looks after his own children separately, and gives them separate instruction of the sort which he thinks best. The training in things which are of common interest should be the same for all.**
>
> —Aristotle, *Politics*

As you can see, the idea that public education is essential to a democratic society had its origins in ancient Greece.

 **Checkpoint** What reforms encouraged the growth of democracy in Athens?

**Main Idea**
Athens used a form of democracy in which citizens played a direct role in making government decisions.

## How Athenian Democracy Worked

The reforms of Greek leaders produced a golden age of democracy, during which Athens had no government bureaucracy, or civil servants. Citizens ran all parts of the government. The most important were the assembly, the council, and the courts.

**The Assembly** The assembly was the main political body of Athens. It met 40 times a year on a rocky hillside above the city. All free adult male citizens could attend assembly meetings. Everyone in attendance had the right to speak at these meetings, from the poorest farmer to the richest aristocrat.

The assembly was a large body. The law required that 6,000 citizens be present at each session in order to conduct business. When important issues came up for discussion, citizens traveled from all parts of the city-state to cast their votes. The assembly also elected ten generals to serve as military and political leaders.

**The Council** A 500-person council was the second key component of the Athenian government. The council helped decide which issues should come before the assembly. Within the council, a smaller rotating group of 50 people helped manage the daily affairs of government.

Members of the council were chosen by lot, or at random, from among the citizens. This method of choosing members meant that every male citizen had an equal chance of being appointed to the council. Council members held office for one year and received payment for their service to the government.

**The Courts** The government's third key component was the court system. The Athenian court system had a series of courts to decide different types of cases. There were eight different courts. Most Athenian courts did not have judges or lawyers. Juries made up of citizens ran the courts and decided cases.

Athenian juries were much larger than the juries that serve today. Anywhere from several hundred to several thousand people might have served on a single jury! Having so many jurors discouraged bribery. These large juries made their decisions by a vote of the majority.

**Direct and Representative Democracy** As you can see, Athenian democracy depended on active citizen involvement. Citizens attended the assembly, served on the council, and acted as jury members. A political system in which citizens participate directly in government decision making is called a **direct democracy.** Direct democracy worked in Athens because the city-state was small and because of the commitment and hard work of its citizens.

**Ancient and Modern Juries**

Modern juries (left), though smaller than those of Athens, still help decide court cases today. Athenian jurors used water clocks (top right) to monitor the time given to speakers addressing the jury. Jurors handed in one of two disks (bottom right) in order to register a verdict of guilty or innocent. **Critical Thinking: Clarify Problems** *Why might Athenian juries have wanted to limit the time given to speakers during court sessions?*

Compare and contrast the current government of the United States with Athenian democracy. What clue words from the text help you make this comparison and contrast?

Direct democracy is less practical in large countries like the United States. Citizens of such countries live too far apart to meet together regularly in huge assemblies. For this reason, most democracies today are representative democracies. In a **representative democracy,** the citizens elect others to represent them in government. In the United States, for example, citizens elect representatives to pass laws and run the governments at the local, state, and national levels.

A modern representative democracy is both larger and more complicated than the direct democracy of ancient Athens. Some features of a democracy may vary from one country to another. However, such a government is still based on the principle of rule by the people.

**Checkpoint** How did the assembly provide Athenians with a direct role in government decisions?

**Looking Back and Ahead** In this section, you have learned about the development of democracy in Athens. You learned that the citizens of Athens played a direct role in government. In the next section, you will read about a different system: the oligarchy of Sparta.

# Section 2 Check Your Progress

**Progress Monitoring** ⏻**nline**
**For:** Self-test with instant help
**Visit:** PHSchool.com
**Web Code:** mwa-5142

 **Standards Review** H-SS: 6.4.3; E-LA: Reading 6.2.2

## Comprehension and Critical Thinking

1. **(a) Explain** What were two key reforms that helped the growth of democracy in Athens?
**(b) Link Past and Present** How are the effects of such reforms still seen in democratic governments today?

2. **(a) List** What were the three main components of the democracy of Athens?
**(b) Explain Problem** Why do you think few modern governments use a direct democracy like that of ancient Athens?

## ⏻ Reading Skill

3. **Identify Comparison and Contrast** Read the last two paragraphs under the heading Social and Economic Factors, on page 395. Compare and contrast your education with that of a student in Athens.

## Vocabulary *Builder*

Read each sentence below. If the sentence is true, write YES. If the sentence is not true, write NO and explain WHY.

4. The <u>major</u> reform had far less impact than other, more important reforms.

5. The citizens could fill their <u>leisure</u> time by performing civic duties.

## Writing

6. Use the text from this section to create an outline organizing important main ideas and details that you have learned about Athenian democracy.

# Citizen Heroes

**History-Social Science** 6.4.8 Describe the enduring contributions of important Greek figures in the arts and sciences (e.g., Hypatia, Socrates, Plato, Aristotle, Euclid, Thucydides).

| Respect | Caring | Responsibility | Fairness | Honesty | Civic Virtue |

# SOCRATES PHILOSOPHER AND TEACHER

**Honesty is an important trait for both people and governments. In ancient Greece, the philosopher and teacher Socrates taught that living justly and honestly was the way to happiness.**

**Socrates** valued truth and honesty above all. "False words are not only evil in themselves, but they infect the soul with evil," he said.

Socrates taught his students to discover truths by questioning things. This teaching method eventually got him into trouble. He was accused of misleading young people and speaking against the gods. He received a death sentence. While in prison, he was given the chance to escape. "I will not break the law to save my life," he said. So, he was given poison and died.

## Connect to Today

**Shirin Ebadi** was born in Iran and has become well known as a judge, lawyer, and teacher. She has been recognized for her work to protect human rights, particularly those of women and children, in her home country.

Ebadi has often exhibited honesty in her work on behalf of Iran's citizens. She has frequently stood up for her beliefs against the government of Iran, and like Socrates, has even been imprisoned for her honesty.

## *Analyze* CITIZEN HEROES

What are some of the ways that you might demonstrate honesty in your life? Work with a small group of classmates to make a list of situations in which honesty would be an important trait. For instance, you might describe a time you found money or an object that you returned to its owner.

## Section

# 3 Oligarchy in Sparta

### Standards Preview

**H-SS 6.4.6** Compare and contrast life in Athens and Sparta, with emphasis on their roles in the Persian and Peloponnesian Wars.

**E-LA Reading 6.2.2** Analyze text that uses the compare-and-contrast organizational pattern.

## Reading Preview

### Reading Skill

**Analyze Comparison and Contrast Structures** You will notice that comparisons and contrasts of Sparta and Athens appear throughout this section. Although information about Athens has appeared in previous sections, the government and social structures of both societies are discussed in Section 3. As you read about Sparta, consider how each main idea relates to what you already know about Athens.

### Vocabulary *Builder*

**High-Use Words**
**abandon** (uh BAN duhn), p. 404
**oblige** (uh BLĪJ), p. 404

**Key Terms and People**
ephor (EHF or), p. 401
military state (MIHL uh tehr ee stayt), p. 402
barracks (BAR uhks), p. 403
Thucydides (thoo SIHD ih deez), p. 405

**Background Knowledge** Following the example of Athens, a number of Greek city-states adopted democratic rule. However, Sparta took a different approach to government. It developed an oligarchy with a strong military foundation. In this section, you will read about the government and society of Sparta, and how they differed from those of Athens.

## The Spartan State

**Main Idea**
Sparta had an oligarchical government and worked to conquer other regions, such as Messenia.

As you have read in Chapter 13, Sparta was a city-state on the Peloponnesian Peninsula. Dorian invaders founded Sparta around 950 B.C. Unlike the Athenians, Spartans had little interest in trade and commerce. Because it was inland, Sparta never became a sea power. Neither did it become a democracy.

**Spartan Government** At first, the government of Sparta looked much like other oligarchies. At the head of the government sat two kings. These kings had probably descended from the two oldest clans in Spartan society.

The kings headed Sparta's main governing body, the council of elders. They also served as military leaders. A Spartan army seldom marched into battle without one of its kings as its leader.

In addition to these kings, the council of elders included 28 men over the age of 60. Members were elected to the council for life. Together, they made up the true governing body of Sparta.

Unlike the citizens of Athens, Spartans played little part in politics. Sparta did have an assembly made up of all free adult males, but it was much smaller than that of Athens. Only about 9,000 citizens sat in the Spartan assembly, whereas around 43,000 citizens belonged to the assembly in Athens.

The Spartan assembly also had far less power than did the Athenian assembly. It could pass laws, but only with the council's approval. However, it did have the power to elect five officials known as ephors. An **ephor** was an official who worked as a government watchdog. The ephors made sure that the kings and the council acted within the limits of Spartan law. Ephors could even remove a king who broke the law. Unlike a king, an ephor could serve for only one year.

**Life in Sparta**
This image shows how Sparta may have appeared in ancient times. **Critical Thinking: Distinguish Verifiable Information** *How might a modern artist verify information shown in an image such as this? What information might be left to the artist's interpretation?*

**Spartan Conquests** Athens turned to trade to solve its population problems. Sparta turned to conquest. After conquering a region, the Spartans took over its farmland to raise food for themselves.

In one region, Messenia, the Spartans took a more extreme approach. They forced most of the local population to become agricultural slaves, called helots. The helots did not belong to individual owners. Instead, they belonged to Sparta as a whole. They were forced to farm the land and turn over half the food they raised to Sparta.

At first, this solution to the population problem seemed to work well for Sparta. The helots produced enough food to support the Spartans. As a result, citizens of Sparta could lead comfortable lives, without having to work for a living.

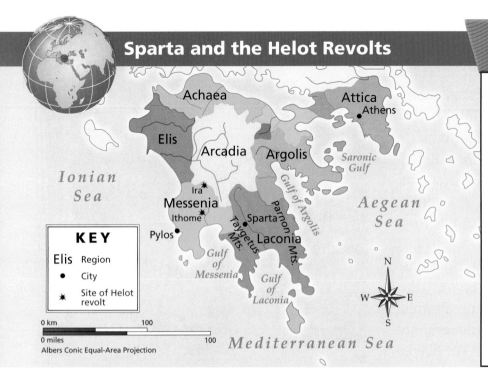

**MAP MASTER™**
*Skills Activity*

After conquering the neighboring region of Messenia, Sparta faced revolts from the enslaved helot population.

**(a) Locate** What was one location at which the helots staged a revolt?

**(b) Draw Conclusions** Why might Messenia's location have made it a valuable region for Sparta to conquer?

**MapMaster ⬤nline**

**For:** Interactive map
**Visit:** PHSchool.com
**Web Code:** mwp-5143

**Helot Revolts** As enslaved workers, the helots had no legal rights. They were expected to work hard for the Spartans. Yet, they received very little in return, often barely enough to survive.

Eventually, the helots rose up against the Spartans. In the early 600s B.C., they launched a series of violent revolts that lasted for years. Although the Spartans managed to put down the revolts, they lived in fear of further unrest. The helots outnumbered them by as many as ten to one. The Spartans feared that, given the chance, the helots would surely rise up against them once again.

The Spartans faced a difficult choice. They could give up control of the helots and the food they produced, or they could strengthen their control by turning Sparta into a military state. A **military state** is a state that is organized primarily for the purpose of waging war.

The Spartans chose the second option. Every year, the ephors declared war on the helots. This gave Spartans the right to kill any helot without fear of punishment. At the same time, the Spartans formed a secret police force to watch over the helots. The helots were forced to wear dog-skin caps to mark their low status. Helots who protested such treatment might be subject to beatings or even harsher punishments.

**Checkpoint** Why did Sparta feel it was necessary to conquer other regions?

# A Disciplined Society

The Spartans firmly believed in the rule of law. Because of their history of conquest and their need to control the helots, they believed just as firmly in military discipline. They organized their society along military lines. Their society held no place for the arts, literature, or luxury goods. Even today, the word Spartan means highly disciplined or lacking in comfort.

**Spartan Education** From an early age, Spartan males trained for military service. At seven, they were taken away from their homes for schooling at state expense. They lived in **barracks, or military housing,** with other young boys.

Unlike students in Athens, Spartan boys did not receive a well-rounded education. They spent most of their time exercising, hunting, and training with weapons. They were not taught to think for themselves, but rather to obey orders. The later Greek scholar Plutarch wrote of the Spartans:

> **❝They learned to read and write for purely practical reasons. But all other forms of education they banned from the country. . . . All their education was directed toward prompt obedience to authority, stout endurance of hardship, and victory or death in battle.❞**
>
> —Plutarch, *The Ancient Customs of the Spartans*

Students were not given enough to eat so that they would learn to steal food while marching as soldiers. To be caught stealing, however, led to punishment and disgrace. A famous Spartan story tells of a boy who stole a fox and then hid it under his clothing when he was discovered. Rather than confess, the boy kept the fox hidden while it clawed him to death.

At the age of 18, young men began a two-year program of military training to become part of a phalanx. During this time, the trainees were allowed to marry. But they were given little time with their wives. After graduating, they spent the next ten years living in barracks as members of a military unit.

**Main Idea**
Spartans lived in a rigid society based on military discipline.

**E-LA 6.2.2 Analyze Comparisons and Contrasts**

How were Athenian education and Spartan education alike? How were they different?

**Spartan Warriors**
The bronze statue pictured above may have been a representation of a Spartan soldier.
**Critical Thinking: Apply Information**
*What features of this statue suggest that the artist valued military discipline and strength?*

## Governments of Athens and Sparta

### Athens
- Large assembly as main political body
- Members of council chosen at random to serve one-year terms
- Courts run by large citizen juries

(overlap)
- Assemblies made up of free adult males
- Governments included smaller councils

### Sparta
- Government led by two kings
- Smaller and less powerful assembly than in Athens
- Council members elected for life
- Ephors monitored kings and council

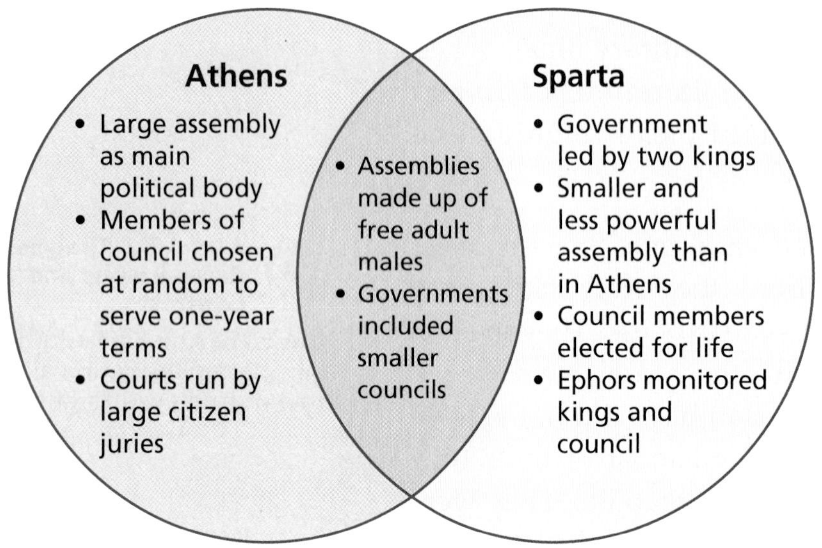

**Reading Diagrams**

This Venn diagram shows important similarities and differences between the governments of Athens and Sparta.

(a) **Read a Diagram** What was one characteristic shared by both governments?

(b) **Organize Information** How might you organize an essay that presented the information contained in this diagram?

**Equals and Inferiors** At age 30, Spartan men left the army, but they soon faced another test. In order to become full citizens, they had to gain entry to a men's club of former soldiers. If they failed, they became "inferiors" who would never gain citizenship and would live as outcasts from society.

Former soldiers who won election to a men's club became known as "equals." An equal received full citizen rights. This included membership in the assembly and the right to a piece of state-owned land worked by helots. At age 60, an equal became a candidate for election to the council of elders.

**Spartan Women** Life proved almost as disciplined for Spartan women. Like men, women were expected to be strong and vigorous. They were encouraged to stay fit so that they could have healthy babies who would make good soldiers. Sickly babies were not accepted in this society. The government ordered that they be <u>abandoned</u> on hillsides to die.

Spartan women had a good deal of freedom and responsibility. With their husbands often away at military camp, wives had control over their households. They were <u>obliged</u> to raise their children according to Spartan values. By doing so, they gained rights that other women in Greece did not have.

**Vocabulary** *Builder*
<u>abandon</u> (uh BAN duhn) *v.* to leave, as in danger, out of necessity; desert

**Vocabulary** *Builder*
<u>oblige</u> (uh BLĪJ) *v.* to compel by moral, legal, or physical force; constrain

**Fear of Change** All of the discipline and training in Spartan life helped create a powerful army and a stable government. But it also produced a society that feared change. The Spartans valued people who fit in, rather than those who stood out. Individual skills and talents held less importance than membership in a group.

Unlike the Spartans, the Athenians valued individual expression and new ideas. As a result, Athens was open to growth and change. Athenian democracy evolved over time. Sparta's rigid oligarchy and society changed very little. These differences led the Greek historian Thucydides to describe Athenians as "addicted to innovation." In contrast, he viewed the Spartans as "having a genius for keeping what you have got."

 **Checkpoint** How did Sparta's rigid society affect the lives of women?

**Looking Back and Ahead** In this section, you have learned that Sparta created an oligarchy with a strong military foundation. You also learned that the Spartans were highly disciplined and fearful of change. In the next chapter, you will read about Greek religion, culture, and thought.

## Section 3 Check Your Progress

**Progress Monitoring Online**
**For:** Self-test with instant help
**Visit:** PHSchool.com
**Web Code:** mwa-5143

**Standards Review** H-SS: 6.4.6; E-LA: Reading 6.2.2

### Comprehension and Critical Thinking

1. **(a) Recall** Who were the helots, and what region did they inhabit?
   **(b) Evaluate Information** How did the status of the helots reflect the values of Spartan society?

2. **(a) Describe** How was Spartan society organized?
   **(b) Draw Conclusions** How might such an organization increase citizens' loyalty to Sparta?

### Reading Skill

3. **Analyze Comparison and Contrast Structures** Review the text below the heading Fear of Change, on page 405. How does this text present its comparisons and contrasts of Athenian and Spartan society?

### Vocabulary Builder

4. Write two definitions for each word: ephor, military state, barracks. First write a formal definition for your teacher. Second, write a definition in everyday English for a classmate.

### Writing

5. Explain how you might construct a strong opening paragraph for an essay on life in ancient Spartan society. You may describe your thesis statement and identify some of the important themes to which your paragraph would refer.

# Analysis Skills: Distinguish Relevant From Irrelevant Information

Our world is filled with many different types of information. As a result, when you want to learn about one particular topic, you must narrow your focus. Search only for the information that is *relevant*, or directly related, to your topic.

**Chapter Standards**

**History-Social Science**

**Research, Evidence, and Point of View 3** Students distinguish relevant from irrelevant information, essential from incidental information, and verifiable from unverifiable information in historical narratives and stories.

> **❝**Pericles was born into the best families of Athens, both on his father's and mother's side. He received a good education from his teachers, including the philosopher Zeno. . . . One day, Pericles was in the marketplace of Athens doing business. All day long some noisy pest followed him around, yelling at him and calling him names. He even followed Pericles home. Throughout this ordeal, Pericles stayed calm. It was dark by the time Pericles arrived home. So he gave orders for one of his servants to take a torch and guide this pest safely back to wherever he lived. Some people said that Pericles was only trying to fool the public with a false front of virtue. But Zeno replied that if Pericles were faking virtue, they should do the same.**❞**
>
> —from Plutarch's *Lives*

**Learn the Skill** *Follow these steps to distinguish relevant from irrelevant information.*

1. **Identify your focus or topic.** By clearly defining your topic, you can better determine which pieces of information will be relevant or irrelevant.

2. **Locate sources and read about the topic.** Based on the topic you identified, select a number of sources that will likely offer information on this topic. You may find sources online or in your school's media center.

3. **Identify the information that is relevant to your topic.** Scan your sources to find passages that may relate to your topic. Then, read these passages closely to determine whether or not they provide relevant information.

4. **Identify the information that is irrelevant to your topic.** Irrelevant information, such as anecdotes, may be interesting, but it is not central to the topic.

**Practice the Skill** *Answer the following questions about the passage above.*

1. **Identify your focus or topic.** What types of information would you look for to prepare a report about Pericles' character?

2. **Locate sources and read about the topic.** (a) What is the source of the passage above? (b) What other types of sources might offer relevant information about the topic above?

3. **Identify the information that is relevant to your topic.** (a) What is one piece of relevant information found in this passage? (b) What does this information tell you about Pericles' character?

4. **Identify the information that is irrelevant to your topic.** Give one detail from the passage that is irrelevant to the topic.

**Apply the Skill**
*See page 409 of the Review and Assessment.*

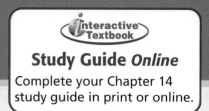

**Study Guide** *Online*
Complete your Chapter 14
study guide in print or online.

## Chapter Summary  H-SS: 6.4.2, 6.4.3, 6.4.6

### Section 1 Political Changes in Greece

- Early Greek city-states were often controlled by governments called oligarchies, in which small groups of aristocrats held power.

- Tyrannies, or governments run by one strong ruler, replaced some Greek oligarchies.

- In Athens, citizens began to take a more active role in government, as the city-state moved toward democracy.

### Section 2 Democracy in Athens

- Leaders such as Cleisthenes and Pericles carried out reforms that aided the development of Athenian democracy.

- Athens' democratic government included a large assembly, a 500-member council, and a court system with citizen juries.

- Athens used a system of government called direct democracy, in which citizens take part directly in government decision making.

### Section 3 Oligarchy in Sparta

- The city-state Sparta featured an oligarchical government led by two kings.

- To overcome their population problems, Spartans carried out conquests of areas such as Messenia.

- The society of Sparta was based on military discipline and did not value growth and change.

**Greek voting tablet**

## Standards Practice  H-SS: 6.4.2, 6.4.3, 6.4.6

## Vocabulary *Builder*

### High-Use Words

Read each sentence below. If the sentence is true, write YES. If the sentence is not true, write NO and explain WHY.

1. The government of Athens was **eventually** an oligarchy, before later becoming a democracy.

2. Solon **granted** new rights to citizens of Athens.

3. Spartan families were ordered to **abandon** sickly babies.

4. Women in Sparta were **obliged** to act with complete freedom from Spartan rules and values.

### Key Terms

Answer the following questions in complete sentences that show your understanding of the Key Terms.

1. What segment of Greek society held power in an oligarchy?

2. Why did many tyrannies last for only a short time?

3. What led Athens to begin moving toward democracy?

4. How did juries take part in the government of Athens?

##  Apply Reading Skills

**Analyze Comparisons and Contrasts** Refer back to the title of this chapter. Then, review the structure and organization of the chapter and its three sections. How does the chapter organize its comparisons and contrasts of the societies of ancient Athens and Sparta?

## Comprehension and Critical Thinking

1. **(a) List** What were the three major forms of government in ancient Greek city-states?
   **(b) Analyze Cause and Effect** How did military developments in ancient Greece cause ordinary citizens to gain more rights?
   **(c) Draw Conclusions** Which system of government do you think gave citizens the best opportunities to improve their lives? Explain.

2. **(a) Recall** What was the main political body in Athens' government?
   **(b) Evaluate Information** How did this body represent the Athenian system of direct democracy?
   **(c) Clarify Problems** What types of problems do you think might arise in such a political body?

3. **(a) Recall** Which group rose up against Spartan rule in the early 600s B.C.?
   **(b) Identify Alternatives** What were the Spartans' options for responding to this situation?
   **(c) Identify Costs** How did the outcome of these events affect the way Sparta was governed?

4. **(a) Summarize** How did Spartan education prepare boys for life in Spartan society?
   **(b) Contrast** In what ways did the lives of men and women in Sparta differ?

## Researching

**The Growth of Democracy** In the late 500s B.C., democracy began to develop in the city-state of Athens. As a result, Athens is sometimes called the birthplace of democracy. In this activity, you will use the library media center to research and report on the growth of Athenian democracy. Choose a task below to work on. When you are done, share your work with the class. Make a list of the resources you used to go with your presentation.

**Government Official:** Suppose that you have just been chosen to serve as a member of Athens' 500-member council. Write a journal entry in which you describe the responsibilities and activities of your new position.

**Economist:** Several economic factors proved important to the growth of democracy in Athens. Make a flowchart that identifies some of these important factors and shows how they affected Athens' democratic government.

> **Researching Online**
> **For:** Help in starting this activity
> **Visit:** PHSchool.com
> **Web Code:** mwe-5143

## Writing

1. **Write a paragraph on the following topic.** The city-states of Athens and Sparta had different forms of government and different sets of values underlying their societies.
   **Your paragraph should:**
   - contain a clear topic sentence.
   - support you explanation with accurate evidence.
   - use clear transition words.

2. **Write a short narrative.** Suppose you were selected to serve on a jury in ancient Athens. Briefly describe your experience in court.

# Apply Analysis Skills

Suppose you have been instructed to write an essay on the following topic: How did citizens take part in Athens' government? Use the text at right to respond to the following items.

1. What is the focus of this passage?

2. In what source might you find such information?

3. What is one detail from the passage that would be relevant to the topic above?

4. Identify one piece of information from the passage that is irrelevant to your topic.

> ❝Athens' government required its citizens to take an active role in civic affairs. All free adult male citizens were called upon to attend meetings of the assembly. In some ways, this body functioned like the United States' Congress of today. Athenians also served in the council and sat on juries. The United States government of today does not have a body exactly like Athens' council. Athenian juries were much larger than those we find in today's courtrooms.❞

# Test Yourself

1. The Greek city-state form of government evolved from oligarchy to tyranny to
   A empire.
   B federalism.
   C democracy.
   D military rule.

Refer to the quotation below to answer Question 2.

2. This quotation suggests that a citizen is someone who

> *"We do not say that a man who takes no interest in politics is a man who minds his own business. We say he has no business here at all."*

   A immigrates from another country.
   B is not entitled to a free public education.
   C must be employed in order to vote.
   D has responsibilities within a political community.

3. Athenian society was innovative, whereas Spartan society was
   A free.
   B rigid.
   C creative.
   D democratic.

Refer to the image below to answer Question 4.
4. This image shows a modern example of which part of the government of Athens?

   A phalanx
   B jury
   C ephors
   D assembly

5. Who wrote a code of law that treated the poor very harshly?
   A Draco
   B Solon
   C Pericles
   D Cleisthenes

# 15

# Greek Religion, Arts, and Learning (700 B.C.–300 B.C.)

## Prepare to Read

### Chapter Standards

**History-Social Science**
**6.4** Students analyze the geographic, political, economic, religious, and social structures of the early civilizations of Ancient Greece.

**Section 1,** pp. 414–419

### Greek Mythology and Religion

**What You Will Learn**

The religious practices of the people of ancient Greece were based on legends and stories of their past and the epics of Homer. They honored their gods in many ways during the course of everyday life.

**Section 2,** pp. 422–427

### Greek Art and Literature

The Greeks made important artistic contributions in fields such as architecture, sculpture, and literature.

**Section 3,** pp. 428–433

### Greek Learning

Ancient Greek scholars helped develop many important areas of study, such as philosophy, history, science, mathematics, and medicine. Many of their ideas are still important today.

Greek theater mask

**700s B.C.**
Homer writes the
*Iliad* and *Odyssey.*

**Chapter Events**

**750 B.C.**

**600 B.C.**

**450 B.C.**

**Other Events**

**700s B.C.** Piye invades Hermopolis.

**587 B.C.** Nebuchadnezzar's armies destroy Jerusalem.

The large Greek statues shown here are part of the Acropolis in Athens.

**400s B.C.**
The Parthenon is built in Athens.

**399 B.C.**
Socrates is sentenced to death.

**About 300 B.C.**
Euclid writes about geometry in his book *Elements.*

**450 B.C.**

**300 B.C.**

**150 B.C.**

**272 B.C.** Asoka becomes India's third Mauryan emperor.

**206 B.C.** The Han Dynasty of China is founded.

# How to Read History

## History Reading Skill

### *Previewing* Figurative Language and Words With Multiple Meanings

When you read, you will often encounter words that have more than one meaning. At times, words may also be given figurative meanings, or meanings different from their dictionary definitions. Use strategies such as those outlined below to help you correctly define these types of words.

**Chapter Standards**

**English-Language Arts**

**Reading 6.1.2** Identify and interpret figurative language and words with multiple meanings.

---

**❶** Read the sentence in which the word appears. What can you learn about how the word is used?

Soon, **plays** became a *central activity at festivals.*

> Here the word *plays* refers to stories acted on a stage. That is different from the way the word is used in the following sentence.

The Greek child **plays** *games with her friends.*

> The word *plays* now refers to taking part in an activity that you enjoy.

Knowledge of the different meanings of a word and context clues can help you identify how a word is used.

---

**❷** Sometimes figurative language can be used to help determine the meaning of a word.

The **polis** was the framework of Greek life.

> The meaning of the familiar words can help you figure out the meaning of the unfamiliar word. You can determine that polis (a city state) was the center or main focus (framework) of the social structure of ancient Greece.

# Vocabulary *Builder*

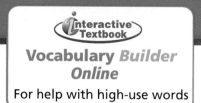
## *Previewing* High-Use Academic Words

| High-Use Word | Definition | Sample Sentence About History |
|---|---|---|
| **supreme** (suh PREEM) (Section 1, p. 415) | *adj.* highest in rank, power, or authority; dominant | The <u>supreme</u> ruler became the most powerful person in the nation. |
| **feature** (FEE cher) (Section 1, p. 418) | *n.* distinct or outstanding part, quality, or characteristic of something | Ancestor worship was an important <u>feature</u> of ancient Chinese religion. |
| **individual** (ihn duh VIHJ oo uhl) (Section 2, p. 425) | *adj.* existing as a single, separate thing or being | An <u>individual</u> ruler stood at the top of Egyptian society. |
| **culture** (KUHL cher) (Section 2, p. 426) | *n.* ideas, customs, skills, or arts of a people or group that are passed along through generations | Literature and the arts played an important role in the <u>culture</u> of the ancient Chinese. |
| **method** (MEHTH uhd) (Section 3, p. 429) | *n.* way of doing anything; procedure or process | Ancient scholars developed a <u>method</u> for studying the natural world. |
| **foundation** (fown DAY shuhn) (Section 3, p. 431) | *n.* fundamental principle on which something is founded; basis | The teachings of the Budda were the <u>foundation</u> of Buddhism. |

## *Previewing* Key Terms and People

**Aristotle**

deity, p. 414
muse, p. 416
mythology, p. 416
Homer, p. 417
Odysseus, p. 417

oracle, p. 419
frieze, p. 424
pediment, p. 424
lyric poetry, p. 425
chorus, p. 425

Sappho, p. 425
drama, p. 425
Sophocles, p. 426
Aesop, p. 426
reason, p. 429

logic, p. 429
Plato, p. 429
academy, p. 429
Thucydides, p. 430
Aristotle, p. 432

### Standards Preview

**H-SS 6.4.4** Explain the significance of Greek mythology to the everyday life of people in the region and how Greek literature continues to permeate our literature and language today, drawing from Greek mythology and epics, such as Homer's *Iliad* and *Odyssey*, and from *Aesop's Fables.*

**E-LA Reading 6.1.2** Identify and interpret figurative language and words with multiple meanings.

## Reading Preview

### Reading Skill

**Identify Words With Multiple Meanings** When you read a word that has multiple meanings, think of all the definitions you know for it. What do they tell you about the word? Then use context for clues to choose the correct meaning.

### Vocabulary *Builder*

**High-Use Words**
supreme (suh PREEM), p. 415
feature (FEE cher), p. 418

**Key Terms and People**
deity (DEE uh tee), p. 414
muse (myooz), p. 416
mythology (mih THAHL uh jee), p. 416
Homer (HOH muhr), p. 417
Odysseus (oh DIHS ee uhs), p. 417
oracle (OR uh kuhl), p. 419

**Background Knowledge** The ancient Greeks never became unified into one state. They lived apart from one another in small city-states and colonies. They did, however, become united by their language, religion, and traditional stories. In this chapter, you will learn about the significance of Greek religion and stories about gods and history.

## Greek Religious Beliefs

**Main Idea**
Ancient Greek religious practices had a basis in Greek mythology and reflected a belief in many gods.

In some ways, Greek religious practices were similar to those found in other ancient cultures. The Greeks were polytheists who believed in many gods, or deities. A deity is a being with supernatural powers. Like other agricultural peoples, the Greeks believed that gods and spirits were at work all around them.

Unlike the gods of Egypt or India, however, the Greek deities looked like ordinary people. Greek gods did not take the forms of animals or beings with many heads or arms. Most Greek deities looked like attractive, athletic men or women.

**The Gods of Mount Olympus**  The Greeks believed that their major gods lived on Mount Olympus, a mountain in northern Greece. Zeus was the <u>supreme</u> ruler of the gods, as well as the lord of the sky and the god of rain. He threw his main weapon, a thunderbolt, at those who displeased him. His wife, Hera, protected married women and their households.

Zeus had two brothers. The first, Poseidon, was the god of the sea. A quarrelsome god, when he was angry Poseidon could make the earth shake and the seas churn. Zeus' second brother, Hades, ruled the underworld. Hades was a greedy god, always looking for more dead people to add to his domain.

Other major gods included Apollo, god of the arts, prophecy, and healing, and Ares, the god of war. Artemis had charge of the woods and hunting. Aphrodite was goddess of love and beauty, and Demeter oversaw farming and the harvest.

**Vocabulary** *Builder*
<u>supreme</u> (suh PREEM) *adj.* highest in rank, power, or authority; dominant

## Gods and Goddesses of Mount Olympus

| God or Goddess | Characteristics |
| --- | --- |
| Zeus | Ruler of the gods; lord of the sky and god of rain; husband of Hera |
| Hera | Protector of married women and their households; wife of Zeus |
| Poseidon | God of the sea; brother of Zeus |
| Hades | God of the underworld; brother of Zeus |
| Apollo | God of the arts and healing; twin brother of Artemis |
| Ares | God of war |
| Artemis | Goddess of the woods and hunting; twin sister of Apollo |
| Aphrodite | Goddess of love and beauty |
| Demeter | Goddess of farming and the harvest |
| Athena | Goddess of war, reason, and craft arts |

### Reading Charts

Ancient Greek writings described the god's home atop Mount Olympus as a place with clear, pure air, where storms never occurred.

**(a) Read a Chart**  Which goddess was the twin sister of Apollo?

**(b) Evaluate Information**  Why might the people of ancient Greece have viewed their many gods as having human characteristics?

Athena was a favorite deity of many Greeks. According to one myth, she gave the Greeks a very useful gift—the olive tree. She was the guardian of the city of Athens and a patron of crafts such as weaving and pottery. The Greeks believed that Athena often appeared to help them in times of war. She was fierce and brave in battle. But she would fight only to protect the Greek city-states from outside enemies.

Minor gods were believed to live on Olympus as well. One was Eros, god of love. Others included the Muses, a group of nine sisters. They inspired poets, historians, scientists, and musicians. Today, the word **muse** is often used to refer to the inspiration for a creative artist. The word *museum* originally meant "the place of the Muses."

**E-LA 6.1.2 Identify Words with Multiple Meanings**

*Minor* can mean both "less important" and "under the age of legal adulthood." Which meaning is used in this paragraph?

### Greek Mythology
The Greeks created no Bible or Vedas to explain their religion. Instead, they based most of their religious beliefs on their mythology. **Mythology is the collection of stories that people tell about their history and their gods.**

The Greeks used mythology to answer questions about the world around them. Some myths explained the changing of the seasons. Others explained why so much trouble existed in the world. Still others tried to explain human behavior.

Greek mythology also included stories about heroes. One such story told of a hero named Hercules. He was famous for his amazing strength and courage. Like many characters in Greek myths, Hercules was only half human. His mother was human, but his father was Zeus. However, being Zeus' son did not protect Hercules from suffering. According to the myths, Zeus' jealous wife, Hera, cast a spell on Hercules that drove him mad and made him kill his beloved wife and sons.

In Greek mythology, gods and goddesses behaved very much like ordinary people. They fell in love, got married, and had children. They liked to celebrate and play tricks. They also grew jealous and became angry. As a result, these deities seemed very real to the Greeks.

**Statue of Hercules**
This bronze statue shows the mythological Greek hero, Hercules. **Critical Thinking: Evaluate Information** *What features of this statue suggest that Hercules was a figure of great strength?*

**Homer's Epics** Two great epic poems provided another source of Greek religious beliefs. As you read in Chapter 12, the *Iliad* and the *Odyssey* told stories of ancient times. They were the work of the poet Homer, who lived in the eighth century B.C., although the stories themselves were much older.

Homer's stories may have been based on real events. Mycenaean Greeks and Trojans may have gone to war over land or trade. To later Greeks, however, what really happened was less important than what Homer imagined might have happened.

Earlier stories had stated that the Trojan War began with a quarrel among Hera, Athena, and Aphrodite over who was the most beautiful. In both the *Iliad* and *Odyssey*, the gods often took part in human affairs. During the war, some gods sided with the Greeks, others with the Trojans. After the war, different gods often influenced the fate of Odysseus and his companions.

Homer's epics reflected the Greeks' belief that the gods controlled much of their lives, while also portraying human characters such as Odysseus as crafty and intelligent. As Odysseus says in the *Odyssey*:

**Odysseus and the Sirens**
This image shows an episode from Homer's *Odyssey*, in which Odysseus avoids the call of the Sirens, who tried to lure sailors' ships to danger with their singing. **Critical Thinking: Draw Inferences** *Why might artists have chosen to show scenes from Homer's work in their art?*

**❝Of all creatures that breathe and walk on the earth there is nothing more helpless than a man. . . .
   For he thinks that he will never suffer misfortune in future days, while the gods grant him courage, and his knees have spring in them. But when the blessed gods bring sad days upon him, against his will he must suffer it with enduring spirit.❞**

—Homer, *Odyssey*

**Checkpoint** **What were the two main sources of Greek religious beliefs?**

# Religion in Everyday Life

Greek myths and Homer's epics shaped the Greeks' identity—their idea of what it meant to be Greek. They saw little separation between the gods' lives and their own. As a result, public and private religious rituals were part of everyday life. Families had household shrines. Public meetings began with prayers and animal sacrifices. Although women did not participate in the government of the polis, their participation in its religious ceremonies was essential.

**Main Idea**
Religious practices such as visiting temples and holding festivals and games were an important part of ancient Greeks' everyday lives.

Each city-state built temples to its favorite deities. At specific times, citizens made sacrifices to those gods in front of their temples. People offered gold, cakes and wine, or prized animals such as bulls. They asked the gods for favors, such as good crops or good health.

**Festivals and Games** Greeks also honored the gods publicly with festivals and games. Poets and musicians competed to offer the best songs. Later, as you will read in Section 2, writers presented their best plays.

Athletic contests were sometimes a <u>feature</u> of religious rituals. Athletes dedicated their skill and strength to the gods. They competed in boxing, wrestling, and running and threw the javelin and discus. They also took part in chariot and horse races.

The leading competitions brought together athletes from many city-states. City-states at war would stop fighting during the games. The most famous competitions were the Olympic games, which honored Zeus. These games took place every four years at Olympia. A huge gold and ivory statue of Zeus stood in a temple at the Olympic site. Archaeologists have found the ruins of the temple, as well as a large stadium there.

Winners in the games were given a wreath of leaves. Like modern athletes, winners became heroes to many ordinary citizens in Greece. Often, wealthy aristocrats supported these athletes. In addition, cities awarded valuable gifts to their winning athletes. Athens and other cities even gave Olympic winners free meals for life.

**Sacred Places** Because many people believed that the gods lived in Greece, they considered many places in the landscape to be sacred. Groves of trees, springs, and other places were thought to be home to various gods and spirits. The Muses, for example, had several favorite mountains.

**Vocabulary** *Builder*

<u>feature</u> (FEE cher) *n.* distinct or outstanding part, quality, or characteristic of something

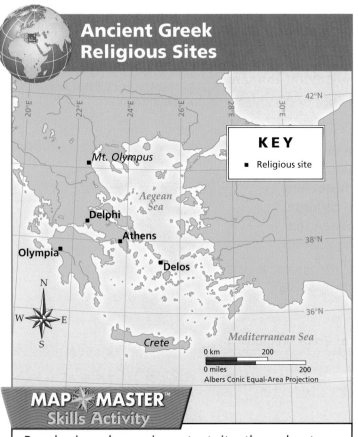

**Ancient Greek Religious Sites**

**KEY**

■ Religious site

**MAP★MASTER**
*Skills Activity*

People viewed many important sites throughout Greece as sacred.

**(a) Locate** Which of the religious sites shown on the map was located the farthest north?

**(b) Compare** What similarities can you draw between the locations of two or more of the religious sites shown?

**MapMaster** ⬤nline

**For:** Interactive map
**Visit:** PHSchool.com
**Web Code:** mwp-5151

A great temple to Apollo stood at Delphi, a religious center on Mount Parnassus. The Greeks believed that a priestess known as the Delphic oracle lived there. An **oracle** is a person who predicts what will happen in the future. People traveled to Delphi from all over Greece to ask the priestess questions about the future. The oracle was famous for answering with puzzling statements that could be interpreted in several ways.

The tourists who visit Delphi today no longer come looking for an oracle. The Greek religion died out long ago, but the myths and epics inspired by those ancient beliefs are still read today. Books and movies often borrow plots from Greek myths. The reason is simple. Religious ideas have changed since the days of ancient Greece, but good stories will always hold people's interest.

 **Checkpoint** What part did athletic games play in Greek religion?

**Looking Back and Ahead** In this section, you have learned about the gods of ancient Greece, as well as the significance of mythology and Homer's epics in Greek life. In the next section, you will read about the arts of ancient Greece.

## Section 1 Check Your Progress

**Progress Monitoring** Online
**For:** Self-test with instant help
**Visit:** PHSchool.com
**Web Code:** mwa-5151

**Standards Review** H-SS: 6.4.4; E-LA: Reading 6.1.2

### Comprehension and Critical Thinking

**1. (a) List** Name and describe the qualities of three major Greek gods or goddesses.
**(b) Compare and Contrast** How did the gods of Greek mythology resemble those of other ancient peoples? How did they differ?

**2. (a) Recall** What types of activities took place during Greek religious festivals?
**(b) Draw Inferences** What do those activities suggest about the Greeks' attitudes toward their gods?

### Reading Skill

**3. Identify Words with Multiple Meanings** Read the following sentence: "They asked the gods for favors, such as good crops or good health." Which word has multiple meanings? Explain which meaning applies to this sentence.

### Vocabulary *Builder*

Read each sentence below. If the sentence is true, write YES. If the sentence is not true, write NO and explain WHY.

**4.** The ancient Greeks believed that Eros was the supreme ruler of the gods.

**5.** Stories about heroes were an important feature of Greek mythology.

### Writing

**6.** Make a list of important ideas that you might include in an opening paragraph for an essay on ancient Greek religious beliefs.

## Literature

# Arachne
by Alice Low (born in 1926)

## Prepare to Read

### Standards Preview

**H-SS 6.4.4** Explain the significance of Greek mythology to the everyday life of people in the region and how Greek literature continues to permeate our literature and language today, drawing from Greek mythology and epics, such as Homer's *Iliad* and *Odyssey*, and from *Aesop's Fables*.

**E-LA Reading 6.3.6** Identify and analyze features of themes conveyed through characters, actions, and images.

## Reading Skill

**Analyze Theme** In a story, the characters' traits and their actions often provide clues to the *theme*, or message, of the work. For example, when a villain in a story commits a crime and is caught, the theme might be "crime does not pay." As you read the myth, look for the theme suggested by the characters and their actions.

## Vocabulary *Builder*

As you read this literature selection, look for the following underlined words:

**conceited** (kuhn SEET ihd) *adj.* showing too much pride in your abilities, appearance, etc.

**impious** (IHM pee uhs) *adj.* lacking respect, especially for gods or sacred things

**pitied** (PIHT eed) *v.* felt sorry for

**BACKGROUND**

The goddess Athena taught women the art of spinning and weaving. One day she heard that a mortal named Arachne thought her own weaving was superior to Athena's. Furious, Athena set off to visit Arachne.

**Athena changes Arachne into a spider.**

Athena flew down to earth disguised as an old woman. She went to Arachne's hut, where wood nymphs were watching in wonder as Arachne wove an intricate pattern out of rainbow-colored threads. "I warn you," Athena said to Arachne. "Do not dare to compete with a goddess. Indeed, I advise you to ask Athena's pardon for what you said."

But Arachne said to the old woman, "I *am* the finest weaver in the world. Everybody knows that. If Athena does not believe it, let her come here and have a weaving contest with me. I am not afraid of her."

Then Athena revealed herself as a shining goddess and said, "I am Athena, and I accept your challenge. Let us begin."

Arachne paled, but she did not back down, so certain was she of her talents.

Athena and Arachne set up their looms and went to work, using every shade of every color thread, and gold and silver threads, as well. They both wove so quickly and skillfully that their shuttles seemed to fly, in and out, up and down, back and forth. The wood nymphs ran from one weaver to the other, exclaiming over the beautiful work of each.

Athena wove into her cloth scenes showing the powerful gods displeased with mortals who had challenged them. *This is a further warning to that <u>conceited</u> Arachne!* she said to herself. *If she does not give up, she will be sorry!*

But Arachne was lost in her own weaving and did not even notice her rival's work. Furthermore, Arachne chose to weave scenes that showed the gods' weaknesses, such as Zeus turning himself into a bull and carrying off Europa. When Athena saw these scenes she was outraged, not only because they showed the gods in a poor light, but also because Arachne's woven web was every bit as fine as hers.

*I'll not be outdone by a mere mortal,* thought Athena, *and a bold, <u>impious</u> one at that!* And she took her shuttle and slashed Arachne's web to shreds. Then Athena touched Arachne's forehead, causing Arachne to feel guilty and ashamed.

Arachne felt so guilty and ashamed that she made a noose out of one of her strongest threads. Then she hanged herself with it.

When Athena saw poor Arachne hanging there, she <u>pitied</u> her a little. She sprinkled her with a magic liquid and said, "You shall not die, Arachne. Instead you shall be changed into a spider, hanging by a thread and weaving your web forever."

And Arachne shrank into a tiny spider. First her nose and ears fell off, and then her fingers turned into legs. What was left of her became her body, out of which she spins and spins the thread for her web.

—From *Greek Gods and Heroes,* by Alice Low.
©1995, MacMillan Publishing Company.

✔ **Checkpoint**  **What did Arachne say and do that angered Athena?**

**BACKGROUND**

In Greek mythology, Zeus fell in love often. He sometimes used tricks to catch the women he was interested in. In one story, he turned himself into a bull and flew away with the surprised Europa on his back.

**E-LA 3.6  Analyze Theme**

Reading Skill  Think about Arachne's words and actions at the beginning of the story. What would you say is her strongest character trait? Based on that information, what do you think is the message, or theme of the myth?

## Analyze LITERATURE

Greek myths often explained things in nature. This myth about Arachne explains why spiders weave webs. Think about other animals that do unusual things. Choose one such animal, and brainstorm an idea for a myth that explains this trait or behavior. Write a paragraph that details your idea.

If you liked this story about Arachne, you might want to read other Greek myths in *D'Aulaire's Book of Greek Myths* by Ingri D'Aulaire and Edgar Parin D'Aulaire. *Yearling Books, 1992*

# Section 2
# Greek Art and Literature

## Standards Preview

**H-SS 6.4.8** Describe the enduring contributions of important Greek figures in the arts and sciences (e.g., Hypatia, Socrates, Plato, Aristotle, Euclid, Thucydides).

**E-LA Reading 6.1.2** Identify and interpret figurative language and words with multiple meanings.

## Reading Preview

### Reading Skill

**Interpret Figurative Language** Figurative language can help paint a picture for readers by using one idea to stand for another. For example, the sentence "My mind wandered," uses the picture of one's mind moving slowly without a purpose to convey the idea that the speaker did not concentrate on something. Examine such language as you find it in the text.

### Vocabulary *Builder*

**High-Use Words**
individual (ihn duh VIHJ oo uhl), p. 425
culture (KUHL cher), p. 426

**Key Terms and People**
frieze (freez), p. 424
pediment (PEHD ih muhnt), p. 424
lyric poetry (LIHR ihk POH uh tree), p. 425
chorus (KOR uhs), p. 425
Sappho (SAF oh), p. 425
drama (DRAH muh), p. 425
Sophocles (SAHF uh kleez), p. 426
Aesop (EE suhp), p. 426

**Background Knowledge** The Greeks appreciated beautiful things. They also believed that anything worth doing was worth doing well. In this section, you will read about the enduring contributions the Greeks made in the arts and literature.

**Main Idea**
Ancient Greeks made many lasting contributions to arts such as sculpture and architecture.

## Art and Architecture

The Greeks were highly skilled in many arts. Whether making a pot, carving a statue, or designing a temple, they created works that have been admired for generations.

**Painted Pottery** The ancient Greeks became famous for their beautiful painted pottery. Greek potters made vases, drinking cups, jars, and bowls in many graceful shapes. People used some of these vessels at home to store wine, water, oil, and perfume. Other vessels served mainly as decoration. For example, winning athletes often received fine painted vases as prizes.

Greek artists developed two main techniques of vase painting known as "black figure" and "red figure" painting. These terms refer to the colors of the figures on a painted vase, in contrast with the background. The paintings on vases often showed scenes from myths or from Homer's epics. Other paintings showed scenes from Greek life, such as warriors fighting battles or people playing games.

**Sculpture**   The Greeks were also expert at sculpture. Huge statues of gods and goddesses stood in shrines and temples. Carved scenes decorated temple walls. Sculptors created such works for public display and to pay tribute to the gods.

The main subject of Greek sculpture was the human figure. "The world is full of wonders," said the writer Sophocles, "but nothing is more wonderful than man." To the Greeks, nothing had more beauty than a strong, athletic human body. Sculptors tried to show that ideal of beauty in their statues of both gods and humans. The perfect beauty of classic Greek sculpture has inspired artists for centuries.

**Ancient Greek Arts**
The ancient Greek vase (left) uses "black figure" painting to show a hunter carrying the animals he has caught. The Greek sculpture (right) shows Penelope, a character from the *Odyssey.* **Critical Thinking: Apply Information** *What makes these items good examples of Greek pottery and sculpture?*

**Influential Architecture**

The influence of Greek architecture, such as that of the Parthenon, can be seen in structures such as the United States Supreme Court building (right). **Critical Thinking: Apply Information** *What features of Greek architecture do these two buildings share?*

## Architecture

Greek architects also sought perfection in their work. The temples and public buildings they created are copied by architects to this day. Civic buildings, banks, and monuments all over the world show the influence of Greek architectural styles.

The most famous building of ancient Greece is the Parthenon. The Greeks built this temple to Athena more than 2,400 years ago. The architects Ictinus and Callicrates worked to design the structure. It stands on the Acropolis, the central hill of Athens. In ancient times, a huge gold and ivory statue of Athena stood inside the temple. It was made by Phidias, Greece's most famous sculptor.

In many ways, the Parthenon was typical of classical Greek architecture. Although made of stone, the building did not appear heavy. Graceful marble columns supported the roof. Above the columns, a carved **frieze, or horizontal band,** ran around the entire building. Carvings on the frieze told stories drawn from mythology. Other carvings decorated the **pediment, a triangular section that rose above the main entrance.**

People today think of Greek buildings and statues as dazzling white marble works of art. In ancient times, however, people painted these works in bright colors. Statues had red lips and hair and wore colorful clothing. Over time, those colors have faded and washed away.

 **Checkpoint** **What features were typical of classical Greek architecture?**

# Literature

Like the other arts, Greek literature was linked with religion. As you have read, religious festivals often included poetry and plays.

**Lyric Poetry**  The epic poems of Homer retold long stories. Later Greek poets wrote shorter poems. Performers often sang these poems while playing a stringed instrument known as a lyre. These poetic songs became known as **lyric poetry.** Lyric poems often expressed a personal viewpoint.

Lyric poetry was spoken or sung at religious festivals and weddings. One person might perform certain poems as a solo. Other poems were presented by a **chorus, or a group of people who sang and danced.** A chorus of young men or women represented the voice of the people praising the gods.

Greeks wrote lyric poetry on many different subjects. The poet Pindar, for example, wrote poems praising victorious athletes. The warrior Alcaeus wrote poems about politics and war. In contrast, Sappho wrote about human emotions, as in this verse:

> **Some say a host of horsemen is the most beautiful thing on the black earth, some say a host of foot-soldiers, some, a fleet of ships; but I say it is whatever one loves.**
>
> —Sappho, "To Anaktoria"

**Greek Drama**  Modern theater grew out of ancient Greek religious festivals. The word drama, which means a play or performance on stage, is a Greek word. The words *theater, tragedy, comedy,* and *scene* also come from the Greek language. Greek theaters like that on page 426 were built outdoors on hillsides. The audience sat on the slopes surrounding a flat, round stage.

Greek drama developed from choral performances honoring the god Dionysus. In those early plays, a few <u>individual</u> actors took on the roles of characters. The chorus made comments on the action and advised the characters. Wealthy citizens often funded the training and costumes of the chorus.

In time, plays became a central feature at festivals. At these events, prizes were awarded for the best play, the best chorus, and the best actor. Men portrayed all of the characters in Greek drama. They wore wigs and masks to play women's parts.

**Main Idea**
Greek literary works, including poems, plays, and fables, still influence writers to this day.

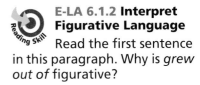

**E-LA 6.1.2 Interpret Figurative Language**  Read the first sentence in this paragraph. Why is *grew out of* figurative?

**Vocabulary** *Builder*
**individual** (ihn duh VIHJ oo uhl)
*adj.* existing as a single, separate thing or being

**Theater in Ancient Greece**

These images show a Greek theater and a mask worn by actors in an ancient drama. **Critical Thinking: Draw Inferences** *Why might Greek theaters such as this one have been built with steep rows facing a flat stage?*

**Vocabulary** *Builder*

<u>culture</u> (KUHL cher) *n.* ideas, customs, skills, or arts of a people or group that are passed along through generations

**Tragedy and Comedy** Greek dramatists wrote two types of plays: tragedy and comedy. The plot of a tragedy often came from mythology or Homer's poems. Tragedies often traced the downfall of heroic figures caught in violent conflict with their family, their city, or the gods. In the tragedy *Antigone* by **Sophocles,** the chorus gives this advice to the audience:

> **❝There is no happiness where there is no wisdom;**
> **No wisdom but in submission to the gods.**
> **Big words are always punished,**
> **And proud men in old age learn to be wise.❞**
>
> —Sophocles, *Antigone*

In contrast to tragedies, Greek comedies, or humorous plays, dealt with current events. They made humorous observations about Greek <u>culture</u>, society, and politicians. Comedies sometimes made serious points, such as protests against war. Aristophanes was perhaps the most famous comic playwright. Two of his comedies, *The Frogs* and *Lysistrata,* are still performed today.

**Fables** In addition to literary works, the Greeks also created fables, or stories that teach a lesson. The most famous are called *Aesop's Fables.* According to some legends, **Aesop** was an Ethiopian slave who lived on the Greek island of Samos during the sixth century B.C. Later in life one of his masters freed him as a reward for his learning and wit. Aesop then traveled widely around the Mediterranean, the Middle East, and Asia, collecting and retelling his fables.

Collections of fables had become popular as early as the fourth century B.C. They included stories such as "Androcles and the Lion" and "The Ant and the Grasshopper." Many sayings from *Aesop's Fables* have become a part of our language today, such as "crying 'wolf'," and, from the fable on this page, "sour grapes."

> **One hot summer's day a fox was strolling through an orchard when he saw a bunch of grapes ripening on a high vine. "Just the thing to quench my thirst," he said. Drawing back a few paces, he took a run and a jump, and just missed the bunch. Again and again he tried to reach the tempting treat, but at last had to give it up. He walked away with his nose in the air, saying: "I am sure the grapes are sour."**
>
> **It is easy to despise what you cannot get.**
>
> —Aesop's Fables, "The Fox and the Grapes"

**Primary** Sources

See "Greek Mythology: Aesop's Fables" in the Reference Section at the back of the book.

 **Checkpoint** What were the two main types of Greek drama?

**Looking Back and Ahead** In this section, you have read about the art and architecture of ancient Greece. You also have learned about the lyric poetry, drama, and fables written by the Greeks. In the next section, you will explore Greek science and philosophy.

# Section 2 Check Your Progress

**Progress Monitoring** Online

**For:** Self-test with instant help
**Visit:** PHSchool.com
**Web Code:** mwa-5152

**Standards Review** H-SS: 6.4.8; E-LA: Reading 6.1.2

## Comprehension and Critical Thinking

1. (a) **Recall** What was the Parthenon?
   (b) **Link Past and Present** How can the influence of such structures be seen in more modern buildings?

2. (a) **Explain** What is lyric poetry?
   (b) **Apply Information** How was lyric poetry related to religion in ancient Greece?

## Reading Skill

3. **Interpret Figurative Language** The phrase "sour grapes" is from the fable on page 427. Briefly explain why the phrase is figurative language and what it means.

## Vocabulary *Builder*

4. Draw a table with four rows and three columns. In the first column, list the following key terms from this section: frieze, pediment, and chorus. In the next column, write the definition of each word. In the last column, make a small illustration that shows the meaning of the word.

## Writing

5. Write a simple outline showing how you might organize the body of a research paper on ancient Greek drama.

**Standards Preview**

**H-SS 6.4.8** Describe the enduring contributions of important Greek figures in the arts and sciences (e.g., Hypatia, Socrates, Plato, Aristotle, Euclid, Thucydides).

**E-LA Reading 6.1.2** Identify and interpret figurative language and words with multiple meanings.

## Reading Preview

### Reading Skill

**Words With Multiple Meanings** The correct definitions of many words with multiple meanings can be determined by identifying where the word is placed in a sentence. Use grammar clues to help you determine whether such a word is an adjective, noun, verb, and so on. This can help you choose a definition that matches the word's role in the sentence.

### Vocabulary *Builder*

**High-Use Words**
method (MEHTH uhd), p. 429
foundation (fown DAY shuhn), p. 431

**Key Terms and People**
reason (REE zuhn), p. 429
logic (LAHJ ihk), p. 429
Plato (PLAYT oh), p. 429
academy (uh KAD uh mee), p. 429
Thucydides (thoo SIHD ih deez), p. 430
Aristotle (AR ihs taht l), p. 432

**Background Knowledge** The ancient Greeks appreciated knowledge as much as they did beauty. They were curious about their world. That curiosity led them to found five important areas of learning: philosophy, history, science, mathematics, and medicine. In this section, you will read about the Greeks' enduring contributions to these fields of knowledge.

**Main Idea**
Greek scholars made important advancements in the study of both philosophy and history.

## Philosophy and History

As you have read in Chapter 11, Chinese thinkers were among the world's first philosophers. Their goal was to pursue wisdom. Greek philosophers had the same goal. In fact, the word *philosophy* comes from Greek words meaning "love of wisdom."

**The Origins of Greek Philosophy** The Greeks began their search for wisdom with the same questions the Chinese had asked. What is the nature of the universe? What is a good life? The Greeks, however, took their search a step further. They also asked: How do we know what is real? How can we determine what is true?

The Greeks believed that they could determine what is real and true by using reason. **Reason** is the power to think in a clear manner. To increase their thinking power, the Greeks developed a system of reasoning known as logic. Logical thinking involves a step-by-step <u>method</u> of thinking through a problem or question.

**Socrates and Plato** Several important philosophers made their homes in Athens. Socrates, whom you read about in Chapter 14, drifted around Athens in a tattered coat. Wherever he went, people came up to talk with him. In these discussions, Socrates asked question after question to make people think clearly about things. Today, this question-and-answer method of teaching is called the Socratic method, and is used to instruct students in a variety of subjects.

Socrates often challenged accepted beliefs. Eventually, this got him into trouble with Athenian leaders. They charged him with corrupting the young by encouraging them to consider new ideas, as well as not believing in the gods the city recognized. In the trial that followed, Socrates defended himself saying:

> **❝I have never set up as any man's teacher. But if anyone, young or old, is eager to hear me . . . I never grudge [deny] him the opportunity. . . . I am ready to answer questions for rich and poor alike . . . If any given one of these people becomes a good citizen or a bad one, I cannot fairly be held responsible.❞**
>
> —Socrates, quoted in Plato's *Apology*

Fairly or not, Socrates was sentenced to death in 399 B.C. He died after being ordered to drink a poison made from the hemlock plant.

Socrates did not write down his ideas. He left that task to his student **Plato.** In a series of conversations called dialogues, Plato demonstrated how Socrates used his teaching methods to guide people to think logically. Plato went on to found a school of philosophy called the Academy. Today, the word academy often means a school devoted to a particular subject.

**Student Becomes Teacher**
Plato's Academy educated students in subjects such as philosophy and mathematics for about 140 years. **Critical Thinking: Evaluate Information** *How does this image reflect Plato's work as a philosopher and teacher?*

**School of Athens**
This painting by the Italian Renaissance painter Raphael shows many well-known Greek scholars, including philosophers, mathematicians, and scientists, from different time periods. **Critical Thinking: Evaluate Information** *What do you think Raphael hoped to say about Greek learning by grouping these people together in this painting?*

**History** *Interactive*
**Meet the figures of Raphael's School of Athens**
**Visit:** PHSchool.com
**Web Code:** mwp-5153

**Greek Historians** The Greeks' search for wisdom also led them to study the past. In other civilizations, such as China, historians wrote down what happened year by year. The Greek historians did more than record events. They investigated not only what happened in the past but also why these events took place.

The Greek writer Herodotus is often called "the father of history" because he wrote *The Histories,* the first known narrative of history. Herodotus was also one of the first known writers to examine historical events critically, looking for their causes and effects. Born about 484 B.C., Herodotus lived during the Persian Wars, a time of conflict between the Greeks and Persians. That conflict, and the cultures of both peoples, is the subject of *The Histories.* You will read more about Herodotus and the Persian Wars in Chapter 16.

The second great Greek historian was an Athenian named Thucydides. Born in 460 B.C., Thucydides also lived during a time of conflict, this one between Athens and Sparta. This war is known as the Peloponnesian War. Thucydides served as a naval commander in the war, then began writing his history of the war while the events were fresh in people's memories. Before writing about a battle, he would visit the battle site and interview people who had been present. He hoped that his history would not only be accurate, but also would serve as "an aid to the interpretation of the future" so that people would not repeat the mistakes of the past.

**E-LA 6.1.2 Words with Multiple Meanings**
*Reading Skill*
What is the part of speech of the word *present* in this paragraph? How does this provide a clue to the word's meaning?

✔**Checkpoint** How did Socrates use logic in his teaching?

# Science and Medicine

Most ancient peoples assumed that the gods caused everything from the rising of the sun to everyday illnesses. While most Greeks had these beliefs, they began to look for natural causes of such events. Like modern scientists, they first made observations of nature. They then formed hypotheses, or logical guesses, to explain what they had observed. Many of their hypotheses were later proved wrong. Nonetheless, their way of thinking represented something new in the ancient world. It laid the <u>foundations</u> of modern science, mathematics, and medicine.

**The Natural Sciences**  Greek philosophers began the scientific study of nature. These early scientists believed that natural laws, not the whims of gods, governed the universe. Identifying and explaining those laws became their challenge.

One of the first scientific thinkers was a philosopher named Thales of Miletus. Thales began his study of nature by asking this basic question: What are all things made of? His answer, water, was not correct. In fact, he believed that the earth was a flat disk that floated on water. However, it inspired other thinkers to develop better answers. For example, the philosopher Democritus said that the universe was made up of tiny particles that could not be split. He called them "atoms."

Thales also asked questions such as: How big is Earth? What is its shape? What holds it up in space? In each case, he based his answer on his observations of nature.

**Vocabulary** *Builder*
<u>foundation</u> (fown DAY shuhn) *n.* fundamental principle on which something is founded; basis

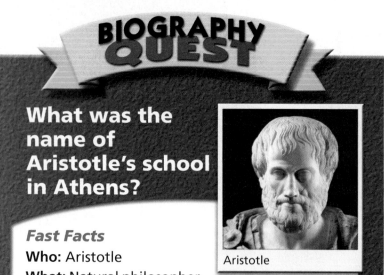

# BIOGRAPHY QUEST

## What was the name of Aristotle's school in Athens?

Aristotle

### Fast Facts

**Who:** Aristotle
**What:** Natural philosopher and teacher
**When:** 384 B.C.–322 B.C.
**Where:** Greece
**Why important:** Aristotle's writings and teachings made major contributions to many different fields of study.

### Fast Find

**How:** Go online to find out the name of the school Aristotle opened, and how this name reflected his style of teaching.

**Biography Online**

**For:** More about Aristotle
**Visit:** PHSchool.com
**Web Code:** mwe-5153

The most famous natural philosopher was the scholar **Aristotle.** He was born in 384 B.C. and studied at Plato's Academy. Aristotle was interested in all kinds of knowledge. He collected and analyzed data about plants, animals, and rocks. He studied mathematics and logic. He wrote about government, poetry, politics, and drama. A modern historian summarized Aristotle's work this way:

> **❝He was a great collector and classifier of data. . . . What he wrote provided the framework for the discussion of biology, physics, mathematics, logic, literary criticism, aesthetics, psychology, ethics, and politics for two thousand years.❞**
>
> —J. M. Roberts, *History of the World*

**Mathematics** The Greeks first discovered many basic concepts in mathematics. Pythagoras of Samos was an early Greek mathematician. Pythagoras thought that numbers were the key to understanding the universe. Geometry students of today still learn the Pythagorean theorem, which bears his name. A theorem is a statement in mathematics that can be proved to be true.

Euclid, another important mathematician, lived about 300 B.C. Euclid brought together all that was known about geometry in his book *Elements*. This work still forms the basis of many modern geometry textbooks.

**Medicine** The Greeks also made contributions in the field of medicine. Greek doctors looked for natural causes of illnesses instead of blaming them on the gods. Their success at treating patients brought them fame throughout the Mediterranean world.

Hippocrates became the best-known Greek doctor. He also wrote many medical books and ran a school that trained new doctors. Hippocrates taught his students to diagnose patients by asking them questions about their illnesses and observing their symptoms.

He also had them swear the following oath, in which they promised to use their medical knowledge in ethical ways.

**"I will prescribe treatment for the good of my patients according to my ability . . . and never do harm to anyone. To please no one will I prescribe a deadly drug nor give advice which may cause his death. . . . In every house where I come I will enter only for the good of my patients. . . . All that I learn from my patients . . . I will keep secret. If I keep this oath faithfully, may I enjoy my life and practice my art, respected by all men and in all times. "**

—Hippocrates, The Hippocratic Oath

The ethics of the Hippocratic Oath still guide doctors today.

 **Checkpoint** How were Greek ideas about nature and medicine different from those of other ancient people?

**Looking Back and Ahead** In this section, you have read about the Greeks' enduring contributions in philosophy, history, science, mathematics, and medicine. In the next chapter, you will read about wars between Greece and Persia and learn how Greek culture spread far beyond Greece itself.

---

## Section 3 Check Your Progress

**Progress Monitoring** Online
**For:** Self-test with instant help
**Visit:** PHSchool.com
**Web Code:** mwa-5153

 **Standards Review** H-SS: 6.4.8; E-LA: Reading 6.1.2

### Comprehension and Critical Thinking

**1. (a) Explain** What were the main goals of Greek philosophers and historians?
**(b) Analyze Cause and Effect** How did those goals affect the methods of Socrates and Thucydides?

**2. (a) Identify** What fields did Greek scientific thinkers explore?
**(b) Draw Conclusions** In what way were their efforts important for modern science?

### Reading Skill

**3. Words with Multiple Meanings** Read the following sentence. Then, explain the meaning of the word *interest* and identify at least one alternate meaning for the word: Aristotle had <u>interest</u> in all kinds of knowledge.

### Vocabulary *Builder*

**4.** Write two definitions for each word: reason, logic, academy. First, write a formal definition for your teacher. Second, write a definition in everyday English for a classmate.

### Writing

**5.** Choose one topic on Greek learning discussed in this section. Then, make a list of important points you would cover in the body of an essay on this topic.

History is more than just a list of facts and events. It also involves the ways in which these facts and events are viewed, or interpreted. Historians look beyond the facts to find the meanings in history. To do this, they use interpretation.

**Chapter Standards**

**History-Social Science**

**Historical Interpretation 5** Students recognize that interpretations of history are subject to change as new information is uncovered.

> Today, putting someone to death for asking questions seems terribly unjust. But the jury that found Socrates guilty would not agree. They saw Socrates as a threat to the values that made Athens great. In one sense they were right. Socrates represented a new type of person in the Greek world. Athens was not the center of his identity. In its place, he put his own sense of what is good and true. This shift from loyalty to the polis to loyalty to self would have far-reaching effects in the Greek world.
>
> —Diane Hart

**Learn the Skill** *Follow these steps to identify historical interpretation.*

1. **Identify the topic, time period, and historian.** This information will help you analyze a historian's interpretation. For example, a modern historian will interpret events differently than an ancient one.

2. **Identify the facts.** Remember, facts are statements that can be proven true. Historians will use facts as the building blocks of their interpretations.

3. **Consider how the historian has interpreted the facts and events.** Try to determine the meaning the historian has found in them. What did the historian think was interesting or important? Did the historian talk about the effects of the facts and events on history?

**Practice the Skill** *Answer the following questions about the passage above.*

1. **Identify the topic, time period, and historian.**
   **(a)** What is the topic of this passage?
   **(b)** What time period is being discussed?
   **(c)** Did an ancient or modern historian write the passage?

2. **Identify the facts.** Identify three facts in the passage.

3. **Consider how the historian has interpreted the facts and events. (a)** How did the historian think modern people would feel about Socrates' punishment? **(b)** What change in the Greek world did the historian think that Socrates represented? **(c)** Why did the historian think this change was important?

**Apply the Skill**
*See page 437 of the Review and Assessment.*

**Study Guide *Online***
Complete your Chapter 15 study guide in print or online.

## Chapter Summary  H-SS: 6.4.4, 6.4.8

### Section 1 Greek Mythology and Religion

• The people of ancient Greece worshiped many gods, who they believed influenced the world around them.

• Greek religious practices were based upon Greek mythology and the epics of Homer.

• People in ancient Greece practiced their religion in many ways, such as building temples and participating in festivals.

### Section 2 Greek Art and Literature

• Greek artists became known for the beauty of their work. Ancient Greek architecture continues to influence architects today.

• Lyric poetry and drama were important parts of the literature of ancient Greece.

• The Greeks enjoyed collections of fables such as those of Aesop.

### Section 3 Greek Learning

• Greek philosophers, such as Socrates and Plato used reason to help them determine what is real and true.

• Historians in ancient Greece began to examine why historical events took place in addition to recording the events themselves.

• Greek scholars made important advances in the natural sciences, mathematics, and medicine.

**Greek architecture**

## Standards Practice  H-SS: 6.4.4, 6.4.8

## Vocabulary *Builder*

### High-Use Words

Read each sentence below. If the sentence is true, write YES. If the sentence is not true, write NO and explain WHY.

1. The **individual** singer performed the poem as a solo.

2. Religious practices were an important part of Greek **culture**.

3. The Greeks used a logical **method** to make guesses about the actions of the gods.

4. Greek scholars established the **foundation** of modern medicine.

### Key Terms

Complete each of the following sentences so that the second part further explains the first part and clearly shows your understanding of the highlighted word.

1. The people of ancient Greece believed in many deities; _____.

2. A key basis of Greek religious belief was mythology; _____.

3. Ancient Greeks often visited an oracle; _____.

4. Many lyric poems were read by a chorus; _____.

## Apply Reading Skills

**Figurative Language and Words with Multiple Meanings** Read the following sentence: "Parents to the world, the gods were sometimes stern and sometimes forgiving." Explain the figurative language in this sentence. Define the two meanings of stern. Which is used in this sentence?

## Comprehension and Critical Thinking

1. **(a) Identify** Who was the ruler of the ancient Greek gods?
   **(b) Apply Information** How did Homer's epics reflect the Greeks' beliefs that the gods were at work all around them?
   **(c) Draw Conclusions** How did the Greeks' religious beliefs affect the way in which they viewed their landscape?

2. **(a) List** Name three types of Greek literature.
   **(b) Link Past and Present** What are two ways in which Greek literature and drama have influenced literature and language of today?

3. **(a) Explain** How did Plato contribute to the study of philosophy?
   **(b) Identify Benefits** Which of Plato's contributions do you think most benefits present-day students and scholars?

4. **(a) Recall** How did Hippocrates advance the study of medicine?
   **(b) Compare** In what ways were Hippocrates' methods similar to those of other ancient Greek scholars?
   **(c) Explain Problem** What problems might Hippocrates have hoped to prevent by asking his students to swear the Hippocratic Oath?

## Researching

**A Time of Accomplishment** The ancient Greek civilization became known for its rich culture and accomplishments in many different fields of study. In this activity, you will use the Internet and library media center to research and report on the culture and achievements of this period. Choose a task below to work on. Share your work with the class by giving a short oral presentation. Make a list of the resources you used to go with your presentation.

**Artist:** Create a poster describing the performance of lyric poetry in ancient Greece. Your poster should include text and visual aids on topics such as the lyre, performers of lyric poetry, and the reasons for its performance.

**Historian:** Research Thucydides' method for writing about history, and choose a historical event you might study using this method. Then, make a historian's notebook, listing places you would visit, people you would interview, and questions you might ask to learn more about the event.

> **Researching Online**
> **For:** Help in starting this activity
> **Visit:** PHSchool.com
> **Web Code:** mwd-5153

## Writing

1. **Write a paragraph on the following topic.** The people of ancient Greece tried to explain their world in several different ways. Discuss how the Greeks' approach to explaining their world changed over time.
   **Your paragraph should:**
   • contain a clear topic sentence.
   • use transition words, as needed.
   • offer evidence to support your explanation.

2. **Write a short narrative.** Suppose you lived in ancient Greece and were attending your first play. Write a short narrative about the event.

## Apply Analysis Skills

**Use the text from Section 3 at right to answer the following questions.**

1. What is the topic of this passage of text?

2. What three facts about this topic are contained in the text?

3. Who is the modern historian listed that wrote about this topic?

4. How would you summarize the historian's interpretation of the topic?

The most famous natural philosopher was the scholar Aristotle. He was born in 384 B.C. and studied at Plato's Academy. Aristotle had interest in all kinds of knowledge. He collected and analyzed data about plants, animals, and rocks. He studied mathematics and logic. He wrote about government, poetry, politics, and drama. A modern historian summarized Aristotle's work this way:

**"**He was a great collector and classifier of data. . . . What he wrote provided the framework for the discussion of biology, physics, mathematics, logic, literary criticism, aesthetics, psychology, ethics, and politics for two thousand years.**"**

—J. M. Roberts, *History of the World*

## Test Yourself

**Refer to the reading below to answer Question 1.**

1. **How does this passage illustrate the type of poetry often performed in ancient Greece?**

*"Some say a host of horsemen is the most beautiful thing on the black earth, some say a host of foot-soldiers, some, a fleet of ships; but I say it is whatever one loves."*

—Sappho, "To Anaktoria"

A It focuses on victorious athletes.

B It retells a long story.

C It expresses a personal viewpoint.

D It presents political ideas and reforms.

2. **Which of the following was not a major form of literature or drama in ancient Greece?**

A poetry

B tragedy

C comedy

D autobiography

**Refer to the image below to answer Question 3.**

3. **People of ancient Greece gathered here to**

A worship the goddess Athena.

B watch the performance of a play.

C study the natural sciences.

D practice medicine.

4. **Which of the following statements is correct?**

A Euclid became famous for his work in geometry.

B Aesop was a well-known epic poet.

C Plato recorded the ideas of Thucydides.

D Aristotle developed many features of Greek architecture.

## Chapter 16

# Greece and Persia

(600 B.C.–30 B.C.)

## Prepare to Read

 **Chapter Standards**

### History-Social Science

**6.4** Students analyze the geographic, political, economic, religious, and social structures of the early civilizations of Ancient Greece.

**6.4.5** Outline the founding, expansion, and political organization of the Persian Empire.

 **What You Will Learn**

**Section 1,** pp. 442–448

### The Persian Empire

The rulers of the Persian empire balanced local self-government with central power to govern their vast territory.

**Section 2,** pp. 449–453

### The Persian Wars

The Persian king Darius intended to conquer all of Greece. The Athenians and Spartans worked together to defend themselves against the Persians.

**Section 3,** pp. 456–460

### The Peloponnesian Wars

Although together they defeated the Persians, Athens and Sparta fought between themselves in the 27-year-long Peloponnesian War.

**Section 4,** pp. 461–465

### The Empire of Alexander the Great

The Greek city-states were finally united under one rule by Alexander the Great. His conquests spread Greek culture east toward India and south into Egypt.

**An ancient statue on the Greek island of Delos**

**559 B.C.**
Cyrus begins his reign of Persia.

**431 B.C.**
The Peloponnesian War begins.

**Chapter Events**

**Other Events**

**800 B.C.**

**600 B.C.**

**400 B.C.**

**663 B.C.** Assyrian troops invade Egypt.

**587 B.C.** Nebuchadnezzar destroys Jerusalem.

## Where and When?
From 600 B.C. through 325 B.C. the powerful Greek and Persian empires expanded throughout Europe and Asia.

A staircase at the Persian capital Persepolis shows people bringing gifts for the King of Persia.

**325 B.C.**
Alexander the Great conquers territory stretching to India.

**30 B.C.**
The Hellenistic period ends.

**400 B.C.**

**200 B.C.**

**B.C./A.D.**

**272 B.C.** Asoka is India's third Mauryan emperor.

**221 B.C.** Qin forces unite northern China.

Greece and Persia    **439**

## History Reading Skill

*Previewing* **Connect and Clarify Main Ideas**

As you read the new ideas and information in this textbook, try to find ways to connect the information to what you already know. Look for ways to connect text ideas to graphic information, to ideas from other sections, and to information from outside sources. Read the primary source below.

 **Chapter Standards**

**English-Language Arts**

**Reading 6.2.3** Connect and clarify main ideas by identifying their relationships to other sources and related topics.

> This is the main idea. You can connect this to earlier reading in Chapter 14 about democracy in Athens. You can also think about what you have learned from the textbook and outside sources about class differences.

> Here the author develops the main idea. He tells why democracy only benefits one group of people.

"Now in discussing the Athenian constitution, I cannot praise this method of running the state because it prefers the masses to the upper classes and respectable citizens. . . . In this way, however, the state ensures that democracy will continue. The common masses naturally lack self-control. They are weak, wicked, and uneducated. As a result, the laws they pass will be inferior because they are only meant to benefit the masses. The government acts in its own best interests by allowing the mob a voice. Anyone who wishes rises and speaks, and as a member of the mob he discovers what is to his own advantage and that of those like him.

—from *Aristotle and Xenophon on Democracy and Oligarchy*

Ask these questions as you look for ways to clarify and connect ideas:

• What is the main idea?
• How is it developed?
• How does this information help you understand class differences in ancient Greece?

# Vocabulary *Builder*

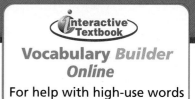

**interactive Textbook**

**Vocabulary *Builder* Online**

For help with high-use words

## *Previewing* High-Use Academic Words

| High-Use Word | Definition | Sample Sentence About History |
|---|---|---|
| **authority** (uh THOHR uh tee), (Section 1, p. 445) | *n.* power or right to give commands, take action, or make final decisions | The emperor had the <u>authority</u> to make people obey the laws. |
| **policy** (PAHL uh see), (Section 2, p. 449) | *n.* principle, plan, or course of action | The civil service had a <u>policy</u> that forbade employees from working in their own communities. |
| **consult** (kuhn SUHLT), (Section 2, p. 452) | *v.* to seek an opinion from or ask the advice of | The king <u>consulted</u> his generals before attacking. |
| **supreme** (suh PREEM), (Section 3, p. 456) | *adj.* highest in rank, power, or authority | The <u>supreme</u> court is the highest court in the country. |
| **launch** (lawnch), (Section 3, p. 459) | *v.* to send forth with some force; to set in operation | The military campaign was <u>launched</u> during the early morning hours. |
| **acquire** (uh KWĪR), (Section 4, p. 465) | *v.* to get or gain by one's actions or efforts | Neither country <u>acquired</u> any new lands as a result of the war. |
| **irrigate** (EER uh gayt) (Section 4, p. 465) | *v.* to bring water to; to water or moisten | The farmers had to <u>irrigate</u> their land in order to produce crops. |

## *Previewing* Key Terms and People

Philip

Cyrus the Great, p. 442

Herodotus, p. 442

reign, p. 443

Croesus, p. 443

Darius the Great, p. 444

Pheidippides, p. 450

Xerxes, p. 450

King Leonides, p. 452

Themistocles, p. 452

Pericles, p. 453

rival, p. 456

rivalry, p. 456

ally, p. 456

truce, p. 459

Philip, p. 461

Alexander the Great, p. 462

cultural diffusion, p. 464

Archimedes, p. 465

**Standards Preview**

**H-SS 6.4.5** Outline the founding, expansion, and political organization of the Persian Empire.

**E-LA Reading 6.2.3** Connect and clarify main ideas by identifying their relationship to other sources and related topics.

## Reading Preview

 **Reading Skill**

**Summarize Main Ideas** The first step in connecting main ideas to one another is to summarize those ideas. Remember that to summarize you must find the idea that connects the key information or details in a reading. Sometimes that idea is stated in a sentence, but sometimes you must piece it together by asking: What is this paragraph mostly about?

**Vocabulary** *Builder*

**High-Use Words**
authority (uh THOHR uh tee), p. 445

**Key Terms and People**
Cyrus the Great (sī ruhs thuh grayt), p. 442
Herodotus (huh RAHD uh tuhs), p. 442
reign (rayn), p. 443
Croesus (KRA suhs), p. 443
Darius the Great (duh RĪ uhs thuh grayt), p. 444

**Background Knowledge**   Across the Aegean Sea from Greece lay the Persian Empire. In contrast to the Greek city-states, which were governed by citizens, Persia was ruled by a powerful monarch. In this section, you will read about the founding, expansion, and government of the Persian Empire.

**Main Idea**
Cyrus the Great conquered many peoples and greatly expanded the Persian Empire.

## The Rise of the Persian Empire

The heart of ancient Persia was the high plateau of Iran. The Persians shared this plateau with the Medes. Both groups were Aryans, like the people who came to control India. Today this region is the country of Iran. The name *Iran* comes from the word "Aryan."

**Cyrus the Great**   The founder of the Persian empire was a ruler known as Cyrus the Great. He was born in 584 B.C. and had a typical Persian boyhood. The Greek historian Herodotus reported that like all Persian boys, Cyrus was taught "to manage a horse, to shoot with a bow, and to speak the truth."

Cyrus began his reign, or rule in 559 B.C. He quickly united the many Persian tribes. Then, he conquered the Medes. Unlike most conquerors, Cyrus was generous to defeated peoples. Rather than replace officials in the Mede government with Persians, Cyrus kept the Medes in their jobs. This policy of tolerance for different peoples and cultures became a pattern in the Persian Empire. As Herodotus observed, "No nation has ever been more ready than the Persians to admit foreign customs."

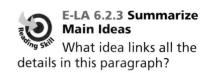

E-LA 6.2.3 **Summarize Main Ideas**
What idea links all the details in this paragraph?

**The Fall of Lydia**   Once in power, Cyrus began to expand his empire. His first target was Lydia, a country near the city-states of Ionia. Croesus, a king famous for his immense wealth, ruled Lydia. Croesus was just as eager as Cyrus to build an empire. But before going to war, Croesus consulted the oracle at Delphi. To ensure a favorable response, Croesus showered the temple at Delphi with gold and jewels. Then, he asked the oracle whether he should go to war against the Persians. The oracle replied that Croesus would "destroy a great empire."

According to Herodotus, Croesus "was overjoyed" with the Oracle's reply. He was also "fully confident of destroying the power of Cyrus." As a result, he went to war, certain that he would win a great victory. Instead, he suffered a terrible defeat. Only then did Croesus fully understand the oracle's reply. He would indeed destroy a great empire, but that empire would be his own.

**The Riches of Croesus**
King Croesus is shown in his court with some of the riches he gained through his many conquests. **Critical Thinking: Explain Problem** *How did the reply that Croesus received from the Oracle at Delphi show that the response could be understood in more than one way?*

**Expanding the Empire** From Lydia, Cyrus moved on to Ionia. One by one, the Greek city-states of Ionia fell to Persian forces. Next, Cyrus marched east toward India. Before long, his empire stretched halfway across the Asian continent.

This rapid expansion was made possible by Persia's huge standing army. A standing army is a permanent army of professional soldiers. The core of this army was a handpicked force of 10,000 soldiers known as the "Immortals."

**The Conquest of Babylonia** Cyrus' last conquest was of the Babylonian Empire. Cyrus treated the defeated Babylonians well. As a result, he won the loyalty of their leaders. Cyrus also won the loyalty of another group in Babylonia: the Jews. The Jews missed Judea, their homeland. As you have learned in Chapter 5, Cyrus not only let the Jews return home, but he also sent them back with treasures that had been looted from the temple in Jerusalem. He also gave the Jews money to rebuild their temple, which the Babylonians had destroyed.

**Further Expansion of Persia** Cyrus' successor was his son Cambyses (kam BĪ sehz). The reign of Cambyses began with his conquest of Egypt. When he tried to conquer Kush, he failed. Cambyses marched his army toward Kush without any food or supplies. Soon, his men were forced to eat their pack animals. But Cambyses did not turn back. Before long, his men had nothing to eat but one another. "One man in ten was chosen by lot to be the victim," Herodotus wrote. Only then did Cambyses abandon his invasion of Kush.

The next Persian ruler was known as **Darius the Great.** Under his rule, Persia became a huge empire. The map on page 445 shows the Persian Empire at its height.

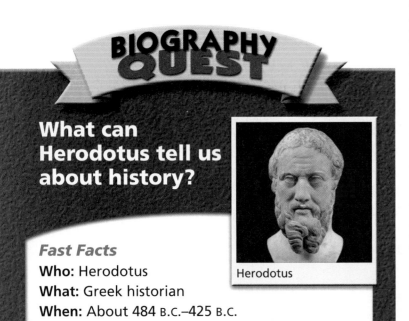

# BIOGRAPHY QUEST

## What can Herodotus tell us about history?

Herodotus

### Fast Facts

**Who:** Herodotus
**What:** Greek historian
**When:** About 484 B.C.–425 B.C.
**Where:** Asia Minor
**Why important:** Herodotus was influenced by the epic poet, Homer. Herodotus differs from Homer in the way he retold reliable, often first-hand information.

### Fast Find

**How:** Go online to find out what Herodotus wrote about the Persian Empire.

**Biography Online**

**For:** More about Herodotus
**Visit:** PHSchool.com
**Web Code:** mwe-5161

✓**Checkpoint** How did Cyrus the Great differ from previous Persian rulers?

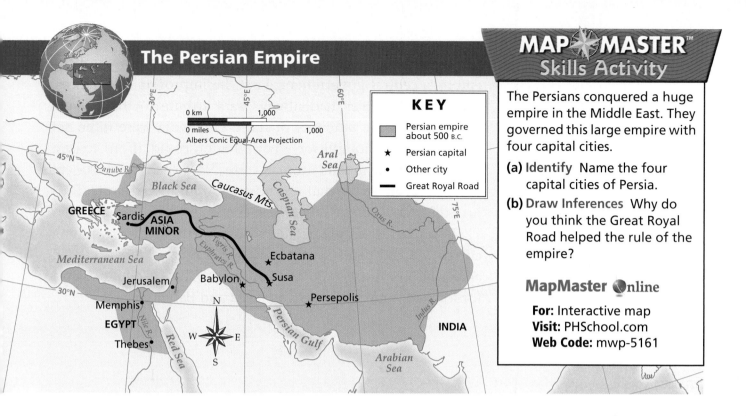

**KEY**

Persian empire about 500 B.C.
★ Persian capital
• Other city
━ Great Royal Road

0 km 1,000
0 miles 1,000
Albers Conic Equal-Area Projection

**MAP MASTER**
**Skills Activity**

The Persians conquered a huge empire in the Middle East. They governed this large empire with four capital cities.

**(a) Identify** Name the four capital cities of Persia.

**(b) Draw Inferences** Why do you think the Great Royal Road helped the rule of the empire?

**MapMaster Online**

**For:** Interactive map
**Visit:** PHSchool.com
**Web Code:** mwp-5161

# Organization of the Empire

After the Persians had conquered this vast multicultural empire, they had to keep it together. Multicultural means made up of different people and cultures. One approach would have been to follow the example of China's first emperor. As you read in Chapter 12, Shi Huangdi tried to unify China by imposing uniform laws and standards across his empire. The Persians, however, followed a different approach. They created a political organization that balanced local self-government and central power.

**Local Self-government** Darius divided his empire into provinces known as satrapies. The leading official in each Persian province was called a satrap. He was usually a Persian noble. Other officials, however, came from the upper classes of the local people. Most of the laws they enforced were local laws. This meant that, for example, Greeks ran the city-states of Ionia and Jews ran Jerusalem.

The satraps had a great deal of <u>authority</u> in their provinces. To keep them from becoming too independent, Darius sent each one a secretary who acted as the king's spy. He reported directly to Darius about affairs in each satrapy, or province governed by a satrap.

**Main Idea**
The Persian rulers efficiently balanced local self-government with central power to govern their empire.

**Vocabulary** *Builder*
<u>authority</u> (uh THOHR uh tee) *n.* power or right to give commands, take action, or make final decisions

**Central Power** Darius also increased the power of the empire's central government. First, he improved its finances. Conquered peoples had always sent tribute to the Persian emperor. But the amounts of these payments were often set without much thought for what a region could afford to pay. Darius created a much fairer tax code. Now, each province sent tribute according to what it produced. With this revenue, Darius built a new capital city at Persepolis.

To unify his empire economically, Darius created common currency. Gold coins stamped with his image were accepted across his empire as payment for goods. This made it possible for Ionia to trade with faraway India and Babylonia.

### Persepolis: Persia's Political Center

Darius the Great began building the new capital city of Persepolis in about 518 B.C. His son and successor, Xerxes completed the project between 486–465 B.C. Today, archaeologists have uncovered most of the city's ruins.
**Critical Thinking: Apply Information** *In what ways did Persepolis contribute to Persia's political organization?*

**History** *Interactive*
**Tour the Persian Capital Persepolis**
**Visit:** PHSchool.com
**Web Code:** mwp-5165

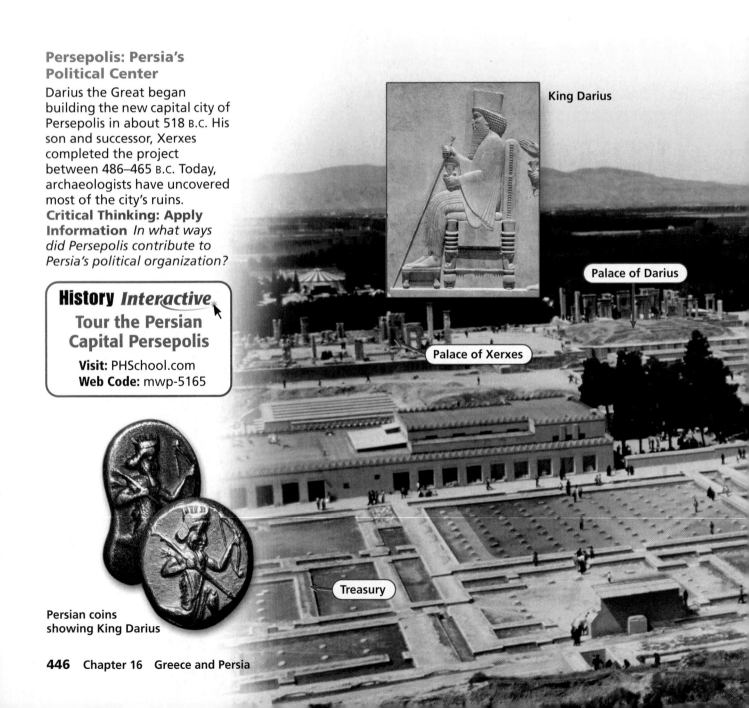

King Darius

Palace of Darius

Palace of Xerxes

Treasury

Persian coins showing King Darius

**The Royal Roads** Darius used some of his great wealth to build roads across his empire. Armies, government officials, and royal messengers travelled on these roads. So, too, did trade goods, tribute, and taxes. The most famous road was the Royal Road, (about 1,500–1,800 miles long) which ran from Sardis in Lydia to Susa in Babylonia. The map on page 445 shows the distance between these cities and the vastness of the empire. According to Herodotus, it took three months to carry a message from one city to the other. Postal stations were located a day's ride apart along the way. Messengers and fresh horses waited at each station to take the message on to the next station.

Stairway to Audience Hall

Audience Hall

Throne Hall, or Hall of Hundred Columns

"Neither snow, nor rain, nor heat, nor gloom of night stays these couriers from the swift completion of their appointed rounds."

**Postal Service**
This unofficial motto of the U.S. Postal Service can be seen in many post offices around the country. **Critical Thinking: Link Past and Present** *How does this unofficial motto compare with what Herodotus wrote describing the Persian postal service?*

This method of carrying messages was successful. As a result, the Persian postal service was the fastest communication system in the ancient world. Herodotus wrote:

**❝Nothing on earth travels faster than do these messengers as the Persians have organized them. . . . Neither snow nor rain, heat nor darkness prevents these riders from covering the distance allotted to them at full speed.❞**

—Herodotus, *The Histories*

More than 2,000 years later, Herodotus' description inspired postal officials in the United States. The words shown at left are considered the unofficial motto of the United States Postal Service.

**Checkpoint** How was the government of the Persian Empire organized?

**Looking Back and Ahead** In this section, you have read about the rise of the Persian Empire. You have seen how it became the largest empire the world had ever known. In the next section, you will learn how this expansion set the stage for war with the Greeks.

## Section 1 Check Your Progress

**Progress Monitoring** Online
**For:** Self-test with instant help
**Visit:** PHSchool.com
**Web Code:** mwa-5161

**Standards Review** H-SS: 6.4.5; E-LA: Reading 6.2.3

**Comprehension and Critical Thinking**

1. **(a) Explain** How did Cyrus unify the Medes and the Persians into one empire?
   **(b) Compare** How does this compare with the policy followed by Darius?

2. **(a) List** List two ways that Darius spent the money that came to him from taxes.
   **(b) Identify Benefits** How did this spending help unify the empire?

**Reading Skill**

3. **Summarize Main Ideas** Read the second paragraph under Local Self-government on page 445. Summarize the main idea.

**Vocabulary** *Builder*
Answer the following questions in complete sentences that show your understanding of the Key People.

4. How far did the empire of Cyrus the Great extend?

5. How did Herodotus describe Croesus' reply from the oracle at Delphi?

6. How did Darius the Great govern his empire?

**Writing**

7. Draft a paragraph describing how the Persians ruled their vast empire. Then, revise your paragraph to make sure that all details support the main topic.

## Section

# 2 The Persian Wars

 **Standards Preview**

**H-SS 6.4.6** Compare and contrast life in Athens and Sparta, with emphasis on their roles in the Persian and Peloponnesian Wars.

**E-LA Reading 6.2.3** Connect and clarify main ideas by identifying their relationships to other sources and related topics.

## Reading Preview

 **Reading Skill**

**Connect Main Ideas to Graphics** This textbook includes many maps, which are especially useful in understanding events from history. They help you see the relationship between places, as well as the movement of people, armies, and commerce. Use maps to clarify the main ideas found in the text, such as by tracing the path an army took.

**Vocabulary** *Builder*

**High-Use Words**
policy (PAHL uh see), p. 450
consult (kuhn SUHLT), p. 452

**Key People**
Pheidippides (fī DIHP ih deez), p. 450
Xerxes (ZERK seez), p. 450
King Leonidas (kihng lee AHN uh duhs), p. 452
Themistocles (thuh MIS tuh kleez), p. 452
Pericles (PER uh kleez), p. 453

**Background Knowledge** The Greeks were at war for much of their history. Often, the city-states fought one another. Then a threat from outside forced the quarreling states to unite for a time. In this section, you will read how the Greeks fought two wars with the Persian Empire.

## The First Persian War

You have read that Cyrus the Great conquered the Greek city-states of Ionia. The Ionians hated Persian rule and Persian taxes. In 499 B.C., the Ionians rebelled against Persia and asked Athens for help. Athens sent 20 shiploads of soldiers to assist the rebels. After burning the Persian city of Sardis, the Athenians returned home.

Persian troops soon recaptured the Ionian cities, burning some to the ground. They punished the Ionian leaders harshly. Darius, king of Persia, was angry. By helping Ionia, the mainland Greeks had dared to defy his power. His revenge would be to conquer all of Greece.

**Main Idea**
The Persian king Darius intended to conquer all of Greece, but the Athenians and Ionians worked together to defend themselves against the Persians.

**E-LA 6.2.3 Connect Main Ideas to Graphics**

Look at the map on page 451. How does it help you understand the Athenians' fear of attack?

**Vocabulary** *Builder*

<u>policy</u> (PAHL uh see) *n.* principle, plan, or course of action

**Main Idea**
The Persians and the Greeks fought another major war, which ended with another defeat for the Persians.

**The Invasion of Greece**   In 490 B.C., about 20,000 Persian soldiers set sail for Greece. They easily captured several Greek islands in the Aegean Sea. Then, they moved on toward the Greek mainland. They landed near the plain of Marathon, just 26 miles from Athens. This flat plain seemed like the perfect battleground for the Persian cavalry, or soldiers on horseback.

In Athens, citizens debated what to do next. Should they adopt a <u>policy</u> of defense and stay locked up behind their city walls? Or should they march out and meet the Persians at Marathon? A vote was taken in the assembly. The decision was to attack at once.

**The Battle of Marathon**   A small force of 10,000 Athenian infantry, or foot soldiers, rushed to Marathon. What they saw there made them pause. The plain was swarming with Persian infantry and cavalry. The Athenians were outnumbered by at least two to one. In addition, they had no archers or cavalry.

After some debate, the Athenians voted to attack the next day. At dawn, Greek phalanxes charged across the plain at a run. The astonished Persians found themselves attacked on all sides. As the Greeks closed in, the Persians fled to their ships. It was an amazing victory for Greece.

According to Herodotus, the victorious soldiers wanted leaders in Athens to hear the good news quickly. Their fastest runner, Pheidippides, had just returned from carrying a message to distant Sparta. Although he was exhausted from that journey, Pheidippides set out for Athens. On reaching the city, he gasped out the message. "Rejoice! We have won." Then he collapsed and died. Today to honor both the battle and Pheidippides, marathon runners still cover the same distance of about 26 miles Pheidippides ran nearly 2,500 years ago.

✔**Checkpoint**   **Why did Darius go to war against Athens?**

# The Second Persian War

The defeat at Marathon made Darius more determined than ever to conquer Greece. But before he could launch another attack, Darius died. It was left to his son Xerxes to punish the Greeks.

## Xerxes Crosses the Hellespont

In 480 B.C., Xerxes assembled a huge invasion force. Herodotus wrote:

> **The army was indeed immense—far greater than any other in recorded history. . . . There was not a nation in Asia that he did not take with him against Greece. . . . Some nations provided ships, others . . . infantry units . . . cavalry . . . transport vessels and . . . warships for floating bridges.**
>
> —Herodotus, *The Histories*

Rather than take his huge army across the sea in ships, Xerxes planned to march it across the Hellespont. This narrow strait divides Europe and Asia and is known today as the Dardanelles. Xerxes had his engineers rope warships together to form a floating bridge across the Hellespont. Then a violent storm smashed the ships to bits. "Xerxes was very angry," wrote Herodotus, "and gave orders that the Hellespont should receive three hundred lashes." After whipping the sea, the Persians built a new and stronger bridge. Xerxes then led an army of an estimated 100,000 men into Greece.

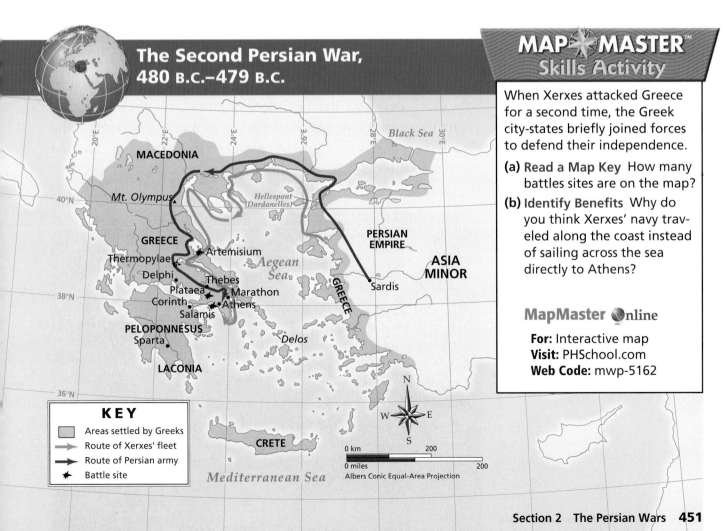

## The Second Persian War, 480 B.C.–479 B.C.

**MAP MASTER™**
**Skills Activity**

When Xerxes attacked Greece for a second time, the Greek city-states briefly joined forces to defend their independence.

**(a) Read a Map Key** How many battles sites are on the map?

**(b) Identify Benefits** Why do you think Xerxes' navy traveled along the coast instead of sailing across the sea directly to Athens?

**MapMaster ●nline**

**For:** Interactive map
**Visit:** PHSchool.com
**Web Code:** mwp-5162

**KEY**
- Areas settled by Greeks
- → Route of Xerxes' fleet
- → Route of Persian army
- ★ Battle site

0 km 200
0 miles 200
Albers Conic Equal-Area Projection

### The Battle of Thermopylae

To many Greeks, the Persians seemed unstoppable. The Spartans did not agree. Led by King Leonidas, a small Spartan force tried to stop the Persians at a narrow mountain pass known as Thermopylae.

The Spartans held off the invaders for several days. Then a traitor showed the Persians another path through the mountains. Attacked from both sides, 300 Spartans chose death over defeat. Herodotus wrote that when their weapons were gone, they fought on "with their hands and teeth" until every man was killed.

**Vocabulary** *Builder*

<u>consult</u> (kuhn SUHLT) *v.* to seek an opinion from or ask the advice of

### The "Wooden Walls" of Athens

Meanwhile, the terrified Athenians <u>consulted</u> the Oracle at Delphi. As usual, the Oracle's words were puzzling. It said that "wooden walls" could save the Athenians.

Many Athenians thought that the Oracle's words meant city walls. A leader named Themistocles, however, convinced Athens that "wooden walls" meant ships. When the Persians reached Athens, they found it, the harbor, and the nearby strait empty. The Athenians had fled by ship to nearby islands. The Persians burned the city, including the temples on the Acropolis.

### The Battle of Salamis

A few days later, Xerxes had his throne set on a hill near Athens. The hill overlooked a narrow strait between the island of Salamis and the mainland. From this point, he planned to watch his fleet destroy the Greek navy. Xerxes had good reason to feel confident. He had 1,200 warships, compared with the Greeks' 380 ships.

**The Battle of Salamis**
The Battle of Salamis was a turning point for the Greeks in the Persian Wars. **Critical Thinking: Explain Problem** *What problem did the Persian army face in the Battle of Salamis?*

Themistocles, however, had set a trap. He kept his fleet hidden while Persian ships filled the narrow strait. Then, the Greeks attacked. They rammed the crowded Persian ships, splintering their hulls and oars. Soon the strait was choked with broken ships, making it impossible for the Persians to escape. By nightfall, the Persians had lost more than 200 ships, compared with just 40 for the Greeks. Rather than lose the rest of his fleet, Xerxes sailed for home.

**A "Golden Age" for Athens** Athenians celebrated their victory by introducing a "golden age" of art and learning. Pericles led the way with a program for rebuilding the city. In the years after the Persian Wars, Athenians created marvels of art and architecture, including the Parthenon. They also enjoyed a golden age of philosophy, science, and literature.

**Checkpoint** What event ended the Second Persian War?

**Looking Back and Ahead** In this section, you have read how the Persians tried to conquer Greece. You have learned that Athenians and Spartans worked together to defend the Greeks. In the next section, you will learn how their victory led to a new and more terrible war.

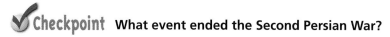

## Section 2 Check Your Progress

**Progress Monitoring** Online
**For:** Self-test with instant help
**Visit:** PHSchool.com
**Web Code:** mwa-5162

**Standards Review** H-SS: 6.4.6; E-LA: Reading 6.2.3

### Comprehension and Critical Thinking

**1. (a) Explain** Why was the victory at Marathon significant in the First Persian War?
**(b) Analyze Cause and Effect** How did this war lead to the Second Persian War?

**2. (a) Recall** What happened at the battle of Thermopylae?
**(b) Draw Conclusions** What did the Greek victory at Salamis show about the Greeks' ability in war?

### Reading Skill

**3. Connect Main Ideas to Graphics** Choose a map or an image from this section. Write one or two sentences connecting information from the map or visual to the main ideas of the nearby text.

### Vocabulary Builder

Read each sentence below. If the sentence is true, write YES. If the sentence is not true, write NO and explain WHY.
**4.** A policy is a plan or course of action.

**5.** When you consult with someone, you do not want to hear what he or she has to say.

### Writing

**6.** Write three sentences about one of the Persian Wars described in this chapter, giving just the details of the battles. Then, revise your paragraphs to include mention of at least one individual who was important to the war.

# The Greek Soldier

**History-Social Science**

**6.4.6** Compare and contrast life in Athens and Sparta, with emphasis on their roles in the Persian and Peloponnesian Wars.

Warfare was a normal part of Greek life. The city-states frequently fought one another. During the Persian Wars, however, the city-states united to fight against a common enemy. Then the city-states fought one another again, during the Peloponnesian War. In Athens, boys between the ages of 18 and 20 trained as soldiers. In Sparta, training began much earlier. Boys aged as young as 7 were taken from their families to live in army barracks. Their lives were dedicated to learning the arts of war.

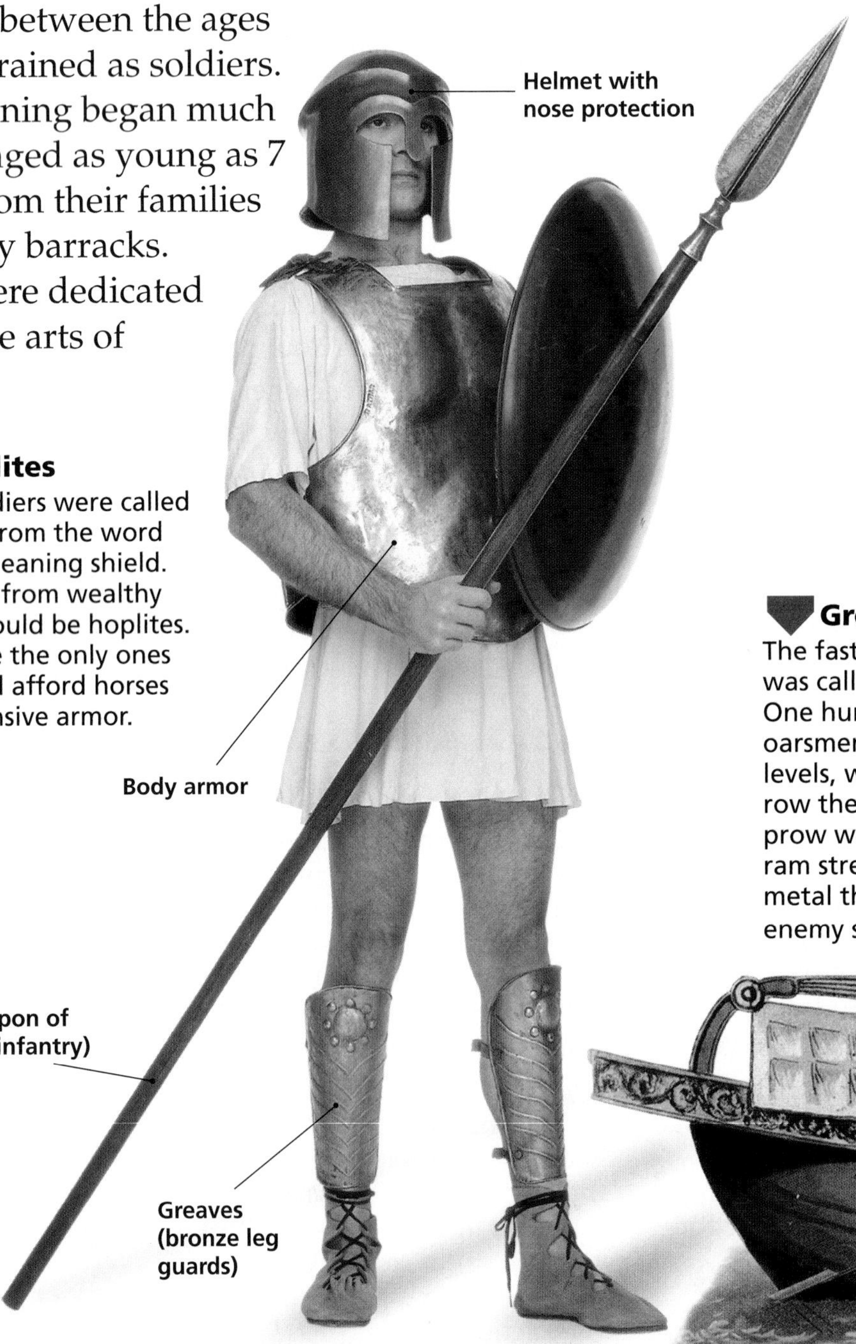

**Helmet with nose protection**

## ▶ Hoplites

Greek soldiers were called hoplites, from the word *hoplon*, meaning shield. Only men from wealthy families could be hoplites. They were the only ones who could afford horses and expensive armor.

**Body armor**

## ▼ Greek Warships

The fastest Greek ship was called a trireme. One hundred seventy oarsmen, on three levels, were needed to row the ship. At the prow was a pointed ram strengthened with metal that could sink enemy ships.

**Spear (main weapon of the Greek infantry)**

**Greaves (bronze leg guards)**

**Spartan Warriors in Training**
Spartan warriors were well known for their strength and speed on the battlefield. This image shows young Spartans exercising on a racecourse.

**Time for Play**
Greek soldiers, such as those shown on this vase, took time off from fighting by enjoying board games. Chess, backgammon, and games similar to Snakes and Ladders, shown here, have been played for more than 2,000 years.

## Analyze LIFE AT THE TIME

You are a soldier from Athens. You are talking with a soldier from Sparta after a Persian War battle. Are you arguing? Celebrating? Comparing your training or your skill in battle? Write down the conversation the two of you have.

# 3 The Peloponnesian Wars

**H-SS 6.4.6** Compare and contrast life in Athens and Sparta, with emphasis on their roles in the Persian and Peloponnesian Wars.

**E-LA Reading 6.2.3** Connect and clarify main ideas by identifying their relationships to other sources and related topics.

## Reading Preview

### Reading Skill

**Connect Main Ideas to Related Reading** The topics and main ideas in each section in this textbook present parts of the larger chapter topic. Look for ways to connect the main ideas of a chapter's section in order to better understand the overall topic.

### Vocabulary *Builder*

**High-Use Words**
supreme (suh PREEM), p. 456
launch (lawnch), p. 459

**Key Terms**
rival (RĪ vuhl), p. 456
rivalry (RĪ vuhl ree), p. 456
ally (AL lī), p. 456
truce (troos), p. 459

---

**Background Knowledge** The end of the Persian Wars did not bring peace to Greece. Although the Greek city-states had worked together to defeat Persia, they were still **rivals, or competitors.** In this section, you will read how the **rivalry, or competition** between Athens and Sparta led to a conflict known as the Peloponnesian War.

**Main Idea**
Both the Delian League, supported by Athens, and the Peloponnesian League, supported by Sparta, grew in power.

**Vocabulary *Builder***
supreme (suh PREEM) *adj.* highest in rank, power, or authority

## Athens Builds an Empire

Athens and Sparta had led the fight against Persia. After the defeat of Xerxes, both remained strong. The powerful navy of Athens made it the strongest sea power in Greece. Sparta, however, had the strongest army on land. As a result, each city-state thought it should be the <u>supreme</u> power in Greece.

**The Delian League** Soon after the war, Athens began to form an alliance with other city-states. An alliance is an organization of nations or other groups formed to achieve a goal. The members of an alliance are called **allies.** Because Athens and its allies met together on the island of Delos, their alliance was known as the Delian League. Members promised to protect each other from Persia and provide ships or money for defense.

The Delian League had about 150 members. All of the allies were supposed to be equal. However, from the start Athens played a major role in the League. Athens was by far the most powerful member. Athenian ships made it safe for Greeks to travel and ship goods by sea, which helped trade. Still, the smaller members of the League came to resent the power held by Athens.

**An Athenian Empire**   Before long, Athens was running the Delian League more like an empire than an alliance. Athens used its position of leadership to build an Athenian empire. City-states near Athens were no longer asked to join the League—they were forced to. Furthermore, member city-states could not leave the League. According to the Greek historian Thucydides, when the city-state Naxos left the League, "the Athenians made war on the place. After a siege (attack) Naxos was forced back to allegiance." Naxos was the first member to try to leave. Other members also tried.

Rather than contribute ships, the city-states near Athens were ordered to send money, which Athens would use to build up its navy. Even when there was no fighting, Athens still demanded money contributions and ships. Of course, such actions increased bad feelings between Athens and the member city-states.

In 454 B.C., Athenian leaders moved the League's treasury from Delos to Athens. Money from League members was then used to rebuild the city. The Parthenon was funded in this way.

**The Lions of Delos**
This island of Delos was the birthplace of the god Apollo, according to Greek mythology. Ancient marble lions, once numbering 16, were dedicated to Apollo in the seventh century B.C. **Critical Thinking: Distinguish Relevant Information** *Locate the island of Delos on the map on page 451. Why was it a good location for meetings of the Delian League? Explain.*

How does the alliance between Sparta and Athens in the Persian Wars help explain the formation of the Delian and Peloponnesian leagues in the years that followed?

**Main Idea**

Athens and Sparta fought against each other in the Peloponnesian War.

**The Peloponnesian War**

In this illustration, Greek and Spartan soldiers prepare for battle. **Critical Thinking: Apply Information** *What does this illustration tell you about the way in which Greek and Spartan soldiers fought?*

**The Peloponnesian League** In the 500s B.C., the Spartans formed their own alliance with other city-states on the Peloponnesian Peninsula. It is known today as the Peloponnesian League. They did this to increase their power on the Peloponnesian Peninsula and to protect Sparta from the city-states that opposed its expansion.

In most Greek city-states the wealthier citizens wanted an oligarchic government, requiring a certain level of wealth for participation in government. The less-wealthy citizens, however, wanted a more broad-based, democratic form of government. Athens supported democratic government in the cities of the Delian League, but Sparta supported an oligarchic government in the cities of the Peloponnesian League.

In 433 B.C., Athens placed a ban on trade with Megara, a member of the Peloponnesian League. This greatly angered Sparta and its allies who got ready for war. Athens and its allies did the same.

✔**Checkpoint**  **Why did Athens start the Delian League?**

# Athens and Sparta at War

War between Athens and Sparta broke out in 431 B.C. Known as the Peloponnesian War, fighting between the two groups continued on and off for 27 years.

458

**The Siege of Athens** The Peloponnesian War began when an army led by Sparta marched into Athenian territory. Pericles, the leader of Athens, ordered farmers living in the Athenian countryside to move inside the walled city.

The Spartans settled down around Athens for a long siege. The goal of a siege is to force the enemy to surrender by cutting off its food and other supplies. Athenians had prepared for just such an event by building two tall walls to line the four-and-one-half-mile road to the port city. While these Long Walls stood, Athenians could supply their city by sea.

**A Deadly Plague** The Athenians resisted the Spartan siege for more than a year. Then, a deadly plague broke out. Thousands of people died. To avoid the plague, the Spartans left the region around Athens. But the war continued. The Athenian navy attacked coastal cities. The Spartan army controlled the land. In 421 B.C., both sides agreed to a **truce, or an agreement by warring parties to stop fighting while they discuss peace terms.** However, the truce did not last long.

**The Defeat of Athens** Athens <u>launched</u> a military invasion of Sicily, which had many Greek colonies. With help from Sparta, the people of Sicily destroyed the Athenian forces.

**Primary** Sources

See "*The Peloponnesian War,*" in the Reference Section at the back of this book.

**Vocabulary *Builder***
launch (lawnch) *v.* to send forth with some force; to set in operation

## Ancient Greek Alliances

| | The Peloponnesian League | The Delian League |
|---|---|---|
| Date founded | 500s B.C. | 478 B.C. |
| Leading city-state | Sparta | Athens |
| Form of government | Oligarchy | Democracy, but later becomes an Athenian empire |
| Reason for alliance | Formed to increase Sparta's power on the Peloponnesian peninsula and to protect it from city-states that opposed Sparta's expansion | Formed to protect members of the alliance from Persia |

**Reading Charts**

After defeating the Persians, ancient Greece did not become a unified nation. However, Sparta and Athens led alliances that included almost all of the city-states in ancient Greece.

(a) **Read a Chart** Which league member changed its form of government? What was its new form?

(b) **Distinguish Relevant Information** How were the reasons for forming each league similar? How were they different?

In 405 B.C., Sparta defeated the once-great Athenian navy in the Hellespont with its own fleet. Then, the Spartans attacked Athens itself.

Again, the Athenians resisted the attack. With its new navy, Sparta was able to keep food from reaching Athens by sea. After a year, Athens was forced to give up its empire and tear down its Long Walls. Its democratic government was replaced by an oligarchy. The golden age of Athens was over.

The Peloponnesian War hurt all of the city-states. Cities were destroyed. Governments fell. Trade dropped. Yet, little seems to have been learned from this conflict. Instead of uniting, the city-states continued to fight each other. Greek culture was still vital and creative, but the best days of ancient Greece now lay in the past, not the future.

 **Checkpoint** What military strengths did Athens and Sparta have?

**Looking Back and Ahead** In this section, you have read about the Peloponnesian War. In the next section, you will read about the leader who finally united the Greek city-states under one rule.

**The Athenian Navy**
This relief, or part of a flat sculpture that stands out, shows a Greek battleship. **Critical Thinking: Frame Questions** *Write a question that can be answered by using this image and the text in this subsection.*

---

## Section 3 Check Your Progress

**Progress Monitoring** Online
**For:** Self-test with instant help
**Visit:** PHSchool.com
**Web Code:** mwa-5163

**Standards Review** H-SS: 6.4.6; E-LA: Reading 6.2.3

### Comprehension and Critical Thinking

1. (a) **Describe** Describe the relationship between Athens and other members of the Delian League.
   (b) **Compare** What were the major differences in the goals of members of the Delian League and those of the Peloponnesian League?

2. (a) **Explain** What event was the turning point in the Peloponnesian War?
   (b) **Analyze Cause and Effect** What were the long-term effects of the Peloponnesian War on Greece?

### Reading Skill

3. **Connect Main Ideas to Related Reading** In Chapter 14, you learned that Sparta had a tradition of military leadership, while Athens had a more democratic leadership. How does this knowledge help you understand each city-state's actions in the Peloponnesian Wars?

### Vocabulary *Builder*

4. Write two definitions for each word: supreme; launch. First write a formal definition for your teacher. Second, write a definition in everyday English for a classmate.

### Writing

5. Prepare an outline for a short essay about a battle of the Peloponnesian War. Use the Internet, the school library, and other research documents to gather information.

# The Empire of Alexander the Great

**Standards Preview**

**H-SS 6.4.7** Trace the rise of Alexander the Great and the spread of Greek culture eastward and into Egypt.

**E-LA Reading 6.2.3** Connect and clarify main ideas by identifying their relationships to other sources and related topics.

## Reading Preview

 **Reading Skill**

**Connect Main Ideas to Other Sources** You will use many sources as you study history. It is important to connect the information in this textbook with information from these other sources. One important source in the study of history is the atlas, which shows you where nations are and may include information about their culture, government, and language.

### Vocabulary *Builder*

**High-Use Words**
<u>acquire</u> (uh KWĪR), p. 465
<u>irrigate</u> (EER uh gayt), p. 465

**Key Terms and People**
Philip (FIHL ihp), p. 461
Alexander the Great (al ihg ZAN duhr thuh grayt), p. 462
cultural diffusion (KUHL cher uhl dih FYOO zhuhn), p. 464
Archimedes (ahr kuh MEE deez), p. 465

**Background Knowledge** After the Peloponnesian War, the Greek city-states continued their quarrels. To the north, however, a new power was rising: the kingdom of Macedonia. In this section, you will read how a Macedonian leader conquered a vast new empire. You will also learn how his conquests spread Greek culture across that empire.

## The Rise of Macedonia

Macedonia was a kingdom just north of Greece. Most Greeks thought of the Macedonians as barbarians. At the time of the Peloponnesian War, Macedonia was part of the Persian Empire. But Persian power was beginning to decline. By the 300s B.C., Persia could no longer control all of its provinces.

**Philip of Macedon** In 359 B.C., a brilliant and ambitious leader named Philip gained control of Macedonia. Philip was quick to take advantage of Persia's weakness. He united the Macedonians into a strong state. He knew a strong army was needed to achieve his goals. He built a superb standing army and then expanded his rule into Greece.

**Main Idea**
By 338 B.C. Philip of Macedon controlled all of Greece.

**King Philip of Macedon**
Philip hoped to unite Greece. Eventually he controlled all of Greece. **Critical Thinking: Apply Information** *How did Philip use diplomacy to gain control of Greece?*

**Main Idea**
The Greek city-states were finally united under one rule by Alexander the Great. In time, he extended the empire as far east as India.

**E-LA 6.2.3 Connect Main Ideas to Other Sources**
Find the Hellespont (now the Dardanelles) in an atlas. What does its location tell you about Alexander's fighting capacities?

In building his army, Philip borrowed methods that had worked well for others and then improved on them. Like the Greeks, Philip organized his infantry into phalanxes. Then he armed each man with an 18-foot-long pike. The Macedonian pike was much longer than the spears used by the Greeks.

**The Conquest of Greece**  Philip combined force with diplomacy in his conquest of Greece. First, he tried to win the loyalty of each city-state with diplomacy. When these tactics did not work, he went to war.

By 338 B.C., Philip controlled all of Greece. The city-states were allowed to keep their own governments. But they were expected to support Macedonia in a new war against Persia. Before that war could begin, however, Philip was assassinated, or killed.

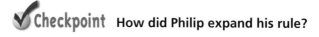
✔**Checkpoint**  **How did Philip expand his rule?**

# Alexander Conquers His World

Philip's successor was his 20-year-old son, **Alexander,** who was as brilliant as his father. As a boy, Alexander's favorite book was a copy of the *Iliad,* given to him by his teacher, the philosopher Aristotle. Alexander wanted to be like the book's hero, Achilles. This ambition would lead him to conquer his world.

**Securing Greece**  Alexander's first task was to secure control of Greece. Some city-states had seen the death of Philip as a chance to regain their independence. Alexander quickly crushed these revolts. To discourage future rebellions, he burned the city-state of Thebes to the ground. With Greece secure, Alexander turned eastward. In 334 B.C., he took his army of 30,000 foot soldiers and 5,500 cavalry troops across the Hellespont into Asia.

**The Gordian Knot**  Within a few weeks, Alexander had freed the Ionian city-states from Persian rule. From there, he moved on to Persian cities. One of these conquests was the city of Gordium. It was famous for a complicated rope knot. A peasant named Gordius was said to have created this knot long ago. According to Greek myths, whoever untied the knot would rule Asia. But all who had tried had failed.

Legends were told about Alexander and the Gordian knot. The most famous version says that he first tried to untie the knot, but failed. He then sliced through the knot with his sword, saying that he had fulfilled the legend. Today, the expression "cutting the Gordian knot" means finding a simple solution to a hard problem.

## From Egypt to India

Alexander's army moved south as far as Egypt. The Egyptians were happy to be freed from Persian rule. They welcomed Alexander as a liberator. Before leaving Egypt, he founded the city of Alexandria on the edge of the Nile delta. From Egypt, Alexander headed back toward Persia. By the end of 330 B.C., he had captured all of the Persian capitals.

Next, Alexander led his army into India. His forces reached the mouth of the Indus River in the summer of 325 B.C. The map on page 544 shows the immense size of Alexander's empire.

## The Death of Alexander

By the time he returned to Mesopotamia, Alexander was weak and ill from war injuries. In 323 b.c., he died of a fever in Babylon. He was not quite 33 years old. In many places, people viewed Alexander as a god. Whatever their beliefs, people from Egypt to India mourned the death of the man they called Alexander the Great.

✔ **Checkpoint**  **How was Alexander able to build a vast empire?**

**Alexander the Great**
This mosaic detail shows Alexander the Great in battle.
**Critical Thinking: Detect Points of View** *Why do you think that some people viewed Alexander as a god?*

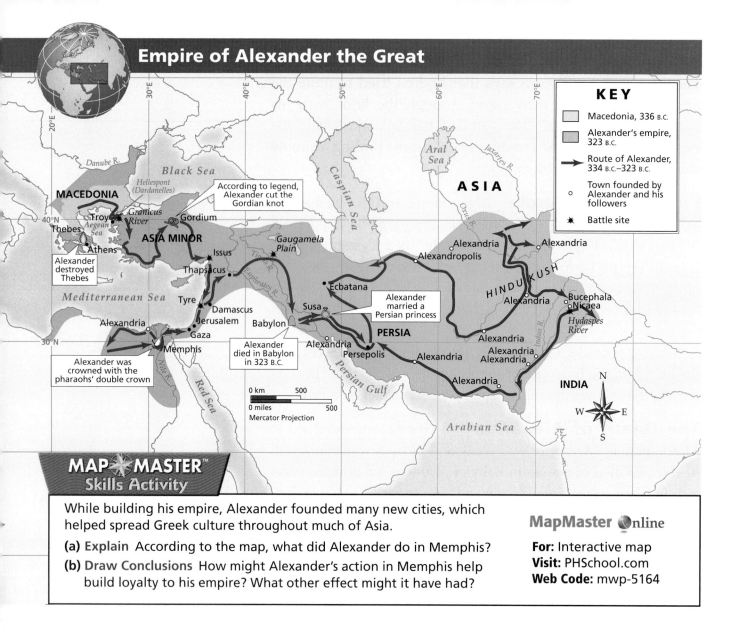

**KEY**

- Macedonia, 336 B.C.
- Alexander's empire, 323 B.C.
- Route of Alexander, 334 B.C.–323 B.C.
- Town founded by Alexander and his followers
- Battle site

**MAP MASTER**
*Skills Activity*

While building his empire, Alexander founded many new cities, which helped spread Greek culture throughout much of Asia.

**(a) Explain** According to the map, what did Alexander do in Memphis?

**(b) Draw Conclusions** How might Alexander's action in Memphis help build loyalty to his empire? What other effect might it have had?

**MapMaster Online**

**For:** Interactive map
**Visit:** PHSchool.com
**Web Code:** mwp-5164

**Main Idea**
Greek culture spread east toward India and south into Egypt due to Alexander the Great's conquests.

# The Spread of Greek Culture

After his death, Alexander's generals divided the empire into three large Greek kingdoms. Alexander's greatest legacy was a new form of Greek culture called Hellenistic, or Greek-like. *Hellenistic* is taken from the Greeks' own word for themselves: Hellenes. The Hellenistic period lasted from Alexander's time until about 30 B.C.

**Hellenistic Culture and Learning** Wherever Alexander's armies went, they took Greek culture with them. The spread of culture from one center to other places in this way is known as **cultural diffusion.** In Egypt, Alexander worshiped Egyptian gods while introducing Greek games and poetry. In Persia, he dressed like a Persian and married a Persian princess.

Greek became the language in the three kingdoms. In cities such as Alexandria in Egypt and Antioch in Asia Minor, people read Homer, watched Greek dramas, and attended Greek festivals.

New centers of Greek learning also appeared. The most famous was the Library of Alexandria, founded by the Hellenistic rulers of Egypt. Their goal was to <u>acquire</u> a copy of every book in the world. Their collection grew over the years to about 500,000 titles.

Hellenistic scholars continued the work of earlier Greek thinkers. An inventor and mathematician named **Archimedes** studied at Alexandria. Archimedes had an incredibly inventive mind. He made important contributions to mathematics. At the same time, he created many useful inventions. One of them, the Archimedean screw, is still used today to lift water for <u>irrigation</u> or for draining swamps.

**Checkpoint** **Why did Greek culture continue to spread?**

**Looking Back and Ahead** In this section, you have read how Alexander conquered an enormous empire. His conquests spread Greek culture east toward India and south into Egypt. In the next unit, you will meet another group of empire builders—the Romans.

**Vocabulary** *Builder*
<u>acquire</u> (uh KWĪR) *v.* to get or gain by one's actions or efforts

**Vocabulary** *Builder*
<u>irrigate</u> (EER uh gayt) *v.* to bring water to; to water or moisten

---

## Section 4 Check Your Progress

**Progress Monitoring** ⬤nline
**For:** Self-test with instant help
**Visit:** PHSchool.com
**Web Code:** mwa-5164

**Standards Review** H-SS: 6.4.7; E-LA: Reading 6.2.3

### Comprehension and Critical Thinking

1. **(a) Explain** Describe the main target of Alexander's invasions.
   **(b) Draw Conclusions** How did Philip of Macedon's political and military efforts make it possible for Alexander's conquests to be successful?
2. **(a) Identify** Where did Greek culture spread during the Hellenistic period?
   **(b) Apply Information** How did Hellenistic culture resemble Greek culture?

### Reading Skill

3. **Connect Main Ideas to Other Sources** Reread the section The Gordian Knot on page 462. Gordium was located near the modern city of Ankara. Find this city in the atlas. Who governs it now? Is it any of the empires that ruled in Alexander's time?

### Vocabulary *Builder*

Answer the following question in a complete sentence that shows your understanding of the Key Term.

4. How did Alexander the Great encourage cultural diffusion?

### Writing

5. Use research sources such as the school library, the Internet, and other resources to gather information for a short essay on the conquests of Alexander the Great. Prepare a short bibliography to identify the resources you would use.

# Recognize Error and Oversight in History

Everyone makes mistakes. Some mistakes result from bad judgment. Others result from oversight, or not paying attention. Many mistakes are not very important. In some cases, however, error and oversight can change the course of history.

**Chapter Standards**

**History-Social Science**

**Historical Interpretation 4** Students recognize the role of chance, oversight, and error in history.

> **❝**Cambyses . . . set out on his march against the Kush without making any provision for the feeding of his army. . . . Like a senseless madman . . . he began his march. Before he had traveled one-fifth of the distance, all the army's food was gone. The men were forced to eat the pack animals, which were soon gone also. If at this time, Cambyses . . . had confessed himself in the wrong, and led his army back, he would have done the wisest thing that he could . . . But . . . he . . . continued to march forward. So long as the earth gave them anything, the soldiers lived by eating the grass and herbs. But when they came to the bare sand, a portion of them were guilty of a horrid deed. By tens they cast lots for a man, who was slain to be the food of the others. When Cambyses heard of these doings . . . he gave up his attack on Kush. . . . **❞**

—from *The History of Herodotus*, Book 3, 440 B.C.

**Learn the Skill** *Follow these steps to identify the role of error and oversight in history.*

1. **Identify the topic.** What is the passage about? Where and when do the events take place?

2. **Identify the errors and oversights.** What mistakes were made? Who made them? Did the mistakes result from bad judgment or from oversight?

3. **Identify the effects of the errors and oversights.** Think about the results that each mistake caused. For example, suppose a military leader made a huge error in judgment and it made his country lose a war. The effect could be that the country is taken over by its enemies.

**Practice the Skill** *Use the passage above to answer the following questions.*

1. **Identify the topic. (a)** Where were Cambyses and his troops going? **(b)** What was Cambyses trying to accomplish?

2. **Identify the errors and oversights. (a)** What mistakes did Cambyses make before he started the journey? **(b)** What mistake did Cambyses make after he discovered his first mistakes?

3. **Identify the effects of the errors and oversights. (a)** Did Cambyses accomplish his goal? **(b)** How might history have been different if Cambyses had not made the mistakes he did?

**Apply the Skill**
See page 469 of the Chapter Assessment.

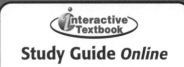

## Chapter Summary  H-SS: 6.4, 6.4.5, 6.4.6, 6.4.7

### Section 1  The Persian Empire

- The rulers of the Persian Empire set up an efficient political organization.
- The Persian Empire balanced local self-government with central government in order to govern their vast territory.

### Section 2  The Persian Wars

- The Persian king Darius intended to conquer all of Greece.
- The Athenians and Spartans worked together to defend themselves against the Persians.

### Section 3  The Peloponnesian Wars

- Athens and its allies form the Delian League. Sparta forms the Peloponnesian League with its allies.
- Although together they defeated the Persians, Athens and Sparta fought against each other in the 27-year-long Peloponnesian War.

### Section 4  The Empire of Alexander the Great

- The Greek city-states were finally united under one rule by Alexander the Great.
- Alexander the Great's conquests spread Greek culture east toward India and south into Egypt.

## Standards Practice  H-SS: 6.4, 6.4.5, 6.4.6, 6.4.7

## Vocabulary *Builder*

### High-Use Words

Decide whether each underlined word is used correctly. If it is, explain why. If not, rewrite the rest of the sentence to make it logical.

1. The emperor's **authority** prevented him from making laws or decisions.

2. The generals **consulted** one another before attacking their enemy.

3. The **supreme** court is the lowest-ranking court in the country.

4. Both nations **acquired**, or gave up, new land after the war.

5. The farmers dried out their crops with **irrigation**.

### Key Terms

Answer the following questions in complete sentences that show your understanding of the Key Terms and People.

1. Explain how Cyrus the Great and Croesus dominated their people during each of their reigns.

2. What role did Herodotus play during the Persian and Peloponnesian wars?

3. How did both Darius the Great and Alexander the Great expand each of their empires?

4. How did Hellenistic culture spread through cultural diffusion?

##  Apply Reading Skills

**Connect and Clarify Main Ideas** Write a statement that connects the main ideas of Section 1, The Persian Empire, and Section 4, The Empire of Alexander the Great.

## Comprehension and Critical Thinking

1. **(a) Identify** Who was the founder and first king of the Persian Empire?
   **(b) Describe** What territory did he and his successors add to the empire?
   **(c) Distinguish Relevant Information** How did Cyrus the Great exhibit tolerance for the peoples he conquered?

2. **(a) List** Which Persian rulers went to war against the Greeks?
   **(b) Analyze Cause and Effect** Which battle led to the second Persian War? How?

3. **(a) Explain** How were the Greeks able to win the Battle of Salamis?
   **(b) Apply Information** Describe the effects of the Battle of Salamis on the Greeks and the Persians.

4. **(a) Recall** How did the Athenians defend themselves against Sparta's attack?
   **(b) Apply Information** What part did Persia play in the final defeat of Athens?
   **(c) Draw Inferences** Do you think Athens would have been defeated had they not invaded Sicily? Explain.

5. **(a) Explain** How was Philip of Macedon able to gain power in Greece?
   **(b) Compare** How did Alexander the Great's conquests compare with those of Cyrus and Darius?

## Researching

**Alexander the Great** Much has been written about the contributions of Alexander the Great to world history in general and to Greek culture in particular. In this activity, you will use the Internet, the library media center, and other resources to report on a contribution made by Alexander the Great. Share your work with the class on "Alexander the Great" Day. Make a list of the resources you used to go with your presentation.

**Historians:** Write several paragraphs that detail how Alexander helped spread Hellenistic culture throughout the world. Include in your writing issues he might have faced in achieving this goal and examples of his legacy.

**Journalist:** From your research, create a front page of a newspaper that reports on Alexander's travels and conquests.

> **Researching Online**
> **For:** Help in starting this activity
> **Visit:** PHSchool.com
> **Web Code:** mwe-5165

## Writing

1. **Write a paragraph on the following topic.** Describe the military strategies used by the Spartans against the Greeks in the Peloponnesian War.
   **Your paragraph should:**
   • Contain information from your text and other resources.
   • Use proper citations when listing all your sources.

2. **Write a short narrative.** Cyrus the Great is meeting with his government officials after his conquest of Babylonia. Write a short narrative describing his remarks to his officials about the advantages of ruling with tolerance.

**H-SS:** HI 4; 6.4, 6.4.5, 6.4.6, 6.4.7

# Apply Analysis Skills

Use the paragraph on page 443 entitled The Fall of Lydia to answer these questions.

1. What was the goal of Cyrus the Great?

2. What goal did Croesus have?

3. What error in judgment did Croesus make?

4. Did Croesus accomplish his goal?

5. How might history have been different if Croesus had not made his errors of judgment and mistakes?

# Test Yourself

1. **As the Persians founded and expanded their empire, they**
   A forced conquered peoples to adopt their language, customs, and religion.
   B established provinces connected by roads and a common currency.
   C appointed Immortals as tax collectors for the emperor.
   D elected Greeks as satraps in all of the provinces.

**Refer to the map below to answer Question 2.**

2. **According to the map, the Persian Empire extended from**

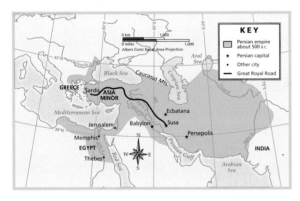

   A the Aral Sea in the south to the Mediterranean Sea in the east.
   B the Mediterranean Sea in the west, to the Red Sea in the north, to India in the east.
   C Greece in the west, to India in the east, and to Egypt in the south.
   D Asia Minor in the east, to India in the west, to Thebes in the south.

**Refer to the quotation below to answer Question 3.**

3. **According to Herodotus, how did Xerxes intend to defeat the Greeks?**

*"The army was indeed immense—far greater than any other in recorded history. . . . There was not a nation in Asia that he did not take with him against Greece."*

   A With diplomacy
   B With bribes and diplomacy
   C With military strength
   D With armies from Egypt

4. **After the Peloponnesian War,**
   A Pericles was killed by the Spartans.
   B Athenian democracy was replaced by an oligarchy.
   C Sparta had the strongest navy and Athens had the strongest army.
   D Sparta led the Delian League and Athens led the Peloponnesian League.

5. **Which statement regarding Hellenistic culture is correct?**
   A Egyptian culture dominated the empire.
   B Athens was the center of Greek learning.
   C Each kingdom had a different official language and government.
   D People from Persia, Greece, and Egypt acquired aspects of each other's cultures.

# Writing Workshop

## Research Paper, Part 2

### ▶ Introduction

As you learned in the Writing Workshop for Unit 4, when you create a research paper, you gather information about a subject from several different sources. You organize this information and present it to your readers in a carefully developed paper. A research paper should have the following characteristics:

- A topic that can be researched
- Information from several different sources
- A thesis statement expressing an idea about the topic, based on the research
- A paper that presents the information and identifies the sources used

**Assignment** On the following pages, you will review what you learned in the previous Writing Workshop about planning and gathering information for a research paper. Then you will learn how to write the paper itself. You will get step-by-step instructions. Each step will include an example from research about the theater of ancient Greece.

Read the instructions and the examples. Then, follow each step to plan a research paper on this topic:

**The Culture of Ancient Greece**

### ▶ Planning and Doing Your Research

**Focus your topic and do research.** Begin by narrowing your research topic to something you can cover effectively in the space you have. For example, if you were writing about the ancient Greek theater, you might think about specific topics such as the architecture of the theater, the plays, actors' masks and costumes, and so on.

To locate sources about your topic, visit the library. Check the card catalogue and the tables of contents and indexes of the books you find. Search the Internet, using various key words.

**History-Social Science**

**6.4** Students analyze the geographic, political, economic, religious, and social structures of the early civilizations of Ancient Greece.

**English-Language Arts**

**Writing 6.2.3** Write research reports.

For a review of the steps in the writing process, see the **Historian's Toolkit,** *Write Like a Historian.*

In taking notes, paraphrase important statements, and summarize longer sections. Copy quotations exactly, always giving credit to the writer. (To review these steps, see the Writing Workshop in Unit 4.)

You will often be asked to write comparison-and-contrast essays. Make sure that you understand which items you are supposed to write about before you begin.

**Gather details.** Look for facts, descriptions, and examples that explain and support your thesis. Write down the facts you may be able to use, as well as the reference information for the places in which you found them.

**Create a working thesis.** After you have taken some notes from your sources, write a sentence expressing an idea about your topic. This "working thesis" can be changed as you do more research and thinking, but it should guide your work.

> **Sample working thesis:** "Although there are some similarities, the experience of going to an ancient Greek theater was quite different from that of attending a play today."

## ▶ Outlining

**Decide how to organize your writing.** When you have your information and your thesis, you need to decide on a method of organization that works for your topic. If you are discussing something from the past, you could compare and contrast it with something from the present. If you are focusing on a particular event or process, you could use chronological organization. If you are discussing several related items, you could organize them in ascending order of importance.

Creating an outline can help you stay organized when you have a great deal of material to present. An outline shows the bare-bones structure of your paper. List the major topics and their subtopics. (A subtopic is one smaller part of a topic. For example, in a section about the audience area of the ancient Greek theaters, one subtopic might be the number of people who could fit into the audience.) On the following page is part of an outline for a research paper on Greek theater.

> **Sample assignment:**
> "Describe the characteristics of ancient Greek theaters that were different from theaters today." Note that this assignment limits the topic so that you do not have to describe the characteristics that are the same as those of theaters today, such as actors, seating, and scripts.

Skene was a building behind the stage.
(http://academic.reed.edu/humanities/110Tech/Theater.html)

Skene started out as a simple building for the actors to use. (Hornblower, p. 709)

Source information
Englert, Walter. "Ancient Greek Theatre."
(http://academic.reed.edu/humanities/110Tech/Theater.html)

Hornblower, Simon, and Spawforth, Antony, eds. The Oxford Companion to Classical Civilization. Oxford, Great Britain University Press, 1998.

# Writing Workshop *continued*

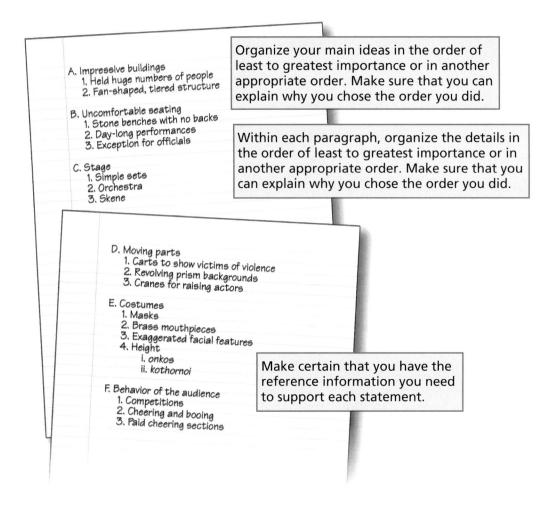

A. Impressive buildings
  1. Held huge numbers of people
  2. Fan-shaped, tiered structure

B. Uncomfortable seating
  1. Stone benches with no backs
  2. Day-long performances
  3. Exception for officials

C. Stage
  1. Simple sets
  2. Orchestra
  3. Skene

D. Moving parts
  1. Carts to show victims of violence
  2. Revolving prism backgrounds
  3. Cranes for raising actors

E. Costumes
  1. Masks
  2. Brass mouthpieces
  3. Exaggerated facial features
  4. Height
    i. onkos
    ii. kothornoi

F. Behavior of the audience
  1. Competitions
  2. Cheering and booing
  3. Paid cheering sections

> Organize your main ideas in the order of least to greatest importance or in another appropriate order. Make sure that you can explain why you chose the order you did.

> Within each paragraph, organize the details in the order of least to greatest importance or in another appropriate order. Make sure that you can explain why you chose the order you did.

> Make certain that you have the reference information you need to support each statement.

## ▶ Writing the First Draft

**Write your introduction.** Write an introductory paragraph that catches your audience's attention. Set up your research topic, indicating what aspects of the topic you will cover. Lead up to your thesis statement.

**Support your thesis with examples and details.** Now write the body of your paper, presenting the best information that you found in your research. Use your outline as a guide. Writing a topic sentence for each paragraph will help you stay on target. Use transitions to keep the relationships between your ideas clear.

**Write a strong conclusion.** In your final paragraph, review the ground that you have covered. Then state what you found most interesting, moving, or surprising about what you learned.

## ▶ Student Model

Read the following model of a research paper about ancient Greek theater. Notice how it includes the characteristics you have learned about.

### The Ancient Greek Theater: A Very Different Experience

Athenians loved the theater. It was so popular, in fact, that an Athenian leader had a theater built in honor of the god Dionysus. Every year during the festival of Dionysus plays were performed at this theater from morning until dusk. Although there are some similarities, the experience of going to an ancient Greek theater was quite different from that of attending a play today.

Greek theaters were very impressive buildings. They were intended both to honor the gods and to hold huge numbers of people. The theater built for Dionysus held as many as 14,000 people. Ancient writings indicate that these theaters were fan-shaped structures of tiers or steps.

At first theaters were made of wood, but later they were constructed from stone. Greek theaters were not built for comfort. Audience seats were stone benches with no backs. If theatergoers were lucky, the people sitting in the row behind let them lean on their legs for support. Religious and civic officials, however, sat in the front of the theater and had special seats with backs.

The stage was also different from those in today's theaters. Modern theaters often have elaborate scenery that moves with the push of a button. Greek stages were simpler. The front of the stage, called the orchestra, was for a chorus of people. A structure called a skene stood at the rear of the stage. It represented the setting of the story. It may have also been a place for actors to wait or change.

The Greek stage did have some moving parts. It was against Greek custom to show violence on a stage. Instead,

*Include a thesis statement that expresses an idea about a topic based on your resesearch.*

*Each paragraph begins with a topic sentence. The sentences that follow contain supporting details.*

*Are the main points organized by least important to most important order?*

actors were wheeled onto the stage on a wooden structure. They posed to create a still picture suggesting that a murder or a battle had occurred. Theaters also had revolving structures shaped like a prism. They had different backgrounds painted on them to show scene changes. To represent gods coming down to Earth, the Greeks used cranes to move actors up and down from the stage.

Probably the most startling difference between the ancient Greek theater and the modern theater is costuming. Greek players wore masks fitted with brass mouthpieces that helped their voices to carry. The facial features of the masks were exaggerated so that people in the farthest seats could understand the play. Actors also had to be tall enough to be easily seen. Actors increased their height by wearing an onkos. This device was a projection on top of the head. Actors also wore kothornoi, or thick-soled shoes, to add height.

Another big difference between ancient and modern theaters was the behavior of the audience. Plays were performed as part of a competition at a religious festival.

In some ways, audiences treated plays as if they were competitive games. If an actor was not very good, he might be booed off the stage. If he was extremely unpopular, he might have food or even rocks thrown at him.

The ancient Greek theaters had a very different atmosphere from that of modern theaters. For the audience, and actors both, the theatre was physically challenging. Audiences did not shrug off a poor performance. Unlike attending a modern theatrical performance, going to the Greek theater was rather like going to a sporting event.

The last paragraph restates the thesis and summarizes the key information.

# ▶ Revising

After completing your draft, read it again carefully to find ways to make your writing better.

## Revise to heighten interest and clarify research
- Does the first paragraph capture the reader's attention?
- Can you describe anything in greater detail?
- Is every piece of information clear?
- Are the relationships between ideas clear? Can you add any transitions to make these relationships clearer?

## Revise to meet standard English conventions
- Are all sentences complete, with a subject and a verb?
- Are spelling, capitalization, and punctuation correct?

## Revise to meet research-paper conventions
- Have you properly identified all of your sources?
- Are all quotations clearly marked, with credit given to the original writer or speaker?

*Theaters also had revolving structures shaped like a prism. ~~They~~ These structures had different backgrounds painted on them to show scene changes. To represent gods ~~or heroes~~ coming down to Earth, the Greeks used cranes to move actors up and down from the stage.*

# ▶ Rubric for Self-Assessment

*Evaluate your essay using this rating scale.*

|  | Score 4 | Score 3 | Score 2 | Score 1 |
|---|---|---|---|---|
| **Topic** | Is appropriate for a research paper, requires outside research | Is appropriate for a research paper, requires outside research | Is barely appropriate for a research paper, is too broad (or too narrow) | Is not appropriate for a research paper |
| **Sources** | Uses a variety of appropriate sources | Uses several appropriate sources | Uses only one or two sources | Uses no outside sources |
| **Organization** | Follows an appropriate organization; makes relationships between the ideas clear | Shows clear organization; clear relationships between most ideas | Shows unclear organization; unclear connections between some ideas | Shows lack of organizational strategy |
| **Presentation** | Presents interesting, concrete and detailed facts, examples, and relevant information | Presents research information relevant to the topic | Research information is not in sufficient depth or detail | Presents little outside information; does not provide details to support ideas |
| **Use of Language** | Varies sentence structure and vocabulary; very few mechanical errors | Uses some variety in sentence structure and vocabulary; a few mechanical errors | Uses limited sentence variety, does not vary vocabulary; includes mechanical errors | Writes incomplete sentences; uses language poorly; many mechanical errors |
| **References** | Provides appropriate sources for all information; provides appropriate details in requested format | Provides appropriate sources for all information; small problems with format of references | Fails to provide appropriate sources for some facts; most references provide appropriate detail | Few or no references provided |

# Unit 6

 **Quick View** Video

**Discovery School Video** View *Ancient Rome* for a quick preview of the main ideas of this unit.

**The Roman Colosseum**

# Ancient Rome

Latium,
1000 B.C.

The Roman Empire,
44 B.C.

Galilee,
4 B.C.

## *Think* like a historian

The map above shows the area in which the civilization
of ancient Rome developed. Rome grew from a small
collection of villages to a large empire.

**As you read this unit, think about this question:**
*Why do some empires have a greater influence on the
world than others?*

Chapter
# 17 The Roman Republic
## (1000 B.C.–287 B.C.)

## Prepare to Read

 **Chapter Standards**

### History-Social Science
**6.7** Students analyze the geographic, political, economic, religious, and social structures during the development of Rome.

 **What You Will Learn**

**Section 1,** pp. 482–486

**On the Banks of the Tiber**

Rome grew from a group of small villages on the Italian Peninsula along the Tiber River. Several founding myths describe the city's beginnings.

**Section 2,** pp. 487–492

**Rise of the Roman Republic**

Following a period of rule by the Etruscans, the Roman Republic was established. Over time, power struggles between upper and lower class citizens moved Rome toward a more democratic government.

**Section 3,** pp. 493–497

**The Government of the Republic**

The government of the Roman Republic had three branches. The Roman constitution and other later reforms helped citizens gain additional rights.

**Section 4,** pp. 498–502

**Roman Society**

Family relationships were an important part of Rome's social structure. Roman virtues and religion also influenced the society of the Republic.

Statue of Minerva

**About 1000 B.C.**
Latins settle in Latium.

**About 600 B.C.**
Etruscans expand into Latium.

Chapter Events

**1000 B.C.**

**800 B.C.**

**600 B.C.**

Other Events

**About 1000 B.C.** King David rules Judea and Israel.

**700 B.C.** India has many Aryan kingdoms.

## Where and When?
About 3,000 years ago, Rome was established along the banks of the Tiber River.

The Forum once served as the center of government and business in ancient Rome.

**509** B.C.
Romans overthrow Etruscan king and establish the Roman Republic.

**287** B.C.
The Lex Hortensia passes.

**600** B.C.

**400** B.C.

**200** B.C.

**508** B.C. Cleisthenes gains power in Athens.

**221** B.C. Qin forces unite China under their rule.

## History Reading Skill

### *Previewing* **Recognize and Use Words with Latin Origins**

Many English words trace their roots to Latin, the language of the ancient Romans. Knowledge of these roots will help you build meaning for English words. Also, some words and phrases from Latin have been added to English in their original form. The chart below lists both Latin word roots and common phrases. Recognizing the origins and meanings of these words will help you use them accurately.

**Chapter Standards**
**English-Language Arts**
**Reading 6.1.3** Recognize the origins and meanings of frequently used foreign words in English and use these words accurately in speaking and writing.

## Latin Roots and Sayings

| Latin Root | Meaning | English Words |
|---|---|---|
| loc | place | located, location |
| portio | share, part | portion |
| orig | beginning | origins, original |
| sign | mark | signify, significance |
| scandere | jump | descendants (includes *de-* = "down") |
| volv | roll | evolved, revolt |
| dict | speak, say | predict, indicated, dictator |
| pop | people | population |
| pater | father | patron, patricians, patriarchal, paterfamilias |
| spec | see | aspect, respect, expect |
| partiri | to divide | tripartite |
| tri | three | |
| magister | chief, director | magistrate |
| legis | law | legislature |

| Latin Saying | English Meaning |
|---|---|
| et cetera | and other things of the same type, the rest |
| vice versa | with the order of meaning reversed |
| per capita | per person |
| de facto | something automatically accepted |
| mea culpa | my fault, my mistake |

# Vocabulary *Builder*

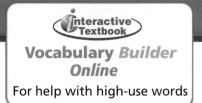

**Vocabulary *Builder* Online**
For help with high-use words

## *Previewing* High-Use Academic Words

| High-Use Word | Definition | Sample Sentence About History |
|---|---|---|
| **link** (lihngk) (Section 1, p. 485) | *v.* to join together with or as with a link | Historians have been able to link some events in legends to historical events. |
| **role** (rohl) (Section 1, p. 485) | *n.* function or office assumed by someone or something | Trade played an important role in the growth of the city. |
| **adapt** (uh DAPT) (Section 2, p. 488) | *v.* to make fit or suitable by changing or adjusting | The civilization survived because people adapted to their environment. |
| **initial** (ih NIHSH uhl) (Section 2, p. 491) | *adj.* having to do with, indicating, or occurring at the beginning | While the soldiers' initial efforts proved unsuccessful, they later won the battle. |
| **focus** (FOH kuhs) (Section 3, p. 493) | *v.* to direct one's thoughts or efforts; concentrate | The government chose to focus on only the most important problems facing the nation. |
| **theory** (THEE uh ree) (Section 3, p. 497) | *n.* branch of art or science consisting of principles and methods rather than of its practice | The citizens agreed to the reforms in theory, yet they chose not to act upon the new laws. |
| **indicate** (IHN dih kayt) (Section 4, p. 500) | *v.* to direct attention to; point out | Archaeological evidence indicates the civilization developed new skills. |

## *Previewing* Key Terms and People

arable land, p. 483
arid, p. 483
Virgil, p. 484
divine, p. 484
navigate, p. 486

republic, p. 489
consul, p. 489
patrician, p. 490
plebeian, p. 490
debt bondage, p. 491

tribune, p. 491
tripartite, p. 493
dictator, p. 494
Cincinnatus, p. 494

veto, p. 495
constitution, p. 495
checks and balances, p. 496

patriarchal, p. 498
clan, p. 500
gravitas, p. 501
civic virtue, p. 501

The Roman Republic **481**

Section 1

# On the Banks of the Tiber

##  Standards Preview

**H-SS 6.7.1** Identify the location and describe the rise of the Roman Republic, including the importance of such mythical and historical figures as Aeneas, Romulus and Remus, Cincinnatus, Julius Caesar, and Cicero.

**E-LA Reading 6.1.3** Recognize the origins and meanings of frequently used foreign words in English and use these words accurately in speaking and writing.

## Reading Preview

### Reading Skill

**Recognize Latin Word Origins** Many words with Latin roots are highlighted in this chapter. When you read one of these words, find it in the chart on page 480. Use the chart to find the meaning of the word's Latin root, and consider how that meaning connects to the definition of the English word.

### Vocabulary *Builder*

**High-Use Words**
link (lihngk), p. 485
role (rohl), p. 485

**Key Terms and People**
arable land (AR uh buhl land), p. 483
arid (AR ihd), p. 483
Virgil (VER juhl), p. 484
divine (duh VĪN), p. 484
navigate (NAV uh gayt), p. 486

**Background Knowledge** In the 500s B.C., a small settlement was established on the banks of the Tiber River in what is now Italy. Its people called it Rome. In time, this settlement would become a great city and the center of a mighty empire that spread across a vast area of land. As in Greece, geography played a key role in the development of Rome. In this section, you will read about Rome's location and origins, as well as the factors that helped it develop from a collection of small villages into a major city.

**Main Idea**
Rome developed from a small settlement along the Tiber River.

## The Location of Rome

As you can see on the map on page 483, Rome is located near the center of the Italian Peninsula. This boot-shaped finger of land extends from southern Europe into the Mediterranean Sea. A high mountain range called the Alps separates the peninsula from the rest of Europe. Several rivers that begin in these mountains flow across the peninsula and reach the Mediterranean Sea. Another long mountain range, the Apennines, runs down the center of this area. This range stretches for more than 850 miles, reaching the "toe" of the Italian Peninsula.

**482** Chapter 17 The Roman Republic

## Rome's Geographic Setting

In some ways, the geography of the Italian Peninsula is similar to that of Greece. Both enjoy a Mediterranean climate with mild winters and warm, dry summers. Both possess natural harbors, and both feature locations well-suited to trading with the lands surrounding the Mediterranean Sea. The two areas are also linked by land with the rest of Europe.

However, several important differences between the two areas do exist. Despite its many mountains, the Italian Peninsula has a less rugged landscape than Greece. This made it easier for Rome to unite the peninsula under its rule. The peninsula also has several large plains, especially in the north. This gave it more arable land, or land suited for farming, than Greece. In fact, crops such as grains, vegetables, and olives still grow in the region today. In addition, the Italian Peninsula has several navigable rivers. Since ancient times, these rivers have provided both water and transportation routes to people who live in the area.

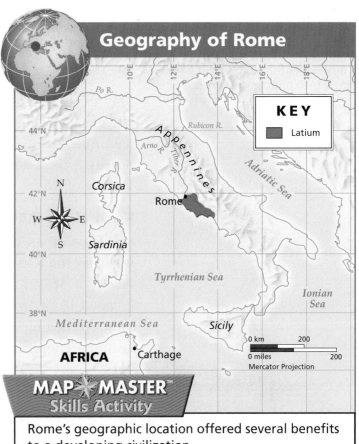

**Geography of Rome**

KEY

Latium

MAP MASTER™
Skills Activity

Rome's geographic location offered several benefits to a developing civilization.

**(a) Locate** In what direction would a person travel from Rome to reach the Adriatic Sea?

**(b) Apply Information** How might early settlers in this area have improved travel over land?

MapMaster Online

**For:** Interactive map
**Visit:** PHSchool.com
**Web Code:** mwp-6171

**The Tiber River**  One such river is the Tiber. The Tiber River stretches for more than 250 miles, making it the second longest river in present-day Italy. The waters of the Tiber eventually flow into the Tyrrhenian Sea after passing through Rome. It drains the west-central portion of present-day Italy, a region called Latium (LAY shee uhm). Today, Latium is rather arid, or dry. But in ancient times, it was green and lush. Many volcanoes dot this region. Ash from the eruptions of these volcanoes helped create fertile soil used for farming.

Just before reaching the sea, the Tiber flows through an area of low hills. It was here, on the banks of the Tiber, that Rome was founded.

 **Checkpoint**  How did Rome's location support its development of agriculture?

# The Origins of Rome

**Main Idea**
Rome's location allowed it to grow into a large city with natural defenses and access to major trade routes.

Around 1000 B.C., a people called the Latins settled in Latium. Eventually they founded a village on Palatine Hill, one of seven hills on the east bank of the Tiber River, about fifteen miles from the sea. Later, other villages were settled on nearby hills. Eventually, these hilltop villages would become the city of Rome.

**Founding Myths** The Romans had two myths regarding their city's origins. One appears in the *Aeneid,* an epic poem by the Roman poet **Virgil.** This poem describes the journey of a Trojan warrior named Aeneas. It says that Aeneas escaped from Troy after its defeat by the Greeks in the Trojan War. According to Virgil, Aeneas traveled until he reached Latium. There, he married a Latin princess and founded a town near the mouth of the Tiber. Eventually, his descendants founded Rome. Because of its patriotic portrayal of Rome and its origins, this myth became well known and Virgil was considered the national poet of Rome.

The second myth concerns two of Aeneas' descendants, a pair of twins named Romulus and Remus. This myth can be traced back to at least 300 B.C. and includes characteristics of both Greek and Roman mythology. Like Hercules, the twins were said to be born of a human mother and a **divine, meaning god or godlike,** father, the god Mars. A jealous uncle had the babies placed in a basket and thrown into the Tiber. The boys were saved from death by a she-wolf and then raised by a shepherd.

When they were grown, Romulus and Remus set out to found a new city. They could not agree, however, on the best location for their city. In the heat of this dispute, Romulus killed Remus. He then founded Rome on Palatine Hill, naming the city after himself and becoming the first king of Rome.

## BIOGRAPHY QUEST

### What caused Virgil to stop writing the *Aeneid*?

Virgil

**Fast Facts**

**Who:** Virgil
**What:** Roman poet
**When:** 70 B.C.–19 B.C.
**Where:** Rome
**Why important:** Virgil's epic poem, the *Aeneid,* celebrates the values and achievements of ancient Rome. The poem has also proven influential to many later poets.

**Fast Find**

**How:** Go online to find out how long Virgil spent writing the *Aeneid,* and how he came to stop his work on the poem.

**Biography**
**Online**

**For:** More about Virgil
**Visit:** PHSchool.com
**Web Code:** mwe-6171

Legend states that Palatine Hill was the location at which Romulus and Remus had been rescued and raised. During several later time periods, Palatine Hill served as the home for many of Rome's most prominent citizens.

Rome's founding myths have little basis in fact. But they do signify something about the Roman people. From early times, they believed that Rome was destined for greatness. They wanted to <u>link</u> its history to gods and legendary heroes. They did so by creating myths that would glorify Rome's beginnings as well as its founders.

**Vocabulary** *Builder*
<u>link</u> (lihngk) *v.* to join together with or as with a link

**Growth of the City**   For many years, Rome remained a collection of tiny villages. Eventually, these villages began to grow together, and by 600 B.C., the villages had formed a single city covering the seven hills on the banks of the Tiber. By this time, Rome's population had increased to around 80,000 people.

Rome's location played a key <u>role</u> in its growth. A Roman author named Cicero wrote that

**E-LA 6.1.3 Recognize Latin Word Origins**   How does the Latin root *loc* relate to an important word in this section?

**Vocabulary** *Builder*
<u>role</u> (rohl) *n.* function or office assumed by someone or something

> **The location [Romulus] chose for the city . . . was unbelievably favorable. . . . It seems to me that even then, Romulus foresaw that this city would sometime be the seat and home of [a great empire]. For practically no city situated in any other part of Italy could have been better able to command such economic advantages.**
>
> —Cicero, *On the Commonwealth*

**Tiber River**
The Tiber River continues to flow through the modern city of Rome. **Critical Thinking: Identify Costs** *How might the depth of the Tiber have been a cost as well as a benefit to the early Romans?*

The city's hills provided the Romans with a natural defense against attack. They could farm the fields below and then retreat to their hilltop homes for safety in times of war. Its location on the Tiber River provided access to a nearby port. Despite the river's shallow depth of only 7 to 20 feet, small boats could **navigate,** or make their way, by river to the sea. Romans also used the river to transport trade goods such as grain. However, because the river was too fast and dangerous for large boats, Rome could not be attacked by large seagoing ships.

Rome was also located on key trade routes. The Tiber Valley provided a natural east-west route for trade. In addition, several north-south trade routes crossed the Tiber just south of Rome. Salt from along the Tiber River, as well as iron found nearby, were some of the items sent along these trade routes. Each of these factors contributed to help Rome grow and prosper.

✔**Checkpoint** How did geography help shape the development of Rome?

**Looking Back and Ahead** In this section, you have read about the location and origins of Rome. In the next section, you will learn about the development of Roman government.

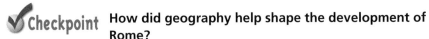

**Section 1 Check Your Progress**

**Progress Monitoring** ⏸Online
**For:** Self-test with instant help
**Visit:** PHSchool.com
**Web Code:** mwa-6171

 **Standards Review** H-SS: 6.7.1; E-LA: Reading 6.1.3

**Comprehension and Critical Thinking**

1. **(a) Recall** Where was Rome located?
   **(b) Explain Problem** What disadvantages might this location have presented to the growing settlement?

2. **(a) Describe** Describe the myths that tell of Rome's founding.
   **(b) Detect Point of View** How did these myths shape the way Romans felt about their history?

**Reading Skill**

3. **Recognize Latin Word Origins** What is the Latin root of the word *descendants*? Explain how this root relates to the meaning of the word—people who come from a specific ancestor.

**Vocabulary** *Builder*
Complete each of the following sentences so that the second part further explains the first part and clearly shows your understanding of the highlighted word.

4. The Italian Peninsula had a great deal of arable land; _____.

5. Hercules' father was believed to be divine; _____.

6. The Tiber River proved deep enough for small boats to navigate; _____.

**Writing**

7. Think of a controversial issue, such as the best location for a new settlement. Then, brainstorm a list of arguments that could support each side of the issue you choose.

# Rise of the Roman Republic

## Standards Preview

**H-SS 6.7.1** Identify the location and describe the rise of the Roman Republic, including the importance of such mythical and historical figures as Aeneas, Romulus and Remus, Cincinnatus, Julius Caesar, and Cicero.

**E-LA Reading 6.1.3** Recognize the origins and meanings of frequently used foreign words in English and use these words accurately in speaking and writing.

## Reading Preview

 **Reading Skill**

**Analyze Latin Word Origins** When you find a word with a Latin root, think about ways in which the root meaning could apply to the modern word. For example, the word *signify* includes the root *sign*, meaning "mark." In the phrase "but they do signify something about the Roman people," the root suggests a meaning such as "make a mark about," but we read it as "tell something important about."

**Vocabulary *Builder***

**High-Use Words**
<u>adapt</u> (uh DAPT), p. 488
<u>initial</u> (ih NIHSH uhl), p. 491

**Key Terms and People**
republic (rih PUHB lihk), p. 489
consul (KAHN suhl), p. 489
patrician (puh TRIHSH uhn), p. 490
plebeian (plih BEE uhn), p. 490
debt bondage (deht BAHN dihj), p. 491
tribune (TRIHB yoon), p. 491

**Background Knowledge** In ancient Greece, governments of city-states evolved from monarchy to oligarchy and democracy. You have read that such changes gave ordinary citizens a greater say in government matters. As you will read in this section, a similar evolution of government took place in Rome. As in Greece, this evolution allowed common people to play a more important role in government.

## From Monarchy to Oligarchy

The first rulers of Rome were kings. According to tradition, Rome had seven kings. Some of these rulers, like Romulus, were legendary. Historians do not know whether they really existed, but some evidence suggests that the last three kings of Rome did exist. These monarchs are known as the Etruscan kings.

**The Etruscan Kings** The people known as Etruscans lived just north of Latium, in a region called Etruria. The Etruscans had an older and more advanced culture than that of the Romans.

**Main Idea**
The Roman Republic was established after the people of Rome overthrew the Etruscan kings.

## Early Alphabets

| Early Greek | Etruscan | Early Latin | Modern |
|:---:|:---:|:---:|:---:|
| ◁ | A | ⋏ | A |
| ٦ | ) | ⟨ | C |
| ⅃ | ⅂ | Ɛ | E |
| ᗺ | ᗺ | H | H |
| ⟨ | I | I | I |
| ⋏ | ⋏ | K | K |
| ﻟ | Ч | Ν | N |
| ⌐ | ⌐ | ⌐ | P |
| ٩ | ٩ | R | R |
| ✕ | ⊤ | ⊤ | T |

### Reading Tables

This table traces the development of several modern letters from the early Greek, Etruscan, and early Latin alphabets.

**(a) Read a Table** What Etruscan character eventually evolved into our modern letter *H*?

**(b) Compare** How is the development of the modern alphabet similar to the way in which Chinese writing developed?

The Etruscans were great artists, builders, and sailors. They traveled to other lands around the Mediterranean, trading goods, ideas, and customs. In the process, they learned many things from other cultures, including the Greek culture.

Around 600 B.C., the Etruscans expanded into Latium. An Etruscan leader known as Tarquin the Elder gained control of Rome and became its king. The throne later passed to two other Etruscan monarchs. Each monarch had broad powers, serving as head of the army, chief priest, and supreme judge.

The Etruscan kings ruled with the consent of Rome's wealthy aristocrats. These aristocrats formed a body called the Senate. This body advised the king on important matters. In addition, there was an assembly made up of all citizens who could bear arms. The king could consult the assembly if he chose to, but the assembly had no real power.

**Etruscan Improvements** The Etruscan kings brought many changes to Rome, including a writing system adapted from the Greek alphabet. It became the basis of the Latin alphabet, which we use today. The kings also brought a strong military tradition to Rome. Their military organization, based on the phalanx, would later aid Roman expansion.

**Vocabulary *Builder***
**adapt** (uh DAPT) *v.* to make fit or suitable by changing or adjusting

The Etruscans also improved the city. They drained the low marshy area between the seven hills so that people could live there. They created a sewer system to carry away wastewater. They laid out new streets in a rectangular, or grid, pattern. They taught the Romans how to pave their streets with cobblestones. The Etruscans also introduced the use of the stone arch in construction in order to support heavy structures such as bridges.

Further, the Etruscans brought their gods and religious practices to Rome. One ritual, called augury, was used to predict the future. Special priests, called augurs, used various methods to read the will of the gods. One method involved observing the flight patterns of birds. Another called for examining animal intestines. Augury remained an important part of Roman culture.

Despite this strong Etruscan influence, the Romans never abandoned their own culture. For example, they continued to speak their own language—Latin.

## Formation of the Republic
The Romans eventually grew tired of Etruscan rule. The third Etruscan king, known as Tarquin the Proud, was a harsh ruler. His policies finally caused the people of Rome to lead a revolt. In 509 B.C., the Romans overthrew the king and established the Roman Republic. A **republic** is a government in which citizens have the right to vote and elect officials.

The word *republic* comes from the Latin term *res publica*, which means "public things" or "public affairs." Although citizens had a role in civic life, the government of the early republic was not a democracy. It was an oligarchy with its own special features.

In the early republic, two officials called consuls took over the jobs once done by the king. The **consuls** stood as the highest officials in the Roman government. They kept the appearance of great power, but their authority proved limited. The aristocratic Senate held most of the power. It passed laws and ran the government. Although the assembly still existed, it also became controlled by aristocrats. You will read more about the development and structure of the republican government in the next section.

**Logo of the Republic**
The letters SPQR in this symbol stand for the Latin phrase *Senatus Populusque Romanus,* which means "the Senate and the people of Rome." The logo represented the Republic on items such as buildings and coins. **Critical Thinking: Link Past and Present** *What symbol is used to represent countries today?*

 **Checkpoint** **How did the government of Rome move from a monarchy to a republic?**

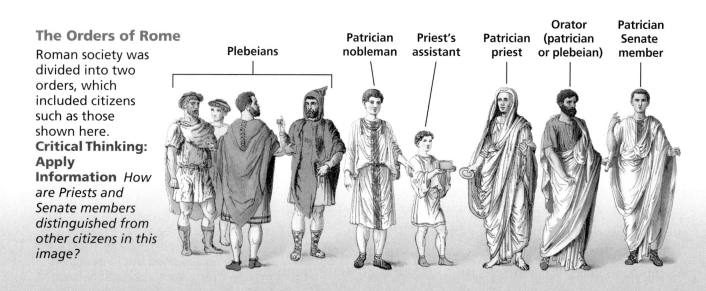

**The Orders of Rome**
Roman society was divided into two orders, which included citizens such as those shown here. **Critical Thinking: Apply Information** *How are Priests and Senate members distinguished from other citizens in this image?*

Plebeians

Patrician nobleman

Priest's assistant

Patrician priest

Orator (patrician or plebeian)

Patrician Senate member

**Main Idea**
Conflicts between social classes brought government reforms to the Roman Republic.

**E-LA 6.1.3 Analyze Latin Word Origins**
*Reading Skill* How does the meaning of the word *population* relate to its Latin origins?

# The Struggle of the Orders

Even before the rise of the Republic, Rome was divided into two main groups called orders. One order was made up of patricians. Patricians represented the upper class of Roman society. The word patrician comes from the Latin term *pater,* which means "father." Patricians took great pride in belonging to noble families with famous or influential ancestors.

The other order included the plebeians, or the common people of Rome. This word also comes from a Latin root, *plebs.* The plebeians made up around 90 percent of the population. Some were wealthy, but most were ordinary farmers, artisans, and workers. Eventually, differences between the orders resulted in a conflict called the Struggle of the Orders.

**Patricians and Plebeians** The organization of Roman society and government strongly favored the patricians. The patricians ran the government through their control of the Senate. They also acted as the leaders of Rome's social and economic life.

The plebeians, in contrast, had little power or influence in government. They could not hold political office, nor could they serve as priests. This meant that they could not perform religious rituals, like augury, that were a key part of political life. Even wealthy plebeians could not advance politically by marrying a patrician. Marriage between the orders was prohibited.

Plebeians also had little influence on Rome's economic life. Most worked as poor peasant farmers and owned very little land.

In poor harvest years, many had to take out loans just to survive. If a plebeian failed to pay his debt, the patrician who made the loan could sell the debtor into slavery. This practice of enslaving people who cannot pay their debts is known as debt bondage. During the initial years of the republic, debt bondage became common. As a result, life for many plebeians became worse than it had been under the old monarchy.

**Vocabulary Builder**
initial (ih NIHSH uhl) *adj.* having to do with, indicating, or occurring at the beginning

**The Plebeians Rebel**   Before long, however, the plebeians began to rebel. At first, they carried out random acts of violence against patricians. However, they later realized that although the patricians could govern Rome alone, they could not defend it without the service of plebeian soldiers.

In 494 B.C., plebeian soldiers went on strike. They refused to serve until they received a voice in government. The Republic was beginning to expand its control of lands near the city. Because these conquests were likely to fail without plebeian soldiers, the patricians began to listen to plebeian demands.

One of these demands called for a plebeian assembly with real power. In 471 B.C., an assembly of common people, known as the Tribal Assembly, became part of Rome's government. The top officials of the plebeian assembly were called tribunes. They represented plebeian interests in civic affairs. They also had the power to block laws they viewed as unfair to the common people.

**The Twelve Tables**   Two decades later, the plebeians won another major reform. This reform concerned Rome's legal system. At that time, Roman law consisted of ancient customs. None of these customs was written down. This allowed judges to choose which laws to follow and which to ignore. Plebeians demanded a written law code.

In 450 B.C. the government issued the Republic's first written law code. It became known as the Twelve Tables because it was written on twelve tablets. The new code listed rights and duties of Roman citizens, such as the right to take anyone to court.

## Contents of the Twelve Tables

| Table | Subject |
| --- | --- |
| 1 | Courts and trials |
| 2 | Trials (continued) |
| 3 | Debt |
| 4 | Family rights |
| 5 | Legal guardians and inheritance |
| 6 | Gaining and possessing property |
| 7 | Land rights |
| 8 | Unlawful acts and penalties |
| 9 | Laws on government |
| 10 | Laws on religion |
| 11 | Additional laws |
| 12 | Additional laws |

**Written Laws**
This table lists the main subjects of each of the Twelve Tables. **Critical Thinking: Apply Information** *Which of the Twelve Tables would have likely included laws about the relationships between fathers and sons?*

**Roman Fasces**
A fasces was carried by Roman officials as a symbol of their authority and power to punish. **Critical Thinking: Detect Points of View** *What are two different ways in which Roman citizens might have viewed this symbol?*

Other laws, such as those listed below, concerned family, property, crime, and punishment:

- A father shall have absolute power over his children.
- Things sold and delivered shall not become the property of the buyer until he has paid the seller.
- A person committing burglary in the night may be lawfully killed. A thief in the daytime may not be killed unless he carried a weapon.
- No one shall be put to death except after trial.

Despite these reforms, the Roman Republic still concentrated governing power in the hands of patricians. However, Rome was gradually moving toward a more democratic system of government.

 **Checkpoint** **What conflicts existed between the social classes?**

**Looking Back and Ahead** In this section, you have read about the shift in Roman government from monarchy to oligarchy and the rise of the Republic. In the next section, you will learn more about the structure of the Roman government, as well as important ideas contained in the Roman Constitution.

---

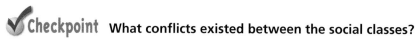

## Section 2 Check Your Progress

**Progress Monitoring Online**
**For:** Self-test with instant help
**Visit:** PHSchool.com
**Web Code:** mwa-6172

**Standards Review** H-SS: 6.7.1; E-LA: Reading 6.1.3

### Comprehension and Critical Thinking

1. **(a) Identify** Who were the first rulers of Rome?
   **(b) Analyze Cause and Effect** How did their period of rule lead to the formation of the Roman Republic?

2. **(a) Explain** Which order made up most of Roman society?
   **(b) Evaluate Information** Why do you think this fact proved important in the reforms that changed Roman society?

### Reading Skill

3. **Analyze Latin Word Origins** Read the sentence below. Then use Latin word origins and context to explain the meaning of *revolt:* His policies finally caused a revolt.

### Vocabulary *Builder*

Read each sentence below. If the sentence is true, write YES. If the sentence is not true, write NO and explain WHY.

4. The Etruscan alphabet <u>adapted</u> today's modern alphabet.

5. The lives of many plebeians became worse during the Roman Republic's <u>initial</u> years.

### Writing

6. Brainstorm a brief list of ideas you might include in a persuasive essay in which you argue that the plebeians had a right to demand reforms in the Roman -government.

# The Government of the Republic

**Standards Preview**

**H-SS 6.7.2** Describe the government of the Roman Republic and its significance (e.g., written constitution and tripartite government, checks and balances, civic duty).

**E-LA Reading 6.1.3** Recognize the origins and meanings of frequently used foreign words in English and use these words accurately in speaking and writing.

## Reading Preview

 **Reading Skill**

**Use Latin Words in Speaking and Writing** Identifying the Latin roots of words gives you a better understanding of what the words mean. This will help you use these words correctly when speaking and writing. Practice creating your own sentences that use the highlighted words in this section. Remember that context often adjusts the meaning of the Latin root to its modern usage.

**Vocabulary** *Builder*

**High-Use Words**
focus (FOH kuhs), p. 493
theory (THEE uh ree), p. 497

**Key Terms and People**
tripartite (trī PAHR tīt), p. 493
dictator (DIHK tayt uhr), p. 494
Cincinnatus (sihn suh NAYT uhs), p. 494
veto (VEE toh), p. 495
constitution (kahn stuh TOO shuhn), p. 495
checks and balances (cheks and BAL uhns uhz), p. 496

**Background Knowledge** Over time, the Roman Republic became more democratic. However, it also maintained elements of monarchy and oligarchy. In this section, you will read more about the government of Rome.

## Tripartite Government

The Republic had a **tripartite,** *or three-part,* government. The three main parts were the magistrates, Senate, and assemblies. They reflected three types of rule: monarchy, oligarchy, and democracy. A Greek scholar of Rome's government wrote:

> **❝For if we were to <u>focus</u> on the power of the consuls it would appear to be altogether monarchical and kingly in nature. If, however, we were to focus on the powers of the Senate, it would appear to be a government under the control of an aristocracy. And yet if one were to look at the powers enjoyed by the people, it would seem plain that it was democratic in nature.❞**
>
> —Polybius, *Histories*

**Main Idea**
The government of the Roman Republic included three branches.

**Vocabulary** *Builder*
focus (FOH kuhs) *v.* to direct one's thoughts or efforts; concentrate

**E-LA 6.1.3 Use Latin Word Origins in Speaking and Writing**

How might you explain to a classmate the link between the definition of *magistrate* and the word's Latin root?

**The Magistrates** The magistrates were the main officials of the Roman Republic. They represented the tradition of monarchy. Two consuls served as the top magistrates. They were elected for one-year terms. The consuls led the government and the army, while also acting as judges and high priests. In effect, they occupied the ruling position once held by the king. But each consul had the power to block the other's decisions, so they had to work together to get things done.

When the consuls left for war, they sometimes appointed a dictator to serve in their place. A **dictator** is a ruler with unlimited power. This word comes from the Latin term for "to say," because the dictator's word was considered law.

Consuls appointed dictators for six-month periods, but the dictators could serve for less time. For example, during a war in 458 B.C. the consuls appointed a farmer-soldier named **Cincinnatus** to serve as dictator. According to legend, Cincinnatus raised an army, defeated the enemy, and handed power back to the consuls, all in just 16 days.

In addition to consuls, Rome also had other magistrates. These lower officials managed specific areas of government, such as the collection of taxes or the maintenance of roads.

**The Senate** The Senate was the second branch of the Roman government. It represented the tradition of oligarchy. In the Republic, the Senate continued to advise the consuls. It also controlled state finances and passed laws.

The original Roman Senate had 300 members who served for life. They came from the oldest and richest patrician families in Rome. Over time, the entrance of wealthy plebeians caused the Senate to grow, though it remained a symbol of oligarchy.

**The Assemblies** Two assemblies made up the third branch of the government. These two groups represented the democratic element of the Roman Republic.

The Centuriate Assembly developed from a system that placed all men in classes according to how much military equipment they could provide. Wealthy patricians gained more votes than plebeians who could afford less equipment.

In the Tribal Assembly, the plebeians were in charge. Over time, this assembly became a powerful force in Rome's government. It elected the tribunes, who had veto power over the other branches. A **veto** is the power to reject a proposed action or law. The term *veto* means "I forbid."

✓**Checkpoint** **What were the branches of Roman government?**

# The Roman Constitution

The powers of these branches were adjusted according to the Roman constitution. A **constitution** is a set of laws and principles that form the basis for a government. While that of the United States is a single, written document, the Roman constitution included laws and practices that formed over time.

**Main Idea**
The Roman constitution set forth important principles of government.

**Roman and United States Senates**

The Senate of the Roman Republic (left) met in a chamber arranged similarly to that of the United States Senate (right). The members of both bodies sit in semicircular rows facing the front of their chambers. **Critical Thinking: Evaluate Information** *Why might groups such as these arrange their meeting places in this way?*

**History** *Interactive*
**Visit the Roman and United States Senates**
**Visit:** PHSchool.com
**Web Code:** mwp-6173

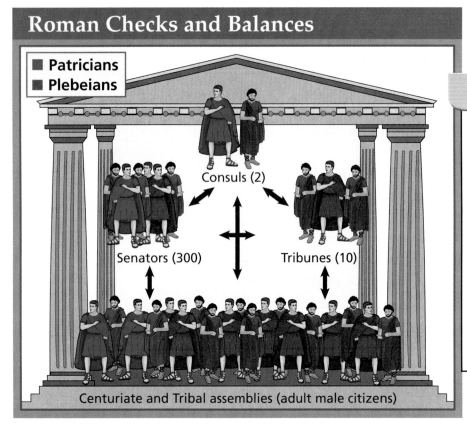

## Roman Checks and Balances

- Patricians
- Plebeians

Consuls (2)

Senators (300)

Tribunes (10)

Centuriate and Tribal assemblies (adult male citizens)

### Reading Graphs

The arrows on this picture graph indicate the checks and balances that the various parts of the Roman government had on one another.

**(a) Read a Graph** What color is used to represent the plebeians in this graph?

**(b) Apply Information** What part of the system of checks and balances is indicated by the arrow between the senators and tribunes?

**Checks and Balances** The basic principles of the Roman constitution evolved during the Struggle of the Orders. One principle was Rome's system of checks and balances. **Checks and balances** represent a means for keeping any one branch of a government from gaining more power than the others. In this way, no one branch can become too powerful. This principle remains a key feature of the United States system of government today.

The Roman system of checks and balances worked in a number of ways. For example, only the Senate could pass a law, but the tribunes could veto any law passed by the Senate. Similarly, each consul had the power to veto an act of the other.

**The Rule of Law** A second basic principle of the Roman Constitution was the rule of law. With the passage of the Twelve Tables, Romans accepted the idea that they should be ruled by written laws, rather than the by whims of judges.

Over time, Roman law changed to give more rights to the common people. In 445 B.C., the law code was altered to allow plebeians to marry patricians. In 367 B.C., another law required one consul to be a plebeian. In later years, laws prohibited debt bondage and allowed plebeians to become priests.

**The Lex Hortensia** In 287 B.C., plebeians won a great victory with the passage of a law called the Lex Hortensia. This law gave the Tribal Assembly the power to pass laws without the approval of the Senate or consuls.

With this change, the Roman Republic became a democracy— at least in <u>theory</u>. In reality, the patricians still dominated the government. Members of the old aristocracy controlled the Senate and held most of the magistrate positions. They also dominated the Centuriate Assembly and held great influence over the Tribal Assembly.

Despite these class differences, most Roman citizens remained loyal to the Republic. As long as plebeians had the right to vote in their assembly, they felt they had a role in the system.

 **Checkpoint** **What were the principles of the Roman constitution?**

**Looking Back and Ahead** In this section, you have read about the government of the Roman Republic. You learned that it had three branches representing three types of government: monarchy, oligarchy, and democracy. In the next section, you will read more about Roman society and values.

**Vocabulary** *Builder*
**theory** (THEE uh ree) *n.* branch of art or science consisting of principles and methods rather than of its practice

---

## Section 3 Check Your Progress

**Progress Monitoring** **Online**
**For:** Self-test with instant help
**Visit:** PHSchool.com
**Web Code:** mwa-6173

**Standards Review** **H-SS:** 6.7.2; **E-LA: Reading** 6.1.3

**Comprehension and Critical Thinking**

**1. (a) List** What three types of rule did the branches of Roman government represent?
**(b) Draw Inferences** Why do you think the Romans might have set up the government in this way?

**2. (a) Link Past and Present** How did the Roman constitution differ from the constitution of the United States?
**(b) Draw Conclusions** Do you think this would have made the Roman constitution easier or more difficult to change? Explain.

**Reading Skill**
**3. Use Latin Word Origins in Speaking and Writing** Explain the Latin word origins of the word *tripartite.* Then use the word in a sentence that describes the structure of the Roman Republic's government.

**Vocabulary** *Builder*
Answer the following questions in complete sentences to show your understanding of the Key Terms.
**4.** What was the role of a dictator in the government of the republic?

**5.** Who had veto power over the other branches of government in the republic?

**6.** What was Rome's system of checks and balances?

**Writing**
**7.** Make a short outline showing details that could support a persuasive essay arguing that the government of the Roman Republic was most influenced by the tradition of either monarchy, oligarchy, or democracy.

 **Standards Preview**

**H-SS 6.7** Students analyze the geographic, political, economic, religious, and social structures during the development of Rome.

**E-LA Reading 6.1.3** Recognize the origins and meanings of frequently used foreign words in English and use these words accurately in speaking and writing.

## Reading Preview

 **Reading Skill**

**Recognize Common Latin Terms** Many Latin phrases still appear in English in their original form. For example, economic reports use the term *per capita,* which literally means "per person." A report that says "Americans eat more hamburgers *per capita* than people elsewhere," discusses the number of hamburgers each American eats. Becoming familiar with such phrases will help you to accurately interpret this type of information.

## Vocabulary *Builder*

**High-Use Word**
indicate (IHN dih kayt), p. 500

**Key Terms and People**
patriarchal (pay tree AHR kuhl), p. 498
clan (klan), p. 500
gravitas (GRAV ih tahs), p. 501
civic virtue (SIH vihk VER choo), p. 501

**Background Knowledge** You have read that citizens of Rome were divided into two social orders, the patricians and plebeians. In this section, you will read more about Roman society and the values and religious beliefs of the Roman people.

**Main Idea**
Family relationships were an important part of Rome's social structure.

## Social Traditions

Roman society was deeply traditional. Although Rome changed over time, the Romans held firm to customs and traditions of the past. The most important of these traditions was a focus on family. Family ties formed strong bonds within Roman society.

**The Role of Men** The Roman family was **patriarchal.** This means that it centered around men, with descent traced through male family members. The father or grandfather in a Roman family was called the paterfamilias, or head of household. His place in the family resembled the king's place in the old monarchy.

As head of the household, a father had absolute, or unlimited, power. He owned all of the family property. He had total control over his wife, children, and slaves. He could sell his children into slavery, or even kill them if he chose. When a father died, his eldest son became the new paterfamilias. If a father had no son, his wife and daughters came under the control of his closest male relative.

In practice, a father's power was limited by custom and tradition. Custom called for men to show proper respect for others, including their families. A man who treated his family poorly was not admired.

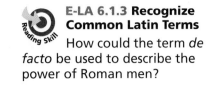
E-LA 6.1.3 **Recognize Common Latin Terms** How could the term *de facto* be used to describe the power of Roman men?

**The Role of Women** Legally, Roman women enjoyed a significant advantage over women in Greece because they could own personal property. Although Roman law required that women have male guardians throughout their lives, women in Rome actually had a great deal of control over their property.

The most important role of Roman women was to bear children and raise them to honor traditional values. The ideal woman was a faithful wife and mother, devoted to her home and family.

As Rome grew in wealth, the role of patrician women changed. Slaves took over much of the household work. Wealthy women gained more freedom to go out in public. Some came to have influence in the political affairs of Rome. Women could not, however, vote or hold public office.

**Growing Up** Children growing up in wealthy families received a primary education. Girls left school by the age of 13, after which they were expected to learn household skills at home. Boys attended secondary school until the age of 16. At that point, they became men. They were given a man's toga and haircut and their first shave. They also became Roman citizens.

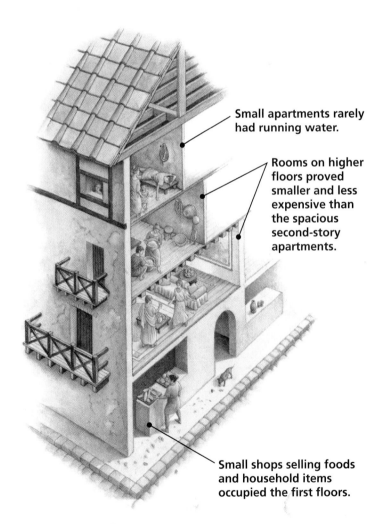

Small apartments rarely had running water.

Rooms on higher floors proved smaller and less expensive than the spacious second-story apartments.

Small shops selling foods and household items occupied the first floors.

**Roman Families**
Many Roman families lived in apartment homes called *insulas.* **Critical Thinking: Analyze Cause and Effect** *What might have caused the people of Rome to set up shops selling food on the first floors of buildings like this?*

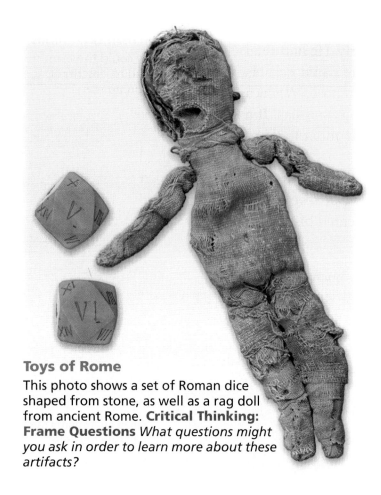

**Toys of Rome**
This photo shows a set of Roman dice shaped from stone, as well as a rag doll from ancient Rome. **Critical Thinking: Frame Questions** *What questions might you ask in order to learn more about these artifacts?*

**Vocabulary** *Builder*
indicate (IHN dih kayt) *v.* to direct attention to; point out

Poor children had very different childhoods. Their families could not afford an education. Most poor children did not learn to read or write. As soon as they became old enough, they went to work alongside their parents.

**Family History** Family history held much importance for the Romans. Wealthy families sometimes kept wax masks or portraits of their ancestors in the home. Most people made regular visits to family graves to honor the dead. Burials were important events that included complicated rituals. At times, people hired actors to wear the death masks of important ancestors.

A man's name reflected his family history. Every Roman family belonged to a clan. A clan was a group of families descended from a common ancestor. A man's personal name came first, followed by his clan name and family name. For example, the Roman leader Marcus Tullius Cicero came from the Tullius clan. Cicero was his family name.

Unmarried women had just two names. A girl's first name was a feminine version of her father's clan name, such as Claudia for Claudius. Her second name indicated her place in the family. The first daughter would be Claudia *Maior,* which meant the "greater" or "older." The next daughter would be Claudia *Secunda,* which meant the "second." When a woman married, she added her husband's family name to her own.

**Patrons and Clients** Another important tradition in Roman society involved the relationships between patrons and clients. Patrons were patricians or wealthy plebeians, and clients were usually poorer plebeians. Patrons offered assistance to clients in return for their political support.

The patron-client relationship began in the early days of the Republic. It offered a way for patricians to help less fortunate people and receive something in return. Patrons provided money and other forms of aid, such as help in legal matters. In return, clients supported the political careers of their patrons.

A client of one patron might even act as the patron of another, less fortunate client. Eventually, these patron-client relationships became deeply woven into the fabric of Roman society.

 **Checkpoint** **What family relationships influenced Rome's social structure?**

# Roman Values

Loyalty represented a key value in Roman society. Romans expected people to remain loyal to their families, their patrons, and Rome. They were also supposed to show courage, strength, and devotion to the gods. These values brought order to Roman society and strengthened the Roman Republic.

**The Virtues** The Romans especially admired two key virtues in their leaders. The first virtue was **gravitas,** or a serious and dignified way of behaving. The word *gravitas* also suggests a powerful force, as in the force of gravity. The Romans believed that a leader with gravitas had to be taken seriously. Such a leader's words and actions held significance, and he inspired feelings of trust and respect.

The second virtue was called civic virtue. For Romans, **civic virtue** meant loving their country more than themselves. Today it usually means a willingness to serve one's country. Romans believed that the main purpose of a republican government was to promote the welfare of all citizens, whether rich or poor. They showed a willingness to put aside their own interests to work for the common good. In times of peace, this meant participating in civic affairs. In times of war, it meant fighting for their country.

**Roman Religion** Rome had an established, official religion. The top officials of the Roman government also served as priests. Religious rituals always accompanied important events.

The Romans worshiped hundreds of gods. Many of these gods were adopted from the Greek and Etruscan religions. Others were ancient Italian spirits of the home and countryside. Later, when Rome grew into an empire, people began to view its emperors as gods. Worship of the emperor became an expression of loyalty toward Rome.

The Romans believed that gods lived in sacred spots, such as trees and rocks. But they also built temples meant to house their most important gods. The main gods of Rome were Jupiter, Juno, Mars, and Minerva.

**Gods and Goddesses**
This statue depicts the Roman goddess Minerva, who has often been associated with the Greek goddess Athena.
**Critical Thinking: Evaluate Information** *How were the Greek and Roman religions the same?*

Like the Greeks, the Romans attributed human forms and qualities to their gods. Jupiter, the sky god, was a proud and terrifying figure. Depictions often showed him holding a thunderbolt. A peacock symbolized his wife Juno, the goddess of women. Minerva, the goddess of wisdom, was often shown dressed in armor.

Romans feared the gods and tried to win their favor. They prayed to the gods and made offerings of food, money, or other goods. They also sacrificed animals, such as birds or cattle.

Romans worshiped in public at the great temples, but they also had home shrines. At these shrines, Romans prayed to the household spirits that they believed shaped daily life. Among these spirits were the *lares*. These were the spirits of the family's ancestors. Romans believed that the *lares* could protect a home from evil.

✔ Checkpoint **Why were some virtues strongly admired in Roman society?**

## Looking Back and Ahead
In this section, you have read about Roman traditions and values, such as family and patron-client relationships. You also have learned about important features of Roman religion. In the next chapter, you will read about the growth of the Roman Empire.

---

## Section 4 Check Your Progress

**Progress Monitoring** Online
**For:** Self-test with instant help
**Visit:** PHSchool.com
**Web Code:** mwa-6174

**Standards Review** H-SS: 6.7; E-LA: Reading 6.1.3

### Comprehension and Critical Thinking
1. (a) **Recall** Who acted as the head of a typical Roman household?
(b) **Analyze Cause and Effect** How did this tradition affect the Roman family?

2. (a) **Identify** What were the two key virtues that Romans admired in their leaders?
(b) **Link Past and Present** How are these virtues similar to and different from the qualities we look for in government leaders of today?

### Reading Skill
3. **Recognize Common Latin Terms** Review the text on page 501. Then tell what a Roman might say if he or she failed to demonstrate a key virtue. Use the term *mea culpa* in your response.

### Vocabulary *Builder*
Read the sentence below. If the sentence is true, write YES. If the sentence is not true, write NO and explain WHY.

4. A Roman man's middle name <u>indicated</u> his clan.

### Writing
5. Create a graphic organizer and use it to gather information for a persuasive essay. Suppose that the topic of this essay will be that Roman women held a higher status in their society than did Greek women.

# Citizen Heroes

**History-Social Science** 6.7.1 Identify the location and describe the rise of the Roman Republic, including the importance of such mythical and historical figures as Aeneas, Romulus and Remus, Cincinnatus, Julius Caesar, and Cicero.

| Respect | Caring | Responsibility | Fairness | Honesty | Civic Virtue |

# CINCINNATUS
### FARMER AND SOLDIER

**Holding a public office and serving in the military both demonstrate civic virtue. In ancient Rome, Cincinnatus did both of these things during a time of crisis.**

**Cincinnatus** was working on his farm when government messengers arrived. They asked him to go to Rome to hear the Senate's instructions. The ancient Roman historian Livy wrote, "This naturally surprised him, and asking if all were well, he told his wife Racilia to run to their cottage and fetch his toga. The toga was brought, and wiping the grimy sweat from his hands and face he put it on. At once the [messengers] saluted him, with congratulations, as Dictator. . . ."

Cincinnatus answered the call to duty during a time of war. He raised and led an army that defeated the Romans' enemy.

## Connect to Today

The **National Guard** is a part of the United States Armed Forces made up of ordinary citizens who can be called to duty in times of emergency. Just as Cincinnatus was called to serve the government of ancient Rome during a difficult time, these citizens demonstrate this same type of civic virtue.

Many members of the National Guard balance their service with responsibilities to their jobs, schools, and families. National Guard troops often serve actively during natural disasters in their states or times of war for the nation.

## *Analyze* CITIZEN HEROES

A motto of the United States National Guard begins, "Civilian in Peace, Soldier in War . . . of security and honor for three centuries I have been the custodian . . . I am the Guard!" Write a brief paragraph that explains whether you think Cincinnatus would have agreed with this statement.

Many everyday activities call for you to follow instructions. You follow instructions when you fill out applications for things, such as library cards. You also follow instructions when you take tests or prepare special foods. In ancient Rome, you might have followed the instructions below to cook mice for dinner.

**Chapter Standards**

**History-Social Science**

Reading 6.2.5 Follow multiple-step instructions for preparing applications (e.g., for a public library card, bank savings account, sports club, league membership).

## Glazed Dormice

**Ingredients:**

4 dormice (often found behind doors)     salt and pepper
honey     poppy seeds

1. Skin the dormice.
2. Roast them in a hot oven until brown.
3. Cover them in honey.
4. Roll them in poppy seeds, and add salt and pepper to taste.
5. Return them to the oven and cook them until poppy seeds are brown.

**Learn the Skill** *Follow these steps to learn how to carry out multi-step instructions.*

1. **Preview the instructions.** Instructions often have many steps. You might need to complete some steps well before you complete others, or you might need to gather materials. Do not begin until you have read the complete series of instructions.

2. **Gather your materials.** At times, you may need only a pencil or pen to complete the various steps. At other times, you may need many ingredients or tools. Gather the items you need to complete the instructions.

3. **Follow the instructions to complete the process.** Make sure you perform the steps in the correct order.

4. **Review the instructions after you have finished.** Read through the instructions again to make sure that you did not leave out any important steps.

**Practice the Skill** *Answer the following questions using the recipe above.*

1. **Preview the instructions. (a)** What will you be making by following these instructions? **(b)** How many steps does the recipe have?

2. **Gather your materials. (a)** What ingredients will you need for this recipe? **(b)** What other items might you need?

3. **Follow the instructions to complete the process. (a)** What is the first step of the recipe? **(b)** What might happen if you completed step 3 before completing step 2?

4. **Review the instructions after you have finished. (a)** What might happen if you left out step 5? **(b)** How might you determine whether you have followed the recipe correctly?

**Apply the Skill**

*See page 507 of the Review and Assessment.*

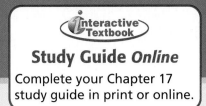

**Study Guide** *Online*
Complete your Chapter 17
study guide in print or online.

## Chapter Summary  H-SS: 6.7, 6.7.1, 6.7.2

### Section 1 On the Banks of the Tiber

- Rome was settled along the Tiber River in the Italian Peninsula during the 500s B.C.
- Romans developed myths to explain the city's founding.
- The location of Rome allowed the settlement to grow. It provided natural defenses, nearby farmland, and access to key trade routes.

### Section 2 Rise of the Roman Republic

- The earliest rulers of Rome were kings. Etruscan rule introduced new trade goods, ideas, and customs to Rome.
- After becoming tired of Etruscan rule, the Romans overthrew the third Etruscan king. They then established the Roman Republic.
- Roman society included two social classes. Struggles between these classes led Rome to move toward a more democratic form of government.

### Section 3 The Government of the Republic

- The government of the Roman Republic had three branches. These branches represented monarchy, oligarchy, and democracy.
- The Roman constitution was a series of laws and practices that formed the basis of government in Rome.
- A system of checks and balances and the rule of law were among the important principles of the Roman constitution.

### Section 4 Roman Society

- Roman society placed much importance on traditions, such as family relationships.
- The relationships between patrons and clients also helped form the social structure of Rome.
- Roman society valued traits such as gravitas and civic virtue. Religion in ancient Rome involved the worship of many gods, both in public and at home.

## Standards Practice  H-SS: 6.7, 6.7.1, 6.7.2

# Vocabulary *Builder*

### High-Use Words

Decide whether each underlined word is used correctly. If it is, explain why. If not, rewrite the rest of the sentence to make it logical.

1. The growth of Rome was **linked** to the city's location on the Tiber River.

2. The poet Virgil played a **role** in shaping the founding myths of Rome.

3. Rome's senate **focused** on representing the interests of Rome's poor citizens.

4. The Lex Hortensia allowed patricians to dominate Rome's government in **theory**.

### Key Terms

Answer the following questions in complete sentences that show your understanding of the Key Terms.

1. Why is the present-day land of Latium considered arid?

2. How did debt bondage affect the lives of citizens in ancient Rome?

3. Why did consuls sometimes appoint dictators to lead the republic's government?

4. How were Roman families patriarchal?

## Apply Reading Skills

**Recognize and Use Words with Latin Origins** Choose three words from the chart on page 480. Explain their Latin origins and use them in a sentence about life in ancient Rome.

## Comprehension and Critical Thinking

**1. (a) List** What were three important features of Rome's location?
**(b) Apply Information** How did these features contribute to Rome's growth?
**(c) Link Past and Present** Do you think these features would also be important to cities today? Why or why not?

**2. (a) Recall** What was the Struggle of the Orders?
**(b) Analyze Cause and Effect** What caused this struggle to take place?
**(c) Evaluate Information** How did this event bring changes to Rome?

**3. (a) Identify** Name the three branches of government in the Roman Republic.
**(b) Organize Information** How did these branches work together to form a stable government?
**(c) Detect Points of View** Why would plebeians have supported the passage of the Lex Hortensia?

**4. (a) Describe** How was the Roman family organized?
**(b) Apply Information** What evidence suggests that family ties were important to the Romans?
**(c) Draw Conclusions** In what ways was the Roman family similar to the Roman Republic?

## Researching

**The Roman Landscape** Rome's geographic location was an important factor in the early growth of the city. In this activity, you will use the Internet and the library media center to research and report on this location. Choose a task below to work on. Share your completed project with your class by giving a brief oral presentation. Make a list of the resources you used to go with your presentation.

**Geographers:** Make an illustrated map of the area in which Rome developed. Place on your map symbols to represent important geographic features, such as plains or rivers.

**Economists:** The Tiber River and several nearby ports contributed to economic growth in Rome. Create a table that identifies other important settlements whose economies benefited from locations near major rivers.

---

**Researching Online**
**For:** Help in starting this activity
**Visit:** PHSchool.com
**Web Code:** mwe-6174

---

## Writing

**1. Write a paragraph on the following topic.** Patron-client relationships became an important part of society in the Roman Republic. Explain whether you think patrons or clients benefited more from these relationships.
**Your paragraph should:**
- include a thesis statement expressing your opinion on the topic.
- list arguments supporting and opposing your position.
- feature a strong conclusion.

**2. Write a short narrative.** Imagine you are an early citizen of Rome. Write a short narrative explaining how the founding story makes you feel about Rome.

# Apply Analysis Skills

Use the recipe for an ancient Roman sauce used to season meat or fish at right, to answer the following questions.

1. What food will you make by following the steps of this recipe?

2. What materials will you need to complete the steps listed?

3. What additional task must you complete before following the second step of the recipe?

4. How might the final product change if you did not mix it daily as directed?

## Garum

Ingredients: fatty fish (ex. sardines), dried herbs, salt

1. Place a layer of dried herbs, such as oregano or dill, at the bottom of a large container.

2. Add a layer of fish (with the bones removed) on top of herbs.

3. Add a layer of salt about two finger lengths high. Repeat these layers until the container has been filled.

4. Place the container in the sun for 7 days. After that time, mix the sauce each day for 20 days until it has become liquid.

# Test Yourself

1. **Which of the following statements is true?**
   A Aeneas was an early king of Rome.
   B Patricians and plebeians were equal.
   C Cicero and Cincinnatus served as consuls.
   D The Alps separate the Italian Peninsula from western Europe.

**Refer to the image below to answer Question 2.**

2. **The image above is a logo representing**
   A Romulus and Remus.
   B the Etruscan kings of Rome.
   C the Centuriate Assembly.
   D the Roman Republic.

3. **The early Roman Republic**
   A granted plebeian women the right to vote.
   B forbid citizens from taking part in civic life.
   C featured two consuls and a Senate.
   D had a democratic form of government.

**Refer to the reading below to answer Question 4.**

4. **What feature of the Roman Republic government does Polybius describe in this quotation?**

> *"Not even the Romans themselves could say for certain whether their system of government was aristocratic in its general nature, or democratic, or monarchial."*
>
> —Polybius, *Histories*

   A the tripartite structure
   B the rule of the law
   C the system of checks and balances
   D the value of gravitas

5. **Which of the following ideas was NOT a part of the constitution of the Roman Republic?**
   A Priests must demonstrate civic virtue.
   B Citizens should not be governed by the whims of judges.
   C No single part of the government should become too powerful.
   D Each consul could veto an act of the other.

## Prepare to Read

**Chapter Standards**

### History-Social Science
**6.7** Students analyze the geographic, political, economic, religious, and social structures during the development of Rome.

**Section 1,** pp. 512–517

**The Conquest of an Empire**

### What You Will Learn

The Romans built their empire on strong military force and diplomacy. They fought wars with Carthage, then experienced serious social problems which would lead to the downfall of the Republic.

**Section 2,** pp. 518–523

**The Pax Romana**

Julius Caesar ruled Rome as "Dictator for Life." After his death in 44 B.C., Caesar's adopted son Octavian became emperor. The empire experienced peace and prosperity.

**Section 3,** pp. 526–529

**Commerce and Culture**

The Romans encouraged economic growth and the spread of culture during Octavian's rule. The empire spread over much of Europe, the Middle East, and northern Africa.

A Roman gladiator

**493 B.C.**
The Romans form the Latin League.

**264 B.C.**
The First Punic War begins.

**Chapter Events**

**750 B.C.**

**500 B.C.**

**250 B.C.**

**Other Events**

**About 587 B.C.**
Jerusalem destroyed.

**272 B.C.** Asoka becomes India's third Mauryan emperor.

A statue of Emperor Augustus in a Roman Amphitheatre

**27 B.C.**
The Pax Romana begins.

**A.D. 180**
The Pax Romana ends.

250 B.C.

B.C./A.D.

A.D. 250

**206 B.C.** Liu Bang founds the Han Dynasty.

**First century B.C.** Meroë becomes a major producer of iron.

# How to Read History

 **History Reading Skill**

*Previewing* **Analyze Comparisons and Contrasts**

The study of history frequently involves comparisons and contrasts. You will learn about important differences between cultures, as well as the ways in which people of different times and places are similar. The passage below from Polybius's *Histories* contains transition words that signal a compare-and-contrast organizational pattern.

 **Chapter Standards**
**English-Language Arts**
**Reading 6.2.2** Analyze text that uses the compare-and-contrast organizational pattern.

In this passage, Polybius discusses the concept of bravery. He uses a compare-and-contrast pattern to describe brave and cowardly people. Analyzing such comparisons and contrasts will help you understand the main points of similar passages.

Everyone thinks about the meaning of duty, which is the beginning and end of justice. **Similarly**, again, **when any man is first in defending his fellows from danger** . . . it is natural that he should receive marks of favor and honor from the people, **while the man who acts in the opposite manner** will meet with disapproval and dislike. From this again some idea of what is dishonorable and what is noble and of what makes up the **difference** is likely to arise among the people; and **noble conduct** will be admired and imitated because it is advantageous, **while** **base conduct** will be avoided.

—*Polybius, Histories*

Transition words, such as *similarly* and *while*, often indicate a compare-and-contrast structure. Words such as *difference* also suggest that the author will be contrasting two or more things.

Ask these questions as you analyze compare-and-contrast patterns:

- Why do writers use the compare-and-contrast pattern?
- How do transitional words and phrases help organize a comparison or contrast?
- How do the comparisons and contrasts in this passage relate to its main idea?

# Vocabulary *Builder*

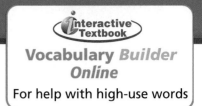

## *Previewing* High-Use Academic Words

| High-Use Word | Definition | Sample Sentence About History |
|---|---|---|
| **treaty** (TREET ee) (Section 1, p. 513) | *n.* written agreement between two peoples or nations | The Romans signed a peace treaty with the nations they conquered. |
| **estate** (eh STAYT) (Section 1, p. 516) | *n.* individually owned large property maintained by great wealth | Wealthy landowners bought slaves to work on their huge estates. |
| **reform** (rih FORM) (Section 1, p. 517) | *n.* a movement aimed at removing political or social abuses | Many important reforms were enacted, but some failed. |
| **adapt** (uh DAHPT) (Section 2, p. 518) | *v.* to fit; to make fit or suitable by changing or adjusting | The soldiers adapted to the mountainous region by breaking formation. |
| **promote** (proh MOHT) (Section 2, p. 519) | *v.* to raise or advance to a higher position or rank | The captain was promoted because of his bravery in battle. |
| **scheme** (skeem) (Section 2, p. 523) | *n.* a carefully arranged plan of action | The senators had a scheme to take over the rule of the senate. |
| **construction** (kuhn STRUHK shuhn) (Section 3, p. 527) | *n.* the act or process of building or constructing | People celebrated when the construction of the temple was complete. |
| **network** (NEHT werk) (Section 3, p. 527) | *n.* an arrangement or system of things such as roads or canals that connect or cross | The vast trade network was important to the nation's growth. |

## *Previewing* Key Terms and People

stable currency

tactic, p. 513
Hannibal, p. 514
Spartacus, p. 516

Julius Caesar, p. 518
Cicero, p. 520
Augustus (Octavian), p. 521

Pax Romana, p. 521
stable currency, p. 528
Greco-Roman culture, p. 528

Cicero

**H-SS 6.7.3** Identify the location of and the political and geographic reasons for the growth of Roman territories and expansion of the empire, including how the empire fostered economic growth through the use of currency and trade routes.

**E-LA Reading 6.2.2** Analyze text that uses the compare-and-contrast organizational pattern.

## Reading Preview

 **Reading Skill**

**Analyze Contrasts** Place names and event names can help you identify elements to contrast. Find the places and events discussed in a text. Often, these places will be discussed in one section in order to highlight relationships between them. Consider the information provided about the places, then analyze it by categories such as *location, type of government, military capacity,* or *date.*

## Vocabulary *Builder*

**High-Use Words**
treaty (TREET ee), p. 513
estate (eh STAYT), p. 516
reform (rih FORM), p. 517

**Key Terms and People**
tactic (TAHK tihk), p. 513
Hannibal (HAN uh buhl), p. 514
Spartacus (SPAHRT uh kuhs), p. 516

**Background Knowledge** In the early days of the Republic, Rome controlled just a small region in central Italy. Other peoples occupied the rest of the Italian peninsula. In this section, you will read about the expansion of the Roman Republic into a great power. You will also see how Roman conquests created problems for the Republic.

## The Growth of the Republic

**Main Idea**
The Romans built an empire based on a strong military force as well as diplomacy.

The Romans overthrew their last king in 509 B.C. Then, in 493 B.C., they formed an alliance with other peoples in Latium. This alliance was called the Latin League. First Rome and its allies drove the Etruscans out of central Italy. Then, as the map on page 515 shows, the Romans gradually took control of the rest of the Italian peninsula. During this time, the Romans developed the foundations on which they would build an empire. One foundation was a strong military force. The other foundation on which they built their empire was good diplomacy.

**The Roman Army**   As you have read in Chapter 17, military service was expected of Rome's male citizens. At first, military campaigns were short. A campaign is a military operation with a specific goal, such as the capture of a city. Unpaid citizen-soldiers left their farms to fight for a few weeks and then returned home.

As the area controlled by Romans expanded, campaigns stretched from weeks into months. Farmers could not be away from home for so long and still raise crops. The government then began to pay its fighting men. The result was a professional army of career soldiers.

The basic unit of the Roman army was the legion. A legion had from 4,500 to 5,000 heavily armed citizens. Most served as infantry, or foot soldiers, but a legion also had officers and specialists, such as blacksmiths or engineers. Soldiers served for 20 to 25 years. At the end of that time, they were given land to settle on. Often that land was in newly conquered areas.

At first, Romans organized their infantry into long, unbroken lines. This tactic worked well on flat plains. A tactic is a method used to achieve a short-term goal, such as winning a battle. But it did not work in hills, where long lines were hard to maintain.

The Romans solved this problem by dividing each legion into groups of soldiers called maniples. Each maniple had around 100 soldiers. On flat plains, maniples could form a solid battle line. But in rough country, each maniple could move and fight on its own. This flexibility gave the Roman legions a great advantage over most enemies.

**Roman Diplomacy**   The Romans combined military strength with diplomacy. Once they conquered a region, the Romans tried to turn its people into allies. They offered to defeated groups peace and many of the advantages of Roman citizenship. In exchange, the Romans asked for loyalty and support.

Defeated peoples were asked to sign peace <u>treaties</u> with the Republic. In these treaties, they agreed "to have the same friends and enemies as the Roman people." They also agreed to provide troops to Rome, which helped make the Roman army the largest military force in the Mediterranean region.

✔ Checkpoint   **How did the Romans use diplomacy to build their empire?**

**Roman Soldier**
Soldiers in ancient Rome wore protective gear that allowed them to fight in close combat. **Critical Thinking: Draw Conclusions** *Based on this image, why do you think Roman soldiers had a difficult time on long marches?*

**Vocabulary** *Builder*
<u>treaty</u> (TREET ee) *n.* written agreement between two peoples or nations

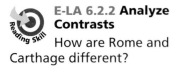

**E-LA 6.2.2 Analyze Contrasts**
How are Rome and Carthage different?

**Permanent Army Camps**
Roman armies usually built temporary camps that they took apart each morning when they moved on. Pictured here, however, is an illustration of a permanent fort that the army built on the empire's frontiers.
**Critical Thinking: Apply Information** *Why did the Roman army need permanent forts on its frontiers?*

# The Punic Wars

Rome's military strength was tested in a series of wars with Carthage, a city founded by Phoenician sea traders in North Africa. The Romans called this conflict the Punic Wars. "Punic" came from *Poeni*, the Latin word for Phoenician.

**The First Punic War**   Rome and Carthage were alike in many ways. Both began as cities, and both grew into empires. While Rome was busy conquering Italy, Carthage gained control of Spain and islands in the Mediterranean Sea.

The First Punic War began in 264 B.C., when Rome sent troops to Sicily, an island claimed by Carthage. Sicily lies just off the southern tip of Italy. The war ended more than 20 years later when Carthage agreed to turn over Sicily to the Romans.

**The Second Punic War**   A brilliant general from Carthage named Hannibal launched the Second Punic War. In the spring of 218 B.C., Hannibal left Spain with an army of about 40,000 soldiers and about 40 war elephants. His plan was to invade northern Italy, where he hoped to find allies who would help him conquer Rome. By fall, Hannibal's army had reached the Alps, the high mountain range that separates Italy from the rest of Europe. Hannibal reached Italy with only a few elephants and about half his army. However, local people who hated Roman rule had joined him along the way.

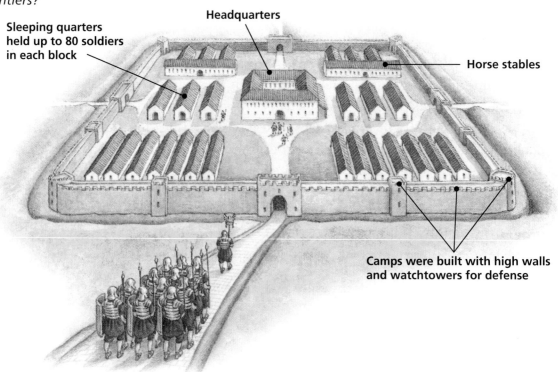

Headquarters

Sleeping quarters held up to 80 soldiers in each block

Horse stables

Camps were built with high walls and watchtowers for defense

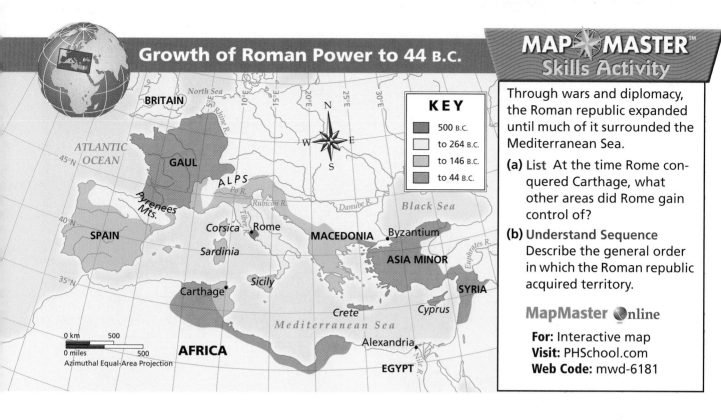

BRITAIN
North Sea
ATLANTIC OCEAN
45°N
GAUL
ALPS
Rhine R.
Po R.
Pyrenees Mts.
Rubicon R.
Danube R.
Black Sea
40°N
SPAIN
Corsica
Tiber R.
Rome
MACEDONIA
Byzantium
ASIA MINOR
Euphrates R.
Sardinia
35°N
SYRIA
Carthage
Sicily
Cyprus
Crete
Mediterranean Sea
Alexandria
AFRICA
Nile R.
EGYPT

0 km    500
0 miles    500
Azimuthal Equal-Area Projection

KEY
- 500 B.C.
- to 264 B.C.
- to 146 B.C.
- to 44 B.C.

Through wars and diplomacy, the Roman republic expanded until much of it surrounded the Mediterranean Sea.

**(a) List** At the time Rome conquered Carthage, what other areas did Rome gain control of?

**(b) Understand Sequence** Describe the general order in which the Roman republic acquired territory.

**MapMaster** ●nline

**For:** Interactive map
**Visit:** PHSchool.com
**Web Code:** mwd-6181

Hannibal's army marched south through Italy, winning battle after battle. The Romans' worst defeat came at a fort called Cannae in southern Italy. There Hannibal's cavalry surrounded the Roman army, killing more than 45,000 men.

During this time, the Romans were building a navy. In 204 B.C., a Roman general named Scipio sailed to Carthage with a large army. Only then did Hannibal finally abandon Italy and return home. In 202 B.C., Hannibal's forces suffered a disastrous defeat at Zama, a town south of Carthage.

A year later Carthage asked for peace. Rome agreed. But many Romans remained suspicious of Carthage. For years after the war ended, a Senator named Cato the Elder ended every speech with these words: "Carthage must be destroyed."

**The Third Punic War** The Third Punic War erupted in 149 B.C. This time, Roman leaders vowed to end the power of Carthage forever. Roman troops burned the city to the ground and sold its people into slavery. Legends say that the Romans even plowed salt into the ground where Carthage had stood so that nothing would ever grow there again.

The destruction of Carthage gave the Roman Republic control of the western Mediterranean. Next, it sent its armies eastward toward Greece and Southwest Asia. By about 133 B.C., the Romans ruled much of the Mediterranean region.

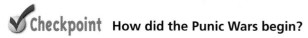 **Checkpoint** How did the Punic Wars begin?

How do we know about daily life in Ancient Rome? Paintings such as this tell us that wealthy Romans lived a far different lifestyle than ordinary Romans. **Critical Thinking: Frame Questions** *What questions would you ask a wealthy Roman family about their daily activities?*

## Explore More Video

**Discovery School Video** View *Daily Life in Ancient Rome* to learn more about how people lived in ancient Rome.

**Main Idea**
Serious social problems would eventually lead to the downfall of the Roman Republic.

**Vocabulary** *Builder*
estate (eh STAYT) *n.* individually owned large property maintained by great wealth

# Growing Pains

The growth of its empire brought great wealth and power to the city of Rome. But not all Romans benefited equally from these gains. Some Romans became rich and powerful. Others sank into poverty and slavery. The growing gap between these groups created serious problems for the Republic.

**Social Unrest and Revolts** As Rome's empire expanded, food was brought into the city from distant territories. As the food supply increased, prices fell. Low prices were disastrous for farmers, many of whom were not able to make a living off their small plots. They had little choice but to sell to rich landowners.

At the same time, large numbers of prisoners-of-war, now slaves, came to Italy. Rather than hire landless farmers to work their growing estates, wealthy landowners bought slaves. Therefore, farmers ended up with no land and no jobs. These farmers became part of a growing class of poor, jobless Romans. From time to time, slaves organized revolts. The most famous revolt was led by an enslaved soldier named Spartacus.

In 73 B.C., Spartacus organized an army of about 70,000 slaves who had escaped. After a few early victories, his army was crushed by Roman troops. More than 6,000 slaves were executed as punishment for rebelling.

**Political Violence**   Unrest spilled into politics as well. In 133 B.C., a tribune named Tiberius Gracchus proposed breaking up large estates and dividing the land among the poor. Before he could carry out this <u>reform</u>, Tiberius was murdered in an election riot along with 300 of his followers. When his brother Gaius Gracchus promoted similar reforms, he too was murdered.

Reform efforts died with the Gracchus brothers. And while no one knew it yet, Rome's republican form of government was about to die as well.

 **Checkpoint** **What factors created serious social problems for the Republic?**

**Looking Back and Ahead**   In this section, you have read about the expansion of Roman power throughout the Mediterranean region. You have seen how rapid growth created problems for the Roman Republic. In the next section, you will learn how the Republic became an empire ruled by one man.

**Vocabulary** *Builder*
<u>reform</u> (rih FORM) *n.* a movement aimed at removing political or social abuses

---

## Section 1 Check Your Progress

**Progress Monitoring** Online
**For:** Self-test with instant help
**Visit:** PHSchool.com
**Web Code:** mwa-6181

**Standards Review**   H-SS: 6.7.3; E-LA: Reading 6.2.2

**Comprehension and Critical Thinking**

1. **(a) Identify** Who did the Romans consider their main enemies in Italy?
   **(b) Evaluate Information** Why was this group a threat to Rome?

2. **(a) Describe** What was Hannibal's plan for invading Italy?
   **(b) Explain Problems** What difficulties did Hannibal face?

**Reading Skill**

3. **Analyze Contrasts** Read the subsections about the Romans and the Carthaginians in the Punic Wars. Contrast the way Romans and Carthaginians fought wars.

**Vocabulary** *Builder*

4. Write two definitions for each term: <u>treaty</u>, <u>estate</u>, <u>reform</u>. First write a formal definition for your teacher. Second, write a definition in everyday English for a classmate.

**Writing**

5. Write a paragraph describing how both military strength and diplomacy were essential elements in Rome's growth. Begin your paragraph with a strong topic sentence. Develop your paragraph further with supporting information. End with a concluding sentence.

# 2 The Pax Romana

**H-SS 6.7.4** Discuss the influence of Julius Caesar and Augustus in Rome's transition from republic to empire.

**E-LA Reading 6.2.2** Analyze text that uses the compare-and-contrast organizational pattern.

## Reading Preview

 **Reading Skill**

**Analyze Comparisons and Contrasts** Text structure offers a clear clue to comparisons and contrasts. Headings tell you who is discussed in each section. The text then gives you the details you need for comparison and contrast. List each person discussed in the section on a sheet of paper, then note details about that person.

**Vocabulary** *Builder*

**High-Use Words**
adapt (uh DAHPT), p. 518
promote (proh MOHT), p. 519
scheme (skeem), p. 523

**Key Terms and People**
Julius Caesar (JOOL yuhs SEE zuhr), p. 518
Cicero (SIS uh roh), p. 520
Augustus (ah GUHS tuhs) (Octavian) (ahk TAY vee uhn), p. 521
Pax Romana (PAHKS roh MAH nuh), p. 521

**Vocabulary** *Builder*

adapt (uh DAHPT) *v.* to fit; to make fit or suitable by changing or adjusting

**Main Idea**
Julius Caesar ruled Rome as "Dictator for Life" until his assassination in 44 B.C.

**Background Knowledge** Rome's republican form of government had been created to run a city and to keep one individual from gaining too much power. Romans tried to adapt that government to fit the needs of an empire. But as you will read, they did not succeed. As the empire grew, so did the ambitions of Roman leaders. Their ambitions would lead to the fall of the Roman Republic.

## The Fall of the Republic

The long years of war taught ambitious Romans an important lesson. The way to wealth and power was to gain control of an army. A victorious general could make himself fabulously rich from his conquests. Furthermore, he could rely on the support of his soldiers in his efforts to gain political power. Several men followed this path to power in the republic. None was more successful than a daring and popular patrician named **Julius Caesar.**

**Caesar Conquers Gaul** Julius Caesar was born into a well-established noble family. He began his rise to power by running for public offices. But Caesar knew that military victories were the best way to win the support of the Roman people. In 59 B.C., Caesar took command of Roman forces fighting in Gaul, which lay to the north of Italy in what is today France and Belgium.

Caesar launched an eight-year campaign of conquest in Gaul. After that, he invaded Britain. He recorded these events in a book called the *Gallic Wars.* The *Gallic Wars* is a work of both history and of propaganda. Propaganda is information that is spread for the purpose of <u>promoting</u> a cause. The cause Caesar was promoting was himself. The *Gallic Wars* portrayed Caesar and his victories as great and glorious. His enemies, in contrast, were characterized as barbarians with no sense of honor or honesty.

**Primary** Sources

See "Republic to Empire: Julius Caesar" in the Reference Section at the back of this book.

**Vocabulary** *Builder*
<u>promote</u> (proh MOHT) *v.* to raise or advance to a higher position or rank

**Crossing the Rubicon** While Caesar was in Gaul, his ambitious rivals gained control of the Roman senate. In 49 B.C., the senate ordered Caesar to give up his command and return to Rome. If he refused, he would be declared an "enemy of the state."

Caesar faced a difficult decision. He could obey the senate and risk being put on trial when he returned to Rome. Or he could march south and risk plunging the Republic into civil war.

The moment of decision came when Caesar and his legions came to the Rubicon River, which marked the southern border of Gaul. An ancient law prevented any general from crossing this stream into Italy with an army. To do so would be an act of treason against Rome. A Roman historian wrote that Caesar paused at the river. According to the story, a man suddenly blew on a trumpet to give the signal to advance. Caesar and his troops then crossed the Rubicon.

**Caesar Crosses the Rubicon**
Julius Caesar and his army crossed the Rubicon River south into Italy, risking another civil war. **Critical Thinking: Detect Points of View** *Why do you think Caesar chose to cross the Rubicon?*

# BIOGRAPHY QUEST

## Was Cicero right about Caesar?

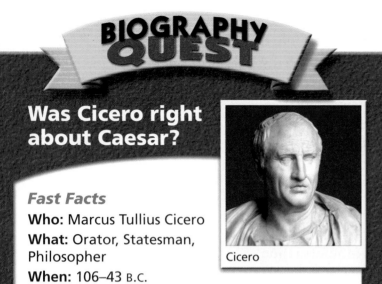

Cicero

### Fast Facts

**Who:** Marcus Tullius Cicero
**What:** Orator, Statesman, Philosopher
**When:** 106–43 B.C.
**Where:** Rome
**Why important:** Cicero spoke out against Julius Caesar's rise to "Dictator for Life."

### Fast Find

**How:** Go online to find out whether Cicero's warnings about Casear becoming Rome's "Dictator for Life" came true.

**Biography Online**
**For:** More about Cicero
**Visit:** PHSchool.com
**Web Code:** mwe-6182

**Dictator for Life** Caesar's crossing of the Rubicon triggered a yearlong civil war. But by 47 B.C., he was master of Rome and all of its territories. As he wrote after one of his victories, *"Veni, vidi, vici,"* which means, in Latin, "I came, I saw, I conquered."

Caesar had great plans to reform government of the empire. He restored order to the city of Rome, lowered taxes, and gave farmland to retired soldiers and the poor. He reorganized the calendar, naming the month of July for himself. His supporters in the senate gave him the power to carry out these reforms by naming him "dictator for life."

This was too much for those who supported the Republic. To them, a "dictator for life" sounded very much like a king. The popular lawyer and philosopher, Cicero, warned the senators that Caesar's rise to power would signal the weakening of the senate itself. "Do you see," Cicero wrote, "the kind of man into whose hands the state has fallen?" On March 15, 44 B.C., a date the Romans called the "Ides of March," several senators stabbed Julius Caesar to death as he entered the senate.

✓**Checkpoint** **Why did some Romans fear Julius Caesar?**

## Augustus: The First Emperor

**Main Idea**
Julius Caesar's adopted son Octavian ruled the Roman Empire during a long period of peace and prosperity.

Caesar's assassination plunged the empire into another civil war. During that conflict, Caesar's adopted son Octavian hunted down the assassins. In 31 B.C., after 14 years of war, Octavian became the master of the Roman world. He later wrote:

❝I often waged war, civil and foreign, on the earth and sea, in the whole wide world. As victor I spared all the citizens who sought pardon. As for foreign nations, those which I was able to safely forgive, I preferred to preserve than to destroy.❞

—Octavian, *The Deeds of the Divine Augustus*

## Octavian Becomes Augustus

Unlike Caesar, Octavian ruled like an emperor, but called himself "first citizen." In 27 B.C., he came to the senate to give up all his offices. The senators begged him to stay and granted him the title **Augustus,** which meant "great and holy one." After that, Octavian was known as Augustus.

Augustus ruled the Roman Empire for more than 40 years. He used power carefully and well. His rule began a long period of peace and prosperity known as the **Pax Romana,** or the "Roman peace."

## Ruling the Empire

Augustus reduced the number of legions in his army from 60 to 28. He paid soldiers of those legions enough to guarantee their loyalty. Augustus made another major change in the army. In the past, soldiers had to be Roman citizens. Augustus allowed men in the provinces to join the army as well. After 25 years of army service, the provincial soldiers could become Roman citizens. He then opened up the senate to all men, not just members of old patrician families.

Augustus made changes to the government of the provinces as well. Augustus replaced greedy officials with honest ones. He paid his officials good salaries so that they would not be tempted to steal from the people.

**E-LA 6.2.2 Analyze Comparisons and Contrasts**

Use a chart with headings *Caesar* and *Augustus.* Tell how these leaders are the same and how they are different.

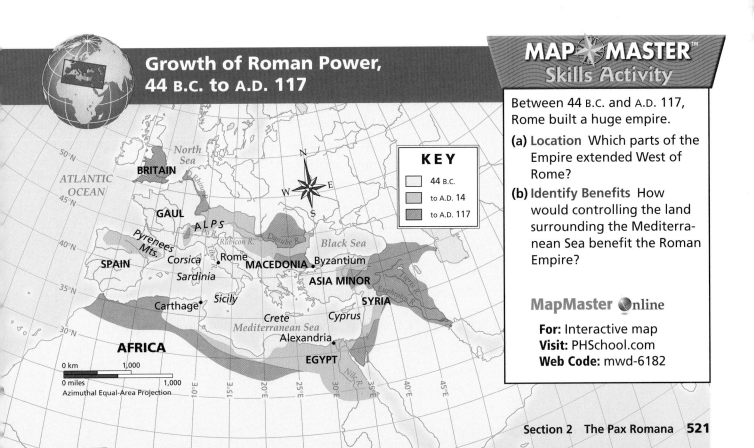

**Growth of Roman Power, 44 B.C. to A.D. 117**

**KEY**
- 44 B.C.
- to A.D. 14
- to A.D. 117

**MAP MASTER™ Skills Activity**

Between 44 B.C. and A.D. 117, Rome built a huge empire.

**(a) Location** Which parts of the Empire extended West of Rome?

**(b) Identify Benefits** How would controlling the land surrounding the Mediterranean Sea benefit the Roman Empire?

**MapMaster Online**

**For:** Interactive map
**Visit:** PHSchool.com
**Web Code:** mwd-6182

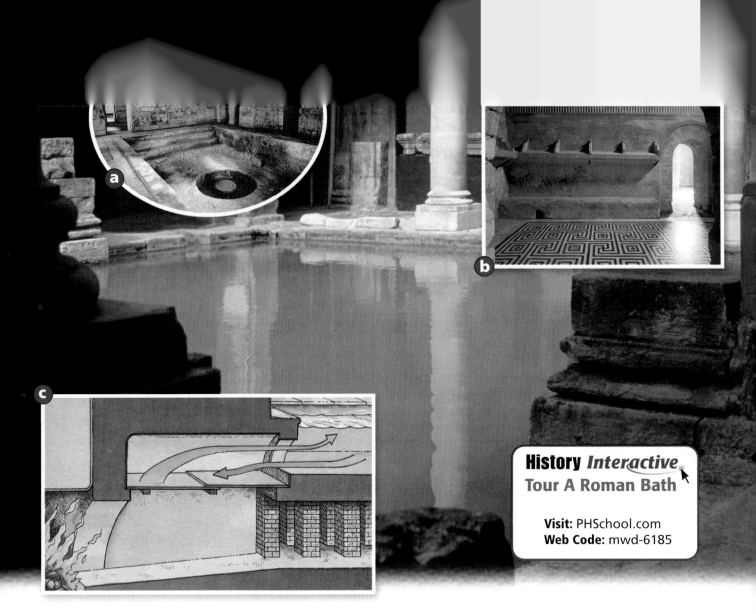

**A Roman Bath**

The images here show the interior of three different Roman baths.

**ⓐ** An empty pool

**ⓑ** An outer room, or dressing room, with elaborate ceramic tile flooring

**ⓒ** This illustration shows how water was circulated underneath the pool to keep the bath hot.

**Critical Thinking: Frame Questions** *What questions would you ask Emperor Augustus about the public baths?*

**History** *Interactive*
Tour A Roman Bath

**Visit:** PHSchool.com
**Web Code:** mwd-6185

**The City of Marble** Augustus began a building program in Rome. Since it was the capital of a great empire, Augustus thought it should look like one, too. He brought in huge amounts of white marble from nearby hills to build new theaters, palaces, and shrines. He also rebuilt the Roman Forum into a center of business and government. "I found Rome a city of brick," Augustus said, "and left it one of marble."

Augustus improved life for ordinary Romans. He provided the poor with jobs, better housing, and free grain. He organized a fire protection force. He also had a large public bath built that was free to all Romans.

**The Succession Problem** As Augustus got older, he faced a new problem. Who would his successor be? Rome had no traditional process for choosing an emperor who would be accepted as legitimate.

Augustus solved the problem by choosing his stepson Tiberius to succeed him. Tiberius ruled the empire well for more than 20 years. The next family member to become emperor—the great-grandson of Augustus, Caligula—was a disaster. Both cruel and insane, Caligula was assassinated after threatening to kill members of the senate.

The question of succession would always be a problem. Inside the imperial palace, people <u>schemed</u> and even murdered their own relatives to become the next emperor. Usually, the final decision was made by the Roman army. This fact led the emperor Severus to advise his sons, "Enrich the soldiers and scorn all other men." The result was a mixed series of good and bad emperors.

**Vocabulary** *Builder*
<u>scheme</u> (skeem) *n.* a carefully arranged plan of action

✔**Checkpoint** How did Augustus rule Rome?

**Looking Back and Ahead** In this section, you have read about the transition of Rome from a republic to an empire. You have also learned about the impact of Julius Caesar and Augustus on Roman history. In the next section, you will learn about commerce and culture during the Pax Romana.

---

## Section 2 Check Your Progress

**Progress Monitoring** Online
**For:** Self-test with instant help
**Visit:** PHSchool.com
**Web Code:** mwa-6182

 **Standards Review** H-SS: 6.7.4; E-LA: Reading 6.2.2

**Comprehension and Critical Thinking**
1. **(a) List** What changes did Caesar make when he was dictator?
   **(b) Draw Inferences** How do you think most Romans felt when Caesar was assassinated?
2. **(a) Recall** Why did Augustus call himself "First Citizen?"
   **(b) Apply Information** How did Augustus' rule lay the foundation for a stable government?

**Reading Skill**
3. **Analyze Comparisons and Contrasts** Choose any two leaders discussed in Section 2. Create a chart to list their features. Then tell how they are the same and different.

**Vocabulary** *Builder*
Read each sentence below. If the sentence is true, write YES. If the sentence is not true, write NO and explain WHY.
4. In the *Gallic Wars*, Julius Caesar portrayed his enemies as honorable people.

5. Cicero opposed Caesar's claim as "Emperor for Life."
6. Augustus chose his stepson Caligula to succeed him.

**Writing**
7. Write a paragraph about one of the topics from this section. As you write, develop your thesis statement for the paragraph from the supporting information you will include about that topic.

# Roman Sport

Emperors such as Augustus and those who followed paid for lavish public entertainments. These entertainments displayed the emperors' wealth and power and made them more popular. People flocked by the thousands to the chariot races and the theater. They also went to the hugely popular "games." These were shows in which people watched killing and bloodshed for fun.

**History-Social Science**
**6.7** Students analyze the geographic, political, economic, religious, and social structures during the development of Rome.

Passageways, cells, and machinery formed a maze beneath the arena.

### Circus Maximus
Ancient Romans loved to spend "a day at the races." The Circus Maximus was built in the sixth century B.C., and was used for almost 1,000 years. Up to 300,000 people could watch the chariot races there.

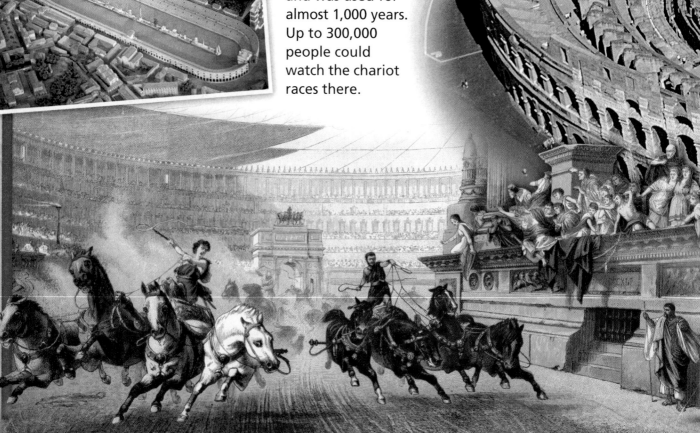

## Gladiators

Gladiators were the men who fought in the "games." Most of them were slaves or criminals who were trained in special schools. "We who are about to die salute you!" they shouted to the emperor, and the fighting began. Sometimes gladiators fought each other. Sometimes they fought animals. If a gladiator was lucky, he survived to win his freedom.

A fight to the death

The outside was decorated with statues.

Arches held the weight of the stands.

## The Colosseum

The emperor Titus opened the Colosseum in A.D. 80. It held about 50,000 people. In the arena, men and wild animals fought to the death. The arena could even be filled with water, so that men could fight "sea battles" in small ships.

## Analyze LIFE AT THE TIME

Today, we also have racetracks and colosseums. However, the activities that take place in them are very different from those that took place in ancient Rome. Write a paragraph that compares modern and ancient racetracks and colosseums, and their activities.

# 3 Commerce and Culture

**H-SS 6.7.3** Identify the location of and the political and geographic reasons for the growth of Roman territories and expansion of the empire, including how the empire fostered economic growth through the use of currency and trade routes.

**E-LA Reading 6.2.2** Analyze text that uses the compare-and-contrast organizational pattern.

## Reading Preview

### Reading Skill

**Analyze Comparisons** Signal words will help you identify elements for comparisons. For example, the word *however* in the next sentence signals a comparison. "In the *Gallic Wars,* Caesar writes about his victories as great and glorious. His enemies, however, are characterized as barbarians with no sense of honor or honesty."

### Vocabulary *Builder*

**High-Use Words**
<u>construction</u> (kuhn STRUHK shuhn), p. 527
<u>network</u> (NEHT werk), p. 527

**Key Terms**
stable currency (STAY buhl KER uhn see), p. 528
Greco-Roman (GREK oh ROH muhn) culture, p. 528

**Background Knowledge** The history of the Roman Empire reads like a story of endless wars. Even during the Pax Romana, there was fighting on the frontiers. Still, most people lived in peace. In this section, you will learn how the Romans encouraged economic growth and the spread of culture.

**Main Idea**
Economic growth and colonization helped the Roman Empire expand during the Pax Romana.

## Economic Growth

The Pax Romana was a time of economic growth for the empire. The long peace lasted from 27 B.C. to A.D. 180. During that time, no nation was powerful enough to attack the empire. The Romans kept the peoples in their empire from fighting one another. As a result, an estimated 60 million people were able to farm, trade, and do business in peace.

**The Roman Economy** Farming was the foundation of the Roman economy. The most important crop was grain grown by farmers in Italy and in the provinces. Farmers paid their taxes in grain. The city of Rome was a huge market for grain, olive oil, and other farm products. Grain also was shipped to Rome's widespread armies for its soldiers to eat.

In return, money flowed from Rome to the provinces. Provincial farmers grew rich from trade with Rome. Many used their new wealth to help their own regions. They built schools, temples, and public baths. That, in turn, helped local cities grow.

Craft industries were part of the Roman economy. Skilled craftsworkers produced wool and linen cloth, glass and pottery, metalwork, and ships. The construction industry was important as well. Huge building projects required marble slabs, terra cotta tiles, lead pipe for plumbing, and other building materials.

**Commerce and Trade** These goods were moved peacefully throughout the empire. Since Romans controlled the Mediterranean, shipping goods by sea was safe. Ships carried wheat from Egypt to Italy. They carried wine, olive oil, and pottery to Europe and the Greek islands.

The Romans linked their empire together with a vast network of paved roads. Roman roads were often built for military purposes, so legions could move quickly. But goods also traveled on Roman roads. As trade increased, provincial cities became centers of industry and commerce. Some Roman trade routes extended well beyond the empire. Red pottery was exported west to Britain and east to India. Silver bowls and bronzeware were shipped to Russia and northern Europe. Romans also imported luxury goods such as silk from as far away as China.

**Vocabulary** *Builder*
underline construction (kuhn STRUHK shuhn) *n.* the act or process of building or constructing

**Vocabulary** *Builder*
underline network (NEHT werk) *n.* an arrangement or system of things such as roads, canals, etc., that connect or cross

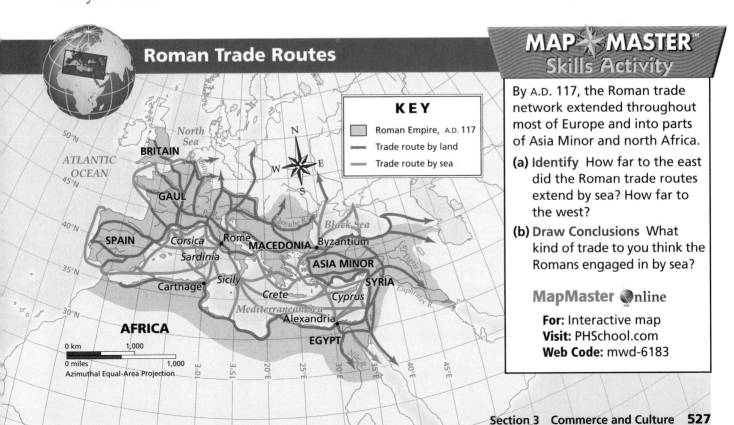

**Roman Trade Routes**

**KEY**
- Roman Empire, A.D. 117
- Trade route by land
- Trade route by sea

**MAP MASTER**
*Skills Activity*

By A.D. 117, the Roman trade network extended throughout most of Europe and into parts of Asia Minor and north Africa.

**(a) Identify** How far to the east did the Roman trade routes extend by sea? How far to the west?

**(b) Draw Conclusions** What kind of trade to you think the Romans engaged in by sea?

**MapMaster** Online

**For:** Interactive map
**Visit:** PHSchool.com
**Web Code:** mwd-6183

## Roman Coins

| | | | |
|---|---|---|---|
| **Coin** | | | |
| **Meaning** | Strength and power of the State | Roman Navy | Caesar's rise to power and eventual fall of the Republic |

### Reading Tables

Roman coins at one time had an important meaning beyond their money value. Coins were used to share pictures and messages. Images placed on Roman coins helped rulers spread political messages to their subjects.

**(a) Read a Table** What does the image of a ship mean when seen on a Roman coin?

**(b) Compare** How do Roman coins compare with coins that we use today? How are they similar? How are they different?

**A Stable Currency** Economic growth in the empire was helped by the creation of a stable currency, which is currency that does not change much in value over time. As a result, stable currency is more quickly and widely accepted in trade and commerce.

After taking power, Augustus issued a new currency in the form of coins. The main coin was the gold denarius. A silver denarius was worth twelve times less than a gold one. The value of the denarius remained stable as long as it contained the same amount of gold or silver year after year.

As Augustus had hoped, Roman coins were soon accepted throughout the empire. This made it far easier to conduct trade over long distances than in the past.

Augustus also used his coins as a kind of political advertisement. The designs on Roman coins often pictured the emperor himself or his building projects. Most people would never visit Rome, but they could see pictures of its great buildings on their money.

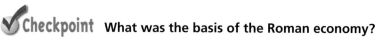 **Checkpoint** What was the basis of the Roman economy?

## Greco-Roman Culture

**Main Idea**
Greco-Roman culture spread throughout the Roman Empire as the empire expanded.

As Rome expanded its empire, wealthy Romans came to admire Greek culture. Greek books were copied and sold widely. An educated Roman learned to read both Latin and Greek. This coming together of Greek and Roman cultural traditions produced what historians today call **Greco-Roman culture.**

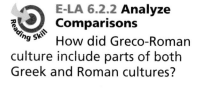 **E-LA 6.2.2 Analyze Comparisons**
How did Greco-Roman culture include parts of both Greek and Roman cultures?

**Roman Colonies** In general, Roman rulers allowed people in the provinces to follow their own customs and culture. However, emperors encouraged the spread of Greco-Roman culture in many ways. One way was by establishing colonies in distant lands. Augustus founded more than 100 colonies in Gaul, Spain, and North Africa. Most of the people who settled in these colonies longed for the pleasures of their homeland. As a result, cities far from Italy had temples, public baths, and a central public forum for meeting or gathering.

**Roman Citizenship** Emperors also spread Greco-Roman culture by expanding Roman citizenship. By A.D. 212, almost everyone in the empire was a Roman citizen. As citizens, they lived under Roman law. They used Roman courts to settle disputes. Citizens served in the Roman army.

Roman soldiers helped spread Greco-Roman culture as well. Many soldiers were sent to the far reaches of the empire. They often married local women and settled where they had served. In this way, distant military outposts grew into Roman towns and cities. These towns and cities in faraway places soon held buildings and other architecture that made them look like Roman towns and cities.

 **Checkpoint** **How were colonies important to the spread of Roman culture?**

**Looking Back and Ahead** In this section, you have read about the growth of the Roman economy during the Pax Romana. You have also learned about the spread of Greco-Roman culture throughout the Roman empire. In the next chapter, you will read about a new religion that got its start in one of Rome's least peaceful provinces.

---

**Section 3 Check Your Progress**

**Progress Monitoring** ●nline
**For:** Self-test with instant help
**Visit:** PHSchool.com
**Web Code:** mwa-6183

 **Standards Review** **H-SS:** 6.7.3; **E-LA:** Reading 6.2.2

**Comprehension and Critical Thinking**

1. **(a) List** What products were important in Roman trade and commerce?
   **(b) Identify Costs** How did building projects affect the Roman economy?

2. **(a) Explain** How did Greek culture affect Roman culture and education?
   **(b) Draw Inferences** Why might a landowner in a provincial city adopt Roman culture?

**⊙ Reading Skill**

3. **Analyze Comparisons** Read this sentence: "An educated Roman had to speak both Greek and Latin well." Compare the importance of Greek and Latin languages to Romans. Identify the signal word that helps you.

**Vocabulary** *Builder*
Complete each of the following sentences so that the second part further explains the first part and clearly shows your understanding of the highlighted word.

4. Economic growth in the Roman empire was helped by the creation of a stable currency; _____.

5. Greco-Roman culture spread throughout the empire; _____.

**Writing**

6. Write a paragraph describing either Roman commerce or culture. Before you begin, narrow the focus of your paragraph by choosing only the most relevant supporting information.

To evaluate historical evidence correctly, you must be able to identify *bias*. Bias means having strong beliefs that prejudice someone's point of view.

The following is from Julius Caesar's *The Civil Wars*, which describes a war battle.

**Chapter Standards**

**History-Social Science**

Reading 6.2.8 Note instances of unsupported inferences, fallacious reasoning, persuasion, and propaganda in text.

> **"**But the enemy, lacking all honor, only waited for a time and an opportunity for fraud and treachery (lies and tricks). And after . . . some days . . . at noon . . . they burst out from the gates, and the wind being high and favorable to them, they set fire to our works. And the wind spread it in such a way that, in an instant, [many parts of our defense] caught the flames and were destroyed before we knew how it happened. . . . Our men . . . laid hold on such arms as they could find. Some rushed from the camp; an attack was made on the enemy. But they were prevented, by arrows and engines from the walls, from pursuing them when they fled. They returned to their walls and there, without fear, set the . . . brick tower on fire. Thus, by the perfidy (betrayal) of the enemy . . . the labor of many months was destroyed in a moment. **"**
>
> —Julius Caesar, *The Civil Wars*

**Learn the Skill** *Follow these steps to identify bias.*

1. **Judge whether any information is incorrect or left out.** Sometimes all the information given is correct. However, information that would support a different view might be left out.

2. **Look for exaggeration, and for emotional words that sound good or bad.** Such words often reflect opinions.

3. **Identify who expresses the bias and why.** The person presenting the biased view usually has a reason for doing so.

4. **State the bias in your own words.** Make a statement that summarizes the bias.

**Practice the Skill** *Use the passage above to answer the following questions.*

1. **Judge whether any information is incorrect or left out.** What information do you think is missing in this passage?

2. **Look for exaggeration, and for emotional words that sound good or bad.** How does the author use exaggeration in this passage?

3. **Identify who expresses the bias and why.** Why does the author use bias?

4. **State the bias in your own words.** Write a sentence that summarizes the bias.

**Apply the Skill**
*See page 533 of the Review and Assessment.*

**interactive Textbook**

**Study Guide Online**
Complete your Chapter 18 study guide in print or online.

## Chapter Summary   H-SS: 6.7; 6.7.3; 6.7.4

### Section 1   The Conquest of an Empire

- Rome's military strength, as well as diplomacy, helped the empire succeed.
- Rome fought against Carthage in three wars known as the Punic Wars.
- Social problems led to the downfall of Rome.

### Section 2   The Pax Romana

- Julius Caesar ruled Rome as "Dictator for Life" until his assassination in 44 B.C.
- Caesar's adopted son Octavian ruled the Roman Empire during a long period of peace and prosperity.

### Section 3   Commerce and Culture

- Economic growth and colonization helped the Roman Empire expand during the Pax Romana.
- Greco-Roman culture spread throughout the Roman Empire as the empire expanded.

**A Roman chariot race**

## Standards Practice   H-SS: 6.7; 6.7.3; 6.7.4

## Vocabulary *Builder*

### High-Use Words

Decide whether each underlined word is used correctly. If it is, explain why. If not, rewrite the rest of the sentence to make it logical.

1. The Romans would sign **treaties** with peoples whom they defeated.

2. Roman **estates** were used to house the prisoners of war.

3. The government tries to correct political or social abuses through **reforms**.

4. The soldier was **promoted** because he disobeyed his captain's orders.

5. They knew that the **scheme** was not planned.

### Key Terms

Answer the following questions in complete sentences that show your understanding of the Key Terms.

1. What tactic did the Roman army use when traveling through hilly countryside?

2. How did a stable currency help the Roman empire's economic growth?

3. How did expanding Roman citizenship help spread Greco-Roman culture?

##  Apply Reading Skills

**Analyze Comparisons and Contrasts** Write a sentence comparing two elements of the Roman Empire such as the differences among social classes or the rule by different emperors. Write a second sentence contrasting two elements of the Roman Empire. Use a signal word in at least one of your sentences.

## Comprehension and Critical Thinking

1. **(a) Explain** How did Rome gain control of both the western and eastern Mediterranean region?
   **(b) Analyze Cause and Effect** How did wars directly affect the Roman economy?

2. **(a) Recall** Why did some senators decide to assassinate Julius Caesar?
   **(b) Compare** How did Augustus gain power without offending the Senate as Caesar had done?

3. **(a) List** Who were the emperors who came after Augustus?
   **(b) Draw Conclusions** Why do you think family members were chosen as successors?

4. **(a) Recall** Why was Roman currency stable during the reign of Augustus?
   **(b) Draw Inferences** Why did Augustus use coins for his political advertisement?

## Researching

**The Colosseum** The Roman Colosseum is a popular place for people visiting Rome. It has provided a great deal of information to people seeking to learn more about Roman civilization. In this activity you will use the Internet, the school library, and other resources to report on a particular feature of the Colosseum. Share your work with the class on "Roman Colosseum" day. Make a list of the resources you used to go with your presentation.

**Historian:** Trace the Colosseum's use through the years. Create a time line showing various stages and uses during the "life" of this great architectural ruin.

**Government Officials:** From the point of view of a Roman government official, use your imagination to create a calendar of events taking place in the Colosseum during one month.

> **Researching Online**
> **For:** Help in starting this activity
> **Visit:** PHSchool.com
> **Web Code:** mwe-6184

## Writing

1. **Write a paragraph on the following topic.** The Roman army was the strongest and finest-trained army in the world. Choose only the most relevant supporting information to include in your paragraph.
   **Your paragraph should:**
   • include a thesis statement.
   • offer details to support your thesis.
   • include relevant supporting information that supports your thesis statement.

2. **Write a short narrative.** Take the part of a Roman soldier who is at a faraway fort. Write a short narrative to your family describing life on the frontier of the Roman empire.

# Apply Analysis Skills

**Use the quotation at right by Octavian to answer these questions.**

1. What information do you think Octavian may have left out of this passage? Why do you think that it was omitted?

2. Does Octavian use exaggeration or emotional words in the quotation? Explain.

3. Do you think Octavian shows bias in this quotation? Explain.

4. Rewrite the quotation to eliminate any bias, exaggeration, or emotional words.

> **"** I often waged war, civil and foreign, on the earth and sea, in the whole wide world. As victor I spared all the citizens who sought pardon. As for foreign nations, those which I was able to safely forgive, I preferred to preserve than to destroy. **"**

# Test Yourself

1. **When the Romans defeated Carthage, they**
   A gained control of the western Mediterranean.
   B gave Hannibal control of Sicily.
   C gave farmland to the poor.
   D gained control of the eastern Mediterranean.

**Refer to the image below to answer Question 2.**

2. **Why does this image represent Rome's change from republic to empire?**
   A Caesar began cutting taxes.
   B The army moved further north.
   C Caesar reorganized the calendar.
   D Caesar crossed the Rubicon into Italy, risking civil war.

3. **Which statement is true?**
   A The Roman Republic had a large and prosperous middle class.
   B The Gracchus brothers had a land reform law passed by the Senate.
   C The Romans turned conquered people into loyal citizens and soldiers.
   D Spartacus and his army of escaped slaves overthrew the Roman Republic.

**Refer to the quotation below to answer Question 4.**

> *"In my nineteenth year, on my own initiative and at my own expense, I raised an army with which I set free the state. . . . I drove the men who slaughtered my father into exile with a legal order, punishing their crime."*

4. **The quotation illustrates how Octavian**
   A began the Pax Romana.
   B began his quest for revenge and power.
   C guaranteed the loyalty of the soldiers in the legions.
   D tricked the Senate into granting him the title of Augustus.

## Chapter
# 19 Christianity
### (63 B.C.–A.D. 395)

## Prepare to Read

### Chapter Standards

**History-Social Science**
**6.7** Students analyze the geographic, political, economic, religious, and social structures during the development of Rome.

| | **What You Will Learn** |
|---|---|
| **Section 1,** pp. 538–544 | |
| **The Origins of Christianity** | During the Roman control of Galilee and Judea, a young teacher attracted many followers before he was arrested and executed. |
| **Section 2,** pp. 545–549 | |
| **The Beliefs of Christianity** | Christian beliefs are drawn from the teachings of Jesus and his apostles, as recorded in the New Testament. |
| **Section 3,** pp. 552–553 | |
| **The Spread of Christianity** | While facing great challenges, early Christians spread their beliefs across the empire. |

Early Christian Carving

**63 B.C.**
The Romans control Jerusalem

**Between 7 B.C. and 4 B.C.**
Jesus is born.

Chapter Events

Other Events

**200 B.C.**   **100 B.C.**   **B.C./A.D.**   **A.D. 100**

**185 B.C.** Maurya Empire comes to an end.

**A.D. 64** A great fire destroys much of Rome

Large crowds followed Jesus as he preached near the Sea of Galilee

**A.D. 313**
Roman Emperor Constantine ends persecution of Christians.

**A.D. 395**
Christianity is the established religion of the Roman Empire.

A.D. 100

A.D. 200

A.D. 300

A.D. 400

**About A.D. 250** Mayan culture begins to flourish in Meso–America.

A.D. 330 Samudra Gupta expands his empire in India.

# How to Read History

## History Reading Skill

### *Previewing* Clues to Determine Meaning

As your readings become more complex, you will come across more and more unfamiliar words. These words may be directly explained in the text, but often you will need to figure them out on your own. You can use many different clues from the surrounding words and sentences. Study the strategies below for ideas.

**Chapter Standards**

**English-Language Arts**

**Reading 6.1.4** Monitor expository text for unknown words or words with novel meanings by using word, sentence, and paragraph clues to determine meaning.

**1** In this example, a nearby sentence contains a synonym that suggests a meaning for the unfamiliar word.

Starting from Spain, Hannibal's <u>route</u> would cross the rugged Alps. The <u>journey</u> across the snowy Alps was terrifying.

> Unfamiliar Word

> Familiar synonym

**2** In this sentence, two adjectives are used together to describe Augustus. Knowing the meaning of one adjective can help you determine the meaning of the related word.

The Senate gave him the title Augustus, which means "<u>majestic</u> and <u>honored</u>."

> Less familiar word

> Related word offers clue

**3** Here, description and examples nearby give you clues to the meaning of an unfamiliar word.

> Unfamiliar Word

Red pottery was <u>exported</u> as far as <u>Britain in the west and India in the east.</u> Silver bowls and bronzeware went <u>to Russia</u> and <u>northern Europe.</u> Merchants <u>even reached parts of Africa and Asia.</u>

> Clues to the meaning of *exported*

# Vocabulary *Builder*

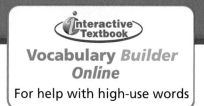
**Interactive Textbook**

**Vocabulary** *Builder*
**Online**
For help with high-use words

## *Previewing* **High-Use Academic Words**

| High-Use Word | Definition | Sample Sentence About History |
|---|---|---|
| **occupy** (AH kyuh pī) (section 1, p. 538) | *v.* to live in and take control of a place, especially by military force | Roman soldiers occupied cities in conquered lands. |
| **conflict** (KAHN flikt) (section 1, p. 539) | *n.* strong disagreement between people or groups | City-states such as Greece and Sparta often had conflicts. |
| **foundation** (fown DAY shun) (section 2, p. 540) | *n.* the basic idea from which something develops | The scientific advances of ancient Greece provided a foundation for many Roman accomplishments. |
| **distinct** (dihs TIHNKT) (Section 2, p. 547) | *adj.* clearly divided | The rights of Roman citizens helped keep them distinct from the peoples they had conquered. |
| **reject** (rih JEHKT) (Section 3, p. 553) | *v.* to refuse to accept | Some officials in Rome rejected Julius Caesar's leadership. |
| **factor** (FAK tuhr) (section 3, p. 555) | *n.* something that causes or helps cause a situation | Caesar's military success was one factor in his popularity. |

## *Previewing* **Key Terms and People**

**Peter**

messiah, p. 538
Herod, p. 538
baptism, p. 539
resurrection, p. 539

Jesus, p. 540
disciple, p. 541
Pontius Pilate, p. 542
crucifixion, p. 542

apostle, p. 545
parable, p. 546
epistle, p. 546
persecute, p. 552

Peter, p. 552
Paul, p. 552
conversion, p. 554
martyr, p. 556

**Pontius Pilate**

# 1 The Origins of Christianity

## Standards Preview

**H-SS 6.7.5** Trace the migration of Jews around the Mediterranean region and the effects of their conflict with the Romans, including the Romans' restrictions on their right to live in Jerusalem.

**H-SS 6.7.6** Note the origins of Christianity in the Jewish Messianic prophecies, the life and teachings of Jesus of Nazareth as described in the New Testament, and the contribution of St. Paul the Apostle to the definition and spread of Christian beliefs (e.g., belief in the Trinity, resurrection, salvation).

## Reading Preview

### Reading Skill

**Use Sentence Clues** Look for clues in sentences surrounding unfamiliar words. These clues could be descriptions that suggest a meaning for the unfamiliar word. Ask yourself what meaning would fit the descriptions. Insert that meaning in place of the unfamiliar word, and read the sentence to yourself. If it makes sense, you are probably close to the meaning of the unfamiliar word.

**E-LA Reading 6.1.4**

### Vocabulary *Builder*

**High-Use Words**
occupy (AH kyuh pī), p. 538
conflict (KAHN flihkt), p. 539

**Key Terms and People**
messiah (muh SĪ uh), p. 538
Herod (HAIR uhd), p. 538
baptism (BAP tih zuhm), p. 539
resurrection (reh zuh REHK shuhn), p. 539
Jesus (JEE zuhs), p. 540
disciple (dih SI puhl), p. 541
Pontius Pilate (PAHN chuhs PĪ laht), p. 542
crucifixion (kroo suh FIHK shuhn), p. 542

**Background Knowledge** Not all of the peoples ruled by Rome accepted Roman domination. In this section, you will read about Jewish unrest under the Romans. You will also learn about a spiritual leader who arose during troubled times.

**Main Idea**
Starting in 63 B.C., the Romans occupied Jewish territories that were divided by religious and political views.

**Vocabulary *Builder***
occupy (AH kyuh pī) *v.* to take control of a place, especially by military force

## The Jews Under Roman Rule

By 63 B.C., the Romans controlled the region that included Jerusalem. The people there were divided in many ways.

**Political Divisions** Many Jews resented Roman rule. They saw the Romans as foreign unbelievers <u>occupying</u> their land. Some Jews believed that they should resist the Romans. Others hoped that God would send a great leader called the messiah, which means anointed leader. They hoped that Messiah would drive the Romans from their homeland.

Some Jews, however, accepted Roman rule. They accepted Herod, a non-Jew whom the Romans made king in 37 B.C.

**Religious Divisions** The Jews under Roman rule were also divided by religious differences. Some of the priests focused on protecting the temple, even when they needed the Romans' help to do so. Other groups moved into desert caves where they could be left alone. Many of these groups practiced baptism, or immersion in water, as a sign of spiritual cleansing.

One very influential group was the Pharisees (FAR uh sees). These were educated people who respected the Torah and the teachings of the rabbis. The Pharisees also believed in the resurrection, the idea that a godly person who dies will be raised from the dead and live with God forever.

Many of the poorer Jews respected the beliefs of the Pharisees. Unfortunately, it was hard for them to keep all of the rules that the Pharisees said they should.

Conflicts among these groups paved the way for further unrest.

✔Checkpoint **How did different groups of Jews react to Roman rule?**

**E-LA 6.1.4 Use Sentence Clues** What does *rabbi* mean? What clues did you use?

**Vocabulary *Builder***
**conflict** (KAHN flikt) *n.* strong disagreement between people or groups

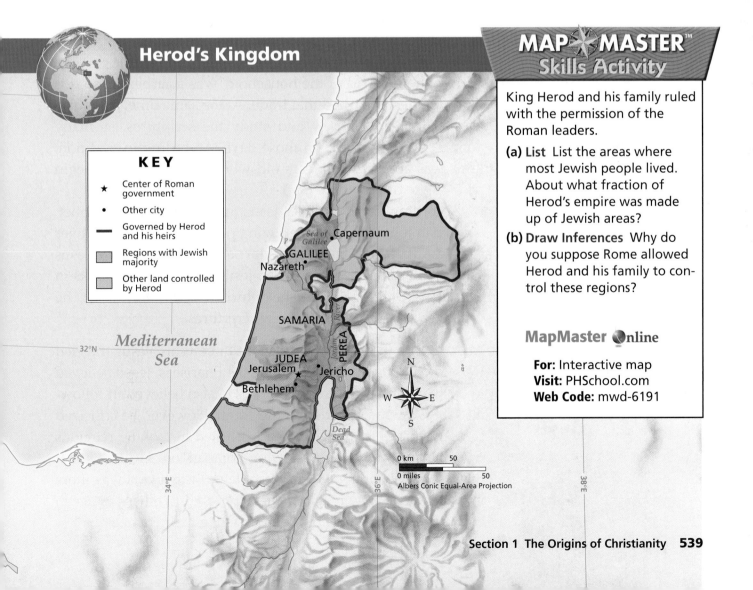

**Herod's Kingdom**

**KEY**

★ Center of Roman government

• Other city

— Governed by Herod and his heirs

▨ Regions with Jewish majority

▨ Other land controlled by Herod

Capernaum
Sea of Galilee
GALILEE
Nazareth
SAMARIA
Jordan River
PEREA
JUDEA
Jerusalem ★  Jericho
Bethlehem
Dead Sea
Mediterranean Sea
32°N
34°E
36°E
38°E

N
W E
S

0 km 50
0 miles 50
Albers Conic Equal-Area Projection

**MAP✷MASTER™**
**Skills Activity**

King Herod and his family ruled with the permission of the Roman leaders.

**(a) List** List the areas where most Jewish people lived. About what fraction of Herod's empire was made up of Jewish areas?

**(b) Draw Inferences** Why do you suppose Rome allowed Herod and his family to control these regions?

**MapMaster ⏺nline**

**For:** Interactive map
**Visit:** PHSchool.com
**Web Code:** mwd-6191

# The Life and Teachings of Jesus

During these years of conflict, a teacher from the northern province of Galilee (GA luh lee) began to attract a following and cause some to wonder whether the messiah had come. This teacher was named after the ancient Jewish leader Joshua, whose name meant "God helps." Most English speakers today call him Jesus.

### A Childhood in Galilee

Most of what we know about Jesus comes from the writings of early Christians, especially from the Gospels. These are four early Christian writings that tell about events in the life of Jesus and record some of his teachings.

According to the Gospels, Jesus was a descendant of King David. He was even born in the town of David's birth—Bethlehem (BEHTH lih hehm). Many historians believe that Jesus was born between 7 and 4 B.C., just before King Herod died and the Romans divided his kingdom into separate provinces.

One of those provinces was Galilee, several days' journey north of Jerusalem. While Jesus was very young, his family moved there, to the town of Nazareth (NA zuh ruhth).

Joseph, the head of the household, was a carpenter, so it is likely that Jesus learned that trade. At the same time, Jesus also learned to read Hebrew and study the scriptures, as many young Jewish boys did in those days. According to tradition, Jesus was about thirty years old when he left home to begin speaking to others about God.

According to the Gospels, Jesus first went to see a prophet, his cousin John. John was baptizing people in the Jordan River as a sign that they wanted to start a new spiritual life. Jesus asked John to baptize him. Then Jesus spent several weeks in the desert praying. When he returned from the desert, he began teaching from the Hebrew scriptures.

### Jesus the Teacher

For about three years, Jesus traveled from town to town, teaching. Like the Pharisees, Jesus believed in one God and in the resurrection. He also believed in following God's law, as recorded in the Torah. However, he criticized some Pharisees who were more interested in looking religious than in doing right and showing compassion. He told them that how they felt about other people in their hearts was more important than how religious they appeared to others. He even encouraged people to show compassion to their enemies.

As this painting illustrates,
Jesus often taught people as
he was traveling. **Critical
Thinking: Detect Points of
View** *Did the artist believe
that Jesus was an important
person? Defend your answer
with information from the
painting.*

According to the Gospel of Matthew, Jesus told his listeners:

**❝You have heard that it was said, 'You shall love your
neighbor and hate your enemy.' But I say to you,
Love your enemies . . . so that you may show your-
selves true sons of your Father in heaven, for he
makes his sun rise on bad and good alike. . . . You
are to be perfect, as your heavenly Father is.❞**

—Matthew 5:43–48

According to the Gospels, even people who disagreed with
Jesus were impressed with the things he said. Then word
spread that he was healing sick people who came to him for
help. The crowds grew. Many began to wonder whether Jesus
was the messiah.

**Understanding Jesus' Words** Sometimes Jesus said
things that people found hard to understand. For example, Jesus
told religious leaders that just following religious rules was not
enough. Showing compassion to others is important too.

According to the Gospels, Jesus called God his father and
made statements such as "I and the Father are one." Many
people were shocked at such statements.

Sometimes Jesus even shocked his **disciples,** who were his
close followers. In the last few weeks of his life, he told them
that he would soon be killed, but that he would be resurrected.
His disciples expected him to lead an army and drive out the
Romans. They became upset when he talked about dying.

✔**Checkpoint** **Why did Jesus' teachings appeal to many people?**

# Opposition to Jesus

According to the Gospels, Jesus had many followers, including some of the religious leaders. However, other leaders began to be nervous about his popularity.

**Jesus Makes Enemies** Leaders in Judea began to worry that Jesus or his followers might cause problems. Jesus had already angered some religious leaders by saying that simply appearing religious did not please God. Jesus angered other leaders when he criticized the way money was being handled in the temple.

Jesus also made some people in the government nervous. One of those leaders was Antipas (AN tuh puhs), one of King Herod's sons. Antipas was ruler of Galilee, but he spent much of his time in Jerusalem. Antipas began to see Jesus as a threat. Other leaders began to fear that Jesus or his followers would start a revolt against the Roman Empire. If that happened, they feared, the Romans might destroy the city and the temple.

Finally, Jesus made his last trip to Jerusalem to observe the Passover feast. For a few days, he sat in the temple, talking to crowds and answering questions. Some leaders began looking for a way to take Jesus prisoner without making the crowds angry.

**Arrest, Trial, and Death** Finally, the enemies of Jesus learned where he could be arrested away from the crowds. According to the Gospels, Jesus was put on trial not once but four times. He was questioned first by some of the religious leaders. Then he was sent to the Roman governor, Pontius Pilate. Pilate learned that Jesus was from Galilee, so he sent Jesus to Antipas. However, Antipas sent Jesus back to Pilate without ruling on his case.

Finally Pilate gave in to pressure and sentenced Jesus to die by crucifixion. This was a method of execution practiced by the Romans. The victim was nailed or tied to a large wooden cross and left to hang until dead. This form of punishment was very painful. It caused death by slow suffocation. Normally, crucifixion was reserved for the worst criminals.

After Jesus died, his body was taken down from the cross. A religious feast day was approaching, so there was no time to prepare his body for burial according to Jewish custom. Instead, his body was wrapped in cloth and laid in a tomb. A heavy stone was rolled into the doorway of the tomb. The Romans sealed the tomb and posted guards around it.

## Jesus' Last Week

Jesus and his followers traveled to Jerusalem. He spent several days teaching in the temple before he was arrested. The illustrations on this page show events of that week, as recorded in the Gospels. **Critical Thinking: Draw Conclusions** *How do you think Jesus' followers reacted as the events shown on this page occurred? Explain.*

**1 The Last Supper** Jesus celebrated the Passover feast with his disciples. He warned them about events that would soon take place.

**2 The Mount of Olives** Jesus spent several hours in prayer in the Garden of Gethsemane. Then he was taken prisoner.

**3 Trial before Pilate** The Roman ruler Pontius Pilate questioned Jesus twice.

**4 Carrying the Cross** Jesus carried his own cross to the place where the Romans would execute him.

**5 The Pieta** This sculpture by Michelangelo shows Jesus' mother Mary holding her son's body after he was taken down from the cross.

**The Resurrection**
Many disciples of Jesus claimed that they saw him alive after his death and burial. **Critical Thinking: Draw Inferences** *Would the disciples of Jesus have continued to spread his teaching if they had not believed in his resurrection? Why or why not?*

**The Resurrection** According to the Gospels, some women who were disciples visited the tomb the following Sunday morning. They were bringing spices and ointments to anoint the body of Jesus for burial. But the women found the guards gone and the tomb empty. They ran to tell the other disciples.

The Gospels describe several occasions during which Jesus appeared to his followers as a living person. The last time that they saw Jesus, he told them to go into the world, share his teachings, and make disciples.

His disciples believed that Jesus had been resurrected, and that he was indeed the Messiah. The Greek word for Messiah is "Christ," so the disciples of Jesus eventually came to be called Christians. The religion that was based on the teachings of Jesus came to be called Christianity.

 **Checkpoint** **Why did some leaders see Jesus as a threat?**

**Looking Back and Ahead** In this section, you have read about Roman rule and about religious differences among Jews. You have also learned about the life of Jesus and the origins of Christianity. In the next section, you will learn more about Christian beliefs.

---

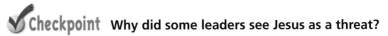

**Section 1** **Check Your Progress**

**Progress Monitoring** ⏺nline
**For:** Self-test with instant help
**Visit:** PHSchool.com
**Web Code:** mwa-6191

**Standards Review** H-SS: 6.7.5; 6.7.6; E-LA: Reading 6.1.4

**Comprehension and Critical Thinking**

1. **(a) Explain** Why did some Jews resist Roman rule?
   **(b) Apply Information** Why do you think some Jews chose to wait for Messiah to resist Roman rule?

2. **(a) Identify** On what issues did Jesus agree with the Pharisees?
   **(b) Draw Inferences** Why did those agreements fail to keep most of the Pharisees on Jesus' side?

⟳ **Reading Skill**

3. **Use Sentence Clues** Reread this sentence from the section: Jesus angered other leaders when he criticized the way money was being handled in the temple. How does the sentence help you understand what the word *criticized* means?

**Vocabulary** *Builder*

4. Write two definitions for each word: <u>occupy</u>, <u>conflict</u>. First, write a formal definition for your teacher. Second, write a definition in everyday English for a classmate.

**Writing**

5. Plan a paragraph describing ways that Roman rule affected the Jews between 100 B.C. and A.D. 100. Start by making a list of details from this chapter. Then divide your list into different categories such as political, religious, and cultural.

# 2 The Beliefs of Christianity

**Standards Preview**

**H-SS 6.7.6** Note the origins of Christianity in the Jewish Messianic prophecies, the life and teachings of Jesus of Nazareth as described in the New Testament, and the contribution of St. Paul the Apostle to the definition and spread of Christian beliefs (e.g., belief in the Trinity, resurrection, salvation).

**E-LA Reading 6.1.4** Monitor expository text for unknown words or words with novel meanings by using word, sentence, and paragraph clues to determine meaning.

## Reading Preview

 **Reading Skill**

**Use Related Words to Determine Meaning** Sometimes you will find clues in related words. These could be unfamiliar parts of speech formed from a familiar word. For example, the unfamiliar word *crucifixion* is related to the familiar word *cross.* Use the familiar word to build meaning. Also look for antonyms—words with opposite meanings—that can suggest meaning. Use signal words such as *but* or *unlike* to spot antonyms.

**Vocabulary *Builder***

**High-Use Words**
**foundation** (fown DAY shun), p. 545
**distinct** (dihs TIHNKT), p. 547

**Key Terms**
apostle (uh PAH suhl), p. 545
parable (PAR uh buhl), p. 546
epistle (ih PIH suhl), p. 546

**Background Knowledge** The crucifixion of Jesus shocked his disciples, but his resurrection filled them with hope. Now certain that Jesus was the Messiah, they set out to share his teachings with the world, beginning in Jerusalem. In this section, you will learn about these teachings and other basic beliefs of Christianity.

## Early Christian Writings

During his life, Jesus chose twelve apostles, disciples who would be sent out to spread his teachings. The original apostles had all known Jesus and heard him preach. Most of them became leaders in the early Christian community. But as Christianity spread, church leaders wanted new leaders and new churches to know the words and actions of Jesus. So they began writing them down. Together with letters from early church leaders, these writings became the <u>foundation</u> for most Christian teaching.

**Main Idea**
As Christians wrote down the teachings of early church leaders, the New Testament of the Christian Bible began to take form.

**Vocabulary *Builder***
**foundation** (fown DAY shun) *n.* a basic idea from which something develops

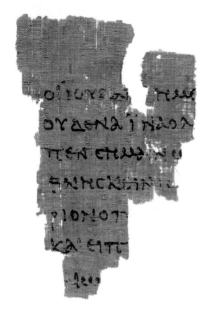

**An Early Manuscript**
This fragment of the Gospel of John was found in Egypt. This copy was probably created within a century after the original Gospel was written. **Critical Thinking: Evaluate Information** *Why might such evidence be important to people who are studying the history of the early church?*

**Main Idea**
Christians believe that Jesus is God's son and that he was sent to become a sacrifice for sin.

**The New Testament** The early church collected the writings of the apostles and other church leaders. Soon church leaders realized that some of these writings should be preserved for all Christians to use. These writings became what Christians today call the New Testament. Together, the Hebrew scriptures and the New Testament make up the Christian Bible.

The first four books of the New Testament are the Gospels. The Gospels describe the life and teaching of Jesus from four different points of view. So the Gospels do not all describe the same events in exactly the same way. But together, they create a powerful portrayal of Jesus and his teachings.

Many of these teachings are presented in the form of parables. A **parable** is a story with a religious moral. Jesus often used parables to explain important lessons.

Most of the books of the New Testament are **epistles.** These are letters to the churches that apostles and other early leaders wrote. Most epistles were written to explain Christian teachings or to solve problems in the church.

The last book of the New Testament, Revelation, is written like an epistle. However, Revelation focuses on future events. It uses complicated images that resemble the writings of some Old Testament prophets.

 **Checkpoint** **What kinds of books make up the New Testament?**

## Christian Teachings

Since the Bible was first written down, Christians have used it as a source for their teachings. Over the years, religious leaders have differed over some details of those teachings. Some groups of Christians also respect the writings and opinions of later Christian leaders. But most practicing Christians today still hold to the same basic beliefs as the early Christians.

**Beliefs About Jesus** You have already read about some of the most important Christian beliefs. To the early Christians, the resurrection proved that Jesus was God as well as a man and that everything Jesus had said was true. They believed that Jesus had come to Earth to show people how to find God. They also believed that his death was no accident. Instead, they believed that Jesus took the punishment for the wrong things they had done. Because of this, God could forgive them. The resurrection of Jesus also proved that his disciples would one day be resurrected as well.

**The Soul and Salvation** Two other key beliefs in Christianity concern the soul and its salvation from sin. Christians believe that everyone has a soul, or spirit. The human soul is <u>distinct</u> from the body and lives on after death. But to a Christian, what happens to the soul after death depends on how that person has lived and whether that person believes in Jesus.

According to Christian belief, every person does wrong things that hurt others. Murder, stealing, and telling lies about other people are examples of sins. Christians believe that sin separates people from the presence of God. They believe that people need for God to forgive their sins so that their souls can live on in the presence of God after they die.

Many ancient peoples offered sacrifices, such as bulls or goats, to have their sins forgiven. But Christians believe that Jesus became the sacrifice for the sins of everyone. They believe that people who are truly sorry for their sins and choose to follow Jesus can be forgiven.

Christians also believe that when they die, their souls will live on in the presence of God. In the future, they will also be resurrected and live with Jesus forever.

**Vocabulary** *Builder*
<u>distinct</u> (dihs TIHNKT) *adj.* different or separate

**E-LA 6.1.4 Use Related Words to Determine Meaning**

What does the word *forgiven* mean? Does the use of the word *forgive* in the previous sentence give you a clue?

## Christian Symbols

| | |
|---|---|
| ✝ | The cross represents Jesus' sacrifice for people's sins. It is the primary symbol of Christianity. |
| 🐟 | Early Christians used the Greek word for fish, *ichthus*, as an abbreviation for the phrase "Jesus Christ, God's Son, Savior." Jesus also called his apostles "fishers of men." |
| ⚓ | The anchor contains a hidden cross symbol. It also symbolizes spiritual safety. |
| ☧ | The Chi-Rho displays the first two letters of the Greek word for "Christ." |
| ◉ | The three interlocking circles stand for the unity of the Father, the Son, and the Holy Spirit. |
| 🕊 | The dove represents God's Spirit descending gently on Jesus' followers. |

**Reading Tables**

The earliest Christians were Jews, who did not believe in creating pictures of religious leaders. Instead, they used symbols to communicate their faith. This practice continued as Gentiles became Christians. Some of these symbols were used in many parts of the Roman Empire.

**(a) Read a Table** What language helped the fish symbol and the chi rho become important to early Christians?

**(b) Draw Conclusions** Do you believe that these symbols still mean what they meant to early Christians? Explain.

**Compassion at Work**
Tabitha was an early Christian who made clothing for people who could not afford to buy it. **Critical Thinking: Link Past and Present** *What are some ways in which people show compassion today?*

## Following Jesus' Teachings

Christians believe that they should lead their lives based on the teachings of Jesus.

Many of the teachings of Jesus concern ethics, or issues of right and wrong and of how to treat people. The most important of those teachings is to love God and one another. Jesus said:

> **You shall love the Lord your God with all your heart, and with all your soul, and with all your mind." This is the great and first commandment. And a second is like it. "You shall love your neighbor as yourself.**
>
> —Matthew 22:37–39

Jesus taught that all people are equal in the eyes of God. In fact, Jesus preached that God was especially concerned for poor and humble people. According to the Gospel of Matthew, he began one of his most famous sermons with these words:

> **Blessed are the meek, for they shall inherit the earth. Blessed are those who hunger and thirst for righteousness [justice], for they shall be satisfied. Blessed are the merciful, for they shall obtain mercy. Blessed are the pure in heart, for they shall see God. Blessed are the peacemakers, for they shall be called sons of God.**
>
> —Matthew 5:5–9

In addition to telling people how they should live, Jesus also told people that he was important to their salvation. He said:

> **I am the way, the truth, and the life: no man comes to the Father, but by me.**
>
> —John 14:6

To some people, Christianity simply means a religion that follows the ethical teaching of Jesus. But for most Christians throughout history, Christianity has also meant believing in Jesus, in his sacrifice for other people's sins, and in his resurrection.

**The Trinity** Like Jews, Christians believe in one God. But most Christians believe that this one God is revealed in three persons, whom they call God the Father, God the Son, and God the Holy Spirit. This idea of three persons in one God is known as the Trinity.

Christians believe that God the Father created the universe. They believe that Jesus existed with the Father long before he became man. In addition, they believe that he returned to the Father's side after the resurrection.

Although the Spirit of God is mentioned in the Torah, the Jews did not consider the Spirit as a separate person from the Father. Early Christians considered the Spirit as a unique part of God. To them, the Spirit allowed them to sense the presence of God even while Jesus was physically removed from Earth.

 **Checkpoint** How does the idea of the Trinity differ from Jewish beliefs about God?

**Looking Back and Ahead** In this section, you have read about the writings and basic beliefs of early Christians. In the next section, you will read about the spread of Christianity through the Roman Empire.

**Representing the Trinity**
Christians often use symbols such as this sign of three overlapping circles to symbolize the three persons in one God. **Critical Thinking: Draw Inferences** *Why do you think that the circles are shown linked instead of one on top of the other?*

---

## Section 2 Check Your Progress

**Progress Monitoring** Online
**For:** Self-test with instant help
**Visit:** PHSchool.com
**Web Code:** mwa-6192

 **Standards Review** H-SS: 6.7.6; E-LA: Reading 6.1.4

**Comprehension and Critical Thinking**

**1. (a) Recall** Why were the Gospels written?
**(b) Draw Conclusions** Why might the individual Gospels differ in some ways?

**2. (a) Explain** What was the main message of Jesus' teachings?
**(b) Apply Information** Which kinds of people probably responded first to these teachings? Explain.

**Reading Skill**

**3. Use Related Words to Determine Meaning** Read this sentence: "Blessed are the peacemakers, for they shall be called sons of God." What does peacemaker mean? What clue did you use?

**Vocabulary** *Builder*

Read each sentence below. If the sentence is true, write YES. If the sentence is not true, write NO and explain WHY.

**4.** Rome divided King Herod's land into <u>distinct</u> provinces after he died.

**5.** The New Testament provides a <u>foundation</u> for the Christian faith.

**Writing**

**6.** Outline a paragraph about Christian beliefs. First, make a list of Christian beliefs using what you have read in this section. Decide how you could group these beliefs into different categories, such as beliefs about God and beliefs about salvation. After you have organized your list, use this information in your outline.

# The Good Samaritan

from The Gospel According to Luke 10:25–37

## Prepare to Read

 **Standards Preview**

**H-SS 6.7.6** Note the origins of Christianity in the Jewish Messianic prophecies, the life and teachings of Jesus of Nazareth.

**E-LA Reading 6.3.8** Critique the credibility of characterization and the degree to which a plot is contrived or realistic.

### Reading Skill

**Analyze Credibility** If something is *credible*, it is believable. A credible story has characters you can believe in and relate to. It has a realistic plot. The following selection is a parable or a short simple story that teaches a lesson. As you read the parable, ask yourself whether its characters and plot are credible.

### Vocabulary *Builder*

As you read this literature selection, look for the following underlined words:

**Levite** (LEE vīt) *n.* religious worker

**Samaritan** (suh MAIR ih tuhn) *n.* member of a religious and ethnic group, originally from Samaria

**denarii** (dih NAIR ee) *n.* ancient Roman coins

> **BACKGROUND**
> The disciple Luke tells this story about Jesus. As the story begins, Jesus is talking to a group of people, including a lawyer who is an expert in the laws of the Jewish religion.

Ａnd behold, a certain lawyer stood up and tested ... [Jesus], saying, "Teacher, what shall I do to inherit eternal life?"

[Jesus] ... said to him, "What is written in the law? What is your reading of it?"

So ... [the lawyer] answered and said, "'You shall love the Lord your God with all your heart, with all your soul, with all your strength, and with all your mind,' and 'your neighbor as yourself.'"

And ... [Jesus] said to him, "You have answered rightly; do this and you will live."

But he, wanting to justify himself, said to Jesus, "And who is my neighbor?"

Then Jesus answered and said: "A certain man went down from Jerusalem to Jericho, and fell among thieves, who stripped him of his clothing, wounded him, and departed, leaving him half dead.

"Now by chance a certain priest came down that road. And when he saw him, he passed by on the other side.

> **BACKGROUND**
> This is one of the many parables that Jesus used to teach a religious moral.

"Likewise a <u>Levite</u>, when he arrived at the place, came and looked, and passed by on the other side.

"But a certain <u>Samaritan</u>, as he journeyed, came where he was. And when he saw him, he had compassion on him, and went to him and bandaged his wounds, pouring on oil and wine; and he set him on his own animal, brought him to an inn, and took care of him.

"On the next day, when he departed, he took out two <u>denarii</u>, gave them to the innkeeper, and said to him, 'Take care of him; and whatever more you spend, when I come again, I will repay you.'

"So which of these three do you think was neighbor to him who fell among the thieves?"

And . . . [the lawyer] said, "He who showed mercy on him." Then Jesus said to him, "Go and do likewise."

—From *Holy Bible: The New King James Version* ©1982 by Thomas Nelson, Inc. American Bible Society New York.

✓ **Checkpoint** **What does this story teach about the meaning of the word *neighbor*?**

▶ **BACKGROUND**
The Jews and the Samaritans did not get along. Though they were not at war, these groups rarely had anything to do with each other.

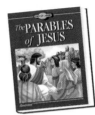

If you liked this parable, you might like to read others. Some parables to start with include "The Sower," "The Prodigal Son," "The Lost Sheep," and "The Unforgiving Servant." They can all be found in the Gospels of the New Testament, or in *The Parables of Jesus* by Ellyn Sanna. *Barbour Pub, Inc., 2000*

Jesus used a story about a Samaritan helping a Jew to explain how Jesus' followers should treat other people.

**E-LA 6.3.8 Analyze Credibility**

Think about the parable that Jesus told. Are the characters believable? Was the plot realistic? Explain your answer.

*Analyze* **LITERATURE**

A "good Samaritan" has come to mean a person who offers help to strangers who are having difficulties.

Have you ever read about or known someone who could be considered a "good Samaritan"? Write a paragraph about that person.

**Standards Preview**

**H-SS 6.7.7** Describe the circumstances that led to the spread of Christianity in Europe and other Roman territories.

**E-LA Reading 6.1.4** Monitor expository text for unknown words or words with novel meanings by using word, sentence, and paragraph clues to determine meaning.

## Reading Preview

 **Reading Skill**

**Use Surrounding Clues to Determine Meaning** Clues to determine meaning may be found in other sentences of a paragraph. These sometimes contain synonyms—words with similar meanings—that help you define unfamiliar words. Look also for examples that help to define unfamiliar words.

### Vocabulary *Builder*

**High-Use Words**
reject (rih JEHKT), p. 553
factor (FAK tuhr), p. 555

**Key Terms and People**
persecute (PUR sih kyoot), p. 552
Peter (PEET ur), p. 552
Paul (pawl), p. 552
Gentile (JEHN tīl), p. 553
conversion (kuhn VUR zhuhn), p. 554
martyr (MAHR tur), p. 556

**Background Knowledge** From its beginnings in Jerusalem, Christianity spread to other lands. In this section, you will read about the growth of the Christian religion. You will learn about the difficulties and successes of the early church.

**Main Idea**
With the help of leaders such as Peter and Paul, the early church spread beyond Jerusalem until it included more non-Jews than Jews.

## The Early Christians

The first Christians faced great challenges. Like Jesus, they were often **persecuted, or treated unfairly for their beliefs.** Leaders such as the apostles **Peter** and **Paul** led them through this difficult time.

**Peter** After the death of Jesus, the apostle Peter became the leader of the disciples. According to the Bible, Peter's Jewish name was Simon. But Jesus had recognized Simon's rock-like loyalty. So he called him "Rock," which is *petra* in Greek.

Later other apostles and disciples became important leaders in the church as well. The actions of some of the apostles are recorded in the Book of the Acts of the Apostles. Acts, as it is sometimes called, is the fifth book in the New Testament.

**Jews or Gentiles**   Despite their disagreements with Jewish leaders, the first Christians still considered themselves Jews. They respected most Jewish customs. They read the Hebrew Bible and went to the temple to pray. According to Acts, thousands of Jews in Jerusalem became Christians before the first Gentile, or non-Jew, was reported as joining. Even some of the Jewish priests and leaders became Christians. But most Jewish leaders in Jerusalem told their followers to <u>reject</u> Christian beliefs.

At first, one of the greatest Jewish teachers, Gamaliel (guh MAY lee uhl), advised other leaders not to bring violence against the Christians. But as Christianity continued to grow throughout all levels of society, other leaders, unlike Gamaliel, decided that it was time to take action. They began arresting Christians and treating them cruelly. As the apostles and other Christian leaders fled from Jerusalem, they began sharing their beliefs with people in other places.

Now people from all sorts of backgrounds were hearing the apostles' message. Although Christianity continued to grow in Jerusalem, other regions were beginning to see more and more Gentiles becoming Christians.

**Vocabulary** *Builder*
<u>reject</u> (rih JEHKT) *v.* to refuse to accept

**Christians at Temple**
The earliest Christians were Jews who continued to participate in Jewish worship. This painting shows Peter and another apostle speaking outside the temple at Jerusalem. **Critical Thinking: Draw Conclusions** *Why might some religious leaders have been uneasy about Peter's message?*

**The Conversion of Saul**   One of the people who was persecuting Christians was Saul of Tarsus (TAHR suhs). Saul was a student of the Jewish teacher Gamaliel. However, unlike Gamaliel, Saul believed that Christians should be arrested and punished for their faith.

According to Acts, Saul even traveled outside Jerusalem to find and arrest Christians. On one of these trips, he had an experience that led to his conversion to Christianity. A conversion is a heartfelt change in one's opinions or beliefs, especially in religion. After his conversion, Saul told many people that he had seen the risen Jesus and spoken to him. He also said that Jesus had told him to take the message of Jesus to the Gentiles. Saul spent the rest of his life doing just that.

**The Travels of Paul**   Several years after his conversion, Saul believed that God was telling him to take a trip to bring the teachings of Jesus to many other people. After he began a journey to Cyprus (SI pruhs), Saul became better known by his Greek name, Paul. Paul and his friends started churches in Cyprus and Asia Minor (modern-day Turkey) and then returned.

Eventually, Paul traveled through Greece and many other countries. Wherever Paul went, he started churches and made disciples. He was arrested for his faith several times. Once he was taken in chains all the way from Jerusalem to Rome.

Paul used his time in prison to write epistles, usually to churches he had started. Some of the churches were having problems because people were spreading teachings that disagreed with those of Paul and the other apostles. So Paul's epistles explained some Christian beliefs in great detail. Paul reminded his disciples that Jesus is God and that they were saved through faith in Jesus and his sacrifice. He also described the resurrection in more detail than any other New Testament writer.

At the same time, Paul helped spread the belief that Gentiles did not need to follow all of the Jewish customs to become Christians, although they did need to live moral lives and stay away from worshipping other gods. Christians respected and used the Hebrew scriptures. But as more Gentiles came into the church, the church's connection to Judaism became weaker.

 **Checkpoint**   Why did the earliest Christians share their beliefs with Jews before they shared them with Gentiles?

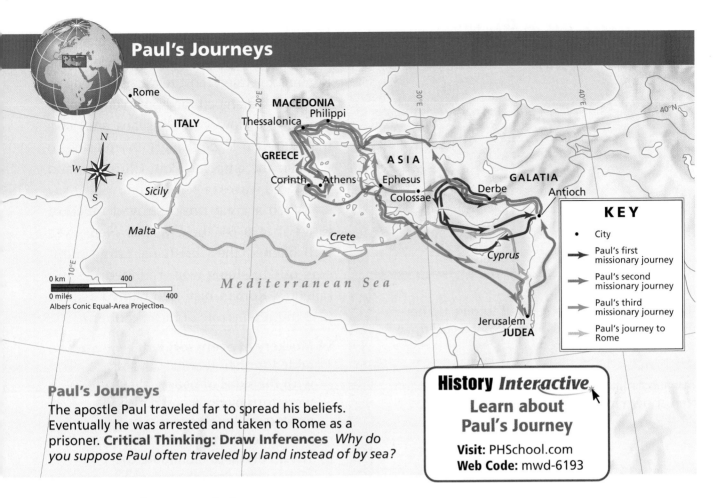

## Paul's Journeys

**KEY**

- • City
- ──▶ Paul's first missionary journey
- ──▶ Paul's second missionary journey
- ──▶ Paul's third missionary journey
- ──▶ Paul's journey to Rome

**Paul's Journeys**
The apostle Paul traveled far to spread his beliefs. Eventually he was arrested and taken to Rome as a prisoner. **Critical Thinking: Draw Inferences** *Why do you suppose Paul often traveled by land instead of by sea?*

**History Interactive**
**Learn about Paul's Journey**
**Visit:** PHSchool.com
**Web Code:** mwd-6193

# A Growing Faith

Led by apostles such as Peter and Paul, the followers of Jesus carried Christian beliefs to many parts of the ancient world, including Europe, Mesopotamia, Persia, and North Africa.

**Reasons for Growth**   Several <u>factors</u> assisted the spread of Christianity. These included Roman roads, which made it easy for people and ideas to move across the empire. The Pax Romana helped as well by making it safer for Christians to travel.

Another factor was a common language. Most civilized people spoke Greek in addition to their own language. Apostles like Paul could speak in Greek throughout the Roman Empire and still be understood. The books of the New Testament were also written in Greek.

The ideas of Christianity also appealed to many people. People who no longer believed in polytheism were attracted to the monotheistic aspect of Christianity. Other people were glad to hear that everyone was equal in God's sight, whether they were slave or free, male or female, Jew or Gentile.

**Main Idea**
In spite of resistance from Roman officials, Christianity spread across the Roman Empire.

**Vocabulary *Builder***
**factor** (FAK tuhr) *n.* something that causes or helps cause

## How is Cecilia remembered?

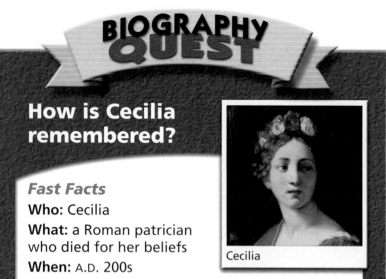

Cecilia

**Fast Facts**

**Who:** Cecilia

**What:** a Roman patrician who died for her beliefs

**When:** A.D. 200s

**Where:** Rome

**Why Important:** Cecilia refused to give up her faith, even after her husband was executed.

**Fast Find**

**How:** Go online to find out what art form is often shown in paintings of Cecilia.

**Biography Online**

**For:** More about Cecilia
**Visit:** PHSchool.com
**Web Code:** mwd-6194

**Primary Sources**

See the Letters of Pliny and Trajan in the Reference Section at the back of this book.

**Roman Persecution** The growth of Christianity worried Roman officials. The Romans tolerated most religions, as long as everyone worshiped the Roman emperor as a god, too. However, Christians and Jews made Roman leaders angry by refusing to worship the emperor. Both Christians and Jews faced waves of persecution.

When a great fire destroyed much of Rome in A.D. 64, the Emperor Nero (NEE roh) blamed the Christians. Large numbers of Christians were rounded up and killed. A Roman historian named Tacitus (TAS uht uhs) wrote of the executions:

**❝Mockery of every sort was added to their deaths. Covered with the skins of beasts, they were torn by dogs and perished, or were nailed to crosses, or were doomed to the flames. These served to illuminate the night when daylight failed.❞**

—Tacitus, *Annals*

In A.D. 72, the Roman emperor Titus destroyed Jerusalem to put down a Jewish rebellion. Jews and Christians were scattered further throughout the Roman world.

Although the emperor Trajan later tried to be a little more fair to Christians, waves of persecution scared some people away from Christianity. However it caused others to bond in their faith. It also produced Christian **martyrs, or people who are remembered because they were put to death for their beliefs.** The courage of the martyrs strengthened the faith of many other Christians.

**The End of Persecution** After Nero, persecutions continued, off and on, until the reign of the Emperor Constantine (KAHN stuhn teen).

According to tradition, Constantine had a powerful dream in 312, just before a key battle. His dream told him to fight under the sign of the cross. After winning the battle, Constantine ended the persecutions of Christians in 313. By 395, Christianity was the established religion of the Roman Empire.

Eventually, Rome became the center of the Latin-speaking church in Western Europe. However, religious leaders in Athens, Greece continued to lead Greek-speaking Christians in Eastern Europe and Asia. The two branches of Christianity gradually grew farther apart. Physical distances and disagreements about religious practices also contributed to the division. In A.D. 1054, the Eastern and Western churches separated permanently.

Later divisions came about because individual Christians disagreed with church leadership about specific practices and beliefs. Today there are many branches of Christianity. However, most people who consider themselves Christian today share the basic beliefs of the earliest Christians.

Today, there are about two billion people who follow some form of Christian teaching. Together, they make up about one third of the world's population.

 **Checkpoint** **What factors helped Christianity spread through the Roman Empire?**

**Looking Back and Ahead**  In this section, you read about the spread of Christianity across the Roman Empire. In the next chapter, you will read about Roman achievements.

**E-LA 6.1.4 Use Surrounding Clues to Determine Meaning**
What does *division* mean? What clues did you use?

---

## Section 3 Check Your Progress

**Progress Monitoring** **Online**
**For:** Self-test with instant help
**Visit:** PHSchool.com
**Web Code:** mwa-6193

 **Standards Review**  H-SS: 6.7.7; E-LA: Reading 6.1.4

### Comprehension and Critical Thinking

**1. (a) Identify** Who was Paul?
**(b) Evaluate Information** Why do you think Paul's epistles became part of the Bible?

**2. (a) Explain** How did the Romans treat the early Christians?
**(b) Draw Inferences** Why do you think Rome eventually became the center of Christianity in Western Europe?

### Reading Skill

**3. Use Surrounding Clues to Determine Meaning** Read the following sentence: The courage of the martyrs strengthened the faith of many other Christians. What clues would help you determine the meaning of the word *courage* in this sentence?

### Vocabulary *Builder*

**4.** Write two definitions for each word: reject, factor. First, write a formal definition for your teacher. Second, write a definition in everyday English for a classmate.

### Writing

**5.** Plan a paragraph that will address one reason Christianity spread so quickly throughout the Roman Empire. Think of an opening sentence or two that would make the topic seem important to the reader. Consider relating the topic to something that is important today, such as how fast ideas spread over the Internet.

# Analyze an Artifact

Artifacts tell a great deal about the people who made them and about the time in which they were made. You can not always get to a museum to see artifacts. However, you can find photos and descriptions of them in books, in magazines, and on the Internet.

**Chapter Standards**

**History-Social Science**

**Reading 6.2.1** Identify the structural features of popular media (e.g., newspapers, magazines, online information) and use the features to obtain information.

Early Christian Carving, not dated

Christian Tomb Carving, from between A.D. 100–300

**Learn the Skill** *Follow these steps to learn how to analyze artifacts.*

1. **Identify the artifact.** Artifacts are usually displayed with labels and descriptions.

2. **Identify what the artifact shows and its date.** Look at the photo on the left. Although there is no date on it, archaeologists know that it is from the early Christian era. They know that because of the symbol *chi* (X) *-rho* (P).

3. **Analyze the details in the artifact.** What details stand out? Are there other symbols that contain meanings? Other than the symbols, is there anything to tell you what this artifact was used for?

4. **Decide what else the artifact tells you.** Based on your study of the artifact, can you draw any conclusions about early Christian beliefs or practices?

**Practice the Skill** *Use the photo of the artifact on the right to answer the following questions.*

1. **Identify the artifact.** What kind of artifact is shown in the photo?

2. **Identify what the artifact shows and its date.** (a) What symbols are shown on the artifact? (b) When was the artifact made?

3. **Analyze the details in the artifact.** What do the symbols and other markings tell you about the artifact and what it was used for?

4. **Decide what else the artifact tells you.** From your study of the artifact, can you draw any conclusions about early Christian beliefs or practices?

**Apply the Skill**

*See page 561 of the Chapter Assessment.*

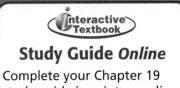

**Study Guide** *Online*
Complete your Chapter 19 study guide in print or online.

## Chapter Summary  H-SS: 6.7.5, 6.7.6, 6.7.7

### Section 1 The Origins of Christianity

• During the Roman occupation of Jerusalem a Jewish teacher named Jesus became popular.

• Jesus was crucified but his followers believed that he was resurrected.

### Section 2 The Beliefs of Christianity

• Christians follow the teachings of the early church, as they were recorded in the New Testament.

• Christians believe that Jesus is God and that he died so people could be forgiven for their sins.

### Section 3 The Spread of Christianity

• Apostles such as Peter and Paul helped spread the new faith across the Roman empire.

• In spite of persecution, the faith continued to grow.

• Today there are many branches of Christianity.

**The Last Supper**

## Standards Practice  H-SS: 6.7.5, 6.7.6, 6.7.7

## Vocabulary *Builder*

### High-Use Words

Decide whether each underlined word is used correctly. If it is, explain why. If not, rewrite the rest of the sentence to make it logical.

1. Roman troops would seldom **occupy** a conquered city.

2. Different political and religious views led to **conflict** among Jews during and after the reign of King Herod.

3. Most Christians **reject** the idea of the Trinity.

4. The Christians in Western Europe and the Christians in Eastern Europe and Asia eventually became two **distinct** branches of Christianity.

### Key Terms

Answer the following questions in complete sentences that show your understanding of the key terms.

1. Why were some disciples of Jesus also called apostles?

2. How did the Roman troops practice crucifixion?

3. How does a parable get its point across?

4. Why did some early Christians became martyrs?

5. Why are the New Testament writings important to Christians?

## Apply Reading Skills

**Using Clues to Determine Meanings** In the following passage from page 556, what does the word *worship* mean?

> The Romans tolerated most religions, as long as everyone also <u>worshiped</u> the Roman emperor as a god, too. However, Christians and Jews made Roman leaders angry by refusing to <u>worship</u> the emperor.

What clues in the passage help you determine the meaning?

## Comprehension and Critical Thinking

**1. (a) Recall** When and where did Jesus live?
**(b) Analyze Information** Why did some people think that Jesus was the Messiah?
**(c) Identify Cause and Effect** Why was he executed? What effects did that have?

**2. (a) Describe** What is the New Testament?
**(b) Summarize** Describe the writing of the New Testament.
**(c) Link Past and Present** How important is the New Testament to Christianity today?

**3. (a) Explain** What challenges did early Christians face?
**(b) Analyze Information** How did they respond to those challenges?
**(c) Draw Conclusions** Why did persecution cause some Christians to grow even stronger in their faith?

## Researching

**The Effects of Christianity** As Christianity spread, the ideas and even the language of Christians found their way through the Roman Empire. For example, the New Testament brought many Greek terms into the Latin language. Christian symbols and subjects began to appear in Roman art and literature. Report on one way that Christianity affected the culture of Rome by choosing a task below to work on. Share your work with the class.

**Art Historians:** Look for Roman artwork made between A.D. 100 and A.D. 600 that includes Christian symbols or subjects. Write a report explaining why you believe they were used so often.

**Linguists:** Look up words in the English language that are related to the Greek words *ekklesia, baptizeia,* and *christos* and the related Latin words *ecclesia, baptizare,* and *christus.* Write sentence definitions for at least four of the words you find.

**Researching Online**

**For:** Help in starting this activity
**Visit:** PHSchool.com
**Web Code:** mwd-6195

## Writing

**1. Write a paragraph on the following topic.** How did conditions in the Roman Empire both contribute to and work against the rise of Christianity?
**Your paragraph should:**
- describe the conditions of the Roman Empire during the rise of Christianity.
- give specific examples of the ways in which these conditions helped and prevented the spread of Christianity

**2. Write a short narrative.** Imagine you were a citizen in ancient Rome, and you heard that people were coming to arrest your neighbors for being Christians. Write a short narrative describing how you would respond.

**Progress Monitoring** ⬤nline
**For:** Self-test with instant help
**Visit:** PHSchool.com
**Web Code:** mwa-6194

## Apply Analysis Skills

**Use the photograph and caption at the right to answer these skills.**

**Roman Flask, from A.D. 300–400**

1. Identify the artifact. What kind of artifact is shown in the photo?

2. Identify what the artifact shows and its date.

3. Analyze the details in the artifact.

4. Decide what else the artifact tells you. Based on your study of the artifact, can you draw any conclusions about early Christian beliefs or practices?

## Test Yourself

1. **Which statement is NOT true?**
   A Some Jews believed Jesus was Messiah.
   B Jews migrated throughout the Roman Empire.
   C The Jewish people were content under Roman rule.
   D The Romans destroyed Jerusalem in A.D. 72.

**Refer to the quote below to answer Question 2.**

> *"I have been beaten . . . by the Romans, . . . stoned, . . . shipwrecked, . . . in danger from rivers, . . . robbers, . . . my own people, . . . the heathen [unbelievers], . . . in the city, . . . in the desert, . . . at sea, . . . from false brothers, through toil and hardship, . . . often without food, and exposed to cold."*

2. **To what does the above quote refer?**
   A Jesus' Sermon on the Mount
   B Paul's life as a Christian missionary
   C Emperor Nero's persecution of Christians
   D Peter's life before he converted to Christianity

3. **Both Christians and Jews believe in**
   A one God and the Hebrew Bible.
   B the teachings of the apostles.
   C the Trinity.
   D the New Testament.

4. **Paul wrote epistles for every reason below except**
   A to explain Christian teachings.
   B to solve problems in the early church.
   C to explain the resurrection.
   D to convince non-Christians to join the church.

**Refer to the image below to answer Question 5.**

5. **This ancient New Testament fragment is important because**
   A it shows that the New Testament was originally written in Hebrew.
   B we have no other copies of the Gospel of John.
   C it shows that Christian writings spread rapidly to other countries.
   D it was found in North America.

### Chapter 20

# Roman Achievements

(A.D. 80–A.D. 476)

## Prepare to Read

 **Chapter Standards**

**History-Social Science**
**6.7** Students analyze the geographic, political, economic, religious, and social structures during the development of Rome.

**Section 1,** pp. 566–571

**Roman Arts and Engineering**

**Section 2,** pp. 572–577

**Literature, Language, and Law**

**Section 3,** pp. 578–584

**The Decline of the Roman Empire**

### ✔ What You Will Learn

The Romans produced a style of art and architecture modeled on Greek works. Roman inventions included new types of roads, water systems, and advances in science and technology.

Roman writers used both Greek and Latin to create a lasting legacy of poems, songs, and other literature. The Roman type of government had a great influence on modern political and legal systems.

Unstable government, high taxes, rising prices, splitting the empire in two, and attacks by invaders all contributed to the fall of the Roman Empire.

Roman census-taker

| Chapter Events | A.D. **80**<br>The Colosseum is<br>built in Rome. | A.D. **180**<br>The Pax Romana<br>ended. | |
|---|---|---|---|
| Other Events | B.C./A.D.<br>A.D. **70** Romans destroy the<br>Second Temple in Jerusalem. | A.D.<br>**125**<br>A.D. **First century** Buddhism<br>spreads to China from India. | A.D.<br>**250** |

A Roman aqueduct, or waterway, in present-day Spain.

**A.D. 284**
Diocletian divides the Roman Empire.

**A.D. 476**
The Roman Empire falls.

**A.D. 250**

**A.D. 375**

**A.D. 500**

**About A.D. 250** Mayan culture begins to flourish in Mesoamerica.

**A.D. 395** Christianity is the established religion of the Roman Empire.

# How to Read History

## History Reading Skill

### *Previewing* Make Reasonable Assertions

Sometimes writers state their ideas directly. Other times you have to read between the lines or piece together a puzzle to figure out what a text means. Clues in the text often suggest an idea. Look at the strategies below to learn how to find and use these clues.

**Chapter Standards**

**English-Language Arts**

Reading 6.2.7 Make reasonable assertions about a text through accurate, supporting citations.

Look at the sample text below. Read it carefully. Then study the questions and answers below to learn about making reasonable assertions.

Jesus grew up in Nazareth. As a young man he worked as a carpenter. After his baptism, Jesus spent weeks wandering in the desert and praying to God. When he returned from the desert, he began to live the life of a prophet.

1. **Did Jesus live the same life after his baptism and desert experience as he did before?**

   *No, he did not. He lived as a prophet afterward, but not before.*

2. **In your life, what usually needs to happen for you to change the way you live every day?**

   *Usually, you must have an experience that strongly affects you.*

3. **What assertion can you make from reading the text above?**

   *Jesus was strongly affected by his baptism and by his experiences in the desert.*

4. **What evidence can you use to support your assertion?**

   • *You read that Jesus changed his life after the baptism and desert experience.*
   • *You can use your personal knowledge of an important event that changed your life or the life of someone you know.*

---

**Text Clues + Personal Knowledge = Reasonable Assertion**

---

# Vocabulary *Builder*

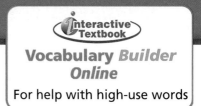

**interactive Textbook**
**Vocabulary** *Builder*
**Online**
For help with high-use words

## *Previewing* High-Use Academic Words

| High-Use Word | Definition | Sample Sentence About History |
|---|---|---|
| **communication** (kuh MYOO nuh kay shuhn) (Section 1, p. 569) | *n.* the act of giving or exchanging information, signals, or messages | The Persian postal system greatly improved <u>communication</u> in the empire. |
| **impress** (ihm PRES) (Section 1, p. 570) | *v.* to have a marked effect on the mind or emotions | Scholars and scribes <u>impressed</u> their rulers with their vast knowledge. |
| **founder** (FOWN duhr) (Section 2, p. 575) | *n.* person who founds, or establishes something | The <u>founder</u> of the ancient city ordered a statue of himself to be built in the center of the city. |
| **code** (kohd) (Section 2, p. 576) | *n.* a set of written rules or laws | Hammurabi's <u>Code</u> was an important set of laws. |
| **income** (IHN kuhm) (Section 3, p. 579) | *n.* the money that you earn from working | People had to pay taxes according to their <u>income</u>. |
| **invade** (ihn VAYD) (Section 3, p. 582) | *v.* to enter forcibly or with hostility; come into as an enemy | Warring tribes <u>invaded</u> the northern and eastern borders of the country. |

## *Previewing* Key Terms and People

**Cicero**

mosaic, p. 566
concrete, p. 567
aqueduct, p. 569
Claudius Ptolemy, p. 570
Hypatia, p. 570

dissect, p. 571
Augustus, p. 573
patriotism, p. 573
Virgil, p. 573
Horace, p. 574

Livy, p. 574
Cicero, p. 574
oratory, p. 574
civil law, p. 576
Marcus Aurelius, p. 578

corrupt, p. 579
money supply, p. 579
inflation, p. 580
Diocletian, p. 580
Constantine, p. 580

# Roman Arts and Engineering

**H-SS 6.7.8** Discuss the legacies of Roman art and architecture, technology and science, literature, language, and law.

**E-LA Reading 6.2.7** Make reasonable assertions about a text through accurate, supporting citations.

## Reading Preview

 **Reading Skill**

**Make Assertions** As you read, ask yourself what assertions you could make about the text. Ask: What could I add to explain the facts provided? For example, Chapter 19 tells you that many people came to hear Jesus speak, and that the Roman government disliked him. You could add a sentence that says: Jesus affected people powerfully, both positively and negatively.

**Vocabulary** *Builder*

**High-Use Words**
communication (kuh MYOO nuh kay shuhn), p. 569
impress (ihm PRES), p. 570

**Key Terms and People**
mosaic (moh ZAY ihk), p. 566
concrete (KAWN kreet), p. 567
aqueduct (AK wuh dukt), p. 569
Claudius Ptolemy (KLAW dee uhs TAHL uh mee), p. 570
Hypatia (hi PAY shee uh), p. 570
dissect (di SEKT), p. 571

**Background Knowledge** Legacies from Roman civilization are a part of modern life. Many public buildings today, for example, look much like those built by Augustus. Builders today still use materials invented by the Romans. In this section, you will read about Roman achievements in art, architecture, technology, and science.

**Main Idea**
The Romans produced a unique and lasting style of art and architecture modeled on Greek works.

## Art and Architecture

Greek art and architecture had a great influence on the Romans. But the Romans did not simply copy the Greeks. They constructed buildings and created artwork that fitted Roman needs and tastes.

**Painting and Sculpture** Art filled many homes and public buildings in Roman towns. Floors were decorated with colorful mosaics. A mosaic is a design formed with small tiles of glass, stone, or pottery. Many homes also had decorative wall murals.

Sculpture was popular as well. Statues of gods and important officials stood in markets, temples, and other public places. In contrast to Greek artists who tried to show perfect beauty, the Romans were more realistic. They showed their subjects as real people.

Skillful artisans used various materials to make beautiful everyday objects. They crafted vases and jars of blue glass and mirrors of polished silver. Animal bone was used in combs and pins. Romans wore jewelry made of silver, gold, and gems.

**Buildings and Bridges** Roman architects also based their designs on Greek models. These architects went on to devise new building materials and methods. One innovation was the invention of concrete. **Concrete is a building material made by mixing small stones and sand with limestone, clay, and water.** The thick, soupy mixture is then poured into forms, where it hardens.

Concrete was lighter and easier to work with than stone. Workers needed less skill to pour concrete than to carve stone. Using this new material, workers were able to design large open structures covered with domes. One of the most famous examples is the Pantheon, which you can see on this page.

**The Pantheon**
The Pantheon—built as a temple in Rome from A.D. 118 to A.D. 126—later became a Catholic church. The Pantheon is one large circular room above which is a dome with a circular "eye," or window. **Critical Thinking: Link Past and Present** *What modern buildings have large domes?*

Concrete was also used to build Rome's Colosseum. This huge outdoor arena opened in A.D. 80. About 50,000 people could watch gladiator battles, wild beast hunts, and criminals being put to death from its stands. The arena could also be filled with water for make-believe sea battles.

A rounded arch is the most typical feature of Roman structures. The arch appears in many forms. Huge "triumphal arches" were built over roadways for parades to honor generals and emperors. The walls of the Colosseum are a series of arches. All across the empire, Roman soldiers and engineers built sturdy bridges supported by rounded arches.

✔ **Checkpoint** **What new methods did Roman builders use?**

## Technology and Science

The Romans were a practical people. They excelled at using technology to improve daily life. Some of the roads, bridges, and water systems they built are still in use today.

**Roman Roads** "All roads lead to Rome" is an old saying. In ancient Italy, it was true. Major roads extended to and from the city of Rome like the spokes of a wheel. More than 50,000 miles of straight, paved roads crisscrossed the empire. The roads linked cities and military forts. Roman roads were built to last a long time. In fact, some modern highways follow these ancient routes.

**E-LA 6.2.7 Make Assertions**
What sentence about the Roman military could you add to this paragraph to explain why the Romans built so many triumphal arches?

**Main Idea**
Roman inventions included new types of roads, water systems, and advances in science and technology.

**All Roads Lead to Rome, c. 150 B.C.**

Luni
Lucca
Pistoia
via Cassia
via Clodia
via Aurelia
Chiusi
via Flaminia
via Salaria
Ancona

*Adriatic Sea*

**KEY**
• City
— Road ("via")

Chieti
via Claudia
via Tiburtina
Rome
Ostia
via Appia
via Latina
*Tyrrhenian Sea (Mediterranean Sea)*
Terracina
Capua
Benevento
Naples
via Appia
Venosa

0 km 100
0 miles 100
Mercator Projection

Roman roads were built mainly to move the army quickly from place to place. Military engineers traveled with the army, as did architects, stonemasons, and surveyors. When not fighting, Roman soldiers turned to road building.

All Roman roads followed the same general pattern. Most were completely straight. A layer of large flat stones was laid in the bottom of the roadbed. Smaller stones and gravel were laid on top of that foundation. The surface of the road was covered with paving stones, crushed rock, or concrete. Roads had a slight hump in the middle so that water would drain during storms.

Smooth, all-weather roads were a considerable improvement over dirt paths. These roads sped up <u>communication</u> throughout the empire. Messengers on horseback could travel up to 75 miles a day on Roman roads, making government and trade more efficient. Roads also made it possible for people to travel and see the world.

**Water Systems** Roman engineers designed elaborate water systems to supply towns with clean water. They built hundreds of miles of canals and aqueducts to move water from mountain springs to the plains below. An **aqueduct** is a structure for carrying water across land. Roman aqueducts looked like long bridges. Water ran on one level in a covered channel. A second level served as a road. Some Roman aqueducts are still used today.

**Vocabulary** *Builder*
<u>communication</u> (kuh MYOO nuh kay shuhn) *n.* the act of giving or exchanging information, signals, or messages

**Roman Roads**
Roman roads were constructed as straight as possible, mainly for the army. **Critical Thinking: Identify Benefits** *Besides helping the army, how did roads help the Roman economy?*

**History** *Interactive*
**Travel along a Roman road**

**Visit:** PHSchool.com
**Web Code:** mwp-6201

An ancient Roman road

Laborers build a paved Roman road.

Once in the city, water flowed into a system of lead pipes. Some pipes ran to public fountains in the streets. Most people got their water from these sources. Wealthier people had water piped directly into their homes. Other pipes supplied the public baths found in every city. In these bathhouses, heating systems under the floors supplied warm or hot water to different soaking pools.

Roman engineers also built sewer systems to carry waste away from their cities. Visitors to Roman towns were <u>impressed</u> by how clean these towns and cities were. In fact, Roman water and sewer systems would not be equaled until modern times.

**Vocabulary** *Builder*

**impress** (ihm PRES) *v.* to have a marked effect on the mind or emotions

**Science** Under Roman rule, science and mathematics continued to develop. One important scientist of this time influenced how people viewed the universe for the next 1,200 years.

He was a Greek astronomer and mathematician named **Claudius Ptolemy** (KLAW dee uhs TAHL uh mee).

Ptolemy wrote a famous book on astronomy called the *Almagest*. In that book, he used mathematics to show that Earth is the center of the universe. The sun, moon, and other planets, he said, revolve around Earth. Although Ptolemy's theory of Earth being the center of the universe was not correct, it was thought to be true for many centuries.

In Chapter 16, you read about the center of Greco-Roman science in Alexandria, Egypt. One of the most popular scholars there during this time was **Hypatia** (hi PAY shee uh). She was a teacher of philosophy, astronomy, mathematics, and religion. Some people in Alexandria, however, including their new bishop, were suspicious of science. This bishop murdered Hypatia. Today Hypatia is remembered as the first woman to be noted for excellence in mathematics. You can read more about Hypatia in the Biography Quest feature on this page.

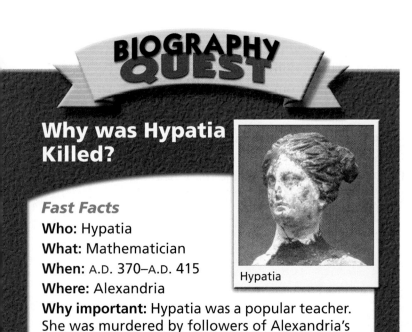

# BIOGRAPHY QUEST

## Why was Hypatia Killed?

Hypatia

### Fast Facts

**Who:** Hypatia
**What:** Mathematician
**When:** A.D. 370–A.D. 415
**Where:** Alexandria
**Why important:** Hypatia was a popular teacher. She was murdered by followers of Alexandria's new bishop.

### Fast Find

**How:** Go online to find out more about Hypatia's contributions to mathematics, astronomy, philosophy, and religion.

**Biography** Online

**For:** More about Hypatia
**Visit:** PHSchool.com
**Web Code:** mwe-6201

**Medicine** During the rule of the Caesars, physicians continued to make advances in medicine. The best-known physician in the Roman Empire was a Greek doctor named Claudius Galen. Early in his career, Galen's patients were gladiators. From that experience he learned a great deal about taking care of wounds. Later he became the physician of three emperors.

Galen is remembered today for his use of experiments to expand medical knowledge. He carefully dissected, or cut open, animals such as monkeys, pigs, sheep, and goats to study how bodies function. He was the first to discover that arteries and veins carry blood, not air, as had been believed for hundreds of years. Doctors used Galen's writings on anatomy for more than a thousand years.

 **Checkpoint** How did the Romans improve water systems and roads?

**Looking Back and Ahead** In this section, you have read about Roman achievements in art, architecture, and technology. You have also read about science and medicine in the Roman Empire. In the next section, you will read about the legacy of Roman literature, language, and law.

**Roman Medical Instruments**
The Romans expanded medical knowledge by using instruments such as these to cut open and study animals. **Critical Thinking: Analyze Cause and Effect** *How would studying animals help advance medical knowledge for humans?*

---

## Section 1 Check Your Progress

**Progress Monitoring** Online
**For:** Self-test with instant help
**Visit:** PHSchool.com
**Web Code:** mwa-6201

 **Standards Review** H-SS: 6.7.8; E-LA: Reading 6.2.7

**Comprehension and Critical Thinking**
1. **(a) Recall** What advantages did concrete have over stone as a building material?
   **(b) Identify Benefits** What did the Romans use concrete for?
2. **(a) Explain** What was the main purpose of Roman roads?
   **(b) Compare** Why was it more practical for Romans than for Greeks to build roads?

**Reading Skill**
3. **Make Assertions** Read the first paragraph under Buildings and Bridges. What words could you use to describe the Romans based on their accomplishments?

**Vocabulary** *Builder*
4. Write two definitions for each word: mosaic, concrete, aqueduct, dissect. First write a formal definition for your teacher. Second, write a definition in everyday English for a classmate.

**Writing**
5. Write a paragraph describing the pictures of Roman roads on pages 568 and 569. Begin your paragraph with a topic sentence. Introduce each point with an appropriate transition word.

**Standards Preview**

**H-SS 6.7.8** Discuss the legacies of Roman art and architecture, technology and science, literature, language, and law.

**E-LA Reading 6.2.7** Make reasonable assertions about a text through accurate, supporting citations.

## Reading Preview

 **Reading Skill**

**Use Supporting Citations** Information from the text can help you make reasonable assertions. This information is called supporting citations. A citation is a quote or piece of evidence from the text. Look at descriptive words in the text. Look at the actions people take and the choices that they make. All of this helps you make assertions about people and events.

**Vocabulary** *Builder*

**High-Use Words**
founder (FOWN duhr), p. 575
code (kohd), p. 576

**Key Terms and People**
Augustus (ah GUHS tuhs), p. 573
patriotism (PAY tree uh tiz uhm), p. 573
Virgil (VUHR juhl), p. 573
Horace (HOHR uhs), p. 574
Livy (LIHV ee), p. 574
Cicero (SIS uh roh), p. 574
oratory (OR uh tohr ee), p. 574
civil (SIHV uhl) law, p. 576

**Background Knowledge** As you have read in the previous section, Roman artists, architects, and writers adapted Greek models to Roman tastes. In law and government, however, the Romans took several steps forward. In this section, you will read about Roman literature and the lasting influence of the Latin language. You will also learn about the legacy of Roman law and government and how Roman law has influenced the law in this country.

**Main Idea**
Roman writers used both Greek and Latin to create a lasting legacy of literature.

## Literature and Language

Greek was once the language of the Mediterranean world. Later, Latin became the language of the Western Roman Empire. Greek remained the language of the Eastern Roman Empire. Educated Romans studied both languages. Scholars and philosophers often wrote in Greek, as did many early Christian writers.

## A Golden Age of Latin Literature

The reign of Augustus began a golden age of literature in Latin. After years of civil war, the empire was at peace. Rome became a center for culture. Augustus himself encouraged writers and artists.

Roman writers often followed Greek models. They wrote poetry, tragedies, comedies, and histories. Roman literature had different themes, or central ideas. One common theme was patriotism, or a feeling of love and support for one's country. Patriotic writers described the glories of Roman history.

## The Poet Virgil

One of the greatest writers of this time was the poet Virgil. As you have read in Chapter 17, Virgil wrote an epic poem about the founding of Rome called the *Aeneid*. Virgil modeled the *Aeneid* on Homer's epics. It tells the story of the Trojan hero Aeneas (ih NEE uhs), the legendary founder of Rome. In the poem, Aeneas embarks on a journey to the underworld to see his dead father. His father shows him a vision of Rome and describes the heroes who will make it great:

> **Behold the Romans . . .**
> **The race to come. One promise have you heard**
> **Over and over: here is its fulfillment,**
> **The son of a god, Augustus Caesar, founder**
> **Of a new age of gold . . . he will extend his empire**
> **Beyond the Indies, beyond the normal measure**
> **Of years and constellations, where high Atlas**
> **Turns on his shoulders the star-studded world.**
>
> —Virgil, *Aeneid*

In Greek mythology, Atlas was the god of heavy burdens. As punishment for waging war against him, the god Zeus sentenced Atlas to carry the earth and the heavens on his shoulders forever.

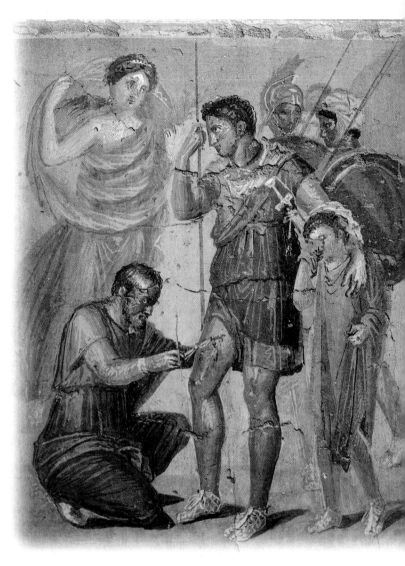

**Aeneas, Legendary Founder of Rome**
This image of Aeneas is from the *Aeneid*. Aeneas was wounded on his journey to the underworld to see his father. **Critical Thinking: Frame Questions** *What questions might Aeneas have asked his father about his vision of Rome?*

**Cicero**

The famous Roman speaker Cicero helped Latin become the language of learning in Europe. **Critical Thinking: Evaluate Information** *How did Cicero contribute to people's knowledge of Latin?*

**E-LA 6.2.7 Use Supporting Citations** Support the following assertion with text evidence: Latin has been an enduring language.

## Other Roman Writers

Horace was another much-loved Roman poet. He is best known for a collection of poems called *odes*. Some are about friendship, love, and everyday pleasures. Others give advice. "Be brief," he advised writers. "More ought to be scratched out than left."

Livy wrote Roman history. Livy's histories are colorful and patriotic. They show Roman heroes as Romans liked to see them. In his history of the Punic Wars, Livy portrays Romans as practical, honest, just, and respectful toward the gods.

The writer and statesman Cicero was famous for his oratory and essays. **Oratory** is the art of making great speeches. Cicero translated into Latin ideas and terms that had before been expressed only in Greek. He so improved Latin that it served for centuries as Europe's language of learning. Even after Latin died out as a spoken language, scholars in many countries used Latin to communicate with each other.

Few people read Latin today, but the wisdom of Roman authors lives on in sayings that have become part of our language. Here are a few examples:

"Love conquers all."—Virgil

"It is quality, not quantity, that matters."—Seneca

"There is no place like home."—Cicero

"No sooner said than done."—Quintus Ennius

"The remedy is worse than the disease."—Publius Syrus

"My heart was in my mouth."—Petronius

"He who desires peace should prepare for war."—Vegetius

## The Legacy of Latin

Although Latin is seldom spoken today, it is far from being a "dead" language. Roman soldiers took their language to many parts of Europe. Over time, forms of Latin replaced the local languages. Today, millions of people speak Romance languages, or languages based on Roman Latin. Spanish is the most widespread Romance language. It is spoken in more than 40 countries. Italian, French, Portuguese, and Romanian are also Romance languages.

English is not a Romance language, but it has a Latin legacy. We use the Roman alphabet, and a few extra letters, to write English. Many English words have Latin roots. Scientists still use Latin to give precise names to plants and animals.

✔ **Checkpoint** What themes were important in Roman literature?

# Roman Law and Government

The idea of democracy comes from the people of ancient Greece, yet no modern government is like that of ancient Athens. By contrast, the Romans who borrowed and absorbed ideas from other peoples, including the Greeks, greatly influenced modern political and legal systems.

**Republican Government**   The <u>founders</u> of the United States greatly admired the Roman Republic. Like the ancient Romans, the Americans had just freed themselves from rule by a king. And, like the Romans, they believed that people could and should rule themselves.

When the founders met to write a constitution for the United States, they borrowed many ideas from ancient Rome. One of these was a republican form of government. As you recall, a republic is a government in which citizens elect their leaders and lawmakers. The upper house of the United States Congress is called the senate after the ancient Roman senate.

Another idea that the founders borrowed from the Romans was a system of checks and balances. Like a Roman tribune, the president of the United States has the power to veto a law passed by Congress.

**Main Idea**
The Roman type of government had a great influence on modern political and legal systems.

**Vocabulary** *Builder*
**founder** (FOWN duhr) *n.* person who founds, or establishes something

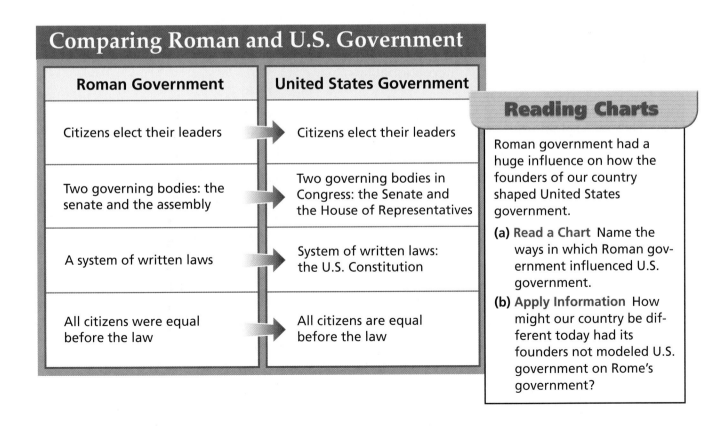

## Comparing Roman and U.S. Government

| Roman Government | United States Government |
|---|---|
| Citizens elect their leaders | Citizens elect their leaders |
| Two governing bodies: the senate and the assembly | Two governing bodies in Congress: the Senate and the House of Representatives |
| A system of written laws | System of written laws: the U.S. Constitution |
| All citizens were equal before the law | All citizens are equal before the law |

**Reading Charts**

Roman government had a huge influence on how the founders of our country shaped United States government.

**(a) Read a Chart** Name the ways in which Roman government influenced U.S. government.

**(b) Apply Information** How might our country be different today had its founders not modeled U.S. government on Rome's government?

**Roman Citizenship**
The bronze copy of a document, above left, granted full citizenship to people serving in the Roman army. The relief sculpture, above right, shows a census-taker with Roman citizens. **Critical Thinking: Apply Information** *Do you think the census-taker would count women in ancient Rome? Explain.*

**Vocabulary** *Builder*
<u>code</u> (kohd) *n.* a set of written rules or laws

## Citizenship

The Greeks invented the idea of citizenship, but they limited citizenship to those people born in a particular city-state. The Romans greatly expanded this idea by granting citizenship to most people living across their empire. Excluded from citizenship were women and slaves. Romans, Greeks, Gauls, Egyptians, and others all shared the same legal rights as citizens.

As the empire grew, the Romans made special laws for dealing with noncitizens. Such laws were needed to set rules for trade and commerce. These special laws made up the Roman "law of nations." They became the basis for modern international law.

## The Rule of Law

The Sumerians created the first known law <u>codes</u>. However, the Romans took the rule of law further by setting up a court system with judges, lawyers, and juries.

As you read earlier, the Twelve Tables issued in 451 B.C. established Rome's first law code. Over time, the civil law, or body of laws affecting citizens, grew. Yet even as the law code changed, it continued to be based on the concept of justice. The word *justice* comes from the Latin word for law.

Equally important was the Roman belief that laws should be applied equally to all people. Cicero asked:

> **What sort of thing is the civil law? It is of a sort that cannot be bent by influence or broken by power or spoiled by money.**
>
> —Cicero

Roman law had the strongest influence in countries that were once Roman provinces. The modern law codes of Italy, France, and Spain all have deep roots in Roman law. The same is true for the many nations that were once colonies of these countries. Listed below are some of the basic concepts of justice that have been handed down to us from Roman law.

- People should not be punished for what they think.
- People should not be taken by force from their homes.
- A person accused of a crime has a right to a trial.
- A person accused of a crime should be considered innocent until proved guilty.
- In handing down punishment, the age and experience of the guilty person should be considered.

 **Checkpoint** **How has Roman law influenced modern political systems?**

**Looking Back and Ahead** In this section, you have read about the legacies of Roman literature, language, government, and law. Still, the glorious Roman civilization did not last. In the next section, you will read about the decline of the Roman Empire.

## Section 2 Check Your Progress

**Progress Monitoring** ●nline
**For:** Self-test with instant help
**Visit:** PHSchool.com
**Web Code:** mwa-6202

 **Standards Review** H-SS: 6.7.8; E-LA: Reading 6.2.7

### Comprehension and Critical Thinking

**1. (a) Explain** What was the theme of Virgil's *Aeneid*?
**(b) Apply Information** What do you think is the most lasting legacy of the Latin language? Explain.

**2. (a) Recall** Where did the Roman law system have the strongest influence?
**(b) Draw Inferences** Why did Rome have different law codes for citizens and non-citizens?

### Reading Skill
**3. Use Supporting Citations** Read the final paragraph under A Golden Age of Latin Literature. Support the following assertion with text evidence: Romans liked to see their heroes as successful soldiers and larger-than-life figures.

### Vocabulary *Builder*
Read each sentence below. If the sentence is true, write YES. If the sentence is not true, write NO and explain WHY.

**4.** A founder is someone who joins an organization that is already established.

**5.** A set of written laws or rules is also called a code.

### Writing
**6.** Write a paragraph describing the information presented in the chart on page 575. Begin your paragraph with a topic sentence about the influences of Roman government on U.S. government.

## Section 3 The Decline of the Roman Empire

**Standards Preview**

**H-SS 6.7.1** Students analyze the causes and effects of the vast expansion and ultimate disintegration of the Roman Empire.

**E-LA Reading 6.2.7** Make reasonable assertions about a text through accurate, supporting citations.

### Reading Preview

 **Reading Skill**

**Use Personal Evidence** Often, you must add clues from your personal experience or knowledge to text evidence in order to make assertions. In particular, when making assertions about the behavior of people or nations, you need to think about what makes people behave this way. Ask yourself: What would I do in this situation? How have I seen others behave in similar situations?

**Vocabulary** *Builder*

**High-Use Words**
income (IHN kuhm), p. 579
invade (ihn VAYD), p. 582

**Key Terms and People**
Marcus Aurelius (MARK uhs uh REE lih uhs), p. 578
corrupt (kuh RUPT), p. 579
money supply (MUHN ee suh PLY), p. 579
inflation (ihn FLAY shuhn), p. 580
Diocletian (dī uh KLEE shuhn), p. 580
Constantine (KAWN stuhn teen), p. 580

**Background Knowledge** For centuries, the Roman Empire was rich and powerful. Greco-Roman culture spread widely. But with the end of the Pax Romana, the glory of the empire began to fade. In this section, you will read about the causes of the ultimate, or final, disintegration of the empire. Disintegration means breaking into smaller pieces.

## Political and Economic Troubles

**Main Idea**
Unstable government, high taxes, rising prices, and splitting the empire in two all contributed to the fall of the Roman Empire.

The Pax Romana ended in A.D. 180 with the death of the emperor **Marcus Aurelius.** He was the last of five powerful emperors who had kept the empire strong and united. By the end of his reign, however, there were signs of trouble ahead. "Our history now plunges," wrote the historian Cassius Dio, "from a kingdom of gold to one of iron and rust." In fact, Rome's "plunge" was a long, slow decline of more than 200 years.

**Unstable Government**   The decline began with a series of weak emperors. Marcus Aurelius was followed by his son Commodus. Commodus was so corrupt, or dishonest, that Cassius Dio described him as "a greater curse to the Romans than any plague or crime." In the 50 years after A.D. 235, there were 21 emperors! All were chosen by the army, and all but one met violent deaths. During this period of unstable government, struggles for power triggered a series of civil wars.

**High Taxes**   The civil wars created enormous economic problems. Wars cost money. To get that money, one emperor after another raised taxes. However, few people had high enough <u>incomes</u> to pay what they owed.

One reason for people's inability to pay their taxes was that the empire's supply of gold and silver coins was declining. Wealthy Romans paid for imported goods with Roman coins, and more gold and silver coins left the empire than could be replaced.

**Price Inflation**   Emperors tried to increase the money supply by issuing coins made of less precious metals. The money supply is the total amount of money in an economy. The denarius, once made of silver, was made of copper with a thin silver coating.

**E-LA 6.2.7 Use Personal Evidence**
Why do you think these kinds of leaders had problems like those described in this section? Use your knowledge to link it to the text.

**Vocabulary** *Builder*
<u>income</u> (IHN kuhm) *n.* the money that you earn from working

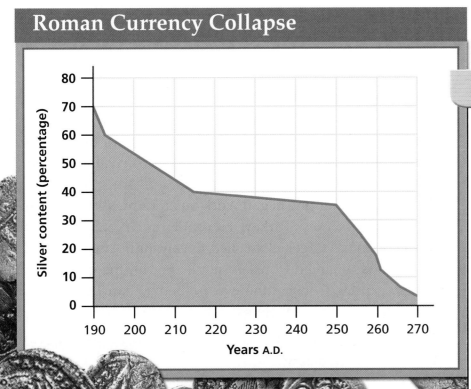

**Roman Currency Collapse**

*Silver content (percentage)* vs *Years A.D.*

**Reading Graphs**

During his reign, Augustus established the system of currency used by the Roman Empire. This currency system existed until the middle of the third century A.D.

**(a) Read a Graph** Between which years did the silver content in Roman currency remain relatively stable?

**(b) Draw Conclusions** Why do you think the empire issued bronze coins that had a thin layer of silver instead of coins made entirely of bronze?

When merchants realized that coins were being made of less precious metals, they raised their prices. The result was **inflation,** or a general rise in the cost of goods. A bag of wheat that had cost one denarius a century earlier rose in price to 200 denarii.

Inflation hurt commerce. It also made difficult the government's task of supplying the army. As money lost its value, tax collectors began seizing food, clothing, wagons, and other valuable and necessary goods as payment of taxes.

**Diocletian Divides the Empire**  Finally, in 284, the empire got a capable leader in the emperor Diocletian (dī uh KLEE shuhn). Over many years, Diocletian reorganized the imperial government from top to bottom. He doubled the size of the army. He greatly increased the number of magistrates. Because no one person could rule all of these officials, he split the empire into two parts—the Eastern Roman Empire and the Western Roman Empire. Each part was ruled by its own emperor. Diocletian also made each emperor responsible for choosing his own successor.

Diocletian's reforms looked good on paper, but they were expensive to carry out. To raise money to pay all the added soldiers and officials, Diocletian raised taxes still higher. Farmers who could not pay their taxes could be sold into slavery. This threat led many farmers to abandon the countryside for urban areas. The loss of farms further weakened the empire's already struggling economy.

**Constantine's New Capital**  Diocletian's effort to solve the succession problem also failed. After his death, rival leaders again fought for control of the empire. In time, a military officer named Constantine defeated his rivals to become sole ruler.

In 330, Constantine began work on an impressive new capital in what is now Turkey. He built his "New Rome" on the site of an old Greek city called Byzantium. After his death, the city was renamed Constantinople. For all the grandeur of his new capital, Constantine was no better than Diocletian at solving the empire's problems.

✔ **Checkpoint**  How did dividing the empire in two add to Rome's problems?

**The Emperor Constantine**
Constantine ruled the Eastern Roman Empire from 306 through 337. The next ten emperors succeeding him honored Constantine by calling themselves "Constantine." **Critical Thinking: Distinguish Facts from Opinions** *Was Constantine a popular emperor? Explain.*

# The Collapse of the Empire

Unstable government and economic problems weakened the Roman Empire from within. At the same time, the empire was also being attacked along its borders by peoples the Romans viewed as "barbarians." The most serious threats came from the Germanic peoples of Eastern Europe.

**The Germans**   Two great rivers, the Rhine and the Danube, marked the northern and eastern boundaries of the Roman Empire in Europe. Romans called the peoples living across those frontiers Germans. The Germans were, in fact, many different groups, such as the Franks, Vandals, Visigoths, and Goths. The Roman historian Tacitus described the Germans in this way:

> ❝They all have fierce blue eyes, reddish hair, and large bodies fit only for sudden exertion (action). . . . The universal dress in Germany is a cloak fastened with a brooch or, failing that, a thorn. . . . They also wear the skins of wild animals.❞
>
> —P. Cornelius Tacitus, *Germania*

**Main Idea**
The Roman Empire fell after attacks by Germanic tribes and other invaders further weakened the empire.

**Attila the Hun**
This image shows Attila the Hun, a fierce warrior who led his bands on raids through Europe. **Critical Thinking: Explain Problems** *How did the invasion of the Huns contribute to the decline of the Roman Empire?*

**Vocabulary** *Builder*
<u>invade</u> (ihn VAYD) *v.* to enter forcibly or with hostility; come into as an enemy

By the time of Constantine, thousands of Germans had joined the Roman army. Having Germans in the army was both good and bad for the empire. Army service made the Germans seem more like true Romans. But few Germans developed the same loyalty to the empire that Romans felt.

**Barbarians on the Move** The crisis that would test the Roman Empire's border legions was triggered by nomadic warriors from Central Asia known to the Romans as Huns. This same group was known in China as the Xiongnu. You read in Chapter 12 about the Emperor Wudi's struggle against the Xiongnu. As the Chinese knew all too well, the Huns were great horsemen. They moved quickly and fought fiercely.

In the 300s, the Huns conquered northern China. Then they turned west toward Europe. As the Huns thundered across the continent, terrified Germans fled in terror. By 376, some Germans had reached the Danube River. In 376 the Goths crossed the Danube, entering the empire. When the Romans tried to drive the Goths back, the Romans were badly defeated. Other groups followed. One by one, the western provinces were taken over by peoples who set up their own Germanic kingdoms.

**The Fall of Rome** In time, Rome itself came under attack. Visigoths <u>invaded</u> Rome in 410 and looted the city. In 455, Vandals attacked Rome a second time. Their raid was so destructive that we now use the word "vandalize."

Rome never recovered from these attacks. In 476, German army officers replaced the last emperor of Rome with a Visigothic general named Odoacer (oh doh AY ser). At that point, Italy, too, became a Germanic kingdom.

Historians have used the date 476 to mark the fall of the Roman Empire. But that year was little different from the ones before or after. Roman peace, order, and government had collapsed long before that date.

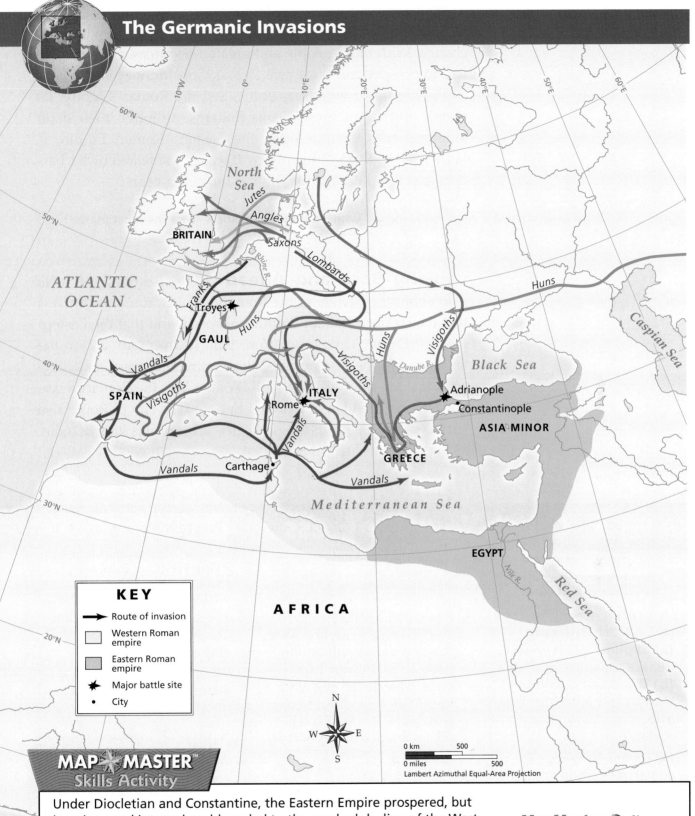

# The Germanic Invasions

North Sea
Jutes
Angles
BRITAIN
Saxons
Lombards
ATLANTIC OCEAN
Rhine R.
Franks
Troyes
GAUL
Huns
Huns
Vandals
SPAIN
Visigoths
Rome
ITALY
Vandals
Vandals
Carthage
Vandals
GREECE
Visigoths
Huns
Danube R.
Visigoths
Huns
Black Sea
Adrianople
Constantinople
ASIA MINOR
Caspian Sea
Mediterranean Sea
EGYPT
Nile R.
Red Sea
AFRICA

**KEY**
→ Route of invasion
▢ Western Roman empire
▢ Eastern Roman empire
★ Major battle site
• City

N
W E
S

0 km    500
0 miles    500
Lambert Azimuthal Equal-Area Projection

## MAP MASTER™
### Skills Activity

Under Diocletian and Constantine, the Eastern Empire prospered, but invasions and internal problems led to the gradual decline of the West.

**(a) Locate** From which direction did the Saxons first invade Britain?

**(b) Draw Conclusions** Foreign invasions hurt the Western Roman Empire more than they did the Eastern Roman Empire. How does the map help you draw that conclusion?

**MapMaster Online**

**For:** Interactive map
**Visit:** PHSchool.com
**Web Code:** mwp-6203

In the Eastern Roman Empire, life also went on with little change. With more people and greater resources, cities continued to prosper and trade was strong. Constantinople survived as the capital of what was still called the Roman Empire. Its people still saw themselves as Romans, although their main language was Greek. Today the Eastern Roman Empire is known as the Byzantine Empire. It was not defeated by barbarians, and it would last for another thousand years.

✔ **Checkpoint** Which barbarian invaders were the most feared? Explain.

**Looking Back and Ahead** In this section, you have read about the decline of the Roman Empire. You have learned that the Western Roman Empire collapsed, and that the Eastern Roman Empire lived on. You will learn more about the legacies of Rome that survived the empire's collapse. These legacies include the Christian faith, Roman law, the Romance languages, and the idea of a united Europe. The city of Rome also survived. Because of its long and great history, it is known today as the "Eternal City."

## Section 3 Check Your Progress

**Progress Monitoring Online**
For: Self-test with instant help
Visit: PHSchool.com
Web Code: mwa-6203

 **Standards Review** H-SS: 6.7.1; E-LA: Reading 6.2.7

### Comprehension and Critical Thinking

**1. (a) Explain** What were Rome's economic problems?
**(b) Draw Conclusions** How did economic problems affect the poor in Roman society?

**2. (a) Recall** Why did Diocletian divide the Roman Empire?
**(b) Draw Inferences** Why do you think the Eastern Roman Empire continued to prosper?

### ⤺ Reading Skill

**3. Use Personal Evidence** Read the first paragraph under High Taxes. In your experience, how do people with less in life feel about people with more in life? Explain your evidence and link it to the text.

### Vocabulary *Builder*

Read each sentence below. If the sentence is true, write YES. If the sentence is not true, write NO and explain WHY.
**4.** The final disintegration of the Roman Empire was caused by the Pax Romana.

**5.** The son of Marcus Aurelius, Commodus, was a corrupt emperor.

**6.** When Rome's money supply increased, the lower price of goods created inflation.

### Writing

**7.** Write a paragraph in which you take a position on the rule of Diocletian. Did his reforms help the Roman Empire? State your opinion in your topic sentence. Revise the paragraph to clearly state your point of view.

# Citizen Heroes

 **History-Social Science 6.7** Students analyze the geographic, political, economic, religious, and social structures during the development of Rome.

| Respect | Caring | Responsibility | Fairness | Honesty | Civic Virtue |
|---------|--------|----------------|----------|---------|--------------|

# Fabiola *Caring for the Needy*

**Good citizens care about the welfare of others. In Ancient Rome, a patrician named Fabiola devoted her life to caring for the sick and poor.**

**Fabiola** was a wealthy patrician during the declining years of the Roman Empire. A devout Christian, she spent her time and money caring for the needy of Rome.

Fabiola used her wealth to establish a public hospital in Rome. She did not wait for the sick to come to the hospital. Instead, she went out on the streets, found people in need of care, and carried them to the hospital herself. Fabiola worked tirelessly, giving the patients food and clothing as well as medicine. When she died in A.D. 399, thousands of grateful people came to her funeral.

## Connect to Today

**Mother Teresa** was a Catholic nun. As a young woman, she moved to India to take care of the people she called "the poorest of the poor." Mother Teresa treated and lived among people whom no one else would help. She opened medical clinics, shelters, homes for the poor and sick, orphanages, and schools. In 1979, she won the Nobel Peace Prize.

Mother Teresa never stopped working. She once said, "The other day I dreamed that I was at the gates of heaven. . . . And St. Peter said, 'Go back to Earth, there are no slums up here.'"

### *Analyze* CITIZEN HEROES

How can you show caring in your community? List at least five ways. Your list should include ways to show caring for people. It could also include ways to show caring for animals and the environment.

When governments are in trouble, their leaders must decide what to do. To make good decisions, leaders must consider the available choices, or options. Knowing how leaders make decisions will help you understand history.

### Chapter Standards
**History-Social Science**

**Historical Interpretation 6** Students interpret basic indicators of economic performance and conduct cost-benefit analyses of economic and political issues.

Constantine was emperor of both the Eastern and Western Roman Empires. At the time, Rome was the capital. Constantine had an important decision to make: should he build a new capital in Byzantium?

There were many benefits to doing this. For one thing, Constantine was a Christian. If he built a new city, he could fill it with Christian churches. He could establish a new senate, and make other changes in government.

Byzantium was in a good location for military defense, and was also an established trade center.

There would be costs in moving to Byzantium, though. Constantine would have to impose high taxes to pay for all the new buildings. Moving the center of power to the East would impact the West because it could hurt its economy and weaken its government and defenses.

Constantine decided to build a new capital in Byzantium. This important decision would affect the history of the world.

**Learn the Skill** *Follow these steps to analyze the decision-making process.*

1. **Identify the decision that has to be made.** A decision often starts with a problem. For example: How can I make my government stronger? How can I improve the economy?

2. **List the options.** Making a decision involves making choices. Listing options is a good way to start the decision-making process.

3. **Evaluate, or judge, each option.** What are the benefits and costs of each option?

4. **Choose the option that seems best.** A good decision involves choosing the best option. The best option may not be perfect, but its benefits will outweigh its costs.

**Practice the Skill** *Use the passage above to answer the following questions.*

1. **Identify the decision that has to be made.** What decision was Constantine considering?

2. **List the options.** What options did Constantine have?

3. **Evaluate, or judge, each option. (a)** What would the benefits of moving the capital be? **(b)** What might the costs be?

4. **Choose the option that seems best.** What choice did Constantine make?

**Apply the Skill**
*See page 589 of the Review and Assessment.*

## Chapter Summary  H-SS: 6.7.8; 6.7.1

### Section 1 Roman Arts and Engineering

- Roman art and architecture was modeled on Greek works.
- New types of roads, water systems, and advances in science, medicine, and technology improved the Romans' daily life.

### Section 2 Literature, Language, and Law

- Rome's legacy of literature was based on both Greek and Latin.
- Roman government and law influenced modern political and legal systems.

### Section 3 The Decline of the Roman Empire

- Many internal problems contributed to the fall of the Roman Empire.
- Attacks by invaders further weakened the empire.

**Constantinople**

## Standards Practice H-SS: 6.7.8; 6.7.1

## Vocabulary *Builder*

### High-Use Words

Decide whether each underlined word is used correctly. If it is, explain why. If not, rewrite the rest of the sentence to make it logical.

1. Visitors to Roman cities were **impressed** by the lack of sewer and water systems.

2. The Romans improved on the Sumerians' law **codes**.

3. **Income** is money that you have to pay for government services.

4. The Visigoths **invaded**, or quickly left, Rome in A.D. 410.

### Key Terms

Answer the following questions in complete sentences that show your understanding of the Key Terms.

1. What was the main use of an aqueduct?

2. What did Galen do when he dissected animals for medical study?

3. If someone is skilled in oratory, what does he or she do well?

4. How did Rome's money supply affect inflation?

## Apply Reading Skills

**Make Reasonable Assertions** Read the subsection Roman Roads in Section 1. Make reasonable assertions about the Romans' approach to road construction based on text clues and, if possible, personal evidence. Explain your supporting evidence.

## Comprehension and Critical Thinking

**1. (a) Recall** What were typical features of Roman architecture?
**(b) Compare** How did the Romans adapt Greek styles to fit their needs?

**2. (a) Describe** What are the Romance languages? Give two examples.
**(b) Analyze Cause and Effect** How did these languages develop, and where did they spread?
**(c) Compare** Compare the spread of Romance languages with the influence of the Roman legal system.

**3. (a) Explain** What types of internal problems did the Roman Empire have?
**(b) Recall** What threatened the Empire from outside?
**(c) Apply Information** Why was it increasingly difficult for the Roman army to defend the empire?

## Researching

**The Fall of the Western Roman Empire**
The year A.D. 476 is generally considered to be when the Western Roman Empire "fell." In this activity you will use the Internet and the library media center to research other events in world history that occurred near this date. Choose a task below to work on. Share your work with the class. Make a list of the resources you used to go with your presentation.

**Musician:** Compose a song that describes the event or events you have researched that occurred near A.D. 476. Be sure to link this date in history with the fall of the Western Roman Empire. Perform several lines of the song for your class.

**Journalist:** Create several newspaper headlines and one or two stories that describe the events you have researched that occurred near A.D. 476. Remember to link this date in history with the fall of the Western Roman Empire.

---

**Researching Online**
**For:** Help in starting this activity
**Visit:** PHSchool.com
**Web Code:** mwe-6204

---

## Writing

**1. Write a paragraph on the following topic.** The Roman influence occurs in many aspects of life in the United States today, including art, architecture, literature, government, and law. Choose one of these legacies to write about in detail.
**Your paragraph should:**
- state a thesis or purpose for writing.
- explain why the legacy that you have chosen is important to life in the United States today.
- offer evidence, or details to support your choice.
- revise your paragraph and include a strong summary statement.

**2. Write a short narrative.** Imagine that you lived in the Eastern Roman Empire during the time of the Emperor Constantine. Write a short narrative describing to your family a speech you have just heard Constantine present.

**Progress Monitoring @nline**
**For:** Self-test with instant help
**Visit:** PHSchool.com
**Web Code:** mwa-6204

# Analysis Skills Practice

**Use the section on page 575 titled Republican Government to answer these questions.**

1. What decision did the founders of the United States have to make?

2. List the options for government that the founders had.

3. What benefits would the new U.S. government have if it followed Roman ways of government?

4. What type of government did the founders choose?

# Test Yourself

**Use the image below to answer Question 1.**

1. **Why are aqueducts good examples of Roman architecture?**
   A because they were made of concrete and had rounded arches
   B because they carried water across land
   C because they had mosaic floors
   D because they were small and compact in design

2. **Which statement is true?**
   A Ptolemy built the Pantheon.
   B English is a Romance language.
   C Roman government was a direct democracy.
   D Galen discovered that arteries and veins carry blood.

3. **Which statement is NOT true?**
   A The Romans invented the idea of citizenship.
   B Roman law had a strong influence in former provinces.
   C The Romans set up a court system with judges, lawyers, and juries.
   D The Roman law of nations is the basis for modern international law.

4. **Emperor Diocletian reorganized the government and**
   A reduced taxes.
   B built Constantinople.
   C abolished slavery for debt.
   D divided the Roman Empire into two parts.

**Use the quotation below to answer Question 5.**

5. **What were some of the causes for the decline of the Roman Empire?**

> *"Our history now plunges from a kingdom of gold to one of iron and rust."*

   A patriotic writers died out
   B the Byzantine Empire collapsed
   C unstable government, high taxes, and inflation
   D cooperation between the Huns and the Germanic groups

# Writing Workshop

## Persuasive Composition

**History-Social Science**

**6.7** Students analyze the geographic, political, economic, religious, and social structures during the development of Rome.

**English-Language Arts**

**Writing 6.2.5** Write persuasive compositions.

For a review of the steps in the writing process, see the Historian's Toolkit, *Write Like a Historian*

### ▶ Introduction

In a persuasive composition, you express an opinion about an issue and try to convince your reader to agree with you. A persuasive essay should have the following characteristics.

- The thesis statement should express your opinion about a topic.

- Details, examples, and reasons should support your opinion.

- Tone and language should win the reader over.

**Assignment** On the following pages, you will learn how to write a persuasive essay. The instructions include an example from an essay expressing an opinion about Julius Caesar.

Read the instructions and the examples. Then, follow each step to plan and write a 500–700 word essay on this topic:

**What is the most important lesson we can learn from the Roman Empire?**

### ▶ Prewriting

**Find a topic you have an opinion about.** A persuasive essay presents an opinion, or judgment, about an issue. Persuasive writing does not deal with factual questions that can be settled by checking sources. Instead, persuasive writing deals with questions that can inspire conflicting opinions. For example, "Was Julius Caesar a danger to the Roman Republic?" is a matter of opinion.

**Create a working thesis expressing an informed opinion.** An informed opinion is a judgment that is based on fact and careful thinking. Gather information about your topic. Think about all sides of the issue. Then make your own judgment. Write out your opinion clearly.

**Brainstorm for supporting information.** Find facts and reasons that support your opinion. One supporting fact would be "Julius Caesar was popular among the Romans." A supporting reason would be "Because Caesar was popular, the Romans might have made him king, ending the Republic."

**Sample assignment:** "What is the most important lesson we can learn from the Roman Empire?" Note that saying something is "most important" is a statement of opinion, not a statement of fact. However, this topic is far too broad to be used for a thesis. Part of your challenge will be to narrow your topic to a thesis you can discuss in a short paper.

**Think about opposing arguments.** Your essay will be more persuasive if you take account of arguments someone could make *against* your opinion. Think about how to deal with such arguments.

**Create a working thesis.** After you review your notes, write a sentence that states your main point. This "working thesis" may change, but it should guide your drafting.

> **Sample working thesis:**
> "Julius Caesar was a threat to the Roman Republic."

## ▶ Drafting

**Decide how to organize your writing.** Focus on the reasons that support your opinion. Plan paragraphs that develop each of these reasons with facts, examples, and logic.

A. Caesar valued personal glory over his duty to the Republic.
  1. In 49 B.C. he crossed the Rubicon with his army against orders of the Senate.
  2. He knew that his actions would cause a civil war.

B. Caesar also let himself be declared dictator for life.
  1. Ordinarily, dictators only ruled Rome during wars.
  2. The Senators saw dictatorship as the opposite of democracy.

C. Although Caesar was popular, he did not have what the people wanted.

> **Organize major and minor points.** List details that support each major point.

> **Address opposing arguments.** When you deal with opposing arguments, it shows the reader that you have looked at both sides of the question. Be sure to state the opposing argument in such a way that it is clear that you do not agree with the argument. You can do this by the way you put your sentences together or by the transitions you use.

**Introduce your thesis.** Draft an introductory paragraph that sets up the issue you will be writing about.

**Support your thesis with examples and details.** Write paragraphs presenting details that support your opinion.

**Use a persuasive tone.** Present your ideas firmly but politely. Do not insult opinions that are different from your own.

**Write a strong conclusion.** In your final paragraph, restate your opinion. Explain why the issue is important.

## ▶ Student Model

Read the following model of a persuasive essay.
Notice how it includes the characteristics you
have learned.

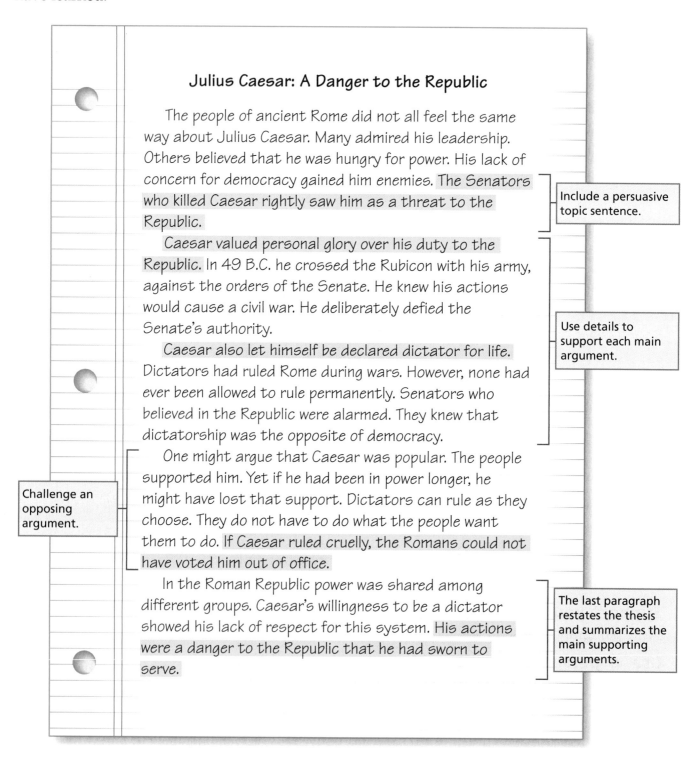

### Julius Caesar: A Danger to the Republic

The people of ancient Rome did not all feel the same
way about Julius Caesar. Many admired his leadership.
Others believed that he was hungry for power. His lack of
concern for democracy gained him enemies. The Senators
who killed Caesar rightly saw him as a threat to the
Republic.

Caesar valued personal glory over his duty to the
Republic. In 49 B.C. he crossed the Rubicon with his army,
against the orders of the Senate. He knew his actions
would cause a civil war. He deliberately defied the
Senate's authority.

Caesar also let himself be declared dictator for life.
Dictators had ruled Rome during wars. However, none had
ever been allowed to rule permanently. Senators who
believed in the Republic were alarmed. They knew that
dictatorship was the opposite of democracy.

One might argue that Caesar was popular. The people
supported him. Yet if he had been in power longer, he
might have lost that support. Dictators can rule as they
choose. They do not have to do what the people want
them to do. If Caesar ruled cruelly, the Romans could not
have voted him out of office.

In the Roman Republic power was shared among
different groups. Caesar's willingness to be a dictator
showed his lack of respect for this system. His actions
were a danger to the Republic that he had sworn to
serve.

*Annotations:*

Include a persuasive topic sentence.

Use details to support each main argument.

Challenge an opposing argument.

The last paragraph restates the thesis and summarizes the main supporting arguments.

## ▶ Revising

After completing your draft, read it again carefully to find ways to make your writing better.

### Revise to strengthen your thesis and support
- Does the thesis state your opinion clearly and strongly?
- Does each paragraph support that opinion?
- Are the reasons you present logical? Are they all supported by convincing facts, details, and examples?

### Revise to be more convincing
- Is the tone of the essay firm but tactful?
- Are the opposing arguments answered effectively and respectfully?
- Does the essay end by making the reader believe the importance of the opinion?

### Revise to meet standard English conventions
- Are all sentences complete, with a subject and a verb?
- Are spelling, capitalization, and punctuation correct?

One might argue that Caesar was
popular, the people supported him.
Yet if he had been in power longer,
he might have lost that support.
Dictators can rule as they chose.
They do not have to do what the
people want them to do.

## ▶ Rubric for Self-Assessment

*Evaluate your persuasive essay using this rating scale.*

|  | Score 4 | Score 3 | Score 2 | Score 1 |
|---|---|---|---|---|
| **Organization** | Supports the thesis with a series of paragraphs guided by a reason stated in a topic sentence; uses effective organization | Uses a reasonably clear organization to present the supporting information | Chooses an organization not suited to the topic | Shows lack of organizational strategy |
| **Presentation** | Supports the opinion effectively with many relevant facts, details, or examples; links all information to the opinion being supported | Supports the opinion adequately with several facts, details, or examples; links most information to the opinion being supported | Does not support the opinion adequately; does not link supporting information to the opinion | Does not provide facts, details, or examples to support the opinion |
| **Use of Language** | Varies sentence structure and vocabulary successfully; includes very few mechanical errors | Uses some variety in sentence structure and vocabulary; includes very few mechanical errors | Uses the same types of sentences without varying them; does not vary vocabulary; includes many mechanical errors | Writes incomplete sentences; uses language poorly; sounds confused; includes many mechanical errors |

# Reference

## Table of Contents

# **Primary** Sources

# Ancestors: In Search of Human Origins
by Donald Johanson, Lenora Johanson, and Blake Edgar

## Prepare to Read

**Standards Preview**

**H-SS 6.1** Students describe what is known through archaeological studies of the early physical and cultural development of humankind from the Paleolithic era to the agricultural revolution.

**Research, Evidence, and Point of View**

**1** Students frame questions that can be answered by historical study and research.

### Background

One of the great questions in archaeology is how did the first tool-using humans make a living. At present, not enough is known about early humans to be sure. However, this big question has led to smaller questions that can be answered by study and research. In this excerpt, archaeologist Donald Johanson describes such research. It was carried out at a game ranch in South Africa.

### Vocabulary *Builder*

**carcass** (KAR kuhs) *n.* dead body

**blind** (BLIND) *n.* hiding place for hunters

**hominid** (HAW mih nihdz) *n.* early human

**viscera** (VIH suh ruh) *n.* internal organs

**connoisseur** (kon uh SIHR) *n.* expert

One night Herb Friedl, our hunter guide, took an impala [antelope] carcass and tied it to a bush not far from our camp. Then he turned on a tape of wild-animal sounds to lure hyenas. . . .

Right on schedule, five hyenas appeared out of nowhere. We watched them tear through the carcass. . . . After we filmed the hyenas feeding, we frightened them away and retrieved the carcass.

The next morning, on the edge of a plain as large as a football field, Rob and I sat in a blind watching the same impala carcass. . . .

Impalas drinking at a watering hole.

After three hours of watching and waiting, we saw a black-and-chestnut-colored bateleur eagle descend upon the remains. The eagle clasped the impala with its talons and began tearing flesh off the carcass with its down-curved beak.

Suddenly, a group of white-headed vultures appeared. The eagle flew off and the vultures covered the carcass, squabbling and jostling for space. Within ten minutes the vultures stripped off all the remaining flesh. . . .

Rising out of our blind, Rob and I approached the carcass. Had we been hominids searching for food, the sight of vultures circling and descending would have lured us here. The birds flew off noisily as soon as they sensed us coming. That meant our ancestors probably had little trouble chasing this carnivore, at least, from a kill. We found a devastated carcass. Skin sagged over empty space that had once held flesh. . . .

I looked at it dubiously. "What's left on this thing to eat?"

"There's a great meal here for the taking if you know what to do," Rob cried with enthusiasm I could not share. "But you can't process a carcass of this size or larger with your hands. You'll need stone tools to get to the nutrients."

Rob grabbed one of the bloody limb bones and laid it on a flat rock . . . He took a battered piece of quartz out of his backpack to use as his hammerstone. The hammerstone is a bone breaker, one of the essential elements of the earliest tool kit. . . .

Rob delivered a sharp blow to each end of the impala leg bone and then twisted it with his hands. The bone splintered into jagged, spiral fragments and an eight-inch rod of pink marrow slid out. "Not counting the <u>viscera</u>, the marrow bones are the major source of fat in a healthy animal," he said. "Lion and leopard kills usually have plenty of marrow left on them."

"How nutritious a meal does marrow make?" I asked.

Rob has calculated that a healthy, well-fed adult impala would yield 1,500 calories worth of marrow from the twelve major limb bones. . . .

A hyena and vultures surround a carcass

"It's a full meal, all right," he said. . . "and it only takes about ten minutes to process."

"The first fast food?"

"A great food source, isn't it?" Rob said with a <u>connoisseur's</u> relish. "There's no other way you could get so many calories so fast out here."

I was powerfully struck by just how much marrow there was and how many nutrients it provided. These limb bones were the power bars of the past.

Source: *Ancestors: In Search of Human Origins,* Donald Johanson, Lenora Johanson, and Blake Edgar

## Analyze Primary Sources: *Frame Questions*

1. Good historical questions inspire interesting research. Read the questions below. Which one do you think led to Donald Johanson's experiment with Rob Blumenschine?
   A  How many calories are in the bone marrow of an antelope?
   B  Was it possible for early humans to live by scavenging food?
   C  What kinds of stone tools did early humans have in their tool kit?
   D  Did early humans prefer eating bone marrow to fresh meat?

2. Not all historical questions can be answered by study and research. Reread the questions at left. Which one do you think may never be answered? Explain your choice.

3. Think of a good question that you think Johanson and Blumenschine could answer about scavenging if they had more research.

# Primary Source

# A Student's Life in Sumer

## Prepare to Read

**Standards Preview**

**H-SS 6.2** Students analyze the geographic, political, economic, religious, and social structures of the early civilizations of Mesopotamia, Egypt, and Kush.

**Research, Evidence, and Point of View**
**3** Students distinguish relevant from irrelevant information, essential from incidental information, and verifiable from unverifiable information in historical narratives and stories.

### Background

Archaeologists excavated documents in the form of essays written by a schoolteacher about 2000 B.C. The essays describe the life of a student in ancient Sumer. These documents are important because they are written history. Primary documents—such as essays, diaries, and journals—give historians important information about the past.

As you read excerpts from the essay "School Days," think about the information that you can gather about school life in ancient Sumer.

### Vocabulary *Builder*

**punctuality** (puhnk choo AL ih tee) *n.* being on time; promptness

**curtsy** (KERT see) *n.* a bow of respect

**loiter** (LOI ter) *v.* stop and play along the way

I recited my tablet, ate my lunch, prepared my (new) tablet, wrote it, finished it; then my model tablets were brought to me; and in the afternoon my exercise tablets were brought to me. When school was dismissed, I went home, entered the house, and found my father sitting there. I explained . . . my exercise tablets to my father, . . . recited my tablet to him, and he was delighted. . . .

[The schoolboy then gives the servants the following orders.] I am thirsty, give me water to drink; I am hungry, give me bread to eat; wash my feet, set up (my) bed, I want to go to sleep. Wake me early in the morning, I must not be late. . . .

When I arose early in the morning, I faced my mother and said to her: "Give me my lunch, I want to go to school!" My mother gave me two rolls, and I set out. . . .

In school the fellow in charge of <u>punctuality</u> said: "Why are you late?" Afraid and with a pounding heart, I entered before my teacher and made a respectful <u>curtsy</u>.

My headmaster read my tablet, said: "There is something missing,". . . The fellow in charge of neatness said: "You <u>loitered</u> in the street and did not straighten up your clothes," The fellow in charge of silence said: "Why did you talk without permission?". . .The fellow in charge of good behavior said: "Why did you rise without permission?". . .The fellow in charge of Sumerian said: "Why didn't you speak Sumerian?. . ."

[The teacher speaks to the schoolboy.] Young fellow, (because) you hated not my words, neglected them not, (may you) complete the scribal [writer's] art from beginning to end. Because you . . . paid me a salary larger than my efforts (deserve), (and) have honored me, . . . may your exercises contain no faults. Of your brothers, may you be their leader; of your friends may you be their chief; may you rank the highest among the schoolboys. . . . You have carried out well the school's activities, you are a man of learning.

Source: "School Days," Anonymous Author

Ancient scribes

## Analyze Primary Sources: *Distinguish Relevant Information*

1. Which parts of the essay about a student's life in ancient Sumer could a historian verify?

2. Which statements in this essay would not be useful to a historian who wants to write an article about education in ancient Sumer?

3. What information in this essay would be essential for someone who is studying ancient teaching methods?

4. Historians learn about the past by studying written documents. By studying the written language, historians learn about ideas that are important to a society. Think of a question that a historian might ask about Sumerian society from reading the essay.

# Psalm 23
# Selections from the Book of Proverbs

## Prepare to Read

**Standards Preview**

**H-SS 6.3** Students analyze the geographic, political, economic, religious, and social structures of the Ancient Hebrews.

**Research, Evidence, and Point of View**

**3** Students distinguish relevant from irrelevant information, essential from incidental information, and verifiable from unverifiable information in historical narratives and stories.

### Background

The Book of Psalms and the Book of Proverbs are both part of the Hebrew Bible. According to Hebrew tradition, David is given credit for many of the songs in the Book of Psalms. In Psalm 23, David compares the God of Israel to a shepherd watching over his sheep.

Solomon, the son of David, is given credit for many of the poems and sayings in the Book of Proverbs. The collection touches on how to live an honest, responsible life. Following Psalm 23 are some selections from the Book of Proverbs.

### Vocabulary *Builder*

**righteousness** (RĪ chuhs nehs) *n.* doing right; just

**anoint** (uh NOINT) *v.* to put oil on someone's head or body

**boast** (bohst) *v.* to speak highly of oneself or what one owns

**entice** (ihn TĪCE) *v.* to persuade someone to do something by offering them something nice

## Psalm 23

The Lord is my shepherd;
　　I shall not want.
He maketh me to lie down in green pastures:
　　He leadeth me beside the still waters.
He restoreth my soul;
　　He leadeth me in the paths of <u>righteousness</u> for His
　　name's sake.
Yea, though I walk through the valley of the shadow of death,
　　I will fear no evil, for thou art with me;
　　Thy rod and staff they comfort me.
Thou preparest a table before me in the presence of mine enemies:
　　thou <u>anointest</u> my head with oil;
　　my cup runneth over.
Surely goodness and mercy shall follow me all the days of my life;
　　and I will dwell in the house of the LORD forever.

*Source:* The Bible

# Selections from the Book of Proverbs

<u>Boast</u> not thyself of to-morrow, for thou knowest not what a day may bring forth.

My son, if sinners shall <u>entice</u> thee, consent not to them.

Let another man praise thee, and not thine own mouth; a stranger and not thine own lips.

A good name is rather to be chosen than great riches, and loving favor rather than silver and gold.

The rich and the poor meet together; the Lord is the maker of them all.

My son, forget not my law, and let thy heart keep my commandments.

Train a child in the way he should go; and when he is old, he will not depart from it.

*Source:* The Bible

**A shepherd watches over his sheep**

## Analyze Primary Sources: *Distinguish Relevant Information*

1. Which lines in the psalm would be useful to a historian who is studying the way sheep were tended in ancient Israel?

2. The word translated "LORD" in the first verse is a name that is only used for the God of Israel. What might that indicate about the author of this psalm?

3. Which lines in the psalm remind you that the "sheep" in the psalm is a person and not an actual sheep?

4. How might a historian verify whether the shepherding practices mentioned in the psalm were common in Israel during the time of David?

5. Why might a historian credit Solomon with gathering parts of the collection of the Book of Proverbs?

6. What important values were taught to children during this time?

7. Why might this information be important to historians?

# Primary Source

# Mauryan Empire: Asoka's Political and Moral Achievements

## Prepare to Read

**Standards Preview**

**H-SS 6.5** Students analyze the geographic, political, economic, religious, and social structures of the early civilizations of India.

**Research, Evidence, and Point of View**

**3** Students distinguish relevant from irrelevant information, essential from incidental information, and verifiable from unverifiable information in historical narratives and stories.

### Background

Asoka became the third king of the Mauryan Empire about 272 B.C. As a young man, he had the reputation of being fierce, cruel, and aggressive. Today, he is known as one of the world's greatest rulers.

Asoka began studying the teachings of Buddhism before he became emperor; however, he did not take the religion's teachings of peace and harmony seriously until he had fought in the battle of Kalinga. This excerpt describes how that battle changed Asoka's life.

### Vocabulary *Builder*

**hilarious** (hih LAIR ee uhs) *adj.* noisy and cheerful

**pomp** (pahmp) *n.* all the impressive clothes, decorations, music, etc. that are traditional for an important public ceremony

**turmoil** (TER moil) *n.* a state of confusion and trouble

**annex** (a NEHKS) *n.* join or add to a larger thing

**humanity** (hyoo MAN ih tee) *n.* people

**jubilation** (jyoo bih LAY shuhn) *n.* happy celebration; rejoicing

**illuminate** (ih LOO mih nayt) *v.* light up; make bright

I t happened in about 261 B.C. . . . Since early morning, men, women, and children had been gathering in large numbers . . . . They were in a <u>hilarious</u> mood as this was their first opportunity to welcome Emperor Asoka after his victory in the Kalinga war. The city of Pataliputra wore a festive look with national flags fluttering high in the sky all along the main highway leading to the place of the public meeting.

There seemed nothing surprising in this exhibition of <u>pomp</u> and show by the . . . citizens of the Mauryan Empire. The victory in the Kalinga war was an achievement of which they could be justly proud. As a result of their ultimate victory, the people of Magadha had almost forgotten the troubles and <u>turmoils</u> through which they had to pass when the war was on. The Jawans, who had accomplished heroic deeds and were instrumental in <u>annexing</u> Kalinga, were expecting high awards . . . for their . . . bravery. . . .

At last, Asoka accompanied by the Buddhist Sage, Moggaliputta Tissa arrived on the scene and the vast mass of <u>humanity</u> burst into cries of joy. When the King . . . ascended the rostrum especially erected for the purpose, the public <u>jubilation</u> cooled down. And when Asoka arose to deliver his address, all eyes turned toward him; there was pin-drop silence. The people thought that they were now going to get a pat from the royalty for their deeds of gallantry and supreme sacrifices.

But they were disillusioned when the king started speaking in an entirely different tone. He said, "Brothers and Sisters, after the victory in the Kalinga war we have assembled here today for the first time. Perhaps you have come here to celebrate the victory with high expectations. But . . . I am unable to celebrate this occasion in the way you might have liked. I am fully conscious of the hardships faced and the sacrifices made by all of you in turning the scales in our favor in the Kalinga war. I am indeed thankful to you all for the help and cooperation you gave to government in the shape of men and material. I am, however, ashamed of the large-scale destruction brought about by the Kalinga war. . . . Moggaliputta Tissa has removed darkness from my eyes and <u>illuminated</u> my mind. I have now fully realized that for the sake of self-glory, for the sake of territorial expansion and for the sake of humiliating others, it is a crime . . . to massacre thousands . . . to destroy . . . the property of others . . . and to uproot a large number of people from their . . . homes. It is such a crime which can never be pardoned . . . The horrible results of this mass destruction and untold misery have served as an eye-opener to me. I am grateful . . . to Moggaliputta Tissa due to whose kind guidance I have found solace [comfort] in the Teachings of the Compassionate Buddha."

"Since the message of . . . the Buddha stands for peace and universal brotherhood," Asoka declared . . . "from today onward . . . I shall endeavor to win the hearts . . . of my empire, by persuasion and love instead of by the use of force and sword."

Source: *Asoka the Great*, D. C. Ahir

**Asoka**

## Analyze Primary Sources: *Distinguish Relevant Information*

1. Which statements in Asoka's speech can help you to understand his point of view on the Kalinga war?

2. Which statements in this excerpt would be relevant to a historian studying the results of the battle of Kalinga?

3. Which statements in this excerpt would not be useful in determining the people's reaction to Asoka's speech?

4. How did Asoka's study of Buddhism affect the people of the Mauryan Empire?

# Chinese Politics: Confucius and Good Government

## Prepare to Read

**Standards Preview**

**H-SS 6.6** Students analyze the geographic, political, economic, religious, and social structures of the early civilizations of China.

**Research, Evidence, and Point of View**
**5** Students detect the different historical points of view on historical events and determine the context in which historical statements were made (the questions asked, sources used, author's perspectives).

### Background
Born in China in 551 B.C., Confucius became a Chinese philosopher and teacher. His ideas on education and government had a profound impact on Chinese society for many centuries.

In this selection from *The Analects*, Confucius discusses his philosophy of good government.

### Vocabulary *Builder*
**beneficent** (beh NEHF uh schnt) *adj.* doing things to help people; generous
**expenditure** (ehk SPEHN dih chur) *n.* the amount of money that a person or government spends
**covetous** (KUHV ih tus) *adj.* having a very strong desire to have something that someone else has
**benevolent** (beh NEHV uh lent) *adj.* kindly
**awe** (aw) *n.* a feeling of great respect and admiration for someone or something
**propriety** (proh PRI ih tee) *n.* proper behavior

Tzu-chang asked Confucius, saying, "In what way should a person in authority act in order that he may conduct government properly?" The Master replied, "Let him honor the five excellent, and banish away the four bad, things; then may he conduct government properly." Tzu-chang said, "What are meant by the five excellent things?" The Master said, "When the person in authority is <u>beneficent</u> without great <u>expenditure</u>; when he gives tasks [to] the people without their complaining; when he [tries to get] what he desires without being <u>covetous</u>; when he maintains a dignified ease without being proud; when he is majestic without being fierce."

Tzu-chang said, "What is meant by being beneficent without great expenditure?" The Master replied, "When the person in authority makes more beneficial to the people the things from which they naturally derive benefit; is not this being beneficent without great expenditure? When he chooses the labors which are proper, and makes them labor on them, who will [complain]? When his desires are set on <u>benevolent</u> government, and he secures it, who will accuse him of covetousness? Whether he has to do with many people or few, or with things great or small, he does not dare to indicate any disrespect; is not this to maintain a dignified ease without any pride? He adjusts his clothes and cap, and throws a dignity into his looks, so that, thus dignified, he is looked at with <u>awe</u>; is not this to be majestic without being fierce?"

Tzu-chang then asked, "What are meant by the four bad things?" The Master said, "To put the people to death without having instructed them; this is called cruelty. To require from them, suddenly, the full [sum] of work, without having given them warning; this is called oppression. To issue orders as if without urgency, at first, and when the time comes, to insist on them with severity; this is called injury. And, generally, in the giving pay or rewards to men, to do it in a stingy way; this is called acting the part of a mere official."

The Master said, "Without recognizing the laws of Heaven, it is impossible to be a superior man."

"Without an acquaintance with the rules of <u>propriety</u>, it is impossible for the character to be established."

"Without knowing the force of words, it is impossible to know men."

Source: *The Analects,*
Confucius

**Confucius**

## Analyze Primary Sources: *Detect Point of View*

1. The question Confucius tries to answer in this excerpt concerns

   A a leader's ability to persuade others

   B a leader's decision to govern fairly

   C the qualities that a good leader needs

   D the importance of being a proud leader

2. What is Confucius's viewpoint on how to govern?

   A The best leaders work to meet their own desires.

   B It is important to be proud and fierce.

   C The best leaders understand human nature.

   D The best leaders know that people should work hard.

3. Who was Confucius trying to persuade with his argument? Do you think he succeeded? Explain.

# Qin Dynasty: The Achievements of Shi Huangdi

## Prepare to Read

 **Standards Preview**

**H-SS 6.6** Students analyze the geographic, political, economic, religious, and social structures of the early civilizations of China.

**Research, Evidence, and Point of View**

**4** Students assess the credibility of primary and secondary sources and draw sound conclusions from them.

### Background

Shi Huangdi ruled as emperor of China during the Qin Dynasty from 221–210 B.C. He is best known as the first emperor to unify China.

Sima Qian, the grand historian of the Han Dynasty, collected many sources from the Qin Dynasty that he included in his book *The Records of the Grand Historian*. In the excerpt, Sima Qian quotes an inscription found on a memorial that Shi Huangdi built.

### Vocabulary *Builder*

<u>inaugurate</u> (in AW gyoo rayt) *v.* to install in office with a ceremony

<u>pacify</u> (PAS ih fy) *v.* make calm; quiet down

<u>diligently</u> (DIHL uh jehnt lee) *adv.* with a lot of care and effort

<u>uniform</u> (YOO nuh form) *adj.* always the same

A new age is <u>inaugurated</u> by the Emperor;
Rules and measures are rectified, . . .
Human affairs are made clear
And there is harmony between fathers and
    sons.
The Emperor in his [wise ways] [kindness]
    and justice
Has made all laws and principles
    [understandable].

He set forth to <u>pacify</u> the east,
To inspect officers and men;
This great task accomplished
He visited the coast.
Great are the Emperor's achievements,
Men attend <u>diligently</u> to basic tasks,
Farming is encouraged, . . .

All the common people prosper;
All men under the sky
Toil with a single purpose;
Tools and measures are made <u>uniform</u>,
The written script is standardized;
Wherever the sun and moon shine,

Wherever one can go by boat or by carriage,
Men carry out their orders
And satisfy their desires;
For our Emperor in [keeping] with the time
Has regulated local customs,
Made waterways and divided up the land.
Caring for the common people,
He works day and night without rest;
He defines the laws, leaving nothing in
    doubt,

Making known what is forbidden.
The local officials have their duties,
Administration is smoothly carried out,
All is done correctly, all according to plan.
The Emperor in his wisdom
Inspects all four quarters of his
   [kingdom] . . . .

Source: *The Records of the Grand Historian,*
Sima Qian

**Shi Huangdi**

## Analyze Primary Sources: *Draw Conclusions*

1. According to Huangdi's memorial, during his reign

   A citizens no longer paid taxes

   B many new lands were conquered

   C ordinary citizens lived well

   D cruel governors ruled the land

2. How might historians describe the time of Huangdi's rule?

   A a time of great economic growth

   B a time when decisions favored the wealthy

   C a time of social unrest

   D a time of warring states

3. Should historians trust the list of accomplishments written on the memorial when they write about Shi Huangdi? Why or why not?

4. What questions might historians want to ask about the source before accepting the inscription as an accurate description of Shi Huangdi's accomplishments?

# Greek Mythology: Aesop's Fables

## Prepare to Read

**Standards Preview**

**H-SS 6.4** Students analyze the geographic, political, economic, religious, and social structures of the early civilizations of Ancient Greece.

**Research, Evidence, and Point of View**

**3** Students distinguish relevant from irrelevant information, essential from incidental information, and verifiable from unverifiable information in historical narratives and stories.

### Background

Fables are stories that offer advice, instruction, and moral lessons. They contain hidden messages that are told in story form. Usually, the main characters are animals. Aesop, a Greek slave, is known for his popular fables that were passed down through oral tradition. In 300 B.C., his fables were written down and put into a collection by an Athenian named Demetrius of Phaleron.

### Vocabulary *Builder*

**coup** (KOO) *n.* something that you do that is successful and impressive

**deliberately** (duh LIHB uh ruht lee) *adv.* done in a way that is intended or planned

**impudence** (IHM pyood ehns) *n.* showing no shame

**eloquence** (EHL oh kwens) *n.* ability to express oneself with grace

### Honesty Is the Best Policy

"A man who was cutting wood on a riverside lost his axe in the water. There was no help for it; so he sat down on the bank and began to cry. Hermes appeared and inquired what was the matter. Feeling sorry for the man, he dived into the river, brought up a gold axe, and asked him if that was the one he had lost. When the woodcutter said that it was not, Hermes dived again and fetched up a silver one. The man said that was not his either. So he went down a third time and came up with the woodcutter's own axe. 'That's the right one,' he said; and Hermes was so delighted with his honesty that he made him a present of the other two axes as well. When the woodman rejoined his mates and told them his experience, one of them thought he would bring off a similar <u>coup</u>. He went to the river, <u>deliberately</u> threw his axe into it, and then sat down and wept [cried]. Hermes appeared again; and on hearing the cause of his tears, he dived in, produced a gold axe as before, and asked if it was the one that had been lost. 'Yes, it is indeed,' the man joyfully exclaimed. The god was so shocked at his…<u>impudence</u>, that, far from giving him the gold axe, he did not even restore his own to him."

## The Fox and the Goat

"A fox tumbled into a water tank and could not get out. Along came a thirsty goat, and seeing the fox asked him if the water was good. The fox jumped at the chance. He sang the praises of the water with all the <u>eloquence</u> at his command and urged the goat to come down. The goat was so thirsty that he went down without stopping to think and drank his fill. Then they began to consider how they were to get up again. 'I have a good idea,' said the fox, 'that is, if you are willing to do something to help us both. Be so kind as to place your forefeet against the wall and hold up your horns straight up. Then I can nip up, and pull you up too.' The goat was glad enough to go along with the suggestion. The fox moved easily over his haunches, shoulders, and horns, reached the edge of the tank, and began to make off. The goat complained that he had broken their [agreement]. But he only came back to say: 'You have more hairs in your beard than brains in your head, my friend. Otherwise, you wouldn't have gone down without thinking how you were going to get up.'"

Source: *Aesop's Fables,*
Translated by S. A. Handford

The fox

## Analyze Primary Sources: *Distinguish Essential Information*

1. How does the fable "Honesty is the Best Policy" use characters to give essential information?

   A The second woodcutter is described as a wise man.

   B Hermes makes an important observation.

   C The first woodcutter talks to his friends.

   D Hermes appears before each woodcutter.

2. How does the appearance of the fox in the second fable add to the lesson taught?

   A Foxes and goats are usually together in most stories.

   B Foxes are usually shown as clever and tricky.

   C Goats are usually shown as clever and tricky.

   D The goat is always tricked in most stories.

3. Which statements in each fable are essential to understanding the moral of the story?

4. What information in Aesop's Fables would be relevant to the study of Greek mythology?

# Primary Source

## The Peloponnesian War: The Plague in Athens

### Prepare to Read

**Standards Preview**

**H-SS 6.4** Students analyze the geographic, political, economic, religious, and social structures of the early civilizations of Ancient Greece.

**Research, Evidence, and Point of View**
**4** Students assess the credibility of primary and secondary sources and draw conclusions from them.

### Background

The Peloponnesian War, fought between Athens and Sparta, broke out in 431 B.C. Thucydides wrote the *History of the Peloponnesian War,* which includes eyewitness accounts of the war and a description of the plague of Athens. Thucydides contracted the plague, but he recovered to write a detailed account of the tragedy.

### Vocabulary *Builder*

**devastation** (dehv uh STAY shuhn) *n.* very bad damage or complete destruction
**virulent** (VIR uh lehnt) *adj.* poisonous; deadly
**unprecedented** (uhn PREHS uh dehnt ehd) *adj.* never having happened before
**calamity** (kuh LAM ih tee) *n.* a great misfortune such as a flood or fire

At the beginning of the following summer the Peloponnesians and their allies . . . invaded Attica, again under the command of the Spartan King Archidamus. . . . Taking up their positions, they set about the <u>devastation</u> of the country.

They had not been many days in Attica before the plague first broke out among the Athenians. Previously attacks of the plague had been reported from many other places in the neighborhood of Lemnos and elsewhere, but there was no record of the disease being so <u>virulent</u> anywhere else or causing so many deaths as it did in Athens. . . .

The plague originated, so they say, in Ethiopia in upper Egypt, and spread from there into Egypt itself and Libya and much of the territory of the King of Persia. In the city of Athens it appeared suddenly, and the first cases were among the population of Piraeus, where there were no wells at that time, so that

it was supposed by them that the Peloponnesians had poisoned the reservoirs. Later, however, it appeared also in the upper city, and by this time the deaths were greatly increasing in number. . . .

Words indeed fail one when one tries to give a general picture of this disease; and as for the sufferings of individuals, they seemed almost beyond the capacity of human nature to endure. Here in particular is a point where this plague showed itself to be something quite different from ordinary diseases: though there were many dead bodies lying about unburied, the birds and animals that eat human flesh either did not come near them or, if they did taste the flesh, died of it afterwards. . . .

A factor which made matters much worse than they were already was the removal of people from the country into the city, and this particularly affected the incomers. There were no houses for them, and, living as they did during the hot season in badly ventilated huts, they died like flies. . . . For the catastrophe was so overwhelming that men, not knowing what would happen next to them, became indifferent to every rule of religion or of law. . . .

[Also] Athens owed to the plague the beginnings of a state of <u>unprecedented</u> lawlessness. Seeing how quick and abrupt were the changes of fortune which came to the rich who suddenly died and to those who had previously been penniless but now inherited their wealth, people now began openly to venture [take a chance] on acts of self-indulgence which before then they used to keep dark. . . . No fear of god or law of man had a restraining influence.

This, then, was the <u>calamity</u> which fell upon Athens. . . . At this time of distress people naturally recalled old oracles, and among them was a verse which the old men claimed had been delivered in the past and which said:

*War with the Dorians comes, and a death will come at the same time.*

. . . What was actually happening seemed to fit in well with the words of this oracle . . . the plague broke out directly after the Peloponnesian invasion, and never affected the Peloponnese at all, or not seriously; its full force was felt at Athens. . . ."

Source: *History of the Peloponnesian War,*
Thucydides

**Soldiers preparing for battle**

## Analyze Primary Sources: *Draw Conclusions*

1. What question was Thucydides trying to answer in this excerpt?

2. What does Thucydides tell the reader about his sources?

3. What is Thucydides' point of view on the events described in this excerpt?

4. What conclusions can you draw regarding the impact of the plague on Athenian society?

# Primary Source

# Republic to Empire: Julius Caesar

## Prepare to Read

### Standards Preview

**H-SS 6.7** Students analyze the geographic, political, economic, religious, and social structures during the development of Rome.

**Research, Evidence, and Point of View**

**2** Students distinguish fact from opinion in historical narratives and stories.

### Background

Julius Caesar remains a colorful and controversial historical figure. His achievements are many. Caesar served the Roman Republic as an accomplished orator, politician, general, and statesman.

In *Lives of the Caesars*, Roman historian Suetonius writes about Julius Caesar's life and character.

### Vocabulary *Builder*

**desist** (dih SIST) *v.* to stop doing something

**perpetuity** (pehr peh TOO ih tee) *n.* for all future time

**arrogance** (AIR oh gans) *n.* too much pride

**insolence** (IHN suh lehns) *n.* insulting behavior

---

When people spoke of him critically, he was content to urge in public that they should <u>desist</u>. He was able to carry with good grace the harm to his reputation caused by the most [unflattering or unkind] book written by Aulus and Caecina and the highly abusive poems of Pitholaus.

However, other things he did and said outweighed these, so that it is thought he abused his power and was justly killed. Not only did he accept excessive honors—one consulship after another, the dictatorship in <u>perpetuity</u>, responsibility for morals, as well as the . . . title "Father of his Fatherland," a statue displayed with those of the kings, and a raised seat at the theater—he even allowed privileges to be given to him which were greater than is right for mortals: a golden seat in the senate house and in front of the speaker's platform, a chariot . . . in the procession for the circus games, temples, altars, statues placed beside those of the gods . . . and a month of the year named after him. Indeed there were no honors which he did not either give to someone or receive as he willed.

His public sayings, as recorded by Titus Ampius, were characterized by equal <u>arrogance</u>: "The republic is nothing—just a name, without substance or form. . . ." "Men should now have more consideration in speaking with me and regard what I say as law." Such was the level of <u>insolence</u> he reached. . . .

. . . At the time of the Latin Festival he was returning to the city, among . . . demonstrations by the people, one member of the crowd had placed a laurel crown, bound with a white ribbon, on his statue and the tribunes . . . had given orders that the ribbon should be removed from the crown and that the man should be thrown into chains. Caesar, regretting, perhaps, that the reference to kingship had met with such a poor reception, or else, as he claimed, that he had been robbed of the glory to be had from refusing the honor, took the tribunes severely to task and deprived them of their authority. And after that time he was never able to shake off the rumor that his ambition was to take the title of king, even though, when the common people greeted him as king, he replied that he was not King but Caesar. . . .

Source: *Lives of the Caesars,* Suetonius

**Caesar crosses the Rubicon**

## Analyze Primary Sources: *Distinguish Facts From Opinions*

1. Which statements in this excerpt about Julius Caesar are facts?

2. Read the following passage. Which statements are facts and which are opinions?

   His public sayings, as recorded by Titus Ampius, were characterized by equal arrogance [self-importance]: "The republic is nothing—just a name, without substance or form. . . ." "Men should now have more consideration in speaking with me and regard what I say as law."

3. What opinion do you think Suetonius had of Julius Caesar?

4. What can historians learn from this historical narrative?

# The Government of the Roman Empire: The Persecution of Christians

## Prepare to Read

 **Standards Preview**

**H-SS 6.7** Students analyze the geographic, political, economic, religious, and social structures during the development of Rome.

**Research, Evidence, and Point of View**

**5** Students detect the different historical points of view on historical events and determine the context in which the historical statements were made (the questions asked, sources used, author's perspectives).

### Background

The Romans were tolerant of different religions. However, all Roman citizens had to honor the Roman gods and pay homage to the emperor. Christians, who worshiped only one god, often faced persecution. In the following letters, Pliny, a Roman governor, asks the emperor Trajan for advice about how to deal with the Christians.

### Vocabulary *Builder*

**repentance** (rih PEHN tens) *n.* sorrow for doing wrong

**denounce** (dih NOWNCE) *v.* accuse; give information against

**folly** (FAHL lee) *n.* being foolish; unwise behavior

**edict** (EE dihkt) *n.* a decree or order proclaimed by an authority that has the force of law

**warrant** (WOR ihnt) *v.* to be a good enough reason for something

## Pliny to Emperor Trajan

. . . I have never participated in trials of Christians. I therefore do not know what offenses it is the practice to punish or investigate, and to what extent. And I have been not a little hesitant as to whether there should be any distinction on account of age or no difference between the very young and the more mature; whether pardon is to be granted for repentance or, if a man has once been a Christian, it does him no good to have ceased to be one; whether the name itself, even without offenses, or only the offenses associated with the name are to be punished.

Meanwhile, in the case of those who were denounced to me as Christians, I have observed the following procedure: I [questioned] these as to whether they were Christians; those who confessed I interrogated a second and a third time, threatening them with punishment; those who persisted I ordered executed. For I had no doubt that, whatever the nature of their beliefs, . . . [they] surely deserved to be punished. There were others possessed of the same folly; but because they were Roman citizens, I signed an order for them to be transferred to Rome.

Soon accusations spread, as usually happens, because of the proceedings going on, and several incidents occurred. An anonymous [written by an unknown person] document was published containing the names of many persons. Those who denied that they were or had been Christians, when they prayed to the gods in words dictated by me, offered prayer . . . to your image, which I had ordered to be brought for this purpose together with statues of the gods, and moreover . . . none of . . .

those who are really Christians, it is said, can be forced to do—these I thought should be discharged. Others named by the informer declared that they were Christians, but then denied it, asserting that they had been but had ceased to be, some three years before, others many years, some as much as twenty-five years. They all worshiped your image and the statues of the gods, and cursed Christ.

They asserted, however . . . their fault . . . had been that they were accustomed to meet on a fixed day before dawn and sing . . . a hymn to Christ as to a god, and to bind themselves by oath. . . . When this was over, it was their custom to depart and to assemble again to partake of food. . . . Even this, they agreed to, they had ceased to do after my <u>edict</u> by which, in agreement with your instructions, I had forbidden political associations. . . . I discovered nothing but . . . excessive superstition.

I therefore postponed the investigation and hastened to consult you. For the matter seemed to me to <u>warrant</u> consulting you, especially because of the number involved. For many persons of every age, every rank, and also of both sexes are and will be endangered. For . . . this superstition has spread not only to the cities but also to the villages and farms. But it seems possible to check and cure it. It is certainly quite clear that . . . the established religious rites, long neglected, are being resumed. . . . Hence it is easy to imagine what a great number of people can be reformed if an opportunity for repentance is given.

Pliny

Emperor Trajan

## Trajan to Pliny

You observed proper procedure, my dear Pliny, in sifting the cases of those who had been denounced [formally accused] to you as Christians. For it is not possible to lay down any general rule to serve as a kind of fixed standard. They are not to be sought [gone after] out; if they are denounced and proved guilty, they are to be punished, with this reservation, that whoever denies that he is a Christian and really proves it—that is, by worshiping our gods—even though he was under suspicion in the past, shall obtain pardon through repentance. But anonymously posted accusations ought to have no place in any prosecution. For this is . . . out of keeping with the spirit of our age.

Source: *Ancestors: Medieval Sourcebook: Pliny on the Christians*

## Analyze Primary Sources: *Detect Point of View*

1. What problem was Pliny trying to solve in this excerpt?
2. What is Trajan's point of view on the prosecution of the Christians?
3. What information does Pliny give about his sources in the letter?
4. How might historians use these letters?

# For Further Reference

You will find numerous sources quoted in this textbook. The list on the following pages gives information about where you might find more information on those quoted passages.

**HT1** McCullough, David. *Why History?* New York: Simon & Schuster, 1996.

**83** Kramer, Samuel Noah. *Cradle of Civilization.* New York: Time-Life Books, 1967.

**85** Kramer, Samuel Noah. *The Sumerians: Their History, Cultures, and Character.* Chicago: University of Chicago Press, 1963.

**103** Brook, Lester. *Great Civilizations of Africa.* New York: Peter Bedrick Books, 1988.

**104** Healy, Mark. *Warrior Pharaoh: Ramses II and the Battle of Qadesh.* Oxford: Osprey Publishing, 2000.

**139** *The Holy Bible, Containing the Old and New Testaments: King James Version.* National Publishing Company, 2000 .

**141** *The Holy Bible, Containing the Old and New Testaments: King James Version.* National Publishing Company, 2000.

**168** Kalidasa, *Loom of Time: A Selection of His Plays and Poems.* Translated by Chandra Rajan. New York: Penguin Group, 1990.

**180** Time-Life Books Editors. *Barbarian Tides: 1500 BC–600 BC.* New York: Time-Life Custom Publishing, 1992.

**194** *Upanishads.* Translated by Patrick Olivelle. New York: Oxford University Press, 1993.

**198** *The Bhagavad Gita.* Translated by Barbara Stoler-Miller. New York: Columbia University Press, 1986.

**222** Nelson, Walter Henry. *Buddha: His Life and Teaching.* Itasca: Putnam Publishing, 2000.

**230** Wangu, Madhu Baaz. *Buddhism (World Religions Series).* New York: Facts on File, 1993.

**247** Kautilya. *The Arthashastra.* New Delhi: Penguin Books India, 1992.

**255** Hsien, Fa. *Record of the Buddhistic Kingdoms Being an Account by the Chinese Monk Fa-Hsien of His Travels in India.* Translated by James Legge. Whitefish: Kessinger Publishing, 2004.

**256** Kalidasa, *The Complete Works of Kalidasa.* New Delhi: Sahitya Akademi, 1997.

**288** *China: Readings on the Middle Kingdom.* Leon Hellerman and Alan L. Stein, editors. New York: Washington Square Press, 1971.

**301** Minford, John, and Lau, Joseph S. M. *Classical Chinese Literature.* New York: Columbia University Press, 2000.

**302** Ebrey, Patricia Buckley, ed. *Chinese Civilization and Society: A Source Book.* New York: Free Press, 1981.

**307** Confucius. *The Analects.* New York: Penguin USA, 1998.

**308** Confucius. *The Analects.* New York: Penguin USA, 1998.

**310** Confucius. *The Analects.* New York: Penguin USA, 1998.

**313** Ni, Maoshing. *The Yellow Emperor's Classic of Medicine: A New Translation of the Neijing Suwen with Commentary.* Halifax: Shambhala Press, 1995.

**330** Tzu, Sun, and Yang, Shang. *The Art of War/The Book of Lord Shang (Wordsworth Classics of World Literature).* Translated by J.J.L. Duyvendak and Robert Wilkinson. Hertfordshire: Wordsworth Publishing, 1999.

**335** Qian, Sima. *Records of the Grand Historian.* Translated by Burton Watson. New York: Columbia University Press, 1993.

**342** Swann, Dennis. *Pan Chao: Foremost Woman Scholar of China (Michigan Classics in Chinese Studies).* Ann Arbor: University of Michigan Center for Chinese Studies, 2001.

**367** Homer. *The Iliad.* Translated by Robert Fitzgerald. Anchor Books/Doubleday, 1974.

**368** McNeil, William H. *A History of the Human Community* (Prentice Hall: Englewood Cliffs, NJ, 1987).

**373** Xenophon. *Oeconomicus VII–XIII Bristol Greek Texts Series.* Bristol: Bristol Classical Texts, 1995.

**380** Graham, Craig, Kagan, Donald, and Ozment, Turner. *The Heritage of World Civilizations.* Upper Saddle River: Prentice Hall Higher Education Division, Pearson Education, 1999.

**380** Homer. *The Odyssey.* Translated by Martin Hammond. London: Duckworth Publishing, 2000.

**391** Plutarch. *The Lives of the Noble Grecians and Romans.* Translated by John Dryden and Arthur Hugh Clough. New York: Modern Library, 1957.

**394** Thucydides. *Pericles' Funeral Oration: Thucydides History of the Peloponnesian War.* New York: Modern Library, 1982.

**396** Thucydides. *Pericles' Funeral Oration: Thucydides History of the Peloponnesian War.* New York: Modern Library, 1982.

**398** Aristotle. *The Politics.* Translated by T. A. Sinclair and Trevor Saunders. New York: Penguin Classics, 1992.

**405** Talbert, Richard J. A. *Plutarch on Sparta.* New York: Penguin USA, 1998.

**419** Homer. *The Odyssey.* Translated by Martin Hammond. London: Duckworth Publishing, 2000.

**419** Barnstone, Willis. *Greek Lyric Poetry.* New York: Bantam Books, 1962.

**428** Sophocles. *Antigone, Oedipus the King, Electra (Oxford World's Classics).* Translated/edited by Edith Hall and H.D.F. Kitto. New York: Oxford University Press, 1998.

**429** *Aesop's Fables.* Translated and edited by S. A. Handford and Brian Robb. London: Puffin Books, 1996.

**431** Plato. *Apology.* Wauconda: Bolchazy-Carducci Publishers, 1997.

**434** Roberts, J. M. *History of the World to 1500.* New York: Knopf Publishers, 1976.

**435** Lloyd, G.E.R. *Hippocratic Writings.* New York: Penguin Books, 1984.

**485** Cicero, Marcus Tullius. *On the Commonwealth and On the Laws (Cambridge Texts in the History of Political Thought).* New York: Cambridge University Press, 1999.

**493** Polybius. *Polybius Histories.* Cambridge: Harvard University Press, 1979.

**521** **On-line:** Augustus, translated by Thomas Bushnell. "The Deeds of the Divine Augustus," Internet Classics Archive. **Print:** Southern, Pat. *Augustus (Roman Imperial Biographies).* London: Routledge Books, 2001.

**530** Herodotus. *The Histories (Penguin Classics).* Edited by John Marincola and Aubrey De Selincourt. New York: Penguin Books, 2003.

**532** Herodotus. *The Histories (Penguin Classics).* Edited by John Marincola and Aubrey De Selincourt. New York: Penguin Books, 2003.

**541** *The Holy Bible, Containing the Old and New Testaments: King James Version.* National Publishing Company, 2000.

**556** Tacitus, Cornelius. *The Annals of Imperial Rome (Penguin Classics).* New York: Penguin Books, 1956.

**573** Virgil. *The Aeneid (Penguin Classics).* Edited by W. F. Jackson Knight. New York: Penguin Books, 1956.

**574** Dryden, John. *Virgil's Aeneid (Penguin Classics).* New York: Penguin Books, 1997.

**574** Sullivan, David, and Veyne, Paul. *Seneca: The Life of a Stoic.* London: Routledge Books, 2002.

**574** Everett, Anthony. *Cicero: The Life and Times of Rome's Greatest Politician.* New York: Random House Trade Paperbacks, 2003.

**574** Ennius, Quintus, and Steuart, Ethel M. *The Annals of Quintus Ennius.* Oxford: Clarendon Press, 1912.

**574** Gibbon, Edward. *The History of the Decline and Fall of the Roman Empire (Penguin Classics).* New York: Penguin Books, 2001.

**576** Everett, Anthony. *Cicero: The Life and Times of Rome's Greatest Politician.* New York: Random House Trade Paperbacks, 2003.

**581** Tacitus, Cornelius. *The Agricola and the Germania (Penguin Classics).* New York: Penguin Books, 1971.

# English and Spanish Glossary

## A

**abandon** (uh BAN duhn) to leave, as in danger or out of necessity; desert (p. 404)
*abandonar* dejar, por peligro, por necesidad; desamparar

**academy** (uh KAD uh mee) school devoted to a particular subject (p. 429)
*academia* escuela dedicada a una materia en particular

**accompany** (uh KUHM puh nee) to go along with (p. 114)
*acompañar* ir junto con

**accomplish** (uh KAHM plihsh) to do; to succeed in doing; to complete (p. 330)
*lograr* hacer, tener éxito al hacer algo; terminar

**accurate** (AK yoor iht) correct; without mistakes (p. 121)
*exacto* correcto; sin errores

**acquire** (uh KWĪR) to get or gain by one's actions or efforts (p. 465)
*adquirir* obtener o ganar por medio de acciones o esfuerzos propios

**acropolis** (uh KRAHP uh lihs) upper part of a city (p. 367)
*acrópolis* la parte más alta de la ciudad

**adapt** (uh DAPT) to change a way of life; to make fit or suitable by changing or adjusting (pp. 20, 488, 572)
*adaptarse* cambiar su forma de vivir; hacer adecuado o idóneo por medio de cambios o ajustes

**afterlife** (AF tuhr līfe) life after death (p. 113)
*vida venidera* vida después de la muerte

**ahimsa** (uh HIHM sah) belief that one should not injure any living thing (p. 250)
*ahimsa* creencia en que no se debe lastimar a ningún ser vivo

**ally** (AL lī) member of an alliance (p. 458)
*aliado* integrante de una alianza

**alphabet** (AL fuh beht) small set of letters or symbols each of which stands for a single sound (p. 79)
*alfabeto* conjunto pequeño de símbolos o letras, cada una de las cuales representa un solo sonido

**anarchy** (AN uhr kee) disorder and confusion (p. 305)
*anarquía* desorden y confusión

**anatomy** (uh NAT uh mee) study of the body and its organs (p. 121)
*anatomía* estudio del cuerpo y sus órganos

**ancestor worship** (AN sehs tuhr WER shihp) practice of honoring the spirits of the dead (p. 304)
*culto a los antepasados* práctica que consiste en honrar los espíritus de los muertos

**annex** (uh NEHKS) to add (p. 377)
*anexar* agregar

**annual** (AN yoo uhl) taking place every year (p. 98)
*anual* que ocurre cada año

**apostle** (uh PAH suhl) disciple who would be sent out to spread Jesus' teachings (p. 545)
*apóstol* discípulo que sería enviado a difundir las enseñanzas de Jesús

**appealing** (uh PEEL ihng) attractive or interesting (p. 235)
*atrayente* que atrae o es interesante

**aqueduct** (AK wuh dukt) structure for carrying water across land (p. 569)
*acueducto* estructura que se usa para transportar agua a través del terreno

**arable land** (AR uh buhl land) land suitable for farming (p. 483)
*tierras de cultivo* terreno propio para la agricultura

**archaeology** (ahr kee AHL uh jee) study of human life in the past through examination of the things that people left behind (p. 6)

**arqueología** estudio de la vida humana en el pasado mediante la examinación de cosas u objetos que han dejado las personas

**architecture** (AHR kuh tehk cher) building design (p. 51)
*arquitectura* diseño de construcciones

**arid** (AR ihd) dry (p. 483)
*árido* seco

**aristocrat** (uh RIHS tuh krat) upper-class, wealthy landowner (p. 367)
*aristócrata* terrateniente rico y de clase alta

**artifact** (AHRT uh fakt) object made and used by humans (p. 7)
*artefacto* objeto elaborado y usado por seres humanos

**artisan** (AHRT uh zan) skilled worker who practices a trade or handicraft (p. 102)
*artesano* trabajador calificado que practica un oficio o artesanía

**ascetic** (uh SEHT ihk) person who practices extreme self-denial as part of a religious life (p. 220)
*asceta* persona que practica la negación extrema de sí mismo como parte de su vida religiosa

**assembly** (uh SEHM blee) group of persons who gather together for a common purpose (p. 393)
*asamblea* grupo de personas que se reúnen para un fin común

**astronomy** (uh STRAHN uh mee) study of stars and planets (p. 50)
*astronomía* estudio de las estrellas y los planetas

**authority** (uh THOR uh tee) right to control other people; power or right to give commands, take action, or make final decisions (pp. 100, 447)
*autoridad* derecho a controlar a otras personas; poder o derecho de dar órdenes, realizar acciones o tomar decisiones finales

**aware** (uh WEHR) realizing that something is true, exists, or is happening (p. 225)
*consciente* que se da cuenta de que algo es verdad, existe o está ocurriendo

## B

**baptism** (BAP tihz uhm) immersion in water (p. 539)
*bautizo* inmersión en agua

**barbarian** (bahr BER ee uhn) person without civilization (p. 82)
*bárbaro* persona no civilizada

**barracks** (BAR uhks) military housing (p. 403)
*cuartel* viviendas militares

**barter** (BAHR tuhr) trading system in which people exchange goods directly without using money (p. 70)
*trueque* sistema de comercio en el que las personas intercambian productos directamente sin usar dinero

**benefit** (BEHN uh fiht) good effect or advantage (p. 35)
*beneficio* buen efecto o ventaja

**bodhisattva** (boh dih SUHT vuh) enlightened ones who return to Earth after death to help others (p. 233)
*bodhisatva* iluminado que regresa a la Tierra después de su muerte para ayudar a otros

**bond** (bahnd) uniting or binding force; tie; to join together (pp. 303, 556)
*vínculo* fuerza que une o liga; lazo

**Brahman** (BRAH muhn) one supreme God (p. 194)
*Brahma* un dios supremo

**Brahmanism** (BRAH muhn ihz uhm) Vedic age religion (p. 193)
*brahmanismo* religión de la era Védica

**Buddhism** (BOO dihz uhm) religion based on the teachings of Siddhartha Gautama (p. 218)
*budismo* religión que se basa en las enseñanzas de Siddhartha Gautama

**bureaucracy** (byu RAH kruh see) system of government based on fixed rules carried out by appointed officials (p. 246)
*burocracia* sistema de gobierno que se basa en reglas fijas cuya ejecución está a cargo de funcionarios designados

## C

**capable** (KAY puh buhl) having the skill, power, or intelligence to do something; having ability; able to do things well; skilled (pp. 291, 306)
*competente* que tiene capacidad; que sabe hacer bien las cosas; diestro

**capacity** (kuh PAS ih tee) ability to do something (p. 371)
*capacidad* habilidad para hacer algo

**caste** (kast) fixed social class into which a person is born (p. 181)
*casta* clase social fija en la que ha nacido una persona

**caste system** (kast SIHS tuhm) social structure in which social class is inherited from one's parents (p. 181)
*sistema de castas* estructura social donde la clase social se hereda de los padres

**cataract** (KAT uh rakt) rocky rapids (p. 97)
*catarata* rápidos entre rocas

**cavalry** (KAV uhl ree) soldiers on horseback (p. 291)
*caballería* soldados montados a caballo

**central planning** (SEHN truhl PLAN ihng) planning carried out by a single strong government (p. 172)
*planificación central* planificación que lleva a cabo un único gobierno poderoso

**challenge** (CHAL uhnj) difficult task that needs special effort (p. 100)
*prueba* tarea difícil que exige un esfuerzo especial

**channel** (CHAN uhl) tubelike passage for liquids (p. 281)
*canal* paso en forma de tubo para líquidos

**chaos** (KAY ahs) total disorder and confusion (p. 289)
*caos* desorden y confusión totales

**chariot** (CHAR ee uht) wheeled war vehicle (p. 82)
*carro* vehículo de guerra con ruedas

**checks and balances** (cheks and BAL uhns ehz) means of keeping any one branch of a government from gaining more power than the others (p. 496)
*controles y equilibrio* medio para impedir que una rama cualquiera del gobierno adquiera más poder que las demás

**chorus** (KOR uhs) group of people who sing and dance (p. 425)
*coro* grupo de personas que canta y baila

**circumstances** (SER kuhm stan sehz) surrounding conditions (p. 255)
*circunstancias* condiciones que rodean una situación

**citizenship** (SIHT uh zuhn shihp) membership in a political community (p. 391)
*ciudadanía* pertenencia a una comunidad política

**city-state** (SIH tee stayt) city and the surrounding land and villages it controls (p. 69)
*ciudad-estado* ciudad y las tierras y aldeas bajo su dominio

**civic virtue** (SIH vihk VER choo) loving one's country more than oneself; willingness to serve one's country (p. 501)
*virtud cívica* amar a su país más que a uno mismo; disposición a servir al propio país

**civilization** (sihv ih luh ZAY shuhn) society that has cities, a well-organized government, and workers with specialized job skills (p. 42)
*civilización* sociedad que tiene ciudades, un gobierno bien organizado y trabajadores con destrezas laborales especializadas

# English and Spanish Glossary (continued)

civil law                                                                                    cultural diffusion

**civil law** (SIHV uhl law) body of
laws affecting citizens (p. 576)
***civil leyes*** conjunto de leyes
que afectan a los ciudadanos
de un país

**clan** (klan) group of families
descended from a common
ancestor (p. 500)
***clan*** grupo de familias que
descienden de un antepasado
común

**classical age** (KLAS ih kuhl ayj)
time of great advances that
affected the culture for
centuries to come (p. 254)
***época clásica*** período de
grandes adelantos que
influyeron en la cultura a lo
largo de muchos siglos
subsiguientes

**code** (kohd) set of written rules
or laws (p. 576)
***código*** conjunto de normas o
leyes escritas

**collapse** (kuh LAPS) act of breaking down, failing, or giving
way (p. 174)
***colapso*** acción de derrum-
barse, fracasar o ceder

**commandment** (kuh MAND
muhnt) order to do something
(p. 135)
***mandamiento*** orden de hacer
algo

**commerce** (KAHM ers) buying
and selling goods and services
(p. 106)
***comercio*** compra y venta de
bienes y servicios

**communication** (kuh myoo nih
KAY shuhn) act of giving or
exchanging information,
signals, or messages (p. 569)
***comunicación*** acción de dar o
intercambiar información,
señales o mensajes

**compassion** (kuhm PASH uhn)
loving concern for others (p.
232)
***compasión*** preocupación
desinteresada por otras
personas

**conclude** (kuh KLOOD) to decide
by reasoning (p. 313)

**concluir** decidir por razonamiento

**concrete** (KAHN kreet) building
material made by mixing small
stones and sand with limestone, clay, and water (p. 567)
***concreto*** material de construcción hecho de la mexcla de
piedras pequeñas y arena con
piedra caliza, arcilla y agua

**conduct** (KAHN duhkt) way that
one acts; behavior (p. 315)
***conducta*** forma de actuar;
comportamiento

**conflict** (KAHN flihkt) fight or
disagreement; strong disagreement between people or
groups (pp. 250, 539)
***conflicto*** lucha o desacuerdo;
fuerte desacuerdo entre
personas o grupos

**Confucianism** (kuhn FYOO shuhn
ihz uhm) teachings of
Confucius (p. 307)
***confucianismo*** enseñanzas de
Confucio

**conquest** (KAHN kwehst) result of
defeating and controlling
another person or group (p.
82)
***conquista*** tiene lugar cuando
una persona vence y domina a
otra

**consist** (kuhn SIHST) to be formed
or made up of (p. 167)
***consistir*** estar formado o
compuesto de algo

**constitution** (kahn stuh TOO
shuhn) set of laws and principles that form the basis for a
government (p. 495)
***constitución*** conjunto de
leyes y principios que son la
base de un gobierno

**construction** (kuhn STRUHK
shuhn) act or process of building or constructing (p. 527)
***construcción*** acción o proceso
de edificar

**consul** (KAHN suhl) one of several
of the highest officials in the
Roman government (p. 489)
***cónsul*** uno de varios
funcionarios de más alto rango
en el gobierno romano

**consult** (kuhn SUHLT) to seek an
opinion from or to ask the
advice of (p. 452)
***consultar*** pedir una opinión o
consejo

**contribute** (kuhn TRIHB yoot) to
help or give to an important
cause (p. 370)
***contribuir*** ayudar o donar a
una causa importante

**conversion** (kuhn VUHR zhuhn)
heartfelt change in one's
opinions or beliefs, especially
in religion (p. 554)
***conversión*** cambio sincero de
las opiniones o creencias
personales, en particular en
materia de religión

**corrupt** (kuh RUHPT) dishonest
(p. 579)
***corrupto*** deshonesto

**covenant** (KUH vuh nuhnt)
binding agreement (p. 134)
***pacto*** acuerdo jurídico

**crucifixion** (kroo suh FIHK shuhn)
act of nailing or tying a victim
to a large wooden cross and
leaving the person to hang
until dead (p. 542)
***crucifixión*** acción de clavar o
atar a una víctima a una cruz
grande de madera y dejarla
colgada hasta morir

**cultivation** (kuhl tuh VAY shuhn)
growing of grain and other
crops (p. 275)
***cultivo*** siembra y cuidado del
desarrollo de granos y otras
plantas

**cultural borrowing** (KUHL chuhr
uhl BAHR oh ihng) transfer of
ideas or customs from one
culture to another (p. 77)
***préstamo cultural*** transferen-
cia de ideas o costumbres de
una cultura a otra

**cultural diffusion** (KUHL chuhr
uhl dih FYOO zhuhn) spread of
culture from one center to
other places (p. 466)
***difusión cultural*** propa-
gación de la cultura de un
centro a otros lugares

**620**    Reference Section

**culture** (KUHL chuhr) way of life, ideas, customs, skills of a people or group that are passed along through generations (p. 13)
*cultura* estilo de vida, costumbres, destrezas, etc., de un pueblo o grupo que se trasmiten de generación en generación; ideas

**cuneiform** (kyoo NEE uh form) written language of Sumer (p. 76)
*cuneiforme* lenguaje escrito de Sumeria

**cycle** (SĪ kuhl) related events that happen again and again in the same order (p. 220)
*ciclo* sucesos relacionados que ocurren una y otra vez en el mismo orden

## D

**Dao** (dow) "a way," "a road," or "the way of nature" (p. 314)
*Tao* "una vía", "un camino" o "el modo de la naturaleza"

**Daoism** (DOW ihz uhm) ancient Chinese philosophy that emphasizes a simple and natural life (p. 312)
*taoísmo* antigua filosofía china que hace hincapié en una vida sencilla y natural

**debate** (dee BAYT) discussion or argument on a subject that people express different opinions about (p. 19)
*debate* sobre el cual la gente expresa diferentes opiniones; discusión acerca de un asunto

**debt bondage** (deht BAHN dihj) practice of enslaving people who cannot pay their debts (p. 491)
*servidumbre por deudas* práctica de esclavizar a las personas que no pueden pagar sus deudas

**decimal system** (DEHS uh muhl SIHS tuhm) counting system based on units of 10 (p. 258)
*sistema decimal* sistema de conteo que se basa en unidades de 10

**deity** (DEE uh tee) being with supernatural powers (p. 414)
*deidad* ser con poderes sobrenaturales

**delta** (DEHL tuh) area of soil deposited at the mouth of a river (p. 98)
*delta* área cubierta de suelo depositado en la desembocadura de un río

**democracy** (dih MAHK ruh see) rule by the people (p. 390)
*democracia* gobierno en el que participa el pueblo

**descendant** (dee SEHN dehnt) someone related to a person who lived a long time ago (p. 134)
*descendiente* persona emparentada con otra que vivió hace mucho tiempo

**dharma** (DAHR muh) what Hindus call living a moral life (p. 197)
*dharma* lo que los hindúes conocen como una vida moralmente buena

**Diaspora** (dī AS puh ruh) communities of Jews living away from their ancient homeland (p. 147)
*Diáspora* comunidades de judíos que viven lejos de su antigua patria

**dictator** (DIHK tayt uhr) ruler with unlimited power (p. 494)
*dictador* gobernante con poderes ilimitados

**dike** (dīk) wall to hold back water (p. 281)
*dique* muro que sirve para contener agua

**direct democracy** (duh REHKT dih MAHK ruh see) political system in which citizens participate directly in government decision making (p. 397)
*democracia directa* sistema político en el que los ciudadanos participan directamente en las decisiones del gobierno

**disciple** (dih SĪ puhl) close follower of Jesus (p. 541)

*discípulo* seguidor cercano de Jesús

**dissect** (dī SEKT) to cut open (p. 571)
*disecar* hacer un corte para abrir

**distinct** (dihs TIHNKT) different or separate (p. 547)
*definido* diferente o aparte

**divine** (duh VĪN) meaning god or godlike (p. 484)
*divino* referente o parecido a un dios

**domesticate** (doh MEHS tih kayt) to change the behavior of a population of animals or plants in ways that are useful for humans (p. 33)
*domesticar* cambiar el comportamiento de una población de animales o plantas de forma que sean útiles para los seres humanos

**double-crop** (DUHB uhl krahp) to raise two crops on the same land within a year (p. 98)
*cultivo doble* obtener dos cosechas de un mismo terreno en un solo año

**drain** (drayn) to empty the waters of a river or stream (p. 275)
*desaguar* vaciar las aguas de un río o arroyo

**drama** (DRAH muh) play or performance on stage (p. 425)
*drama* obra de teatro o representación en un escenario

**dynasty** (DĪ nuhs tee) ruling family (p. 281)
*dinastía* familia gobernante

## E

**economy** (ih KAHN uh mee) production, distribution, and use of goods and services (p. 41)
*economía* producción, distribución y uso de bienes y servicios

**efficient** (eh FIHSH uhnt) working well (p. 246)
*eficiente* que trabaja bien

**empire** (EHM pīr) group of countries or peoples ruled by one government (p. 82)
*imperio* grupo de países o pueblos sometidos a un solo gobierno

**enable** (ehn AY buhl) to make possible (p. 361)
*posibilitar* hacer posible

**enlightenment** (ehn LĪT uhn muhnt) state of perfect wisdom (p. 221)
*iluminación* estado de sabiduría perfecta

**environment** (ehn VĪ ruhn muhnt) surroundings (p. 20)
*medio ambiente* entorno; alrededores

**ephor** (EHF or) official who works as a government watchdog (p. 401)
*efor* funcionario que actuaba como guardián al servicio del gobierno

**epic poem** (EHP ihk POH uhm) long story of heroes and history told in verse (p. 194)
*poema épico* relato largo en verso sobre héroes e historia

**epistle** (ee PIHS uhl) letter written to the churches founded by apostles and other early leaders of the Christian church (p. 546)
*epístola* carta a las iglesias escrita por un apóstol u otro de los primeros dirigentes de la iglesia cristiana

**establish** (uh STAB lihsh) to set up; to start (p. 101)
*establecer* montar; poner en marcha

**established religion** (uh STAB lihsht rih LIHJ uhn) set of religious beliefs shared by everyone in a society (p. 44)
*religión establecida* conjunto de creencias religiosas que comparten todos los miembros de una sociedad

**estate** (eh STAYT) plots of land; individually owned large property maintained by great wealth (pp. 370, 516)
*finca* extensión de tierras; propiedad grande que pertenece a una sola persona y cuyo mantenimiento exige mucho dinero

**ethical** (EHTH ih kuhl) behavior based on ideas of right and wrong (p. 132)
*ético* comportamiento que se basa en las ideas de lo que está bien y lo que está mal

**ethnic group** (EHTH nihk groop) group of people who share a distinctive culture and a sense of identity (p. 204)
*grupo étnico* grupo de personas que comparten una cultura distintiva y un sentido de identidad

**exile** (EHK sīl) separation from one's homeland (p. 146)
*exilio* separación de la tierra donde uno nació

**expand** (ehk SPAND) to become or make larger in size or scope (p. 109)
*expandir* hacer más grande en cuanto a tamaño o alcance

**expedition** (ehks puh DIHSH uhn) journey or trip taken for a special purpose (p. 107)
*expedición* viaje o recorrido que se hace con un propósito especial

**export** (ehk SPORT) to send goods to another land for sale (p. 172)
*exportar* enviar productos a otro país para venderlos

**expose** (ehk SPOHZ) to allow to be seen; to reveal; to display (p. 21)
*exponer* permitir que algo sea visto; revelar; exhibir

**extended family** (ehk STEHN dihd FAM uh lee) family with several generations living together (p. 301)
*familia extensa* familia en la que viven juntas varias generaciones

# F

**fable** (FAY buhl) short story with a moral, or lesson, at the end (p. 256)
*fábula* relato corto con una moraleja o lección al final

**feature** (FEE cher) distinct or outstanding part, quality, or characteristic of something (p. 418)
*rasgo* parte, cualidad o característica definida o sobresaliente de algo

**fertile** (FERT uhl) producing vegetation or crops abundantly (p. 168)
*fértil* que produce vegetación o cosechas en abundancia

**filial piety** (FIHL ee uhl PĪ uh tee) unending devotion of children, especially sons, to their parents and family (p. 309)
*piedad filial* la devoción sin límite de los niños, en especial los hijos, a sus padres y familia

**fleet** (fleet) group of ships (p. 379)
*flota* grupo de barcos

**focus** (FOH kuhs) to direct one's thoughts or efforts; to concentrate (p. 493)
*enfocar* dirigir los pensamientos o esfuerzos propios; concentrar

**fossil** (FAHS uhl) remains or imprints of living things that existed millions of years ago (p. 7)
*fósil* restos o huellas de seres vivos que existieron hace millones de años

**found** (fownd) to start a city or an organization (p. 40)
*fundar* dar comienzo a una ciudad o a una organización

**foundation** (fown DAY shuhn) basic idea, principle, or situation; fundamental principle on which something is founded; basis (pp. 342, 431)
*fundamento* idea, principio o situación básica; principio fundamental sobre el que se funda algo; base

**founder** (FOWN duhr) person who founds, or establishes, something (p. 575)
*fundador* persona que funda o establece algo

**frieze** (freez) horizontal band (p. 424)
*friso* banda horizontal

# G

**generation** (jehn uhr AY shuhn) group of family members born and living at about the same time (p. 300)
*generación* grupo de miembros de una familia que nacieron y viven aproximadamente al mismo tiempo

**granary** (GRAN uh ree) special building used to hold grain (p. 172)
*granero* edificio especial donde se guarda grano

**gravitas** (GRAV ih tahs) serious, dignified way of behaving (p. 501)
*gravedad* modo de comportarse con seriedad y dignidad

**gravity** (GRAV ih tee) force that tends to draw all bodies in Earth's sphere toward the center of Earth (p. 501)
*gravedad* fuerza que tiende a atraer hacia el centro de la Tierra todos los cuerpos que se hallan en la esfera terrestre

**Greco-Roman culture** (GREK oh ROH muhn KUHL chuhr) coming together of Greek and Roman cultural traditions (p. 528)
*cultura grecorromana* encuentro de las tradiciones culturales griega y romana

**guru** (GOO roo) thinker and teacher (p. 194)
*gurú* pensador y maestro

# H

**helot** (HEHL uht) conquered person (p. 377)
*helot* persona conquistada

**hieroglyph** (HĪ er oh glihf) symbol that can represent a word, an idea, or a sound (p. 50)
*jeroglífico* símbolo que representa una palabra, idea o sonido

**Hindu-Arabic numerals** (HIHN doo AR uh bihk NOO muhr uhlz) numerals 0 through 9 (p. 258)
*números indoarábigos* los números del 0 al 9

**Hinduism** (HIHN doo ihz uhm) religion of the people of India (p. 192)
*hinduismo* religión de los pueblos de India

**Homo sapiens** (HOH moh SAY pee ehnz) first modern humans (p. 14)
*Homo sapiens* los primeros seres humanos modernos

**hunter-gatherers** (HUHNT er GATH er erz) people who lived by hunting small animals and gathering plants (p. 12)
*cazadores recolectores* personas que vivían de cazar animales pequeños y recolectar plantas

# I

**ideograph** (ihd ee oh GRAF) symbol for a word (p. 284)
*ideograma* símbolo que representa una palabra

**import** (ihm PORT) to bring goods in from another land (p. 172)
*importar* traer productos de otro país

**impress** (ihm PREHS) to have a marked effect on the mind or emotions (p. 570)
*impresionar* producir un importante efecto en la mente o emociones de otra persona

**impressive** (ihm PREHS ihv) causing admiration (p. 51)
*impresionante* que provoca admiración

**income** (IHN kuhm) money that you earn from working (p. 579)
*ingreso* dinero que se gana por hacer un trabajo

**individual** (ihn duh VIHJ oo uhl) existing as a single, separate thing or being (p. 425)
*individual* que existe como una sola cosa o ser separado de los demás

**inflation** (ihn FLAY shuhn) general rise in the cost of goods (p. 580)
*inflación* aumento general en el costo de los bienes

**initial** (ih NIHSH uhl) having to do with, indicating, or occurring at the beginning (p. 491)
*inicial* que tiene que ver con, indica u ocurre en el comienzo

**innovation** (ihn uh VAY shuhn) new way of doing something (p. 12)
*innovación* forma nueva de hacer ciertas cosas

**intelligent** (ihn TEHL uh juhnt) having or using intelligence (p. 15)
*inteligente* que tiene inteligencia o la usa

**interior** (in TIR ee uhr) area of land away from the coast (p. 97)
*interior* área de tierra alejada de la costa

**interpret** (ihn TER pruht) to explain the meaning of; to make understandable (p. 284)
*interpretar* explicar el significado de algo; hacer comprensible

**invade** (ihn VAYD) to enter forcibly or with hostility; to come into as an enemy (p. 582)
*invadir* entrar de manera forzada o con hostilidad; entrar como enemigo

**irrigate** (IR uh gayt) to bring water to; to water or moisten (p. 467)
*irrigar* llevar agua a un lugar; regar o humedecer

**irrigation** (ir uh GAY shuhn) system for watering crops (p. 68)
*irrigación* sistema para regar cultivos

**isthmus** (IHS muhs) narrow strip of land that connects two larger bodies of land (p. 360)
*istmo* franja estrecha de tierra que comunica dos masas más grandes de tierra

Judaism

material

## J

**Judaism** (JOO day ihz uhm) religion of the Jewish people (p. 133)
*judaísmo* religión de los judíos

**judge** (juhj) among the Israelites, a warrior or prophet who could inspire an army of volunteers to defend their land (p. 143)
*juez* entre los israelitas, guerrero o profeta capaz de servir de inspiración a un ejército de voluntarios para defender su tierra

**jury** (JOOR ee) group of people who hear evidence and decide a court case (p. 394)
*jurado* grupo de personas que atienden a las pruebas y deciden sobre una causa judicial

**justice** (JUHS tihs) fair treatment (p. 142)
*justicia* trato equitativo

## K

**karma** (KAHR muh) sum of a person's actions and consequences, words, and thoughts (p. 199)
*karma* suma de los actos, palabras y pensamientos de una persona y de sus consecuencias

**kingship** (KIHNG shihp) government headed by a king (p. 73)
*reino* gobierno encabezado por un rey

## L

**launch** (lawnch) to send forth with some force; to set in operation (p. 459)
*lanzar* propulsar con cierta fuerza; comenzar el funcionamiento

**law code** (law kohd) written set of laws (p. 74)
*código jurídico* conjunto de leyes

**layer** (LAY uhr) single thickness, coat, or fold (p. 7)
*capa* espesor, recubrimiento o pliegue individual

**legal** (LEE guhl) created by, based upon, or authorized by the law (p. 501)
*legal* referente a, creado por, basado en o autorizado por la ley

**Legalism** (LEE guhl ihz uhm) belief that a strong legal system, not moral values, was the key to social order in China (p. 305)
*legalismo* creencia de que un sistema jurídico fuerte, y no los valores morales, fue la clave del orden social en China

**leisure** (LEE zhuhr) free and unoccupied; spare time (p. 395)
*ocioso* libre y sin ocupación; tiempo de sobra

**link** (lihngk) to join together with or as with a link (p. 485)
*enlazar* unir con o como con un lazo

**location** (loh KAY shuhn) particular place or position (p. 359)
*ubicación* lugar en particular o posición

**loess** (LOH ehs) fine yellow dust (p. 275)
*loess* polvo amarillo fino

**logic** (LAHJ ihk) system of reasoning (p. 429)
*lógica* sistema de razonamiento

**luxury** (LUHK shuh ree) something expensive that you want but do not need (p. 219)
*lujo* algo costoso que uno desea pero no necesita

**luxury goods** (LUHK shuh ree gudz) goods that people do not need, but that make life more enjoyable in some way (p. 107)
*artículos de lujo* productos que la gente no necesita, pero que hacen la vida más placentera de alguna forma

**lyric poetry** (LIHR ihk POH uh tree) poetic songs (p. 425)
*poesía lírica* cantos poéticos

## M

**mainland** (MAYN land) part of a country that is attached to a continent, as compared to its offshore islands (p. 360)
*tierra firme* parte de un país que forma parte de un continente, a diferencia de sus islas del litoral

**maintain** (mayn TAYN) to provide what is needed to make something continue; to keep in good condition (pp. 44, 251)
*dar mantenimiento* suministrar lo que se necesita para que algo continúe; conservar en buenas condiciones

**magistrate** (MAJ ihs trayt) main official of the Roman Republic (p. 494)
*magistrado* funcionario principal de la República Romana

**major** (MAY juhr) greater in importance or rank (p. 394)
*principal* de mayor importancia o rango

**Mandate of Heaven** (MAN dayt uhv HEHV uhn) Chinese belief that heaven was a supreme force of nature that gave dynasties the right to rule (p. 287)
*Mandato del Cielo* los chinos creían que el cielo era una fuerza suprema de la naturaleza que confería a las dinastías el derecho a gobernar

**martyr** (MAHRT uhr) person who is remembered because of being put to death for his or her beliefs (p. 556)
*mártir* persona a la que se recuerda porque perdió la vida por sus creencias

**material** (muh TIR ee uhl) what a thing is, or may be, made of (p. 8)
*material* aquello de lo que una cosa está o puede estar hecha

**medical** (MEHD ih kuhl) relating to medicine and the treatment of disease or injury (p. 258)
*médico* referente a la medicina y al tratamiento de las enfermedades o lesiones

**meditate** (MEHD uh tayt) to calm or empty the mind, often by focusing on a single object (p. 220)
*meditar* calmar o vaciar la mente, con frecuencia concentrándose en un solo objeto

**Mediterranean climate** (mehd uh tuh RAY nee uhn CLĪ muht) climate that features mild, wet winters and hot, dry summers (p. 361)
*clima mediterráneo* clima en el que los inviernos son húmedos y templados, y los veranos son calurosos y secos

**messiah** (muh SĪ uh) anointed leader (p. 538)
*mesías* dirigente ungido

**metallurgy** (MEHT uh ler jee) science that deals with extracting metal from ore and using it to create useful objects (p. 259)
*metalurgia* ciencia que se ocupa de la extracción de metales de las menas y de su uso para elaborar objetos útiles

**method** (MEHTH uhd) way of doing anything; procedure; process (p. 429)
*método* forma de hacer cualquier cosa; modo; procedimiento; proceso

**migrate** (MĪ grayt) to move from one place to another; to change location (p. 206)
*emigrar* mudarse de un lugar a otro; cambiar de ubicación

**migration** (mī GRAY shuhn) movement of people from their homeland to other places; the movement of a large group from one area to another (pp. 19, 364)
*migración* movimiento de personas de su tierra natal a otros lugares; movimiento de un grupo grande de una región a otra

**military state** (MIHL uh tehr ee stayt) state that is organized primarily for the purpose of waging war (p. 402)
*estado militar* estado organizado principalmente con la finalidad de hacer la guerra

**missionary** (MIHSH uhn ehr ee) person who goes to another place to teach about his or her religion (p. 231)
*misionero* persona que va a otro lugar a enseñar su religión

**modify** (MAHD uh fī) to change or alter (p. 33)
*modificar* cambiar o alterar

**moksha** (MAHK shuh) to release from life (p. 197)
*moksha* liberar de la vida

**monarchy** (MAHN ahr kee) government headed by a king or queen (p. 364)
*monarquía* gobierno encabezado por un rey o reina

**monastery** (MAHN uh stehr ee) home of a religious community (p. 226)
*monasterio* hogar de una comunidad religiosa

**money supply** (MUHN ee suh PLĪ) total amount of money in an economy (p. 579)
*masa monetaria* cantidad total de dinero en una economía

**monk** (muhngk) man who lives in a monastery (p. 226)
*monje* hombre que vive en un monasterio

**monotheism** (MAHN oh thee ihz uhm) belief that there is only one God (p. 132)
*monoteísmo* creencia de que hay un solo Dios

**monsoon** (mahn SOON) seasonal wind pattern (p. 168)
*monzón* modalidad estacional de los vientos

**mosaic** (moh ZAY ihk) design formed with small tiles of glass, stone, or pottery (p. 566)
*mosaico* diseño formado con

pequeños pedazos de cristal, piedras o cerámica

**mummy** (MUH mee) dead body preserved by a special process (p. 113)
*momia* cadáver conservado mediante un procedimiento especial

**muse** (myooz) often refers to the inspiration for a creative artist (p. 416)
*musa* se suele usar para referirse a la inspiración de un artista creativo

**mythology** (mih THAHL uh jee) collection of stories that people tell about their history and their gods (p. 416)
*mitología* conjunto de relatos que los pueblos cuentan acerca de su historia y de sus dioses

## N

**natural barrier** (NACH er uhl BEHR ee er) geographic feature that makes travel and communication difficult or dangerous (p. 167)
*barrera natural* accidente geográfico que dificulta o hace peligrosos los viajes y la comunicación

**navigate** (NAV uh gayt) to make one's way (p. 486)
*navegar* avanzar en un recorrido

**Neanderthals** (nee AN der thawlz) group of people that appeared in Europe and parts of Asia about 200,000 years ago (p. 14)
*neandertales* grupo de gente que apareció en Europa y en partes de Asia hace unos 200,000 años

**network** (NEHT werk) arrangement or system of things, such as roads and canals, that connect with or cross one another (p. 527)
*red* arreglo o sistema de comunicación como caminos y canales, que se enlazan o se cruzan unas con otras

**nirvana** (nihr VAH nuh) state of blissful peace without desire or suffering (p. 226)
***nirvana*** estado de paz gozosa sin deseos ni sufrimiento

**nomad** (NOH mad) person who moves from place to place with the seasons (p. 13)
***nómada*** persona que se trasladaba de un lugar a otro con las estaciones

**nun** (nuhn) woman who lives in a religious community (p. 226)
***monja*** mujer que vive en una comunidad religiosa

**oblige** (uh BLĪJ) to compel by moral, legal, or physical force; to constrain (p. 404)
***compeler*** obligar por medio de la fuerza moral, jurídica o física; obligar

**occupy** (AH kyoo pī) to live, to exist, or to stay in a particular place (p. 341)
***ocupar*** vivir, existir o permanecer en un lugar en particular

**oligarchy** (AHL ih gahr kee) government in which most political power is held by a small segment of society (p. 388)
***oligarquía*** gobierno en el que un segmento pequeño de la sociedad posee casi todo el poder político

**oracle** (OR uh kuhl) person who predicts what will happen in the future (p. 419)
***oráculo*** persona que predice lo que ocurrirá en el futuro

**oracle bones** (AWR uh kuhl bohnz) animal bones carved with written characters, which were used to tell the future (p. 284)
***huesos de oráculo*** huesos de animal con caracteres grabados, los cuales se usaban para predecir el futuro

**oratory** (OR uh tor ee) art of making great speeches (p. 574)
***oratoria*** arte de dar grandes discursos

## P

**papyrus** (puh PĪ ruhs) reed that grows along the Nile (p. 123)
***papiro*** junco que crece a lo largo del Nilo

**parable** (PAR uh buhl) story with a religious moral (p. 546)
***parábola*** relato con moraleja religiosa

**patriarchal** (pay tree AHR kuhl) refers to a society centered around men, with descent traced through male family members (p. 498)
***patriarcal*** se refere a una sociedad centrada en torno a hombres, cuya ascendencia se sigue a través de los integrantes varones de la familia

**patrician** (puh TRIHSH uhn) member of the upper class of Roman society (p. 490)
***patricio*** miembro de la clase más alta de la sociedad romana

**patriotism** (PAY tree uh tihz uhm) feeling of love and support for one's country (p. 573)
***patriotismo*** sentimiento de amor y apoyo al país propio

**Pax Romana** (pahks roh MAH nuh) long period of peace and prosperity in the Roman Empire (p. 521)
***Pax Romana*** largo período de paz y prosperidad en el Imperio Romano

**pediment** (PEHD ih muhnt) in architecture, a triangular section that rises above the main entrance (p. 424)
***frontón*** en arquitectura, sección triangular que se alza por encima de la entrada principal

**peninsula** (puh NIHN suh luh) body of land surrounded on three sides by water (p. 359)
***península*** masa de tierra rodeada de agua en tres de sus costados

**persecute** (PUR sih kyoot) to treat someone unfairly for his or her beliefs (p. 552)

***perseguir*** tratar injustamente a alguien por sus creencias

**phalanx** (FAY langks) formation of heavily armed soldiers who move together as a unit (p. 389)
***falange*** formación de soldados fuertemente armados que se movían juntos como una unidad

**pharaoh** (FAIR oh) ruler of Egypt (p. 101)
***faraón*** gobernante de Egipto

**philosophy** (fih LAHS uh fee) set of beliefs about how to live (p. 312)
***filosofía*** conjunto de creencias acerca de cómo se debe vivir

**pictograph** (PIHK tuh graf) picture that represents an object (p. 78)
***pictografía*** imágenes que representan objetos

**pilgrim** (PIHL grihm) someone who travels to a shrine or sacred place (p. 208)
***peregrino*** persona que viaja a un santuario o lugar sagrado

**plebeian** (plih BEE uhn) common people of Rome (p. 490)
***plebeyo*** habitante común de Roma

**policy** (PAHL uh see) principle, plan, or course of action pursued by a government or an organization (p. 329)
***política*** principio, plan o método de acción que sigue un gobierno u organización

**politics** (PAHL uh tihks) art and practice of government (p. 367)
***política*** arte y práctica de gobernar

**polytheism** (PAHL ih thee ihz uhm) worship of many gods (p. 72)
***politeísmo*** culto a muchos dioses

**populate** (PAHP yuh layt) become inhabitants of (p. 18)
***poblar*** convertirse en habitantes de

**population** (pahp yuh LAY shuhn) number of people (p. 69)
***población*** número de habitantes

**predict** (pree DIHKH) to say in advance what one believes will happen (p. 73)
**predecir** decir anticipadamente lo que uno piensa que ocurrirá

**prehistory** (pree HIHS tuh ree) time before written records (p. 6)
**prehistoria** tiempos anteriores a la existencia de registros escritos

**previous** (PREE vee uhs) happening or existing before a particular event, time, or thing (p. 227)
**previo** que ocurre o existe antes de un acontecimiento, momento o cosa en particular

**principle** (PRIHN suh puhl) rule of conduct (p. 310)
**principio** regla de conducta

**promote** (proh MOHT) to raise or advance to a higher position or rank (p. 519)
**ascender** elevar o avanzar a una posición o rango más elevado

**prophet** (PRAHF iht) person chosen by God to bring truth to a ruler and the people (p. 139)
**profeta** persona elegida por Dios para llevar la verdad a un gobernante y al pueblo

**province** (PRAHV ihns) district or region of a country with its own government bureaucracy (p. 247)
**provincia** distrito o región de un país que tiene su propia burocracia gubernamental

**pyramid** (PIR uh mihd) structure with a flat base and sides shaped like triangles (p. 51)
**pirámide** estructura de base plana y lados con forma de triángulo

## R

**rabbi** (RAB ī) teacher (p. 147)
**rabino** maestro

**reason** (REE zuhn) power to think in a clear manner (p. 429)
**razón** poder de pensar con claridad

**reform** (rih FORM) movement aimed at removing political or social abuses (p. 517)
**reforma** movimiento encaminado a acabar con los abusos políticos o sociales

**reincarnation** (ree ihn kahr NAY shuhn) rebirth of a soul in a new body (p. 198)
**reencarnación** renacimiento de un alma en un cuerpo nuevo

**reject** (rih JEHKT) to refuse to accept, believe in, or agree with something (pp. 223, 553)
**rechazar** negarse a aceptar, creer o estar de acuerdo con algo

**rely** (rih LĪ) to depend on (p. 171)
**contar con** depender de

**representative democracy** (rehp ruh ZEHN tuh tihv dih MAHK ruh see) government in which citizens elect others to represent them in government (p. 398)
**democracia representativa** gobierno en el cual los ciudadanos eligen a personas que los representan en el gobierno

**republic** (rih PUHB lihk) government in which citizens have the right to vote and elect officials (p. 489)
**república** gobierno en el que los ciudadanos tienen derecho a votar y a elegir funcionarios

**resource** (REE sors) supply of something that can be used as needed (p. 42)
**recurso** abasto de algo que se puede usar según se necesite

**resurrection** (reh zuh REHK shuhn) idea that a godly person who dies will be raised from the dead and live with God forever (p. 539)
**resurección** idea de que una persona piadosa que ha muerto se alzará de entre los muertos y vivirá con Dios para siempre

**revolution** (rehv uh LOO shuhn) complete change in ways of thinking, working, or living (p. 36)
**revolución** cambio total en las formas de pensar, trabajar y vivir

**ritual** (RIHCH yoo uhl) ceremony enacted in the same way time after time; set of actions done in a specific way (pp. 101, 140)
**ritual** ceremonia que se celebra del mismo modo una y otra vez; conjunto de acciones que se llevan a cabo de una forma específica

**rival** (RĪ vuhl) competitor (p. 458)
**rival** competidor

**rivalry** (RĪ vuhl ree) competition (p. 458)
**rivalidad** competencia

**river system** (RIHV er SIHS tuhm) main river and all of its branches (p. 167)
**sistema fluvial** río importante y todos sus ramales

**role** (rohl) function or office assumed by someone or something (p. 485)
**papel** función o cargo que asume una persona o cosa

## S

**saint** (saynt) someone who is very good, kind, or patient (p. 221)
**santo** persona muy bondadosa, amable o paciente

**salvation** (sal VAY shuhn) escape; saved (p. 220)
**salvación** escape; asegurado

**scheme** (skeem) carefully arranged, systematic program of action (p. 523)
**plan** programa de acción sistemático arreglado cuidadosamente

**scribe** (skrīb) person trained to write and keep records in ancient times (p. 72)
**escriba** persona capacitada para escribir y llevar registros en la antigüedad

**scriptures** (SKRIHP chuhrz) sacred writings (p. 138)
**escrituras** escritos sagrados

**sculpture** (SKUHLP cher) statue made of clay, stone, or other material (p. 120)
**escultura** figura de arcilla, piedra u otros materiales

**sect** (sehkt) smaller religious group that has broken away from a larger established religion (p. 205)
**secta** grupo religioso más pequeño que se ha separado de una religión establecida más grande

**shift** (shihft) to replace by another or others; to change or exchange (p. 180)
**mudar** sustituir por otro u otros; cambiar o intercambiar

**shrine** (shrīn) place of worship that is often dedicated to a sacred object or person (p. 205)
**santuario** lugar de culto que suele estar consagrado a un objeto sagrado o persona

**site** (sīt) location for building (p. 378)
**emplazamiento** lugar para construir

**slavery** (SLAY vuhr ee) ownership and control of other people as property (p. 371)
**esclavitud** posesión y control de otras personas en calidad de propiedad

**social class** (SOH shuhl klas) a certain group of people that occupy rank or level in society (p. 44)
**clase social** grupo que ocupa un cierto rango o nivel en la sociedad

**source** (sors) place where something begins (p. 97)
**fuente** lugar donde algo comienza

**specialize** (SPEHSH uhl īz) to spend most of the time working at a craft (p. 37)
**especializarse** dedicar la mayor parte del tiempo a trabajar en un oficio

**stable currency** (STAY buhl KER uhn see) currency that does not change much in value over time (p. 528)
**divisa estable** divisa o moneda cuyo valor no cambia mucho con el paso del tiempo

**status** (STAT uhs) person's rank or position in a society (p. 370)
**condición social** rango o posición de una persona en una sociedad

**steppe** (stehp) dry grass-covered plain (p. 276)
**estepa** llanura seca cubierta de pastos

**strategy** (STRAT uh jee) long-term plan for achieving a goal (p. 245)
**estrategia** plan de largo plazo para alcanzar una meta

**structure** (STRUHK cher) how parts connect to form a whole (p. 49)
**estructura** forma en que las partes se unen para formar un todo

**subcontinent** (SUHB kahnt uhn uhnt) large landmass that is smaller than a continent (p. 166)
**subcontinente** masa continental grande más pequeña que un continente

**subject** (SUHB jehkt) people under a ruler's control (p. 247)
**súbdito** persona bajo el dominio de un gobernante

**supreme** (suh PREEM) highest in rank, power, or authority; dominant (p. 415)
**supremo** lo que ocupa el lugar más alto en cuanto a rango, poder, autoridad; dominante

**surplus** (SER pluhs) more than what is needed (p. 37)
**superávit** más de lo necesario

**symbol** (SIHM buhl) written or printed mark, letter, or abbreviation that stands for something else (p. 15)
**símbolo** marca, letra o abreviatura escrita o impresa que representa otra cosa

**synagogue** (SIH nuh gahg) meeting place (p. 147)
**sinagoga** lugar de reunión

## T

**tactic** (TAK tihk) method used to achieve a short-term goal, such as winning a battle (p. 513)
**táctica** método para alcanzar una meta de corto plazo, por ejemplo, ganar una batalla

**technology** (tehk NAH luh jee) application of human intelligence to problems to create new and better ways of doing things (p. 74)
**tecnología** aplicación de la inteligencia humana a los problemas para idear formas nuevas y mejores de hacer las cosas

**tenant farmer** (TEHN uhnt FAHR muhr) person who pays rent, in either money or crops, to farm another person's land (p. 370)
**agricultor arrendatario** persona que paga un alquiler, ya sea en dinero o en producto cosechado, por cultivar las tierras de otra persona

**terrify** (TEHR uh fī) to frighten greatly (p. 245)
**aterrorizar** asustar mucho

**text** (tehkst) words in a piece of writing (p. 192)
**texto** palabras de un escrito

**theory** (THEE uh ree) branch of an art or science consisting of a knowledge of its principles and methods rather than of its practice (p. 497)
**teoría** rama de un arte o ciencia que consiste en el conocimiento de sus principios y métodos más que de su práctica

**tolerance** (TAHL er uhns) willingness to respect different beliefs and customs (p. 251)
**tolerancia** disposición a respetar las diferentes creencias y costumbres

**Torah** (TOH ruh) sacred books of Judaism that are also called the Law of Moses (pp. 133, 139)
*tora* libros que se conocen también como la Ley de Moisés

**trading post** (TRAYD ihng pohst) trade center (p. 378)
*factoría* centro de comercio

**tradition** (truh DIHSH uhn) long-established custom or practice (p. 196)
*tradición* costumbre o práctica establecida de largo tiempo atrás

**traditional** (truh DIHSH uh nuhl) of, handed down by, or following tradition (p. 300)
*tradicional* referente a, transmitido por o que sigue la tradición

**traditional arts** (truh DIHSH uh nuhl ahrts) arts of China, including painting, sculpture, and poetry (p. 343)
*artes tradicionales* artes de China que incluyen pintura, escultura y poesía

**treaty** (TREET ee) written agreement between two peoples or nations (p. 513)
*tratado* convenio por escrito entre dos pueblos o naciones

**tribune** (TRIHB yoon) top officials of the plebeian assembly in Rome (p. 491)
*tribuno* funcionario de la más alta categoría en la asamblea de plebeyos en Roma

**tributary** (TRIHB yoo ter ee) river or stream that flows into a larger river (p. 276)
*afluente* río o arroyo que desemboca en un río más grande

**tribute** (TRIHB yoot) payment made by a conquered people to a stronger power (p. 108)
*tributo* pago que hace un pueblo conquistado a una potencia más fuerte

**tripartite** (trī PAHR tīt) divided into three parts (p. 493)

*tripartita* de tres partes

**truce** (troos) agreement by warring parties to stop fighting while they discuss peace terms (p. 461)
*tregua* acuerdo de las partes en guerra de dejar de pelear mientras se tratan los términos de la paz

**tyranny** (TIHR uh nee) government run by a single strong ruler (p. 390)
*tiranía* gobierno dirigido por un único gobernante poderoso

**underworld** (UHN der wuhrld) world of the dead (p. 112)
*averno* el mundo de los muertos

**untouchable** (uhn TUHCH uh buhl) class of workers below the Sudras in India (p. 182)
*intocables* clase de trabajadores que se hallan por debajo de los sudras en India

**value** (VAL yoo) ideal thought to be worthwhile by a person or group (p. 300)
*valor* pensamiento ideal considerado como valioso por una persona o grupo

**veto** (VEE toh) power to reject a proposed action or law (p. 495)
*veto* poder para rechazar una acción o ley propuesta

**virtue** (VER choo) good quality (p. 232)
*virtud* cualidad aceptable

**warlord** (WAWR lawrd) military ruler of a small state (p. 289)
*caudillo* gobernante militar de un estado pequeño

**welfare** (WEHL fair) health, comfort, or happiness; state of health and comfort (pp. 230, 251)

*bienestar* salud, comodidad o felicidad; estado de salud y comodidad

**yin and yang** (yihn and yahng) two great forces at work in the universe (p. 313)
*yin y yang* dos grandes fuerzas que actúan en el universo

Page numbers in italics refer to illustrations. The letter refers to a map *(m)*; chart, diagram, table *(c)*; graph *(g)*; or picture *(p)*.

# E

# F

   

# Acknowledgments

## Staff Credits

The people who made up the *Ancient Civilizations* team—representing Design Services, Editorial, Editorial Services, Manufacturing and Inventory Planning, Marketing, Marketing Services, Market Research, Online Services and Multimedia Development, Production Services, Project Office, and Publishing Processes—are listed below. Bold type denotes the core team members.

**Margaret Antonini, Renee Beach,** Kerry Lyn Buckley, Doreen Galbraith, **Jennifer Hafley,** Kristan Hoskins, **John Kingston,** Marian Manners, **Kathy Mercandetti,** Xavier W. Niz, Matt Raycroft, **Maureen Raymond,** Kirsten Richert, **Gerry Schrenk, Elizabeth Torjussen**

## Additional Credits

Gregory Abrom, Susan Andariese, Michele Angelucci, Rosalyn Arcilla, Rachel Avenia-Prol, Penny Baker, Claudio Barriga, Lois Brown, Justin Contursi, Paul DelSignore, Lisa Ferrari, Joseph Galka, Catalina Gavilanes, Michael Ginsberg, Florrie Gadson, Monduane Harris, Beth Hyslip, Karen Mancinelli, Daniela Mastria, Michael McLaughlin, Mark Michelson, Terri Mitchell, Art Mkrtchyan, Ken Myett, Meg Montgomery, Raymond Parenteau, Bruce Rolff, Andrew Roney, Rachel Ross, Lloyd Sabin, Mildred Schulte, Ann Shea, Frank Tangredi, Rachel Winter, Helen Young

## Charts

gdps: HT20; HRS: HT 23; Keithley and Associates: HT2, HT3, HT6, HT7, HT21, HT22, HT24, HT25, HT26, HT27

## Atlas Art

Keithley and Associates

## Maps

All maps created by Mapping Specialists Limited

## Photos

**Cover & title page:** Araldo De Luca/White Star SRL; **A2 t,** Natalie Pecht/Alamy; **A2 b,** John Warden/SuperStock; **A3 t,** © Macduff Everton/CORBIS; **A3 b,** Getty Images; **A8 b,** PhotoDisc, Inc./Getty Images; **A8 t,** © Michael Sewell/Peter Arnold, Inc.; **A9 t,** Tim Davis/Photo Researchers, Inc.; **A10 b,** CORBIS; **A10 t,** Scala/Art Resource, NY; **A11 t,** © Asian Art & Archeology, Inc./CORBIS; **A11 b,** The Granger Collection, New York; **A12 t,** National Archaeological Museum; **A13 b,** CORBIS; **A13 b,** Philip Baird/www.anthroarcheart.org; **A13 t,** © Free Agents limited/CORBIS; **A14 t,** ©Porterfield-Chickering/Art Resource, NY; **A14 b,** Werner Forman/Art Resource, NY; **A15 t,** Geoff Brightling/© Dorling Kindersley, Courtesy of the Pitt Rivers Museum, University of Oxford; **A15 b,** CORBIS/Bettmann; **A15 m,** CORBIS/Bettmann; **viii,** Paul Solomon/Woodfin Camp & Associates; **ix bl,** www.kamat.com; **ix br,** Jeremy Horner/Corbis; **x,** The Image Bank/Getty Images, Inc.; **xi b,** Zephyr Picture/Index Stock Imagery; **xi cl,** Dorling Kindersley/The British Museum; **xii,** Ted Grant/Masterfile; **xiv bl,** Bridgeman Art Library; **xiv br,** The Art Archive/Bibliothèque des Arts Décoratifs Paris/Dagli Orti; **xx br,** The Granger Collection, New York; **xv l,** Richard Bonson/Dorling Kindersley; **xv b,** David Sutherland/Stone-Allstock/Getty Images, Inc.; **xvii r,** Dorling Kindersley; **xvii l,** Roger Phillips/Dorling Kindersley; **xvii cl,** Dorling Kindersley/Butser Ancient Farm; **xvii cr,** Don Farrall/Getty Images, Inc.; **HT 1,** Scala/Art Resource, NY; **HT 2 tr,** Dave King/© Dorling Kindersley, Courtesy of The Museum of London; **HT 2 tl,** Philip Baird/www.anthroarcheart.org; **HT 3,** BananaStock/PictureQuest; **HT 4,** Pearson Education; **HT 5,** © Michael Newman/PhotoEdit Inc.; **HT 6,** Getty Images; **HT 7,** © David Young-Wolff/PhotoEdit Inc.; **HT 10,** Wolfgang Kaehler Photography; **HT 12,** Silver Burdett Ginn; **HT 16,** Getty Images; **HT 17,** © Dean Conger/CORBIS; **HT 18,** Gavin Hellier/Robert Harding World Imagery; **HT 19,** © Royalty-Free/CORBIS; **HT 25,** © Jeff Greenberg/PhotoEdit Inc.; **HT 26,** Lawrence Migdale/Pix; **1,** David Noton/naturepl.com; **2,** Dorling Kindersley/Natural History Museum; **3,** Beth Wald/Aurora & Quanta Productions, Inc.; **4,** Doug Pensinger/Getty Images, Inc.; **5,** Bettmann/Corbis; **7,** National Science Foundation; **9 cl,** Patrick Robert/MPFT/Corbis; **9 c,** John Reader/Science Photo Library/Photo Researchers, Inc.; **9 bc,** Robert F. Sisson/National Geographic Image Collection; **9 cr,** Bettmann/Corbis; **10,** The Natural History Museum, London; **13 cr,** Dorling Kindersley/Natural History Museum; **13 c,** Dorling Kindersley/Pitt Rivers Museum; **13 b,** Dave King/Dorling Kindersley; **17,** Archivo Iconografico, S.A./Corbis; **20,** Richard Hook/Dorling Kindersley; **21 bl,** Dorling Kindersley; **21 cr,** Dorling Kindersley/The Natural History Museum, London; **21 br,** Gianni Dagli Orti/Corbis; **22 tl,** Dorling Kindersley/The Natural History Museum, London; **22 tr,** Charles Walker/Topfoto/The Image Works; **25,** Richard Hook/Dorling Kindersley; **27,** Dorling Kindersley/Pitt Rivers Museum; **28,** Scala/Art Resource, NY; **29,** Paolo Koch/Photo Researchers, Inc.; **31,** Rakoczy/Art Resource, NY; **33,** Hans Georg Roth/Corbis; **34 tc,** Dorling Kindersley/Butser Ancient Farm; **34 tr,** Dorling Kindersley; **34 cl,** Roger Phillips/Dorling Kindersley; **34 cr,** Don Farrall/Getty Images, Inc.; **36 tr,** Chris Forsey/Dorling Kindersley; **36 cl,** Yann Arthus-Bertrand/Corbis; **38 bl,** Dorling Kindersley/Museum of London; **38 br,** Dorling Kindersley/Museum of London; **38–39 c,** Corel Professional Photos CD-ROM(tm); **39 tl,** Mary Evans Picture Library; **39 b,** Dorling Kindersley/Museum of London; **39 cr,** Dorling Kindersley/Museum of London; **41 cr,** Scala/Art Resource, NY; **41 b,** Nik Wheeler/Corbis; **43,** Mary Evans Picture Library; **48 c,** Macduff Everton/Corbis; **48–49 c,** Christopher Evans/National Geographic Image Collection; **49 cl,** Werner Forman/Art Resource, NY; **49 cr,** Werner Forman/Art Resource, NY; **50,** Scala/Art Resource, NY; **53,** Nik Wheeler/Corbis; **55,** Dorling Kindersley/Museum of London; **60–61 c,** Paul Solomon/Woodfin Camp & Associates; **60–61 bkgd,** Roger Markham Smith/Getty Images, Inc.; **62,** Iraq Museum, Baghdad, Iraq/Bridgeman Art Library; **63,** George Gerster/Photo Researchers, Inc.; **70,** Gianni Dagli Orti/Corbis; **72,** Gianni Dagli Orti/Corbis; **73,** The Granger Collection, New York; **74,** HIP/Scala/Art Resource, NY; **75,** Erich Lessing/Art Resource, NY; **77 bl,** The Ashmolean Museum, Oxford, UK/Bridgeman Art Library; **77 br,** Southwest Palace, Nineveh, Iraq, Ancient Art and Architecture Collection Ltd./Bridgeman Art Library; **78 c,** Erich Lessing/Art Resource, NY; **78 br,** Louvre, Paris, France/Bridgeman Art Library; **79 cl,** Charles & Josette Lenars/Corbis; **79 br,** Dorling Kindersley/The British Museum; **82,** Scala/Art Resource, NY; **83 br,** Iraq Museum, Baghdad, Iraq/Bridgeman Art Library; **83 b,** Erich Lessing/Art Resource, NY; **83 cl,** The Art Archive/Musée du Louvre, Paris/Dagli Orti; **85,** Erich Lessing/Art Resource, NY; **87 tl,** Louvre, Paris, France/Bridgeman Art Library; **87 bl,** Bettmann/Corbis; **87 c,** Louvre, Paris, France/Bridgeman Art Library; **91,** Ashmolean Museum, Oxford, UK/Bridgeman Art Library; **92,** The Egyptian Museum, Cairo; **93,** David Sutherland/Stone-Allstock/Getty Images, Inc.; **98,** Wolfgang Kaehler Photography; **101,** Scala/Art Resource, NY; **103,** Giraudon/Art Resource, NY; **104,** Michael Melford, Inc./Getty Images, Inc.; **105,** Egyptian National Museum, Cairo, Egypt/Bridgeman Art Library; **108,** The Metropolitan Museum of Art; **109,** The Egyptian Museum, Cairo, Egypt; **110,** Werner Forman/Corbis; **112,** Dorling Kindersley/The British Museum; **113 bl,** Dorling Kindersley/The British Museum; **113 bc,** Kingston Lacy, Dorset, UK, National Trust Photographic Library/Derrick E. Witty/Bridgeman Art Library; **113 br,** Max Alexander/Dorling Kindersley; **113 bc,** Doug Scott/AGE Fotostock America, Inc.; **114,** Dorling Kindersley/The British Museum; **115,** Werner Forman/Art Resource, NY; **116 c,** Erich Lessing/Art Resource, NY; **116 bl,** Dorling Kindersley/The British Museum; **117,** Giraudon/Art Resource, NY; **119 c,** Richard Bonson/Dorling Kindersley; **119 bkgd,** David Sutherland/Getty Images, Inc.; **120,** Paul W. Liebhardt; **121,** The Art Archive/Ragab Papyrus Institute, Cairo/Dagli Orti; **122 c,** The Granger Collection, New York; **122 tr,** EMG Education Management Group/Pearson Education; **122 bkgd,** Peter Johnson/Corbis; **127,** David Sutherland/Getty Images, Inc.; **128,** Richard Nowitz/Corbis; **129,** Erich Lessing/Art Resource, NY; **131 bc,** Andy Crawford/Dorling Kindersley; **131 br,** The Art Archive/Bibliothèque des Arts Décoratifs Paris/Dagli Orti; **131 bl,** Mitch Hrdlicka/Getty Images, Inc.; **133,** Archivo Iconografico, S.A./Corbis; **135,** The Jewish Museum, NY/Art Resource,

NY; **136 bl,** Erich Lessing/Art Resource, NY; **136 bc,** Peter Dennis/ Dorling Kindersley; **136 br,** Alistair Duncan/Dorling Kindersley; **139,** Dorling Kindersley/Jewish Museum; **140 tc,** Andy Crawford/Dorling Kindersley; **140 tr,** Andy Crawford/Dorling Kindersley; **140 tl,** Andy Crawford/Dorling Kindersley; **141,** PonkaWonka; **142,** Andy Crawford/Dorling Kindersley; **144,** The Art Archive/Bibliothèque des Arts Décoratifs, Paris/Dagli Orti; **147,** Mitch Hrdlicka/Getty Images, Inc.; **149,** Skjold Photographs; **151 tr,** Charles Walker/Topfoto/The Image Works; **153,** PonkaWonka; **155,** Dorling Kindersley/Jewish Museum, NY; **160–161c,** Jeremy Horner/Corbis; **162,** Dorling Kindersley; **163,** Galen Rowell/Corbis; **165 bl,** Brian Brake/Photo Researchers, Inc.; **165 br,** Francis & Donna Caldwell/Affordable Photo/AGPix.com; **169,** Brian Brake/Photo Researchers, Inc.; **171,** Diego Lezama Orezzoli/Corbis; **172,** Dorling Kindersley; **173 tl,** Adam Woolfitt/Robert Harding World Imagery; **173 tc,** Prentice Hall School Division; **173 tr,** Archivo Iconografico S.A./Corbis; **173 cl,** Max Alexander/Dorling Kindersley; **173 c,** Roger Phillips/Dorling Kindersley; **174,** Dorling Kindersley/National Museum of New Delhi; **176 c,** Dorling Kindersley; **176–176b,** Corel Professional Photos CD-ROM(tm); **177 tr,** Borromeo/Art Resource, NY; **177 tl,** Copyright J.M. Kenoyer; **177 cr,** Photo by J.M. Kenoyer, courtesy Department of Archaeology and Museums, Government of Pakistan; **177 c,** Photo by J.M. Kenoyer, courtesy Department of Archaeology and Museums, Government of Pakistan; **181 cr,** Hulton Archive/Getty Images, Inc.; **181 c,** Ric Ergenbright/Corbis; **181 bl,** Jeremy Horner/Getty Images, Inc.; **181 br,** Dinodia/Omni-Photo Communications; **185,** Dorling Kindersley/National Museum of New Delhi; **187,** Archivo Iconografico S.A./Corbis; **188,** Royalty Free/Corbis; **189,** Robyn Jones/Lonely Planet Images; **191 bl,** SEF/Art Resource, NY; **191 cr,** Richard I'Anson/Lonely Planet Images; **193,** Arvind Garg/Corbis; **194,** Courtesy Lysa Oeters; **197,** Victoria & Albert Museum, London/Art Resource, NY; **200 t,** Greg Elms/Lonely Planet Images; **200 cl,** Paul Beinssen/Lonely Planet Images; **203 tr,** Paul Beinssen/Lonely Planet Images; **205 br,** SEF/Art Resource, NY; **205 bc,** Royalty Free/Corbis; **205 cl,** Scala/Art Resource, NY; **208,** Arko Datta/AFP/Getty Images, Inc.; **211,** Pearson Education; **213,** Greg Elms/Lonely Planet Images; **214,** Dorling Kindersley/Powell Cotton Museum; **215,** PhotoDisc/Getty Images, Inc.; **217 bl,** www.worldreligions.co.uk<http://www.worldreligions.co.uk>; **217 cr,** Alison Wright/Corbis; **219,** The Art Archive/Musée Guimet Paris/Dagli Orti; **220,** Dorling Kindersley/Gables; **221,** www.worldreligions.co.uk <http://www.worldreligions.co.uk>; **222,** Dorling Kindersley/Powell Cotton Museum; **224,** www.worldreligions.co.uk <http://www.worldreligions.co.uk>; **225,** Brian A. Vikander/Corbis; **226,** George Gerster/Comstock Images; **228 b,** Luca I. Tettoni/Corbis; **228 bkgd,** PhotoDisc; **229 tc,** Richard A. Cooke/Corbis; **229 tr,** Alison Wright/Corbis; **229 c,** Barnabas Kindersley/Dorling Kindersley; **229 b,** Dorling Kindersley/Buddha Padipa Temple, Wimbledon; **233,** Scala/Art Resource, NY; **234 bkgd,** David Cumming; Eye Ubiquitous/ Corbis; **234 tc,** Richard I'Anson/Lonely Planet Images; **234 cr,** Amit Pashricha/Dorling Kindersley; **234 tr,** Lindsay Hebberd/Corbis; **237,** Scala/Art Resource, NY; **239,** www.worldreligions.co.uk<http:// www.worldreligions.co.uk>; **240,** Lauria Nandangarh, Bihar, India/ Bridgeman Art Library; **241,** Edifice/Corbis; **243 bl,** www.kamat.com; **243 br,** Philip Baird/www.anthroarcheart.org; **246,** Burstein Collection/ Corbis; **247,** Scala/Art Resource, NY; **248,** www.kamat.com; **250,** Adam Woolfitt/Corbis; **252,** Sarnath, Uttar Pradesh, India/Bridgeman Art Library; **253 cl,** Philip Baird/www.anthroarcheart.org; **253 cr,** Najlah Feanny/Corbis; **253 bkgd,** Adam Woolfitt/Corbis; **257 tl,** Dorling Kindersley; **257 tc,** Dorling Kindersley; **257 c,** Andy Crawford/ Dorling Kindersley; **257 bc,** Andy Crawford/Dorling Kindersley; **258,** Lindsay Hebberd/Corbis; **259,** Dinesh Khanna/Dorling Kindersley; **261,** Scala/Art Resource, NY; **263,** Edifice/Corbis; **268–269c,** The Image Bank/Getty Images, Inc.; **270,** Asian Art & Archaeology, Inc./Corbis; **271,** Corbis; **273,** Lowell Georgia/Corbis; **276 tl,** Craig Lovell/Corbis; **279 b,** Casey Krimmel; **281,** Julia Waterlow; Eye Ubiquitous/Corbis; **282,** The Granger Collection, New York; **283 tl,** ChinaStock/Wang Deying; **283 cr,** Asian Art & Archaeology, Inc./Corbis; **285,** Lowell Georgia/Corbis; **288,** Giraudon/Art Resource, NY; **289,** ChinaStock; **290 t,** ChinaStock; **290 br,** Kimbell Art Museum/Corbis; **290 cr,** The British Museum; **290 bc,** Dorling Kindersley; **293,** Giraudon/Art

Resource, NY; **296,** The Ashmolean Museum; **297,** ChinaStock; **299 br,** ChinaStock; **299 bl,** Bridgeman Art Library; **301,** Stapleton Collection/Corbis; **303,** The Ashmolean Museum; **304,** Dorling Kindersley/The Glasgow Museum; **307,** The Art Archive/Bibliothèque National, Paris/Marc Charmet; **308 bl,** Pixtal/AGE Fotostock America; **308 c,** Courtesy of The General Libraries, The University of Texas at Austin; **308 br,** Alamy Images; **311 bkgd,** Alamy Images; **311 tr,** Bridgeman Art Library; **311 bl,** Peter Turnley/Corbis; **313,** ChinaStock; **314 t,** Dave G. Houser/Corbis; **314 cl,** PhotoDisc/Getty Images, Inc.; **315,** Werner Forman/Corbis; **316,** The Art Archive/The British Museum; **319,** The Art Archive/Bibliothèque National Paris/Marc Charmet; **321,** PhotoDisc/Getty Images, Inc.; **322,** Erich Lessing/Art Resource, NY; **323,** Juliet Coombe/Lonely Planet Images; **325 br,** Asian Art & Archaeology, Inc./Corbis; **325 bl,** The Granger Collection, New York; **327,** The Granger Collection, New York; **328,** Russell Barnett/Dorling Kindersley; **329,** Stone/AllStock/Getty Images, Inc.; **330,** Erich Lessing/Art Resource, NY; **331,** The Art Archive/ Bibliothèque National Paris; **332,** Scala/Art Resource, NY; **336,** ChinaStock; **337,** Geoff Brightling/Dorling Kindersley; **338 cl,** Giraudon/Art Resource, NY; **338 bc,** PhotoDisc/Getty Images, Inc.; **338 bl,** Dorling Kindersley/Courtesy of the Pitt Rivers Museum, University of Oxford; **339 bc,** Dorling Kindersley/Courtesy of the Pitt Rivers Museum, University of Oxford; **339 tr,** Asian Art & Archaeology, Inc./Corbis; **341,** Historical Picture Archive/Corbis; **343 cl,** Asian Art & Archaeology, Inc./Corbis; **343 cr,** Wolfgang Kaehler/Corbis; **343 b,** Burstein Collection/Corbis; **344 tl,** Alan Hills and Geoff Brightling/Dorling Kindersley; **344 tr,** Geoff Brightling/Dorling Kindersley; **345 tl,** Dorling Kindersley/Courtesy of the Pitt Rivers Museum, University of Oxford; **345 tc,** ChinaStock; **345 tr,** Dorling Kindersley/Science Museum; **347,** Asian Art & Archaeology, Inc./Corbis; **349,** Burstein Collection/Corbis; **352–353c,** Zephyr Picture/Index Stock Imagery, Inc.; **354,** SuperStock; **355,** Wolfgang Kaehler/Corbis; **360,** Erich Lessing/Art Resource, NY; **361,** Martyn Chillmaid/Robert Harding Picture Library; **362,** The Granger Collection, New York; **364,** Gilles Mermet/Art Resource, NY; **365,** Bettmann/Corbis; **367,** Rob Matheson/Corbis; **368,** Nick Nicolls/ Dorling Kindersley; **371,** Liz McAulay/Dorling Kindersley; **372,** Bildarchiv Preussischer Kulturbesitz/Art Resource, NY; **374 bl,** Dorling Kindersley/The British Museum; **374 cr,** Dorling Kindersley/The British Museum; **374 tr,** Dorling Kindersley/The British Museum; **374–375 bkgd,** Corel Professional Photos CD-ROM(tm); **375 t,** The Granger Collection, New York; **375 bc,** Dorling Kindersley/The British Museum; **377,** Bettmann/Corbis; **379,** SuperStock; **383,** Rob Matheson/Corbis; **384,** Foto Marburg/Art Resource, NY; **385,** North Wind Picture Archives; **387 bl,** The Art Archive/Agora Museum, Athens/Dagli Orti; **387 br,** Alan Klehr/Getty Images, Inc.; **389,** Bettmann/Corbis; **390,** Martin von Wagner Museum der Universität Würzburg, Photo: K. Oehrlein; **392,** The Art Archive/Agora Museum, Athens/Dagli Orti; **394,** Dorling Kindersley/The British Museum; **395 t,** Susan Muhlhauser/Time Life Pictures/Getty Images, Inc.; **395 tc,** David Swift; **395 tl,** David Swift; **395 tr,** David Swift; **397 bl,** Alan Klehr/ Stone/Getty Images, Inc.; **397 br,** The Art Archive/Agora Museum Athens/Dagli Orti; **399 cr,** HIP/Scala/Art Resource, NY; **399 cl,** Kaveh Kazemi/Corbis; **399 bkgd,** PhotoDisc; **401,** Mary Evans Picture Library; **403,** Foto Marburg/Art Resource, NY; **407,** The Art Archive/ Agora Museum, Athens/Dagli Orti; **409,** Alan Klehr/Stone/Getty Images, Inc.; **410,** Prentice Hall School Division; **411,** SuperStock; **413,** The Art Archive/Muséo Nazionale Romano, Rome/Dagli Orti; **415,** Dodwell, Edward (1767–1832) The Stapleton Collection, UK/ Bridgeman Art Library; **416,** Erich Lessing/Art Resource, NY; **417,** Erich Lessing/Art Resource, NY; **420,** The Granger Collection, New York; **423 br,** Scala/Art Resource, NY; **423 bl,** Dorling Kindersley/The British Museum; **424 tl,** Courtesy Martha Hall, Mazer Photography; **424 tr,** Royalty Free/Corbis; **426 t,** Christine Osborne/Corbis; **426 cl,** Prentice Hall School Division; **429,** Scala/Art Resource, NY; **431,** Scala/Art Resource, NY; **432,** The Art Archive/Muséo Nazionale Romano, Rome/Dagli Orti; **435,** Courtesy Martha Hall /Mazer Photography; **437,** Christine Osborne/Corbis; **438,** Charles Walker/Topfoto/The Image Works; **439,** Corbis; **441,** The Granger Collection, New York; **443,** Erich Lessing/Art Resource, NY; **444,**

Bildarchive Preussischer Kulturbesitz/Art Resource, NY; **446 c,** Gianni Dagli Orti/Corbis; **446 bl,** The Art Archive/The British Museum/Eileen Tweedy; **446–447 b,** Patrick Ben Luke Syder/Lonely Planet Images; **447,** Keren Su/Corbis; **452,** Bettmann/Corbis; **454,** Liz McAulay/Dorling Kindersley; **454–455 bkgd,** PhotoDisc; **454–455 b,** The Art Archive/Biblioteca Braidense, Milan/Dagli Orti; **455 cr,** De Antonia/Musei Vaticani; **455 t,** The Granger Collection, New York; **455 c,** The British Museum; **457,** Charles Walker/Topfoto/The Image Works; **458–459 b,** Jose Miralles/S.I. International; **460,** The Art Archive/Archaeological Museum, Venice/Dagli Orti; **462,** The Granger Collection, New York; **463,** Araldo de Luca/Corbis; **476–477 bkgd,** Ted Grant/Masterfile; **478,** Giraudon/Bridgeman Art Library; **479,** David Noton/Taxi/Getty Images, Inc.; **484,** Roger Wood/Corbis; **485,** Mary Evans Picture Library; **486,** Alinari/Art Resource, NY; **490,** Mary Evans Picture Library; **492 cl,** The Granger Collection, New York; **492 tl,** Dorling Kindersley/The British Museum; **494,** Scala / Art Resource, N.Y.; **495,** Corbis Sygma; **499,** Russell Barnett/Dorling Kindersley; **500 tc,** Dorling Kindersley/The British Museum; **500 tl,** Dorling Kindersley/The British Museum; **501,** Giraudon/Bridgeman Art Library; **503 cr,** Tom Uhlman Photography; **503 bkgd,** Corel Professional Photos CD-ROM(tm); **503 bl,** Mike Okoniewski / The Image Works; **507,** John Woodcock/Dorling Kindersley; **508,** Bettmann/Corbis; **509,** Sandro Vannini/Corbis; **511,** Araldo de Luca/Corbis; **513,** Dorling Kindersley; **514,** Russell Barnett/Dorling Kindersley; **516,** Mary Evans Picture Library; **519,** The Granger Collection, New York; **520,** Araldo de Luca/Corbis; **522 cl,** Peter Bull/Dorling Kindersley; **522 tr,** Mimmo Jodice/Corbis; **522 t,** Jan Butchofsky-Houser/Corbis; **522 tl,** The Art Archive/Dagli Orti; **524 cl,** Simon James/Dorling Kindersley; **524 b,** Hulton Archive/Getty Images, Inc.; **524–525 c,** Alinari/Art Resource, NY; **524–525 bkgd,** PhotoDisc/Getty Images, Inc.; **525,** Bettmann/Corbis; **531,** Hulton Archive/Getty Images, Inc.; **533,** The Granger Collection, New York; **534,** Scala/Art Resource, NY; **535,** Réunion des Musée Nationaux/Art Resource, NY; **537 br,** Peter Dennis/Dorling Kindersley; **537 bl,** Cameraphoto/Art Resource, NY; **541,** SuperStock; **543 bl,** Mary Evans Picture Library; **543 c,** Cameraphoto/Art Resource, NY; **543 bkgd,** Dorling Kindersley; **543 br,** Jack Novak/SuperStock; **543 t,** Giraudon/Bridgeman Art Library; **544,** Mary Evans Picture Library; **546,** Reproduction by Courtesy of the University Librarian and Director, John Rylans University Library, The University of Manchester; **548,** Historical Picture Archive/Corbis; **549,** The Crosiers/Gene Plaisted, OSC; P.O. BOX 500, Onamia MN 56359; **551 b,** Peter Dennis/Dorling Kindersley; **553,** Peter Dennis/Dorling Kindersley; **556,** National Gallery Collection; By kind permission of the Trustees of the National Gallery, London/Corbis; **558 cl,** Scala/Art Resource, NY; **558 cr,** Erich Lessing/Art Resource, NY; **559,** Giraudon/Bridgeman Art Library; **561 tr,** The British Museum, London, UK/Bridgeman Art Library; **561 br,** Reproduction by Courtesy of the University Librarian and Director, John Rylans University Library, The University of Manchester; **562,** The Art Archive/Musée du Louvre, Paris/Dagli Orti; **563,** Garry Adams/Index Stock Imagery; **565,** Araldo de Luca/Corbis; **567,** Vanni/Art Resource, NY; **568–569b,** Buddy Mays/Corbis; **569 br,** Eric Thomas/Dorling Kindersley; **570,** Ancient Art and Architecture Collection Ltd./Bridgeman Art Library; **571,** Dorling Kindersley; **573,** The Art Archive/Archaeological Museum, Naples/Dagli Orti; **574,** Araldo de Luca/Corbis; **576 tl,** Christi Graham and Nick Nicholls/Dorling Kindersley; **576 tr,** The Art Archive/Musée du Louvre, Paris / Dagli Orti; **579,** Richard T. Nowitz/Corbis; **580,** The Art Archive/Hagia Sophia, Istanbul/Dagli Orti; **581,** Christie's Images/Corbis; **582,** Bettmann/Corbis; **585 cr,** SuperStock; **585 bl,** Topham/The Image Works; **585 bkgd,** PhotoDisc; **587,** Christie's Images/Corbis; **589 cl,** Garry Adams/Index Stock Imagery; **594,** © Martin Harvey/Peter Arnold, Inc.; **596,** Garry Adams/Index Stock Imagery; **597,** © Gallo Images/CORBIS; **599,** Southwest Palace, Nineveh, Iraq, Ancient Art and Architecture Collection Ltd./Bridgeman Art Library; **601,** Philip Baird/www.anthroarcheart.org; **605,** Bridgeman Art Library; **607,** The Granger Collection, New York; **609,** Roger Perrin/Private Collection/Bridgeman Art Library; **611,** Jose Miralles/S.I. International; **613,** The Granger Collection, New York; **615 l,** The Granger Collection, New York; **615 r,** Bibliothèque Nationale, Paris, France, Giraudon/The Bridgeman Art Library, London/New York

## Text Credits

Grateful acknowledgment is made to the following for copyrighted material:

### Oxford University Press, Inc.
From *Lives of the Caesars* by Suetonius. Copyright © 2000 by Catharine Edwards. Used by permission of Oxford University Press. All rights reserved.

### Penguin Books Ltd., London
From *History of the Peloponnesian War* by Thucydides Translated by Rex Warner. Translation copyright © Rex Warner, 1954. Used by permission of Penguin Books. All rights reserved.

### American Bible Society
From The Book of Daniel from THE HOLY BIBLE (KING JAMES VERSION) containing the Old and New Testaments. Copyright © 1992 by Ashley Bryan. Used by permission of American Bible Society.

### American Bible Society
The Parable of the Good Samaritan from HOLY BIBLE: THE NEW KING JAMES VERSION. Copyright © 1982 by Thomas Nelson, Inc. Used by permission of the American Bible Society. All rights reserved.

### Clarion Books
From MAROO OF THE WINTER CAVES by Ann Turnbull. Copyright © 1984 by Ann Turnbull. Reprinted by permission of Clarion Books, a Houghton Mifflin Company. All rights reserved.

### Unwin Hyman Limited
From *The Analects of Confucius*. Translated and annotated by Arthur Waley. Copyright © 1938 by George Allen and Unwin Ltd. Used by permission of George Allen & Unwin Ltd.

### Madhur Jaffrey
From *Seasons of Splendour: Tales, Myths & Legends of India* by Madhur Jaffrey from *HOW GANESH GOT HIS ELEPHANT HEAD*. Copyright © 1985 Madhur Jaffrey. Used by permission of Atheneum Books for Young Readers. All rights reserved.

### School Specialty, Inc.
*The Bird and the Sea* by Tao Tao Liu Sanders from *DRAGONS, GODS & SPIRITS*. Copyright © 1980 by Eurobook Limited. Used by permission of Peter Bedrick Books, published by agreement with Eurobook Ltd. All rights reserved.

### Simon & Schuster Books for Young Readers
Arachne by Alice Low from *THE MACMILLAN BOOK OF GREEK GODS AND HEROES*. Copyright © 1985 by Macmillan Publishing Company. Reprinted with the permission of Simon & Schuster Books For Young Readers, an imprint of Simon & Schuster Children's Publishing Division. All rights reserved.

### India Sourcebook
"The Rains" by Kalidasa from *The India Sourcebook,* edited by Don and Jean Johnson, 1992. Supported in part, by a grant from the Mid-Atlantic Association for Asian Studies.

### Villard Books
From *Ancestors: In Search of Human Origins* by Donald and Leonora Johanson and Blake Edgar. Copyright © 1994 by Donald and Leonora Johanson and Blake Edgar. Used by permission of Villard Books a registered trademark of Random House, Inc. All rights reserved.

### The University of Chicago Press
From *The Sumerians: Their History, Culture, and Character* by Samuel Noah Kramer. Copyright © 1963 by The University of Chicago Press. Used by permission of The University of Chicago Press.

### Dorling Kindersley Ltd.
From *Asoka the Great* by D.C. Ahir. Copyright © 1995 by D.C. Ahir. Used by permission of Dorling Kindersley Ltd. All rights reserved.

**Commercial Press (H.K.) Ltd.**
From *The Records of the Grand Historian* by Sima Qian Ssuma Ch'ien. Copyright © 1974 by Commercial Press, Hong Kong. Used by permission of Commercial Press.

**TIME Consumer Marketing, Time Inc.**
From *Cradle of Civilization* by Samuel Noah Kramer. Copyright © 1967 reprinted 1971 by Time Inc. Used by permission of Time Inc. All rights reserved.

**Bantam Books**
From *The Bhagavad-Gita* translated by Barbara Stoler Miller. Copyright © 1986 by Barbara Stoler Miller. Used by permission of Bantam Books, a division of Random House, Inc. All rights reserved.

**Interlink Publishing Company**
From *A Traveller's History of India* by Sinharaja Tammita-Delgoda. Print Copyright © 1995 by Sinharaja Tammita-Delgoda. Used by permission of Interlink Publishing Group, Inc. All rights reserved.

**TIME Consumer Marketing, Time Inc.**
From *The World's Greatest Religions* by the Editorial Staff of LIFE. Copyright © 1958 by Time, Inc. Used by permission of Time Inc. All rights reserved.

**The Free Press**
From I Beg of You, Chung Tzu by Shijing from *CHINESE CIVILIZATION AND SOCIETY* by Patricia Buckley Ebrey. Copyright © 1981 by The Free Press. Reprinted with the permission of The Free Press, a Division of Simon & Schuster Adult Publishing Group. All rights reserved.

**Hackett Publishing Company**
From To Anaktoria from *An Anthology in Translation* by A.M. Miller. Copyright © 1996. Used by permission of Hackett Publishing Company.

**Lockman Foundation**
From The New American Standard Bible, Psalm 23. Copyright © 1973 by The Lockman Foundation. Used by permission of the Lockman Foundation (www.lockman.org).

**Note:** Every effort has been made to locate the copyright owner of material reprinted in this book. Omissions brought to our attention will be corrected in subsequent editions.